*One World*
*Many Cultures*

# One World Many Cultures

---

## STUART HIRSCHBERG

RUTGERS: THE STATE UNIVERSITY
OF NEW JERSEY, NEWARK

MACMILLAN PUBLISHING COMPANY
NEW YORK

Editor: Eben Ludlow
Production Supervisor: Charlotte Hyland
Production Manager: Pamela Kennedy Oborski
Cover Designer: Robert Freese
Cover photographs: Clockwise from left—© Thomas Hopker, © R. & S. Michaud, © M. & E. Berheim, © Homer Sykes, © Lindsey Hebberd, and © Adam Woolfitt/all Woodfin Camp and Assoc., Inc.

This book was set in Palatino Type by Digitype, Inc., and was printed and bound by Book Press. The cover was printed by New England Book Components, Inc.

Acknowledgments appear on pages 695–701, which constitute a continuation of the copyright page.

Macmillan Publishing Company
866 Third Avenue, New York, New York 10022

Macmillan Publishing Company is part of the Maxwell Communication Group of Companies.

LIBRARY OF CONGRESS CATALOGING-IN-PUBLICATION DATA

One world, many cultures / [compiled by] Stuart Hirschberg.
        p.   cm.
     Includes indexes.
     ISBN 0-02-354775-8 (pbk.)
     1. College readers.  2. English language—Rhetoric.  3. Readers—
Intercultural communication.  I. Hirschberg, Stuart.
PE1417.057  1992           91-10862
808'.0427—dc20             CIP

Printing:  1 2 3 4 5 6 7     Year:  2 3 4 5 6 7 8

For Jerzy Kosinski
(1933–1991)

P.E.N. pal, with thanks for his many acts
of kindness and generosity

# *Preface*

*One World, Many Cultures* is a global, contemporary reader with an international and multicultural focus that offers an exciting alternative for freshman composition courses.

In nine thematic chapters, seventy-four readings by internationally recognized writers from forty countries explore cultural differences and displacement in relation to race, class, gender, region, and nation. *One World, Many Cultures* also reflects timely issues generated by political changes in Eastern Europe and by the war in the Persian Gulf. The selections challenge readers to see similarities between their own experiences and the experiences of others in radically different cultural circumstances. Compelling and provocative writings by authors from the Caribbean, Africa, Asia, Europe, and Central America reflect the cultural and ethnic heritage of many students.

The fifty-one nonfiction selections include diaries, essays, journalists' reports, interviews, autobiographies, scholarly articles, prison memoirs, and speeches. These and the twenty-three short stories (over half of which are fact-based) encourage readers to perceive the relationship between a wide range of experiences in different cultures with corresponding experiences writers have had within the United States. *One World, Many Cultures* also provides a rich sampling of accounts (forty-four in all) by writers who are native to the cultures they describe, allowing the reader to hear authentic voices rather than filtered journalistic reports.

# Chapter Descriptions

The nine chapters move from the most personal sphere of family life, through adolescent turning points, male and female relationships, the responsibilities of working, and the conflicts of class and race to more encompassing social dimensions. The readings examine the struggles of individuals against government powers, the problems that arise from exile, the difficulty of understanding unfamiliar social customs, and the human consequences of war.

Chapter 1, "The Family in Different Cultures," introduces families in rural Ireland, the Soviet Union, turn-of-the-century Japan, the Quiché Indians of Guatemala, communist China, and, within the United States, in a second-generation Chinese American family. These selections illustrate that the "family," however defined (as a single-parent household, nuclear family, or the extended family of an entire community), serves the role of passing on the mores and values of a particular culture to the next generation.

Chapter 2, "Turning Points," provides insights into both formal and informal rites of passage and initiation ceremonies in the lives of young people in Ireland, Borneo, Kenya, Egypt, and the Sudan, and contrasts their experiences with being initiated into the United States Marine Corps and coming of age in the Chicano barrio of East Los Angeles.

Chapter 3, "How Culture Shapes Gender Roles," explores the role culture plays in shaping sexual identity. Readers can gain insight into how gender roles are culturally conditioned rather than biologically determined. The extent to which sex role expectations differ from culture to culture can be seen in societies as diverse as those of Bali, Pakistan, the !Kung of Botswana, the Congo, Israel, and Canada.

Chapter 4, "How Work Creates Identity," explores work as a universal human experience through which we define ourselves and others. The role culture plays in shaping attitudes toward work can be seen in the different values of Amish farmers in Ohio, a Singapore stock exchange speculator, and a successful Korean immigrant who began as a wig peddler. We can share the work experiences of an English pilot who tells of her pioneering solo flight across the Atlantic, a typical Japanese "salaryman," a Chinese martial-arts master exchanging instruction for English lessons, and a French worker with a most unusual occupation.

Chapter 5, "Class Conflicts," takes up the crucial and often unrecognized relationships between race, sense of identity, and class through readings that explore positions of power and powerlessness. Selections include Gloria Steinem's analysis of the relationship of social class to power, Jo Goodwin Parker's poignant revelation of exactly what it means to be poor in the southern United States, and Krishnan Varma's story of homelessness and survival, set in modern-day Calcutta. The voices heard are those of men and women of many races and several nations, including an interview conducted by Studs Terkel with a former president of the Ku Klux Klan who became a civil rights activist, Josef Škvorecký's story exploring racial hypocrisy and class consciousness in Soviet-dominated Czechoslovakia, and Toi Derricotte's journal entries as one of the first blacks to move into an upper middle-class New Jersey neighborhood. Unusual perspectives on class issues are provided by Ivan Karp's analysis of how the Marx Brothers' movies reflected immigrant rebellion against upper-class values, and Dino Buzzati's parable exploring the fatal attraction to wealth and social status among Italy's post-World War II generation.

Chapter 6, "The State and the Individual," looks at the resilience and courage of ordinary citizens pitted against state tyranny in Castro's Cuba, the China of Mao Tse-tung and Tiananmen Square, Soviet-dominated Poland, and Cambodia under the Khmer Rouge. We hear the voices of writers of conscience and survivors of oppressive regimes in Argentina, Iraq under Saddam Hussein, Kenya during British colonial rule, and South Africa under apartheid. We learn of the challenge posed by the recent freedom in Czechoslovakia and in other countries in Eastern Europe.

Chapter 7, "Strangers in a Strange Land," explores the condition of exiles—whether refugees, immigrants, or travelers—who are caught between two cultures, but are at home in neither. The need of those who have left "home" to make sense of their lives in a new place is a theme explored by Edward Said, V. S. Naipaul, Nicholasa Mohr, Joan Didion, Le Ly Hayslip, David Whitman, Jamaica Kincaid, Salman Rushdie, and Bharati Mukherjee.

Chapter 8, "The Role Customs Play in Different Cultures," focuses on the role that ritual, religion, and belief play in shaping social behavior. The decisive influence of cultural values is explored through analyses of how the concept of being "on time" varies from culture to culture, how the Japanese have adapted baseball, the role aggression plays among the Yạnomamö Indians in Brazil, and the reasons for French and American cultural misunderstandings. We gain insight into the role customs play in accounts of a Kiowa Indian Sun Dance in Wyoming, nude beaches along the Yugoslavian coast, Mexican fiestas, zombification in Haiti, and a terrifying tribal ritual in Botswana.

Chapter 9, "The Impact of War," addresses the ultimate consequences of cross-cultural conflict—war. George Orwell describes his experiences as a soldier during the Spanish Civil War. Then, Everett C. Hughes, a sociologist, tells of visiting Germany after World War II to probe the underlying social forces responsible for the concentration camps. Different perspectives of participants and survivors are explored in an interview with the pilot who led the squadron that dropped the first atomic bomb on Hiroshima, Kyōko Hayashi's story based on her experience of being exposed to the atomic bomb in Nagasaki, and Panos Ioannides's fact-based story set during the Greek Cypriot struggle against the British. A set of selections dramatizes the impact of the Vietnam War on the soldiers who fought it and the dehumanizing effects on both Vietnamese and American civilians. A concluding selection by a military historian, Trevor N. Dupuy, analyzes the military strategies that proved so successful in Operation Desert Storm.

## Editorial Apparatus

Chapter introductions discuss the theme of each chapter as related to the individual selections. Biographical sketches preceding each selection give background information on the writer's life and identify the cultural, historical, and personal context in which the selection was written. Background information on countries represented by multiple selections (e.g., Botswana, Brazil, China, Czechoslovakia, France, India, Ireland, Japan, the Soviet Union, and Vietnam) are keyed to the subject of each reading.

### END-OF-SELECTION QUESTIONS

The questions that follow each of the selections are designed to encourage readers to discover relationships between personal experiences and the ideas in the text, to explore points of agreement and areas of conflict sparked by the viewpoints of the authors, and to provide ideas for further research and inquiry.

The first set of questions, "Evaluating the Text," asks readers to think critically about the content, meaning, and purpose of the selections and to evaluate the author's rhetorical strategy, voice projected in relationship to his or her audience, evidence cited, and underlying assumptions.

Questions labeled "Exploring Different Perspectives" focus on relationships between readings within each chapter that illuminate differences and similarities between cultures. These questions encourage readers to make connections between diverse cultures, to understand the writer's values and beliefs, to enter into the viewpoints of others, and to understand how culture shapes perception and a sense of self.

Questions in "Extending Viewpoints through Writing" invite readers to extend their thinking by seeing wider relationships between themselves and others through writing of many different kinds, including personal or expressive as well as expository, persuasive writing and more formal research papers.

Questions following each chapter, "Connecting Cultures," challenge readers to make connections and comparisons between selections within the chapter and throughout the book. These questions provide opportunities to consider additional cross-cultural perspectives on a single issue or to explore a particular topic in depth.

A rhetorical index, a geographical index, and a map of the world identifying countries mentioned in the selections are included to allow the text to accommodate a variety of teaching approaches.

## Instructor's Manual

An *Instructor's Manual* provides guidelines for using the text, supplemental bibliographies of books and periodicals, suggested answers to questions in the text, and a filmography for instructors who wish to use films and videos connected to particular selections.

## Acknowledgments

No expression of thanks can adequately convey my appreciation for the sound advice of my editor, Eben W. Ludlow. I owe a particular debt of gratitude to all those teachers of composition who offered thoughtful comments and have given this book the benefit of their scholarship and teaching experience. I would very much like to thank the instructors who reviewed the various stages of the manuscript, including Nancy K. Barry, Luther College; George Otte, Baruch College; Linda Palumbo, Cerritos College; Joan Rothstein-Vandergriff, University of Missouri-Kansas City; and Winifred Wood, Wellesley College.

For their dedication and skill, I owe much to the able staff at Macmillan, especially to Wendy Conn, John Sollami, Luanne Dreyer Elliott, Pamela Kennedy Oborski, Robert Freese, and Scott Rubin. I am most grateful to Charlotte Hyland for her outstanding work as Production Supervisor. Heartfelt thanks also to my permissions editor/wife, Terry, for making it possible to present some of the most compelling readings to ever appear in an anthology.

# Contents

*One World*
*Many Cultures*

# 1

# *The Family in Different Cultures*

The structure of the family is subject to a wide range of economic and social influences in different cultures. For example, child care in China is a vastly different enterprise from what it is in American society because of the enormous differences in economic circumstances and political systems. Yet the family in different cultures still serves its age-old role of nurturing, protecting, and instilling values and social mores. The variety of family structures depicted by writers of many different nationalities offers insight into how the concept of the family is modified according to the constraints, beliefs, and needs of particular societies.

Andrew Cherlin and Frank F. Furstenberg, Jr., in "The American Family in the Year 2000," attempt to identify how currents of social change will result in families very different from those experienced by our parents or grandparents. In a story set in rural Ireland, William Trevor, in "Teresa's Wedding," depicts the pressures a young couple experience as they prepare for their forthcoming marriage. The difficulties Soviet women face in receiving sex education, contraceptive devices, and health care during pregnancy is the subject of Francine du Plessix Gray's report, "Sex and Birth." A fascinating glimpse into communal life in Russia's heartland is offered by Boris Yeltsin in "Childhood in Russia." Natsume Soseki provides insight into the life of a Japanese family from a most unusual viewpoint. Rigoberta Menchu, in "Birth Ceremonies," offers a unique perspective on the significance of rituals and ceremonies performed to usher a newborn baby into the Guatemalan Indian community. The way child-care programs in China are set up to instill collective values of cooperation and sharing is explored by Bruce Dollar in "Child Care in China." The pressures on second-generation Chinese children to succeed are treated with candor and wit in "Jing-Mei Woo: Two Kinds," from Amy Tan's *The Joy Luck Club.*

Andrew Cherlin and
Frank F. Furstenberg, Jr.

# The American Family in the Year 2000

---

*This article originally appeared in* The Futurist, June 1983. *The authors, both sociologists, attempt to predict what family life in America will look like in the year 2000. Andrew J. Cherlin is professor of sociology at Johns Hopkins University and is the author of* Marriage, Divorce, Remarriage *(1981) and (with Frank F. Fustenberg, Jr.)* The New American Grandparent *(1986). Frank F. Furstenberg, Jr., is professor of sociology at the University of Pennsylvania. His books include* The Changing American Family and Public Policy *(1988),* Unplanned Parenthood: The Social Consequences of Teenage Child-Bearing *(1976), and* Adolescent Mothers in Later Life *(1989). By analyzing present trends, Cherlin and Furstenberg project a growing diversity in family forms and foresee more single-parent families and greater numbers of families of remarriages.*

- At current rates, half of all American marriages begun in the early 1980s will end in divorce.
- The number of unmarried couples living together has more than tripled since 1970.
- One out of four children is not living with both parents.

1    The list could go on and on. Teenage pregnancies: up. Adolescent suicides: up. The birthrate: down. Over the past decade, popular and scholarly commentators have cited a seemingly endless wave of grim statistics about the shape of the American family. The trends have caused a number of concerned Americans to wonder if the family, as we know it, will survive the twentieth century.

2    And yet, other observers ask us to consider more positive developments:

- Seventy-eight percent of all adults in a recent national survey said they get "a great deal" of satisfaction from their family lives; only 3 percent said "a little" or "none."
- Two-thirds of the married adults in the same survey said they

were "very happy" with their marriages; only 3 percent said "not too happy."

- In another recent survey of parents of children in their middle years, 88 percent said that if they had to do it over, they would choose to have children again.
- The vast majority of the children (71 percent) characterized their family life as "close and intimate."

Family ties are still important and strong, the optimists argue, and the predictions of the demise of the family are greatly exaggerated.  3

Neither the dire pessimists who believe that the family is falling apart  4
nor the unbridled optimists who claim that the family has never been in better shape provide an accurate picture of family life in the near future. But these trends indicate that what we have come to view as the "traditional" family will no longer predominate.

## Diverse Family Forms

In the future, we should expect to see a growing amount of diversity in  5
family forms, with fewer Americans spending most of their life in a simple "nuclear" family consisting of husband, wife, and children. By the year 2000, three kinds of families will dominate the personal lives of most Americans: families of first marriages, single-parent families, and families of remarriages.

In first-marriage families, both spouses will be in a first marriage,  6
frequently begun after living alone for a time or following a period of cohabitation. Most of these couples will have one, two, or less frequently, three children.

A sizable minority, however, will remain childless. Demographer  7
Charles F. Westoff predicts that about one-fourth of all women currently in their childbearing years will never bear children, a greater number of childless women than at any time in U.S. history.

One other important shift: In a large majority of these families, both  8
the husband and the wife will be employed outside the home. In 1940 only about one out of seven married women worked outside the home; today the proportion is one out of two. We expect this proportion to continue to rise, although not as fast as it did in the past decade or two.

## Single-Parent Families

The second major type of family can be formed in two ways. Most are  9
formed by a marital separation, and the rest by births to unmarried women. About half of all marriages will end in divorce at current rates, and we doubt that the rates will fall substantially in the near future.

When the couple is childless, the formerly married partners are likely  10
to set up independent households and resume life as singles. The high

rate of divorce is one of the reasons why more men and women are living in single-person households than ever before.

11    But three-fifths of all divorces involve couples with children living at home. In at least nine out of ten cases, the wife retains custody of the children after a separation.

12    Although joint custody has received a lot of attention in the press and in legal circles, national data show that it is still uncommon. Moreover, it is likely to remain the exception rather than the rule because most ex-spouses can't get along well enough to manage raising their children together. In fact, a national survey of children aged 11 to 16 conducted by one of the authors demonstrated that fathers have little contact with their children after a divorce. About half of the children whose parents had divorced hadn't seen their father in the last year; only one out of six had managed to see their father an average of once a week. If the current rate of divorce persists, about half of all children will spend some time in a single-parent family before they reach 18.

13    Much has been written about the psychological effects on children of living with one parent, but the literature has not yet proved that any lasting negative effects occur. One effect, however, does occur with regularity: Women who head single-parent families typically experience a sharp decline in their income relative to before their divorce. Husbands usually do not experience a decline. Many divorced women have difficulty reentering the job market after a long absence; others find that their low-paying clerical or service-worker jobs aren't adequate to support a family. . . .

## Families of Remarriages

14    The experience of living as a single parent is temporary for many divorced women, especially in the middle class. Three out of four divorced people remarry, and about half of these marriages occur within three years of the divorce.

15    Remarriage does much to solve the economic problems that many single-parent families face because it typically adds a male income. Remarriage also relieves a single parent of the multiple burdens of running and supporting a household by herself.

16    But remarriage also frequently involves blending together two families into one, a difficult process that is complicated by the absence of clear-cut ground rules for how to accomplish the merger. Families formed by remarriages can become quite complex, with children from either spouse's previous marriage or from the new marriage and with numerous sets of grandparents, stepgrandparents, and other kin and quasi-kin.

17    The divorce rate for remarriages is modestly higher than for first marriages, but many couples and their children adjust successfully to their remarriage and, when asked, consider their new marriage to be a big improvement over their previous one. . . .

## Convergence and Divergence

The family lives of Americans vary according to such factors as class, ethnicity, religion, and region. But recent evidence suggests a convergence among these groups in many features of family life. The clearest example is in childbearing, where the differences between Catholics and non-Catholics or between Southerners and Northerners are much smaller than they were 20 years ago. We expect this process of convergence to continue, although it will fall far short of eliminating all social class and subcultural differences. 18

The experiences of blacks and whites also have converged in many respects, such as in fertility and in patterns of premarital sexual behavior, over the past few decades. But with respect to marriage, blacks and whites have diverged markedly since about 1960. 19

Black families in the United States always have had strong ties to a large network of extended kin. But in addition, blacks, like whites, relied on a relatively stable bond between husbands and wives. But over the past several decades—and especially since 1960—the proportion of black families maintained by a woman has increased sharply; currently, the proportion exceeds four in ten. In addition, more young black women are having children out of wedlock; in the late 1970s about two out of three black women who gave birth to a first child were unmarried. 20

These trends mean that we must qualify our previously stated conclusion that marriage will remain central to family life. This conclusion holds for Americans in general. For many low-income blacks, however, marriage is likely to be less important than the continuing ties to a larger network of kin. 21

Marriage is simply less attractive to a young black woman from a low-income family because of the poor prospects many young black men have for steady employment and because of the availability of alternative sources of support from public-assistance payments and kin. Even though most black women eventually marry, their marriages have a very high probability of ending in separation or divorce. Moreover, they have a lower likelihood of remarrying. 22

Black single-parent families sometimes have been criticized as being "disorganized" or even "pathological." What the critics fail to note is that black single mothers usually are embedded in stable, functioning kin networks. These networks tend to center around female kin—mothers, grandmothers, aunts—but brothers, fathers, and other male kin also may be active. The members of these networks share and exchange goods and services, thus helping to share the burdens of poverty. The lower-class black extended family, then, is characterized by strong ties among a network of kin but fragile ties between husband and wife. The negative aspects of this family system have been exaggerated greatly; yet it need not be romanticized, either. It can be difficult and risky for individuals to leave the network in order to try to make it on their own; 23

thus, it may be hard for individuals to raise themselves out of poverty until the whole network is raised.

## The Disintegrating Family?

24   By now, predictions of the demise of the family are familiar to everyone. Yet the family is a resilient institution that still retains more strength than its harshest critics maintain. There is, for example, no evidence of a large-scale rejection of marriage among Americans. To be sure, many young adults are living together outside of marriage, but the evidence we have about cohabitation suggests that it is not a lifelong alternative to marriage; rather, it appears to be either another stage in the process of courtship and marriage or a transition between first and second marriages.

25   The so-called alternative life-styles that received so much attention in the late 1960s, such as communes and lifelong singlehood, are still very uncommon when we look at the nation as a whole.

26   Young adults today do marry at a somewhat older age, on average, than their parents did. But the average age at marriage today is very similar to what it was throughout the period from 1890 to 1940.

27   To be sure, many of these marriages will end in divorce, but three out of four people who divorce eventually remarry. Americans still seem to desire the intimacy and security that a marital relationship provides.

28   Much of the alarm about the family comes from reactions to the sheer speed at which the institution changed in the last two decades. Between the early 1960s and the mid-1970s, the divorce rate doubled, the marriage rate plunged, the birthrate dropped from a twentieth-century high to an all-time low, premarital sex became accepted, and married women poured into the labor force. But since the mid-1970s the pace of change has slowed. The divorce rate has risen modestly and the birthrate even has increased a bit. We may have entered a period in which American families can adjust to the sharp changes that occurred in the 1960s and early 1970s. We think that, by and large, accommodations will be made as expectations change and institutions are redesigned to take account of changing family practices.

29   Despite the recent difficulties, family ties remain a central part of American life. Many of the changes in family life in the 1960s and 1970s were simply a continuation of long-term trends that have been with us for generations.

30   The birthrate has been declining since the 1820s, the divorce rate has been climbing since at least the Civil War, and over the last half-century a growing number of married women have taken paying jobs. Employment outside the home has been gradually eroding the patriarchal system of values that was a part of our early history, replacing it with a more egalitarian set of values.

31   The only exception occurred during the late 1940s and the 1950s.

After World War II Americans raised during the austerity of depression and war entered adulthood at a time of sustained prosperity. The sudden turnabout in their fortunes led them to marry earlier and have more children than any generation before or since in this century. Because many of us were either parents or children in the baby-boom years following the war, we tend to think that the 1950s typify the way twentieth-century families used to be. But the patterns of marriage and childbearing in the 1950s were an aberration resulting from special historical circumstances; the patterns of the 1960s and 1970s better fit the long-term trends. Barring unforeseen major disruptions, small families, working wives, and impermanent marital ties are likely to remain with us indefinitely.

A range of possible developments could throw our forecasts off the     32
mark. We do not know, for example, how the economy will behave over the next 20 years, or how the family will be affected by technological innovations still at the conception stage. But, we do not envision any dramatic changes in family life resulting solely from technological innovations in the next two decades. . . .

Were we to be transported suddenly to the year 2000, the families we     33
would see would look very recognizable. There would be few unfamiliar forms—not many communes or group marriages, and probably not a large proportion of lifelong singles. Instead, families by and large would continue to center around the bonds between husbands and wives and between parents and children. One could say the same about today's families relative to the 1960s: the forms are not new. What is quite different, comparing the 1960s with the 1980s, or the 1980s with a hypothetical 2000, is the distribution of these forms.

In the early 1960s there were far fewer single-parent families and     34
families formed by remarriages after divorce than is the case today; and in the year 2000 there are likely to be far more single-parent families and families of remarriage than we see now. Moreover, in the early 1960s both spouses were employed in a much smaller percentage of two-parent families; in the year 2000, the percentage with two earners will be greater still. Cohabitation before marriage existed in the 1960s, but it was a frowned-upon, bohemian style of life. Today, it has become widely accepted; it will likely become more common in the future. Yet we have argued that cohabitation is less an alternative to marriage than a precursor to marriage, though we expect to see a modest rise in the number of people who never marry.

## Evaluating the Text

1. How does the unusually high degree of satisfaction people express appear to conflict with statistics on divorce and broken homes? Which of the conclusions Cherlin and Furstenberg draw based on statistics seem to be

the most probable and which seem to be the least probable? Explain your reaction.

2. Evaluate the response of 88 percent of people interviewed who say that if they had to do it over, they would choose to have children again. Discuss the psychological factors that might distort the responses people would give to this question.

3. How are the problems and satisfactions of living in a family with step-siblings different from those experienced in a nuclear family?

4. How would the reaction of a child to new step-siblings be determined by how happy he or she was in the nuclear family before the breakup and subsequent remarriage?

5. On what basis do Cherlin and Furstenberg expect to see differences between family structures in the northern and southern United States and among Catholics as compared to non-Catholics?

6. What cultural assumptions about poor black mothers do the authors seek to correct? What inferences might you draw about the kinds of relationships black children have with their relatives and the capacity of the extended family to share the burdens of poverty?

7. Why, in the authors' view, is cohabitation (living together) a transitional rather than an alternative form of family structure?

8. Evaluate the role of economic motivation in determining how quickly middle-class women tend to remarry. What factors appear to determine the rate of remarriage among men? What do the authors' assumptions seem to be regarding this?

9. In your opinion, what overall impression about the American family in the year 2000 do Cherlin and Furstenberg want to leave with their audience?

## Exploring Different Perspectives

1. Compare the typical family structure in Guatemalan Indian culture (see Rigoberta Menchu, "Birth Ceremonies") with those described by Cherlin and Furstenberg. How would you characterize the forces that create and maintain family life among the Guatemalan Indians, according to Menchu? Evaluate the differences in kinds of sources used as a basis for these accounts. Do you find the statistics Cherlin and Furstenberg use to be more credible, as credible, or less credible as supporting evidence than Menchu's personal account of cultural traditions?

2. How do the goals and values of Irish family life in William Trevor's story ("Teresa's Wedding") compare with the picture you get of family life in America described by Cherlin and Furstenberg? Compare the resources used by Trevor as a fiction writer with those used by Cherlin and Furstenberg as sociologists in creating realistic depictions of family life in the two cultures.

## Extending Viewpoints through Writing

1. If changes Cherlin and Furstenberg project were to occur, how do you think you would like what having a family will mean in the future? Can you think of other kinds of changes that may affect family life? Do you consider having children important in your future? Why or why not?

2. Do you know anyone who has been divorced and remarried? If so, is the second time around working out better than the first, in your view? Compare and contrast experiences of belonging to a nuclear family with comparable experiences in a step-family.
3. Why is custody of children almost always awarded to the mothers of the children? Explain your reactions, and discuss other kinds of arrangements that might prove equally satisfactory, if not better.
4. Discuss some of the pressures that create difficulties in second marriages, such as resistance of children to the new mate, unrealistic expectations of step-parents, and financial equity in treating both sets of children fairly.

# William Trevor

# *Teresa's Wedding*

---

*William Trevor was born in 1928 in Michelstown, County Cork, Ireland. He graduated from Trinity College in 1950 and has worked as an art teacher, a sculptor, and a copywriter for a London advertising agency. The publication of* The Old Boys *in 1964 signaled the emergence of a remarkable talent. In addition to numerous plays for television, radio, and the stage, Trevor has written many acclaimed novels and short story collections, including* The Love Department *(1966);* Angels at the Ritz *(1975), from which "Teresa's Wedding" was taken; and* Fools of Fortune *(1983). Trevor's stories are distinguished by their remarkably accurate rendering of interactions between people in groups, especially families, in Britain and Ireland.*

*The Republic of Ireland occupies all but the northeast corner of the island of Ireland, in the British Isles, and has a population of 3.5 million. Cork, founded in the seventh century, is the second-largest city in the Republic of Ireland. A treaty with Great Britain in 1922 partitioned Ireland into the Irish Free State and the six counties of Ulster in the northeast (whose population now numbers 1.5 million) and precipitated a civil war. The anti-treaty forces were identified with the Irish Republican Army (IRA), a nationalist organization that was defeated at the time but has continued to fight for the unification of Ireland. The ongoing conflict between Irish Roman Catholics and Ulster's Protestants stems from Henry VIII's attempt in 1541 to impose the Protestant Church of Ireland on the predominantly Catholic population. To this day, Ulster's Protestants and Catholics are divided over whether to remain under British rule or join the Republic of Ireland. In 1937, a new constitution was put forward, establishing the sovereign state of Ireland within the British Commonwealth. In 1949, the Republic of Ireland was proclaimed, and the country withdrew from the Commonwealth. The extent to which the lack of choices dramatized by Trevor's story is a fact of Irish life can be seen in the country's seventeen percent unemployment rate, one of the highest in western Europe. William Trevor is one of many prominent Irish writers along with George Bernard Shaw, William Butler Yeats, John Millington Synge, Sean O'Casey, James Joyce, Frank O'Connor, Samuel Beckett, and Brendan Behan, among others, whose works have permanently enriched the English language.*

The remains of the wedding-cake was on top of the piano in Swanton's lounge-bar, beneath a framed advertisement for Power's whiskey. Chas Flynn, the best man, had opened two packets of confetti: it lay thickly on the remains of the wedding-cake, on the surface of the bar and the piano, on the table and the two small chairs that the lounge-bar contained, and on the tattered green and red linoleum.

The wedding guests, themselves covered in confetti, stood in groups. Father Hogan, who had conducted the service in the Church of the Immaculate Conception, stood with Mrs. Atty, the mother of the bride, and Mrs. Cornish, the mother of the bridegroom, and Mrs. Tracy, a sister of Mrs. Atty's.

Mrs. Tracy was the stoutest of the three women, a farmer's widow who lived eight miles from the town. In spite of the jubilant nature of the occasion, she was dressed in black, a colour she had affected since the death of her husband three years ago. Mrs. Atty, bespectacled, with her grey hair in a bun, wore a flowered dress—small yellow and blue blooms that blended easily with the confetti. Mrs. Cornish was in pink, with a pink hat. Father Hogan, a big red-complexioned man, held a tumbler containing whiskey and water in equal measures; his companions sipped Winter's Tale sherry.

Artie Cornish, the bridegroom, drank stout with his friends Eddie Boland and Chas Flynn, who worked in the town's bacon factor, and Screw Doyle, so called because he served behind the counter in Phelan's hardware shop. Artie, who worked in a shop himself—Driscoll's Provisions and Bar—was a freckled man of twenty-eight, six years older than his bride. He was heavily built, his bulk encased now in a suit of navy-blue serge, similar to the suits that all the other men were wearing that morning in Swanton's lounge-bar. In the opinion of Mr. Driscoll, his employer, he was a conscientious shopman, with a good memory for where commodities were kept on the shelves. Customers occasionally found him slow.

The fathers of the bride and bridegroom, Mr. Atty and Mr. Cornish, were talking about greyhounds, keeping close to the bar. They shared a feeling of unease, caused by being in the lounge bar of Swanton's, with women present, on a Saturday morning. "Bring us two more big ones," Mr. Cornish requested of Kevin, a youth behind the bar, hoping that this addition to his consumption of whiskey would relax matters. They wore white carnations in the button-holes of their suits, and stiff white collars which were reddening their necks. Unknown to one another, they shared the same thought: a wish that the bride and groom would soon decide to bring the occasion to an end by going to prepare themselves for their journey to Cork on the half-one bus. Mr. Atty and Mr. Cornish, bald-headed men of fifty-three and fifty-five, had it in mind to spend the remainder of the day in Swanton's lounge-bar, celebrating in their particular way the union of their children.

The bride, who had been Teresa Atty and was now Teresa Cornish, had a round, pretty face and black, pretty hair, and was a month and a half pregnant. She stood in the corner of the lounge with her friends, Philomena Morrissey and Kitty Roche, both of whom had been brides-maids. All three of them were attired in their wedding finery, dresses they had feverishly worked on to get finished in time for the wedding. They planned to alter the dresses and have them dyed so that later on they could go to parties in them, even though parties were rare in the town.

7        "I hope you'll be happy, Teresa," Kitty Roche whispered. "I hope you'll be all right." She couldn't help giggling, even though she didn't want to. She giggled because she'd drunk a glass of gin and Kia-Ora orange,[1] which Screw Doyle had said would steady her. She'd been nervous in the church. She'd tripped twice on the walk down the aisle.

8        "You'll be marrying yourself one of these days," Teresa whispered, her cheeks still glowing after the excitement of the ceremony. "I hope you'll be happy too, Kit."

9        But Kitty Roche, who was asthmatic, did not believe she'd ever marry. She'd be like Miss Levis, the Protestant woman on the Cork road, who'd never got married because of tuberculosis. Or old Hannah Flood, who had a bad hip. And it wasn't just that no one would want to be saddled with a diseased wife: there was also the fact that the asthma caused a recurrent skin complaint on her face and neck and hands.

10       Teresa and Philomena drank glasses of Babycham,[2] and Kitty drank Kia-Ora with water instead of gin in it. They'd known each other all their lives. They'd been to the Presentation Nuns together, they'd taken First Communion together. Even when they'd left the Nuns, when Teresa had gone to work in the Medical Hall and Kitty Roche and Philomena in Keane's drapery, they'd continued to see each other almost every day.

11       "We'll think of you, Teresa," Philomena said. "We'll pray for you." Philomena, plump and pale-haired, had every hope of marrying and had even planned her dress, in light lemony lace, with a Limerick veil.[3] Twice in the last month she'd gone out with Des Foley the vet, and even if he was a few years older than he might be and had a car that smelt of cattle disinfectant, there was more to be said for Des Foley than for many another.

12       Teresa's two sisters, much older than Teresa, stood by the piano and the framed Power's advertisement, between the two windows of the lounge-bar. Agnes, in smart powder-blue, was tall and thin, the older of the two; Loretta, in brown, was small. Their own two marriages, eleven and nine years ago, had been consecrated by Father Hogan in the Church of the Immaculate Conception and celebrated afterwards in this same lounge-bar. Loretta had married a man who was no longer men-

---

[1] A soft drink.
[2] A weak alcoholic beverage containing champagne — "baby champagne."
[3] A veil made of lace from Limerick, Ireland.

tioned because he'd gone to England and had never come back. Agnes had married George Tobin, who was at present sitting outside the lounge-bar in a Ford Prefect in charge of his and Agnes's three small children. The Tobins lived in Cork now, George being the manager of a shoe-shop there. Loretta lived with her parents, like an unmarried daughter again.

"Sickens you," Agnes said. "She's only a kid, marrying a goop like     13
that. She'll be stuck in this dump of a town forever."

Loretta didn't say anything. It was well known that Agnes's own     14
marriage had turned out well: George Tobin was a teetotaller and had no interest in either horses or greyhounds. From where she stood Loretta could see him through the window, sitting patiently in the Ford Prefect, reading a comic to his children. Loretta's marriage had not been consummated.

"Well, though I've said it before I'll say it again," said Father Hogan.     15
"It's a great day for a mother."

Mrs. Atty and Mrs. Cornish politely agreed, without speaking. Mrs.     16
Tracy smiled.

"And for an aunt too, Mrs. Tracy. Naturally enough."     17

Mrs. Tracy smiled again. "A great day," she said.     18

"Ah, I'm happy for Teresa," Father Hogan said. "And for Artie, too,     19
Mrs. Cornish; naturally enough. Aren't they as fine a couple as ever stepped out of this town?"

"Are they leaving the town?" Mrs. Tracy asked, confusion breaking     20
in her face. "I thought Artie was fixed in Driscoll's."

"It's a manner of speaking, Mrs. Tracy," Father Hogan explained.     21
"It's a way of putting the thing. When I was marrying them this morning I looked down at their two faces and I said to myself, 'Isn't it great God gave them life?'"

The three women looked across the lounge, at Teresa standing with     22
her friends Philomena and Kitty Roche, and then at Artie, with Screw Doyle, Eddie Boland and Chas Flynn.

"He has a great career in front of him in Driscoll's," Father Hogan     23
pronounced. "Will Teresa remain on in the Medical Hall, Mrs. Atty?"

Mrs. Atty replied that her daughter would remain for a while in the     24
Medical Hall. It was Father Hogan who had persuaded Artie of his duty when Artie had hesitated. Mrs. Atty and Teresa had gone to him for advice, he'd spoken to Artie and to Mr. and Mrs. Cornish, and the matter had naturally not been mentioned on either side since.

"Will I get you another glassful, Father?" inquired Mrs. Tracy, hold-     25
ing out her hand for the priest's tumbler.

"Well, it isn't every day I'm honoured," said Father Hogan with his     26
smile, putting the tumbler into Mrs. Tracy's hand.

At the bar Mr. Atty and Mr. Cornish drank steadily on. In their corner     27
Teresa and her bridesmaids talked about weddings that had taken place in the Church of the Immaculate Conception in the past, how they had

stood by the railings of the church when they were children, excited by the finery and the men in serge suits. Teresa's sisters whispered, Agnes continuing about the inadequacy of the man Teresa had just married. Loretta whispered without actually forming words. She wished her sister wouldn't go on so because she didn't want to think about any of it, about what had happened to Teresa, and what would happen to her again tonight, in a hotel in Cork. She'd fainted when it had happened to herself, when he'd come at her like a farm animal. She'd fought like a mad thing.

28    It was noisier in the lounge-bar than it had been. The voices of the bridegroom's friends were raised; behind the bar young Kevin had switched on the wireless. *Take my hand,* cooed a soft male voice, *take my whole life too.*

29    "Bedad, there'll be no holding you tonight, Artie," Eddie Boland whispered thickly into the bridegroom's ear. He nudged Artie in the stomach with his elbow, spilling some Guinness. He laughed uproariously.

30    "We're following you in two cars," Screw Doyle said. "We'll be waiting in the double bed for you." Screw Doyle laughed also, striking the floor repeatedly with his left foot, which was a habit of his when excited. At a late hour the night before he'd told Artie that once, after a dance, he'd spent an hour in a field with the girl whom Artie had agreed to marry. "I had a great bloody ride of her," he'd confided.

31    "I'll have a word with Teresa," said Father Hogan, moving away from Teresa's mother, her aunt and Mrs. Cornish. He did not, however, cross the lounge immediately, but paused by the bar, where Mr. Cornish and Mr. Atty were. He put his empty tumbler on the bar itself, and Mr. Atty pushed it towards young Kevin, who at once refilled it.

32    "Well, it's a great day for a father," said Father Hogan. "Aren't they a tip-top credit to each other?"

33    "Who's that, Father?" inquired Mr. Cornish, his eyes a little bleary, sweat hanging from his cheeks.

34    Father Hogan laughed. He put his tumbler on the bar again, and Mr. Cornish pushed it towards young Kevin for another refill.

35    In their corner Philomena confided to Teresa and Kitty Roche that she wouldn't mind marrying Des Foley the vet. She'd had four glasses of Babycham. If he asked her this minute, she said, she'd probably say yes. "Is Chas Flynn nice?" Kitty Roche asked, squinting across at him.

36    On the wireless Petula Clark was singing "Downtown." Eddie Boland was whistling "Mother Macree."[4] "Listen, Screw," Artie said, keeping his voice low although it wasn't necessary. "Is that true? Did you go into a field with Teresa?"

37    Loretta watched while George Tobin in his Ford Prefect turned a page of the comic he was reading to his children. Her sister's voice

---

[4]Respectively, a popular song from the early 1960s and an old Irish folk song.

continued in its abuse of the town and its people, in particular the shopman who had got Teresa pregnant. Agnes hated the town and always had. She'd met George Tobin at a dance in Cork and had said to Loretta that in six months' time she'd be gone from the town for ever. Which was precisely what had happened, except that marriage had made her less nice than she'd been. She'd hated the town in a jolly way once, laughing over it. Now she hardly laughed at all.

"Look at him," she was saying. "I doubt he knows how to hold a knife and fork." 38

Loretta ceased her observation of her sister's husband through the window and regarded Artie Cornish instead. She looked away from him immediately because his face, so quickly replacing the face of George Tobin, had caused in her mind a double image which now brutally persisted. She felt a sickness in her stomach, and closed her eyes and prayed. But the double image remained: George Tobin and Artie Cornish coming at her sisters like two farmyard animals and her sisters fighting to get away. "Dear Jesus," she whispered to herself. "Dear Jesus, help me." 39

"Sure it was only a bit of gas," Screw Doyle assured Artie. "Sure there was no harm done, Artie." 40

In no way did Teresa love him. She had been aware of that when Father Hogan had arranged the marriage, and even before that, when she'd told her mother that she thought she was pregnant and had then mentioned Artie Cornish's name. Artie Cornish was much the same as his friends: you could be walking along a road with Screw Doyle or Artie Cornish and you could hardly tell the difference. There was nothing special about Artie Cornish, except that he always added up the figures twice when he was serving you in Driscoll's. There was nothing bad about him either, any more than there was anything bad about Eddie Boland or Chas Flynn or even Screw Doyle. She'd said privately to Father Hogan that she didn't love him or feel anything for him one way or the other: Father Hogan had replied that in the circumstances all that line of talk was irrelevant.

When she was at the Presentation Convent Teresa had imagined her wedding, and even the celebration in this very lounge-bar. She had imagined everything that had happened that morning, and the things that were happening still. She had imagined herself standing with her bridesmaids as she was standing now, her mother and her aunt drinking sherry, Agnes and Loretta being there too, and other people, and music. Only the bridegroom had been mysterious, some faceless, bodiless presence, beyond imagination. From conversations she had had with Philomena and Kitty Roche, and with her sisters, she knew that they had imagined in a similar way. Yet Agnes had settled for George Tobin because George Tobin was employed in Cork and could take her away from the town. Loretta, who had been married for a matter of weeks, was going to become a nun. 41

Artie ordered more bottles of stout from young Kevin. He didn't want to catch the half-one bus and have to sit beside her all the way to Cork. He didn't want to go to the Lee Hotel when they could just as easily have remained in the town, when he could just as easily have gone in to Driscoll's tomorrow and continued as before. It would have been different if Screw Doyle hadn't said he'd been in a field with her: you could pretend a bit on the bus, and in the hotel, just to make the whole thing go. You could pretend like you'd been pretending ever since Father Hogan had laid down the law, you could make the best of it like Father Hogan had said.

42     He handed a bottle of stout to Chas Flynn and one to Screw Doyle and another to Eddie Boland. He'd ask her about it on the bus. He'd repeat what Screw Doyle had said and ask her if it was true. For all he knew the child she was carrying was Screw Doyle's child and would be born with Screw Doyle's thin nose, and everyone in the town would know when they looked at it. His mother had told him when he was sixteen never to trust a girl, never to get involved, because he'd be caught in the end. He'd get caught because he was easy-going, because he didn't possess the smartness of Screw Doyle and some of the others. "Sure, you might as well marry Teresa as anyone else," his father had said after Father Hogan had called to see them about the matter. His mother had said things would never be the same between them again.

Eddie Boland sat down at the piano and played "Mother Macree," causing Agnes and Loretta to move to the other side of the lounge-bar. In the motor-car outside the Tobin children asked their father what the music was for.

43     "God go with you, girl," Father Hogan said to Teresa, motioning Kitty Roche and Philomena away. "Isn't it a grand thing that's happened, Teresa?" His red-skinned face, with the shiny false teeth so evenly arrayed in it, was close to hers. For a moment she thought he might kiss her, which of course was ridiculous, Father Hogan kissing anyone, even at a wedding celebration.

44     "It's a great day for all of us, girl."

45     When she'd told her mother, her mother said it made her feel sick in her stomach. Her father hit her on the side of the face. Agnes came down specially from Cork to try and sort the matter out. It was then that Loretta had first mentioned becoming a nun.

46     "I want to say two words," said Father Hogan, still standing beside her, but now addressing everyone in the lounge-bar. "Come over here alongside us, Artie. Is there a drop in everyone's glass?"

47     Artie moved across the lounge-bar, with his glass of stout. Mr. Cornish told young Kevin to pour out a few more measures. Eddie Boland stopped playing the piano.

48     "It's only this," said Father Hogan. "I want us all to lift our glasses to Artie and Teresa. May God go with you, the pair of you," he said, lifting his own glass.

"Health, wealth and happiness," proclaimed Mr. Cornish from the 49
bar.

"And an early night," shouted Screw Doyle. "Don't forget to draw 50
the curtains, Artie."

They stood awkwardly, not holding hands, not even touching. Teresa 51
watched while her mother drank the remains of her sherry, and while
her aunt drank and Mrs. Cornish drank. Agnes's face was disdainful, a
calculated reply to the coarseness of Screw Doyle's remarks. Loretta was
staring ahead of her, concentrating her mind on her novitiate. A quick
flush passed over the roughened countenance of Kitty Roche. Philomena
laughed, and all the men in the lounge-bar, except Father Hogan,
laughed.

"That's sufficient of that talk," Father Hogan said with contrived 52
severity. "May you meet happiness halfway," he added, suitably altering
his intonation. "The pair of you, Artie and Teresa."

Noise broke out again after that. Father Hogan shook hands with 53
Teresa and then with Artie. He had a funeral at half-past three, he said:
he'd better go and get his dinner inside him.

"Good-bye, Father," Artie said. "Thanks for doing the job." 54

"God bless the pair of you," said Father Hogan, and went away. 55

"We should be going for the bus," Artie said to her. "It wouldn't do 56
to miss the old bus."

"No, it wouldn't." 57

"I'll see you down there. You'll have to change your clothes." 58

"Yes." 59

"I'll come the way I am." 60

"You're fine the way you are, Artie." 61

He looked at the stout in his glass and didn't raise his eyes from it 62
when he spoke again. "Did Screw Doyle take you into a field, Teresa?"

He hadn't meant to say it then. It was wrong to come out with it like 63
that, in the lounge-bar, with the wedding-cake still there on the piano,
and Teresa still in her wedding-dress, and confetti everywhere. He knew
it was wrong even before the words came out; he knew that the stout
had angered and befuddled him.

"Sorry," he said. "Sorry, Teresa." 64

She shook her head. It didn't matter: it was only to be expected that a 65
man you didn't love and who didn't love you would ask a question like
that at your wedding celebration.

"Yes," she said. "Yes, he did." 66

"He told me. I thought he was codding. I wanted to know." 67

"It's your baby, Artie. The other thing was years ago." 68

He looked at her. Her face was flushed, her eyes had tears in them. 69

"I had too much stout," he said. 70

They stood where Father Hogan had left them, drawn away from 71
their wedding guests. Not knowing where else to look, they looked
together at Father Hogan's black back as he left the lounge-bar, and then
at the perspiring, naked heads of Mr. Cornish and Mr. Atty by the bar.

72    At least they had no illusions, she thought. Nothing worse could happen than what had happened already, after Father Hogan had laid down the law. She wasn't going to get a shock like Loretta had got. She wasn't going to go sour like Agnes had gone when she'd discovered that it wasn't enough just to marry a man for a purpose, in order to escape from a town. Philomena was convincing herself that she'd fallen in love with an elderly vet, and if she got any encouragement Kitty Roche would convince herself that she was mad about anyone at all.

73    For a moment as Teresa stood there, the last moment before she left the lounge-bar, she felt that she and Artie might make some kind of marriage together because there was nothing that could be destroyed, no magic or anything else. He could ask her the question he had asked, while she stood there in her wedding dress: he could ask her and she could truthfully reply, because there was nothing special about the occasion, or the lounge-bar all covered in confetti.

## Evaluating the Text

1. What events have led to Teresa and Artie's wedding? How do each of the families feel about the forthcoming marriage? How does the point of view from which Trevor tells the story encourage the reader to look at the situation objectively while understanding the feelings of the people involved?
2. How would you characterize Teresa and Artie's relationship? How do their feelings toward each other differ?
3. What is the significance of Screw Doyle's past intimacy with Teresa? How do Artie's feelings toward Teresa change when he learns what happened? How does Teresa's response to Artie's accusation change their expectations about getting married?
4. How do Teresa's expectations about marriage contrast with those of the priest, her and Artie's parents, and her sisters and friends?
5. How do the details Trevor uses in characterizing Father Hogan suggest his attitude toward him and toward the role religion plays in people's lives?
6. How do the details Trevor supplies in describing the wedding cake, setting, and songs played on the radio all contribute to establishing the mood of the story?
7. Evaluate the effectiveness with which Trevor presents a broad spectrum of opinions on marriage. Is Trevor sympathetic toward Teresa's predicament? How does the story dramatize the problems of who to marry in an Irish country village? What conclusions might you draw about the closed culture of rural Ireland, the chances of meeting different people, and the need to make a marriage from the available choices? Why would all these factors tend to produce a realistic rather than a romantic view of marriage?

## Exploring Different Perspectives

1. In what way is personal life subordinated to the community in both the small village in Ireland and among Guatemalan Indians (see Rigoberta Menchu's "Birth Ceremonies")? Explore the similarities and differences between the two cultures and the role religion plays in both.

2. Compare the attitudes toward sex in both this story and in Francine du Plessix Gray's account in "Sex and Birth." What culturally based differences between Ireland and Russia can you observe?
3. To what extent is the personal subordinated to communal expectations both in Trevor's story and in Bruce Dollar's "Child Care in China"?

## Extending Viewpoints through Writing

1. What does this story add to your understanding of the pressures couples experience in traditional Irish Catholic culture? To what extent are these pressures similar to or different from pressures experienced by young couples in other cultures?
2. Discuss a time when you were faced with a social or cultural obligation that went against what you personally felt. What did you do, and how did you feel about it?
3. Are you aware of a marriage that started out as Teresa and Artie's did but developed into a much better relationship than one might expect in Teresa and Artie's case?
4. Describe a wedding you attended or witnessed or in which you participated. How was the couple different from or similar to Teresa and Artie in Trevor's story? Describe the event in vivid detail and what made it memorable.

# Francine du Plessix Gray

# *Sex and Birth*

---

*Francine du Plessix Gray introduces us to a new generation of Soviet women battling the archaic Russian bureaucracy, a scandalously inefficient health system, and outmoded attitudes toward sex in this chapter, "Sex and Birth," from* Soviet Women; Walking the Tightrope *(1990). du Plessix Gray's previous books include* Lovers and Tyrants *(1976),* World Without End *(1981), and* Adam and Eve and the City *(1987). She has received the National Catholic Book Award and the National Magazine Award for Best Reporting.*

*A universal health-care system provides free medical care for all citizens in the U.S.S.R. Although the standard of medical care is lower than that in the West, as du Plessix Gray discusses, life expectancy ranges from sixty-four for men to seventy-four years for women. The infant mortality rate averages approximately twenty-five per thousand. There is a ratio of approximately one physician for every 245 people. Whereas medical care is adequate in the major cities, ordinary medicines are not always available, and in the winter of 1990, the United States and other countries air-lifted medical supplies to offset endemic shortages.*

1      The most startling example of *glasnost* I witnessed during my stays in the Soviet Union occurred at a doctor's office in the same city — Tbilisi, Georgia.

2      It occurred in the office of gynecologist Archil Khomassuridze, one of the angriest of the many angry citizens I have recently met in the Soviet Union. The doctor is indignant because he has long fought a futile crusade to establish efficient family planning programs throughout the Soviet Union. He is enraged by the officials in Moscow's Ministry of Health who until recently refused to disseminate any birth control information, arguing that such measures would slow down the nation's birth rate. He is exasperated because until the Gorbachev era, the prudishness imposed on the Soviet press forbade the use of such fundamental words as "menstruation" or "prostitution." Such taboos, in Dr. Khomassuridze's words, have maintained "a level of national ignorance relating to all sexual matters equaled only by the most backward countries — Iraq, Iran."

*(For further background on the U.S.S.R., see pp. 25–26 and on Eastern Europe see p. 294.)

Dr. Khomassuridze had already startled me by stating his estimate of ₃ the amount of abortions performed in the Soviet Union—the highest rate of abortions in the world, *between five and eight abortions for every birth.*

And then, still sitting at his desk—two Georgian journalists were ₄ also attending the meeting—the doctor suddenly accused leading members of his country's Ministry of Health of being *prestupniki,* "criminals," for having allowed abortions to proliferate by opposing birth control programs. "They should be serving time," he said, "for the harm they've done to women's health!"

My Georgian colleagues looked startled, started taking a few notes. ₅ The doctor rose from his desk, walked toward me, and bent over my own notes, making sure that I was spelling the "criminals'" names correctly. "Petrovsky," he enunciated slowly, "Boris Vassilevitch Petrovsky, our former Minister of Health—O—V—S—K—Y—now you've got it right."

He sat down at his desk and repeated: "Criminals, murderers! And ₆ they're still in power up in Moscow, continuing to ruin our national health programs . . . they should serve time for ruining the lives of millions of our women!"

Dr. Khomassuridze is a handsome Georgian in his middle forties who ₇ cares deeply about women's well-being, about the birth of healthier infants, about the need to curb the population explosion on our planet. And sitting in his office in Tbilisi, still in the presence of several of his compatriots, he went on to tell me how he had broken his government's laws for the sake of Soviet women's health:

"Our state laws demand that we write out a *napravlenie,* an official ₈ document, to register every contraceptive device or treatment a woman receives. Well, I decided that this law is harmful in a country as obscurantist as ours. I decided to treat women without this document, anonymously, without even asking their names. We made announcements in the paper to advertise our services, and here we are! No one's punished us yet."

Khomassuridze is a man with a passion for statistics on all matters of ₉ procreation. And after relating his acts of civil disobedience he went on to give me some even more detailed figures on the absence of contraceptive use in the Soviet Union.

"Guess how many women in this country are using some form of ₁₀ birth control—I'm including pills, condoms, IUD's, rhythm, any method available? Only 18 percent. But of this 18 percent, guess how many use decent contemporary methods, the pill, IUD's? Only 5 percent. That's the lowest in the world, lower than Bhutan or India. And what's that percentage right here in Georgia? Hold your breath . . . only 3 percent.

"When will those idiots in Moscow realize that the damage done to ₁₁ our women by abortion is quite equal to the harm done by narcotic addiction, alcoholism," he continued indignantly. "If women knew the harm done them by abortion they would simply abstain from all sexual life, become like nuns. . . ."

12    He leaned forward, angrily striking his desk. "Do you really want to know why so many of our doctors oppose birth control? In many areas of the Soviet Union—Georgia is one of them—much shame is still attached to abortion, and our doctors oppose birth control because they make so much money out of *criminal* abortions performed at home . . .

13    "Bring us our treasures," he curtly commanded one of his interns. Like many lonely crusaders, Khomassuridze has a stern, dictatorial streak. And his assistant, a docile young doctor who addressed his superior with filial deference, immediately presented me with a drawerful of oral contraceptives from East and West Germany, Holland, Hungary, Denmark, Great Britain, Sweden, Norway, Finland.

14    "Foreign aid," Khomassuridze commented dryly, "charitable gifts from abroad. How could you expect us to make decent medications of this kind in the Soviet Union, when we are so backward that half of our condoms still break upon first use? Ah, *Gospozha* Gray, our government is barely beginning to learn what human needs are."

15    Archil Khomassuridze, a very cosmopolitan, multilingual native of Georgia, won the Komsomol Prize for his doctoral dissertation (it is the highest national honor available to any new Doctor of Science) and was the youngest candidate ever to receive that award. He worked for several years as chief gynecologist at a Moscow hospital before returning to his native Tbilisi, where he had been offered the directorship of the Zhordania Institute for Human Reproduction, then a nearly defunct clinic using antiquated methods of curing infertility. Since 1983, Khomassuridze has transformed it into one of the most visionary institutions in the U.S.S.R., and the only Soviet medical center that is a full-fledged member of the World Health Organization.

16    The original headquarters of the Zhordania Institute, a ramshackle three-floor structure a few blocks from Tbilisi's main square, left much to be desired. Khomassuridze took a measure that would have been unthinkable before Gorbachev's *perestroika:* He entered into a joint venture with West German scientists to build new facilities for his center, for which the Germans will provide all building material and technological equipment; in return, Khomassuridze will offer free treatment to all patients sent him by his German colleagues. He will be repaying his debt, in effect, by man-hours of labor, a commodity far cheaper in the Soviet Union than in Western Europe.

17    Khomassuridze's dedication to curing infertility is as passionate as his crusade to lower the nations's appalling abortion rate; he is one of the first scientists in the U.S.S.R. to have experimented with *in vitro* fertilization and artificial insemination. Yet however advanced his techniques, many cultural handicaps still stand in his way. One such obstacle is the widespread machismo of Soviet men, who have traditionally blamed women in any instance of childlessness, overlooking the possibility that men could be at fault.

"Statistics tell us that 60 percent of all infertility is caused by the male [18] partner," Khomassuridze says, "but try to get the average Soviet male to have a sperm count! Easier to teach a bear to thread a needle. Yet another double standard of sexist behavior, our men simply continue to torture their women with guilt feelings for being barren . . ."

National machismo is accrued by the Soviets' deep-rooted puritan- [19] ism, which, according to Khomassuridze, also accounts for phenomenal rates of female frigidity and male impotence. "Do you know that some 70 percent of our women have never had an orgasm? And that over half of the Soviet women polled outrightly state that they detest sexual contact? How can it be otherwise, since parents are embarrassed to tell their young the most basic fundamentals of sexuality, and our school system remains equally silent?" ("In your U.S.A.," he added admiringly, "the rate of female frigidity is only 34 percent.")

Khomassuridze went on to deplore the dearth of basic commodities [20] for female hygiene in his country. There are no sanitary tampons or napkins to be found in the U.S.S.R.; women must resort to wads of cotton, or, on those very frequent occasions when pharmacies run out of cotton, to carefully saved cotton rags. Khomassuridze has begged his "charitable Western friends" for ton loads of Modess and Tampax, and distributes them as prodigally throughout Georgia as he distributes contraceptives.

"It is ridiculous that women should lug huge packages of cotton [21] everywhere, to work, to theater, on trains, and where do they have to throw it but in the toilet; no wonder our Soviet plumbing system is constantly, catastrophically clogged . . . well, perhaps one of the finest results of our *glasnost* will be the manufacture of Tampax."

## Evaluating the Text

1. How does this interview illustrate the new Russian policy of openness or *glasnost*?
2. What factors does Dr. Khomassuridze feel are responsible for producing "a level of national ignorance related to all sexual matters"? What form does this ignorance take?
3. How would you characterize Dr. Khomassuridze? What do the laws that he breaks reveal about Soviet cultural attitudes toward sex and birth?
4. What insights does this article give you about how difficult it is for an individual to make changes that go against the bureaucracy? How would the intractable nature of Soviet bureaucracy illustrate the need for policies of *perestroika*?
5. According to Dr. Khomassuridze, why do physicians in the Soviet province of Georgia have an interest in discouraging women from using contraceptives?
6. How did Gorbachev's policy of *perestroika* bring much-needed reforms to upgrade Soviet scientific facilities?
7. According to Dr. Khomassuridze, what part does the national machismo of Soviet men play in the attitude of Soviet women toward sex and sexual

matters? For example, how is this attitude related to the high rate of female frigidity and high rate of male impotence?

8. What specific details did you find most effective in dramatizing the state of female health care in the Soviet Union? For example, what sanitary products taken for granted in America are unavailable?

9. To what extent would you characterize Dr. Khomassuridze as a reliable and credible source? Does his testimony seem to be sufficient to justify conclusions about the entire system of health care for women in the Soviet Union?

## Exploring Different Perspectives

1. What unexpected similarities can you discover between male attitudes toward women and sex in Ireland as depicted in William Trevor's "Teresa's Wedding" and national machismo in Russia described by du Plessix Gray? What are the underlying cultural assumptions responsible for these attitudes?

2. Why would the abortion policy in the Soviet Union be unacceptable in the Guatemalan Indian culture described by Rigoberta Menchu in "Birth Ceremonies"?

## Extending Viewpoints through Writing

1. Because du Plessix Gray is an outsider interviewing an insider, readers must be careful to discover if she brings any underlying cultural assumptions to the interview that might alter its direction and focus. What is the relationship between du Plessix Gray as an interviewer and her subject, Dr. Khomassuridze?

2. Which of the facts about what life is like for Russian women would be the hardest to accept? Discuss your reactions.

3. In an essay, explore some major differences between America and the Soviet Union as regards national attitudes toward health care, contraception, or any of the other issues discussed in du Plessix Gray's article.

4. As a reporter, du Plessix Gray could have presented her information in a report (as Bruce Dollar does in "Child Care in China"), using information she gained from the interviews with Dr. Khomassuridze. Why do you think she chose to present her information retaining the interview format? After reading Dollar's article to see how he uses information he obtained in interviews, write a short expository essay on health care in the Soviet Union based on du Plessix Gray's interviews with Dr. Khomassuridze.

# Boris Yeltsin

# *Childhood in Russia*

---

*Born in the Russian heartland, near the Ural Mountains, and raised in a communal hut with twenty other families, Boris Yeltsin experienced the hardships of the Soviet system firsthand. His success as an engineer attracted the local Communist Party, and he was appointed district representative. In this post, he was instrumental in alleviating chronic food shortages throughout the region. Mikhail Gorbachev then brought Yeltsin to Moscow as a member of the party elite. Yeltsin's initial support of Gorbachev's* perestroika *program gave way to criticism so severe that he was expelled from the politburo and the party. Yeltsin's comeback began when he won a seat in the National Legislature. The following year, Yeltsin was elected President of the Russian Republic, the largest of the fifteen Soviet Republics. Yeltsin has proposed a "500-day" plan designed to turn the economy of the Russian Republic into a free-market system. "Childhood in Russia" is taken from Yeltsin's 1990* Against the Grain: An Autobiography, *translated by Michael Glenny.*

*The U.S.S.R. came into existence as a result of the Russian Revolution of 1917, in which the Bolsheviks, under Vladimir Ilyich Lenin, seized control of the government from the Czars (derived from the Roman Caesar), who had ruled Russia since the seventeenth century. The U.S.S.R. is the largest country in the world, with the third-largest population. The policy of* glasnost *("openness"), permitting criticism of the government, was introduced by Mikhail Gorbachev after he became General Secretary of the Party in 1985. One of the first results of the changed attitude of the Soviet leadership was the 1987 treaty between the United States and the Soviet Union eliminating intermediate-range nuclear missiles. The new policy of* glasnost *set in motion a dramatic restructuring of the Soviet Union as the Baltic states (Latvia, Estonia, Lithuania) moved toward total political and economic independence from Moscow. The same demands for autonomy in Soviet bloc countries (including Poland, Czechoslovakia, and Hungary) ushered in a period of political and social turmoil that ended forty years of the Communist Party's domination. The historic events in Eastern Europe set the stage for the dismantling of the Berlin wall, which had divided the city since 1961, and the dramatic reunification of East and West Germany. Paradoxically, in the same year (1989) that saw the U.S.S.R.'s first elections, lives of the Russian people worsened dramatically, as deteriorating economic circumstances brought about massive unemployment, food rationing, and ever longer lines for the necessities of life.*

1    I was born on February 1, 1931, in the village of Butko in the Talitsky district of Sverdlovsk province, where all my forebears had lived. They had plowed the land, sown wheat, and passed their lives like all other country people. Among the people in our village there were the Yeltsins, my father's family, and the Starygins, my mother's family. My father married my mother there, and soon I made my appearance in the world —their first child.

2    My mother used to tell me the story of what happened at my baptism. The little church, with its priest, was the only one for the whole district, which consisted of several villages. The birth rate for the area was quite high, but even so the baptismal service was held only once a month. Consequently, that day was a busy one for the priest, and the church was filled to bursting with parents, babies, relatives, and friends. The baptism was conducted in the most primitive fashion: There was a tub full of holy liquid, water seasoned with something or other, in which each baby was completely immersed. The squalling infant was then chistened and given a name, which was entered in the parish register. And of course, as was the custom in villages all over Russia, the parents offered the priest a glass of home-brewed beer, moonshine, or vodka — whatever they could afford.

3    Since my turn did not come until the afternoon, the priest, having drunk many toasts, could barely stand. When my mother, Klavdia Vasilievna, and my father, Nikolai Ignatievich, handed me to him, the priest dropped me into the tub and, being drawn into an argument with a member of the congregation, forgot to take me out. At first, my parents, who were standing at some distance from the baptismal font, didn't know what had happened. When they finally realized what was going on, my mother screamed, leapt forward, and fished me out from somewhere at the bottom of the tub.

4    They then shook the water out of me. The priest was not particularly worried. He said, "Well, if he can survive such an ordeal, it means he's a good, tough lad — and I name him Boris."

5    Thus I became Boris Nikolayevich. I won't say that after that I developed any special affinity for religion; of course not.

6    My childhood was passed during hard times: very bad harvests and no food. We were all forced to join a collective farm — and all of us were treated like peasants. To make matters worse, gangs of outlaws roamed at large, and almost every day we saw shootouts, murders, and robbery.

7    We lived in near poverty, in a small house with one cow. We did have a horse, but when it died, we were left without an animal to pull the plow. In 1935, the situation became more unbearable — even our cow died — and my grandfather, who was over sixty, was forced to go from

house to house, building stoves. Besides being a plowman, he was also a carpenter and cabinetmaker—a complete jack-of-all-trades.

In order to save the family, my father decided to leave the farm to   8
find work on a construction site. It was then Stalin's so-called period of industrialization. He knew that construction workers would be needed for the building of a potash plant at Berezniki in the neighboring province of Perm, so he moved the family there. We all harnessed ourselves to the cart, loaded it with our few possessions, and set off for the railway station—itself a distance of twenty miles.

After we arrived at Berezniki and my father signed on at the con-   9
struction site as a laborer, we were housed in one of the communal huts typical of that time—which, to this day, are still to be found in a few places—built of clapboard, through which drafts whistled relentlessly. The hut had a central corridor and twenty small rooms, naturally without any modern conveniences; there was only an outdoor toilet and water drawn from a well. We were given a few sticks of furniture, and we bought a goat to supply us with milk. My brother and my sister, the youngest, had already been born by then. The six of us, including the goat, slept on the floor, huddled together. From the age of six I was in charge of the household. This meant looking after the younger children —rocking my sister in her cradle and keeping an eye on my brother to see that he didn't misbehave. My other domestic chores were boiling potatoes, washing the dishes, and fetching water from the well.

While my father labored on the building site, my mother, a gentle   10
and kind woman by nature, would help relatives and neighbors by sewing clothes. Every night she would sit down with her sewing—never taking money for her work. She was grateful if someone gave her half a loaf of bread or some other morsel of food.

My father was rough and quick-tempered, just like my grandfather.   11
No doubt they passed these characteristics on to me. My parents constantly argued about me. My father's chief instrument for teaching good behavior was the strap, and he walloped me good and proper for any lapses. Whatever happened in our neighborhood—if a neighbor's apple tree had been robbed or if someone played a nasty trick on the German teacher in school—my father would not say a word but would reach for the strap. My mother would weep and beg him not to touch me. But he would firmly shut the door and tell me to lie down. I would pull up my shirt and lower my trousers. He would lay into me with great thoroughness. I always clenched my teeth and did not make a sound, which infuriated him; then my mother would burst in, snatch the strap away from him, pushing him aside and standing between us. She always defended me.

My father was an inventor, and he was always working on a new   12
idea. One of his ambitions was to invent a machine that would lay bricks. He would sketch it out, rethink it, make calculations, and then produce another set of drawings; it was a kind of will-o'-the-wisp that he was

perpetually chasing. Unfortunately, no one has yet invented such a machine, although even now whole research institutes rack their brains over it. He would constantly describe to me what his machine would be like and how it would work; how it would mix the mortar, lay the bricks, clean off the surface mortar, and move forward. He had worked it all out in his head and drawn the general plan, but he never managed to realize his idea.

13      We lived in that crowded wooden hut for ten years. Strange as it may seem, the people who lived under those conditions somehow managed to be good, friendly neighbors, especially when one considers that there was no sound insulation. If there was a party in the rooms — a birthday or a wedding — everyone could hear it. There was an old wind-up gramophone with only two or three records, and these were shared by the whole hut; I can still remember one song in particular: "Shchors the Red Commander marches on beneath the standard . . ." which the whole hut used to sing. Conversations, quarrels, rows, secrets, laughter —the whole hut could hear everything, and everyone knew everyone else's business.

14      Perhaps it is because I can remember to this day how hard our life was then that I so hate those communal huts. Winter was worst of all. There was nowhere to hide from the cold. Since we had no warm clothes, we would huddle up to the nanny goat to keep warm. We children survived on her milk. She was also our salvation throughout the war.

15      We all earned money on the side. Every summer my mother and I would go out to a nearby collective farm. We would be allotted several acres of meadowland, and we scythed the grass, stacked it, and prepared the hay, half of which went to the collective farm and the other half to us. We would then sell our half and buy bread at exorbitant prices.

16      That was how my childhood was spent. It was a fairly joyless time. There were never any sweets, delicacies, or anything of that sort; we had only one aim in life — to survive.

17      Despite these hardships, I always stood out from the other students —especially because of my energy and drive. From first grade on, I was elected class leader, even though I went to several different schools. I did well at my studies and got top marks in my exams. But my behavior was less praiseworthy. In all my years of school I was the ringleader, always devising some mischief. In fifth grade, for instance, I persuaded the whole class to jump out the first-floor window, and when our unpopular teacher came back, the classroom was empty. She immediately went to the watchman at the main entrance, who told her that no one had left the building. We had hidden in a small yard beside the school. When we returned to the classroom we were given a zero for the day. We protested. We said, "Punish us for our bad behavior, but test us on the lesson — we know it." The headmaster arrived, organized a special class, and questioned us for about two hours. We had learned everything by

heart, and all of us, even the weak pupils, answered every question correctly. In the end, the zeroes were canceled, although we were given the lowest possible mark for behavior.

Another of our adventures took place at the local stream, the Zyr- 18 yanka. In the spring, it would overflow its banks and become a river, and logs were floated down it. I invented a game to see who could run across floating logs to the far bank. The timber tended to flow in a fairly tight mass, so that if you judged it carefully there was a chance of being able to get across — although to do so you needed to be extremely skillful. Step on a log and if it gave the slightest sign of rolling over and you delayed for a second, you would be under water. So you had to move really fast from one log to another, keeping your balance all the time and leaping briskly in order to reach the far bank. The slightest miscalculation and it was into the icy water, with nothing but logs above you, between which you would have to try to push your head and gulp a lungful of air, not sure if you would come out alive.

We also used to have fights, neighborhood against neighborhood, 19 with between sixty and a hundred boys at a time fighting with sticks, cudgels, or fists. I used to take part in these fights, although I always got clobbered. When two solid walls of opponents clashed head-on, however strong you might be, you would always end up with several bumps on your head. I achieved my broken nose, like a boxer's, when someone whacked me with the shaft of a cart. I fell, everything went black, and I thought it was the end. But I came to my senses and was carried home. There were no fatalities in these fights, because although we fought enthusiastically, we observed certain limits.

I was expelled from school once. It happened at my primary school 20 graduation. About six hundred people were gathered in the assembly hall — parents, teachers, and pupils — in an atmosphere of cheerfulness and elation. Everyone was solemnly handed his or her diploma. Everything was going according to plan, when I suddenly stood up and asked permission to speak. My exam results had been excellent, nothing but top marks in every subject, and for that reason I was allowed up on the stage. Everyone thought that I would simply say a few gracious words. Naturally I had some kind words to say to those teachers who had given us valuable instruction that would help us in our lives and who had developed in us the habits of reading and thinking. But then I declared that our homeroom teacher had no right to teach children because she crippled them mentally and psychologically.

That awful woman might hit you with a heavy ruler, she might stand 21 you in the corner, she might humiliate a boy in front of a girl. She even made us clean her house. Once, the class had to collect food scraps from all over the district to feed her pig. It was endless, and some of the children refused to oblige her, but others submitted.

Briefly I described how she mocked her pupils, destroyed their self- 22 confidence, and did everything possible to humiliate every one of us — I went for her tooth and nail. There was an uproar. The whole event was ruined.

23     The next day the school board sent for my father to tell him my diploma was being withdrawn and instead I was to be given a so-called wolf's ticket: a little scrap of white paper that testified to my having completed the required seven years of primary schooling but stated below that I was deprived of the right to acquire a secondary education anywhere in the USSR. My father came home furious and reached for the strap—but at that moment, for the first time, I gripped him by the arm and said, "That's enough. From now on I'm going to educate myself." Never again was I made to stand in the corner all night, and no one ever took the strap to me again.

24     I refused to accept the decision of the school board and took my case up the education hierarchy: first to the district and then to the city education department. I learned for the first time what a local party committee was. I succeeded in getting a commission of inquiry set up, which investigated the work of that teacher and dismissed her from the school. She got exactly what she deserved, and I got my diploma back, although under the heading "Discipline," the word "unsatisfactory" glared out from the line of otherwise perfect grades.

25     I decided not to go back to that school and instead entered the eighth grade at Sverdlovsk's Pushkin School, of which I retain the fondest memories. The staff was excellent; and in Angonina Kohonina we had a superb homeroom teacher.

26     It was then that I began participating in sports. I was fascinated by volleyball and was prepared to play it endlessly. I liked the way the ball obeyed me, that I could return even the most difficult volley. At the same time I took up skiing, gymnastics, decathlon, boxing, and wrestling; I wanted to try my hand at them all, to do absolutely everything well. In the end, volleyball prevailed, and I started playing it seriously. I kept a ball with me all the time, even when I went to bed, when I'd sleep with my hand resting on it. As soon as I woke up I would start practicing by myself—spinning the ball on one finger or bouncing it off the wall and the floor. But because I was missing two fingers on my left hand, I had difficulty catching a ball, and I worked out my own unique method of catching.

27     This is the story of how I lost my two fingers: The Second World War had begun, and some of us who were too young to go to the front made our own pistols and rifles and even a cannon. We decided to steal some grenades in order to learn what was inside them. I volunteered to break into the local church, which was being used as an ammunition dump. That night I crept through three layers of barbed wire, and while the sentry was on the other side of the building, I filed through the mesh on a window and climbed inside. There I took two RGD-33 hand grenades with fuses and managed to make my way back unharmed (the sentry would have fired without warning). We went to a forest about forty

miles away, and this time I volunteered to take the grenades apart. I told the other boys to take cover a hundred yards off; then I put the grenade on a stone, knelt down, and hit it with a hammer. I didn't realize I had to remove the fuse. There was an explosion — and two of my fingers were mangled. The other boys were unharmed. I kept losing consciousness while they took me to town. Gangrene set in. The hospital surgeons cut off the two fingers.

Every summer during my student days I worked to earn pocket money, and I also organized long class hikes. Each trip had a special objective: to find the source of a river, or to get to the mountains. The expeditions usually involved trekking several several hundred miles with knapsacks and living in the forest for several weeks.

The summer after ninth grade, we decided to find the source of the river Yaiva. We spent a long time climbing up through the forest, knowing that the source was somewhere near the crest of the Urals. The food we had taken with us was soon gone, and we lived on what we could find in the forest, mushrooms and berries. The Urals forest is very fertile; one can survive there for a considerable time. Far from any roads, we tramped for a long time through the virgin woodland. Occasionally we came across a little hut used by hunters, where we would spend the night, but more often we built our own brushwood shelter or simply slept in the open.

We did at last find the source of the river — a spring of natural hydrogen sulfide. Turning back, we descended a few miles to the first village, by which time we were pretty worn out. We knew we needed a boat to travel farther. We collected whatever each of us could offer — a knapsack, a shirt, a hat — more or less everything we had to trade for a boat. Then we went to a little cottage and gave our possessions to the owner, in exchange for a small wooden flat-bottomed boat. In this boat we floated downstream; we no longer had the strength to walk. As we were floating along, we suddenly saw a cave in the hillside above us. We decided to stop and explore it. The cave led us on and on, until it suddenly opened out and brought us to a point somewhere deep in the forest. We scouted around but could not figure out where we were. We were lost, and we had lost our boat too. We wandered around for almost a week. We had brought nothing with us from the boat, and since the region turned out to be swampy, with nothing but stunted saplings and undergrowth, it provided us with barely enough to eat, and no fresh water at all. We collected the murky swamp water and sodden moss in a shirt, squeezed it, and drank the liquid that dripped out of the shirt.

We finally managed to make our way back to the river, where we found our boat and were able to calculate our position, but the water we had drunk made us all very ill (eventually we were diagnosed as having typhoid fever). As the expedition leader, I stayed on my feet. I carried all the other boys down to the boat, laid them in the bottom, and, exerting my last ounce of strength to prevent myself from losing consciousness, steered the boat as it drifted downstream. I had only enough energy left to give the others some river water to splash over their faces, which were burning with fever. They lost consciousness, and soon I, too, began to pass out. When we reached a railway bridge that crossed the river, we thought that someone would find us. I moored our boat to the bank and collapsed unconscious. We were seen, picked up, and driven back to town; the school term had begun a month before, and search parties had been looking for us.

32 Typhoid fever kept us in the hospital for nearly three months. They had no medicines for it. My companions on the expedition had decided not to attend tenth grade — our last — that year and to stay on at school for an extra year. But halfway through the school year I began studying on my own at home. I worked day and night, and when the final exams began, I went to school to take them.

33 I arrived at school and was told I couldn't take the exams; there was no provision for home study in the final year. Once again, helped by the fact that this path was already familiar to me, I set off on a well-beaten track: all the local education departments and the party committee. By this time I was a member of the city's volleyball team; fortunately, I was also known as the junior champion in several sports and as volleyball champion of Sverdlovsk province. In the end I was allowed to take the exams as an external student. Admittedly I did not get top marks in all subjects; I was given a four in two subjects, a five in all the others. That was my baggage for the onward journey to higher education.

34 As a boy, I had dreamed of attending an institute of shipbuilding. I had read a number of standard textbooks and tried to understand how ships were built. But gradually I began to be attracted by the profession of civil engineering — no doubt because I had already worked as a building laborer and because my father was in the construction business.

35 But before I could enter the department of civil engineering at Urals Polytechnic Institute, I had to pass one more test — this one administered by my grandfather. He was over seventy by then, a most impressive man, with a long beard and a quirky, original cast of mind. He said to me, "I won't let you go into the building trade until you have built something with your own hands. You can build me a bathhouse. A small one, in the backyard, complete with a changing room."

36 We had never had our own bathhouse, though our neighbors did. Circumstances had always prevented us from building one.

37 My grandfather explained, "You must build it all yourself. My only contribution will be to get the local office of the State Timber Trust to allot you some trees in the forest. From then on you must fell the necessary pine trees, prepare moss for caulking the walls, clean it and dry it; you must carry all the logs from the forest yourself" — it was two miles — "to the place where you're going to build the bathhouse; you must make the foundations and do all the woodworking yourself, all the way up to the roof tree. And I," he said, "will not come anywhere near

you." He was a stubborn old man, obstinate as they come, and he never once came within thirty yards of me. Nor did he lift a finger to help me, even though I found the work incredibly hard. When I had finished the bathhouse, my grandfather solemnly announced that I had passed the test and I now had his full permission to enter the department of civil engineering.

## Evaluating the Text

1. How is the significance of Yeltsin's Christian name related to the circumstances in which he received it?
2. To what extent does Yeltsin's description of what life was like under communal circumstances both on the farm and in the city of Berezniki differ from your conception of the meaning of *communism* (keep in mind the root word *commune*)?
3. How might the stringent circumstances in which the family lived explain why Yeltsin's father was so strict in punishing him for misbehavior of any kind?
4. How would you characterize Yeltsin's attitude toward his parents and siblings?
5. How do you interpret Yeltsin's comments about his father's endeavor to construct an automatic brick-laying machine?
6. What does Yeltsin's decision to publicly castigate a teacher for injurious and unfair treatment of students in front of everyone during the graduation ceremony reveal about him?
7. How was Yeltsin's discovery that he could successfully manipulate the bureaucracy when he was in the seventh grade an important lesson for him?
8. What does his continued persistance in playing volleyball even after having lost two fingers show about his character?
9. How did Yeltsin's leadership abilities emerge during the time he and the other boys got lost in the forest?
10. In your opinion, what was Yeltsin's grandfather hoping to achieve by setting such difficult conditions for Boris before allowing him to enroll in a civil engineering program?
11. What cumulative impression does this chapter from Yeltsin's autobiography convey to you?

## Exploring Different Perspectives

1. What in Yeltsin's background would suggest that he might be an effective reformer for the kind of abuses going on in Russia, described by Francine du Plessix Gray ("Sex and Birth")? What similarities can you discover between Yeltsin and Dr. Khomassuridze?
2. What insight do you gain from Yeltsin's account about what life is like in a communal setting when compared with Rigoberta Menchu's account ("Birth Ceremonies")?
3. How does being a child under communism in Russia differ from or resemble being a child under communism in China as described by Bruce Dollar ("Child Care in China")?

4. How do Yeltsin's motive and skills in getting up in front of his school auditorium differ from those of Jing Mei-Woo in Amy Tan's story ("Jing-Mei Woo: Two Kinds")? What does each hope to achieve?

## Extending Viewpoints through Writing

1. Just as Yeltsin nearly drowned during his baptism, people experience events differently because of where their last name comes in the alphabet. How do people whose last names begin with early letters in the alphabet have different experiences from people whose last names begin with letters close to the end? Discuss experiences you have had attributable to where in the alphabet your last name falls.

2. You might wish to read the rest of Yeltsin's autobiography, *Against the Grain* (1990), to discover how character traits Yeltsin developed in childhood served him in his confrontations with Soviet bureaucracy in general, and Gorbachev in particular, in his rise to being elected President of Russia.

# Natsume Soseki

# *I Am a Cat*

---

*Natsume Soseki (1867–1916) was one of Japan's most distinguished writers. He taught English at Tokyo University and was literary editor of the* Asahi Newspaper. *Considered to be a milestone in Japanese literature,* I Am a Cat *(1905) brought Soseki instant recognition as an incisive observer of Japanese bourgeois life. This work was translated into English by Katsue Shibata and Motomari Kai in 1961. Soseki's work, like that of other twentieth-century Japanese writers, reveals the influence of the West on Japanese life and culture. The first chapter from* I Am a Cat *introduces a professor of English and his family as they appear through the eyes of a cat who has taken up residence in their home.*

*Known historically as the "land of the rising sun" symbolized in the national flag, Japan is made up of four main islands off the coast of east Asia: Honshu (the largest, where the capital Tokyo and major cities are located), Hokkaido, Shikoku, and Kyushu. Two-thirds of Japan's terrain is mountainous, including the most famous peak, Mount Fuji. Earth tremors are a frequent occurrence. Because Japan has few natural resources, and such a small percentage of land is suitable for cultivation, the country must import almost half its food supply and almost all raw materials required for industrial production. Despite this, Japan is one of the most productive industrial nations; its exports of automobiles, electronic equipment, televisions, textiles, chemicals, and machinery have made it an economic superpower. Education is free and compulsory to the age of fifteen, and Japan has an extraordinarily high literacy rate of 99 percent.*

*According to legend, Japan was founded by Emporor Jimmu in 660 B.C. and has had a line of Emperors that continues into the present. The current Emperor, Akihito, succeeded to the throne in 1989 following his father, Hirohito, who was Emperor from 1926. Actual political control of the country from the twelfth to the late nineteenth century was held by fuedal lords, called Shoguns. In 1854, Commadore Matthew Perry reopened contact with Japan after the Shoguns had expelled all foreigners from the country in the seventeenth century. Subsequently, the Shoguns lost power to the emperor, and with the defeat of China in 1895 and victory over Russia in the Russo–*

---

*(For more information on contemporary Japan, see p. 250.)

*Japanese War ending in 1905, the year in which I Am a Cat was written, Japan became a global power.*

1    I am a cat but as yet I have no name.

2    I haven't the faintest idea of where I was born. The first thing I do remember is that I was crying "meow, meow," somewhere in a gloomy damp place. It was there that I met a human being for the first time in my life. Though I found this all out at a later date, I learned that this human being was called a Student, one of the most ferocious of the human race. I also understand that these Students sometimes catch us, cook us and then take to eating us. But at that time, I did not have the slightest idea of all this so I wasn't frightened a bit. When this Student placed me on the palm of his hand and lifted me up lightly, I only had the feeling of floating around. After a while, I got used to this position and looked around. This was probably the first time I had a good look at a so-called "human being." What impressed me as being most strange still remains deeply imbedded in my mind: the face which should have been covered with hair was a slippery thing similar to what I now know to be a teakettle. I have since come across many other cats but none of them are such freaks. Moreover, the center of the Student's face protruded to a great extent, and from the two holes located there, he would often emit smoke. I was extremely annoyed by being choked by this. That this was what they term as tobacco, I came to know only recently.

3    I was snuggled up comfortably in the palm of this Student's hand when, after a while, I started to travel around at a terrific speed. I was unable to find out if the Student was moving or if it was just myself that was in motion, but in any case I became terribly dizzy and a little sick. Just as I was thinking that I couldn't last much longer at this rate, I heard a thud and saw sparks. I remember everything up till that moment but think as hard as I can, I can't recall what took place immediately after this.

4    When I came to, I could not find the Student anywhere. Nor could I find the many cats that had been with me either. Moreover, my dear mother had also disappeared. And the extraordinary thing was that this place, when compared to where I had been before, was extremely bright —ever so bright. I could hardly keep my eyes open. This was because I had been removed from my straw bed and thrown into a bamboo bush.

5    Finally, mustering up my strength, I crawled out from his bamboo grove and found myself before a large pond. I sat on my haunches and tried to take in the situation. I didn't know what to do but suddenly I had an idea. If I could attract some attention by meowing, the Student might come back to me. I commenced but this was to no avail; nobody came.

6    By this time, the wind had picked up and came blowing across the pond. Night was falling. I sensed terrible pangs of hunger. Try as I would, my voice failed me and I felt as if all hope were lost. In any case, I resolved to get myself to a place where there was food and so, with this

decision in mind, I commenced to circle the water by going around to the left.

This was very difficult but at any rate, I forced myself along and eventually came to a locality where I sensed Man. Finding a hole in a broken bamboo fence, I crawled through, having confidence that it was worth the try, and lo! I found myself within somebody's estate. Fate is strange; if that hole had not been there, I might have starved to death by the roadside. It is well said that every tree may offer shelter. For a long time afterwards, I often used this hole for my trips to call on Mi-ke, the tomcat living next door.

Having sneaked into the estate, I was at a loss as to what the next step should be. Darkness had come and my belly cried for food. The cold was bitter and it started to rain. I had no time to fool around any longer so I went in to a room that looked bright and cozy. Coming to think of it now, I had entered somebody's home for the first time. It was there that I was to confront other humans.

The first person I met was the maid Osan. This was a human much worse than the Student. As soon as she saw me, she grabbed me by the neck and threw me outdoors. I sensed I had no chance against her sudden action so I shut my eyes and let things take their course. But I couldn't endure the hunger and the cold any longer. I don't know how many times I was thrown out but because of this, I came to dislike Osan all through. That's one reason why I stole the fish the other day and why I felt so proud of myself.

When the maid was about to throw me out for the last time, the master of the house made his appearance and asked what all the row was about. The maid turned to him with me hanging limp from her hand, and told him that she had repeatedly tried throwing this stray cat out but that it always kept sneaking into the kitchen again — and that she didn't like it at all. The master, twisting his moustache, looked at me for a while and then told the maid to let me in. He then left the room. I took it that the master was a man of few words. The maid, still mad at me, threw me down on the kitchen floor. In such a way, I was able to establish this place as my home.

At first it was very seldom that I got to see my master. He seemed to be a schoolteacher. Coming home from school he'd shut himself up in his study and would hardly come out for the rest of the day. His family thought him to be very studious and my master also made out as if he were. But actually, he wasn't as hard working as they all believed him to be. I'd often sneak up and look into his study only to find him taking a nap. Sometimes I would find him drivelling on the book he had been reading before dozing off.

He was a man with a weak stomach so his skin was somewhat yellowish. He looked parched and inactive, yet he was a great consumer of food. After eating as much as he possibly could, he'd take a dose of Taka-diastase and then open a book. After reading a couple of pages, however, he'd become drowsy and again commence drooling. This was his daily routine. Though I am a cat myself, at times I think that schoolteachers are very fortunate. If I were to be reborn a man, I would, without doubt, become a teacher. If you can keep a job and still sleep as much as my master did, even cats could manage such a profession. But according to my master—and he makes it plain—there's nothing so hard as teaching. Especially when his friends come to visit him, he does a lot of complaining.

13    When I first came to this home, nobody but the master was nice to me. Wherever I went, they would kick me around and I was given no other consideration. The fact that they haven't given me a name even as of today goes to show how much they care for me. That's why I try to stay close to my master.

14    In the morning, when my master reads the papers, I always sit on his lap; and when he takes his nap, I perch on his back. This doesn't mean that he likes it, but then, on the other hand, it doesn't mean that he dislikes it—it has simply become a custom.

15    Experience taught me that it is best for me to sleep on the container for boiled rice in the mornings as it is warm, and on a charcoal-burning foot warmer in the evenings. I generally sleep on the veranda on fine days. But most of all, I like to crawl into the same bed with the children of the house at night. By children, I mean the girls who are five and three years old respectively. They sleep together in the same bed in their own room. In some way or other, I try to slip into their bed and crawl in between them. But if one of them wakes up, then it is terrible. The girls—especially the smaller one—raise an awful cry in the middle of the night and holler, "There's that cat in here again!" At this, my weak-stomached master wakes up and comes in to help them. It was only the other day that he gave me a terrible whipping with a ruler for indulging in this otherwise pleasant custom.

16    In coming to live with human beings, I have had the chance to observe them and the more I do the more I come to the conclusion that they are terribly spoiled, especially the children. When they feel like it, they hold you upside down or cover your head with a bag; and at times, they throw you around or try squeezing you into the cooking range. And on top of that, should you so much as bare a claw to try to stop them, the whole family is after you. The other day, for instance, I tried sharpening my claws just for second on the straw mat of the living room when the Mrs. noticed me. She got furious and from then on, she won't let me in the sitting room. I can be cold and shivering in the kitchen but they never take the trouble to bother about me. When I met Shiro across the street whom I respected, she kept telling me there was nothing as inconsiderate as humans.

17    Only the other day, four cute little kittens were born to Shiro. But the Student who lives with the family threw all four of them into a pond

behind the house on the third day. Shiro told me all this in tears and said that in order for us cats to fulfil parental affection and to have a happy life, we will have to overthrow the human race. Yes, what she said was all very logical. Mi-ke, next door, was extremely furious when I told him about Shiro. He said that humans did not understand the right of possession of others. With us cats, however, the first one that finds the head of a dried sardine or the navel of a gray mullet gets the right to eat it. Should anyone try to violate this rule, we are allowed to use force in order to keep our find. But humans depend on their great strength to take what is legally ours away from us and think it right.

Shiro lives in the home of a soldier and Mi-ke in the home of a lawyer. I live in the home of a schoolteacher and, in comparison, I am far more optimistic about such affairs than either of them. I am satisfied only in trying to live peacefully day after day. I don't believe that the human race will prosper forever so all I have to do is to relax and wait for the time when cats will reign.

Coming to think of the way they act according to their whims — another word for selfishness—I'm going to tell you more about my master. To tell the truth, my master can't do anything well but he likes to stick his nose into everything. Going in for composing *haiku*, he contributes his poems to the *Hototogisu* magazine, or writes some modern poetry for the *Myojo* magazine; or at times, he composes a piece in English, but all grammatically wrong. Then again, he finds himself engrossed in archery or tries singing lyrical plays; or maybe he tries a hand at playing discordant tunes on the violin. What is most disheartening is the fact that he cannot manage any of them well. Though he has a weak stomach, he does his best.

When he enters the toilet, he commences chanting so he is nicknamed "Mr. Mensroom" by his neighbors. Yet, he doesn't mind such things and continues his chanting: "This is Taira-no-Munemori. . . . " Everybody says, "There goes Munemori again," and then bursts out laughing. I don't know exactly what had come over him about a month after I first established myself at his place, but one pay day he came home all excited carrying with him a great big bundle. I couldn't help feeling curious about the contents.

The package happened to contain a set of water colors, brushes and drawing paper. It seems that he had given up lyrical plays and writing verses and was going in for painting. The following day, he shut himself up in his study and without even taking his daily nap, he drew pictures. This continued day after day. But what he drew remained a mystery because others could not even guess what they were. My master finally came to the conclusion that he wasn't as good a painter as he had thought himself to be. One day he came home with a man who considers himself an aesthetic and I heard them talking to each other.

"It's funny but it's difficult to draw as well as you want. When a painting is done by others, it looks so simple. But when you do a work with a brush yourself, it's quite a different thing," said my master. Coming to think of it, he did have plenty of proof to back up his statement.

23    His friend, looking over his gold-rimmed glasses, said, "You can't expect to draw well right from the beginning. In the first place, you can't expect to draw anything just from imagination, and by shutting yourself up in a room at that. Once the famous Italian painter Andrew del Sarto said that to draw, you have to interpret nature in its original form. The stars in the sky, the earth with flowers shining with dew, the flight of birds and the running animals, the ponds with their goldfish, and the black crow in a withered tree — nature is the one great panorama of the living world. How about it? If you want to draw something recognizable, why not do some sketching?"

24    "Did del Sarto really say all those things? I didn't know that. All right, just as you say," said my master with admiration. The eyes behind the gold-rimmed glasses shone, but with scorn.

25    The following day, as I was peacefully enjoying my daily nap on the veranda, my master came out from his study, something quite out of the ordinary, and sat down beside me. Wondering what he was up to, I slit my eyes open just a wee bit and took a look. I found him trying out Andrea del Sarto's theory on me. I could not suppress a smile. Having been encouraged by his friend, my master was using me as a model.

26    I tried to be patient and pretended to continue my nap. I wanted to yawn like anything but when I thought of my master trying his best to sketch me, I felt sorry for him, and so I killed it. He first drew my face in outline and then began to add colors. I'd like to make a confession here: as far as cats are concerned, I have to admit that I'm not one of those you'd call perfect or beautiful; my back, my fur or even my face cannot be considered superior in any way to those of other cats. Yet, even though I may be uncomely, I am hardly as ugly as what my master was painting. In the first place, he shaded my color all wrong. I am really somewhat like a Persian cat, a light gray with a shade of yellow with lacquer-like spots — as can be vouched by anyone. But according to my master's painting, my color was not yellow nor was it black. It wasn't gray or brown. It wasn't even a combination of these colors but something more like a smearing together of many tones. What was most strange about the drawing was that I had no eyes. Of course, I was being sketched while taking a nap so I won't complain too much, but you couldn't even find the location of where they should have been. You couldn't tell if I was a sleeping cat or a blind cat. I thought, way down inside me, that if this is what they called the Andrea del Sarto way of drawing pictures, it wasn't worth a sen.

27    But as to the enthusiasm of my master, I had to bow my head humbly. I couldn't disappoint him by moving but, if you'll excuse my saying so, I had wanted to go outside to relieve myself from a long while back. The muscles of my body commenced fidgeting and I felt that I couldn't hold out much longer. So, trying to excuse myself, I stretched

out my forelegs, gave my neck a little twist and indulged in a long slow yawn. Going this far, there was no need for me to stay still any longer because I had changed my pose. I then stepped outside to accomplish my object.

But my master, in disappointment and rage, shouted from within the room, "You fool!" My master, in abusing others, has the habit of using this expression. "You fool!" This is the best he can manage as he doesn't know any other way to swear. Even though he had not known how long I had endured the urgent call of nature, I still consider him uncivilized for this. If he had ever given me a smile or some other encouragement when I climbed onto his back, I could have forgiven him this time, but the fact is that he never considers my convenience. That he should holler, "You fool!" only because I was about to go and relieve myself was more than I could stand. In the first place, humans take too much for granted. If some power doesn't appear to control them better, there's no telling how far they will go in their excesses.

I could endure their being so self-willed but I've heard many other complaints regarding mankind's lack of virtue, and they are much worse.

Right in back of the house, there is a patch of tea plants. It isn't large but it is nice and sunny. When the children of the house are so noisy that I can't enjoy my naps peacefully or when, because of idleness, my digestion is bad, I usually go out to the tea patch to enjoy the magnanimous surroundings. One lovely autumn day about two o'clock in the afternoon, after taking my after-lunch nap, I took a stroll through this patch. I walked along, smelling each tea plant as I went, until I reached a cryptomeria hedge at the west end.

There I found a large cat sleeping soundly, using a withered chrysanthemum in lieu of a mat. It seemed as if he didn't notice me coming, for he kept snoring loudly. I was overwhelmed at his boldness;—after sneaking into somebody else's yard. He was a big black cat.

The sun, now past midday, cast its brilliant rays upon his body and reflected themselves to give the impression of flames bursting from his soft fur. He had such a big frame that he seemed fit to be called a king of the feline family. He was more than twice my size. Admiration and a feeling of curiosity made me forget the past and the future, and I could only stare at him.

The soft autumn breeze made the branches of the paulawnia above quiver lightly and a couple of leaves came fluttering down upon the thicket of dead chrysanthemums. Then the great "king" opened his eyes. I can still feel the thrill of that moment. The amber light in his eyes shone much brighter than the jewels man holds as precious. He did not move at all. The glance he shot at me concentrated on my small forehead, and he abruptly asked me who I was. The great king's directness betrayed his rudeness. Yet, there was a power in his voice that would have terrified dogs, and I found myself shaking with fear. But thinking it inadvisable not to pay my respects, I said, "I am a cat though, as yet, I don't have any name." I said this while pretending to be at ease but actually my heart was beating away at a terrific speed. Despite my courteous reply, he said, "A cat? You don't say so! Where do you live?" He was extremely audacious.

34    "I live here in the schoolteacher's house."

35    "I thought so. You sure are skinny." Gathering from his rudeness I couldn't imagine him coming from a very good family. But, judging from his plump body, he seemed to be well fed and able to enjoy an easy life. As for myself, I couldn't refrain from asking, "And you are you?"

36    "Me? Huh—I'm Kuro, living at the rickshawman's place."

37    So this was the cat living at the rickshawman's house! He was known in the vicinity as being awfully unruly. Actually he was admired within the home of the rickshawman but, having no education, nobody else befriended him. He was a hoodlum from whom others shied. When I heard him tell me who he was, I felt somewhat uneasy and, at the same time, I felt slightly superior. With the intention of finding out how much learning he had, I asked him some more questions.

38    "I was just wondering which of the two is the greater—the rickshawman or the schoolteacher."

39    "What a question! The rickshawman, naturally. Just take a look at your teacher—he's all skin and bones," he snorted.

40    "You look extremely strong. Most probably, living at the rickshawman's house, you get plenty to eat."

41    "What? I don't go unfed anywhere! Stick with me for a while instead of going around in circles in the tea patch and you'll look better yourself in less than a month."

42    "Sure, some day, maybe. But to me, it seems as though the schoolteacher lives in a bigger house than the rickshawman," I purred.

43    "Huh! What if the house is big? That doesn't mean you get your belly full there, does it?"

44    He seemed extremely irritated and, twitching his pointed ears, he walked away without saying another word. This was my first encounter with Kuro of the house of the rickshawman, but not the last.

45    Since then, we've often talked together. Whenever we do, Kuro always commences bragging, as one living with a rickshawman would.

46    One day, we were lying in the tea patch and indulging in some small talk. As usual, he kept bragging about the adventures he had had, and then he got around to asking me, "By the way, how many rats have you killed?"

47    Intellectually I am much more developed than Kuro but when it comes to using strength and showing bravado, there is no comparison. I was prepared for something like this but when he actually asked me the question, I felt extremely embarrassed. But facts are facts; I could not lie to him: "To tell the truth, I have been wanting to catch one for a long time but the opportunity has never come."

48    Kuro twitched the whiskers which stood out straight from his muzzle and laughed hard. Kuro is conceited, as those who brag usually are, so

when I find him being sarcastic I try to say something to appease him. In this way, I am able to manage him pretty well. Having learned this during our first meeting, I stayed calm when he laughed. I realized that it would be foolish to commit myself now by giving unasked-for reasons. I figured it best, at this stage, to let him brag about his own adventures and so I purred quietly, "Being as old as you are, you've probably caught a lot of rats yourself." I was trying to get him to talk about himself. And, as I had expected, he took the bait.

"Well, can't say a lot—maybe about thirty or forty." He was very     49
proud of this and continued, "I could handle one or two hundred rats alone but when it comes to weasels, they're not to my liking. A weasel once gave me a terrible time."

"So? And what happened?" I chimed in. Kuro blinked several times     50
before he continued. "It was at the time of our annual housecleaning last summer. The master crawled under the veranda to put away a sack of lime, and—what do you think? He surprised a big weasel which came bouncing out."

"Oh?" I pretended to admire him.     51

"As you know, a weasel is only a little bigger than a rat. Thinking him     52
to be just another big mouse, I cornered him in a ditch."

"You did?"     53

"Yeah. Just as I was going in for the *coup-de-grace*—can you imagine     54
what he did? Well, it raised its tail and—ooph! You ought to have taken a whiff. Even now when I see a weasel I get giddy." So saying, he rubbed his nose with one of his paws as if he were still trying to stop the smell. I felt somewhat sorry for him so, with the thought of trying to liven him up a little, I said, "But when it comes to rats, I hardly believe they would have a chance against you. Being such a famous rat catcher, you probably eat nothing else and that's why you're so plump and glossy, I'm sure."

I had said this to get him into a better mood but actually it had the     55
contrary effect. He let a big sigh escape and replied, "When you come to think of it, it's not all fun. Rats are interesting but, you know, there's nobody as crafty as humans in this world. They take all the rats I catch over to the police box. The policeman there doesn't know who actually catches them so he hands my master five sen per head. Because of me, my master has made a neat profit of one yen and fifty sen, but yet he doesn't give me any decent food. Do you know what humans are? Well, I'll tell you. They're men, yes, but thieves at heart."

Even Kuro, who was not any too bright, understood such logic and he     56
bristled his back in anger. I felt somewhat uneasy so I murmured some excuse and went home. It was because of this conversation that I made up my mind never to catch rats. But, on the other hand, neither do I go around hunting for other food. Instead of eating an extravagant dinner, I simply go to sleep. A cat living with a schoolteacher gets to become, in nature, just like a teacher himself. If I'm not careful I might still become just as weak in the stomach as my master.

57      Speaking of my master the schoolteacher, it finally dawned upon him that he could not ever hope to get anywhere with water-color painting. He wrote the following entry in his diary, dated December 1:

> Met a man today at a party. It's said that he's a debauchee and he looked like one. Such individuals are liked by women, so it may be quite proper to say that such people cannot help becoming dissipated. His wife was formerly a geisha girl and I envy him. Most of the people who criticize debauchees generally have no chance to become one themselves. Still, others who claim to be debauchees have no qualifications to become so worldly. They simply force themselves into that position. Just as in the case of my water-color painting, there was absolutely no fear of my making good. But indifferent to others, I might think that I was good at it. If some men are considered worldly only because they drink *sake* at restaurants, frequent geisha houses and stop over for the night, and go through all the necessary motions, then it stands to reason that I should be able to call myself a remarkable painter. But my water-color paintings will never be a success.

58      In regard to this theory, I cannot agree. That a schoolteacher should envy a man who has a wife who was once a geisha shows how foolish and inferior my master is. But his criticism of himself as a water-color painter is unquestionably true. Though my master understands many of his own shortcomings, he cannot get over being terribly conceited. On December 4, he wrote:

> Last night, I attempted another painting but I have finally come to understand that I have no talent. I dreamed that somebody had framed the pictures I have laying around, and had hung them on the wall. Upon seeing them framed, I suddenly thought that I was an excellent painter. I felt happy and kept looking but, when the day dawned, I awoke and again clearly realized that I am still a painter of no talent.

59      Even in his dreams, my master seemed to regret his having given up painting. This is characteristic of a learned man, a frustrated water-color painter and one who can never become a man of the world.

60      The day after my master had had his dream, his friend, the man of arts, came to see him again. The first question he asked my master was "How are the pictures getting along?"

61      My master calmly answered, "According to your advice I'm working hard at sketching. Just as you said, I am finding interesting shapes and detailed changes of colors which I had never noticed before. Due to the fact that artists in Western countries have persisted in sketching, they have reached the development we see today. Yes, all this must be due to Andrea del Sarto." He did not mention what he had written in his diary, but only continued to show his admiration for del Sarto.

The artist scratched his head and commenced to laugh, "That was all 62
a joke, my friend."

"What's that?" My master didn't seem to understand. 63

"Andrea del Sarto is only a person of my own highly imaginative 64
creation. I didn't think you'd take it so seriously. Ha, ha, ha." The artist
was greatly enjoying himself.

Listening to all this from the veranda, I couldn't help wondering what 65
my master would write in his diary about that conversation. This artist
was a person who took great pleasure in fooling others. As if he did not
realize how his joke about Andrea del Sarto hurt my master, he boasted
more: "When playing jokes, some people take them so seriously that
they reveal great comic beauty, and it's a lot of fun. The other day I told a
student that Nicholas Nickleby had advised Gibbon to translate his great
story of the French Revolution from a French textbook and to have it
published under his own name. This student has an extremely good
memory and made a speech at the Japanese Literature Circle quoting
everything I had told him. There were about a hundred people in the
audience and they all listened very attentively. Then there's another
time. One evening, at a gathering of writers, the conversation turned to
Harrison's historical novel *Theophano*. I said that it was one of the best
historical novels ever written, especially the part where the heroine dies.
'That really gives you the creeps'—that's what I said. An author who
was sitting opposite me was one of those types who cannot and will not
say no to anything. He immediately voiced the opinion that that was a
most famous passage. I knew right away that he had never read any
more of the story than I had."

With wide eyes, my nervous and weak-stomached master asked, 66
"What would you have done if the other man had really read the story?"

The artist did not show any excitement. He thought nothing of 67
fooling other people. The only thing that counted was not to be caught in
the act.

"All I would have had to do is to say that I had made a mistake in the 68
title or something to that effect." He kept on laughing. Though this artist
wore a pair of gold-rimmed glasses, he looked somewhat like Kuro of the
rickshawman's.

My master blew a few smoke rings but he had an expression on his 69
face that showed he wouldn't have the nerve to do such a thing. The
artist, with a look in his eyes as if saying, "That's why you can't paint
pictures," only continued. "Jokes are jokes but, getting down to facts, it's
not easy to draw. They say that Leonardo da Vinci once told his pupils to
copy a smear on a wall. That's good advice. Sometimes when you're
gazing at water leaking along the wall in a privy, you see some good
patterns. Copy them carefully and you're bound to get some good
designs."

"You're only trying to fool me again." 70

"No, not this time. Don't you think it's a wonderful idea? Just what 71
da Vinci himself would have suggested."

72     "Just as you say," replied my master, half surrendering. But he still hasn't made any sketches in the privy—at least not yet.

73     Kuro of the rickshawman's wasn't looking well. His glossy fur began to fade and fall out. His eyes, which I formerly compared to amber, began to collect mucus. What was especially noticeable was his lack of energy. When I met him in the tea patch, I asked him how he felt.

74     "I'm still disgusted with the weasel's stink and with the fisherman. The fish seller hit me with a pole again the other day."

75     The red leaves of the maple tree were beginning to show contrast to the green of the pines here and there. The maples shed their foliage like dreams of the past. The fluttering petals of red and white fell from the tea plants one after another until there were none remaining. The sun slanted its rays deeper and deeper into the southern veranda and seldom did a day pass that the late autumn wind didn't blow. I felt as though my napping hours were being shortened.

76     My master still went to school every day and, coming home, he'd still bottle himself up in his study. When he had visitors he'd continue to complain about his job. He hardly ever touched his water colors again. He had discontinued taking Taka-diastase for his indigestion, saying that it didn't do him any good. It was wonderful now that the little girls were attending kindergarten every day but returning home, they'd sing loudly and bounce balls and, at times, they'd still pick me up by the tail.

77     I still had nothing much to eat so I did not become very fat but I was healthy enough. I didn't become sick like Kuro and, as always, I took things as they came. I still didn't try to catch rats, and I still hated Osan, the maid. I still didn't have a name but you can't always have what you want. I resigned myself to continue living here at the home of this schoolteacher as a cat without a name.

## Evaluating the Text

1. From its own perspective, why would a cat assume faces should be covered with hair? Why would it perceive the center of the student's face as protruding to a great extent?
2. How is the cat's process of justifying stealing the fish quite similar to the human characteristic of rationalizing? How do both involve attributing reasons after the fact to justify an action one performed without those reasons being the cause?
3. What chain of events leads to the cat being employed as a subject of his master's sketching?
4. What human character traits are revealed in the master's reaction to his cat's desire to go outside and relieve itself?
5. What standards of behavior can you infer the cat applies to judge the behavior of humans in general and its master in particular? Why is it ironic for a cat to call a human "uncivilized"?

6. What is the purpose of Soseki's description (in paragraph 3) of how the cat realizes it is in violent motion without understanding how it happened? How does this make the reader perceive this event from the cat's point of view? As far as you can tell, what actually did happen to the cat?

7. Normally, we don't think of cats consciously deciding to meow for a specific purpose. What effect does Soseki achieve by attributing consciousness to the cat?

8. What additional insights about the master does the cat provide, which the schoolteacher has concealed from his family? How does the cat's viewpoint complete the picture of the master and show him as he really is, as compared with how he would like to be seen?

9. What assumptions underlie the cat's statement that "the fact that they haven't given me a name even as of today goes to show how much they care for me"?

10. What details in the story suggest that the schoolmaster identifies with the cat in the sense that he too feels like an outsider in his own household?

11. What relationships does the cat have with other cats in the neighborhood? How do the observations of other cats about their masters help create a composite picture of humanity in general, and these two households in particular, from the perspective of their pets?

12. Discuss the subtle or overt resemblances between each of the cats and the characteristics of its owner or the household in which it lives. For example, how is the unnamed cat like the schoolteacher? How is Mi-ke like the lawyer and Kuro like the rickshawman? What similarities show how the unnamed cat grows more and more like his master (in terms of digestion, standards, attitude toward learning, etc.). Which cat does not seem especially similar to its owner?

13. How does the cat manipulate Kuro into talking about his achievements so Kuro will not ask him why he has as yet caught no rats?

14. How does the December 1 entry from the diary show that the master tries to fool himself about the quality of his artistic endeavors? How does jumping from one activity to another (poetry, archery, singing, violin, painting, etc.) relate to his statement that his water-color paintings will never be a success? What are his real motives for pursuing these diverse hobbies?

15. How does the schoolmaster reveal both his naïveté and gullibility when he is taken in by the so-called historical facts concerning Andrea Del Sarto? What assumptions can you make about Soseki's Japanese audience during the early part of the twentieth century simply from the fact that nowhere in this chapter does the author provide the true facts concerning this figure—namely, that Andrea Del Sarto (1486–1531) really was an Italian painter.

## Exploring Different Perspectives

1. In view of the importance that cats have as pets in American families (now outranking dogs as America's favorite pets), do you think the definition of what constitutes a family and how different families are classified by Andrew Cherlin and Frank F. Furstenberg, Jr. ("The American Family in the Year 2000") should be modified?

2. How do both Soseki's story and Amy Tan's "Jing-Mei Woo: Two Kinds" depend on the author's establishing a connection with the reader so that the protagonist's views are taken ironically rather than literally? What are some of the ways Soseki and Tan use to alert the reader?

## Extending Viewpoints through Writing

1. How does the cat's conception of justice differ from that of humans? How might this narrative be interpreted as expressing the relationships between those with power in a culture to those without power?

2. What does the cat's description of how it established itself tell you about the cat's character when compared with the actual circumstances of its arrival? How does Soseki illustrate the all-too-human desire to take credit for what really happened by chance? Draw up a two-column list of events, with the left column consisting of events you caused to happen, and the right, of events that just happened to you. Now try to discover if there is any event on the left side (which you said you caused to happen) that in retrospect had really happened to you. Keep in mind the natural human tendency to take credit for good events and disclaim responsibility for all bad ones — "success has many fathers and failure is an orphan."

3. Take a cat's-eye view of the member of the human species called a "student" by stepping outside the situation and objectively describing traits that distinguish students. Write it from the cat's point of view. If you wish, you can be the student–subject. What are the things students do that distinguish them from other people that might seem improbable if you didn't already know about their practices?

4. What if the cat had observed an activity that we would know as chewing "smokeless" tobacco? How would this activity appear? Write a paragraph mentioning all the details that you, as the cat, would observe (without understanding them as a human would).

5. What actions did a pet of yours ever take that you believed manifested evidence of consciousness, motivation, and intelligence? Describe this action or event, and reply to the objections of someone who would not see this action as evidence of intelligence but simply as your desire to interpret it as such.

6. What could your pet say about you that no other human being knows?

7. Describe the search you went through and final decision you made as to what to name your pet. What does the name reveal about the character traits important to you and your family in bestowing an identity on the animal.

8. Give the cat in this story a name, and explain the reasons behind your choice. Feel free to choose a feminine or masculine name because the cat's sex is never specified.

9. How does family life change before and after the acquisition of a pet? For instance, have you ever observed people addressing one another indirectly through a pet? To what extent do pets function as a buffer, middle-ground, or even a screen onto which people project their real feelings, negative and positive, about each other that they could never express to each other directly?

# Rigoberta Menchu

## *Birth Ceremonies*

Rigoberta Menchu, a Quiché Indian, was born in the hamlet of Chi-
mel, in northwestern Guatemala. Her life reflects experiences common
to Indian communities throughout Central America. She survived a
genocide that destroyed her family and community: Her brother, father, and mother were all killed in acts of savagery after the coming to
power of the Garcia Lucas regime in 1978. "Birth Ceremonies" is
taken from I, Rigoberta Menchu: An Indian Woman in Guatemala
(1983), translated by Ann Wright, a powerful work that speaks of the
struggle to maintain Indian culture and tradition.

 The republic of Guatemala is located in Central America. After
defeating the Quiché (Mayan) Indians in 1523, Spain established a
prosperous colony that lasted until Guatemala gained its independence in 1821. The predominantly Roman Catholic population is
evenly divided between Mayan Indians and Mestizos (a person of
mixed Spanish and Amerindian blood), who Menchu refers to as
ladinos. Politically unstable, Guatemala has been dominated since
the 1970s by ruthless military regimes. Violence in the country caused
many, including Menchu, to flee and live as exiles.

'Whoever may ask where we are, tell them what you know of us
and nothing more.'

—POPOL VUH

'Learn to protect yourselves, by keeping our secret.'

—POPOL VUH

 In our community there is an elected representative, someone who is
highly respected. He's not a king but someone whom the community
looks up to like a father. In our village, my father and mother were the
representatives. Well, then the whole community becomes the children
of the woman who's elected. So, a mother, on her first day of pregnancy
goes with her husband to tell these elected leaders that she's going to
have a child, because the child will not only belong to them but to the
whole community, and must follow as far as he can our ancestors'
traditions. The leaders then pledge the support of the community and
say: 'We will help you, we will be the child's second parents'. They are

known as *abuelos*, 'grandparents' or 'forefathers'. The parents then ask the 'grandparents' to help them find the child some godparents, so that if he's orphaned, he shouldn't be tempted by any of the bad habits our people sometimes fall into. So the 'grandparents' and the parents choose the godparents together. It's also the custom for the pregnant mother's neighbours to visit her every day and take her little things, no matter how simple. They stay and talk to her, and she'll tell them all her problems.

2     Later, when she's in her seventh month, the mother introduces her baby to the natural world, as our customs tell her to. She goes out in the fields or walks over the hills. She also has to show her baby the kind of life she leads, so that if she gets up at three in the morning, does her chores and tends the animals, she does it all the more so when she's pregnant, conscious that the child is taking all this in. She talks to the child continuously from the first moment he's in her stomach, telling him how hard his life will be. It's as if the mother were a guide explaining things to a tourist. She'll say, for instance; 'You must never abuse nature and you must live your life as honestly as I do.' As she works in the fields, she tells her child all the little things about her work. It's a duty to her child that a mother must fulfil. And then, she also has to think of a way of hiding the baby's birth from her other children.

3     When her baby is born, the mother mustn't have her other children round her. The people present should be the husband, the village leaders, and the couple's parents. Three couples. The parents are often away in other places, so if they can't be there, the husband's father and the wife's mother can perhaps make up one pair. If one of the village leaders can't come, one of them should be there to make up a couple with one of the parents. If none of the parents can come, some aunts and uncles should come to represent the family on both sides, because the child is to be part of the community. The birth of a new member is very significant for the community, as it belongs to the community not just to the parents, and that's why three couples (but not just anybody) must be there to receive it. They explain that this child is the fruit of communal love. If the village leader is not a midwife as well, another midwife is called (it might be a grandmother) to receive the child. Our customs don't allow single women to see a birth. But it does happen in times of need. For instance, I was with my sister when she went into labour. Nobody else was at home. This was when we were being heavily persecuted. Well, I didn't exactly see, but I was there when the baby was born.

4     My mother was a midwife from when she was sixteen right up to her death at forty-three. She used to say that a woman hadn't the strength to push the baby out when she's lying down. So what she did with my sister was to hang a rope from the roof and pull her up, because my brother wasn't there to lift her up. My mother helped the baby out with my sister in that position. It's a scandal if an Indian woman goes to hospital and gives birth there. None of our women would agree to that.

Our ancestors would be shocked at many of the things which go on today. Family planning, for example. It's an insult to our culture and a way of swindling the people, to get money out of them.

This is part of the reserve that we've maintained to defend our customs and our culture. Indians have been very careful not to disclose any details of their communities, and the community does not allow them to talk about Indian things. I too must abide by this. This is because many religious people have come among us and drawn a false impression of the Indian world. We also find a *ladino* using Indian clothes very offensive. All this has meant that we keep a lot of things to ourselves and the community doesn't like us telling its secrets. This applies to all our customs. When the Catholic Action[1] arrived, for instance, everyone started going to mass, and praying, but it's not their only religion, not the only way they have of expressing themselves. Anyway, when a baby is born, he's always baptized within the community before he's taken to church. Our people have taken Catholicism as just another channel of expression, not our one and only belief. Our people do the same with other religions. The priests, monks and nuns haven't gained the people's confidence because so many of their things contradict our own customs. For instance, they say; 'You have too much trust in your elected leaders.' But the village elects them *because* they trust them, don't they? The priests say; 'The trouble is you follow those sorcerers,' and speak badly of them. But for our people this is like speaking ill of their own fathers, and they lose faith in the priests. They say; 'Well, they're not from here, they can't understand our world.' So there's not much hope of winning our people's hearts.

To come back to the children, they aren't to know how the baby is born. He's born somewhere hidden away and only the parents know about it. They are told that a baby has arrived and that they can't see their mother for eight days. Later on, the baby's companion, the placenta that is, has to be burned at a special time. If the baby is born at night, the placenta is burned at eight in the morning, and if he's born in the afternoon, it'll be burned at five o'clock. This is out of respect for both the baby and his companion. The placenta is not buried, because the earth is the mother and the father of the child and mustn't be abused by having the placenta buried in it. All these reasons are very important for us. Either the placenta is burned on a log and the ashes left there, or else it is put in the *temascal*. This is a stove which our people use to make vapour baths. It's a small hut made of adobe and inside this hut is another one made of stone, and when we want to have a bath, we light a fire to heat the stones, close the door, and throw water on the stones to produce steam. Well, when the woman is about four months pregnant, she starts taking these baths infused with evergreens, pure natural

---

[1]Association created in 1945 by Monsignor Rafael Gonzalez, to try and control the Indian fraternities of the *Altiplano*.

aromas. There are many plants the community uses for pregnant women, colds, headaches, and things like that. So the pregnant mother takes baths with plants prescribed for her by the midwife or the village leader. The fields are full of plants whose names I don't know in Spanish. Pregnant women use orange and peach leaves a lot for bathing and there's another one we call Saint Mary's leaf which they use. The mother needs these leaves and herbs to relax because she won't be able to rest while she's pregnant since our women go on working just as hard in the fields. So, after work, she takes this calming bath so that she can sleep well, and the baby won't be harmed by her working hard. She's given medicines to take as well. And leaves to feed the child. I believe that in practice (even if this isn't a scientific recommendation) these leaves work very well, because many of them contain vitamins. How else would women who endure hunger and hard work, give birth to healthy babies? I think that these plants have helped our people survive.

7    The purity with which the child comes into the world is protected for eight days. Our customs say that the new-born baby should be alone with his mother in a special place for eight days, without any of her other children. Her only visitors are the people who bring her food. This is the baby's period of integration into the family; he very slowly becomes a member of it. When the child is born, they kill a sheep and there's a little fiesta just for the family. Then the neighbours start coming to visit, and bring presents. They either bring food for the mother, or something for the baby. The mother has to taste all the food her neighbours bring to show her appreciation for their kindness. After the eight days are over, the family counts up how many visitors the mother had, and how many presents were received; things like eggs or food apart from what was brought for the mother, or clothing, small animals, and wood for the fire, or services like carrying water and chopping wood. If, during the eight days, most of the community has called, this is very important, because it means that this child will have a lot of responsibility towards his community when he grows up. The community takes over all the household expenses for these eight days and the family spends nothing.

8    After eight days everything has been received, and another animal is killed as recognition that the child's right to be alone with his mother is over. All the mother's clothes, bedclothes, and everything she used during the birth, are taken away by our elected leader and washed. She can't wash them in the well, so no matter how far away the river is, they must be carried and washed there. The baby's purity is washed away and he's ready to learn the ways of humanity. The mother's bed is moved to a part of the house which has first been washed with water and lime. Lime is sacred. It strengthens the child's bones. I believe this really is true. It gives a child strength to face the world. The mother has a bath in the *temascal* and puts on clean clothes. Then, the whole house is cleaned. The child is also washed and dressed and put into the new bed. Four candles are placed on the corners of the bed to represent the four

corners of the house and show him that this will be his home. They symbolize the respect the child must have for his community, and the responsibility he must feel towards it as a member of a household. The candles are lit and give off an incense which incorporates the child into the world he must live in. When the baby is born, his hands and feet are bound to show him that they are sacred and must only be used to work or do whatever nature meant them to do. They must never steal or abuse the natural world, or show disrespect for any living thing.

After the eight days, his hands and feet are untied and he's now with 9 his mother in the new bed. This means he opens the doors to the other members of the community, because neither the family or the community know him yet. Or rather, they weren't shown the baby when he was born. Now they can all come and kiss him. The neighbours bring another animal, and there's big lunch in the new baby's house for all the community. This is to celebrate his integration 'in the universe', as our parents used to say. Candles will be lit for him and his candle becomes part of the candle of the whole community, which now has one more person, one more member. The whole community is at the ceremony, or at least, if not all of it, then some of it. Candles are lit to represent all the things which belong to the universe—earth, water, sun, and man—and the child's candle is put with them, together with incense (what we call *pom*) and lime—our sacred lime. Then, the parents tell the baby of the suffering of the family he will be joining. With great feeling, they express their sorrow at bringing a child into the world to suffer. To us, suffering is our fate, and the child must be introduced to the sorrows and hardship, but he must learn that despite his suffering, he will be respectful and live through his pain. The child is then entrusted with the responsibility for his community and told to abide by its rules. After the ceremony comes the lunch, and then the neighbours go home. Now, there is only the baptism to come.

When the baby is born, he's given a little bag with a garlic, a bit of 10 lime, salt, and tobacco in it, to hang round his neck. Tobacco is important because it is a sacred plant for Indians. This all means that the child can ward off all the evil things in life. For us, bad things are like spirits, which exist only in our imagination. Something bad, for instance, would be if the child were to turn out to be a gossip—not sincere, truthful, and respectful, as a child should be. It also helps him collect together and preserve all our ancestors' things. That's more or less the idea of the bag—to keep him pure. The bag is put inside the four candles as well, and this represents the promise of the child when he grows up.

When the child is forty days old, there are more speeches, more 11 promises on his behalf, and he becomes a full member of the community. This is his baptism. All the important people of the village are invited and they speak. The parents make a commitment. They promise to teach the child to keep the secrets of our people, so that our culture and customs will be preserved. The village leaders come and offer their experience, their example, and their knowledge of our ancestors. They explain how to preserve our traditions. Then, they promise to be responsible for the child, teach him as he grows up, and see that he follows in their ways. It's also something of a criticism of humanity, and of the many people who have forsaken their traditions. They say almost a prayer, asking that our traditions again enter the spirits of those who have forsaken them. Then, they evoke the names of our ancestors, like Tecun Umán and others who form part of the ceremony, as a kind of chant. They must be remembered as heroes of the Indian peoples. And then they say (I analyse all this later); 'Let no landowner extinguish all this, nor any rich man wipe out our customs. Let our children, be they workers or servants, respect and keep their secrets'. The child is present for all of this, although he's all wrapped up and can scarcely be seen. He is told that he will eat maize and that, naturally, he is already made of maize because his mother ate it while he was forming in her stomach. He must respect the maize; even the grain of maize which has been thrown away, he must pick up. The child will multiply our race, he will replace all those who have died. From this moment, he takes on this responsibility, and is told to live as his 'grandparents' have lived. The parents then reply that their child promises to accomplish all this. So, the village leaders and the parents both make promises on behalf of the child. It's his initiation into the community.

12      The ceremony is very important. It is also when the child is considered a child of God, our one father. We don't actually have the word God but that is what it is, because the one father is the only one we have. To reach this one father, the child must love beans, maize, the earth. The one father is the heart of the sky, that is, the sun. The sun is the father and our mother is the moon. She is a gentle mother. And she lights our way. Our people have many notions about the moon, and about the sun. They are the pillars of the universe.

13      When children reach ten years old, that's the moment when their parents and the village leaders talk to them again. They tell them that they will be young men and women and that one day they will be fathers and mothers. This is actually when they tell the child that he must never abuse his dignity, in the same way his ancestors never abused their dignity. It's also when they remind them that our ancestors were dishonoured by the White Man, by colonization. But they don't tell them the way that it's written down in books, because the majority of Indians can't read or write, and don't even know that they have their own texts. No, they learn it through oral recommendations, the way it has been handed down through the generations. They are told that the Spaniards dishonoured our ancestors' finest sons, and the most humble of them. And it is to honour these humble people that we must keep our secrets. And no-one except we Indians must know. They talk a lot about our ancestors. And the ten-years ceremony is also when our children are reminded that they must respect their elders, even though this is some-

thing their parents have been telling them ever since they were little. For example, if an old person is walking along the street, children should cross over to allow him to pass by. If any of us sees an elderly person, we are obliged to bow and greet them. Everyone does this, even the very youngest. We also show respect to pregnant women. Whenever we make food, we always keep some for any of our neighbours who are pregnant.

When little girls are born, the midwives pierce their ears at the same 14 time as they tie their umbilical cords. The little bags around their necks and the thread used to tie their umbilical cord are both red. Red is very significant for us. It means heat, strength, all living things. It's linked to the sun, which for us is the channel to the one god, the heart of everything, of the universe. So red gives off heat and fire and red things are supposed to give life to the child. At the same time, it asks him to respect living things too. There are no special clothes for the baby. We don't buy anything special beforehand but just use pieces of *corte* to wrap him in.

When a male child is born, there are special celebrations, not because 15 he's male but because of all the hard work and responsibility he'll have as a man. It's not that *machismo* doesn't exist among our people, but it doesn't present a problem for the community because it's so much part of our way of life. The male child is given an extra day alone with his mother. The usual custom is to celebrate a male child by killing a sheep or some chickens. Boys are given more, they get more food because their work is harder and they have more responsibility. At the same time, he is head of the household, not in the bad sense of the word, but because he is responsible for so many things. This doesn't mean girls aren't valued. Their work is hard too and there are other things that are due to them as mothers. Girls are valued because they are part of the earth, which gives us maize, beans, plants and everything we live on. The earth is like a mother which multiplies life. So the girl child will multiply the life of our generation and of our ancestors whom we must respect. The girl and the boy are both integrated into the community in equally important ways, the two are inter-related and compatible. Nevertheless, the community is always happier when a male child is born and the men feel much prouder. The customs, like the tying of the hands and feet, apply to both boys and girls.

Babies are breast-fed. It's much better than any other sort of food. But 16 the important thing is the sense of community. It's something we all share. From the very first day, the baby belongs to the community, not only to the parents and the baby must learn from all of us . . . in fact, we behave just like bourgeois families in that, as soon as the baby is born, we're thinking of his education, of his well-being. But our people feel that the baby's school must be the community itself, that he must learn to live like all the rest of us. The tying of the hands at birth also symbolizes this; that no-one should accumulate things the rest of the community does not have and he must know how to share, to have open hands. The mother must teach the baby to be generous. This way of thinking comes from poverty and suffering. Each child is taught to live like the fellow members of his community.

17    We never eat in front of pregnant women. You can only eat in front of a pregnant woman if you can offer something as well. The fear is that, otherwise, she might abort the baby or that the baby could suffer if she didn't have enough to eat. It doesn't matter whether you know her or not. The important thing is sharing. You have to treat a pregnant woman differently from other women because she is two people. You must treat her with respect so that she recognizes it and conveys this to the baby inside her. You instinctively think she's the image of the baby about to be born. So you love her. Another reason why you must stop and talk to a pregnant woman is because she doesn't have much chance to rest or enjoy herself. She's always worried and depressed. So when she stops and chats a bit, she can relax and feel some relief.

18    When the baby joins the community, with him in the circle of candles — together with his little red bag — he will have his hoe, his machete, his axe and all the tools he will need in life. These will be his playthings. A little girl will have her washing board and all the things she will need when she grows up. She must learn the things of the house, to clean, to wash, and sew her brothers' trousers, for example. The little boy must begin to live like a man, to be responsible and learn to love the work in the fields. The learning is done as a kind of game. When the parents do anything they always explain what it means. This includes learning prayers. This is very important to our people. The mother may say a prayer at any time. Before getting up in the morning, for instance, she thanks the day which is dawning because it might be a very important one for the family. Before lighting the fire, she blesses the wood because that fire is going to cook food for the whole family. Since it's the little girl who is closest to her mother, she learns all of this. Before washing the *nixtamal,* the woman blows on her hands and puts them in the *nixtamal.* She takes everything out and washes it well. She blows on her hands so that her work will bear fruit. She does it before she does the wash as well. She explains all these little details to her daughter, who learns by copying her. With the men it's the same. Before they start work every day, whatever hour of the morning it is, they greet the sun. They remove their hats and talk to the sun before starting to work. Their sons learn to do it too, taking of their little hats to talk to the sun. Naturally, each ethnic group has its own forms of expression. Other groups have different customs from ours. The meaning of their weaving patterns, for example. We realize the others are different in some things, but the one thing we have in common is our culture. Our people are mainly peasants, but there are some people who buy and sell as well. They go into this after they've worked on the land. Sometimes when they come back from working in the *finca,* instead of tending a little plot of land, they'll

start a shop and look for a different sort of life. But if they're used to greeting the sun every morning, they still go on doing it. And they keep all their old customs. Every part of our culture comes from the earth. Our religion comes from the maize and bean harvests which are so vital to our community. So even if a man goes to try and make some money, he never forgets his culture springs from the earth.

As we grow up we have a series of obligations. Our parents teach us to be responsible; just as they have been responsible. The eldest son is responsible for the house. Whatever the father cannot correct is up to the eldest son to correct. He is like a second father to us all and is responsible for our upbringing. The mother is the one who is responsible for keeping an account of what the family eats, and what she has to buy. When a child is ill, she has to get medicine. But the father has to solve a lot of problems too. And each one of us, as we grow up, has our own small area of responsibility. This comes from the promises made for the child when he is born, and from the continuity of our customs. The child can make the promise for himself when his parents have taught him to do it. The mother, who is closest to the children, does this, or sometimes the father. They talk to their children explaining what they have to do and what our ancestors used to do. They don't impose it as a law, but just give the example of what our ancestors have always done. This is how we all learn our own small responsibilities. For example, the little girl begins by carrying water, and the little boy begins by tying up the dogs when the animals are brought into the yard at night, or by fetching a horse which has wandered off. Both girls and boys have their tasks and are told the reasons for doing them. They learn responsibility because if they don't do their little jobs, well, their father has the right to scold them, or even beat them. So, they are very careful about learning to do their jobs well, but the parents are also very careful to explain exactly why the jobs have to be done. The little girl understands the reasons for everything her mother does. For example, when she puts a new earthenware pot on the fire for the first time, she hits it five times with a branch, so that it knows its job is to cook and so that it lasts. When the little girl asks, 'Why did you do that?', her mother says, 'So that it knows what its job is and does it well.' When it's her turn to cook, the little girl does as her mother does. Again this is all bound up with our commitment to maintain our customs and pass on the secrets of our ancestors. The elected fathers of the community explain to us that all these things come down to us from our grandfathers and we must conserve them. Nearly everything we do today is based on what our ancestors did. This is the main purpose of our elected leader — to embody all the values handed down from our ancestors. He is the leader of the community, a father to all our children, and he must lead an exemplary life. Above all, he has a commitment to the whole community. Everything that is done today, is done in memory of those who have passed on.

# Evaluating the Text

1. Discuss the principles that determine how representatives of the community are chosen. What cultural values do these principles reveal?
2. How does the birth of a child represent continuity and the propagation of tradition? In what way is the newborn infant the "property" of the entire village?
3. How do married couples serve to represent the ethic of mutual responsibility and survival of the tribe in a way that unmarried people cannot?
4. How does the Indian perception of non-Indians and *ladinos* as unreliable, untrustworthy betrayers of traditional culture explain the reluctance Indians have toward giving birth in a hospital?
5. How does much of Menchu's narrative depend on the assumption that the *ladino* way of life would represent a denial of nature and tradition?
6. What is the rationale behind the Indian perception of the placenta as a companion to the baby? How does the burning of the placenta rather than its burial reveal a distinctively Guatemalan Indian cultural attitude toward the earth? How is the same attitude expressed in the Indian view of maize?
7. What conflict do you observe between native Indian beliefs and the belief system of Catholic missionaries? What specific aspects of Indian rituals might missionaries fail to understand? How is the Church's attempt to dissuade Indians from electing an elder to lead the village related to their wish to convert Indians to Catholicism?
8. How does the treatment of new-born infants reveal the importance of responsibility to the community and tradition? How is this basic attitude toward life related to the circumstances under which people must live?
9. Discuss how the idea of responsibility or obligation of the child toward the community is related to the role the community plays during the first eight days after the child's birth.
10. How are the "birth ceremonies" organized around the following stages in the ritual: a community pledge of support for the child, an introduction of the as yet unborn child to the daily regimen, a witnessing of the birth by representatives of the tribe, and a sequestering of the child for eight days, during which the house and baby are washed and purified with lime, candles are lit, the child's hands are bound, and the child is introduced to the community and subsequently baptized? Which one of these rituals struck you as the most unusual and interesting?
11. How does Menchu's attitude toward the "birth ceremonies" reveal the importance she places on preserving tradition and keeping faith with the tribal heritage of the Guatemalan Indians?

# Exploring Different Perspectives

1. What similarities can you discover between Menchu's account and Bruce Dollar's description in "Child Care in China"? How do both cultures impress on their children the need to live their lives in a way that fulfills obligations to the community, whether defined as the village or the state?
2. Compare the role played by Catholicism as the central belief of the Irish

community in William Trevor's "Teresa's Wedding" with how it appears from Menchu's perspective, as an alien and peripheral faith, antagonistic to the values of her people.

## Extending Viewpoints through Writing

1. Which aspects of Guatemalan Indian life surprised you by presenting a view quite different from the culture in which you were raised?
2. Describe the rituals or "birth ceremonies" of another ethnic community. What objects are used, what prayers are said, and what are their significance; who attends and what role do they perform? How is the scene decorated or altered through the use of symbols, and what do these symbols mean? How does the ceremony express the specific cultural values of the community?

# Bruce Dollar

# *Child Care in China*

*"Child Care in China" first appeared in* Saturday Review World, *May 1973. Based on extensive interviews he conducted in many early child-care facilities, Bruce Dollar discovered that mother-surrogates play a crucial role in instilling values of cooperation, sharing, and altruism in institutionalized child-care programs in China.*

*The People's Republic of China is ruled by a government established in 1949 after the victory of Mao Zedong (Tse-tung) and his communist forces against the Nationalist forces of Chiang Kai-Chek, who fled to Taiwan and set up a government in exile. Under Mao's leadership, industry was nationalized, and a land reform program, based on collectivization, was introduced. China entered the Korean War against United Nations forces between 1950 and the Armistice of 1953. China's modern history has been characterized by cycles of liberalization followed by violent oppression. In 1957, reaction against the so-called "let a hundred flowers bloom" period led to a crackdown against intellectuals. In 1966, Mao launched the Cultural Revolution to purge the government and society of liberal elements. After Mao's death in 1976, a backlash led to the imprisoning of Mao's wife, Jiang Qing, and three colleagues (the "Gang of Four"). A period of liberalization once again followed, as Deng Xiao Ping came to power in 1977 and adopted more conciliatory economic, social, and political policies. The United States recognized the People's Republic of China as a valid government on January 1, 1979. The pattern re-emerged in June 1989, when government troops were sent into Tiananmen Square to crush the prodemocracy movement. Zhao Ziyang, who had shown sympathy toward the students, was ousted and replaced by hard-liner Jing Zemin. The June events, in which thousands are reported to have died, led to a crackdown and execution of sympathizers throughout China, despite widespread international condemnation.*

1     The old art of China watching is giving way to China witnessing, and one quality of the new China that seems inevitably to impress all recent visitors is the extraordinary vibrancy of Chinese children, from the very youngest to the adolescents, who already tower so noticeably over their

*(For further information on the events of June 3, 1989, in Tiananmen Square, see pp. 344–352.)

grandparents. During my own recent trip within China, my companions and I saw for ourselves the exuberant self-confidence that seems to infuse all Chinese kids, whether they are performing for strangers, participating in a classroom exercise, or playing by themselves.

"Ours is a socialist society; everything is done according to plan." This pronouncement, with which our various Chinese hosts so frequently prefaced their answers to our questions, provides a starting point for understanding how this spirit of exuberance has been achieved. Although Chinese society is largely decentralized to encourage local self-sufficiency and diversification, the whole is knit together by an administrative structure that is more or less uniform from city to city and, somewhat less, from commune (or network of villages) to commune. It is a framework that provides an efficient system of communication and has helped produce a remarkable social cohesion based on commonly held goals and values—which themselves are informed by the teachings of Mao Tse-tung.

The consensus is particularly apparent with respect to the care and training of the young. This is hardly surprising when one considers the enormous stock the Chinese place in producing what they call "revolutionary successors," an apt phrase in a country where revolutionary consciousness has been maintained largely through vivid comparisons with the "bitter past," and where the problem of continuing the revolution into succeeding generations is paramount.

Thus, throughout our visit we constantly encountered—with amazing consistency at various points along a 2,500-mile itinerary—several major ideas about child rearing in the numerous conversations we had with people in child-related institutions: families, nurseries, kindergartens, and schools. These themes—especially the subordination of personal to social needs, respect for productive labor, altruism, cooperation, and the integration of physical with intellectual labor—together describe the kind of citizen China hopes to produce. The techniques employed to achieve these values are in practice virtually from infancy.

During the years before primary school, which begins at the age of seven, a series of public child care facilities is available to parents who wish to use them. In the cities, where patterns are more uniform, a mother's maternity leave (paid) usually terminates 56 days after birth. Since breast-feeding is the rule in China, the mother may then place her child in the nursing room at her place of work. Most work institutions—factories, hospitals, and government offices, for example—provide this facility for their employees. In a typical arrangement the mother has two half hour breaks, plus lunch, to visit and nurse her baby during the work day. After work the baby returns home with the mother.

Nursing rooms provide care for infants up to one and a half years old; then they may be sent to one of the various kinds of nurseries. Some of these are attached to the work place or located in the home neighborhood; they may be open only during the work day, or they may be "live-in" nurseries, where children stay overnight and go home on weekends. Kindergartens, usually located in the residential areas, generally care for children from three and a half to seven years old and may also be either part-time or full-time.

7      In a country in which over 90 percent of all women of working age do work, it might be expected that a similar percentage of children would therefore receive some kind of institutional care. But there are options. The most common is to leave the child in the care of grandparents, who frequently live with the family. Another alternative is to make arrangements with a friend or neighbor. Estimates vary from place to place, but in most cities no more than half the children of nursery school age are in attendance. For kindergarten the figures are higher, especially in the cities, where attendance is over 80 percent.

8      Since child care is decentralized, different localities often make their own arrangements, which may not conform to the usual patterns. This is particularly true of rural areas, where a lack of resources and the persistence of custom probably account for a lower incidence of public child care facilities. One small village we visited, the Sha Shih Yu Brigade in northeast China, had no permanent facility; only during harvest time, when all hands were needed in the fields, was there organized care for small children. A child care center located in a coalmining area near Tangshan, on the other hand, served 314 children divided into at least five separate age groups, from 56 days to six years old.

9      How do these institutions work to socialize the children under their care? And what are they like for the kids? In spite of the diversity in organizational structure, the remarkable similarity from place to place, both in the values espoused and the methods used to inculcate them, seems to support a number of generalizations.

10     One quality that is sure to strike an American observer is the preponderance and the style of group activities. A common example is the "cultural performance," usually presented for visitors. Whether they are songs from a revolutionary opera, dances to celebrate a harvest, or a program of folk melodies played on traditional Chinese instruments, these performances are always presented by groups, and it is impossible to pick out a "star."

11     Although there were exceptions, many early child care facilities we visited seemed rather poorly supplied with the variety of toys and materials that the conventional wisdom in the United States says should be on hand to enrich and enliven a child's environment. Although this may have been due to a simple inability to pay for more equipment, the teachers we spoke to did not seem to consider it a shortcoming. Perhaps this is because Chinese children are generally expected to rely on each other for stimulation—at any rate, this seems to be the effect. The situation provides an interesting contrast to that in the United States,

where the highly desired "rich environment" often means that kids interact with inanimate materials more than they do with other people.

The small children we saw were not without playthings, however. 12 There was always at least one toy for each child—typically a rubber or plastic doll of a worker, a peasant, or a soldier. Rocking horses were also common, as were military toys and playground equipment that could accommodate many children. But in general the emphasis was on group play. One recent American visitor to a Chinese nursery school reports noticing that the blocks seemed awfully heavy for the small children. "Exactly!" beamed the teachers. "That fosters mutual help."

Chinese teachers actively encourage such group behavior as coopera- 13 tion, sharing, and altruism. "We praise a child when he shows concern for others' interests," said one kindergarten teacher. "For example, at meal time teachers give out bowls and chop sticks. If a youngster gets a nicer bowl and gives it to someone else, we praise him for it. Or when the children are asked to select a toy and a child gives the best one to a classmate, we praise that, too."

Even in a competitive situation, this teacher said, helping another is 14 more important than winning. "When the children run in a relay race, sometimes one will fall down, especially if he's small. If another child stops to help him get up or to see if he's all right, even though his own team might fall behind, we encourage this." The approach contrasts markedly with methods used in the Soviet Union, another country that stresses the collective in its child-rearing practices. There, competition is discouraged between individuals but promoted between groups. Each child is made aware of his importance within his group—say, a row in his classroom—and then competes fiercely for the rewards of a group victory. The Chinese seem genuinely to eschew even this form of competition in favor of straightforward mutual help and cooperation.

But how do teachers deal with improper behavior and matters of 15 discipline? Here is how the question was answered in a conversation with three staff members of a full-time kindergarten in Peking:

Q: What kinds of behavior do you discourage in the children?
A: We criticize those who take toys or other things from others. Or if children beat each other—we criticize that.
Q: Exactly how do you handle such a situation—say, two kids fighting?
A: First, the teacher must understand the reason for the fight. For instance, one might have taken a toy from the other, and the second child hit him. In that case, the teacher will criticize both. This criticism is carried out alone, unless it took place in the class; in that case it will be done in front of the class so that all the children will understand that was wrong. Criticism is to make children understand what was wrong and why.

Q: What kind of punishment do you use?

A: There is no punishment.

Q: Well, what if a child were really intractable? Would you use some mild sanction, such as depriving him of some free play time on the playground?

A: (At this point all three women broke into smiles at our incredulity. Waving their hands back and forth to underscore their words, they said): No, no, nothing like that. We believe in persuasion.

Q: Do other children ever participate in criticism?

A: Generally, no. Unless a third child saw what happened — then he'll be asked to tell.

Q: Let's say the incident was unobserved by any third party and the two kids involved give conflicting versions of what happened. Then how does the teacher act?

A: If the teacher finds a contradiction when both tell what happened, she will try to educate the children. She will note that everyone can make a mistake, including teachers. The mistake that led to the fight is not important, she will say, but telling the truth is very important. At this point the children will probably tell the truth.

16    This sounded like fine theory, but it provoked some skepticism among those of us who had been teachers. What about teachers who do not have the patience to use such positive techniques? we asked. How do you deal with teachers who don't observe the school's policy? The reply: "We all — teachers and leadership — have the same goal: to cultivate revolutionary successors. So we all work together and help each other. We study our profession together. We have regular criticism and self-criticism sessions, and sometimes we help each other on specific problems."

17    If we had not already seen many teachers in action here and elsewhere on our trip, we might have been dissatisfied with this answer. But we were constantly struck by the teachers' apparent love for their work in all the early child care institutions we visited. These women, we learned (there were no men), were chosen for their jobs after having shown a particular interest in children, and "sensitivity and love for children" were the criteria most often cited for their recruitment. Credentials were secondary. Since the Cultural Revolution, the amount of training teachers receive has ranged all the way from university graduation to short-term training classes and "learning through practice."

18    Three of us in the group who were especially interested in child rearing and education often asked to see child care centers and schools under normal operating conditions. Our guides accommodated these requests by arranging for us to stay behind after the form tour or make a

low-key visit to a kindergarten, say, without the rest of the group. Some of our most revealing insights occurred during our observation of every-day free playground activities.

One afternoon, for example, at the child care center serving workers 19 of the Fan Ga Chong coal mine area near Tangshan, I spent nearly an hour outside among the four-and-a-half-to-six-year-olds and their teachers, or "nurses." Here was the one place where I saw what might be called a disruptive child—a little boy who, in the United States, would probably have been labeled hyperkinetic and put on Ritalin. While the other 50 or so children busied themselves with various games—rope jumping, drop the handkerchief, tricycle riding, playing with toys and each other—this boy ran constantly from place to place, trying to be in on everything at once and occasionally interfering with someone else's fun. The nurses, who themselves were taking part in the games, were obviously aware of the boy's actions, but they made no fuss over him. Instead, each time he ran by a nurse, she would reach out, place her hand on the back of his head, and gently guide him away from trouble or toward an activity he might like—usually with a few soothing words. Soon he was off again, and once or twice it was necessary to intervene when he began picking on another child. But always the adults acted cheerfully and patiently, and the boy never became a center of attention. His actions were the closest thing to aggressive or disruptive behavior among children that I saw on the entire trip.

After visiting several classrooms at the Pei Hai Kindergarten, a full- 20 time kindergarten located in a park in Peking, I spent an even longer time on the playground watching free play. Once again I was struck by the way teachers enthusiastically joined in. The children, well over a hundred of them, had formed into a variety of play groups. Some played on slides, a merry-go-round, monkey bars, and swings. Some were organized into class-sized groups for games. Others were in smaller groups, jumping rope or kicking a ball around. There were kids in pairs and kids alone. One gleeful little boy, holding aloft a leafy twig, ran, danced, and twirled with it till he fell down from dizziness. And ranging over the whole playground, sweeping past and through everyone else's games, was a whooping pack of boys chasing a soccer ball, a laughing teacher in the lead.

In one group that especially caught my eye, seven or eight girls were 21 jumping rope, taking turns at the ends of a pink plastic rope and lining up to jump one by one. No teacher was with them. They were very absorbed and used chants and songs to accompany each jumper. Several times while I watched, a minor controversy of some kind would erupt and everything would come to a halt. Maybe it concerned whose turn was next on the rope or how many times one had jumped before missing. Whatever it was, the whole group would come together and heatedly debate their points. With no single girl taking charge, they would quickly work out a settlement that seemed to satisfy everyone and then resume their jumping with all the gusto of before. These little girls were good jumpers, incidentally. So good that after a while they attracted an audience: six little boys found chairs, lined them up to form a small gallery, and proceeded to join in the jumping chants, applauding for each jumper. Great fun for all, highly organized, and by all indications spontaneous and undirected by adults.

22    In the United States the growing demand for facilities for the care of infants and preschool children has provoked a chorus of urgent questions: Doesn't a baby need a single individual to relate to and identify with as mother? How can a mother be sure that those to whom she entrusts her child will teach the same values she holds? Isn't it the mother's natural role to care for her own children? What is the effect of institutionalized child care on the family?

23    Obviously, the answers the Chinese have found to these questions are not directly applicable to this country. Yet the insights they provide can be instructive as we seek our own solutions.

24    There is a strong likelihood that the average child in China will undergo "multiple mothering" of some kind. Even if the mother does not choose to leave her infant in the nursing room where she works, chances are the child will wind up in the care of a neighbor or the grandmother. Offsetting this diversity of "mothers," however, is the near-uniform consensus of values and methods of child rearing I have described. This consistency seems to go a long way toward providing young children with the kind of security we in the United States might normally associate only with single mothering.

25    Another aspect of multiple or "shared" mothering, as Ruth Sidel, author of the excellent recent book *Women & Child Care in China*, points out, "is that infants can thrive physically and emotionally if the mother-surrogates are constant, warm, and giving. Babies in China are not subjected to serial mothering; we were repeatedly told that aunties (i.e., nurses) and teachers rarely leave their jobs. And they are warm and loving with the children. The children show none of the lethargy or other intellectual, emotional, or physical problems of institutionalized children. Quite the opposite!"

26    "Everything is planned," and the position of mothers in China is the consequence of a society-wide effort to provide for the economic liberation of women. In keeping with Mao Tse-tung's edict calling for "genuine equality between the sexes," a broad series of programs, including birth control information and prenatal care with maternity leave, in addition to the system of child care facilities, is underway to assume the full participation of women in "building socialism." The objects of unspeakable oppression in prerevolutionary society, Chinese women today

have been thoroughly integrated into the labor force, both in factory and commune. And a growing number of them are entering professions— for example, 50 percent of the medical students are now women.

Despite the enormous progress, even the Chinese will concede that 27 full parity with men is not yet a reality. Top governmental, military, and management posts continue to be mostly male preserves. However, women do wield considerable political and administrative power at the local level, where they often run the smallest governmental units, the . neighborhood revolutionary committees.

But the key to liberation is still economic independence, which de- 28 pends on the availability of work. Since 1971 a new source of work for women has appeared: the so-called housewives' factories. These have been organized locally by women who live in housing areas like the Kung Kiang Workers' Residential Area in Shanghai, and whose hus- bands work in the various nearby factories. As they described it to us, the housewives were looking for ways in which they could contribute pro- ductively to the revolution without having to leave the residential area. So they set up their own light industries in workshops near their homes, and by working full- or part-time were able to produce needed commod- ities, such as flashlight bulbs or men's trousers, while earning extra money for themselves. The entire operation in each case was staffed and run by women.

Since nearly all working-age women in China today work and are no 29 longer economically dependent on their husbands or families, one might well wonder about the effects of these conditions on the family.

By all available evidence the family is thriving in China, and the 30 individual household continues to be the basic social unit. A featured item in every home we visited, as ubiquitous as a portrait of Chairman Mao, was a display of a great many photographs of family members, usually pressed under a piece of glass on top of a bureau or framed on the wall. Our host or hostess would invariably point this out with pride. Signs of active and full participation in family life were everywhere, and all generations were included. A man out with his children is a common sight, as is a child with a grandmother or grandfather.

Parents are obviously revered by children, and so are grandparents. 31 In fact, the complete absence of a "generation gap" is a striking phenom- enon to an American. Not only are grandparents well integrated into family life, but old people who have no family or who are disabled live in well-tended "respect for aged" homes and are given important func- tions that serve the neighborhood.

Far from undermining the family structure, we were repeatedly told, 32 jobs for women and day care for children have made home life easier, having eliminated many former sources of friction and frustration. A major factor here is undoubtedly the mass commitment to working for the betterment of China. Personal gratification seems to derive from each individual's knowledge that he or she makes an important contribution, no matter how small, to the national effort and that the benefits of this contribution, and others like it, will be distributed to all.

## Evaluating the Text

1. How do the practices described by Dollar reflect specific values and beliefs? What can you infer about Chinese culture from the way they bring up their children as described by Dollar?
2. What is Dollar's attitude toward this system? Is he objective? What words and phrases reveal his attitude? Is there anything he doesn't question that you might? Do the conclusions Dollar reaches appear to be based on on-site interviews at a sufficient number of child-care facilities of different kinds?
3. What is the relationship between propaganda, political ideology, and the way children are raised to become citizens of the Chinese state? How are specific practices designed to produce what the government would see as good citizens?
4. To what extent do factories and other workplaces provide facilities for mothers to be with and nurse their infants? How does this policy differ from workplaces in the United States? How do Chinese maternity-leave policies differ from those in America?
5. How is the structure of group activities and performances designed to teach cultural values to children? How is the American concept of standing out from the group an alien one to the Chinese?
6. Why is it significant that Chinese children do without different kinds of toys and for the most part must entertain each other? By contrast, how might the amount and variety of toys given to American children encourage them to expect satisfaction from objects rather than from other people?
7. How do "loss of face," "shame," and guilt before the group play a significant role in shaping the character of Chinese children from their very earliest years? Why is the instilling of these feelings valuable as a social control?
8. Why is it significant that the blocks children play with are purposely made to be too heavy for any single child to pick up and move? How does this teach children the culturally desired values of cooperation, sharing, and altruism?
9. How is Soviet society, from Dollar's perspective, based on an ethic of competition between groups? How does this differ from Chinese society? How does the approach toward competition taken in the United States differ from the approaches used in the Soviet Union and in China?
10. How does the concept of group persuasion play an important role in situations where children need to be disciplined? How do different cultural expectations govern Chinese methods of discipline when compared with methods of corporal punishment approved for use in U.S. schools?
11. What is revealing about the way Chinese teachers handled the disruptive behavior of the hyperkinetic child? How would this child have been classified and treated in the United States? How do the different

assumptions regarding disruptive behavior reveal important differences between the two societies? Keep in mind that hyperkinetic children in the United States are routinely medicated with Ritalin, a powerful psychotropic drug.

12. Why is it significant that Chinese teachers join in games with children rather than simply supervise them? Why is it also significant that children, when unsupervised, manage to settle their own disputes as in the case of the girls jumping rope? How does this approach to teaching differ from the concept of directed play employed in kindergartens and child-care centers in the United States?

13. How might a Chinese teacher respond to Western concerns that a child needs the one-to-one relationship offered by his or her own mother?

14. Why is it important that a single set of cultural values exist, since most children receive "multiple mothering"?

15. What evidence does Dollar present in the final part of his discussion to attempt to correct the impression that relationships between children and their families are minimal? How does this respond to concerns his American readers might have?

## Exploring Different Perspectives

1. Discuss the differences in goals and values between patterns of child rearing described in Dollar's article with those discussed by Andrew Cherlin and Frank F. Furstenberg, Jr., in "The American Family in the Year 2000." How do these differences reflect different cultural expectations as to what children should be like as adults in society?

2. Drawing on Amy Tan's "Jing-Mei Woo: Two Kinds," what are some significant culturally based differences between children raised in China and their second-generation counterparts who have been raised in America by first-generation Chinese parents? Analyze "Jing-Mei Woo: Two Kinds" as an example of this process of being socialized in the context of a new value system.

3. What difference in cultural attitudes toward birth control emerges from this account and Francine du Plessix Gray's interview ("Sex and Birth") with health-care professionals in the Soviet Union? What might explain these differences?

## Extending Viewpoints through Writing

1. In an essay, explore the similarities and differences between U.S. day-care centers and those in China, based on your own experience or those of friends or family. Are there any problems in the United States that could be solved by adopting some of the methods used in China?

2. To what extent do U.S. Saturday-morning television programs aimed at children attempt to instill prosocial communal values of the type described by Dollar in the context of Chinese schooling?

# Amy Tan

# *Jing-Mei Woo: Two Kinds*

---

*Amy Tan was born in Oakland, California, in 1952, two and a half years after her parents immigrated to the United States in 1949, just before the Communist Revolution. She has worked as a consultant to programs for disabled children and as a freelance writer. Of her first visit to China in 1984 she says, "As soon as my feet touched China, I became Chinese."*

*"Jing-Mei Woo: Two Kinds" is from Tan's first book,* The Joy Luck Club *(1989), a work that explores conflicts between different cultures, and generations, of Chinese mothers and daughters in America. This amusing chapter reflects Tan's own experiences of the difficulties created by her mother's expectations that she would become a prodigy, although in real life Tan's parents anticipated that she would become, as she says, "a neurosurgeon by trade and concert pianist by hobby."*

1    My mother believed you could be anything you wanted to be in America. You could open a restaurant. You could work for the government and get good retirement. You could buy a house with almost no money down. You could become rich. You could become instantly famous.

2    "Of course you can be prodigy, too," my mother told me when I was nine. "You can be best anything. What does Auntie Lindo know? Her daughter, she is only best tricky."

3    America was where all my mother's hopes lay. She had come here in 1949 after losing everything in China: her mother and father, her family home, her first husband, and two daughters, twin baby girls. But she never looked back with regret. There were so many ways for things to get better.

We didn't immediately pick the right kind of prodigy. At first my mother thought I could be a Chinese Shirley Temple. We'd watch Shirley's old movies on TV as though they were training films. My mother would poke my arm and say, *"Ni kan"*—You watch. And I would see Shirley tapping her feet, or singing a sailor song, or pursing her lips into a very round O while saying, "Oh my goodness."

---

*(For background information on China, see pp. 60 and 258.)

70

*"Ni kan,"* said my mother as Shirley's eyes flooded with tears. "You 4
already know how. Don't need talent for crying!"

Soon after my mother got this idea about Shirley Temple, she took 5
me to a beauty training school in the Mission district and put me in the
hands of a student who could barely hold the scissors without shaking.
Instead of getting big fat curls, I emerged with an uneven mass of crinkly
black fuzz. My mother dragged me off to the bathroom and tried to wet
down my hair.

"You look like Negro Chinese," she lamented, as if I had done this on 6
purpose.

The instructor of the beauty training school had to lop off these soggy 7
clumps to make my hair even again. "Peter Pan is very popular these
days," the instructor assured my mother. I now had hair the length of a
boy's, with straight-across bangs that hung at a slant two inches above
my eyebrows. I liked the haircut and it made me actually look forward to
my future fame.

In fact, in the beginning, I was just as excited as my mother, maybe 8
even more so. I pictured this prodigy part of me as many different
images, trying each one on for size. I was a dainty ballerina girl standing
by the curtains, waiting to hear the right music that would send me
floating on my tiptoes. I was like the Christ child lifted out of the straw
manger, crying with holy indignity. I was Cinderella stepping from her
pumpkin carriage with sparkly cartoon music filling the air.

In all of my imaginings, I was filled with a sense that I would soon 9
become *perfect.* My mother and father would adore me. I would be
beyond reproach. I would never feel the need to sulk for anything.

But sometimes the prodigy in me became impatient. "If you don't 10
hurry up and get me out of here, I'm disappearing for good," it warned.
"And then you'll always be nothing."

Every night after dinner, my mother and I would sit at the Formica 11
kitchen table. She would present new tests, taking her examples from
stories of amazing children she had read in *Ripley's Believe It or Not,* or
*Good Housekeeping, Reader's Digest,* and a dozen other magazines she
kept in a pile in our bathroom. My mother got these magazines from
people whose houses she cleaned. And since she cleaned many houses
each week, we had a great assortment. She would look through them all,
searching for stories about remarkable children.

The first night she brought out a story about a three-year-old boy 12
who knew the capitals of all the states and even most of the European
countries. A teacher was quoted as saying the little boy could also
pronounce the names of the foreign cities correctly.

"What's the capital of Finland?" my mother asked me, looking at the 13
magazine story.

All I knew was the capital of California, because Sacramento was the 14
name of the street we lived on in Chinatown. "Nairobi!" I guessed,

saying the most foreign word I could think of. She checked to see if that was possibly one way to pronounce "Helsinki" before showing me the answer.

15    The tests got harder—multiplying numbers in my head, finding the queen of hearts in a deck of cards, trying to stand on my head without using my hands, predicting the daily temperatures in Los Angeles, New York, and London.

16    One night I had to look at a page from the Bible for three minutes and then report everything I could remember. "Now Jehoshaphat had riches and honor in abundance and . . . that's all I remember, Ma," I said.

17    And after seeing my mother's disappointed face once again, something inside of me began to die. I hated the tests, the raised hopes and failed expectations. Before going to bed that night, I looked in the mirror above the bathroom sink and when I saw only my face staring back—and that it would always be this ordinary face—I began to cry. Such a sad, ugly girl! I made high-pitched noises like a crazed animal, trying to scratch out the face in the mirror.

18    And then I saw what seemed to be the prodigy side of me—because I had never seen that face before. I looked at my reflection, blinking so I could see more clearly. The girl staring back at me was angry, powerful. This girl and I were the same. I had new thoughts, willful thoughts, or rather thoughts filled with lots of won'ts. I won't let her change me, I promised myself. I won't be what I'm not.

19    So now on nights when my mother presented her tests, I performed listlessly, my head propped on one arm. I pretended to be bored. And I was. I got so bored I started counting the bellows of the foghorns out on the bay while my mother drilled me in other areas. The sound was comforting and reminded me of the cow jumping over the moon. And the next day, I played a game with myself, seeing if my mother would give up on me before eight bellows. After a while I usually counted only one, maybe two bellows at most. At least she was beginning to give up hope.

20    Two or three months had gone by without any mention of my being a prodigy again. And then one day my mother was watching *The Ed Sullivan Show* on TV. The TV was old and the sound kept shorting out. Every time my mother got halfway up from the sofa to adjust the set, the sound would go back on and Ed would be talking. As soon as she sat down, Ed would go silent again. She got up, the TV broke into loud piano music. She sat down. Silence. Up and down, back and forth, quiet and loud. It was like a stiff embraceless dance between her and the TV set. Finally she stood by the set with her hand on the sound dial.

21    She seemed entranced by the music, a little frenzied piano piece with this mesmerizing quality, sort of quick passages and then teasing lilting ones before it returned to the quick playful parts.

22    "*Ni kan*," my mother said, calling me over with hurried hand gestures, "Look here."

I could see why my mother was fascinated by the music. It was being 23
pounded out by a little Chinese girl, about nine years old, with a Peter
Pan haircut. The girl had the sauciness of a Shirley Temple. She was
proudly modest like a proper Chinese child. And she also did this fancy
sweep of a curtsy, so that the fluffy skirt of her white dress cascaded
slowly to the floor like the petals of a large carnation.

In spite of these warning signs, I wasn't worried. Our family had no 24
piano and we couldn't afford to buy one, let alone reams of sheet music
and piano lessons. So I could be generous in my comments when my
mother bad-mouthed the little girl on TV.

"Play note right, but doesn't sound good! No singing sound," com- 25
plained my mother.

"What are you picking on her for?" I said carelessly. "She's pretty 26
good. Maybe she's not the best, but she's trying hard." I knew almost
immediately I would be sorry I said that.

"Just like you," she said. "Not the best. Because you not trying." She 27
gave a little huff as she let go of the sound dial and sat down on the sofa.

The little Chinese girl sat down also to play an encore of "Anitra's 28
Dance" by Grieg. I remember the song, because later on I had to learn
how to play it.

Three days after watching *The Ed Sullivan Show,* my mother told me 29
what my schedule would be for piano lessons and piano practice. She
had talked to Mr. Chong, who lived on the first floor of our apartment
building. Mr. Chong was a retired piano teacher and my mother had
traded housecleaning services for weekly lessons and a piano for me to
practice on every day, two hours a day, from four until six.

When my mother told me this, I felt as though I had been sent to hell. 30
I whined and then kicked my foot a little when I couldn't stand it
anymore.

"Why don't you like me the way I am? I'm *not* a genius! I can't play 31
the piano. And even if I could I wouldn't go on TV if you paid me a
million dollars!" I cried.

My mother slapped me. "Who ask you be genius?" she shouted. 32
"Only ask you be your best. For you sake. You think I want you be
genius? Hnnh! What for! Who ask you!"

"So ungrateful," I heard her mutter in Chinese. "If she had as much 33
talent as she has temper, she would be famous now."

Mr. Chong, whom I secretly nicknamed Old Chong, was very 34
strange, always tapping his fingers to the silent music of an invisible
orchestra. He looked ancient in my eyes. He had lost most of the hair on
top of his head and he wore thick glasses and had eyes that always
looked tired and sleepy. But he must have been younger than I thought,
since he lived with his mother and was not yet married.

I met Old Lady Chong once and that was enough. She had this 35
peculiar smell like a baby that had done something in its pants. And her
fingers felt like a dead person's, like an old peach I once found in the

back of the refrigerator; the skin just slid off the meat when I picked it up.

36     I soon found out why Old Chong had retired from teaching piano. He was deaf. "Like Beethoven!" he shouted to me. "We're both listening only in our head!" And he would start to conduct his frantic silent sonatas.

37     Our lessons went like this. He would open the book and point to different things, explaining their purpose: "Key! Treble! Bass! No sharps or flats! So this is C major! Listen now and play after me!"

38     And then he would play the C scale a few times, a simple chord, and then, as if inspired by an old, unreachable itch, he gradually added more notes and running trills and a pounding bass until the music was really something quite grand.

39     I would play after him, the simple scale, the simple chord, and then I just played some nonsense that sounded like a cat running up and down on top of garbage cans. Old Chong smiled and applauded and then said, "Very good! But now you must learn to keep time!"

40     So that's how I discovered that Old Chong's eyes were too slow to keep up with the wrong notes I was playing. He went through the motions in half-time. To help me keep rhythm, he stood behind me, pushing down on my right shoulder for every beat. He balanced pennies on top of my wrists so I would keep them still as I slowly played scales and arpeggios. He had me curve my hand around an apple and keep that shape when playing chords. He marched stiffly to show me how to make each finger dance up and down, staccato like an obedient little soldier.

41     He taught me all these things, and that was how I also learned I could be lazy and get away with mistakes, lots of mistakes. If I hit the wrong notes because I hadn't practiced enough, I never corrected myself. I just kept playing in rhythm. And Old Chong kept conducting his own private reverie.

42     So maybe I never really gave myself a fair chance. I did pick up the basics pretty quickly, and I might have become a good pianist at that young age. But I was so determined not to try, not to be anybody different that I learned to play only the most ear-splitting preludes, the most discordant hymns.

43     Over the next year, I practiced like this, dutifully in my own way. And then one day I heard my mother and her friend Lindo Jong both talking in a loud bragging tone of voice so others could hear. It was after church, and I was leaning against the brick wall wearing a dress with stiff white petticoats. Auntie Lindo's daughter, Waverly, who was about my age, was standing farther down the wall about five feet away. We had grown up together and shared all the closeness of two sisters squabbling over crayons and dolls. In other words, for the most part, we hated each other. I thought she was snotty. Waverly Jong had gained a certain amount of fame as "Chinatown's Littlest Chinese Chess Champion."

44     "She bring home too many trophy," lamented Auntie Lindo that

Sunday. "All day she play chess. All day I have no time do nothing but dust off her winnings." She threw a scolding look at Waverly, who pretended not to see her.

"You lucky you don't have this problem," said Auntie Lindo with a    45
sigh to my mother.

And my mother squared her shoulders and bragged: "Our problem    46
worser than yours. If we ask Jing-Mei wash dish, she hear nothing but music. It's like you can't stop this natural talent."

And right then, I was determined to put a stop to her foolish pride.    47

A few weeks later, Old Chong and my mother conspired to have me    48
play in a talent show which would be held in the church hall. By then, my parents had saved up enough to buy me a secondhand piano, a black Wurlitzer spinet with a scarred bench. It was the showpiece of our living room.

For the talent show, I was to play a piece called "Pleading Child"    49
from Schumann's *Scenes from Childhood*. It was a simple, moody piece that sounded more difficult than it was. I was supposed to memorize the whole thing, playing the repeat parts twice to make the piece sound longer. But I dawdled over it, playing a few bars and then cheating, looking up to see what notes followed. I never really listened to what I was playing. I daydreamed about being somewhere else, about being someone else.

The part I liked to practice best was the fancy curtsy: right foot out,    50
touch the rose on the carpet with a pointed foot, sweep to the side, left leg bends, look up and smile.

My parents invited all the couples from the Joy Luck Club to witness    51
my debut. Auntie Lindo and Uncle Tin were there. Waverly and her two older brothers had also come. The first two rows were filled with children both younger and older than I was. The littlest ones got to go first. They recited simple nursery rhymes, squawked out tunes on miniature violins, twirled Hula Hoops, pranced in pink ballet tutus, and when they bowed or curtsied, the audience would sigh in unison, "Awww," and then clap enthusiastically.

When my turn came, I was very confident. I remember my childish    52
excitement. It was as if I knew, without a doubt, that the prodigy side of me really did exist. I had no fear whatsoever, no nervousness. I remember thinking to myself, This is it! This is it! I looked out over the audience, at my mother's blank face, my father's yawn, Auntie Lindo's stiff-lipped smile, Waverly's sulky expression. I had on a white dress layered with sheets of lace, and a pink bow in my Peter Pan haircut. As I sat down I envisioned people jumping to their feet and Ed Sullivan rushing up to introduce me to everyone on TV.

And I started to play. It was so beautiful. I was so caught up in how    53
lovely I looked that at first I didn't worry how I would sound. So it was a surprise to me when I hit the first wrong note and I realized something

didn't sound quite right. And then I hit another and another followed that. A chill started at the top of my head and began to trickle down. Yet I couldn't stop playing, as though my hands were bewitched. I kept thinking my fingers would adjust themselves back, like a train switching to the right track. I played this strange jumble through two repeats, the sour notes staying with me all the way to the end.

54    When I stood up, I discovered my legs were shaking. Maybe I had just been nervous and the audience, like Old Chong, had seen me go through the right motions and had not heard anything wrong at all. I swept my right foot out, went down on my knee, looked up and smiled. The room was quiet, except for Old Chong, who was beaming and shouting, "Bravo! Bravo! Well done!" But then I saw my mother's face, her stricken face. The audience clapped weakly, and as I walked back to my chair, with my whole face quivering as I tried not to cry, I heard a little boy whisper loudly to his mother, "That was awful," and the mother whispered back, "Well, she certainly tried."

55    And now I realized how many people were in the audience, the whole world it seemed. I was aware of eyes burning into my back. I felt the shame of my mother and father as they sat stiffly throughout the rest of the show.

56    We could have escaped during intermission. Pride and some strange sense of humor must have anchored my parents to their chairs. And so we watched it all: the eighteen-year-old boy with a fake mustache who did a magic show and juggled flaming hoops while riding a unicycle. The breasted girl with white makeup who sang from *Madame Butterfly* and got honorable mention. And the eleven-year-old boy who won first prize playing a tricky violin song that sounded like a busy bee.

57    After the show, the Hsus, the Jongs, and the St. Clairs from the Joy Luck Club came up to my mother and father.

58    "Lots of talented kids," Auntie Lindo said vaguely, smiling broadly.

59    "That was somethin' else," said my father, and I wondered if he was referring to me in a humorous way, or whether he even remembered what I had done.

60    Waverly looked at me and shrugged her shoulders. "You aren't a genius like me," she said matter-of-factly. And if I hadn't felt so bad, I would have pulled her braids and punched her stomach.

61    But my mother's expression was what devastated me: a quiet, blank look that said she had lost everything. I felt the same way, and it seemed as if everybody were now coming up, like gawkers at the scene of an accident, to see what parts were actually missing. When we got on the bus to go home, my father was humming the busy-bee tune and my mother was silent. I kept thinking she wanted to wait until we got home before shouting at me. But when my father unlocked the door to our apartment, my mother walked in and then went to the back, into the bedroom. No accusations. No blame. And in a way, I felt disappointed. I

had been waiting for her to start shouting, so I could shout back and cry and blame her for all my misery.

I assumed my talent-show fiasco meant I never had to play the piano again. But two days later, after school, my mother came out of the kitchen and saw me watching TV.                                                        62

"Four clock," she reminded me as if it were any other day. I was stunned, as though she were asking me to go through the talent-show torture again. I wedged myself more tightly in front of the TV.             63

"Turn off TV," she called from the kitchen five minutes later.            64

I didn't budge. And then I decided. I didn't have to do what my mother said anymore. I wasn't her slave. This wasn't China. I had listened to her before and look what happened. She was the stupid one.                                                                                   65

She came out from the kitchen and stood in the arched entryway of the living room. "Four clock," she said once again, louder.                 66

"I'm not going to play anymore," I said nonchalantly. "Why should I? I'm not a genius."                                                            67

She walked over and stood in front of the TV. I saw her chest was heaving up and down in an angry way.                                       68

"No!" I said, and I now felt stronger, as if my true self had finally emerged. So this was what had been inside me all along.                 69

"No! I won't!" I screamed.                                                  70

She yanked me by the arm, pulled me off the floor, snapped off the TV. She was frighteningly strong, half pulling, half carrying me toward the piano as I kicked the throw rugs under my feet. She lifted me up and onto the hard bench. I was sobbing by now, looking at her bitterly. Her chest was heaving even more and her mouth was open, smiling crazily as if she were pleased I was crying.                                         71

"You want me to be someone that I'm not!" I sobbed. "I'll never be the kind of daughter you want me to be!"                                    72

"Only two kinds of daughters," she shouted in Chinese. "Those who are obedient and those who follow their own mind! Only one kind of daughter can live in this house. Obedient daughter!"                      73

"Then I wish I wasn't your daughter. I wish you weren't my mother," I shouted. As I said these things I got scared. It felt like worms and toads and slimy things crawling out of my chest, but it also felt good, as if this awful side of me had surfaced, at last.                                     74

"Too late change this," said my mother shrilly.                            75

And I could sense her anger rising to its breaking point. I wanted to see it spill over. And that's when I remembered the babies she had lost in China, the ones we never talked about. "Then I wish I'd never been born!" I shouted. "I wish I were dead! Like them."                          76

It was as if I had said the magic words. Alakazam!—and her face went blank, her mouth closed, her arms went slack, and she backed out        77 of the room, stunned, as if she were blowing away like a small brown leaf, thin, brittle, lifeless.

It was not the only disappointment my mother felt in me. In the years that followed, I failed her so many times, each time asserting my own will, my right to fall short of expectations. I didn't get straight As. I didn't become class president. I didn't get into Stanford. I dropped out of college.

For unlike my mother, I did not believe I could be anything I wanted to be. I could only be me.

And for all those years, we never talked about the disaster at the recital or my terrible accusations afterward at the piano bench. All that remained unchecked, like a betrayal that was now unspeakable. So I never found a way to ask her why she had hoped for something so large that failure was inevitable.

And even worse, I never asked her what frightened me the most: Why had she given up hope?

For after our struggle at the piano, she never mentioned my playing again. The lessons stopped. The lid to the piano was closed, shutting out the dust, my misery, and her dreams.

So she surprised me. A few years ago, she offered to give me the piano, for my thirtieth birthday. I had not played in all those years. I saw the offer as a sign of forgiveness, a tremendous burden removed.

"Are you sure?" I asked shyly. "I mean, won't you and Dad miss it?"

"No, this your piano," she said firmly. "Always your piano. You only one can play."

"Well, I probably can't play anymore," I said. "It's been years."

"You pick up fast," said my mother, as if she knew this was certain. "You have natural talent. You could been genius if you want to."

"No I couldn't."

"You just not trying," said my mother. And she was neither angry nor sad. She said it as if to announce a fact that could never be disproved. "Take it," she said.

But I didn't at first. It was enough that she had offered it to me. And after that, every time I saw it in my parents' living room, standing in front of the bay windows, it made me feel proud, as if it were a shiny trophy I had won back.

Last week I sent a tuner over to my parents' apartment and had the piano reconditioned, for purely sentimental reasons. My mother had died a few months before and I had been getting things in order for my father, a little bit at a time. I put the jewelry in special silk pouches. The sweaters she had knitted in yellow, pink, bright orange — all the colors I hated — I put those in moth-proof boxes. I found some old Chinese silk dresses, the kind with little slits up the sides. I rubbed the old silk against my skin, then wrapped them in tissue and decided to take them home with me.

After I had the piano tuned, I opened the lid and touched the keys. It 90
sounded even richer than I remembered. Really, it was a very good
piano. Inside the bench were the same exercise notes with handwritten
scales, the same secondhand music books with their covers held together
with yellow tape.

I opened up the Schumann book to the dark little piece I had played 91
at the recital. It was on the left-hand side of the page, "Pleading Child."
It looked more difficult than I remembered. I played a few bars, surprised at how easily the notes came back to me.

And the first time, or so it seemed, I noticed the piece on the right- 92
hand side. It was called "Perfectly Contented." I tried to play this one as
well. It had a lighter melody but the same flowing rhythm and turned
out to be quite easy. "Pleading Child" was shorter but slower; "Perfectly
Contented" was longer, but faster. And after I played them both a few
times, I realized they were two halves of the same song.

## Evaluating the Text

1. Why is it so important to Jing-Mei's mother to have her daughter become a
   prodigy of some kind? How does this expectation shape Jing-Mei's early
   childhood? How does Jing-Mei react to the pressure of living up to her
   mother's expectations? Left to her own devices, do you feel she would have
   preferred to be just an ordinary child and not stand out from the crowd?
2. How was it that Jing-Mei did not know that she had little talent for the
   piano? Why weren't her teacher, her mother, or Jing-Mei herself able to
   determine this? Why did it have to get to the point where she gave a
   horrible recital for everyone to realize she couldn't play the piano?
3. Describe the conflict Jing-Mei feels in trying to search for her own identity,
   while at the same time trying to make her mother happy by becoming a
   child prodigy. Do you think Jing-Mei misunderstood her mother and
   transformed her mother's desire for her to "be her best" into the
   expectation that she would become a prodigy?
4. What evidence is there within the story that this account was written many
   years after the events described took place? How do we know that at a
   later point Jing-Mei saw her mother was only trying to do what was best
   for her? What evidence is there that the narrator is much older, has greater
   understanding of what her mother was trying to do, and has more
   compassion toward her mother? How does the different perspective from
   which she remembers the situation enable her to grasp it in a way she
   could not as a child?
5. How does Jing-Mei's treatment of the old piano, which she "reconditioned,
   for purely sentimental reasons," symbolize her attitude toward her
   childhood?
6. How do the two pieces of music mentioned in the story ("Pleading Child"
   and "Perfectly Contented") refer to her role as daughter and to the
   outcome of attempting to fulfill her mother's expectations? In what way do
   these two pieces of music represent different sides of her personality?

# Exploring Different Perspectives

1. Compare the value placed on personal success in this story with Chinese cultural values described in Bruce Dollar's "Child Care in China." How does the concept of a "child prodigy" reflect American values that would be rejected in China?
2. Compare the sources of humor in this story and in Natsume Soseki's chapter from *I Am a Cat.* In each story, how does the author use the naiveté of the main character as a source of humor?

# Extending Viewpoints through Writing

1. What kinds of pressures are children of immigrants under to take advantage of opportunities offered by American society as a way of repaying sacrifices made by their parents?
2. You need not be the child of a first-generation immigrant to experience the kinds of pressures Tan describes. For example, did your parents try to live vicariously through your achievements in Little League or other sports? What experiences have you had that gave you insight into Jing-Mei Woo's dilemma?
3. Were you encouraged or forced to take piano lessons or any other musical instrument when you were a child? Were your experiences similar to or different from those of Jing-Mei Woo?

# CONNECTING CULTURES

## Andrew Cherlin and Frank F. Furstenberg, Jr., "The American Family in the Year 2000"

1. Drawing on the account of Jo Goodwin Parker ("What Is Poverty?" Chapter 5), compare the experience of being poor and white with Cherlin and Furstenberg's description of being poor and black, especially in terms of the role played by the network of "extended kin."
2. What insights do Christy Brown ("The Letter 'A,'" Chapter 2) and Tepilit Ole Saitoti ("The Initiation of a Maasai Warrior," Chapter 2) provide about the role of family life in cultures as diverse as those of the Irish and the Maasai?
3. How might the practice of female circumcision Nawal El Saadawi describes ("Circumcision of Girls," Chapter 2) adversely affect family life in terms of trust and expectations in those societies that practice it?

## William Trevor, "Teresa's Wedding"

4. How do Trevor's and Christy Brown's ("The Letter 'A,'" Chapter 2) portrayal of Irish family life complement each other?
5. Compare the role played by Catholicism in Trevor's story with the religious values of the Amish in Gene Logsdon's "Amish Economics" (Chapter 4).
6. In what way do both Trevor's story and the account by Douchan Gersi ("Initiated into an Iban Tribe of Headhunters," Chapter 2) involve the stripping away of romanticized notions in very different contexts?
7. In what way do the attitudes toward sex and courtship depicted in Trevor's story resemble those described by Tepilit Ole Saitoti ("The Initiation of a Maasai Warrior," Chapter 2)? In what ways do they differ?
8. How do pressures by the outside community produce a marriage in "Teresa's Wedding" and prevent it between an Arab woman and an Israeli man, in David K. Shipler's "The Sin of Love" (Chapter 3)? How do these pressures reflect characteristic values in each culture?

## Francine du Plessix Gray, "Sex and Birth"

9. Drawing on Marilyn French's discussion ("Gender Roles," Chapter 3) of the role culture plays in determining gender roles, analyze the distinctive contribution of Russian culture in shaping the roles of women as described by du Plessix Gray.
10. Compare attitudes toward sex in Russia analyzed by du Plessix Gray with those described by Nawal El Saadawi in Egypt ("Circumcision of Girls," Chapter 2) and Tepilit Ole Saitoti ("The Initiation of a Maasai Warrior," Chapter 2) among the Maasai in Kenya.

## Boris Yeltsin, "Childhood in Russia"

11. Explore the similarities and differences in the relationship between Yeltsin and his grandfather and the protagonist with his grandfather in Tayeb Salih's "A Handful of Dates," Chapter 2).

12. Discuss the differences between Amish communal life (see Gene Logsdon's "A Lesson for the Modern World: Amish Economics," Chapter 4) and the communal life of Yeltsin's childhood in Russia.

13. What common elements can you find between Yeltsin's homeroom teacher and Miss Bontempo in Danny Santiago's "Famous All Over Town" (Chapter 2)? How important a part did gangs play in both Yeltsin's and Rudy's life?

14. Compare what poverty means in the different cultural settings of Russia in the 1930s, the rural South in the United States (see Jo Goodwin Parker's "What Is Poverty?" Chapter 5), and in modern-day Calcutta (see Krishnan Varma's "The Grass-Eaters," Chapter 5).

15. What very different picture emerges of Soviet versus Chinese bureaucracy in Yeltsin's account compared with Shen Tong's account in "Bloody Sunday in Tiananmen Square" (Chapter 6)? What leadership qualities do both Yeltsin and Shen Tong exhibit?

## Natsume Soseki, I Am a Cat

16. Compare and contrast the different treatment accorded the two household pets, the chicken in Nicholasa Mohr's "A Very Special Pet" (Chapter 7) and the unnamed cat in Soseki's novel. How does each pet symbolize the true circumstances of each household? In what way does each story provide insight into a Puerto Rican family who has immigrated to the United States and bourgeois (middle-class) Japanese society in the early 1900s, respectively?

17. How do both Soseki and Jamaica Kincaid ("A Small Place" Chapter 7) provide unusual perspectives on situations not normally seen from their respective points of view? Why are these unusual points of view made more necessary because they represent the viewpoints of those who are powerless within each respective culture (Japan and Antigua)?

18. Compare Soseki's portrait of the Japanese schoolmaster with Mark Salzman's portrayal of Pan as a teacher in "Lessons" (Chapter 4). What differences in personality, methods, and attitudes toward the subjects taught can you observe?

19. How do both Catherine Lim ("Paper" Chapter 4) and Soseki criticize bourgeois social aspirations in Singapore and Japan, respectively?

## Rigoberta Menchu, "Birth Ceremonies"

20. Compare the role played by traditional tribal rituals in Menchu's account with the reemergence of an ancient tribal belief in Bessie Head's "Looking for a Rain God" (Chapter 8). How are attitudes toward children in these two selections connected with superstitions and "magical thinking"?

21. Compare the respective role played by initiation rituals described by Menchu with those described by Nawal El Saadawi ("Circumcision of

Girls," Chapter 2). How, in each case, do the rituals provide insight into the cultural values and the role of women in Middle-Eastern countries and among the Quiché Indians in Guatemala?

22. What elements of Marilyn French's observations about gender roles ("Gender Roles," Chapter 3) in Western culture would hold true for the different sex roles, identified by Menchu, among the Guatemalan Indians?

23. Explore the role played by community in conferring individual identity in both Menchu's account and Gene Logsdon's depiction of Amish life ("Amish Economics," Chapter 4).

24. How do both Menchu's and Ngũgĩ wa Thiong'o's accounts ("Decolonising the Mind," Chapter 6) enhance your understanding of what life is like for a native people living under the domination of a different culture (the *ladino* in Guatemala and the colonial British bureaucracy in Kenya)?

## Bruce Dollar, "Child Care in China"

25. How does Mark Salzman's account ("Lessons," Chapter 4) of being trained by the great Chinese martial arts master, Pan, embody attitudes toward education that complement Dollar's account?

26. How do both Dollar and John Burgess ("A Day in the Life of 'Salaryman'," Chapter 4) shed light on the role conformity plays in shaping the cultural values of Chinese and Japanese societies? How do the pressures to conform take different forms in each society?

## Amy Tan, "Jing-Mei Woo: Two Kinds"

27. How would you compare the aspiration of Rudy's father for his son in Danny Santiago's story ("Famous all over Town," Chapter 2) with the aspiration of Jing-Mei Woo's mother for her daughter? In what way are these desires typical of those of first-generation immigrant parents?

28. How are both Jing-Mei Woo and Christy Brown ("The Letter 'A'," Chapter 2) influenced by their mother's aspirations and expectations?

29. How does Jing-Mei Woo's mother's extreme expectations connect to Edward Said's analysis of the psychological needs characteristic of immigrants, refugees, and exiles ("Reflections On Exile," Chapter 7)? To what extent is the mother's expectation her daughter will gain prominence and acceptance in a new culture a form of compensation to make up for the sacrifices the mother has made in emigrating from China?

30. How does Mark Salzman's account ("Lessons," Chapter 4), describing the kinds of rewards bestowed on Pan, the greatest martial arts master in China, compare with the expectations Jing-Mei Woo's mother has for her daughter if she becomes a successful child prodigy? How do the differences in rewards reflect underlying differences in cultural values between China and America?

# 2

# *Turning Points*

In virtually every society, certain rites or ceremonies are used to signal adulthood. Although many of these occasions are informal, some are quite elaborate and dramatic. The following chapter offers a range of perspectives that illustrate how these turning points are marked by informal and formal rituals across a broad spectrum of cultures. These moments of insight may be private psychological turning points or ceremonies that initiate the individual into adulthood within a community. These crucial moments in which individuals move from childhood innocence to adult awareness often involve learning a particular society's rules governing what should or should not be done under different circumstances, values, knowledge, and expectations as to how the individual should present him- or herself in a wide variety of situations. Because this chapter is rich in a wide variety of perspectives, it invites you to make discoveries about turning points in your own life.

The essays and stories in this chapter focus on the psychological and cultural forces that shape the identity of those who are about to be initiated into their respective communities. From Ireland, we read the moving narrative of Christy Brown, who describes, in "The Letter 'A'," his struggle to communicate signs of intelligence, by drawing the letter "A" with his left foot, after having been diagnosed as hopelessly retarded as the result of cerebral palsy. Henry Allen, in "The Corps," describes how new recruits at Parris Island Marine Boot Camp undergo a modern-day rite of passage. The international French explorer, Douchan Gersi, offers a hair-raising account appropriately titled "Initiated into an Iban Tribe of Headhunters," a first hand narrative based on his experiences in modern-day Borneo. The unexpected consequences of attempting to gain approval from his English teacher and become a good student are the subject of Danny Santiago's vivid portrayal of the Chicano urban experience in "Famous all over Town." In the first autobiographical account ever written by a Maasai, Tepilit Ole Saitoti describes, in "The Initiation of a Maasai Warrior," the circumcision ceremony that served as his rite of passage into adulthood. The internationally renowned Egyptian feminist writer, Nawal El Saadawi, in "Circumcision of Girls," analyzes the cultural prejudices that still encourage the archaic and damaging practice of female circumcision in many countries of the Middle East. Last, the Sudanese writer Tayeb Salih tells a story, "A Handful of Dates," of a moment during the harvest of date palms that permanently alters the relationship between a boy and his grandfather.

# Christy Brown

# *The Letter "A"*

---

*Christy Brown (1932–1981) was born in Dublin, the tenth child in a family of twenty-two. Brown was diagnosed as having cerebral palsy and as being hopelessly retarded. An intense personal struggle and the loving attention and faith of his mother resulted in a surprising degree of rehabilitation. Brown's autobiography,* My Left Foot *(1954), describing his struggle to overcome his massive handicap, was the basis for the 1989 Academy Award-winning film. Brown is also the author of an internationally acclaimed novel,* Down All the Days *(1970). "The Letter 'A'," from his autobiography, describes the crucial moment when he first communicated signs of awareness and intelligence.*

I was born in the Rotunda Hospital,[1] on June 5th, 1932. There were nine children before me and twelve after me, so I myself belong to the middle group. Out of this total of twenty-two, seventeen lived, but four died in infancy, leaving thirteen still to hold the family fort. 1

Mine was a difficult birth, I am told. Both mother and son almost died. A whole army of relations queued up outside the hospital until the small hours of the morning, waiting for news and praying furiously that it would be good. 2

After my birth Mother was sent to recuperate for some weeks and I was kept in the hospital while she was away. I remained there for some time, without name, for I wasn't baptized until my mother was well enough to bring me to church. 3

It was Mother who first saw that there was something wrong with me. I was about four months old at the time. She noticed that my head had a habit of falling backward whenever she tried to feed me. She attempted to correct this by placing her hand on the back of my neck to keep it steady. But when she took it away, back it would drop again. That was the first warning sign. Then she became aware of other defects as I got older. She saw that my hands were clenched nearly all of the time and were inclined to twine behind my back; my mouth couldn't grasp the teat of the bottle because even at that early age my jaws would either lock together tightly, so that it was impossible for her to open them, or they would suddenly become limp and fall loose, dragging my whole 4

---

*(For more background on Ireland, see p. 10.)

[1]*Rotunda Hospital,* a hospital in Dublin, Ireland.

mouth to one side. At six months I could not sit up without having a mountain of pillows around me. At twelve months it was the same.

5 Very worried by this, Mother told my father her fears, and they decided to seek medical advice without any further delay. I was a little over a year old when they began to take me to hospitals and clinics, convinced that there was something definitely wrong with me, something which they could not understand or name, but which was very real and disturbing.

6 Almost every doctor who saw and examined me labeled me a very interesting but also a hopeless case. Many told Mother very gently that I was mentally defective and would remain so. That was a hard blow to a young mother who had already reared five healthy children. The doctors were so very sure of themselves that Mother's faith in me seemed almost an impertinence. They assured her that nothing could be done for me.

7 She refused to accept this truth, the inevitable truth—as it then seemed—that I was beyond cure, beyond saving, even beyond hope. She could not and would not believe that I was an imbecile, as the doctors told her. She had nothing in the world to go by, not a scrap of evidence to support her conviction that, though my body was crippled, my mind was not. In spite of all the doctors and specialists told her, she would not agree. I don't believe she knew why—she just knew, without feeling the smallest shade of doubt.

8 Finding that the doctors could not help in any way beyond telling her not to place her trust in me, or, in other words, to forget I was a human creature, rather to regard me as just something to be fed and washed and then put away again, Mother decided there and then to take matters into her own hands. I was *her* child, and therefore part of the family. No matter how dull and incapable I might grow up to be, she was determined to treat me on the same plane as the others, and not as the "queer one" in the back room who was never spoken of when there were visitors present.

9 That was a momentous decision as far as my future life was concerned. It meant that I would always have my mother on my side to help me fight all the battles that were to come, and to inspire me with new strength when I was almost beaten. But it wasn't easy for her because now the relatives and friends had decided otherwise. They contended that I should be taken kindly, sympathetically, but not seriously. That would be a mistake. "For your own sake," they told her, "don't look to this boy as you would to the others; it would only break your heart in the end." Luckily for me, Mother and Father held out against the lot of them. But Mother wasn't content just to say that I was not an idiot: she set out to prove it, not because of any rigid sense of duty, but out of love. That is why she was so successful.

10 At this time she had the five other children to look after besides the "difficult one," though as yet it was not by any means a full house. They were my brothers, Jim, Tony, and Paddy, and my two sisters, Lily and

Mona, all of them very young, just a year or so between each of them, so that they were almost exactly like steps of stairs.

Four years rolled by and I was now five, and still as helpless as a    11
newly born baby. While my father was out at bricklaying, earning our bread and butter for us, Mother was slowly, patiently pulling down the wall, brick by brick, that seemed to thrust itself between me and the other children, slowly, patiently penetrating beyond the thick curtain that hung over my mind, separating it from theirs. It was hard, heart-breaking work, for often all she got from me in return was a vague smile and perhaps a faint gurgle. I could not speak or even mumble, nor could I sit up without support on my own, let alone take steps. But I wasn't inert or motionless. I seemed, indeed, to be convulsed with movement, wild, stiff, snakelike movement that never left me, except in sleep. My fingers twisted and twitched continually, my arms twined backwards and would often shoot out suddenly this way and that, and my head lolled and sagged sideways. I was a queer, crooked little fellow.

Mother tells me how one day she had been sitting with me for hours    12
in an upstairs room, showing me pictures out of a great big storybook that I had got from Santa Claus last Christmas and telling me the names of the different animals and flowers that were in them, trying without success to get me to repeat them. This had gone on for hours while she talked and laughed with me. Then at the end of it she leaned over me and said gently into my ear:

"Did you like it, Chris? Did you like the bears and the monkeys and    13
all the lovely flowers? Nod your head for yes, like a good boy."

But I could make no sign that I had understood her. Her face was    14
bent over mine hopefully. Suddenly, involuntarily, my queer hand reached up and grasped one of the dark curls that fell in a thick cluster about her neck. Gently she loosened the clenched fingers, though some dark strands were still clutched between them.

Then she turned away from my curious stare and left the room,    15
crying. The door closed behind her. It all seemed hopeless. It looked as though there was some justification for my relatives' contention that I was an idiot and beyond help.

They now spoke of an institution.    16

"Never!" said my mother almost fiercely, when this was suggested to    17
her. "I know my boy is not an idiot; it is his body that is shattered, not his mind. I'm sure of that."

Sure? Yet inwardly, she prayed God would give her some proof of    18
her faith. She knew it was one thing to believe but quite another thing to prove.

I was now five, and still I showed no real sign of intelligence. I    19
showed no apparent interest in things except with my toes — more espe-cially those of my left foot. Although my natural habits were clean, I could not aid myself, but in this respect my father took care of me. I used to lie on my back all the time in the kitchen or, on bright warm days, out

in the garden, a little bundle of crooked muscles and twisted nerves, surrounded by a family that loved me and hoped for me and that made me part of their own warmth and humanity. I was lonely, imprisoned in a world of my own, unable to communicate with others, cut off, separated from them as though a glass wall stood between my existence and theirs, thrusting me beyond the sphere of their lives and activities. I longed to run about and play with the rest, but I was unable to break loose from my bondage.

20    Then, suddenly, it happened! In a moment everything was changed, my future life molded into a definite shape, my mother's faith in me rewarded, and her secret fear changed into open triumph.

21    It happened so quickly, so simply after all the years of waiting and uncertainty, that I can see and feel the whole scene as if it had happened last week. It was the afternoon of a cold, gray December day. The streets outside glistened with snow, the white sparkling flakes stuck and melted on the windowpanes and hung on the boughs of the trees like molten silver. The wind howled dismally, whipping up little whirling columns of snow that rose and fell at every fresh gust. And over all, the dull, murky sky stretched like a dark canopy, a vast infinity of grayness.

22    Inside, all the family were gathered round the big kitchen fire that lit up the little room with a warm glow and made giant shadows dance on the walls and ceiling.

23    In a corner Mona and Paddy were sitting, huddled together, a few torn school primers before them. They were writing down little sums onto an old chipped slate, using a bright piece of yellow chalk. I was close to them, propped up by a few pillows against the wall, watching.

24    It was the chalk that attracted me so much. It was a long, slender stick of vivid yellow. I had never seen anything like it before, and it showed up so well against the black surface of the slate that I was fascinated by it as much as if it had been a stick of gold.

25    Suddenly, I wanted desperately to do what my sister was doing. Then — without thinking or knowing exactly what I was doing, I reached out and took the stick of chalk out of my sister's hand — with my left foot.

26    I do not know why I used my left foot to do this. It is a puzzle to many people as well as to myself, for, although I had displayed a curious interest in my toes at an early age, I had never attempted before this to use either of my feet in any way. They could have been as useless to me as were my hands. That day, however, my left foot, apparently by its own volition, reached out and very impolitely took the chalk out of my sister's hand.

27    I held it tightly between my toes, and, acting on an impulse, made a wild sort of scribble with it on the slate. Next moment I stopped, a bit dazed, surprised, looking down at the stick of yellow chalk stuck between my toes, not knowing what to do with it next, hardly knowing how it got there. Then I looked up and became aware that everyone had

stopped talking and was staring at me silently. Nobody stirred. Mona, her black curls framing her chubby little face, stared at me with great big eyes and open mouth. Across the open hearth, his face lit by flames, sat my father, leaning forward, hands outspread on his knees, his shoulders tense. I felt the sweat break out on my forehead.

My mother came in from the pantry with a steaming pot in her hand. 28 She stopped midway between the table and the fire, feeling the tension flowing through the room. She followed their stare and saw me in the corner. Her eyes looked from my face down to my foot, with the chalk gripped between my toes. She put down the pot.

Then she crossed over to me and knelt down beside me, as she had 29 done so many times before.

"I'll show you what to do with it, Chris," she said, very slowly and in 30 a queer, choked way, her face flushed as if with some inner excitement.

Taking another piece of chalk from Mona, she hesitated, then very 31 deliberately drew, on the floor in front of me, *the single letter "A."*

"Copy that," she said, looking steadily at me. "Copy it, Christy." 32
I couldn't. 33

I looked about me, looked around at the faces that were turned 34 towards me, tense, excited faces that were at that moment frozen, immobile, eager, waiting for a miracle in their midst.

The stillness was profound. The room was full of flame and shadow 35 that danced before my eyes and lulled my taut nerves into a sort of waking sleep. I could hear the sound of the water tap dripping in the pantry, the loud ticking of the clock on the mantel shelf, and the soft hiss and crackle of the logs on the open hearth.

I tried again. I put out my foot and made a wild jerking stab with the 36 chalk which produced a very crooked line and nothing more. Mother held the slate steady for me.

"Try again, Chris," she whispered in my ear. "Again." 37
I did. I stiffened my body and put my left foot out again, for the third 38 time. I drew one side of the letter. I drew half the other side. Then the stick of chalk broke and I was left with a stump. I wanted to fling it away and give up. Then I felt my mother's hand on my shoulder. I tried once more. Out went my foot. I shook, I sweated and strained every muscle. My hands were so tightly clenched that my fingernails bit into the flesh. I set my teeth so hard that I nearly pierced my lower lip. Everything in the room swam till the faces around me were mere patches of white. But — I drew it — *the letter "A."* There it was on the floor before me. Shaky, with awkward, wobbly sides and a very uneven center line. But it *was* the letter "A." I looked up. I saw my mother's face for a moment, tears on her cheeks. Then my father stooped and hoisted me onto his shoulder.

I had done it! It had started — the thing that was to give my mind its 39 chance of expressing itself. True, I couldn't speak with my lips. But now I would speak through something more lasting than spoken words — written words.

40     That one letter, scrawled on the floor with a broken bit of yellow chalk gripped between my toes, was my road to a new world, my key to mental freedom. It was to provide a source of relaxation to the tense, taut thing that was I, which panted for expression behind a twisted mouth.

## Evaluating the Test

1. What unusual signs alerted Christy's mother that he might be physically impaired? What did her response to the doctors' diagnosis reveal about her as a person and her attitude toward Christy?
2. What did Christy's mother hope to achieve by showing him pictures of animals and flowers? How did her friends and relatives react to her decision to treat Christy as if he were capable of mental development? How would Christy's day-to-day treatment have differed if his mother had not treated him as a member of the family?
3. What is the reason the narrative shifts from Christy's mother's perspective to Christy's recollection of the day he was able to form the letter *A* with his left foot?
4. How does Christy structure his narrative, describing the moment he first communicated signs of intelligence, to dramatize what was at stake for himself and for his family?
5. From the point of view of Christy's mother and father and siblings, how did they know that his forming the letter *A* was a sign of intelligence and not merely an imitative gesture?
6. How does the conclusion of this account suggest that this moment had deeper meaning for Christy than it did even for his family? What did this mean to him?

## Exploring Different Perspectives

1. In what way can Brown be considered to be just as courageous in meeting the challenge he faced as Tepilit Ole Saitoti was in exhibiting bravery during his initiation as a Maasai warrior ("The Initiation of a Maasai Warrior").
2. Explore the value of communication as it emerges in Danny Santiago's "Famous All Over Town" and in this account in terms of how society draws conclusions about people's mental capacity based on their ability to communicate. Compare the different meanings that being able to communicate had for Christy and for Rudy in "Famous All Over Town." What underlying similarities between the two can you discover?

## Extending Viewpoints through Writing

1. On any given day, how do you think Christy would have been treated if his mother had not made the decision to treat him as a member of the family? Write two brief accounts analyzing why, over a period of time, the difference in the way he was treated might have been capable of producing the unexpected development Christy describes. Include everyday events such as meals, visits from friends, and the like in your account.

2. If you have seen the 1989 Academy Award-winning film *My Left Foot*, based on Christy Brown's autobiography of the same name, discuss which treatment, film or written account, more effectively dramatized the issues at stake and the feelings of Christy and his family at the moment when he drew the letter *A*.

3. The same stylistic qualities of closely noted detail and studied keen observation of human nature are apparent in his widely acclaimed novel *Down All the Days* (1970). For further research, you may wish to read this novel and write a short analysis of Christy's compelling style.

4. If you have ever been temporarily physically incapacitated, or have a disability, write an essay that will help your audience to understand your plight and the visible and subtle psychological aspects of discrimination that the disabled must endure every day.

# Henry Allen

# *The Corps*

---

*Henry Allen, born in 1941, served in the Marine Corps and is currently a reporter and writer for the* Washington Post. *He is the author of the novel* Fool's Mercy (1982). *"The Corps," originally written in 1971, recounts the grueling experiences of Marine boot camp and sketches in vivid detail the drill instructors who invoke and exploit "primal dread." Allen's report emerged as the distilled core of his experiences as a reporter and a former Marine from over two hundred pages written over seventeen days.*

1    PARRIS ISLAND, S.C. — He is seething, he is rabid, he is wound up tight as a golf ball, with more adrenalin surging through his hypothalamus than a cornered slum rat, he is everything these Marine recruits with their heads shaved to dirty nubs have ever feared or even hoped a drill instructor might be.

2    He is Staff Sgt. Douglas Berry and he is rushing down the squad bay of Receiving Barracks to leap onto a table and brace at parade rest in which none of the recruits, daring glances from the position of attention, can see any more of him under the rake of his campaign hat than his lipless mouth chopping at them like a disaster teletype: WHEN I GIVE YOU THE WORD YOU WILL WALK YOU WILL NOT RUN DOWN THESE STEPS WHERE YOU WILL RUN YOU WILL NOT WALK TO THE YELLOW FOOTMARKS. . . .

3    Outside, Berry's two junior drill instructors, in raincoats over dress greens, sweat in a muggy February drizzle which shrinks the view down to this wooden World War II barracks, to the galvanized Butler hut across the company street, the overground steam pipes, a couple of palmetto trees, the raindrops beading on spitshined black shoes.

4    Sgt. Hudson mans the steps, Sgt. Burley the footmarks. They pace with a mannered strut, like men wearing white tie and tails, their hands folded behind their backs, their jaw muscles flexing. One senses there's none of the wisecracking "See Here, Private Hargrove," or "Sgt. Bilko" Army routine here, no hotshot recruits outsmarting dumb sarge for passes to town.

5    In fact, during his 63 days of training at Parris Island, unless a member of his immediate family dies, a recruit will get no liberty at all. He will also get no talking, no phone calls, no books or magazines, no television, radio or record players, no candy or gum, one movie, one

newspaper a week, and three cigarettes a day. Unless he fouls up, gets sent to the brig or to motivation platoon, and loses the cigarettes.

WHEN I GIVE YOU THE WORD TO MOVE OUT YOU WILL MOVE OUT DO YOU UNDERSTAND ME? 6

Hudson meets the first one at the steps like a rotary mower ripping into a toad, so psyched he's actually dancing on tiptoe, with his face a choleric three-quarters of an inch from the private FASTER PRIVATE FASTER JUST TAKE YOUR DUMB TIME SWEETHEART MOVE! MOVE! as this hog, as recruits are colloquially known, piles out of the barracks in a stumble of new boots, poncho, laundry bag and the worst trouble his young ass has ever been in, no doubt about it when Burley meets him just like Hudson, in an astonishment of rage that roars him all the way down to the right front set of yellow footprints YOU LOCK YOUR BODY AT ATTENTION YOU LOCK YOUR BODY. . . . 7

Or maybe Burley writhes up around this private to hiss in his ear — and Burley is very good at this — *you hate me, don't you, you hate me, private, you'd better hate me because I hate you,* or any of the other litanies drill instructors have been barking and hissing at their charges ever since the first of more than one million Parris Island graduates arrived on this flea-ridden sand barren in 1911. 8

Until there are 60 of them out there in the drizzle with the drill instructors shouting themselves hoarse, 60 volunteers who had heard from countless older brothers and street corner buddies and roommates that it would be exactly like this but they volunteered anyhow, to be Marines. 9

Right now, with lips trembling, eyes shuttling YOU BETTER STOP THAT EYE-BALLING, PRIVATE! fat and forlorn, they look like 60 sex perverts trapped by a lynch mob. They are scared. They are scared as fraternity pledges during a cleverly staged hell week, shaking like boys about to abandon their virginity. 10

It's a primal dread that drill instructors invoke and exploit in eight weeks (soon to revert to the pre-Vietnam 11 weeks) of folk theater, a spectacle staged on the scale of the Passion Play at Oberammergau, an initiation that may be the only true rite of passage to manhood that America hasn't yet scoured away as an anthropological anachronism. 11

Fifteen minutes after that first recruit panicked out of receiving barracks, Berry, Burley and Hudson have stampeded all of them into their new squad bay. While 1st Lt. Roger McElrath lectures them on the vast variety of crimes and punishments on display in the Uniform Code of Military Justice, the D.I.s are hidden in a room called the drill instructor's house, changing their uniforms. Squared-away drill instructors change uniforms up to six times a day. It is no more possible for a drill instructor to appear sweatstained, soiled or wrinkled than a Vatican priest. 12

"Goddam, goddam, goddam," Hudson is saying, over and over. Fresh sweat blisters his brow. All of them are flushed and breathing 13 hard, swearing and fumbling for cigarettes like a roller derby team at half time.

14     "They look good," Berry says, He's baby-faced, actually, earnest with a flair of cynicism, like a professional athlete. "We got 15 brothers (blacks). They'll pick up drill right away. The others can get the rhythm off them. Not too many fatbodies, not too many belligerents. This'll be a good platoon."

15     The problem for D.I.s picking up platoons isn't exhaustion, though, or even getting psyched to that glitter of madness, but "getting too psyched up, so psyched up you might grab a kid to straighten him out and BAM, that's it, it's your stripes," says Gunnery Sgt. Ronald Burns, a drill field veteran who now meets the late night buses hauling recruits in from the Charleston and Savannah airports.

16     Brutality to the Marines is like usury to Jews — a nightmare that threatens their very existence. It is also the leading figment of the Marine mystique and the stock brag of any Parris Island graduate. It is a legend like that of the "Old Corps," which always seems to have ended about three years ago. In the Old Corps, Marines tell each other, there was none of this Standard Operating Procedure (SOP) for recruit training, none of these maltreatment questionnaires and "swoop teams" of inspectors to hamstring the drill instructors.

17     Nothing to keep a D.I. from working over recruits during nightly "thump call," from slamming the whole platoon into "Chinese thinking position," an excruciating calisthenic in which you prop yourself solely on elbows and toes, and not to be confused with other outlawed old favorites such as six-point kneeling, steam engines, dry shaving, blanket parties, smoking under a blanket, the game of Flood and Air Raid, ethnic taunts, profanity, and allowing a recruit to eat all two pounds of the divinity fudge his girlfriend mailed him, eat it in three minutes flat, lover boy, every goddam crumb.

18     All outlawed now and outlawed too back in 1956, when rumors of Truman's plans to merge the Corps into the Army still haunted Marines, and Staff Sgt. Matthew McKeon made very front page in America by leading an unauthorized night march into Ribbon Creek, out behind the rifle range, and six recruits drowned in a mass panic.

19     Since then, enforcement of the SOP has been screwed down tighter every year at both Parris Island and San Diego, a more recent recruit training base that trains enlistees from the western half of the country.

20     The SOP orders drill instructors to instill "instant obedience to orders." It also forbids them on pain of court-martial from touching a recruit, except to adjust a military position.

21     It prescribes 63 days of training which will include: 89 hours on firing the M-14 rifle, 60 hours of drill, 57 hours of physical training (PT), 23 hours of inspections and testing, 12 hours on clothing and equipment, 10 hours on history of the Marine Corps, and 114 hours of "commander's time," to include one hour each night of "free time" for writing and reading letters and doing anything else that does not involve talking,

smoking, eating or leaving the squad bay. There are also endless hours of rifle cleaning, shoe shining, and singing of the Marine Corps hymn:

*From the halls of Montezuma*
*To the shores of Tripoli . . .*

"Parris Island is a game. If you can play by the rules, you do very well," says Lt. Scott Shaffer, a Navy psychologist (the Marines get medical and religious services from the Navy) who interviews a daily parade of bedwetters, attempted suicides, weepers, catatonics and others suspected mentally unfit for the Marine Corps. 22

"It's very behaviorally oriented, like a big Skinner box. You do well, you get rewarded. You do badly and you're punished. Positive and negative reinforcement. Personally, I'd like to see more positive reinforcement (reward)." 23

This doesn't explain, though, why anybody joins in the first place, especially in an age of beer machines in Navy barracks, and Army boot camps that promise you don't have to lose your dignity to get your training. 24

"They join because they want their girl to be proud of them, or their parents, or the gang on the block. Or they want to be proud of themselves. They want to be somebody, want to be able to go home a big, bad-ass Marine," says Gunnery Sgt. Mike "Big Mac" McCormick, who is all of that at 6-feet-4½ and 212 pounds, with five years on Parris Island drilling recruits and training drill instructors. "That's the best lever you've got on that recruit—pride. Next comes fear." 25

But neither pride, fear nor game theory can explain to anyone who has been through Parris Island why he endured those long, dusty, staggering exhaustions of runs, or the standing at attention in chow lines, thumbs locked to trouser seams while sand fleas put on a flying circus in his ears. 26

Or the incessant, insane, "Catch-22" paradoxes—a recruit pumping out jumping jacks, sweating his T-shirt translucent while his D.I. yells "DO YOU WANT TO DO MORE?" and the private, of course, answers "NO, SIR," until he realizes the correct answer is "YES, SIR," and the drill instructor tells him to stop doing any more, of course. 27

Given the fact that there are choices, such as the Air Force, which at least offers job-skill training, it would seem the only reason any human being puts up with Marine boot camp is that he wants to—a horrendous thought, if you're an enlightened believer in the basic rationality and pleasure drives of modern, educated man. 28

Think about it: drill instructors might as well be Pueblo shamans scaring candidates for tribal membership and manhood with nothing but masks and chants. (That wry ferocity drill instructors cultivate, the squinted eyes and the mouth about as generous as a snapping turtle's, and the jutjawed arrogance of their back-of-the-throat voices.) 29

And recruits, swaddled in their new uniforms and shorn of hair, are 30 no more civilized, perhaps, than Australian aborigine boys who are circumcised and wrapped in blankets to be purified and symbolically reborn.

31      In *Man and His Symbols*, Joseph Henderson, a disciple of Carl Jung, states that the archetypal initiation that has pervaded all primitive cultures involves submission (enlistment), symbolic death by ordeal (degradation and physical demands far beyond what the recruit believes possible), and symbolic rebirth as a member of the collective consciousness (the Marine Corps).

32      It all fits, even the fact that the lessons taught at Parris Island involve stress or ceremony but few combat skills, except "instant obedience." The Marines leave the grenade throwing and small unit tactics and camouflage to Camp Lejeune, in North Carolina, where, for the first time, recruits are greeted as "Marine." Rifle firing is strictly on a formal bull's-eye target range, in the official National Rifle Association positions.

33      In fact, drill instructors may gain their extraordinary power from invoking all the archetypal terrors of initiation while never actually threatening the life of the recruit — a threat that would break the bond of trust between recruit and D.I., a bond so strong after only a few weeks that some drill instructors have been able to thump hell out of recruits with no fear they'll turn him in.

34      Like a score of fellow recruits Pvt. John Hedrick, 19, of Lynchburg, Va., answers only "Yessir my drill instructors treat me well, Nossir, there's no maltreatment, Yessir, I'd enlist again if I had it to do over."

35      Of course, there is bound to be some falling away from the faith, apostasies that drill instructors watch for with those quick glares, stalking up and down a row of recruits in a mess hall, say, making sure the hogs or ladies or maggots are popping those heels and squaring those corners.

36      The drill instructors watch because once a recruit sees the whole ritual is just a magic show, he loses both his fear of the D.I., and his motivation. And motivation is what Parris Island is all about. It not only makes you a Marine, not only makes you like it, but also makes you believe in it.

37      ("The worst thumping I ever got was when the D.I. called the retreat from the Chosen reservoir an 'advance to the rear,' and I snickered," says Mike Jerace, who went through Parris Island in 1963.)

38      So secret doubters who stop shouting those yessirs at peak bellow, who stop trembling and panting like a dog in a thunderstorm to crank out one more pull-up, are apt to spend one to 10 days at motivation platoon: Last year, 3,384 of 28,153 Parris Island initiates did time at motivation platoon, and 557 were later discharged from the Marines "for reasons of defective attitude," said Capt. John Woggon, who directs Special Training Branch. (Which, besides motivating recruits who aren't putting out 100 percent, also takes a pound a day off "fatbodies," reconditions hospital discharges, and punishes legal offenders in its Correctional Custody Platoon.)

Motivation platoon is a ferocious speed-up of the carrot-and-stick 39
routine, starting with eight to 20 maddening, grueling miles of speed
march broken only by patriotic lectures and movies about epic Marine
heroisms at Tarawa, Iwo Jima, Khe Sanh . . . Then fight with padded
"pugil sticks" between recruits who may never have been in a fight in
their lives. And finally, lining up sweating and gritty, muscles shrill with
fatigue, for The Ditch.

What happens to most recruits in eight weeks happens to most of 40
motivation platoon in 30 minutes in The Ditch. The Ditch is Parris
Island's last-chance purgatory, 480 meters of sand, mud, barbed wire
and corrugated storm pipe all half-flooded with tidewater that these
recruits will crawl through on their knees and bellies with metal rifle
frames YOU WILL JUMP INTO THIS FIRST WATER OBSTACLE YOU
WILL COMPLETELY IMMERSE YOURSELF YOU WILL THEN CRAWL
ON YOUR KNEES DOWN THAT DITCH YELLING MARINE CORPS
WITH EVERY BREATH YOU BREATHE. . . .

Baptism in a waste-deep mud puddle and the crawl begins. Shaved 41
heads stream mud and water, mouths yaw wide as anatomy displays
gasping MARINE CORPS, MARINE CORPS as they grind their way
down that ditch like nothing so much as Mexican *penitentes* struggling on
their knees for miles to win salvation at the Shrine of Our Lady, the
ultimate prostration, the last plea . . .

Under the frantic frustration of the barbed wire, through the drain- 42
pipes that deliver them into a mock-up of an Indochinese village where
they form up shivering and chanting MARINE CORPS while Staff Sgt.
Sam Michaux pounds time with his boot. Then Michaux delivers the last
speech before the penitents are sent back filthy and exhausted to their
platoons.

"This is the world, sweeties, and your drill instructor wants to help 43
you BUT BY GOD YOU BETTER HELP YOURSELVES because when
the going gets rough, you can't say anymore I'M GONNA TAKE MY
LITTLE RED WAGON AND GO HOME. The next time you think you
can slack off you'd best remember that a HARD HEAD MAKES A SOFT
ASS and yours is GONNA GET KICKED."

Meanwhile, Platoon 220, like another platoon yesterday, and another 44
tomorrow, is just beginning its long initiation back in its barracks, or
"barn," as the drill instructors call it, with its paint-flaked bunks lined up
like stanchions, its bathroom of cement floors and naked squads of
gleaming seatless toilets.

Cardboard placards advertise the Eleven General Orders like reli- 45
gious mottoes in the bare-bulb glare of this drizzly afternoon indoors.
Decades of sweat and pivoting boots have worn the floors to a shine.
Platoon 220's home is shabby but immaculate, like the tin-roof shack of
a "good nigger," like Parris Island itself, in fact, a grim, mundane 3,300
habitable acres on which neatness and thrift are the only aesthetics,
instant obedience the only ethic.

In the next eight weeks, Berry, Burley and Hudson will whipsaw 46

these 60 recruits with reward and punishment. As former Marine com-
mandant Gen. David M. Shoup once said, they will "receive, degrade,
sanitize, immunize, clothe, equip, train, pain, scold, mold, sand and
polish."

47      They will condition this stampede of adolescence until it understands
a great paradox called military fear, a first law of survival that states the
only thing you have to fear is not being scared enough to put up with the
insult and hassle that are any military existence, with the chronic disaster
of war.

48      Platoon 220 will discover the ease and convenience of this tautology
just as they will discover that this fear, bleakness and degradation can
yield a beauty they'll never be able to explain to anyone who hasn't gone
through it and made it.

49      Eight weeks later, for instance, in the lambency of a Southern twilight
in spring, Platoon 220 may fall out on the grinder for close order drill,
which they'll be very good at by then, and they'll feel the cool flutter of
their new tropical uniforms against their legs, and their rifles will flip
from shoulder arms to port arms with one, crisp crash, and they'll lean
back in a limber strut to the singsong of the D.I.'s cadence—a voice
burnished by years of too much fatigue, coffee and cigarettes—the
whole platoon floating across the quiet parade field like a ship at sea.

—March 5, 1972

## Evaluating the Text

1. What purpose is served by depriving the recruits of common items such as
   candy, gum, radios, and records?
2. How does the fact that D.I.s can't be seen sweating widen the gap between
   recruits and D.I.s and make the recruits feel even worse? What assumptions
   about the best way to train recruits does this reveal on the part of the
   Marine Corps?
3. Although "The Corps" is organized to answer the traditional questions in
   journalism of "who, what, where, when, and why," readers might be able
   to infer what Allen's attitude is toward the events he describes. In your
   opinion, what is his attitude?
4. Discuss the techniques Allen uses to bring the reader into the story as
   someone who is being yelled at by the drill instructor. How effective do
   you find this method?
5. What evidence can you cite to demonstrate Allen's use of dialogue to
   create a sense of immediacy and realism?
6. What function do figurative comparisons (such as "fat and forlorn, they
   look like 60 sex perverts trapped by a lynch mob") serve in Allen's
   description? What other examples can you identify?
7. What is the purpose of the ditch? When do recruits encounter it, and why
   is it so effective in changing their behavior?
8. Describe the psychological process of transformation that changes a raw

recruit into a member of the Marine Corps who will respond with "instant obedience to orders," will work smoothly as a member of a unit, and put the good of the corps above self-interests.

## Exploring Different Perspectives

1. In what way are the changes in recruits that Marine boot camp is designed to produce similar to the transformation resulting from the rituals that initiate a Maasai boy into manhood, in Tepilit Ole Saitoti's "The Initiation of a Maasai Warrior?"
2. Compare the stages of Marine boot camp training, described by Allen, to their corresponding aspects in the Maasai ritual initiation of warriors.
3. What unexpected similarities can you discover between Allen's account of Marine boot camp and Douchan Gersi's ordeal (described in "Initiated into an Iban Tribe of Headhunters")? In what ways are both symbolic rites of passage entailing the "death" of the individual and "rebirth" as a member of the "tribe"?
4. Compare the sources Allen drew on in producing this report with Saitoti's or Gersi's first-person narratives. How is the description of each initiation modified according to the role of the writer and the point of view from which the account was written in terms of suspense generated?

## Extending Viewpoints through Writing

1. Describe a situation where you were tested to your limits, either physically or mentally or both. What character traits enabled you to meet the challenge?
2. To what extent do the experiences a pledge undergoes before being admitted as a full member of a fraternity or sorority resemble the rites of passage described by Allen?
3. If you have ever considered a military career, describe your reasons and expectations.
4. If you have seen Stanley Kubrick's film *Full Metal Jacket* (1988), evaluate the extent to which the stages in the life of a Marine boot camp recruit, described by Allen, are accurately portrayed in the movie. Does Kubrick depict additional dimensions to this experience that Allen might not have taken into account? Although they both depict the same events, how does the difference between Allen's treatment and that of Kubrick reflect their different purposes as a journalist and a film director, respectively?

# Douchan Gersi

# *Initiated Into An Iban Tribe of Headhunters*

---

*Douchan Gersi is the producer of the National Geographic television series called* Discovery. *He has traveled extensively throughout the Philippines, New Zealand, the Polynesian and Melanesian Islands, the Sahara Desert, Africa, New Guinea, and Peru. "Initiated into an Iban Tribe of Headhunters," from his book* Explorer *(1987), tells of the harrowing initiation process he underwent to become a member of the Iban Tribe in Borneo.*

*Borneo, the third largest island in the Malay archipelago, is situated southwest of the Philippines and north of Java. The indigenous people of Borneo, or Dyaks, number over one million and occupy the sparsely populated interior, a region of dense jungles and rain forests. The northern portion of the island is Malayasian territory; the southern portion is part of the Republic of Indonesia. Gersi's account introduces us to the mode of life of the Iban, a people whose customs, including intertribal warfare and headhunting, have remained unchanged through the centuries.*

The hopeful man see success where others see shadows and storm.

O. S. Marden

1     Against Tawa's excellent advice I asked the chief if I could become a member of their clan. It took him a while before he could give me an answer, for he had to question the spirits of their ancestors and wait for their reply to appear through different omens: the flight of a blackbird, the auguries of a chick they sacrificed. A few days after the question, the answer came:

2     "Yes . . . but!"

3     The "but" was that I would have to undergo their initiation. Without knowing exactly what physical ordeal was in store, I accepted. I knew I had been through worse and survived. It was to begin in one week.

4     Late at night I was awakened by a girl slipping into my bed. She was sweet and already had a great knowledge of man's morphology. Like all

---

*(For additional information on Indonesia, see p. 159.)

100

the others who came and "visited" me this way every night, she was highly skilled in the arts of love. Among the Iban, only unmarried women offer sexual hospitality, and no one obliged these women to offer me their favors. Sexual freedom ends at marriage. Unfaithfulness — except during yearly fertility celebrations when everything, even incest at times, is permitted — is punished as an offense against their matrimonial laws.

As a sign of respect to family and the elders, sexual hospitality is not openly practiced. The girls always came when my roommates were asleep and left before they awoke. They were free to return or give their place to their girlfriends.

The contrast between the violence of some Iban rituals and the beauty of their art, their sociability, their kindness, and their personal warmth has always fascinated me. I also witnessed that contrast among a tribe of Papuans (who, besides being headhunters, practice cannibalism) and among some African tribes. In fact, tribes devoted to cannibalism and other human sacrifices are often among the most sociable of people, and their art, industry, and trading systems are more advanced than other tribes that don't have these practices.

For my initiation, they had me lie down naked in a four-foot-deep pit filled with giant carnivorous ants. Nothing held me there. At any point I could easily have escaped, but the meaning of this rite of passage was not to kill me. The ritual was intended to test my courage and my will, to symbolically kill me by the pain in order for me to be reborn as a man of courage. I am not sure what their reactions would have been if I had tried to get out of the pit before their signal, but it occurred to me that although the ants might eat a little of my flesh, the Iban offered more dramatic potentials.

Since I wore, as Iban do, a long piece of cloth around my waist and nothing more, I had the ants running all over my body. They were everywhere. The pain of the ants' bites was intense, so I tried to relax to decrease the speed of my circulation and therefore the effects of the poison. But I couldn't help trying to get them away from my face where they were exploring every inch of my skin. I kept my eyes closed, inhaling through my almost closed lips and exhaling through my nose to chase them away from there.

I don't know how long I stayed in the pit, waiting with anguish for the signal which would end my ordeal. As I tried to concentrate on my relaxing, the sound of the beaten gongs and murmurs of the assistants watching me from all around the pit started to disappear into a chaos of pain and loud heartbeat.

Then suddenly I heard Tawa and the chief calling my name. I removed once more the ants wandering on my eyelids before opening my eyes and seeing my friends smiling to indicate that it was over. I got out of the pit on my own, but I needed help to rid myself of the ants, which were determined to eat all my skin. After the men washed my body, the shaman applied an herbal mixture to ease the pain and reduce the swellings. I would have quit and left the village then had I known that the "pit" experience was just the hors d'oeuvre.

11    The second part of the physical test started early the next morning. The chief explained the "game" to me. It was Hide and Go Seek Iban-style. I had to run without any supplies, weapons, or food, and for three days and three nights escape a group of young warriors who would leave the village a few hours after my departure and try to find me. If I were caught, my head would be used in a ceremony. The Iban would have done so without hate. It was simply the rule of their life. Birth and death. A death that always engenders new life.

12    When I asked, "What would happen if someone refused this part of the initiation?" the chief replied that such an idea wasn't possible. Once one had begun, there was no turning back. I knew the rules governing initations among the cultures of tradition but never thought they would be applied to me. Whether or not I survived the initiation, I would be symbolically killed in order to be reborn among them. I had to die from my present time and identity into another life. I was aware that, among some cultures, initiatory ordeals are so arduous that young initiates sometimes really die. These are the risks if one wishes to enter into another world.

13    I was given time to get ready and the game began. I run like hell without a plan or, it seemed to me, a prayer of surviving. Running along a path I had never taken, going I knew not where, I thought about every possible way I could escape from the young warriors. To hide somewhere. But where? Climb a tree and hide in it? Find a hole and squeeze in it? Bury myself under rocks and mud? But all of these seemed impossible. I had a presentiment they would find me anyway. So I ran straight ahead, my head going crazy by dint of searching for a way to safely survive the headhunters.

14    I would prefer staying longer with ants, I thought breathlessly. It was safer to stay among them for a whole day since they were just simple pain and fear compared to what I am about to undergo. I don't want to die.

15    For the first time I realized the real possibility of death—no longer in a romantic way, but rather at the hands of butchers.

16    Ten minutes after leaving the long house, I suddenly heard a call coming from somewhere around me. Still running, I looked all around trying to locate who was calling, and why. At the second call I stopped, cast my gaze about, and saw a woman's head peering out from the bushes. I recognized her as one of my pretty lovers. I hesitated, not knowing if she were part of the hunting party or a goddess come to save me. She called again. I thought, God, what to do? How will I escape from the warriors? As I stood there truly coming into contact with my impossible situation, I began to panic. She called again. With her fingers she showed me what the others would do if they caught me. Her forefinger

traced an invisible line from one side of her throat to the other. If someone was going to kill me, why not her? I joined her and found out she was in a lair. I realized I had entered the place where the tribe's women go to hide during their menstruation. This area is taboo for men. Each woman was her own refuge. Some have shelters made of branches, others deep covered holes hidden behind bushes with enough space to eat and sleep and wait until their time is past.

She invited me to make myself comfortable. That was quite difficult    17
since it was just large enough for one person. But I had no choice. And after all, it was a paradise compared to what I would have undergone had I not by luck crossed this special ground.

Nervously and physically exhausted by my run and fear and despair,    18
I soon fell asleep. Around midnight I woke. She gave me rice and meat. We exchanged a few words. Then it was her turn to sleep.

The time I spent in the lair with my savior went fast. I tried to sleep all    19
day long, an escape from the concerns of my having broken a taboo. And I wondered what would happen to me if the headhunters were to learn where I spent the time of my physical initiation.

Then, when it was safe, I snuck back to the village . . . in triumph. I    20
arrived before the warriors, who congratulated and embraced me when they returned. I was a headhunter at last.

I spent the next two weeks quietly looking at the Iban through new    21
eyes. But strangely enough, instead of the initiation putting me closer to them, it had the opposite effect. I watched them more and more from an anthropological distance: my Iban brothers became an interesting clan whose life I witnessed but did not really share. And then suddenly I was bored and yearned for my own tribe. When Tawa had to go to an outpost to exchange pepper grains for other goods, I took a place aboard his canoe. Two days later I was in a small taxi-boat heading toward Sibu, the first leg in civilization on my voyage home.

I think of them often. I wonder about the man I tried to cure. I think    22
about Tawa and the girl who saved my life, and all the others sitting on the veranda. How long will my adopted village survive before being destroyed like all the others in the way of civilization? And what has become of those who marked my flesh with the joy of their lives and offered me the best of their souls? If they are slowly vanishing from my memories, I know that I am part of the stories they tell. I know that my life among them will be perpetuated until the farthest tomorrow. Now I am a story caught in a living legend of a timeless people.

## Evaluating the Text

1. What do the unusual sexual customs of hospitality bestowed on outsiders suggest about the different cultural values of the Iban? Do these customs

suggest that the initiation would be harsher or milder than Gersi expected? Interpret this episode as it relates to the probable nature of Gersi's forthcoming initiation.

2. In a short paragraph, explain the nature of the "hide-and-go-seek" game that constituted the main test for a candidate. Explain why the use of the lighthearted term *game* is ironic in this context.

3. At what point did Gersi realize that his former ideas about death were based on fantasy and that in the present situation he might in fact be separated from his head? How did this realization change his previous attitudes?

4. How does the reappearance of one of the girls who had earlier paid a nocturnal "visit" to Gersi result in his finding a safe hiding place? What does the nature of the hiding place reveal about the tribe's taboos?

5. In terms of suspense, how effective is it for the reader to learn from Gersi that "I would have quit and left the village then had I known that the 'pit' experience was just the hors d'oeuvre"? How is the narrative shaped so as to put the reader through the same suspenseful moments that Gersi himself experienced?

6. If you can enter into the mind of the Iban, explain in what way the voluntary endurance of the pain of innumerable bites of carnivorous ants could serve as a ritual of symbolic death of the individual and subsequent rebirth as a member of the tribe.

7. Explain in what way the initiation resulted in Gersi feeling quite differently from what he had expected. That is, instead of feeling he was now part of the tribe, he actually felt more distant from them than he had felt before the initiation. To what factors do you attribute this unexpected sense of alienation? What did he discover about his own preconceptions during the initiation that stripped away certain romantic ideas he had about the Iban and the ability of any outsider to truly become a member of the tribe?

## Exploring Different Perspectives

1. In what respects do the "death" and "rebirth" pattern (the death of the initiate's old personal self and his rebirth as a member of the community) of the Iban parallel experiences of recruits in Marine boot camp in Henry Allen's "The Corps"?

2. What similarities can you discover between Tepilit Ole Saitoti's experiences in "The Initiation of a Maasai Warrior" and those of Gersi? What might explain their very different reactions after being initiated? Specifically, why does Gersi feel so isolated after attaining what seemed so desirable at the outset?

## Extending Viewpoints through Writing

1. If you have ever been initiated into a fraternity or sorority or another organization, compare the nature of Gersi's initiation with those you experienced. In particular, try to identify particular stages in these initiations that mark the "death" of the outsider and "rebirth" of the initiated member.

2. Examine any religious ritual such as confirmation in the Catholic Church and analyze it in terms of initiation rites. For example, the ceremony of the

Catholic Church by which one is confirmed as an adult member when one is about fourteen years old follows this pattern with a period of preparation spent the year before confirmation, a ceremony that itself has several stages involving confession, communion, and subsequent confirmation. Candidates are routinely quizzed before confirmation about a knowledge of basic theology and must be sponsored by a member in good standing of the Catholic community. In this ritual, what is the significance of the newly chosen confirmation name? How is it chosen? How does this name represent the new identity candidates have as members of the faith? What responsibilities and obligations are incurred by candidates who complete the confirmation ceremony?

3. Have you ever had an experience of looking forward to being a member of a particular group, and achieving this, only to discover that you felt estranged from the group after you became part of it?

4. What was your reaction to learning that the culture Gersi describes is one that exists today (in Borneo) two days away from taxi-boats and civilization? Would you ever consider undertaking a journey to such a place? Describe the most exotic place you would ever want to visit and explain why you would want to go there.

# Danny Santiago

# *Famous All Over Town*

*Danny Santiago grew up in the Chicano* barrio *of Los Angeles. His stories have been widely acclaimed for their realistic evocation of the Chicano experience. The following chapter is from his first novel,* Famous All Over Town *(1983), which the* New York Times Book Review *called "a classic of the Chicano urban experience." Santiago's authentic voice speaks of the unconscious racism that a Chicano boy confronts as he tries to impress a teacher and turn over a new leaf.*

*The term* Chicano, *short for the Spanish word* mexicanos, *which is sometimes pronounced* mechicanos, *is used to describe Mexican Americans. Migrating first to the United States, legally and illegally, usually as seasonal farm laborers, at least 8.7 million Chicanos now live in the United States, chiefly in Los Angeles and south Texas, many in neighborhoods called* barrios. *Under the leadership of Cesar Chavez, Chicanos became politically active, first through the United Farm Workers (winning victories against large California growers) and later through La Raza Unida, a political party formed in 1970, which has won many local elections. The quest for equal employment opportunities continues to this day.*

1    Next day I woke up before the alarm clock. Daylight Savings was almost over, the sun was tardy and the house was black but I woke up happy because today I would turn over my New Leaf. I was disgusted with the old one.

2    What about that zip gun, man? you might be wondering. Did it go off in my pocket? Did I get caught with it, or what? No is the answer. Did I get rid of it in the nearest trash barrel? And throw away a valuable piece of Shamrock hardware? And be a traitor to Boxer that trusted me? No, señor, I lived through two periods with it burning up my pocket and even carried it home, which won me merit badges with the Jesters even if it costed me two years' growth.

3    So anyway, I ate breakfast in the dark and went out back. The yard looked very different and misterioso at that time of day. A crouching leopard chilled my blood, which turned into an up-ended washtub. The moon hung low over City Hall. My neighbors were all asleep and I was temporary King of Shamrock Street, till I heard my father talking with the chickens. He was always the early bird of the family and preached for us to do the same but when he spotted me in the moonlight he

106

seemed quite cranky that anybody should trespass on his private time of day.

"Qué milagro!" he growled and went in the toledo.                                    4

Shamrock mostly walks to school by Broadway to show our face to    5
the public and because the chicks go that way too, for window-shopping, but today I went by the S.P. tracks which was the shortest road and safest from the Sierra. A steady little breeze blew on my back to help me on my way, which was a hopeful sign. The rails by now were turning pink, night was behind my back and day in front of me and my feet wanted to run. The railroad ties were spaced just right to land on every third one and I ran and ran as if I could run forever, and jumped up in the air and happy little yells and screeches came out of my mouth. Lucky for me, nobody was around to hear. Possibly my father was right, this was the best time of day after all and all my life I had been missing out on it.

It was 6:30 when I got to Audubon. The gates were still locked but I    6
got in through Administration where the custodian was mopping halls. Out back the picnic tables were new-washed and the ground too. The place looked naked, not a single candy paper or Dixie Cup in sight. I dropped a crumpled page out of my notebook to dress it up, then sat down and waited for my tutor.

Who could quite possibly turn out to be some chick. They got better    7
grades than the guys. It might even be some Paddy 9th-grader with blue eyes and stately shape, why not? which would be a new learning experience for me and may be just what I needed to straighten me out. Besides, they claim blondies often get quite interested in dark-skin Latins like myself, though I never quite saw it happen at Audubon Junior High. Whatever, I couldn't afford to show myself a dummy so I opened up my English assignment which slipped my mind last night.

Our text was supposed to be about a certain Mexican kid named    8
Pancho which his father worked for the railroad and his sister María cleaned house for rich old ladies. The story started out in New Mexico where this Pancho specialized mostly in killing rattlesnakes under the baby's crib. They seemed to follow the guy around like a dog, but now Santa Fe has moved the family to Elmsville, Kansas. It's Pancho's first day in his new school but the blondie kids discriminate him and won't let him play on their ball teams so there he is, sitting on the bench. Except Miss Brewster proves very understanding the way teachers are in books and in the ninth inning with bases loaded she gets the bright idea to send him in to pitch. That's where our assignment began so I started reading:

> As Pancho advanced to the "mound," a howl of disapproval arose from his teammates. "Who ever heard of a Mexican pitcher?" the shortstop grumbled. "I quit." "He doesn't even have a baseball mitt," exclaimed the catcher. "Then someone can lend

him his," Miss Brewster retorted. "Thank you, Miss Brewster," said Pancho, "I'd rather do without."

Billy Jasper stepped into the batter's "box." He was the best hitter on his team. Pancho hurled his pitch. Billy swung his famous home run swing. But lo and behold, the ball twisted around his bat like a corkscrew.

"Steerike one!" roared Miss Brewster in tones a Big League umpire well might envy. New hope came to Pancho's teammates.

"Oh boy," cried one of them. "Did you see that "sinker?"

Pancho pitched again. A sharp crack like a pistol shot was heard. It would be a "three-bagger" at least. But Pancho leaped high in the air and caught the ball bare-handed. He then ran nimbly to third base. It was a double play unassisted. The game was over.

"Three cheers for Pancho," his teammates cried. Pancho's "strangeness" was now just a memory. Miss Brewster beamed. "This should be a lesson to us all," she remarked. But Pancho had no time to enjoy his triumph. He had promised his sister María to help her clean house for rich Mrs. Murdock.

The sturdy lad ran all the way up Maple Street and down Persimmon Place and into the banker's spacious driveway. Scarcely noticing the presence of Sheriff Trotter's car parked before the towering white columns, he hurried to the kitchen door. Little did he suspect the painful situation into which he was about to stumble.

9     That ended our chapter and I wasn't sorry. Like always, they then asked ten questions. Number 1 was, "Can you find a good example of foreshadowing in the pages you have just read?" I went looking for one but before I could find it, here comes my tutor. It was no blondie chick, to my disgust, but only Eddie Velasquez from Milflores Street. Eddie was no friend of mine, but in one way you had to give him credit. He was a big success at Audubon, president of this, secretary of that and a straight-A student with horn-rim specs to prove it, but not even Eddie could find any of that foreshadowing my book told me to look out for.

10     "Tell you what, Rudy," he said. "Get up there in class and ask your teacher what the question means."

11     "Ask her shit," I said.

12     "Hold it right there, guy." Eddie waved his finger back and forth in front of my eyes. "How dumb can you get? Ask a question and there's a question you won't have to answer. And teachers love it, Bontempo especially."

13     We all know the type that asks that kind of question, but why start an argument? So I sat on the bench and Eddie stood with one foot on it and told me the Secrets of Success at School. First, look neat and well-combed and always sit up straight and don't stare out the window. Have

pencil and paper on you so you don't have to borrow. Put your hand up every chance you get and give your teacher a pleasant smile when convenient.

"Attitude," Eddie instructed me, "cooperation, guy, that's what gets    14
you grades in English and Social Studies and all those bullshit courses. So let's look at your next question."

"What important lesson does this chapter teach us?" it asked.    15

"Learn to catch barehanded," I suggested.    16

"Wrong," he told me frankly. "They expect something way bigger,    17
like Attitude to Life."

Eddie studied the air.    18

"Here you go," he said. "That chapter teaches us you can't keep a    19
good man down irregardless of his race, how's that? So don't holler if they discriminate you, just be patient and your time will come. Can you remember that? Okay, tell it to Bontempo and there's an A for you every time."

I could remember, but how could I recite it with Pelón in the    20
classroom?

"I know a lot of you guys call me a kiss-up," Eddie went on, "but give    21
me ten years, then come up to my office and we'll see who's kissing whose? CPA, Rudy, Certified Public Accountant, that's where I'm heading. And how'm I going to get up there? Grades, buddy, grades. And school activities don't hurt you any when they're passing out those college scholarships. Like for instance, I'm making service points for tutoring you right now."

"Thanks anyway," I said.    22

"Take one tip from me," he said. "Cut loose from the Jesters. You'll    23
never get nowhere with them guys, except dead or jailed."

I hated to admit it but it made you think. Shamrock had more than its    24
share of early corpses and half our Veteranos ended up in the wrong class of college. Like old San Quentin U. On the other side, there was Eddie. The teachers loved him and right now he was running for Student Body president and had a good chance of winning, it was said, and some, blondie chick would be his secretary.

The chainlink gates were open now. The yard was filling up with    25
voters.

"Figure out those other questions on your own," Eddie told me. "I got    26
to go associate. And hey, since I'm doing you a favor, do me one. Line up the Shamrock vote for me, I could do you guys a lot of favors if I get elected. See you tomorrow, Rudy, same place, same time."

And away went Eddie Velasquez, not walking cool and casual like us,    27
more on the order of a diesel locomotive pounding down the track, one Mexican who was going places and I only wondered if I could go that road too. Yesterday I had done my bit for Shamrock. Today I would do it for me, myself and I, and Miss Bontempo's English class was my testing ground.

28     I'd hoped to be the first student there, to prove my Attitude but of course two Oriental guys were in their seats ahead of me. Possibly they spent the night in there. Miss Bontempo was at the blackboard writing down our Words-We-Live-With. Today they were solid ITES and IGHTS such as right and write, sight, night and kite. She omitted fight, I noticed, and was in a big hurry to finish her list before the class showed up. She never cared to turn her back on us for fear things might go flying.

29     Miss Bontempo was Italian and around twenty-six years old or twenty-four and not too bad-looking when she smiled. The only trouble was, her smile stayed glued on there too long. It got to looking more like a scream. She was fresh out of teacher college and how that lady had changed since the first day of school. She started out preaching Democracy in the Classroom and Everybody Express Yourself, which was a big change for Audubon after all those Don't-drop-a-pin-or-else teachers we were accustomed to. Then one day somebody stole $11 from Miss Bontempo's purse during Nutrition and a couple of windows got broken by mistake. She still talked Democratic ways but as soon as the discussion got interesting she suddenly turned cop on you.

30     So anyway, I sat down very studious to copy out my word list and when I caught Bontempo's eye, I flashed her a grade-A smile. It gave her such a scare she dropped the chalk. When the tardy bell rang, the usual stampede came through the door. Books banged down on desks. A guy from Sierra yanked all the windows open. A Shamrock banged them shut. Then came the usual parade of pencil and paper borrowers till finally something more or less like quiet settled in.

31     "Good morning, people," Miss Bontempo started off. "And how many of you bothered to read today's assignment?"

32     Half the hands went up, my own included, though I could see Miss Bontempo serious doubted me.

33     "Very good. Excellent. Now tell me, class, is reading just some old-fashioned subject we teachers assign to make your lives miserable?" I heard some yesses but my teacher didn't. "Why is it we really need to read well and easily? Can I see hands?"

34     A few went up, not mine. I hate that kind of question but all the Oriental hands were flying.

35     "We read so we can get to college and make money."

36     "Very good, Wah, excellent. Are there any other reasons? Yes, Gloria?"

37     "How could we buy stuff at the store if we can't read the cans?"

38     "Like street signs too, man, not to get lost."

39     "My grandma can read Spanish even!"

40     "That's very nice, Linda," Miss Bontempo said, "and I only wish I could too. Those are all good answers. Excellent, but we read for pleasure too, do we not?"

41     Nobody passed any comments.

42     "A good book can whisk us off to India or deep into past ages, can it

not? Reading takes us out of our little lives and opens whole worlds for us to roam in. Then too, there is another kind of book which gives us insights into our own daily problems and helps us solve them. Our text for instance. Young Pancho and his sister María, are they so very different from the boys and girls seated in this room?"

Slapsy Annie of the Sierra spoke up. "María's working and I wish I was!"          43

"What I mean is," Miss Bontempo said, "they're both Mexican-American young people like so many of us here. We can identify with them, can we not? And learn from their experience. For instance, from Pancho we can see how patience is rewarded when he proves himself. Isn't that the best way for us to deal with Discrimination? And far better than just sulking or shouting our heads off?"          44

She had just killed Eddie's fine speech which I was all primed with. I had to work fast and up went my hand.          45

"Yes, Rudy?" Miss Bontempo sighed.          46

"I don't get that first question," I told her. "What's all this 'foreshadowing' they ask you for?"          47

"Why, that's a very good question, Rudy. Excellent."          48

Pelón gave the back of his hand a fat juicy kiss. My face burned.          49

"I was hoping someone would ask that question," Miss Bontempo said. "This is the first time we've met that useful word. Foreshadowing, can anyone tell me what it means? Class?"          50

Wah said it meant like sunset when it throws your shadow in front of you like walking up Broadway.          51

"Almost," Miss Bontempo agreed. "But here it means that our author is giving us a little hint that something very exciting is about to happen. He FORESHADOWS it. Open your texts to page forty-seven. Do you see the line, 'Little did Pancho suspect . . . '? That's how our author leads us on into the next chapter."          52

"He don't lead me on," Pelón said. "He turns me off, man."          53

"Yes, Richard," which was Pelón's other name. "We all know how hard you are to please."          54

"Oh, indubitably."          55

"You see," Miss Bontempo went on, "the writer is telling us to expect trouble ahead, though none of us can guess just what it will be."          56

My hand was up. I was following Eddie to the letter.          57

"I could guess," I proudly said.          58

Possibly it was the wrong thing to say because I was told to stand up and give the whole class the benefit of my wisdom.          59

"Well, that rich old lady, I bet she's lost her diamond bracelet so of course she claims María stole it and calls the cops on her."          60

Miss Bontempo's smile left her for far-off places.          61

"Rudy, I'm afraid you read the next chapter." I denied it. "Rudy," she sang my name, "you're not being very honest with us, and you're spoiling the story. Nobody could possibly guess that from the text."          62

63 I got quite hot. "Then how come the sheriff's car's in the driveway, huh?" I asked. "And how come in that other chapter Mrs. Murdock bragged about her bracelet unless somebody's gonna steal it? Anybody can guess what happens in these dumb books, where on the television—"

64 "You may be seated, Rudy."

65 Pelón was happy to take over. "Chato's right," he hollered. "And you know something else? Sturdy old Pancho goes and finds that bracelet right where the old lady lost it. In the toledo."

66 A big scream went up from the girls.

67 "In the what?" Miss Bontempo was stupid enough to ask.

68 "The toledo, Oheedo," said Pelón.

69 "Eeee, send him to the Vice, Miss, he's talking dirty about the restroom," Slapsie Annie screamed.

70 "Shut your big mouth," Boxer suggested.

71 Various others had other suggestions.

72 "Quiet! Class, settle down! I won't stand for this!"

73 "Look at Pelón, Miss," Annie yelled. "He just called me THAT WORD!"

74 "I did not."

75 "He made it with his lips. I seen him."

76 "Your mother!"

77 "La tuya!"

78 Annie was off in Spanish. Pelón said several things in both languages. The Sierra backed up Annie. We backed our buddy. A pencil flew. Somebody tossed a book. Miss Bontempo hammered on her desk to establish some kind of Law and Order.

79 "He found it in the toledo," Pelón repeated, "tucked away in a big old raggedy—"

80 Scream scream went the girls.

81 "—roll of toledo paper."

82 "Out!" said Miss Bontempo.

83 "Who? Me?" Pelón asked innocently. "Out where?"

84 "How come?" I asked. "He was only guessing."

85 "You too. Out!"

86 "You're discriminating, lady," Pelón told her. "I'm gonna phone the Mexican consul on you."

87 "Vice-principal!" was Miss Bontempo's answer.

88 She scratched angry words on pink slips and dealt them out to us. The trip was nothing new for Pelón, but believe it or not, this was my first time.

89 "You really set that Bontempo up," Pelón told me in the hall. "Little brother, you done it perfect."

90 I felt quite proud of myself but as we passed by Mr. Pilger's office it bothered me the way my new leaf had withered.

91 "Mr. Beaver is busy," the Vice's secretary informed us. "Wait in the hall."

The happy sound of the paddle could be heard. We waited on the    92
mourner's bench.

"He'll give you a choice," Pelón advised me. "Either the paddle or    93
else he'll send home a note. Take the swats. Beaver has a heavy hand but
your father's hand is heavier."

Pelón popped one of his uncle Ruben's famous pills.    94

"Care for one?" he asked.    95

"Why not?"    96

"Did you hear the news?" he asked me. "We're gonna have it out    97
with Sierra after school. Fat Manuel's gonna meet us across the bridge.
He'll have the arsenal in the back of his car. Are we gonna slaughter
them? Oh, indubitably."

Pelón's pill hopped around in my stomach like a frog. I coughed and    98
almost threw it up.

"What's with you, guy?" Pelón inquired. "Did you swallow wrong?"    99

## Evaluating the Text

1. What can you infer about the gang to which Rudy belongs and the way in which territory is ruled by the Shamrocks, Jesters, and Sierra? Why has being part of a gang been more important to Rudy up to this point than school? What has changed his attitude? What does he now plan to do?
2. Describe the relationship between Rudy and his tutor, Eddie. What does Rudy seek advice from him? What does Eddie hope to gain by being Rudy's tutor? How are they both trying to manipulate the system to their own advantage?
3. What can you infer about the relationships between Irish, Oriental, and Chicano students from comments Rudy makes?
4. What does the excerpt from the assigned story seem to assume about Mexican Americans? Why does Rudy find this portrayal unrealistic and patronizing?
5. If one of the Oriental students rather than Rudy had suggested the probable conclusion to the story, do you think Miss Bontempo would have reacted as she did? In what way does her response to Rudy's genuine insight illustrate her unconscious bigotry toward Chicanos? Why is it ironic that the class is reading a story that is supposed to overcome such attitudes?
6. Why is it ironic that Pelón interprets what Rudy does, and the raucous aftermath, as a superbly orchestrated confrontation with authority, rather than what it really was?
7. What would you say was Santiago's attitude toward the characters in his story, the events he describes, and the effect of what happened on his main character, Rudy?

## Exploring Different Perspectives

1. In both Henry Allen's "The Corps" and in Santiago's story, an important requirement for being admitted into the select group ("Marines" and "good students") involves learning the unwritten rules of giving the "right" answers to the authorities (drill instructors and teachers). Discuss why

giving the right answer is such an important part of initiation rituals that determine whether one is worthy of being admitted into a select group.

2. In what way is belonging to a gang the same for Rudy as being accepted as a Maasai warrior is for Tepilit Ole Saitoti (see "The Initiation of a Maasai Warrior")?

## Extending Viewpoints through Writing

1. How has this encounter with Miss Bontempo been a decisive turning point in Rudy's life? What kind of a future do you predict for him?

2. If you have ever been a member of a gang, describe the significance of the identity of your "street name?" Did you ever decide, as Rudy did, that other things were more important to you after all? What happened?

3. Have you ever had the experience of trying to "psyche" out a teacher? If so, describe the assumptions that guided your attempt to manipulate the teacher. What was the outcome of your endeavors?

4. Rudy assumes that success in school forecasts success in later life. Do you agree or disagree with this assumption? Why or why not? Provide examples to support your views.

5. To what extent do you think Santiago presents a realistic picture of the interaction between teachers and minority students? How would you modify this account to make it more realistic?

6. Describe a situation when a teacher did not see the real you, but reacted instead to some attribute such as sex, race, ethnicity, appearance. What insight does your experience give you into how Rudy felt in his encounter with Miss Bontempo?

# Tepilit Ole Saitoti

# *The Initiation of a Maasai Warrior*

---

*Named for the language they speak—Maa, a distinct, but unwritten African tongue—the Maasai of Kenya and Tanzania, a tall, handsome, and proud people, still live much as they always have, herding cattle, sheep, and goats in and around the Great Rift Valley. This personal narrative is unique—the first autobiographical account written by a Maasai, which vividly documents the importance of the circumcision ceremony that serves as a rite of passage into warrior rank. Tepilit Ole Saitoti studied animal ecology in the United States and has returned to Kenya, where he is active in conservation projects. His experiences formed the basis for a National Geographic Society film,* Man of Serengeti *(1971). This account first appeared in Saitoti's autobiography,* The Worlds of a Maasai Warrior *(1986).*

*The United Republic of Tanzania was formed in 1964 by the union of Tanganyika and Zanzibar. It is bordered on the north by Kenya, Lake Victoria, and Uganda. Fossils discovered by British anthropologist, Louis B. Leakey, at Olduvai Gorge in northeastern Tanzania have been identified as the remains of a direct ancestor of the human species from 1.75 million years ago. Tanzania contains the famed Mount Kilimanjaro, which at 19,340 feet is the highest point in Africa. Tanzania also boasts the highest literacy rate in Africa.*

"Tepilit, circumcision means a sharp knife cutting into the skin of the   1
most sensitive part of your body. You must not budge; don't move a muscle or even blink. You can face only one direction until the operation is completed. The slightest movement on your part will mean you are a coward, incompetent and unworthy to be a Maasai man. Ours has always been a proud family, and we would like to keep it that way. We will not tolerate unnecessary embarrassment, so you had better be ready. If you are not, tell us now so that we will not proceed. Imagine yourself alone remaining uncircumcised like the water youth [white people]. I hear they are not circumcised. Such a thing is not known in Maasailand; therefore, circumcision will have to take place even if it means holding you down until it is completed."

*(For more information on Kenya, see pp. 402–403.)

115

2    My father continued to speak and every one of us kept quiet. "The pain you will feel is symbolic. There is a deeper meaning in all this. Circumcision means a break between childhood and adulthood. For the first time in your life, you are regarded as a grownup, a complete man or woman. You will be expected to give and not just to receive. To protect the family always, not just to be protected yourself. And your wise judgment will for the first time be taken into consideration. No family affairs will be discussed without your being consulted. If you are ready for all these responsibilities, tell us now. Coming into manhood is not simply a matter of growth and maturity. It is a heavy load on your shoulders and especially a burden on the mind. Too much of this — I am done. I have said all I wanted to say. Fellows, if you have anything to add, go ahead and tell your brother, because I am through. I have spoken."

3    After a prolonged silence, one of my half-brothers said awkwardly, "Face it, man . . . it's painful. I won't lie about it, but it is not the end. We all went through it, after all. Only blood will flow, not milk." There was laughter and my father left.

4    My brother Lellia said, "Men, there are many things we must acquire and preparations we must make before the ceremony, and we will need the cooperation and help of all of you. Ostrich feathers for the crown and wax for the arrows must be collected."

5    "Are you *orkirekenyi?*" One of my brothers asked. I quickly replied no, and there was laughter. *Orkirekenyi* is a person who has transgressed sexually. For you must not have sexual intercourse with any circumcised woman before you yourself are circumcised. You must wait until you are circumcised. If you have not waited, you will be fined. Your father, mother, and the circumciser will take a cow from you as punishment.

6    Just before we departed, one of my closest friends said, "If you kick the knife, you will be in trouble." There was laughter. "By the way, if you have decided to kick the circumciser, do it well. Silence him once and for all." "Do it the way you kick a football in school." "That will fix him," another added, and we all laughed our heads off again as we departed.

7    The following month was a month of preparation. I and others collected wax, ostrich feathers, honey to be made into honey beer for the elders to drink on the day of circumcision, and all the other required articles.

8    Three days before the ceremony my head was shaved and I discarded all my belongings, such as my necklaces, garments, spear, and sword. I even had to shave my pubic hair. Circumcision in many ways is similar to Christian baptism. You must put all the sins you have committed during childhood behind and embark as a new person with a different outlook on a new life.

9    The circumciser came the following day and handed the ritual knives to me. He left drinking a calabash of beer. I stared at the knives uneasily.

It was hard to accept that he was going to use them on my organ. I was to sharpen them and protect them from people of ill will who might try to blunt them, thus rendering them inefficient during the ritual and thereby bringing shame on our family. The knives threw a chill down my spine; I was not sure I was sharpening them properly, so I took them to my closest brother for him to check out, and he assured me that the knives were all right. I hid them well and waited.

Tension started building between me and my relatives, most of whom worried that I wouldn't make it through the ceremony valiantly. Some even snarled at me, which was their way of encouraging me. Others threw insults and abusive words my way. My sister Loiyan in particular was more troubled by the whole affair than anyone in the whole family. She had to assume my mother's role during the circumcision. Were I to fail my initiation, she would have to face the consequences. She would be spat upon and even beaten for representing the mother of an unworthy son. The same fate would befall my father, but he seemed unconcerned. He had this weird belief that because I was not particularly handsome, I must be brave. He kept saying, "God is not so bad as to have made him ugly and a coward at the same time." 10

Failure to be brave during circumcision would have other unfortunate consequences: the herd of cattle belonging to the family still in the compound would be beaten until they stampeded; the slaughtered oxen and honey beer prepared during the month before the ritual would go to waste; the initiate's food would be spat upon and he would have to eat it or else get a severe beating. Everyone would call him Olkasiodoi, the knife kicker. 11

Kicking the knife of the circumciser would not help you anyway. If you struggle and try to get away during the ritual, you will be held down until the operation is completed. Such failure of nerve would haunt you in the future. For example, no one will choose a person who kicked the knife for a position of leadership. However, there have been instances in which a person who failed to go through circumcision successfully became very brave afterwards because he was filled with anger over the incident; no one dares to scold him or remind him of it. His agemates, particularly the warriors, will act as if nothing had happened. 12

During the circumcision of a woman, on the other hand, she is allowed to cry as long as she does not hinder the operation. It is common to see a woman crying and kicking during circumcision. Warriors are usually summoned to help hold her down. 13

For woman, circumcision means an end to the company of Maasai warriors. After they recuperate, they soon get married, and often to men twice their age. 14

The closer it came to the hour of truth, the more I was hated, particularly by those closest to me. I was deeply troubled by the withdrawal of all the support I needed. My annoyance turned into anger and resolve. I decided not to budge or blink, even if I were to see my 15 intestines flowing before me. My resolve was hardened when newly circumcised warriors came to sing for me. Their songs were utterly insulting, intended to annoy me further. They tucked their wax arrows under my crotch and rubbed them on my nose. They repeatedly called me names.

16      By the end of the singing, I was fuming. Crying would have meant I was a coward. After midnight they left me alone and I went into the house and tried to sleep but could not. I was exhausted and numb but remained awake all night.

17      At dawn I was summoned once again by the newly circumcised warriors. They piled more and more insults on me. They sang their weird songs with even more vigor and excitement than before. The songs praised warriorhood and encouraged one to achieve it at all costs. The songs continued until the sun shone on the cattle horns clearly. I was summoned to the main cattle gate, in my hand a ritual cowhide from a cow that had been properly slaughtered during my naming ceremony. I went past Loiyan, who was milking a cow, and she muttered something, She was shaking all over. There was so much tension that people could hardly breathe.

18      I laid the hide down and a boy was ordered to pour ice-cold water, known as *engare entolu* (ax water), over my head. It dripped all over my naked body and I shook furiously. In a matter of seconds I was summoned to sit down. A large crowd of boys and men formed a semicircle in front of me; women are not allowed to watch male circumcision and vice-versa. That was the last thing I saw clearly. As soon as I sat down, the circumciser appeared, his knives at the ready. He spread my legs and said, "One cut," a pronouncement necessary to prevent an initiate from claiming that he had been taken by surprise. He splashed a white liquid, a ceremonial paint called *enturoto*, across my face. Almost immediately I felt a spark of pain under my belly as the knife cut through my penis' foreskin. I happened to choose to look in the direction of the operation. I continued to observe the circumciser's fingers working mechanically. The pain became numbness and my lower body felt heavy, as if I were weighed down by a heavy burden. After fifteen minutes or so, a man who had been supporting from behind pointed at something, as if to assist the circumciser. I came to learn later that the circumciser's eyesight had been failing him and that my brothers had been mad at him because the operation had taken longer than was usually necessary. All the same, I remained pinned down until the operation was over. I heard a call for milk to wash the knives, which signaled the end, and soon the ceremony was over.

19      With words of praise, I was told to wake up, but I remained seated. I waited for the customary presents in appreciation of my bravery. My father gave me a cow and so did my brother Lillia. The man who had supported my back and my brother-in-law gave me a heifer. In all I had eight animals given to me. I was carried inside the house to my own bed to recuperate as activities intensified to celebrate my bravery.

I laid on my own bed and bled profusely. The blood must be retained 20
within the bed, for according to Maasai tradition, it must not spill to the
ground. I was drenched in my own blood. I stopped bleeding after about
half an hour but soon was in intolerable pain. I was supposed to squeeze
my organ and force blood to flow out of the wound, but no one had told
me, so the blood coagulated and caused unbearable pain. The circumciser was brought to my aid and showed me what to do, and soon the
pain subsided.

The following morning, I was escorted by a small boy to a nearby 21
valley to walk and relax, allowing my wound to drain. This was common
for everyone who had been circumcised, as well as for women who had
just given birth. Having lost a lot of blood, I was extremely weak. I
walked very slowly, but in spite of my caution I fainted. I tried to hang
on to bushes and shrubs, but I fell, irritating my wound. I came out of
unconsciousness quickly, and the boy who was escorting me never
realized what had happened. I was so scared that I told him to lead me
back home. I could have died without there being anyone around who
could have helped me. From that day on, I was selective of my company
while I was feeble.

In two weeks I was able to walk and was taken to join other newly 22
circumcised boys far away from our settlement. By tradition Maasai
initiates are required to decorate their headdresses with all kinds of
colorful birds they have killed. On our way to the settlement, we hunted
birds and teased girls by shooting them with our wax blunt arrows. We
danced and ate and were well treated wherever we went. We were
protected from the cold and rain during the healing period. We were not
allowed to touch food, as we were regarded as unclean, so whenever we
ate we had to use specially prepared sticks instead. We remained in this
pampered state until our wounds healed and our headdresses were
removed. Our heads were shaved, we discarded our black cloaks and
bird headdresses and embarked as newly shaven warriors, Irkeleani.

As long as I live I will never forget the day my head was shaved and I 23
emerged a man, a Maasai warrior. I felt a sense of control over my
destiny so great that no words can accurately describe it. I now stood
with confidence, pride, and happiness of being, for all around me I was
desired and loved by beautiful, sensuous Maasai maidens. I could now
interact with women and even have sex with them, which I not been
allowed before. I was now regarded as a responsible person.

In the old days, warriors were like gods, and women and men wanted 24
only to be the parent of a warrior. Everything else would be taken care of
as a result. When a poor family had a warrior, they ceased to be poor.
The warrior would go on raids and bring cattle back. The warrior would
defend the family against all odds. When a society respects the individual and displays confidence in him the way the Maasai do their warriors,
the individual can grow to his fullest potential. Whenever there was a
task requiring physical strength or bravery, the Maasai would call upon
their warriors. They hardly ever fall short of what is demanded of them

and so are characterized by pride, confidence, and an extreme sense of freedom. But there is an old saying in Maasai: "You are never a free man until your father dies." In other words, your father is paramount while he is alive and you are obligated to respect him. My father took advantage of this principle and held a tight grip on all his warriors, including myself. He always wanted to know where we all were at any given time. We fought against his restrictions, but without success. I, being the youngest of my father's five warriors, tried even harder to get loose repeatedly, but each time I was punished severely.

25      Roaming the plains with other warriors in pursuit of girls and adventure was a warrior's pastime. We would wander from one settlement to another, singing, wrestling, hunting, and just playing. Often I was ready to risk my father's punishment for this wonderful freedom.

26      One clear day my father sent me to take sick children and one of his wives to the dispensary in the Korongoro Highlands. We rode in the L.S.B. Leakey lorry. We ascended the highlands and were soon attended to in the local hospital. Near the conservation offices I met several acquaintances, and one of them told me of an unusual circumcision that was about to take place in a day or two. All the local warriors and girls were preparing to attend it.

27      The highlands were a lush green from the seasonal rains and the sky was a purple-blue with no clouds in sight. The land was overflowing with milk, and the warriors felt and looked their best, as they always did when there was plenty to eat and drink. Everyone was at ease. The demands the community usually made on warriors during the dry season when water was scarce and wells had to be dug were now not necessary. Herds and flocks were entrusted to youths to look after. The warriors had all the time for themselves. But my father was so strict that even at times like these he still insisted on overworking us in one way or another. He believed that by keeping us busy, he would keep us out of trouble.

28      When I heard about the impending ceremony, I decided to remain behind in the Korongoro Highlands and attend it now that the children had been treated. I knew very well that I would have to make up a story for my father upon my return, but I would worry about that later. I had left my spear at home when I boarded the bus, thinking that I would be coming back that very day. I felt lighter but now regretted having left it behind; I was so used to carrying it wherever I went. In gales of laughter resulting from our continuous teasing of each other, we made our way toward a distant kraal. We walked at a leisurely pace and reveled in the breeze. As usual we talked about the women we desired, among other things.

29      The following day we were joined by a long line of colorfully dressed girls and warriors from the kraal and the neighborhood where we had spent the night, and we left the highland and headed to Ingorienito to the rolling hills on the lower slopes to attend the circumcision ceremony. From there one could see Oldopai Gorge, where my parents lived, and the Inaapi hills in the middle of the Serengeti Plain.

Three girls and a boy were to be initiated on the same day, an    30
unusual occasion. Four oxen were to be slaughtered, and many people
would therefore attend. As we descended, we saw the kraal where the
ceremony would take place. All those people dressed in red seemed from
a distance like flamingos standing in a lake. We could see lines of other
guests heading to the settlements. Warriors made gallant cries of happiness known as *enkiseer*. Our line of warriors and girls responded to their
cries even more gallantly.

In serpentine fashion, we entered the gates of the settlement. Holding    31
spears in our left hands, we warriors walked proudly, taking small steps,
swaying like palm trees, impressing our girls, who walked parallel to us
in another line, and of course the spectators, who gazed at us
approvingly.

We stopped in the center of the kraal and waited to be greeted.    32
Women and children welcomed us. We put our hands on the children's
heads, which is how children are commonly saluted. After the greetings
were completed, we started dancing.

Our singing echoed off the kraal fence and nearby trees. Another line    33
of warriors came up the hill and entered the compound, also singing and
moving slowly toward us. Our singing grew in intensity. Both lines of
warriors moved parallel to each other, and our feet pounded the ground
with style. We stamped vigorously, as if to tell the next line and the
spectators that we were the best.

The singing continued until the hot sun was overhead. We recessed    34
and ate food already prepared for us by other warriors. Roasted meat
was for those who were to eat meat, and milk for the others. By our
tradition, meat and milk must not be consumed at the same time, for this
would be a betrayal of the animal. It was regarded as cruel to consume a
product of the animal that could be obtained while it was alive, such as
milk, and meat, which was only available after the animal had been
killed.

After eating we resumed singing, and I spotted a tall, beautiful *esian-*    35
*kiki* (young maiden) of Masiaya whose family was one of the largest and
richest in our area. She stood very erect and seemed taller than the
rest.

One of her breasts could be seen just above her dress, which was    36
knotted at the shoulder. While I was supposed to dance generally to
please all the spectators, I took it upon myself to please her especially. I
stared at and flirted with her, and she and I danced in unison at times.
We complemented each other very well,

During a break, I introduced myself to the *esiankiki* and told her I    37
would like to see her after the dance. "Won't you need a warrior to escort
you home later when the evening threatens?" I said. She replied, "Perhaps, but the evening is still far away."

I waited patiently. When the dance ended, I saw her departing with a    38
group of other women her age. She gave me a sidelong glance, and I took
that to mean come later and not now. With so many others around, I

would not have been able to confer with her as I would have liked anyway.

39    With another warrior, I wandered around the kraal killing time until the herds returned from pasture. Before the sun dropped out of sight, we departed. As the kraal of the *esiankiki* was in the lowlands, a place called Enkoloa, we descended leisurely, our spears resting on our shoulders.

40    We arrived at the woman's kraal and found that cows were now being milked. One could hear the women trying to appease the cows by singing to them. Singing calms cows down, making it easier to milk them. There were no warriors in the whole kraal except for the two of us. Girls went around into warriors' houses as usual and collected milk for us. I was so eager to go and meet my *esiankiki* that I could hardly wait for nightfall. The warriors' girls were trying hard to be sociable, but my mind was not with them. I found them to be childish, loud, bothersome, and boring.

41    As the only warriors present, we had to keep them company and sing for them, at least for a while, as required by custom. I told the other warrior to sing while I tried to figure out how to approach my *esiankiki*. Still a novice warrior, I was not experienced with women and was in fact still afraid of them. I could flirt from a distance, of course. But sitting down with a woman and trying to seduce her was another matter. I had already tried twice to approach women soon after my circumcision and had failed. I got as far as the door of one woman's house and felt my heart beating like a Congolese drum; breathing became difficult and I had to turn back. Another time I managed to get in the house and succeeded in sitting on the bed, but then I started trembling until the whole bed was shaking, and conversation became difficult. I left the house and the woman, amazed and speechless, and never went back to her again.

42    Tonight I promised myself I would be brave and would not make any silly, ridiculous moves. "I must be mature and not afraid," I kept reminding myself, as I remembered an incident involving one of my relatives when he was still very young and, like me, afraid of women. He went to a woman's house and sat on a stool for a whole hour; he was afraid to awaken her, as his heart was pounding and he was having difficulty breathing.

43    When he finally calmed down, he woke her up, and their conversation went something like this:

44    "Woman, wake up."

45    "Why should I?"

46    "To light the fire."

47    "For what?"

48    "So you can see me."

49    "I already know who you are. Why don't *you* light the fire, as you're nearer to it than me?"

50    "It's your house and it's only proper that you light it yourself."

"I don't feel like it."          51

"At least wake up so we can talk, as I have something to tell you."          52

"Say it."          53

"I need you."          54

"I do not need one-eyed types like yourself."          55

"One-eyed people are people too."          56

"That might be so, but they are not to my taste."          57

They continued talking for quite some time, and the more they spoke,          58
the braver he became. He did not sleep with her that night, but later on
he persisted until he won her over. I doubted whether I was as strong-
willed as he, but the fact that he had met with success encouraged me. I
told my warrior friend where to find me should he need me, and then I
departed.

When I entered the house of my *esiankiki*, I called for the woman of          59
the house, and as luck would have it, my lady responded. She was
waiting for me. I felt better, and I proceeded to talk to her like a
professional. After much talking back and forth, I joined her in bed.

The night was calm, tender, and loving, like most nights after initia-          60
tion ceremonies as big as this one. There must have been a lot of courting
and lovemaking.

Maasai women can be very hard to deal with sometimes. They can          61
simply reject a man outright and refuse to change their minds. Some play
hard to get, but in reality are testing the man to see whether he is worth
their while. Once a friend of mine while still young was powerfully
attracted to a woman nearly his mother's age. He put a bold move on
her. At first the woman could not believe his intention, or rather was
amazed by his courage. The name of the warrior was Ngengeiya, or
Drizzle.

"Drizzle, what do you want?"          62

The warrior stared her right in the eye and said, "You."          63

"For what?"          64

"To make love to you."          65

"I am your mother's age."          66

"The choice was either her or you."          67

This remark took the woman by surprise. She had underestimated          68
the saying "There is no such thing as a young warrior." When you are a
warrior, you are expected to perform bravely in any situation. Your age
and size are immaterial.

"You mean you could really love me like a grown-up man?"          69

"Try me, woman."          70

He moved in on her. Soon the woman started moaning with excite-          71
ment, calling out his name. "Honey Drizzle, Honey Drizzle, you *are* a
man." In a breathy, stammering voice, she said, "A real man."

Her attractiveness made Honey Drizzle ignore her relative old age.          72
The Maasai believe that if an older and a younger person have inter-

course, it is the older person who stands to gain. For instance, it is believed that an older woman having an affair with a young man starts to appear younger and healthier, while the young man grows older and unhealthy.

73          The following day when the initiation rites had ended, I decided to return home. I had offended my father by staying away from home without his consent, so I prepared myself for whatever punishment he might inflict on me. I walked home alone.

## *Evaluating the Text*

1. How is the candidate's life, reputation, and destiny dependent on the bravery he shows during the ceremony? What consequences would his family have to suffer if he were to flinch or shudder?
2. What function does relentless taunting by warriors and those who are newly circumcised serve before the ceremony?
3. What is Tepilit's attitude toward his father? What assumptions about a son's responsibilities account for how Tepilit's father treats him?
4. How are the different stages of the ceremony designed to intertwine the candidate's life with that of his community and ensure a continuation of their values and traditions?
5. What is the significance of Tepilit's throwing away his possessions and shaving his hair three days before the ceremony?
6. Explain the significance of the ceremonial white paint with which the boy is splashed and the fact that after the surgery, milk, rather than water, is used to wash the knives.
7. What is the significance of the bird headdress the candidate must wear and the fact that he is not allowed to touch food during the period of time when he is recovering from the surgery?
8. How does the language Tepilit uses to describe his feelings after the ceremony reflect the idea that he has been reborn into the community?
9. Several Maasai customs reveal the profound symbiotic relationship they have with nature and the animal world. For example, what is the rationale behind their practice of not eating milk and meat together? Why is Tepilit careful not to allow the blood from his wound to spill onto the ground as he lies on his bed bleeding from the surgery?
10. What responsibilities does Tepilit assume, and what privileges is he allowed on successful completion of the ceremony?
11. How is the necessity of learning to distinguish between people who are unreliable and those who are trustworthy one of the first psychological benefits of the initiation?

## *Exploring Different Perspectives*

1. Discuss the similarities and differences between Tepilit's initiation and that of Douchan Gersi in "Initiated into an Iban Tribe of Headhunters." To what extent does Tepilit's status as an "insider," in contrast to Gersi's role as an "outsider," explain their different responses both before and after the initiation ceremonies?

2. Compare and contrast the respective attitudes toward sexual freedom allowed to women before and after marriage among the Maasai in East Africa and among the Iban in Borneo described by Douchan Gersi in "Initiated into an Iban Tribe of Headhunters."
3. What similarities can you discover between the stages in Tepilit's initiation and the training recruits receive to transform them into Marines, as described in Henry Allen's report ("The Corps")? You might focus on how initiates and recruits are treated, each culture's attitude toward possessions, the significance of hair shaving, the role played by songs sung at different stages, what is expected of each as a warrior, weapons displayed and worn, and official warrior dress. How do both ceremonies deepen the bond between the initiate and his "tribe," continue traditions of the community, and enlist warriors who then become responsible for protecting their respective communities?

## Extending Viewpoints through Writing

1. Every culture and society has some form of initiation that its members must undergo to become part of that society. In what way is the Maasai ritual Tepilit describes intended to deepen the bond between the community and the initiate in ways that are quite similar, allowing for cultural differences, to the Bar Mitzvah in Judaism and the confirmation ceremony in Christianity? In an essay, explore how any of these rites of passage affirm the culture, unite the candidate with his or her community, and ensure the continuation of traditions.
2. Despite obvious differences between the Maasai society and contemporary American culture, Tepilit's interactions with his friends and the opposite sex are quite typical of those of any teenage boy. Write an essay exploring these similarities.
3. If you had to choose between being initiated as a warrior into the Maasai in East Africa, as a Marine (Henry Allen's "The Corps"), or into the Iban tribe of headhunters in Borneo (Douchan Gersi's "Initiated into an Iban Tribe of Headhunters"), which would you choose and why? Keep in mind the great differences in the length of time over which the initiation takes place, the respective penalties for not successfully completing the rite of passage, and the privileges and responsibilities that ensue from a successful completion.

# Nawal El Saadawi

# *Circumcision of Girls*

---

*Nawal El Saadawi is an Egyptian physician and feminist writer whose work publicizing the injustices and brutalities to which Arab women are subject is well known throughout the world. Born in the village of Kafrtahla on the banks of the Nile, in 1931, she began her medical practice in rural areas, then in Cairo, and finally became Egypt's Director of Public Health. The publication of her first nonfiction book,* Women and Sex *(1972), resulted in her dismissal from her post by Anwar Sadat, imprisonment, and censorship of her books on the status, psychology, and sexuality of women. Her works are now banned in Egypt, Saudi Arabia, and Libya. The following chapter, "Circumcision of Girls," is from* The Hidden Face of Eve: Women in the Arab World *(1980, translated and edited by Saadawi's husband, Dr. Sherif Hetata), a work depicting the hitherto unpublicized but culturally accepted procedure of female circumcision, a practice to which she herself was subjected at the age of eight.*

*Egypt is a Arab republic in northeastern Africa, bordered by the Mediterranean to the north, Israel and the Red Sea to the east, the Sudan to the south, and Libya to the west. Egypt was the site of one of the earliest civilizations that developed in the Nile valley over 5,000 years ago and flourished until it became part of the Roman Empire in 30 B.C. As always, Egypt depends on the Nile River for maintaining arable lands, and its economy, although weakened in the 1980s by the Arab–Israeli wars, remains primarily agricultural. Under the leadership of Anwar Sadat, in 1979, Egypt became the first Arab nation to sign a peace treaty with Israel. In 1981, Sadat was assassinated by Muslim fundamentalists, and his successor, Hosni Mubarak, has faced the difficult task of dealing with the resurgence of Islamic fundamentalism while moving Egypt into a position of leadership in the Arab world. Egypt joined the United States and other nations in sending troops to Saudi Arabia after the August 1990 invasion of Kuwait by Iraq. Saadawi's analysis reveals the extent to which women's lives in the Middle East are constrained by age-old Islamic laws and customs.*

1    The practice of circumcising girls is still a common procedure in a number of Arab countries such as Egypt, the Sudan, Yemen and some of the Gulf states.

2    The importance given to virginity and an intact hymen in these

126

societies is the reason why female circumcision still remains a very widespread practice despite a growing tendency, especially in urban Egypt, to do away with it as something outdated and harmful. Behind circumcision lies the belief that, by removing parts of girls external genital organs, sexual desire is minimized. This permits a female who has reached the 'dangerous age' of puberty and adolescence to protect her virginity, and therefore her honour, with greater ease. Chastity was imposed on male attendants in the female harem by castration which turned them into inoffensive eunuchs. Similarly female circumcision is meant to preserve the chastity of young girls by reducing their desire for sexual intercourse.

Circumcision is most often performed on female children at the age of seven or eight (before the girl begins to get menstrual periods). On the scene appears the *daya* or local midwife. Two women members of the family grasp the child's thighs on either side and pull them apart to expose the external genital organs and to prevent her from struggling — like trussing a chicken before it is slain. A sharp razor in the hand of the *daya* cuts off the clitoris.

During my period of service as a rural physician, I was called upon many times to treat complications arising from this primitive operation, which very often jeopardized the life of young girls. The ignorant *daya* believed that effective circumcision necessitated a deep cut with the razor to ensure radical amputation of the clitoris, so that no part of the sexually sensitive organ would remain. Severe haemorrhage was therefore a common occurrence and sometimes led to loss of life. The *dayas* had not the slightest notion of asepsis, and inflammatory conditions as a result of the operation were common. Above all, the lifelong psychological shock of this cruel procedure left its imprint on the personality of the child and accompanied her into adolescence, youth and maturity. Sexual frigidity is one of the after-effects which is accentuated by other social and psychological factors that influence the personality and mental make-up of females in Arab societies. Girls are therefore exposed to a whole series of misfortunes as a result of outdated notions and values related to virginity, which still remains the fundamental criterion of a girl's honour. In recent years, however, educated families have begun to realize the harm that is done by the practice of female circumcision.

Nevertheless a majority of families still impose on young female children the barbaric and cruel operation of circumcision. The research that I carried out on a sample of 160 Egyptian girls and women showed that 97.5% of uneducated families still insisted on maintaining the custom, but this percentage dropped to 66.2% among educated families.[1]

When I discussed the matter with these girls and women it transpired that most of them had no idea of the harm done by circumcision, and some of them even thought that it was good for one's health and conducive to cleanliness and 'purity'. (The operation in the common language of the people is in fact called the cleansing or purifying operation.) Despite the fact that the percentage of educated women who have undergone circumcision is only 66.2%, as compared with 97.5% among uneducated women, even the former did not realize the effect that this amputation of the clitoris could have on their psychological and sexual health. The dialogue that occurred between these women and myself would run more or less as follows:

'Have you undergone circumcision?'

'Yes.'

'How old were you at the time?'

'I was a child, about seven or eight years old.'

'Do you remember the details of the operation?'

'Of course. How could I possibly forget?'

'Were you afraid?'

'Very afraid. I hid on top of the cupboard [in other cases she would say under the bed, or in the neighbour's house], but they caught hold of me, and I felt my body tremble in their hands.'

'Did you feel any pain?'

'Very much so, It was like a burning flame and I screamed. My mother held my head so that I could not move it, my aunt caught hold of my right arm and my grandmother took charge of my left. Two strange women whom I had not seen before tried to keep me from moving my thighs by pushing them as far apart as possible. The *daya* sat between these two women, holding a sharp razor in her hand which she used to cut off the clitoris. I was scared and suffered such great pain that I lost consciousness at the flame that seemed to sear me through and through.'

'What happened after the operation?'

'I had severe bodily pains, and remained in bed for several days, unable to move. The pain in my external genital organs led to retention of urine. Every time I wanted to urinate the burning sensation was so unbearable that I could not bring myself to pass water. The wound continued to bleed for some time, and my mother used to change the dressing for me twice a day.'

'What did you feel on discovering that a small organ in your body had been removed?'

'I did not know anything about the operation at the time, except that it was very simple, and that it was done to all girls for purposes of cleanliness, purity and the preservation of a good reputation. It was said that a girl who did not undergo this operation was liable to be talked about by people, her behaviour would become bad, and she would start running after men, with the result that no one would agree to marry her when the time for marriage came. My grandmother told me that the operation had only consisted in the removal of a very small piece of flesh from between my thighs, and that the continued existence of this small piece of flesh in its place would have made me unclean and impure, and would have caused the man whom I would marry to be repelled by me.'

'Did you believe what was said to you?'

'Of course I did. I was happy the day I recovered from the effects of the operation, and felt as though I was rid of something which had to be removed, and so had become clean and pure.'

Those were more or less the answers that I obtained from all those interviewed, whether educated or uneducated. One of them was a medical student from Ein Shams School of Medicine. She was preparing for her final examinations and I expected her answers to be different, but in fact they were almost identical to the others. We had quite a long discussion which I reproduce here as I remember it.

'You are going to be a medical doctor after a few weeks, so how can you believe that cutting off the clitoris from the body of a girl is a healthy procedure, or at least not harmful?'

'This is what I was told by everybody. All the girls in my family have been circumcised. I have studied anatomy and medicine, yet I have never heard any of the professors who taught us explain that the clitoris had any function to fulfil in the body of a woman, neither have I read anything of the kind in the books which deal with the medical subjects I am studying.'

'That is true. To this day medical books do not consider the science of sex as a subject which they should deal with. The organs of a woman worthy of attention are considered to be only those directly related to reproduction, namely the vagina, the uterus and the ovaries. The clitoris, however, is an organ neglected by medicine, just as it is ignored and disdained by society.'

'I remember a student asking the professor one day about the clitoris. The professor went red in the face and answered him curtly, saying that no one was going to ask him about this part of the female body during examinations, since it was of no importance.'

My studies led me to try and find out the effect of circumcision on the girls and women who had been made to undergo it, and to understand what results it had on the psychological and sexual life. The majority of the normal cases I interviewed answered that the operation had no effect on them. To me it was clear that in the face of such questions they were much more ashamed and intimidated than the neurotic cases were. But I did not allow myself to be satisfied with these answers, and would go on to question them closely about their sexual life both before and after the circumcision was done. Once again I will try to reproduce the dialogue that usually occurred.

'Did you experience any change of feeling or of sexual desire after the operation?'

'I was a child and therefore did not feel anything.'

'Did you not experience any sexual desire when you were a child?'

'No, never. Do children experience sexual desire?'

'Children feel pleasure when they touch their sexual organs, and some form of sexual play occurs between them, for example, during the game of bride and bridegroom usually practised under the bed. Have you never played this game with your friends when still a child?'

At these words the young girl or woman would blush, and her eyes would probably refuse to meet mine, in an attempt to hide her confusion. But after the conversation had gone on for some time, and an atmosphere of mutual confidence and understanding had been established, she would begin to recount her childhood memories. She would often refer to the pleasure she had felt when a man of the family permitted himself certain sexual caresses. Sometimes these caresses would be proffered by the domestic servant, the house porter, the private teacher or the neighbour's son. A college student told me that her brother had been wont to caress her sexual organs and that she used to experience acute enjoyment. However after undergoing circumcision she no longer had the same sensation of pleasure. A married woman admitted that during intercourse with her husband she had never experienced the slightest sexual enjoyment, and that her last memories of any form of pleasurable sensation went back twenty years, to the age of six, before she had undergone circumcision. A young girl told me that she had been accustomed to practise masturbation, but had given it up completely after removal of the clitoris at the age of ten.

10    The further our conversations went, and the more I delved into their lives, the more readily they opened themselves up to me and uncovered the secrets of childhood and adolescence, perhaps almost forgotten by them or only vaguely realized.

11    Being both a woman and a medical doctor I was able to obtain confessions from these women and girls which it would be almost impossible, except in very rare cases, for a man to obtain. For the Egyptian woman, accustomed as she is to a very rigid and severe upbringing built on a complete denial of any sexual life before marriage, adamantly refuses to admit that she has ever known, or experienced, anything related to sex before the first touches of her husband. She is therefore ashamed to speak about such things with any man, even the doctor who is treating her.

12    My discussions with some of the psychiatrists who had treated a number of the young girls and women in my sample, led me to conclude that there were many aspects of the life of these neurotic patients that remained unknown to them. This was due either to the fact that the psychiatrist himself had not made the necessary effort to penetrate deeply into the life of the woman he was treating, or to the tendency of the patient herself not to divulge those things which her upbringing made her consider matters not to be discussed freely, especially with a man.

13    In fact the long and varied interchanges I had over the years with the majority of practising psychiatrists in Egypt, my close association with a large number of my medical colleagues during the long periods I spent working in health centres and general or specialized hospitals and, finally, the four years I spent as a member of the National Board of the Syndicate of Medical Professions, have all led me to the firm conclusion that the medical profession in our society is still incapable of under-

standing the fundamental problems with which sick people are burdened, whether they be men or women, but especially if they are women. For the medical profession, like any other profession in society, is governed by the political, social and moral values which predominate, and like other professions is one of the institutions which is utilized more often than not to protect these values and perpetuate them.

Men represent the vast majority in the medical profession, as in most 14 professions. But apart from this, the mentality of women doctors differs little, if at all, from that of the men, and I have known quite a number of them who were even more rigid and backward in outlook than their male colleagues.

A rigid and backward attitude towards most problems, and in partic- 15 ular towards women and sex, predominates in the medical profession, and particularly within the precincts of the medical colleges in the Universities.

Before undertaking my research study on 'Women and Neurosis' at 16 Ein Shams University, I had made a previous attempt to start it at the Kasr El Eini Medical College in the University of Cairo, but had been obliged to give up as a result of the numerous problems I was made to confront. The most important obstacle of all was the overpowering traditionalist mentality that characterized the professors responsible for my research work, and to whom the word 'sex' could only be equated to the word 'shame'. 'Respectable research' therefore could not possibly have sex as its subject, and should under no circumstances think of penetrating into areas even remotely related to it. One of my medical colleagues in the Research Committee advised me not to refer at all to the question of sex in the title of my research paper, when I found myself obliged to shift to Ein Shams University. He warned me that any such reference would most probably lead to fundamental objections which would jeopardize my chances of going ahead with it. I had initially chosen to define my subject as 'Problems that confront the sexual life of modern Egyptian women', but after prolonged negotiations I was prevailed to delete the word 'sexual' and replace it by 'psychological'. Only thus was it possible to circumvent the sensitivities of the professors at the Ein Shams Medical School and obtain their consent to go ahead with the research.

After I observed the very high percentages of women and girls who 17 had been obliged to undergo circumcision, or who had been exposed to different forms of sexual violation or assault in their childhood, I started to look for research undertaken in these two areas, either in the medical colleges or in research institutes, but in vain. Hardly a single medical doctor or researcher had ventured to do any work on these subjects, in view of the sensitive nature of the issues involved. This can also be explained by the fact that most of the research carried out in such institutions is of a formal and superficial nature, since its sole aim is to obtain a degree or promotion. The path of safety is therefore the one to choose, and safety means to avoid carefully all subjects of controversy. No one is therefore prepared to face difficulties with the responsible academic and scientific authorities, or to engage in any form of struggle against them, or their ideas. Nor is anyone prepared to face up to those who lay down the norms of virtue, morals and religious behaviour in society. All the established leaderships in the area related to such matters suffer from a pronounced allergy to the word 'sex', and any of its implications, especially if it happens to be linked to the word 'woman'.

18      Nevertheless I was fortunate enough to discover a small number of medical doctors who had the courage to be different, and therefore to examine some of the problems related to the sexual life of women. I would like to cite, as one of the rare examples, the only research study carried out on the question of female circumcision in Egypt and its harmful effects. This was the joint effort of Dr. Mahmoud Koraim and Dr. Rushdi Ammar, both from Ein Shams Medical College, and which was published in 1965. It is composed of two parts, the first of which was printed under the title *Female Circumcision and Sexual Desire*,[2] and the second, under the title *Complications of Female Circumcision*.[3] The conclusions arrived at as a result of this research study, which covered 651 women circumcised during childhood, may be summarized as follows:

(1) Circumcision is an operation with harmful effects on the health of women, and is the cause of sexual shock to young girls. It reduces the capacity of a woman to reach the peak of her sexual pleasure (i.e., orgasm) and has a definite though lesser effect in reducing sexual desire.

(2) Education helps to limit the extent to which female circumcision is practised, since educated parents have an increasing tendency to refuse the operation for their daughters. On the other hand, uneducated families still go in for female circumcision in submission to prevailing traditions, or in the belief that removal of the clitoris reduces the sexual desire of the girl, and therefore helps to preserve her virginity and chastity after marriage.

(3) There is no truth whatsoever in the idea that female circumcision helps in reducing the incidence of cancerous disease of the external genital organs.

(4) Female circumcision in all its forms and degrees, and in particular the fourth degree known as Pharaonic or Sudanese excision, is accompanied by immediate or delayed complications such as inflammations, haemorrhage, disturbances in the urinary passages, cysts or swellings that can obstruct the urinary flow or the vaginal opening.

(5) Masturbation in circumcised girls is less frequent than was observed by Kinsey in girls who have not undergone this operation.

19      I was able to exchange views with Dr. Mahmoud Koraim during several meetings in Cairo. I learnt from him that he had faced numerous difficulties while undertaking his research, and was the target of bitter criticism from some of his colleagues and from religious leaders who

considered themselves the divinely appointed protectors of morality, and therefore required to shield society from such impious undertakings, which constituted a threat to established values and moral codes.

The findings of my research study coincided with some of the con-  20
clusions arrived at by my two colleagues on a number of points. There is no longer any doubt that circumcision is the source of sexual and psychological shock in the life of the girl, and leads to a varying degree of sexual frigidity according to the woman and her circumstances. Education helps parents realize that this operation is not beneficial, and should be avoided, but I have found that the traditional education given in our schools and universities, whose aim is simply some certificate, or degree, rather than instilling useful knowledge and culture, is not very effective in combating the long-standing, and established traditions that govern Egyptian society, and in particular those related to sex, virginity in girls, and chastity in women. These areas are strongly linked to moral and religious values that have dominated and operated in our society for hundreds of years.

Since circumcision of females aims primarily at ensuring virginity  21
before marriage, and chastity throughout, it is not to be expected that its practice will disappear easily from Egyptian society or within a short period of time. A growing number of educated families are, however, beginning to realize the harm that is done to females by this custom, and are therefore seeking to protect their daughters from being among its victims. Parallel to these changes, the operation itself is no longer performed in the old primitive way, and the more radical degrees approaching, or involving, excision are dying out more rapidly. Nowadays, even in Upper Egypt and the Sudan, the operation is limited to the total, or more commonly the partial, amputation of the clitoris. Nevertheless, while undertaking my research, I was surprised to discover, contrary to what I had previously thought, that even in educated urban families over 50% still consider circumcision as essential to ensure female virginity and chastity.

Many people think that female circumcision only started with the  22
advent of Islam. But as a matter of fact it was well known and widespread in some areas of the world before the Islamic era, including in the Arab peninsula. Mahomet the Prophet tried to oppose this custom since he considered it harmful to the sexual health of the woman. In one of his sayings the advice reported as having been given by him to Om Attiah, a woman who did tattooings and circumcision, runs as follows: 'If you circumcise, take only a small part and refrain from cutting most of the clitoris off . . . The woman will have a bright and happy face, and is more welcome to her husband, if her pleasure is complete.[4]

This means that the circumcision of girls was not originally an Islamic  23
custom, and was not related to monotheistic religions, but was practised in societies with widely varying religious backgrounds, in countries of the East and the West, and among peoples who believed in Christianity,

or in Islam, or were atheistic . . . Circumcision was known in Europe as late as the 19th century, as well as in countries like Egypt, the Sudan, Somaliland, Ethiopia, Kenya, Tanzania, Ghana, Guinea and Nigeria. It was also practised in many Asian countries such as Sri Lanka and Indonesia, and in parts of Latin America. It is recorded as going back far into the past under the Pharaonic Kingdoms of Ancient Egypt, and Herodotus mentioned the existence of female circumcision seven hundred years before Christ was born. This is why the operation as practised in the Sudan is called 'Pharaonic excision'.

24       For many years I tried in vain to find relevant sociological or anthropological studies that would throw some light on the reasons why such a brutal operation is practised on females. However I did discover other practices related to girls and female children which were even more savage. One of them was burying female children alive almost immediately after they were born, or even at a later stage. Other examples are the chastity belt, or closing the aperture of the external genital organs with steel pins and a special iron lock.[5] This last procedure is extremely primitive and very much akin to Sudanese circumcision where the clitoris, external lips and internal lips are completely excised, and the orifice of the genital organs closed with a flap of sheep's intestines leaving only a very small opening barely sufficient to let the tip of the finger in, so that the menstrual and urinary flows are not held back. This opening is slit at the time of marriage and widened to allow penetration of the male sexual organ. It is widened again when a child is born and then narrowed down once more. Complete closure of the aperture is also done on a woman who is divorced, so that she literally becomes a virgin once more and can have no sexual intercourse except in the eventuality of marriage, in which case the opening is restored.

25       In the face of all these strange and complicated procedures aimed at preventing sexual intercourse in women except if controlled by the husband, it is natural that we should ask ourselves why women, in particular, were subjected to such torture and cruel suppression. There seems to be no doubt that society, as represented by its dominant classes and male structure, realized at a very early stage that sexual desire in the female is very powerful, and that women, unless controlled and subjugated by all sorts of measures, will not submit themselves to the moral, social, legal and religious constraints with which they have been surrounded, and in particular the constraints related to monogamy. The patriarchal system, which came into being when society had reached a certain stage of development and which necessitated the imposition of one husband on the woman whereas a man was left free to have several wives, would never have been possible, or have been maintained to this day, without the whole range of cruel and ingenious devices that were used to keep her sexuality in check and limit her sexual relations to only one man, who had to be her husband. This is the reason for the implacable enmity shown by society towards female sexuality, and the weapons used to

resist and subjugate the turbulent force inherent in it. The slightest leniency manifested in facing this 'potential danger' meant that woman would break out of the prison bars to which marriage had confined her, and step over the steely limits of a monogamous relationship to a forbidden intimacy with another man, which would inevitably lead to confusion in succession and inheritance, since there was no guarantee that a strange man's child would not step into the waiting line of descendants. Confusion between the children of the legitimate husband and the outsider lover would mean the unavoidable collapse of the patriarchal family built around the name of the father alone.

History shows us clearly that the father was keen on knowing who his real children were, solely for the purpose of handing down his landed property to them. The patriarchal family, therefore, came into existence mainly for economic reasons. It was necessary for society simultaneously to build up a system of moral and religious values, as well as a legal system capable of protecting and maintaining these economic interests. In the final analysis we can safely say that female circumcision, the chastity belt and other savage practices applied to women are basically the result of the economic interests that govern society. The continued existence of such practices in our society today signifies that these economic interests are still operative. The thousands of *dayas*, nurses, paramedical staff and doctors, who make money out of female circumcision, naturally resist any change in these values and practices which are a source of gain to them. In the Sudan there is a veritable army of *dayas* who earn a livelihood out of the series of operations performed on women, either to excise their external genital organs, or to alternately narrow and widen the outer aperture according to whether the woman is marrying, divorcing, remarrying, having a child or recovering from labour.[6]

Economic factors and, concomitantly, political factors are the basis upon which such customs as female circumcision have grown up. It is important to understand the facts as they really are, the reasons that lie behind them. Many are the people who are not able to distinguish between political and religious factors, or who conceal economic and political motives behind religious arguments in an attempt to hide the real forces that lie at the basis of what happens in society and in history. It has very often been proclaimed that Islam is at the root of female circumcision, and is also responsible for the under-privileged and backward situation of women in Egypt and the Arab countries. Such a contention is not true. If we study Christianity it is easy to see that this religion is much more rigid and orthodox where women are concerned than Islam. Nevertheless, many countries were able to progress rapidly despite the preponderance of Christianity as a religion. This progress was social, economic, scientific and also affected the life and position of women in society.

That is why I firmly believe that the reasons for the lower status of

women in our societies, and the lack of opportunities for progress af-
forded to them, are not due to Islam, but rather to certain economic and
political forces, namely those of foreign imperialism operating mainly
from the outside, and of the reactionary classes operating from the
inside. These two forces cooperate closely and are making a concerted
attempt to misinterpret religion and to utilize it as an instrument of fear,
oppression and exploitation.

29      Religion, if authentic in the principles it stands for, aims at truth,
equality, justice, love and a healthy wholesome life for all people,
whether men or women. There can be no true religion that aims at
disease, mutilation of the bodies of female children, and amputation of
an essential part of their reproductive organs.

30      If religion comes from God, how can it order man to cut off an organ
created by Him as long as that organ is not diseased or deformed? God
does not create the organs of the body haphazardly without a plan. It is
not possible that He should have created the clitoris in woman's body
only in order that it be cut off at an early stage in life. This is a
contradiction into which neither true religion nor the Creator could
possibly fall. If God has created the clitoris as a sexually sensitive organ,
whose sole function seems to be the procurement of sexual pleasure for
women, it follows that He also considers such pleasure for women as
normal and legitimate, and therefore as an integral part of mental health.
The psychic and mental health of women cannot be complete if they do
not experience sexual pleasure.

31      There are still a large number of fathers and mothers who are afraid
of leaving the clitoris intact in the bodies of their daughters. Many a time
they have said to me that circumcision is a safeguard against the mistakes
and deviations into which a girl may be led. This way of thinking is
wrong and even dangerous because what protects a boy or a girl from
making mistakes is not the removal of a small piece of flesh from the
body, but consciousness and understanding of the problems we face, and
a worthwhile aim in life, an aim which gives it meaning and for whose
attainment we exert our mind and energies. The higher the level of
consciousness to which we attain, the closer our aims draw to human
motives and values, and the greater our desire to improve life and its
quality, rather than to indulge ourselves in the mere satisfaction of our
senses and the experience of pleasure, even though these are an essential
part of existence. The most liberated and free of girls, in the true sense of
liberation, are the least preoccupied with sexual questions, since these no
longer represent a problem. On the contrary, a free mind finds room for
numerous interests and the many rich experiences of a cultured life. Girls
that suffer sexual suppression, however, are greatly preoccupied with
men and sex. And it is a common observation that an intelligent and
cultured woman is much less engrossed in matters related to sex and to
men than is the case with ordinary women, who have not got much with
which to fill their lives. Yet at the same time such a woman takes much

more initiative to ensure that she will enjoy sex and experience pleasure, and acts with a greater degree of boldness than others. Once sexual satisfaction is attained, she is able to turn herself fully to other important aspects of life.

In the life of liberated and intelligent women, sex does not occupy a disproportionate position, but rather tends to maintain itself within normal limits. In contrast, ignorance, suppression, fear and all sorts of limitations exaggerate the role of sex in the life of girls and women, and cause it to swell out of all proportion and to end up by occupying the whole, or almost the whole, of their lives.

*Translated and edited by Dr. Sherif Hetata*

## REFERENCES

1. This research study was carried out in the years 1973 and 1974 in the School of Medicine, Ein Shams University, under the title: *Women and Neurosis.*

2. *Female Circumcision and Sexual Desire,* Mahmoud Koraim and Rushdi Ammar, (Ein Shams University Press, Cairo, 1965).

3. *Complications of Female Circumcision,* the same authors, (Cairo, 1965).

4. See *Dawlat El Nissa'a,* Abdel Rahman El Barkouky, first edition, (Renaissance Bookshop, Cairo, 1945).

5. Desmond Morris, *The Naked Ape,* (Corgi, 1967). p. 76.

6. Rose Oldfield, 'Female genital mutilation, fertility control, women's roles, and patrilineage in modern Sudan', *American Ethnologist,* Vol. II, No. 4, November 1975.

## Evaluating the Text

1. Discuss the cultural assumptions underlying the importance ascribed to female virginity in Middle-Eastern cultures. What inferences can you draw about how female sexuality is viewed from Saadawi's analysis?

2. How does the fact that Saadawi herself is a physician who has treated girls suffering the medical complications of circumcision enhance the credibility of her analysis?

3. How would you characterize Saadawi's tone in this article, that is, her attitude toward the subject? What is the relationship between the tone she uses and the purpose of this essay? What words and phrases reveal her attitude to you most clearly?

4. Why does Saadawi find it so distressing that even among the educated (of whom two-thirds have undergone the operation) few women have given up the cultural programming that female circumcision is a purifying or cleansing procedure?

5. What psychological and economic objectives is female circumcision designed to achieve? How, in Saadawi's view, does it function as one of the main methods by which the countries of Sudan, Yemen, Saudi

Arabia, and Libya keep their social structure intact and ensure the transmission of property from one generation to the next?

6. What role do personal narratives and case histories play in authenticating Saadawi's account?

7. Do you believe that the 160 interviews she conducted would be a sample sufficiently large to form the basis for generalizations? Why was the interview with the medical student particularly significant? What harmful psychological effects of female circumcision did Saadawi discover from the interviews she conducted?

8. How does Saadawi's analysis depend on pointing out the distinction the culture draws between so-called utilitarian parts of a woman's body and the clitoris, which is only of value to the woman herself yet is perceived as a threat to the social structure?

9. What prevailing cultural view, unexpectedly strong even among male and female doctors and medical-school professors, made it so difficult for Saadawi to pursue her research?

10. What prevailing beliefs did Koraim and Ammar's study about the supposed medical efficacy of circumcision disclose to be baseless? How does Saadawi use the results of their study in her analysis?

11. How does Saadawi's reference to Muhammad's ("Mahomet") comment support her claim that female circumcision was not originally an Islamic custom? How is this phase of her argument intended to undercut claims by religious leaders that they are simply upholding Islamic religious values?

12. How plausible do you find Saadawi's reasoning to be when she argues that God would not have created an organ in the human body with the sole purpose of having it removed at an early stage of life?

## Exploring Different Perspectives

1. How is circumcision intended to physically and psychologically restrict girls in Middle-Eastern cultures described by Saadawi and to empower and confer authority onto boys among the Maasai in East Africa? Discuss the different culturally defined values attached to circumcision.

2. How are the cultural values attached to circumcision of girls in Maasai culture similar to yet different from the corresponding procedure performed on girls in Middle-East countries? How would you distinguish between the underlying social objectives of both cultures?

## Extending Viewpoints through Writing

1. Compare and contrast the value placed on female virginity in cultures Saadawi is describing in contrast to contemporary American society. What factors do you think explain the differences, and how do these differences reflect the different ways women are viewed in these two cultures?

2. Is there any outdated custom or practice that you would wish to make the case against in contemporary society? Formulate your response as an argument, making sure that you cite evidence and give cogent reasons to support your views. You should also attempt to anticipate the objections opponents to your views might raise and think of responses to each of these possible objections.

3. Drawing on Saadawi's essay, explore the relationship between law and custom and women's freedom of choice. How is the societal practice of female circumcision intended to take the power of choice out of the woman's hands as to what she will do with her body? Discuss possible similarities between this practice and issues arising from the continuing abortion debate in America.

# Tayeb Salih

# *A Handful of Dates*

---

*Tayeb Salih was born in the northern province of the Sudan in 1929. He was head of drama in the BBC's Arabic Service and now works for UNESCO in Paris. His writings include* Season of Migration to the North, *translated by Denys Johnson-Davies (1969), and the collection of a short novel and stories titled* The Wedding of Zein *(1978), from which "A Handful of Dates" (translated from Arabic into English by Denys Johnson-Davies) was taken. This story describes a boy's reaction to the discovery that his grandfather's business practices conflict with the teachings of the Koran, the sacred book of Islam, which Muslims believe contain the divine teachings revealed to the prophet Muhammed.*

*Sudan, the largest country on the African continent, is a republic in the northeast, bordered on the north by Egypt; on the east by the Red Sea and Ethiopia; on the south by Kenya, Uganda, and Zaire; and on the west by Chad and Libya. The population (24.5 million) of the Sudan is divided into three main groups — northerners, who speak Arabic and are Muslims (70 percent); peoples from West Africa; and southerners, who follow traditional animistic beliefs (20 percent). Animism is the belief that natural objects such as rivers and rocks possess a soul or spirit and are alive. Independence from British control was achieved in 1956, although a bloody civil war between Muslims and those who follow animistic beliefs lasted seventeen years and ended only in 1972, after 1.5 million had died. The period of time during which "A Handful of Dates" was written corresponded with a movement that sought to impose Islamic law (sharia) on the whole country. Reaction against this triggered a civil war between Muslims in the north and the members of the Sudan People's Liberation Movement — who desire a secular democratic state, free from control by Islamic law — in the south. This war continues to the present. At least 250,000 people died in 1988 when relief supplies were diverted from reaching drought-affected populations.*

1    I must have been very young at the time. While I don't remember exactly how old I was, I do remember that when people saw me with my

---

*(For further background on the Middle East, see pp. 126 and 480.)

grandfather they would pat me on the head and give my cheek a pinch — things they didn't do to my grandfather. The strange thing was that I never used to go out with my father, rather it was my grandfather who would take me with him wherever he went, except for the mornings when I would go to the mosque to learn the Koran. The mosque, the river and the fields — these were the landmarks in our life. While most of the children of my age grumbled at having to go to the mosque to learn the Koran, I used to love it. The reason was, no doubt, that I was quick at learning by heart and the Sheikh always asked me to stand up and recite the *Chapter of the Merciful* whenever we had visitors, who would pat me on my head and cheek just as people did when they saw me with my grandfather.

Yes, I used to love the mosque, and I loved the river too. Directly we    2
finished our Koran reading in the morning I would throw down my wooden slate and dart off, quick as a genie, to my mother, hurriedly swallow down my breakfast, and run off for a plunge in the river. When tired of swimming about I would sit on the bank and gaze at the strip of water that wound away eastwards and hid behind a thick wood of acacia trees. I loved to give rein to my imagination and picture to myself a tribe of giants living behind that wood, a people tall and thin with white beards and sharp noses, like my grandfather. Before my grandfather ever replied to my many questions he would rub the tip of his nose with his forefinger; as for his beard, it was soft and luxuriant and as white as cotton-wool — never in my life have I seen anything of a purer whiteness or greater beauty. My grandfather must also have been extremely tall, for I never saw anyone in the whole area address him without having to look up at him, nor did I see him enter a house without having to bend so low that I was put in mind of the way the river wound round behind the wood of acacia trees. I loved him and would imagine myself, when I grew to be a man, tall and slender like him, walking along with great strides.

I believe I was his favourite grandchild: no wonder, for my cousins    3
were a stupid bunch and I — so they say — was an intelligent child. I used to know when my grandfather wanted me to laugh, when to be silent; also I would remember the times for his prayers and would bring him his prayer-rug and fill the ewer for his ablutions without his having to ask me. When he had nothing else to do he enjoyed listening to me reciting to him from the Koran in a lilting voice, and I could tell from his face that he was moved.

One day I asked him about our neighbour Masood. I said to my grand-father: 'I fancy you don't like our neighbour Masood?'

To which he answered, having rubbed the tip of his nose: 'He's an    4
indolent man and I don't like such people.'

I said to him: 'What's an indolent man?'    5

My grandfather lowered his head for a moment, then looking across    6 at the wide expanse of field, he said: 'Do you see it stretching out from the edge of the desert up to the Nile bank? A hundred feddans. Do you see all those date palms? And those trees — sant, acacia, and sayal? All this fell into Masood's lap, was inherited by him from his father.'

7     Taking advantage of the silence that had descended upon my grandfather, I turned my gaze from him to the vast area defined by his words. 'I don't care,' I told myself, 'who owns those date palms, those trees or this black, cracked earth — all I know is that it's the arena for my dreams and my playground.'

8     My grandfather then continued: 'Yes, my boy, forty years ago all this belonged to Masood — two-thirds of it is now mine.'

9     This was news to me for I had imagined that the land had belonged to my grandfather ever since God's Creation.

10    'I didn't own a single feddan when I first set foot in this village. Masood was then the owner of all these riches. The position has changed now, though, and I think that before Allah calls to Him I shall have bought the remaining third as well.'

11    I do not know why it was I felt fear at my grandfather's words — and pity for our neighbour Masood. How I wished my grandfather wouldn't do what he'd said! I remembered Masood's singing, his beautiful voice and powerful laugh that resembled the gurgling of water. My grandfather never used to laugh.

12    I asked my grandfather why Masood had sold his land.

13    'Women,' and from the way my grandfather pronounced the word I felt that 'women' was something terrible. 'Masood, my boy, was a much-married man. Each time he married he sold me a feddan or two.' I made the quick calculation that Masood must have married some ninety women. Then I remembered his three wives, his shabby appearance, his lame donkey and its dilapidated saddle, his djellaba with the torn sleeves. I had all but rid my mind of the thoughts that jostled in it when I saw the man approaching us, and my grandfather and I exchanged glances.

14    'We'll be harvesting the dates today,' said Masood. 'Don't you want to be there?'

15    I felt, though, that he did not really want my grandfather to attend. My grandfather, however, jumped to his feet and I saw that his eyes sparkled momentarily with an intense brightness. He pulled me by the hand and we went off to the harvesting of Masood's dates.

16    Someone brought my grandfather a stool covered with an ox-hide, while I remained standing. There was a vast number of people there, but though I knew them all, I found myself for some reason, watching Masood: aloof from the great gathering of people he stood as though it were no concern of his, despite the fact that the date palms to be harvested were his own. Sometimes his attention would be caught by the sound of a huge clump of dates crashing down from on high. Once he shouted up at the boy perched on the very summit of the date palm who

had begun hacking at a clump with his long, sharp sickle: 'Be careful you don't cut the heart of the palm.'

No one paid any attention to what he said and the boy seated at the very summit of the date palm continued, quickly and energetically, to work away at the branch with his sickle till the clump of dates began to drop like something descending from the heavens.

I, however, had begun to think about Masood's phrase 'the heart of the palm'. I pictured the palm tree as something with feeling, something possessed of a heart that throbbed. I remembered Masood's remark to me when he had once seen me playing about with the branch of a young palm tree: 'Palm trees, my boy, like humans, experience joy and suffering.' And I had felt an inward and unreasoned embarrassment.

When I again looked at the expanse of ground stretching before me I saw my young companions swarming like ants around the trunks of the palm trees, gathering up dates and eating most of them. The dates were collected into high mounds. I saw people coming along and weighing them into measuring bins and pouring them into sacks, of which I counted thirty. The crowd of people broke up, except for Hussein the merchant, Mousa the owner of the field next to ours on the east, and two men I'd never seen before.

I heard a low whistling sound and saw that my grandfather had fallen asleep. Then I noticed that Masood had not changed his stance, except that he had placed a stalk in his mouth and was munching at it like someone surfeited with food who doesn't know what to do with the mouthful he still has.

Suddenly my grandfather woke up, jumped to his feet and walked towards the sacks of dates. He was followed by Hussein the merchant, Mousa the owner of the field next to ours, and the two strangers. I glanced at Masood and saw that he was making his way towards us with extreme slowness, like a man who wants to retreat but whose feet insist on going forward. They formed a circle round the sacks of dates and began examining them, some taking a date or two to eat. My grandfather gave me a fistful, which I began munching. I saw Masood filling the palms of both hands with dates and bringing them up close to his nose, then returning them.

Then I saw them dividing up the sacks between them. Hussein the merchant took ten; each of the strangers took five. Mousa the owner of the field next to ours on the eastern side took five, and my grandfather took five. Understanding nothing, I looked at Masood and saw that his eyes were darting about to left and right like two mice that have lost their way home.

'You're still fifty pounds in debt to me,' said my grandfather to Masood. 'We'll talk about it later.'

Hussein called his assistants and they brought along donkeys, the two strangers produced camels, and the sacks of dates were loaded on to them. One of the donkeys let out a braying which set the camels frothing at the mouth and complaining noisily. I felt myself drawing close to Masood, felt my hand stretch out towards him as though I wanted to touch the hem of his garment. I heard him make a noise in his throat like the rasping of a lamb being slaughtered. For some unknown reason, I experienced a sharp sensation of pain in my chest.

24     I ran off into the distance. Hearing my grandfather call after me, I hesitated a little, then continued on my way. I felt at that moment that I hated him. Quickening my pace, it was as though I carried within me a secret I wanted to rid myself of. I reached the river bank near the bend it made behind the wood of acacia trees. Then, without knowing why, I put my finger into my throat and spewed up the dates I'd eaten.

*translated by Denys Johnson-Davies*

## Evaluating the Text

1. What is the role of the "Chapter of the Merciful" of the Koran in the child's reaction to the ensuing events in this story? What inferences might you draw about Salih's view of the Koran from this story?
2. Why does the boy so drastically change his attitude toward his grandfather?
3. Why does the boy wish "my grandfather wouldn't do what he said"? What is it that the grandfather is going to do? What values seem to motivate the boy's wishes, and how do they contrast with those of his grandfather? How does the boy bring a very different set of assumptions to the situation from that of the grandfather? How does this contrast in underlying assumptions explain the boy's disillusionment?
4. How do you know that Salih intends to show that the boy sympathizes with Masood and not with his grandfather?
5. How does the boy's reaction (in making himself vomit the dates he had eaten) relate to his reluctance to become the kind of person his grandfather would wish him to be?

## Exploring Different Perspectives

1. How is the boy's disenchantment with his grandfather very similar to Rudy's disenchantment with Miss Bontempo in Danny Santiago's "Famous all over Town"?
2. How do both Nawal El Saadawi in "Circumcision of Girls" and Salih in this story criticize the dominant value system by showing things from the perspective of those who are powerless?
3. How does the grandfather's view of women in "A Handful of Dates" confirm what Saadawi says is a prevailing social view toward women in the Sudan?

## Extending Viewpoints through Writing

1. Has your attitude ever changed toward a member of your family or a close friend based on a business practice that showed you a side of their nature

you had not known existed? Did you react as strongly as the boy in Salih's story? Did this event permanently alter your relationship? If so, in what way?

2. Analyze how the ideals adults urge children to adopt often backfire when children use these standards to judge adult behavior. Discuss how this theme operates in Salih's story and in Danny Santiago's "Famous All Over Town."

3. Has any major religious text (The Koran, The Old Testament, The New Testament, the Bhagavad Gita, etc.) had as profound an impact in shaping your ideals and attitudes as the Koran did for the boy in "A Handful of Dates"? Discuss your experiences.

# CONNECTING CULTURES

## Christy Brown, "The Letter 'A'"

1. After reading Bruce Dollar's "Child Care in China" (Chapter 1), explain why a child in situations comparable to those of Christy Brown might not receive the intense personal attention devoted to him by his mother.
2. How do both Christy Brown's narrative and the chapter from Natsume Soseki's novel *I Am a Cat* (Chapter 1) rely on the point of view of one who perceives but cannot communicate with others and is discounted as an observer?
3. How do both Panos Ioannides's "Gregory" (Chapter 9) and the second part of Brown's account rely on the story being told in a way that lets the reader directly share the thoughts and feelings of the narrator?

## Henry Allen, "The Corps"

4. Compare the methods of conditioning recruits described by Allen with the techniques of social conditioning described by Bruce Dollar in "Child Care in China" (Chapter 1).
5. What similarities in training techniques, discipline, and morale can you observe between methods used by the drill instructors, described by Allen, and those employed by Pan in Mark Salzman's "Lessons" (Chapter 4)?

## Douchan Gersi, "Initiated into an Iban Tribe of Headhunters"

6. In what way do the methods used to attain their objectives by Gersi on one hand and Napoleon A. Chagnon ("Doing Fieldwork Among the Yąnomanö," Chapter 8) on the other reflect important differences between exploration and the field of anthropology?
7. In what respects is the ritual initiation experienced by Gersi comparable to that described by Rigoberta Menchu in "Birth Ceremonies" (Chapter 1)? How are both ceremonies divisible into clearly identifiable stages?

## Danny Santiago, "Famous All Over Town"

8. Contrast Pan's methods for learning English in Mark Salzman's "Lessons" (Chapter 4) with those encountered by Rudy in "Famous All Over Town."
9. How do both Rudy's experiences and those described by Toi Derricotte (from *The Black Notebooks*," Chapter 5) illustrate the subtle, but nonetheless real, forms that discrimination can take?

10. What insight do you gain from Rudy's desire to learn the language of mainstream America as it sheds light on Ngũgĩ wa Thiong'o's ("Decolonising the Mind," Chapter 6) discussion of how the British sought to suppress the speaking of native African languages in Kenya?

11. Read Raymonde Carroll's ("Minor Accidents," Chapter 8) discussion of how culturally based patterns of difference create the potential for conflict and misunderstanding. Using insights you gain from this article, discuss differences between Anglo and Chicano cultural styles in Santiago's story.

## Tepilit Ole Saitoti, "The Initiation of a Maasai Warrior"

12. How are initiation rituals described by Saitoti and Rigoberta Menchu ("Birth Ceremonies," Chapter 1) designed to integrate the individual into the community?

13. Compare the economic structure of Maasai society in terms of responsibilities, communal ownership, and care of collectively owned herds of cattle with the economic structure of Amish society as portrayed by Gene Logsdon ("A Lesson for the Modern World: Amish Economics," Chapter 4).

## Nawal El Saadawi, "Circumcision of Girls"

14. After reading Marilyn French's "Gender Roles" (Chapter 3), write an essay exploring how cultural pressures toward manipulating body images of women in contemporary America is as damaging, psychologically and physically, as female circumcision is in the Middle East. To what extent are female circumcision and dieting to the point of anorexia culturally conditioned? How do these two phenomena stem from culturally reinforced stereotypes governing women's bodies? How are these stereotypes related to the status of women in Middle Eastern and American cultures?

15. How does Beryl Markham's account ("West with the Night," Chapter 4) suggest what is possible for women in Western culture as compared with possibilities described by Saadawi?

16. How does Saadawi's essay provide a background against which you can better understand accusations directed against Salman Rushdie's depiction ("A Pen Against the Sword," Chapter 7) of women and religious figures in Islamic culture?

## Tayeb Salih, "A Handful of Dates"

17. How does possession of property transform the grandfather in Salih's story in ways that are remarkably similar to the effects of owning property on the wife in Talat Abbasi's "Facing the Light" (Chapter 3)?

18. How do both Salih's story and Nicholasa Mohr's ("A Very Special Pet," Chapter 7) reach crisis points in which children see the actions of adults in a realistic light?

# 3

# *How Culture Shapes Gender Roles*

Culture plays an enormous role in shaping expectations attached to sex roles. This process, sometimes called *socialization*, determines how each of us assimilates our culture's ideas of what it means to act as a male or female. We tend to acquire a sense of our own sexual identity in conjunction with societal expectations. Yet these expectations differ strikingly from culture to culture. For example, in male-dominated Islamic Middle-Eastern societies, the sex roles and relationships between men and women are very different from those in modern industrial societies.

The writers in this chapter address the question of how males and females learn the sex roles they are to play in their respective societies. Marilyn French, in "Gender Roles," explores the extent to which sex role behavior of men and women in Western societies is culturally conditioned and not simply biologically determined. Cultural anthropologist Clifford Geertz, in "Of Cocks and Men," analyzes how cockfighting reflects male sexual identity in Bali. Talat Abbasi's short story "Facing the Light" provides insight into the problematic nature of sex roles in modern Pakistan. Marjorie Shostak, in "Memories of a !Kung Girlhood," lets us hear the voice of Nisa, a !Kung woman, in Botswana, as she remembers important moments in her childhood and marriage. The French writer and pioneer of the women's movement, Simone de Beauvoir, eloquently portrays, in "The Married Woman," the attributes and qualities of this traditionally defined gender role. From the People's Republic of the Congo, Henri Lopes tells the ironic story of "The Esteemed Representative," whose public commitment to women's rights contrasts dramatically with the male chauvinism he reveals in his private life. In David K. Shipler's "The Sin of Love," we see the divisive cultural and political pressures that beset an Arab woman and an Israeli man who wish to marry. Last, Margaret Atwood, the Canadian writer, explores variations in the delicate balance of stability and surprise in relationships between men and women in her story "Happy Endings."

# Marilyn French

# *Gender Roles*

---

*Marilyn French, born in 1929, established herself as a leading figure in contemporary feminism with her compelling depiction of women's subservience to domestic roles in her novel* The Women's Room *(1977). Her other works include* The Bleeding Heart *(1980),* Her Mother's Daughter *(1987), and the acclaimed study of the future of feminism,* Beyond Power: On Women, Men, and Models *(1985), from which "Gender Roles" is taken. French discloses how sex roles are ultimately determined by culture rather than biology.*

Although many people believe it is women who work harder to maintain gender roles, to teach their daughters to be "ladies," and their sons to be "gentlemen," studies have revealed that in late twentieth-century America, men are more concerned than women that their children adopt "proper"—that is, dictated, traditional sex-role behavior.[1] Other studies show that boys have more difficulty accepting their appropriate sex role. David Lynn, who has conducted a number of these studies, attributes boys' difficulties to three sources: lack of male models, the rigidity and harshness of masculine roles, and the negative nature of the requirements.[2] Boys especially appear to suffer from the fact that fathers are absent, whether emotionally or physically, and from the lack of other significant males in their young lives. And the male role in patriarchal society consists, as we have seen, largely of sacrifices—men must give up the hope of happiness, the ideal of home, emotional expressiveness and spontaneity, in order to become members of an elite that values power, wandering isolation, individuality, and discipline (order in obedience).

The fact that the male role does not gratify a boy, does not arise from primary desire but from the secondary desire of wanting to be like other boys or wanting to be a man like others he sees (on television, in films, in comic books, in history books), may account for the rigid, almost ritualistic way in which many adult men "play" their roles. Lynn discovered that boys who lack fathers entirely are more likely to entertain exaggerated and stereotypical images of masculinity than boys who have fathers, no matter how absent or violent.[3]

What Westerners mean when they say they want to make a man out of a boy is that they want a boy to learn that the sacrifices mentioned above are essential, are *the* characteristics of men. And the schools, or

149

gymnasia, or army training camps to which people send boys to "make men of them" specialize in brutalization: rigid discipline, emphasis on physical hardness and strength, and contempt for sensitivity, delicacy, and emotion. Fortunately, not all boys are subjected to such treatment, but no boy escapes knowledge of the severities of "manliness" in our society, and those who feel they have not achieved it live with lingering self-doubt, self-diminishment. On the other hand, those men who score highest on tests of "masculinity" refuse to restrain their aggressiveness even when by expressing it they lose the approval of their community.[4]

4     "Manliness," as defined by patriarchy, means to be or appear to be in control at all times. But remaining in control prevents a person from ever achieving intimacy with another, from ever letting down his guard; it thus precludes easy friendship, fellowship, community. Men may have "buddies," acquaintances with whom they can engage in the ritual competition of banter, sport, or game, but they rarely possess intimate friends. I mentioned before that on tests administered by Carol Gilligan, in which a set of pictures was submitted to male and female subjects, men offered the most violent and threatening narratives as explanations of the photographs showing people close to each other, and the least threatening stories to explain photographs of men in isolation.[5] Shut out from the most nourishing parts of life, men seek what they need in the channels they have been told are "theirs": work, achievement, success. They imagine that success, or the demonstration of "manliness," will bring them love; instead, it often alienates those they love.[6] They feel cheated: and they blame women.

5     And men have, through patriarchal forms, achieved power-in-the-world. Men own 99 percent of the world's property and earn 90 percent of its wages, while producing only 55 percent of the world's food and performing only one-third of the world's work.[7] Men rather exclusively direct the course not just of states and corporations but of culture: religion, arts, education. Despite the assaults of various waves of feminism, men have been able to retain their control over the people, creatures, plants, and even some of the elements of this planet. Many men wish to retain these powers.

6     Yet psychological, sociological, and philosophical studies describe men as deeply unhappy. Writers like Philip Slater, R. D. Laing, Theodore Roszak, for instance, have described men of our time as alienated, fragmented, suffering from anomie, conflict over role, or identity crises.[8] In projective tests like the Rorschach, men from a number of different cultures showed more insecurity and anxiety than women.[9] Men seem to fall ill more frequently than women — at least they lose more work days through illness than women do; they are more vulnerable than women to diseases that are associated with stress; and they die younger.[10] These statistics do not necessarily reflect only biological differences: when more women died in childbirth, men lived longer than women. Part of the reason why men are physically vulnerable is the stress they live with.

And some of that stress is caused by attempting to live up to a definition of manliness that is unattainable for any human.

Sex-role behavior is learned. Whatever qualities we possess "by nature," from our genes, sex role is not among them. If it were, men could not feel and act as differently as they do from culture to culture, and especially from patriarchal society to societies that are not fully patriarchal. The range of behavior within one sex is as great as that between the two sexes; nondeterminist scientists point out that we have no substantive knowledge about the meaning of genetic and hormonal differences between the sexes.[11] The research of John Money and of Hampson and Hampson shows that hermaphrodites who are chromosomally and hormonally of one sex but are raised as if they were the opposite sex lead normal lives, including sex lives, as members of the sex in which they have been reared.[12]

Most men in Western societies work in some form of institution. Institutions breed competitiveness and inculcate an instrumental relation to everything, even personal relationships. One has contacts, not friends. One chooses to cultivate people not (as many women do) because of a sense of rapport with them, but because they might be useful. It also inculcates a focus upward, implicitly teaching men to see life as a power struggle directed at dominance. Men thus tend to see their bosses as masters not only over their working lives but over all of life. Such structures impose dependency, making people feel helpless, powerless; and this in turn arouses rigid, rule-bound behavior, making people act like petty tyrants in the realms which they control. Moreover, the structure is absorbing, and tends to make people regard the other parts of life as secondary. Rosabeth Kanter, who has observed this style in depth, believes it is not a male style but a corporate one; that it is not related to maleness itself, but is a response to the order imposed and the values implicit in large hierarchical organizations.[13]

What is learned can be learned differently. Because men overwhelmingly sit in seats of access to power, there is little possibility of altering the morality of our world unless men are willing to contribute to that alteration, unless men adopt a new set of values. Many men have been reaching toward such a change—witness the many books published in the past two decades offering self-help for men, suggesting broader ways of thinking adapted from Eastern religions, or recounting a personal change toward greater integration of self and of self with world. Whether men desire to change their lives depends upon two major factors: the degree to which they are conscious of misery in their present condition; and the degree of contempt they feel for women. Many enlightened men will be offended by the suggestion that they feel contempt for women at all: but no one in patriarchal society, woman or man, is free from that feeling. If you imagine you are, imagine how you would feel if someone told you you were "womanly," or asked you to dress and act as a woman for a day. You are a rare creature if you are male and do not react with horror.

10      The grounds of this pervasive contempt for women have been suggested throughout this book. Basically, they lie in women's reproductive
functioning, in menstruation, conception and pregnancy, and lactation,
none of which men experience, and all of which men have been taught
to see as disgusting or worse. But only creatures who have been taught to
despise the body would see such things as disgusting; and beings who
urinate, excrete, vomit, exude pus and other issue cannot justify disgust
at menstruation, the production of nourishing milk, and the wondrous
process of pregnancy and birth.

11      If men's disgust with women's reproductive functioning is the basis
on which patriarchy taught contempt, it is women's mothering that
allowed patriarchy to diminish women. For power is irrelevant to mothering, and vice versa. It is received wisdom that women's capacity for
mothering is innate: this alone makes them unfit to participate as full
partners in patriarchal society. Fatherhood, on the other hand, is seen as
hardly biological at all, but as a "cultural phenomenon."[14] This contrasts
conveniently with women's capacity for motherhood, considered as
nonvolitional, making women "naturally" subject to coercion into other
nonvolitional labors.

12      Yet studies show that there is no evidence of an instinctual or biological basis for mothering: there is no harm to infants, or to their mothers, if
the infants are not reared by their biological mothers. There is nothing in
the physiology of the parturient woman that makes her particularly
suited to later child care, nor any instinctual basis for the ability to
perform it. There is no biological or hormonal element differentiating a
male "substitute" mother from a female one.[15] Nor is there any evidence
that exclusive mothering is necessarily better for children than mothering
by a group.[16]

13      Mothering is learned, just as aggression is learned. We often see
among women that those who lacked mothers in their childhood cannot
mother in turn, and are distant or abusive to their children. Among
animals this has been shown frequently. Female animals who were
deprived of their own mothers do not mother their babies but abuse and
sometimes even kill them.[17] If a female baby rat is removed from her
mother just after birth, before the mother has licked the offspring clean,
that baby will not, as a new mother, lick her own off-spring clean.
Education in mothering occurs so early that we confuse it with "instinct," genetically programmed knowledge. But as Erving Goffman
pointed out in another context, "there is no appreciable quid pro quo"
between parents and children; "what is received in one generation is
given in the next."[18] This is true of deprivations as well as of gifts.

14      Although women care for children in all cultures, men actively participate in child care in nonpatriarchal societies. Even in patriarchal ones,
men are involved in rearing children in communities that live on the
land, that work in or near the home. Our present notion of motherhood
is quite recent, having been institutionalized only in the past couple of

centuries—that is, separated from other dimensions of life, conceived of as an occupation, named, circumscribed, and prescribed as women's work, and to some degree regulated.

Exclusive mothering tends to produce more achievement-oriented men, and people with psychologically monogamic tendencies. Dorothy Dinnerstein and Nancy Chodorow, among others, believe it also creates men's dread and resentment of women, and their search as adults for nonthreatening, undemanding, dependent, even infantile women. Dinnerstein hypothesizes that men's pervasive fear of women—a fear she believes is shared by women—arises from the fact that women do most of the early mothering, that we emerge into consciousness facing a woman who appears huge, all-powerful, and awe-ful, in control of all our pleasures, all our pains. Although as we grow, we bury this sense of her and, indeed, belittle her, the sense is triggered when we encounter a mature woman in a position of authority or control. Such a woman arouses a symbolic dread and fear, preconscious emotions.[19] "Psychologists have demonstrated unequivocally that the very fact of being mothered by a woman generates in men conflicts over masculinity, a psychology of male dominance, and a need to be superior to women." As they reject the control of a woman because it seems overpowering, they also come to reject and devalue "feminine" qualities in general.[20] Sidney Bolkowsky suggests that societies that reject mothers may create their own misery, may be "unnatural," and that "precivilized" societies in which a child is raised by a series of "mothers," all offering extended loving contact, display low incidence of the psychological disorders found in "civilized" societies.[21]

A study of Russian and American children demonstrated that the Russian children were better socialized, having been cared for in group centers since infancy; there was more companionship between parents and children, and parents spent more time with their children than the American parents.[22] Collective child-rearing situations—on kibbutzim, in China, in Cuba—seem to produce children who have a greater sense of commitment to and solidarity with a group, less individualism and competitiveness, and who are less likely to form possessive, exclusive adult relationships.[23]

If we want a society that learns early to live together in harmony, collective child rearing is essential. To participate in child rearing would enlarge and enrich men's experience. It would also enlarge and enrich women's by allowing them to participate in both private and public life. Exclusive gender identity is not an expression of natural differences between the sexes but a suppression of natural similarities.[24] The unhappiness of many women would be eliminated or modified if their men provided them with the same nurturance they offer men, if their children had loving fathers, and if they were able to use their other talents in the world. It is even possible, as Gayle Rubin suggests, that if children were raised by people of both sexes, human social and sexual arrangements would be far richer, sexual power would disappear, and with it the Oedipus complex: she believes feminism must call for a revolution in kinship.[25] We cannot now predict what kind of people would result from such an integration, but it is only reasonable to assume that since they would be more integrated within themselves, people would be more content; and since they would be in greater harmony with each other, people would be more peaceful. To assume that contentment and peaceability would produce less brilliance, less art, less uniqueness than our own society possesses is unwarranted: what we would lose is the brilliance, uniqueness, and art that arises from utter isolation, self-hate, and the atrophy of personal qualities. The world as a whole has to be better off with greater integration and harmony.

18     Power has for too long gone unmodified and in defiant disregard of basic human feelings and needs. The exclusion of women from the public world is at once symbolic of its character and a reason for its character. Women are trained for private virtue, men for public power; and the severance between the sexes and the two realms is responsible for much of our irrational thinking and behavior, as Elshtain has shown.[26] In each realm, one is requested to close the eyes to what the other realm is doing and signifies and to connections between the two. *To disconnect virtue from power is to ensure that virtue will be powerless, and licenses power to be without virtue.* Yet there is no position of virtue for anyone who lives in a world as cruel and ugly as our own; nor any position of power for people who do not even know how to live with themselves. As Dietrich Bonhoeffer wrote, "Here and there people flee from public altercation into the sanctuary of private *virtuousness.* But anyone who does this must shut his mouth and his eyes to the injustice around him. Only at the cost of self-deception can he keep himself pure from the contamination arising from *responsible* action."[27] Bonhoeffer, a Catholic priest who persisted in opposing the Nazis, and died while imprisoned by them, was living his morality, not talking it. Those who closet themselves in a fugitive and cloistered virtue must remain adamantly ignorant or confess themselves participants in evil; those who stand only in the world and never gaze at the inner life, at connections among people, at the sharing and bonding that make all life possible, stride off and become the evil. For millennia, men have possessed fairly total worldly control over women. They have owned women, bought and sold them, forbidden them any form of independence at a cost of death. They have enslaved women, treated them as minors, defectives. In some cultures fathers had the right to kill their daughters, husbands their wives. Women's bodies have been imprisoned, removed from their own control, beaten, tortured, destroyed; women's minds have been constrained and deprived of nourishment by morality and enforced ignorance.

19     Yet despite all this control, men have remained anxious. As we have seen, some of the worst vituperation against women occurred in periods

in which men had the greatest control over them. Wife beating does not cease in societies in which law gives men almost total control over women. It is claimed by some that feminism creates a male backlash against women; but no one can point to a culture in which women are subordinate yet are treated well. It seems that women have a choice between having some power over their lives and being hated and feared by men — and being hated and feared and having no power whatever. Whatever position women occupy in a society, men experience them as threatening; however great men's control, they do not feel in control.

Men do not attempt to establish control over women because they hate and fear them; rather, men hate and fear women because they *must* control them, because control over women is essential to their self-definition. Forced to demonstrate superiority, they can do so only by cheating, stacking the deck, by imposing on women deprivations which imprison them in a condition seen as inferior by the male culture.[28]

In hubris, bravado, and self-aggrandizement, men have declared themselves superior to other creatures. So they necessarily hate and fear the one creature who could disprove their claim, and attempt to put her in a position of such dependency that she will fear to do so. There are men who acknowledge this, yet cannot change. Their entire *human* identity rests on a manhood that is defined as control. Such men are in the deepest sense deprived, dehumanized: for they cannot find significance within nature, within their bodies and emotions, as part of a human-natural context. For them, significance is located only in that which transcends the natural context and offers something more enduring than life. Deluded by the notion that power offers what endures, they ignore the fact that nothing endures, not even art, except culture itself — the children we make, and the world each generation in turn makes. Searching for meaning in what is superhuman, men have ignored their humanity, the only possible ground for human meaning.

## NOTES

1. Evelyn Goodenough, "Interests in Persons as an Aspect of Sex Differences in the Early Years," *Genetic Psychological Monograph* 55 (1957):287–323.

2. David Lynn, *Parental and Sex Role Identification: A Theoretical Formulation* (Berkeley, Calif., 1969), p. 24.

3. David Lynn, "A Note on Sex Difference in the Development of Masculine and Feminine Identification," *Psychological Review* 66, 2 (1959):126–135.

4. D. B. Leventhal and K. M. Shember, "Sex Role Adjustment and Non-sanctioned Aggression," *Journal of Experimental Research in Personality* 3 (1969): 283–286.

5. Carol Gilligan, *In a Different Voice* (Cambridge, Mass.: Harvard Univ. Press, 1982), pp. 39–40.

6. Myron Brenton, *The American Male* (New York, 1966), p. 22.

7. Statistics taken from International Labor Organization study presented at the United Nations Women's Conference in Copenhagen, 1980, but reversed.

8. Glennon, Linda M., *Women and Dualism* (New York, 1979), pp. 170–199, discusses some of these complaints.

9. Roy D'Andrade, "Sex Differences and Cultural Institutions," in Eleanor Maccoby, ed. *The Development of Sex Differences* (Stanford, Calif.: Stanford Univ. Press, 1966), p. 202.

10. D'Andrade, "Sex Differences," Maccoby, *Development*, p. 216; David A. Hamburg and Donald Munde, "Sex Hormones in the Development of Sex Differences in Human Behavior," Maccoby, *Development*, p. 19; and Jane E. Brody, "Some Disorders Appear Linked to Being Left-Handed," *New York Times*, April 19, 1983.

11. Rose Lewontin, and Leon Kamin, *Not in Our Genes* (New York: Pantheon, 1984), Chapter Six.

12. John Money, "Sex, Hormones, and Other Variables in Human Eroticism"; J. L. Hampson and Joan G. Hampson, "The Ontogenesis of Sexual Behavior in Man"; both in *Sex and Internal Secretions*, Vol. 2, ed. W. C. Young, (Baltimore, 1961).

13. Rosabeth Moss Kanter, *Men and Women of the Corporation* (New York: Basic Books, 1977), pp. 163, 170, 255ff.

14. See David M. Potter, *American Women and the American Character*, Stetson University Bulletin LXIII (Jan. 1962), p. 21.

15. Nancy Chodorow, *The Reproduction of Mothering* (Berkeley and Los Angeles: Univ. of Calif. Press, 1978), pp. 23–30.

16. Chodorow, *Mothering*, p. 75.

17. Warren Farrell, *The Liberated Man* (New York: Random House, 1974), p. 122.

18. Erving Goffman, "Gender Display," Lionel Tiger and Heather T. Fowler, eds., *Female Hierarchies* (Chicago: Beresford Book Service, 1978), p. 70.

19. Dorothy Dinnerstein, *The Mermaid and the Minotaur* (New York: Harper/Colophon, 1977), especially pp. 188–191.

20. Chodorow, *Mothering*, pp. 75–76, 185, 214; Dinnerstein, *Mermaid*.

21. Sidney Bolkowsky, "The Alpha and Omega of Psychoanalysis," *Psychoanalytic Review* 69 1 (Spring 1982):131–150. See also Stanley Diamond, "The Search for the Primitive," *In Search of the Primitive: A Critique of Civilization* (New Brunswick, N.J.: Transaction Books, 1974), pp. 116–175; and Meyer Fortes, "Mind," *The Institutions of Primitive Society*, ed. E. E. Evans-Pritchard (Glencoe, Ill., 1956), pp. 90–94.

22. Rosalyn F. Baxandall, "Who Shall Care for Our Children? The History and Development of Day Care in the United States," in Jo Freeman, ed., *Women: A Feminist Perspective* (Palo Alto, Calif., Mayfield, 1979), pp. 134–149. The study was conducted by Urie Brofenbrenner, *Two Worlds of Childhood: U.S. and USSR* (New York: Simon & Shuster, 1970).

23. Chodorow, *Mothering*, p. 217.

24. Gayle Rubin, "The Traffic in Women," in Rayna R. Reiter, ed., *Toward an Anthropology of Women* (New York: Monthly Review Press, 1975), p. 180.

25. Rubin, "Traffic," Reiter, *Anthropology*, p. 199.

26. Jean Bethke Elshtain, *Public Man, Private Woman* (Princeton, N.J.: Princeton Univ. Press, 1981), passim.

27. Dietrich Bonhoeffer, *Letters and Papers from Prison*, ed. Eberhard Bethge (New York, 1967), p. 27. The emphasis is Bonhoeffer's.

28. Philip Slater, *The Glory of Hera* (Boston: Beacon Press, 1971), p. 8.

## Evaluating the Text

1. In what way are the kinds of requirements governing male sexual identity so much more difficult, according to French, than for female sexual identity? How does French use the results of David Lynn's research to demonstrate this idea?

2. Evaluate French's claim that "remaining in control" is the single most important defining attribute for male identity. How does this attribute make it less likely that men will form gratifying relationships?

3. What inferences can be drawn from the kinds of interpretive narratives men supply to explain two categories of photographs in a study by Carol Gilligan?

4. How does French use the claim that "men own 99 percent of the world's property and earn 90 percent of its wages, while producing only 55 percent of the world's food and performing only one-third of the world's work" to illustrate her thesis?

5. By what objective criteria does French conclude that men, in many cultures, suffer from being under more stress than women do? How is this stress a result of gender expectations?

6. Why would the fact that the careers of most men are lived out in connection with an institution produce, according to French, a male view of human relationships that is cold, competitive, paranoid, and manipulative?

7. From French's perspective, how do the values of institutionalized society promote hostility toward women? How does patriarchal antagonism toward women, according to French, result from a loathing for the biological processes with which women are identified?

8. What evidence does French offer to support the claim that "mothering" is a culturally defined rather than an innate biological instinct?

9. How does French's hypothesis explaining male antagonism toward mature women depend on assumptions as to how male infants perceive their mothers? In French's view, how would collective child rearing offset the damaging effects of exclusive mothering? How persuasively in your view does she build a case for this? What disadvantages can you think of that French does not mention?

10. What might French hope to achieve by persuading her readers that gender roles are culturally, rather than biologically, determined?

## Exploring Different Perspectives

1. Drawing on French's article, what features of Balinese culture discussed by Clifford Geertz ("Of Cocks and Men") shape expectations attached to masculinity?

2. What gender roles described by French appear in Margaret Atwood's "Happy Endings"?
3. Does Simone de Beauvoir's analysis of the predicament of "The Married Woman" support or contradict French's analysis of gender roles? What features of both can be characterized as distinctly feminist?

## *Extending Viewpoints through Writing*

1. If you are male, evaluate French's analysis of the kinds of cultural pressures men experience. Would you agree with French that men would benefit from being less tied to cultural stereotypes?
2. How is being male in any particular subculture of ethnic community (for example, African-American, Asian, Chicano, Jewish, Irish, etc.) dependent on expectations that are different from those French describes? Give specifics to support your answer.
3. Which, if any, of French's assertions would you dispute? For example, do you feel she is correct when she says "There is nothing in the physiology of the parturient women that makes her particularly suited to later child care, nor any instinctual basis for the ability to perform it. . . . Nor is there any evidence that exclusive mothering is necessarily better for children than mothering by a group"?
4. To what extent does your personal experience support French's theory of the role culture plays in producing sex role differences?

# Clifford Geertz

# *Of Cocks and Men*

---

*Clifford Geertz is an anthropologist who currently is Professor of Social Science at the Institute for Advanced Study at Princeton. Based on his own extensive fieldwork in Java and Bali, Geertz evolved a methodology that depends on analyzing aspects of culture in a creative rather than merely technical manner. This method can be seen in "Of Cocks and Men," an essay from* The Interpretation of Culture *(1973), in which Geertz analyzes the role of cockfighting in defining male sexual identity within Balinese culture. An earlier version of Geertz's analysis of the Balinese cockfight appeared in* Daedalus *(Winter, 1972). Geertz is also the author of* Local Knowledge: Further Essays in Interpretive Anthropology *(1985),* Negara: The Theatre State in Nineteenth-Century Bali *(1980), and* Works and Lives: The Anthropologist as Author *(1988).*

*The island of Bali, along with Sumatra, Java, and areas of Borneo and New Guinea, is part of a chain of 13,700 islands that collectively make up the Republic of Indonesia. As Geertz points out, "Even the very island itself is perceived from its shape as a small, proud cock, poised, neck extended, back taut, tail raised, in eternal challenge to large, feckless, shapeless Java." The Balinese are Hindus within the mainly Muslim nation of Indonesia and are renowned for the elaborate dances, music, sculpture, and rituals such as cockfighting, which endow features of everyday life with mythic, larger-than-life meanings. Geertz's sensitivity to the cultural symbolism of cockfighting is illustrated in the following essay.*

Bali, mainly because it is Bali, is a well-studied place. Its mythology, art, ritual, social organization, patterns of child rearing, forms of law, even styles of trance, have all been microscopically examined for traces of that elusive substance Jane Belo called "The Balinese Temper."[1] But, aside from a few passing remarks, the cockfight has barely been noticed, although as a popular obsession of consuming power it is at least as important a revelation of what being a Balinese "is really like" as these

---

[1] J. Belo, "The Balinese Temper," in *Traditional Balinese Culture*, ed. J. Belo (New York: Books Demand UMI, 1970) (originally published in 1935), pp. 85–110.

*(For additional background on Indonesia, see Borneo, p. 100.)

more celebrated phenomena.[2] As much of America surfaces in a ball park, on a golf links, at a race track, or around a poker table, much of Bali surfaces in a cock ring. For it is only apparently cocks that are fighting there. Actually, it is men.

2      To anyone who has been in Bali any length of time, the deep psychological identification of Balinese men with their cocks is unmistakable. The double entendre here is deliberate. It works in exactly the same way in Balinese as it does in English, even to producing the same tired jokes, strained puns, and uninventive obscenities. Bateson and Mead have even suggested that, in line with Balinese conception of the body as a set of separately animated parts, cocks are viewed as detachable, self-operating penises, ambulant genitals with a life of their own.[3] And while I do not have the kind of unconscious material either to confirm or disconfirm this intriguing notion, the fact that they are masculine symbols par excellence is about as indubitable, and to the Balinese about as evident, as the fact that water runs downhill.

3      The language of everyday moralism is shot through, on the male side of it, with roosterish imagery. *Sabung,* the word for cock (and one which appears in inscriptions as early as A.D. 922), is used metaphorically to mean "hero," "warrior," "champion," "man of parts," "political candidate," "bachelor," "dandy," "lady-killer," or "tough guy." A pompous man whose behavior presumes above his station is compared to a tailless cock who struts about as though he had a large, spectacular one. A desperate man who makes a last, irrational effort to extricate himself from an impossible situation is likened to a dying cock who makes one final lunge at his tormentor to drag him along to a common destruction. A stingy man, who promises much, gives little, and begrudges that, is compared to a cock which, held by the tail, leaps at another without in fact engaging him. A marriageable young man still shy with the opposite sex or someone in a new job anxious to make a good impression is called "a fighting cock caged for the first time."[4] Court trials, wars, political

---

[2]The best discussion of cockfighting is again Bateson and Mead's *Balinese Character,* pp. 24–25, 140; but it, too, is general and abbreviated.

[3]Ibid., pp. 25–26. The cockfight is unusual within Balinese culture in being a single-sex public activity from which the other sex is totally and expressly excluded. Sexual differentiation is culturally extremely played down in Bali and most activities, formal and informal, involve the participation of men and women on equal ground, commonly as linked couples. From religion, to politics, to economics, to kinship, to dress, Bali is a rather "unisex" society, a fact both its customs and its symbolism clearly express. Even in contexts where women do not in fact play much of a role—music, painting, certain agricultural activities—their absence, which is only relative in any case, is more a mere matter of fact than socially enforced. To this general pattern, the cockfight, entirely of, by, and for men (women—at least *Balinese* women—do not even watch), is the most striking exception.

[4]C. Hooykaas, *The Lay of the Jaya Prana* (London, 1958), p. 39. The lay has a stanza (no. 17) which the reluctant bridegroom uses. Jaya Prana, the subject of a Balinese Uriah myth, responds to the lord who has offered him the loveliest of six hundred servant girls: "Godly King, my Lord and Master / I beg you, give me leave to go / such things are not yet in my mind; / like a fighting cock encaged / indeed I am on my mettle / I am alone / as yet the flame has not been fanned."

contests, inheritance disputes, and street arguments are all compared to cockfights.[5] Even the very island itself is perceived from its shape as a small, proud cock, poised, neck extended, back taut, tail raised, in external challenge to large, feckless, shapeless Java.[6]

But the intimacy of men with their cocks is more than metaphorical. 4 Balinese men, or anyway a large majority of Balinese men, spend an enormous amount of time with their favorites, grooming them, feeding them, discussing them, trying them out against one another, or just gazing at them with a mixture of rapt admiration and dreamy self-absorption. Whenever you see a group of Balinese men squatting idly in the council shed or along the road in their hips down, shoulders forward, knees up fashion, half or more of them will have a rooster in his hands, holding it between his thighs, bouncing it gently up and down to strengthen its legs, ruffling its feathers with abstract sensuality, pushing it out against a neighbor's rooster to rouse its spirit, withdrawing it toward his loins to calm it again. Now and then, to get a feel for another bird, a man will fiddle this way with someone else's cock for a while, but usually by moving around to squat in place behind it, rather than just having it passed across to him as though it were merely an animal.

In the houseyard, the high-walled enclosures where the people live, 5 fighting cocks are kept in wicker cages, moved frequently about so as to maintain the optimum balance of sun and shade. They are fed a special diet, which varies somewhat according to individual theories but which is mostly maize, sifted for impurities with far more care than it is when mere humans are going to eat it, and offered to the animal kernel by kernel. Red pepper is stuffed down their beaks and up their anuses to give them spirit. They are bathed in the same ceremonial preparation of tepid water, medicinal herbs, flowers, and onions in which infants are bathed, and for a prize cock just about as often. Their combs are cropped, their plumage dressed, their spurs trimmed, and their legs massaged, and they are inspected for flaws with the squinted concentration of a diamond merchant. A man who has a passion for cocks, an enthusiast in the literal sense of the term, can spend most of his life with them, and even those, the overwhelming majority, whose passion though intense has not entirely run away with them, can and do spend what seems not only to an outsider, but also to themselves, an inordinate amount of time with them. "I am cock crazy," my landlord, a quite ordinary *afficionado* by Balinese standards, used to moan as he went to move another cage, give another bath, or conduct another feeding. "We're all cock crazy."

The madness has some less visible dimensions, however, because 6

---

[5]For these, see V. E. Korn, *Het Adatrecht van Bali*, 2d ed. (The Hague, 1932), index under *toh*.
[6]There is indeed a legend to the effect that the separation of Java and Bali is due to the action of a powerful Javanese religious figure who wished to protect himself against a Balinese culture hero (the ancestor of two Ksatria castes) who was a passionate cockfighting gambler. See C. Hooykaas, *Agama Tirtha* (Amsterdam, 1964), p. 184.

although it is true that cocks are symbolic expressions or magnifications of their owner's self, the narcissistic male ego writ out in Aesopian terms, they are also expressions—and rather more immediate ones—of what the Balinese regard as the direct inversion, aesthetically, morally, and metaphysically, of human status: animality.

7    The Balinese revulsion against any behavior regarded as animal-like can hardly be overstressed. Babies are not allowed to crawl for that reason. Incest, though hardly approved, is a much less horrifying crime than bestiality. (The appropriate punishment for the second is death by drowning, for the first being forced to live like an animal.)[7] Most demons are represented—in sculpture, dance, ritual, myth—in some real or fantastic animal form. The main puberty rite consists in filing the child's teeth so they will not look like animal fangs. Not only defecation but eating is regarded as a disgusting, almost obscene activity, to be conducted hurriedly and privately, because of its association with animality. Even falling down or any form of clumsiness is considered to be bad for these reasons. Aside from cocks and a few domestic animals—oxen, ducks—of no emotional significance, the Balinese are aversive to animals and treat their large number of dogs not merely callously but with a phobic cruelty. In identifying with his cock, the Balinese man is identifying not just with his ideal self, or even his penis, but also, and at the same time, with what he most fears, hates, and ambivalence being what it is, is fascinated by—"The Powers of Darkness."

8    The connection of cocks and cockfighting with such Powers, with the animalistic demons that threaten constantly to invade the small, cleared-off space in which the Balinese have so carefully built their lives and devour its inhabitants, is quite explicit. A cockfight, any cockfight, is in the first instance a blood sacrifice offered, with the appropriate chants and oblations, to the demons in order to pacify their ravenous, cannibal hunger. No temple festival should be conducted until one is made. (If it is omitted, someone will inevitably fall into a trance and command with the voice of an angered spirit that the oversight be immediately corrected.) Collective responses to natural evils—illness, crop failure, volcanic eruptions—almost always involve them. And that famous holiday in Bali, "The Day of Silence" (*Njepi*), when everyone sits silent and immobile all day long in order to avoid contact with a sudden influx of demons chased momentarily out of hell, is preceded the previous day by large-scale cockfights (in this case legal) in almost every village on the island.

9    In the cockfight, man and beast, good and evil, ego and id, the creative power of aroused masculinity and the destructive power of

---

[7] An incestuous couple is forced to wear pig yokes over their necks and crawl to a pig trough and eat with their mouths there. On this, see J. Belo, "Customs Pertaining to Twins in Bali," in *Traditional Balinese Culture*, ed. J. Belo, p. 49; on the abhorrence of animality generally, Bateson and Mead, *Balinese Character*, p. 22.

loosened animality fuse in a bloody drama of hatred, cruelty, violence, and death. It is little wonder that when, as is the invariable rule, the owner of the winning cock takes the carcass of the loser—often torn limb from limb by its enraged owner—home to eat, he does so with a mixture of social embarrassment, moral satisfaction, aesthetic disgust, and cannibal joy. Or that a man who has lost an important fight is sometimes driven to wreck his family shrines and curse the gods, an act of metaphysical (and social) suicide. Or that in seeking earthly analogues for heaven and hell the Balinese compare the former to the mood of a man whose cock has just won, the latter to that of a man whose cock has just lost.

## Evaluating the Text

1. Discuss Geertz's assumption that you can learn as much about a culture from its games as from its official institutions (law, religion, etc.).
2. How is the first paragraph designed to capture the reader's attention?
3. What details in paragraph two emphasize the symbolic dimension of cockfighting in Balinese culture?
4. What details in Geertz's description allow the reader to understand the extent to which the male identity of Balinese men is tied up with how well their birds perform?
5. What is significant about the qualities imputed to the geographical shape of Bali and its relationship to its neighboring island, Java?
6. Why is it significant that fighting cocks receive care and attention equal to that given to human babies?
7. What taboos do the Balinese have relating to animals? How are these taboos and the all-consuming passion for fighting cocks two sides of the same psychological coin?

## Exploring Different Perspectives

1. How does Simone de Beauvoir's ("The Married Woman") analysis shed light on the enforced separation of women in Bali from this central activity in the culture?
2. To what extent might the cockfight in Bali be an expression of the same activity which in !Kung society (see Marjorie Shostak, "Memories of a !Kung Girlhood") appears as hunting?
3. What insights does Marilyn French's ("Gender Roles") analysis of culturally enforced gender roles provide in understanding why cockfighting enables Balinese men to define their idealized masculine selves?

## Extending Viewpoints through Writing

1. What aspects of American culture seem analogous to Balinese cockfighting —where male sexual attitudes are implicated in the activity (football, sports cars, etc.)? How do these cultural pursuits embody idealized masculine traits?

2. Does anything in American culture play the same role for women as cockfighting does for men in Balinese culture?
3. To what extent does bullfighting reveal features of Spanish culture? Try your hand at writing an analysis interpreting the role bullfighting plays in Spanish culture. Discuss whether it fulfills any of the same psychological needs as cockfighting does for men in Bali.
4. Analyze the function any sport plays in its cultural context. For example, you might look at cricket in the West Indies; Gaelic football and hurling in Ireland; kendo (fencing with bamboo poles) in Japan; squash in Pakistan; jai-alai in the Basque region between northern Spain and France; *charreada* (a form of rodeo) in Mexico; ice hockey and lacrosse in Canada; *petanque* (a form of bowling) in France; *taijiquan* (shadow boxing) among senior citizens in Singapore; rugby, snooker (billiards), and darts in England; polo in Argentina; and soccer in Brazil and throughout the world.
5. In a brief essay, write about a recent sporting event, telling what led up to it, details of the match itself, and your reactions.
6. To what extent could football be described as an expression of the stereotyped male "gender role" Marilyn French discusses? Analyze some of the following features of football: its heroics, larger-than-life players, the danger of physical injury and humiliation, "armor" worn by the combatants, the regimentation of drills, formations, and training camps.

# Talat Abbasi

# *Facing the Light*

---

*Talat Abbasi was born in Karachi, a seaport on the southwest coast of Pakistan, and was educated at the London School of Economics. Her stories have appeared in* Feminist Studies, Asian Women's Anthology, *and in* Short Story International. *A recent story, "Going to Baltistan" was published in* Massachusetts Review *(Winter 1988– 1989). Of her short stories, Abbasi observes, "I am on the whole a person of few words. I studied in a convent in Karachi, where the nuns said, 'Economy in everything, including words.'" Abbasi's character- istic sensitivity to gender roles and class in Pakistani culture are revealed in "Facing the Light," a story that explores the moment in a relationship when illusions give way to truth.*

*With India's independence in 1947, the nation of Pakistan was established as a separate Muslim state comprising two regions on either side of India separated by a thousand miles with East Pakistan sharing a border with Burma. The creation of the Indo-Pakistani border was followed by an exodus of seven million Hindus to India and an equal number of Muslims to Pakistan. In 1971, East Pakistan declared its independence and took the name Bangladesh. Pakistan's precarious economic conditions worsened in the 1980s, when millions of refugees fleeing the Soviet invasion of Afghanistan poured into Pakistan. In 1988 Benazir Bhutto became the first woman to govern a Muslim country, a position she held for two years, until she was ousted by a no-confidence vote in the National Assembly because of accusations of nepotism and corruption. She was replaced by Nawaz Sharif in 1990.*

"I wish to be fair to you," he says and the head goes up as it always 1 does when he wishes to be fair to her. And in sympathy, in solidarity, the eyebrows and nose rise to the occasion, positioning themselves upwards. And the mouth tightens into a straight line to underline it all. And together they all say the same thing: And now you may thank us, and now you may thank us. And she, bent over her sewing machine, pricks her finger with its needle which she is pretending to thread and snatches up a tissue, wipes off the drop of blood and tosses it in the direction of

*(For additional information on the lives of women in Muslim countries, see p. 126.)

the maidservant. The woman springs out of the sea of silk and muslin on the Persian carpet, giggles as she catches it, darts across to the wastepaper basket and still giggling, leaps back into the pile of saris. The room is looking like a smuggler's den with trunks and suitcases spilling out hoards of dazzling material. And there is scarcely room to stand let alone sit for rolls of georgette are billowing on the sofa, brocades are draped over chairs and everything is flowing onto the carpet where a clean bedsheet has been spread.

2     The seasons are changing. Another few days and summer will be upon Karachi, stretching endlessly like the desert itself from which hot winds are already rising. The brush with cool weather a memory.

3     So they are right in the midst of sorting out her wardrobe, packing away the heavier silks and satins and unpacking the cool cottons and frothy chiffons and she is instructing the little maidservant — these for washing, these for dry cleaning, that black one throw over to me, I have just the magenta and purple border to liven it up. That petticoat for mending. And this whole lot kicked towards her, all that for throwing out. Yes yes of course that is what she meant — that she could have them all. But no, again no, not this midnight blue chiffon sari, most certainly not. Is she in her senses that she can even ask again? A thousand, twelve hundred rupees for the embroidery alone, for these hundreds of silver sequins — real silver, each one of them, sprinkled all over like stars. And she, whenever she'd worn it, so like a goddess who on a summer night stepping out of heaven had hastily snatched a piece of the star-spangled sky to cover herself with. For after all, that had been the whole idea, she'd designed it herself with herself in mind. And now give it away to a servant? Just like that? Throw it down the drain? Preposterous. How did she dare ask again? How did she dare even think? Yes even if the silver was tarnished, even if every single star had blackened and the sari no more than a shabby rag. Which shouldn't have happened because she herself had packed it away at the end of last season, with these hands, trusting no one, wrapped it up in layer upon layer of muslin, buried it like a mummy, deep inside a steel trunk. Safe, airtight. She's been so certain the Karachi air couldn't possibly get to it and tarnish the silver. But it had and had snuffed out the stars like candles. And now, on her lap, this veil of darkness, dullness.

4     And he chooses that precise moment to rap so loudly with his cane on her bedroom door that the midnight blue sari slithers to her feet, an inky shadow. She quickly bends over her sewing machine, pretending to thread the needle. What's he doing here at this time, jamming the doorway of her bedroom? Never home for dinner why here even before tea? "Malik Sahib," announces the woman as though she needs assistance in recognizing her own husband of twenty-two — three — years. And rushes to evict a stack of summer cotton saris which have usurped the sofa. But he makes an impatient gesture with his hands and remains standing and immediately begins to be fair to her. So anxious is he to be fair to her.

"Go to your quarter," she says to the woman, for she cannot allow    5
him to be fair to her in front of the servants. Not when he's going out of
his way to be fair to her and she can tell that he's going to outdo himself
in fairness today. She can tell by that red flower which has blossomed
overnight upon his chest and is now blazing out of his button hole. She
can tell by that moustache, till yesterday steel grey, stiff as a rod, today
henna red, oiled, curled softly, coaxed gently to a fine point at both
edges. Like a pair of wings dipped in a rosy sunset! And as surely as a
pair of wings ever did fly she can tell that that moustache will fly tonight.

"But the saris . . . " Such a thrill of excitement has shot through    6
her, lighting up the saucer eyes in the dark face as though car headlights
have suddenly flashed in a tunnel. She must stay, she must listen. She
mustn't miss a word of this.

"Later."    7

The woman dares not say another word and hurriedly picks up her    8
slippers at the door.

"Tea in half an hour," she says to the woman so he doesn't spend all
evening being fair to her.

The door is closing after her and he is already stretching himself up to    9
his full height—and beyond—in preparation for ultimate fairness to
her. Striding over, he will come straight to the point. He will not waste
his time blaming her for anything because he realizes that she cannot
help herself. And because she will in any case pay for it, regret it all,
regrets made more bitter by the remembrance of his own decency
throughout, for after all how many men, how many men—but no,
straight to the point. Looming over her, smiling, positively beaming
down at her in anticipation of her shock at his news, he must tell her that
it is too late for regrets. He is leaving. Yes. Leaving and this time it is
final. She heard right. She did not imagine it. But in case she thinks she
did, he will thump the ground with his cane. Three times he will thump
the ground with his cane. And three times the ground reverberates.
Final. Final. Final. Yet he will be fair to her. Indeed more than. He will be
generous. Large hearted.

And so, his chest is swelling, expanding, the petals on it trembling as    10
it grows larger and larger. In any case, he has a position to maintain and
so she will be maintained in the style which she has always been used to
and which—stretching himself further up, risking a launch into space in
his determination to be fair to her—a man in his position can well
afford. Therefore car, house, servants, nothing will change. And looking
down at her as at a pebble he has just flung at the bottom of a well he
reassures her: car, house, servants . . .

Car, house, servants! Tea in five minutes, she should've said. For—    11
car, house, servants—what more was there? Her fault, her mistake, her
stupidity thinking a half hour would be needed, thinking there was so
much to say now when not a word had ever been spoken before.

Is she listening? Is she listening?    12

13    Noises. Just noises. Two prisoners in neighbouring cells and no one on the other side. Hence the tapping noises. One tap for food, two for money. Short taps, sharp taps, clear taps. And please, not too many. Just enough to pull along, I in my cell, you in yours.

14    Has she heard? Car, house, serv . . .

15    The lid crashes down on the sewing machine, the spool of cotton, the thimble, flying to the floor. The other side then! To the far end of the room, to the window, to her big brass bed, there to spread out the sari, all six yards of it, give it another look, every inch of it, one last chance, for surely, surely in the bright light of day, the sun shining directly on it, it would look different. Yes it would, of course it would, everything looks different in the light. So there by the open window, she would see it again, the sparkle of a thousand stars, lost here, in the shadows of the room. It would still be salvaged. Still be saved.

16    He cannot believe this. Getting up, walking away, right in the middle of his being fair to her. Leaving him talking as though to himself, turning her back to him . . .

17    Facing the light. The sari laid out on the bed. The curtains drawn aside. The sun streaming through the window, pouring down the sky-light onto the bed, warming the brass, setting afire the ruby carpet. Yet here too, that veil of darkness, dullness, will not yield but instead spreads its claim everywhere. For now she sees that same layer of darkness, dullness, on everything. Nothing is safe then, for it is in the air, the very air. Nothing escapes. Nothing remains the same. The toughest metals suffer. Brass blackens. Silver loses its luster. Gold dulls. This bed. These bangles. Constantly being polished and repolished. Even these grilles on this window. Painted how long ago? A month? Two? And already here, there, in patches, the rust is cutting through. Everything is being at-tacked. As though an unseen force is snaking its way through the city, choosing its victims, the strongest, the most precious, stalking them, ferreting them out as they lie hidden under paint and polish, shrouded in trunks. Strikes them, robs them of their sparkle, their luster, their very light.

18    . . . as if he isn't there, as if he doesn't exist. Very well then. Out through that door. This instant.

19    And some things you simply cannot keep polishing and repolishing no matter how precious they are. Too fragile, the fabric. It will have to be discarded, thrown away on that heap of old clothes. She will have it after all. She will. There is no help for it, for it is in the air, the very air. And so, still facing the light, she begins to fold the sari.

## Evaluating the Text

1. How does the repetition of the word *fair* contribute to the characterization of the husband seen from the wife's perspective?

2. How does the detail of pricking her finger underscore the puncturing of the illusion she has created of herself as a "goddess"?
3. How would you characterize the relationship of the wife with her maidservant? How is it similar to the relationship she has with her husband? Why does she resent the maid asking for the dress? How does her attitude that giving the sari to the maid is like throwing it down the drain reveal what kind of a person she is?
4. What details suggest that the husband and wife have grown apart over the years and that he may be breaking up with her to marry his mistress?
5. How does Abbasi shed light on the relationship between the husband and wife by using the analogy of the prisoner in a cell, tapping for food and water?
6. At what point does Abbasi shift the narrative so that events appear from the maidservant's perspective? How does this brief shift let the reader see events from another angle?
7. How does Abbasi use natural elements like hot winds and light to represent the corroding forces that undermine the relationship she describes? To what extent does she suggest that this is an objective force changing the traditional role of women as protected, dependent, isolated creatures within Pakistani society?
8. What is the significance of the title, "Facing the Light," and how is it related to the light that tarnishes the silver sequins on the blue sari?
9. How does Abbasi's attitude toward the events she describes express itself in the way she writes? How would you characterize her approach? Is it ironic, wistful, nostalgic, empathetic, bitter?

## Exploring Different Perspectives

1. What similarities can you discover in the husband's attitude toward his wife in Henri Lopes's story ("The Esteemed Representative") and in "Facing the Light"? What different cultural attitudes about the status of women in the Republic of the Congo and in Pakistan can you infer from these stories?
2. How does Simone de Beauvoir's ("The Married Woman") analysis shed light on the dependency and quasi-servitude of married women in Pakistan? Why is the woman in Abbasi's story forced to live a life of isolation?

## Extending Viewpoints through Writing

1. Describe the breakup of a relationship in which you have been involved. Were there any similarities to the situation described in "Facing the Light"?
2. What cultural differences can you observe between separation and divorce as represented in Abbasi's story, which is set in Pakistan and America? Abbasi may be referring to the three-stage process of divorce in Islamic culture in phrases such as "three times" and "Final. Final. Final."
Separation leading to divorce is accompanied by ritual pronouncements by the husband before witnesses ("I divorce you") once every month for three consecutive months. The three months are allotted in case the couple can work out their differences and the marriage can be saved.

3. Rewrite any portion of this story you wish so that events and conversations appear from the maidservant's perspective.

4. Works by Abbasi, Nawal El Sadaawi ("Circumcision of Girls," Chapter 2), Tayeb Salih ("A Handful of Dates," Chapter 2), and Salman Rushdie ("A Pen Against the Sword," Chapter 7), provide insight into the gender roles and the influence of the Koran in shaping expectations for men and women in the Islamic countries of Pakistan, Egypt, the Sudan, and Iran. Drawing on information in these articles, reports, and stories, write an essay comparing and contrasting the expectations and perceptions of men and women in Islamic countries with those in the United States.

# Marjorie Shostak

# *Memories of a !Kung Girlhood*

*Marjorie Shostak initially spent two years, from 1969 to 1971 living and working among the !Kung San of Botswana, as a research assistant on the Harvard Kalahari Desert Project. The !Kung or !Kung bushmen live in southwestern Africa in isolated areas of Botswana (where they make up only 3 percent of the population), Angola, and Namibia. The ! is meant to represent a clicking sound in their language made by the tongue breaking air pockets in different parts of the mouth. Anthropologists have studied this nomadic community with great interest because they are one of the few peoples who live by hunting and gathering rather than by some form of agriculture. After gaining fluency in the language of the !Kung, Shostak returned to Botswana in 1975 for six months to complete the life histories of several women in the tribe. The results of her fieldwork first appeared in* Kalahari Hunter-Gatherers: Studies of the !Kung San and Their Neighbors, *edited by Richard B. Lee and Irven De Vore (1976), and later in* Human Nature, *as "Memories of a !Kung Girlhood" (1978). Shostak's research also served as the basis for the 1983 book* Nisa: The Life and Words of a !Kung Woman. *She currently teaches anthropology at Emory University. In "Memories of a !Kung Girlhood," we hear the remembrances of Nisa, recalling her childhood and marriage.*

I remember when my mother was pregnant with Kumsa. I was still small (about four years old) and I asked, "Mommy, that baby inside you . . . when that baby is born, will it come out from your bellybutton?" She said, "No, it won't come out from there. When you give birth, a baby comes from here." And she pointed to her genitals.

When she gave birth to Kumsa, I wanted the milk she had in her breasts, and when she nursed him, my eyes watched as the milk spilled out. I cried all night . . . cried and cried.

Once when my mother was with him and they were lying down asleep, I took him away from her and put him down on the other side of the hut. Then I lay down beside her. While she slept I squeezed some milk and started to nurse, and nursed and nursed and nursed. Maybe she thought it was him. When she woke and saw me she cried, "Where . . . tell me . . . what did you do with Kumsa? Where is he?"

*(For additional information on Botswana, see p. 598.)

171

# About the !Kung

Nisa is a 50-year-old !Kung woman, one of an estimated 13,000 !Kung San living on the northern fringe of the Kalahari Desert in southern Africa. Much of her life—as daughter, sister, wife, mother, and lover—has been spent in the semi-nomadic pursuit of food and water in the arid savanna.

Like many !Kung, Nisa is a practiced storyteller. The !Kung have no written language with which to record their experiences, and people sit around their fires for hours recounting recent events and those long past. Voices rise and fall, hands move in dramatic gestures, and bird and animal sounds are imitated as stories are told and retold, usually with much exaggeration.

I collected stories of Nisa's life as part of my anthropological effort to record the lives of !Kung women in their own words. Nisa enjoyed working with the machine that "grabs your voice" and the interviews with her produced 25 hours of tape and 425 pages of transcription. The excerpts included here are faithful to her narrative except where awkward or discontinuous passages have been modified or deleted, and where long passages have been shortened.

Although most of Nisa's memories are typical of !Kung life, her early memories, like those of most people, are probably idiosyncratic mixtures of fact and fantasy. Her memories of being hit for taking food are probably not accurate. The !Kung tend to be lenient and indulgent with their children, and researchers have rarely observed any physical punishment or the withholding of food.

Strong feelings of sibling rivalry, like those that Nisa describes, are common. !Kung women wean their children as soon as they find they are pregnant again because they believe the milk belongs to the fetus. Children are not usually weaned until they are three or four years old, which tends to make them resent their younger siblings. Nisa's complaints about being given too little food probably stem from her jealousy of her little brother.

Despite the lack of privacy, !Kung parents are generally discreet in their sexual activity. As children become aware of it, they engage each other in sexual play. Parents say they do not approve of this play but do little to stop it.

Many !Kung girls first marry in their early teens, but these relationships are not consummated until the girls begin menstruating around the age of 16. Early marriages are relatively unstable. Nisa was betrothed twice before marrying Tashay.

The exclamation point at the beginning of !Kung represents one of the many click sounds in the !Kung language. Clicks are made by the tongue breaking air pockets in different parts of the mouth; but the notation for clicks has been eliminated from the translation in all cases except for the name of the !Kung people. Nisa, for instance, should be written as N≠isa.

*Marjorie Shostak*

I told her he was lying down inside the hut. She grabbed me and    4
pushed me hard away from her. I lay there and cried. She took Kumsa,
put him down beside her, and insulted me by cursing my genitals.

"Are you crazy? Nisa-Big Genitals, what's the matter with you? What    5
craziness grabbed you that you took a baby, dropped him somewhere
else, and then lay down beside me and nursed? I thought it was Kumsa."

When my father came home, she told him, "Do you see what kind of    6
mind your daughter has? Hit her! She almost killed Kumsa. This little
baby, this little thing here, she took from my side and dropped him
somewhere else. I was lying here holding him and fell asleep. She came
and took him away, left him by himself, then lay down where he had
been and nursed. Now, hit her!"

I said, "You're lying! Me . . . Daddy, I didn't nurse. Really I didn't. I    7
don't even want her milk anymore."

He said, "If I ever hear of this again, I'll hit you. Now, don't ever do    8
that again!"

I said, "Yes, he's my little brother, isn't he? My little baby brother and    9
I *love* him. I won't do that again. He can nurse all by himself. Daddy,
even if you're not here, I won't try to steal Mommy's breasts. They
belong to my brother."

We lived and lived, and as I kept growing, I started to carry Kumsa    10
around on my shoulders. My heart was happy and I started to love him. I
carried him everywhere. I would play with him for a while, and whenever he started to cry, I'd take him over to mother to nurse. Then I'd take
him back with me and we'd play together again.

That was when Kumsa was still little. But once he was older and    11
started to talk and then to run around, that's when we were mean to
each other all the time. Sometimes we hit each other. Other times I
grabbed him and bit him and said, "Ooooh . . . what is this thing that
has such a horrible face and no brains and is so mean? Why is it so mean
to me when I'm not doing anything to it?" Then he said, "I'm going to *hit*
you!" And I said, "You're just a *baby*! I, I am the one who's going to hit
*you*. Why are you so miserable to me?" I insulted him and he insulted me
and then I insulted him back. We just stayed together and played like
that.

Once, when our father came back carrying meat, we both called out,    12
"Ho, ho. Daddy! Ho, ho, Daddy!" But when I heard him say, "Daddy,
Daddy," I yelled, "Why are you greeting my father? He's *my* father, isn't
he? You can only say, 'Oh, hello Father.'" But he called out, "Ho,
ho . . . Daddy!" I said, "Be quiet! Only *I* will greet him. Is he your
father? I'm going to hit you!"

We fought and argued until Mother finally stopped us. Then we just    13
sat around while she cooked the meat.

This was also when I used to take food. It happened over all kinds of    14
food — sweet *nin* berries or *klaru* bulbs . . . other times it was mongongo nuts. Sometimes before my mother left to go gathering, she'd

leave food inside a leather pouch and hang it high on one of the branches inside the hut.

15 But as soon as she was gone, I'd take some of whatever food was left in the bag. If it was *klaru*, I'd find the biggest bulbs and take them. I'd hang the bag back on the branch and go sit somewhere to eat them.

16 One time I sat down in the shade of a tree while my parents gathered food nearby. As soon as they had moved away from me, I climbed the tree where they had left a pouch hanging, full of *klaru*, and took the bulbs.

17 I had my own little pouch, the one my father had made me, and I took the bulbs and put them in the pouch. Then I climbed down and sat waiting for my parents to return.

18 They came back. "Nisa, you ate the *klaru!*" What do you have to say for yourself?" I said, "Uhn uh, I didn't eat them."

19 I started to cry. Mother hit me and yelled, "Don't take things. You can't seem to understand! I tell you but you don't listen. Don't your ears hear when I talk to you?"

20 I said, "Uhn uh. Mommy's been making me feel bad for too long now. She keeps saying I steal things and hits me so that my skin hurts. I'm going to stay with Grandma!"

21 But when I went to my grandmother, she said, "No, I can't take care of you now. If I try you will be hungry. I am old and just go gathering one day at a time. In the morning I just rest. We would sit together and hunger would kill you. Now go back and sit beside your mother and father."

22 I said, "No, Daddy will hit me. Mommy will hit me. I want to stay with you."

23 So I stayed with her. Then one day she said, "I'm going to bring you back to your mother and father." She took me to them, saying, "Today I'm giving Nisa back to you. But isn't there someone here who will take good care of her? You don't just hit a child like this one. She likes food and likes to eat. All of you are lazy and you've just left her so she hasn't grown well. You've killed this child with hunger. Look at her now, how small she still is."

24 Oh, but my heart was happy! Grandmother was scolding Mother! I had so much happiness in my heart that I laughed and laughed. But then, when Grandmother went home and left me there, I cried and cried.

25 My father started to yell at me. He didn't hit me. His anger usually came out only from his mouth. "You're so senseless! Don't you realize that after you left, everything felt less important? We wanted you to be with us. Yes, even your mother wanted you and missed you. Today, everything will be all right when you stay with us. Your mother will take you where she goes; the two of you will do things together and go gathering together."

26 Then when my father dug *klaru* bulbs, I ate them, and when he dug *chon* bulbs, I ate them. I ate everything they gave me, and I wasn't yelled at any more.

Mother and I often went to the bush together. The two of us would 27
walk until we arrived at a place where she collected food. She'd set me
down in the shade of a tree and dig roots or gather nuts nearby.

Once I left the tree and went to play in the shade of another tree. I 28
saw a tiny steenbok, one that had just been born, hidden in the grass and
among the leaves. It was lying there, its little eye just looking out at me.

I thought, "What should I do?" I shouted, *"Mommy!"* I just stood 29
there and it just lay there looking at me.

Suddenly I knew what to do—I ran at it, trying to grab it. But it 30
jumped up and ran away and I started to chase it. It was running and I
was running and it was crying as it ran. Finally, I got very close and put
my foot in its way, and it fell down. I grabbed its legs and started to carry
it back. It was crying, "Ehn . . . ehn . . . ehn. . . ."

Its mother had been close by and when she heard it call, she came 31
running. As soon as I saw her, I started to run again. I wouldn't give it
back to its mother!

I called out, "Mommy! Come! Help me with this steenbok! Mommy! 32
The steenbok's mother is coming for me! Run! Come! Take this steenbok
from me."

But soon the mother steenbok was no longer following, so I took the 33
baby, held its feet together, and banged it hard against the sand until I
killed it. It was no longer crying; it was dead. I felt wonderfully happy.
My mother came running and I gave it to her to carry.

The two of us spent the rest of the day walking in the bush. While my 34
mother was gathering, I sat in the shade of a tree, waiting and playing
with the dead steenbok. I picked it up. I tried to make it sit up, to open its
eyes. I looked at them. After mother had dug enough *sha* roots, we left
and returned home.

My father had been out hunting that day and had shot a large 35
steenbok with his arrows. He had skinned it and brought it back hanging
on a branch.

"Ho, ho. Daddy killed a steenbok!" I said, "Mommy! Daddy! I'm not 36
going to let anyone have any of *my* steenbok. Now *don't* give it to anyone
else. After you cook it, just my little brother and I will eat it, just the two
of us."

I remember another time when we were traveling from one place to 37
another and the sun was burning. It was the hot, dry season and there
was no water anywhere. The sun was burning! Kumsa had already been
born and I was still small.

After we had been walking a long time, my older brother Dau spotted 38
a beehive. We stopped while he and my father chopped open the tree.
All of us helped take out the honey. I filled my own little container until
it was completely full.

We stayed there, eating the honey, and I found myself getting very 39
thirsty. Then we left and continued to walk, I carrying my honey and my
digging stick. Soon the heat began killing us and we were all dying of
thirst. I started to cry because I wanted water so badly.

40     After a while, we stopped and sat down in the shade of a baobab tree. There was still no water anywhere. We just sat in the shade like that.

41     Finally my father said, "Dau, the rest of the family will stay here under this baobab. But you, take the water containers and get us some water. There's a well not too far away."

42     Dau collected the empty ostrich eggshell containers and the large clay pot and left. I lay there, already dead from thirst and thought, "If I stay with Mommy and Daddy, I'll surely die of thirst. Why don't I follow my big brother and go drink water with him?"

43     With that I jumped up and ran after him, crying out, calling to him, following his tracks. But he didn't hear me. I kept running . . . crying and calling out.

44     Finally, he heard something and turned to see. There I was, "Oh, no!" he said. "Nisa's followed me. What can I do with her now that she's here?" He just stood there and waited for me to catch up. He picked me up and carried me high up on his shoulder, and along we went. He really liked me!

45     The two of us went on together. We walked and walked and walked and walked. Finally, we reached the well. I ran to the water and drank, and soon my heart was happy again. We filled the water containers, put them in a twine mesh sack, and my brother carried it on his back. Then he took me and put me on his shoulder again.

46     We walked the long way back until we arrived at the baobab where our parents were sitting. They drank the water. Then they said, "How well our children have done, bringing us this water! We are alive once again!"

47     We just stayed in the shade of the baobab. Later we left and traveled to another water hole where we settled for a while. My heart was happy . . . eating honey and just living.

48     We lived there, and after some time passed, we saw the first rain clouds. One came near but just hung in the sky. More rain clouds came over and they too just stood there. Then the rain started to spill itself and it came pouring down.

49     The rainy season had finally come. The sun rose and set, and the rain spilled itself and fell and kept falling. It fell without ceasing. Soon the water pans were full. And my heart! My heart within me was happy and we lived and ate meat and mongongo nuts. There was more meat and it was all delicious.

50     And there were caterpillars to eat, those little things that crawl along going "mmm . . . mmmmm . . . mmmmm. . . ." People dug roots and collected nuts and berries and brought home more and more food. There was plenty to eat, and people kept bringing meat back on sticks and hanging it in the trees.

51     My heart was bursting. I ate lots of food and my tail was wagging, always wagging about like a little dog. I'd laugh with my little tail, laugh with a little donkey's laugh, a tiny thing that is. I'd throw my tail one

way and the other, shouting, "Today I'm going to eat caterpillars . . . *cat-er-pillars!*" Some people gave me meat broth to drink, and
others prepared the skins of caterpillars and roasted them for me to eat,
and I ate and ate and ate. Then I went to sleep.

But that night, after everyone was dead asleep, I peed right in my    52
sleeping place. In the morning, when everyone got up, I just lay there.
The sun rose and had set itself high in the sky, and I was still lying there.
I was afraid of people shaming me. Mother said, "Why is Nisa acting like
this and refusing to leave her blankets when the sun is sitting up in the
sky? Oh . . . she has probably wet herself!"

When I did get up, my heart felt miserable. I thought, "I've peed on    53
myself and now everyone's going to laugh at me." I asked one of my
friends, "How come, after I ate all those caterpillars, when I went to
sleep I peed in my bed?" Then I thought, "Tonight, when this day is
over, I'm going to lie down separate from the others. If I pee in my bed
again, won't mother and father hit me?"

When a child sleeps beside her mother, in front, and her father sleeps    54
behind and makes love to her mother, the child watches. Her parents
don't fear her, a small child, because even if the child sees, even if she
hears, she is unaware of what it is her parents are doing. She is still
young and without sense. Perhaps this is the way the child learns. The
child is still senseless, without intelligence, and just watches.

If the child is a little boy, when he plays with other children, he plays    55
sex with them and teaches it to himself, just like a baby rooster teaches
itself. The little girls also learn it by themselves.

Little boys are the first ones to know its sweetness. Yes, a young girl,    56
while she is still a child, her thoughts don't know it. A boy has a penis,
and maybe, while he is still inside his mother's belly, he already knows
about sex.

When you are a child you play at nothing things. You build little huts    57
and play. Then you come back to the village and continue to play. If
people bother you, you get up and play somewhere else.

Once we left a pool of rain water where we had been playing and    58
went to the little huts we had made. We stayed there and played at being
hunters. We went out tracking animals, and when we saw one, we struck
it with our make-believe arrows. We took some leaves and hung them
over a stick and pretended it was meat. Then we carried it back to our
village. When we got back, we stayed there and ate the meat and then
the meat was gone. We went out again, found another animal, and killed
it.

Sometimes the boys asked if we wanted to play a game with our    59
genitals and the girls said no. We said we didn't want to play that game,
but would like to play other games. The boys told us that playing sex was
what playing was all about. That's the way we grew up.

When adults talked to me I listened. Once they told me that when a    60
young woman grows up, she takes a husband. When they first talked to

me about it, I said: "What? What kind of thing am I that I should take a husband? Me, when I grow up, I won't marry. I'll just lie by myself. If I married a man, what would I think I would be doing it for?"

61    My father said: "Nisa, I am old. I am your father and I am old; your mother's old, too. When you get married, you will gather food and give it to your husband to eat. He also will do things for you and give you things you can wear. But if you refuse to take a husband, who will give you food to eat? Who will give you things to have? Who will give you things to wear?"

62    I said to my father and mother, "No. There's no question in my mind—I refuse a husband. I won't take one. Why should I? As I am now, I am still a child and won't marry."

63    Then I said to Mother, "Why don't you marry the man you want for me and sit him down beside Father? Then you'll have two husbands."

64    Mother said: "Stop talking nonsense. I'm not going to marry him; you'll marry him. A husband is what I want to give you. Yet you say I should marry him. Why are you playing with me with this talk?"

65    We just continued to live after that, kept on living and more time passed. One time we went to the village where Old Kantla and his son Tashay were living. My friend Nhuka and I had gone to the water well to get water, and Tashay and his family were there, having just come back from the bush. When Tashay saw me, he decided he wanted to marry me. He called Nhuka over and said, "Nhuka, that young woman, that beautiful young woman . . . what is her name?"

66    Nhuka told him my name was Nisa, and he said, "That young woman . . . I'm going to tell Mother and Father about her. I'm going to ask them if I can marry her."

67    The next evening there was a dance at our village, and Tashay and his parents came. We sang and danced into the night. Later his father said, "We have come here, and now that the dancing is finished, I want to speak to you. Give me your child, the child you gave birth to. Give her to me, and I will give her to my son. Yesterday, while we were at the well, he saw your child. When he returned he told me in the name of what he felt that I should come and ask for her today so I could give her to him."

68    My mother said, "Yes . . . but I didn't give birth to a woman, I bore a child. She doesn't think about marriage, she just doesn't think about the inside of her marriage hut."

69    Then my father said, "Yes, I also conceived that child, and it is true: She just doesn't think about marriage. When she marries a man, she leaves him and marries another man and leaves him and gets up and marries another man and leaves him. She refuses men completely. There are two men whom she has already refused. So when I look at Nisa today, I say she is not a woman."

70    Then Tashay's father said, "Yes, I have listened to what you have

said. That, of course, is the way of a child; it is a child's custom to do that. She gets married many times until one day she likes one man. Then they stay together. That is a child's way."

They talked about the marriage and agreed to it. In the morning 71 Tashay's parents went back to their camp, and we went to sleep. When the morning was late in the sky, his relatives came back. They stayed around and his parents told my aunt and my mother that they should all start building the marriage hut. They began building it together, and everyone was talking and talking. There were a lot of people there. Then all the young men went and brought Tashay to the hut. They stayed around together near the fire. I was at Mother's hut. They told two of my friends to get me. But I said to myself, "Ooooh . . . I'll just run away."

When they came, they couldn't find me. I was already out in the 72 bush, and I just sat there by the base of a tree. Soon I heard Nhuka call out, "Nisa . . . Nisa . . . my friend . . . there are things there that will bite and kill you. Now leave there and come back here."

They came and brought me back. Then they laid me down inside the 73 hut. I cried and cried, and people told me: "A man is not something that kills you; he is someone who marries you, and becomes like your father or your older brother. He kills animals and gives you things to eat. Even tomorrow he would do that. But because you are crying, when he kills an animal, he will eat it himself and won't give you any. Beads, too. He will get some beads, but he won't give them to you. Why are you afraid of your husband and why are you crying?"

I listened and was quiet. Later Tashay lay down by the mouth of the 74 hut, near the fire, and I was inside. He came in only after he thought I was asleep. Then he lay down and slept. I woke while it was still dark and thought, "How am I going to jump over him? How can I get out and go to Mother's hut?" Then I thought, "This person has married me . . . yes." And, I just lay there. Soon the rain came and beat down and it fell until dawn broke.

In the morning, he got up first and sat by the fire. I was frightened. I 75 was so afraid of him, I just lay there and waited for him to go away before I got up.

We lived together a long time and began to learn to like one another 76 before he slept with me. The first time I didn't refuse. I agreed just a little and he lay with me. But the next morning my insides hurt. I took some leaves and wound them around my waist, but it continued to hurt. Later that day I went with the women to gather mongongo nuts. The whole time I thought "Ooooh . . . what has he done to my insides that they feel this way."

That evening we lay down again. But this time I took a leather strap, held my skin apron tightly against me, tied up my genitals with it, and then tied the strap to the hut's frame. I didn't want him to take me again. The two of us lay there and after a while he started to touch me. When he reached my stomach, he felt the leather strap. He felt around to see what it was. He said, "What is this woman doing? Yesterday she lay with me so nicely when I came to her. Why has she tied up her genitals this way?"

78    He sat me up and said, "Nisa . . . Nisa . . . what happened? Why are you doing this?" I didn't answer him.

79    "What are you so afraid of that you tied your genitals?"

80    I said, "I'm not afraid of anything."

81    He said, "No, now tell me what you are afraid of. In the name of what you did, I am asking you."

82    I said, "I refuse because yesterday when you touched me my insides hurt."

83    He said, "Do you see me as someone who kills people? Am I going to eat you? I am not going to kill you. I have married you and I want to make love to you. Have you seen any man who has married a woman and who just lives with her and doesn't have sex with her?"

84    I said, "No, I still refuse it! I refuse sex. Yesterday my insides hurt, that's why."

85    He said, "Mmm. Today you will lie there by yourself. But tomorrow I will take you."

86    The next day I said to him, "Today I'm going to lie here, and if you take me by force, you will have me. You will have me because today I'm just going to lie here. You are obviously looking for some 'food,' but I don't know if the food I have is food at all, because even if you have some, you won't be full."

87    I just lay there and he did his work.

88    We lived and lived, and soon I started to like him. After that I was a grown person and said to myself, "Yes, without doubt, a man sleeps with you. I thought maybe he didn't."

89    We lived on, and then I loved him and he loved me, and I kept on loving him. When he wanted me I didn't refuse and he just slept with me. I thought, "Why have I been so concerned about my genitals? They are after all, not so important. So why was I refusing them?"

90    I thought that and gave myself to him and gave and gave. We lay with one another, and my breasts had grown very large. I had become a woman.

## FOR FURTHER INFORMATION

Lee, Richard, B., and Irven De Vore, eds. *Kalahari Hunter-Gatherers: Studies of the !Kung San and Their Neighbors.* Harvard University Press, 1976.
Lee, Richard B., and Irven De Vore, eds. *Man the Hunter.* Aldine, 1968.
Marshall, Lorna. *The !Kung of Nyae Nyae.* Harvard University Press, 1976.
Shostak, Marjorie. "Life before Horticulture: An African Gathering and Hunting Society." *Horticulture*, Vol. 55, No. 2, 1977.

# Evaluating the Text

1. How would you characterize Nisa's relationships with family members? How does she interact with her mother, father, older brother, baby brother, and grandmother? What explains the changes in her attitude toward her baby brother as she grows up?
2. How is Nisa's narrative shaped to explore important turning points in her childhood and life as a young married woman?
3. What details reveal the extraordinary importance simply getting enough food to eat and enough water to drink plays in the everyday life of the !Kung?
4. How does the episode where she describes killing the baby steenbok reveal her inner conflict about becoming an adult?
5. What details illustrate that the !Kung San are a tribe of hunter-gatherers rather than farmers?
6. What can you infer about the severity of seasonal droughts in Botswana from the occasion when Nisa used an ostrich eggshell for a water container?
7. What is the !Kung San attitude toward sex play among children? In what other ways do children acquire information and expectations about their own gender roles?
8. Describe the circumstances that lead to Nisa's marriage to Tashay. What change in attitude must she undergo before the marriage takes place? What can you infer about the kinds of problems she faces in adapting to the role of married woman in !Kung society? Keep in mind she has left several prospective husbands before Tashay.
9. What picture of Nisa emerges from her recollections?

# Exploring Different Perspectives

1. Drawing on Marilyn French's ("Gender Roles") analysis, discuss how cultural expectations shape the behavior of males and females in !Kung society.
2. Compare the differences in the Balinese attitude toward animals, instincts, and sexuality with those of the !Kung. What might the Balinese think of the explicit sexual games played by !Kung children?

# Extending Viewpoints through Writing

1. In !Kung society, why is it considered insulting to be referred to as "big genitals"? What cultural values and underlying assumptions can you infer from the kinds of sexual insults typically used in a culture?
2. What unexpected similarities can you discover between !Kung and contemporary American society in terms of disciplining children, the role played by grandparents (including their concern that their grandchildren are too thin), sibling rivalry, bed-wetting, playing sexual games, and finding husbands for daughters who are fussy?
3. Nisa's narrative was originally elicited as answers to questions she was asked over a period of time by Shostak. How do recurring motifs in this account suggest the kinds of questions Shostak asked Nisa, and what conclusions might you draw about the relationship between Nisa and Shostak from the answers Nisa gave?

# Simone de Beauvoir

# *The Married Woman*

*Simone de Beauvoir (1908–1986) was born in Paris, studied philoso-phy at the Sorbonne, where she later taught, and is widely regarded as the founder of the contemporary women's movement. De Beauvoir's literary career was interwined with that of the existentialist philoso-pher and writer, Jean-Paul Sartre. Her many illuminating works include* The Second Sex *(1949), an enormously influential work in defining the goals of feminism;* The Mandarins *(1954), winner of the* Prix Goncourt; *and* All Said and Done *(1974), one of several brilliant autobiographical memoirs. In "The Married Woman," from* The Sec-ond Sex *(translated and edited by H. M. Parshley, 1952), de Beauvoir describes with eloquence and profound insight the life of servitude and frustration that is the fate of the married woman.*

1     Few tasks are more like the torture of Sisyphus than housework, with its endless repetition: the clean becomes soiled, the soiled is made clean, over and over, day after day. The housewife wears herself out marking time, she makes nothing, simply perpetuates the present. She never senses conquest of a positive Good, but rather indefinite struggle against negative Evil. A young pupil writes in her essay: "I shall never have house-cleaning day"; she thinks of the future as constant progress toward some unknown summit; but one day, as her mother washes the dishes, it comes over her that both of them will be bound to such rites until death. Eating, sleeping, cleaning—the years no longer rise up toward heaven, they lie spread out ahead, gray and identical. The battle against dust and dirt is never won.

2     Washing, ironing, sweeping, ferreting out rolls of lint from under wardrobes—all this halting of decay is also the denial of life; for time simultaneously creates and destroys, and only its negative aspect con-cerns the housekeeper. Hers is the position of the Manichaeist, regarded philosophically. The essence of Manichaeism is not solely to recognize two principles, the one good, the other evil; it is also to hold that the good is attained through the abolition of evil and not by positive action. In this sense Christianity is hardly Manichaeist in spite of the existence of the devil, for one fights the demon best by devoting oneself to God and

*(For information on France, see p. 265.)

182

not by endeavoring to conquer the evil one directly. Any doctrine of transcendence and liberty subordinates the defeat of evil to progress toward the good. But woman is not called upon to build a better world: her domain is fixed and she has only to keep up the never ending struggle against the evil principles that creep into it; in her war against dust, stains, mud, and dirt she is fighting sin, wrestling with Satan.

But it is a sad fate to be required without respite to repel an enemy instead of working toward positive ends, and very often the housekeeper submits to it in a kind of madness that may verge on perversion, a kind of sado-masochism. The maniac housekeeper wages her furious war against dirt, blaming life itself for the rubbish all living growth entails. When any living being enters her house, her eye gleams with a wicked light: "Wipe your feet, don't tear the place apart, leave that alone!" She wishes those of her household would hardly breathe; everything means more thankless work for her. Severe, preoccupied, always on the watch, she loses *joie de vivre*, she becomes overprudent and avaricious. She shuts out the sunlight, for along with that come insects, germs, and dust, and besides, the sun ruins silk hangings and fades upholstery; she scatters naphthalene, which scents the air. She becomes bitter and disagreeable and hostile to all that lives: the end is sometimes murder.

The healthly young woman will hardly be attracted by so gloomy a vice. Such nervousness and spitefulness are more suited to frigid and frustrated women, old maids, deceived wives, and those whom surly and dictatorial husbands condemn to a solitary and empty existence. I knew an old beldame, once gay and coquettish, who got up at five each morning to go over to her closets; married to a man who neglected her, and isolated on a lonely estate, with but one child, she took to orderly housekeeping as others take to drink. In this insanity the house becomes so neat and clean that one hardly dares live in it; the woman is so busy she forgets her own existence. A household, in fact, with its meticulous and limitless tasks, permits to woman a sado-masochistic flight from herself as she contends madly with the things around her and with herself in a state of distraction and mental vacancy. And this flight may often have a sexual tinge. It is noteworthy that the rage for cleanliness is highest in Holland, where the women are cold, and in puritanical civilizations, which oppose an ideal of neatness and purity to the joys of the flesh. If the Mediterranean Midi lives in a state of joyous filth, it is not only because water is scarce there: love of the flesh and its animality is conducive to toleration of human odor, dirt, and even vermin.

The preparation of food, getting meals, is work more positive in nature and often more agreeable than cleaning. First of all it means marketing, often the bright spot of the day. And gossip on doorsteps, while peeling vegetables, is a gay relief for solitude; to go for water is a great adventure for half-cloistered Mohammedan women; women in markets and stores talk about domestic affairs, with a common interest, feeling themselves members of a group that—for an instant—is opposed to the group of men as the essential to the inessential. Buying is a profound pleasure, a discovery, almost an invention. As Gide says in his *Journal*, the Mohammedans, not knowing gambling, have in its place the discovery of hidden treasure; that is the poetry and the adventure of mercantile civilizations. The housewife knows little of winning in games, but a solid cabbage, a ripe Camembert, are treasures that must be cleverly won from the unwilling storekeeper; the game is to get the best for the least money; economy means not so much helping the budget as winning the game. She is pleased with her passing triumph as she contemplates her well-filled larder.

6      Gas and electricity have killed the magic of fire, but in the country many women still know the joy of kindling live flames from inert wood. With her fire going, woman becomes a sorceress; by a simple movement, as in beating eggs, or through the magic of fire, she effects the transmutation of substances: matter becomes food. There is enchantment in these alchemies, there is poetry in making preserves; the housewife has caught duration in the snare of sugar, she has enclosed life in jars. Cooking is revolution and creation; and a woman can find special satisfaction in a successful cake or a flaky pastry, for not everyone can do it: one must have the gift.

7      Here again the little girl is naturally fond of imitating her elders, making mud pies and the like, and helping roll real dough in the kitchen. But as with other housework, repetition soon spoils these pleasures. The magic of the oven can hardly appeal to Mexican Indian women who spend half their lives preparing tortillas, identical from day to day, from century to century. And it is impossible to go on day after day making a treasure-hunt of the marketing or ecstatically viewing one's highly polished faucets. The male and female writers who lyrically exalt such triumphs are persons who are seldom or never engaged in actual housework. It is tiresome, empty, monotonous, as a career. If, however, the individual who does such work is also a producer, a creative worker, it is as naturally integrated in life as are the organic functions; for this reason housework done by men seems much less dismal; it represents for them merely a negative and inconsequential moment from which they quickly escape. What makes the lot of the wife-servant ungrateful is the division of labor which dooms her completely to the general and the inessential. Dwelling-place and food are useful for life but give it no significance: the immediate goals of the housekeeper are only means, not true ends. She endeavors, naturally, to give some individuality to her work and to make it seem essential. No one else, she thinks, could do her work as well; she has her rites, superstitions, and ways of doing things. But too often her "personal note" is but a vague and meaningless rearrangement of disorder.

8      Woman wastes a great deal of time and effort in such striving for originality and unique perfection; this gives her task its meticulous, disorganized, and endless character and makes it difficult to estimate the

true load of domestic work. Recent studies show that for married women housework averages about thirty hours per week, or three fourths of a working week in employment. This is enormous if done in addition to a paid occupation, little if the woman has nothing else to do. The care of several children will naturally add a good deal to woman's work: a poor mother is often working all the time. Middle-class women who employ help, on the other hand, are almost idle; and they pay for their leisure with ennui. If they lack outside interests, they often multiply and complicate their domestic duties to excess, just to have something to do.

The worst of it all is that this labor does not even tend toward the     9 creation of anything durable. Woman is tempted — and the more so the greater pains she takes — to regard her work as an end in itself. She sighs as she contemplates the perfect cake just out of the oven: "it's a shame to eat it!" It is really too bad to have husband and children tramping with their muddy feet all over her waxed hardwood floors! When things are used they are soiled or destroyed — we have seen how she is tempted to save them from being used; she keeps preserves until they get moldy; she locks up the parlor. But times passes inexorably; provisions attract rats; they become wormy; moths attack blankets and clothing. The world is not a dream carved in stone, it is made of dubious stuff subject to rot; edible material is as equivocal as Dali's fleshy watches: it seems inert, inorganic, but hidden larvae may have changed it into a cadaver. The housewife who loses herself in things becomes dependent, like the things, upon the whole world: linen is scorched, the roast burns, china-ware gets broken; these are absolute disasters, for when things are destroyed, they are gone forever. Permanence and security cannot possible be obtained through them. The pillage and bombs of war threaten one's wardrobes, one's house.

The products of domestic work, then, must necessarily be consumed;    10 a continual renunciation is required of the woman whose operations are completed only in their destruction. For her to acquiesce without regret, these minor holocausts must at least be reflected in someone's joy or pleasure. But since the housekeeper's labor is expended to maintain the *status quo*, the husband, coming into the house, may notice disorder or negligence, but it seems to him that order and neatness come of their own accord. He has a more positive interest in a good meal. The cook's moment of triumph arrives when she puts a successful dish on the table: husband and children receive it with warm approval, not only in words, but by consuming it gleefully. The culinary alchemy then pursues its course, food becomes chyle and blood.

Thus, to maintain living bodies is of more concrete, vital interest than    11 to keep a fine floor in proper condition; the cook's effort is evidently transcended toward the future. If, however, it is better to share in another's free transcendence than to lose oneself in things, it is not less dangerous. The validity of the cook's work is to be found only in the mouths of those around her table; she needs their approbation, demands that they appreciate her dishes and call for second helpings; she is upset if they are not hungry, to the point that one wonders whether the fried potatoes are for her husband or her husband for the fried potatoes. This ambiguity is evident in the general attitude of the housekeeping wife: she takes care of the house for her husband; but she also wants him to spend all he earns for furnishings and an electric refrigerator. She desires to make him happy; but she approves of his activities only in so far as they fall within the frame of happiness she has set up.

12      There have been times when these claims have in general found satisfaction: times when such felicity was also man's ideal, when he was attached above all to his home, to his family, and when even the children chose to be characterized by their parents, their traditions, and their past. At such times she who ruled the home, who presided at the dinner table, was recognized as supreme; and she still plays this resplendent role among certain landed proprietors and wealthy peasants who here and there perpetuate the patriarchal civilization.

13      But on the whole marriage is today a surviving relic of dead ways of life, and the situation of the wife is more ungrateful than formerly, because she still has the same duties but they no longer confer the same rights, privileges, and honors. Man marries today to obtain an anchorage in immanence, but not to be himself confined therein; he wants to have hearth and home while being free to escape therefrom; he settles down but often remains a vagabond at heart; he is not contemptuous of domestic felicity, but he does not make of it an end in itself; repetition bores him; he seeks after novelty, risk, opposition to overcome, companions and friends who take him away from solitude *à deux*. The children, even more than their father, want to escape beyond family limits: life for them lies elsewhere, it is before them; the child always seeks what is different. Woman tries to set up a universe of permanence and continuity; husband and children wish to transcend the situation she creates, which for them is only a given environment. This is why, even if she is loath to admit the precarious nature of the activities to which her whole life is devoted, she is nevertheless led to impose her services by force: she changes from mother and housewife into harsh stepmother and shrew.

14      Thus woman's work within the home gives her no autonomy; it is not directly useful to society, it does not open out on the future, it produces nothing. It takes on meaning and dignity only as it is linked with existent beings who reach out beyond themselves, transcend themselves, toward society in production and action. That is, far from freeing the matron, her occupation makes her dependent upon husband and children; she is justified through them; but in their lives she is only an inessential intermediary. That "obedience" is legally no longer one of her duties in no way changes her situation; for this depends not on the will of the couple but on the very structure of the conjugal group. Woman is not allowed to *do* something positive in her work and in consequence win recognition as a complete person. However respected she may be, she is subordinate, secondary, parasitic. The heavy curse that weighs upon her

consists in this: the very meaning of her life is not in her hands. That is why the successes and the failures of her conjugal life are much more gravely important for her than for her husband; he is first a citizen, a producer, secondly a husband; she is before all, and often exclusively, a wife; her work does not take her out of her situation; it is from the latter, on the contrary, that her work takes its value, high or low. Loving, generously devoted, she will perform her tasks joyously; but they will seem to her mere dull drudgery if she performs them with resentment. In her destiny they will never play more than an inessential role; they will not be a help in the ups and downs of conjugal life. We must go on to see, then, how woman's condition is concretely experienced in life — this condition which is characterized essentially by the "service" of the bed and the "service" of the housekeeping and in which woman finds her place of dignity only in accepting her vassalage.

## Evaluating the Text

1. What characteristics define the life of "The Married Woman," according to de Beauvoir? Why is the legend of Sisyphus an appropriate myth with which to characterize housework?
2. What is de Beauvoir's attitude toward the activities she describes? What radically different set of assumptions underlie her analysis of the extent to which the housewife must subordinate her individuality to time-consuming daily tasks? How did these assumptions form the basis for the feminist movement of which de Beauvoir was the pioneer?
3. In de Beauvoir's view, why is preparing food more intrinsically satisfying than housecleaning?
4. How does de Beauvoir use comparisons drawn with work performed by Mexican Indian women, Muhammedan women, women in Holland, and women living near the Mediterranean to fill out her characterization of the "married woman"? How does women's work reflect the values of the culture in which it is performed?
5. What purpose does de Beauvoir's comparison of the tasks of the married woman with the work that men do outside of the home serve in her overall argument?

## Exploring Different Perspectives

1. How does de Beauvoir's essay provide an additional ironic dimension to the outcome of choice A (the traditional happy ending) described by Atwood in "Happy Endings"?
2. To what extent does Talat Abbasi's story, "Facing the Light," dramatize the predicament of "The Married Woman" in Pakistani culture?

## Extending Viewpoints through Writing

1. Discuss your reaction to de Beauvoir's statement that a woman's work within the home "is not directly useful to society, it does not open out on the future, it produces nothing."

2. How do changes in society since de Beauvoir wrote "The Married Woman"
   (which was published in 1949)—the women's liberation movement,
   reentry of women into the labor force, and higher divorce rates—make her
   observations more or less relevant in the 1990s?
3. In your opinion, are there any positive features or benefits that de Beauvoir
   omits from her characterization of the married woman's life?
4. Drawing on the essays by de Beauvoir, Marilyn French ("Gender Roles")
   and the story by Talat Abbasi ("Facing the Light"), write an essay defining
   *feminism*. Identify the goals of feminism, and discuss any differences in
   approach between these three authors who are known as feminists in their
   respective cultures.

# Henri Lopes

# *The Esteemed Representative*

---

*Henri Lopes, the eminent Congolese writer, was born in 1937 in Kinshasa. After receiving a university education in France, he returned to the Congo Republic to teach history. He was subsequently appointed to the Congo-Brazzaville Government, and held a succession of senior ministerial positions, as Minister of Education, Foreign Affairs, and Finance. Between 1973 and 1974, he served as Prime Minister. In "The Esteemed Representative," from* Tribaliks: Contemporary Congolese Stories *(1971, translated by Andrea Leskes), which won the Grand Prix Litteraire de l'Afrique Noire in 1972, Lopes offers a satirical portrayal of a government official whose private chauvinism toward his wife, daughters, and mistress sharply contrasts with his public rhetoric advocating women's rights.*

*The People's Republic of the Congo, in West central Africa, achieved its independence from France in 1960. Because of its location, the Congo has always played an important role as a center of commerce and transportation connecting inland areas of Africa with the Atlantic Ocean. After a series of coups, a new military regime following socialist policies, led by Colonel Sassou-Nguesso, was installed in 1979 and continues to the present. Lopes's story takes place during the time of turbulent political events when the Congo became the People's Republic of the Congo in 1970. The sentiments voiced by the "the esteemed representative" would have been those heard during this time.*

. . . Colonization has imposed an economic system on us that has  1
reduced our sisters to slaves. At the present stage, it's up to the men to liberate the underprivileged of our society in general, and our women in particular, from this economic servitude.' (Applause.) 'Our women have a right to certain jobs and they must be allowed to hold them. It is unacceptable in an independent country like ours, where thousands of girls are educated, that only the foreigners in our country get jobs as secretaries and saleswomen.' (Applause.) 'Sisters, let us take advantage of the occasion of your conference to publicly ask our National Assembly and our government, "Why the delay?" What is holding up the passage of a law explicitly spelling out that all positions as waitresses in bars and night clubs are to be exclusively reserved for Africans, and prohibited to

Europeans?' (Everyone in the hall rose, and thundering applause drowned out the speaker.) 'The salaries earned by our women in these jobs must be equal to those earned by European women.' (Thunderous applause.) 'Because as was said by — um — um — as was said by — uh — La Fontaine, I believe it was La Fontaine . . .' (Applause.) '. . . As I said, La Fontaine stated, "Equal pay for equal work."' (Thundering applause.) 'It is also time that those fathers, who in the name of tradition still refuse to allow their daughters to continue their schooling, be disillusioned of their prejudices. Women have the same rights as men. Yet some men still refuse to accept this truth. That is why I am turning to you, my sisters, and proclaiming that you women alone must liberate yourselves from masculine tyranny.' (Applause.) 'At the present time, when tribal divisions are strong and men throughout the world are mercilessly killing each other like lunatics, let me say in front of you, up here on this platform, that only women can help us to overcome tribal prejudices and win peace on earth.' (Applause.)

2    Representative Ngouakou-Ngouakou continued to speak in this manner for twenty minutes, watch in hand. When he had finished, he wiped his brow. The crowd in the lecture room at the party headquarters broke out in a frenzied joy. Men and women congratulated each other with slaps on the back, laughed and shouted out, 'Papa Ngouakou-Ngouakou! Is it Papa Ngouakou-Ngouakou?' 'Yes, yes,' responded another part of the room. Some of the women danced in place while the babies they carried on their backs grimaced at being so rudely awakened from their naps.

3    The bodyguard ceremoniously removed the official shoulder sash from the speaker and carried off the folder in which was sandwiched the text of the speech Ngouakou-Ngouakou had just delivered. The excited crowd, given over to rejoicing, could not calm down.

4    At 8 p.m. Ngouakou-Ngouakou returned home. His house-boy hurried to relieve him of his briefcase. He threw himself into an arm chair.

5    'Bouka-Bouka, come say hello to Papa.'

6    The child climbed into his father's lap. Ngouakou-Ngouakou surveyed him proudly, his only son, his seventh child.

7    'Papa, you didn't buy me an Apollo XII.'

8    'What in the world is that?'

9    'Akpa has one. His father bought it for him.'

10    'Emilienne,' shouted Ngouakou-Ngouakou. 'Emilienne!'

11    'She is writing a paper for school,' called her mother from the kitchen.

12    'Writing? A paper? Writing won't teach her how to please her husband. Tell her to bring me my slippers.'

13    'Listen, Ngouakou-Ngouakou. Be a little more understanding of that poor child,' said her mother.

14    'Tell me, woman, since when do wives talk back to their husbands? Are you going to teach me how to bring up my daughter?'

'Here, Papa, here are your slippers,' said Bouka-Bouka. 15

'Thank you, son. At least you think of me. But this is really too much. 16
Are we men going to have to do the work around here now?'

'Emilienne!' 17

Emilienne arrived, all distraught. 18

'Well now, how many times must I call you?' 19

'I'm sorry, Papa. I didn't hear you.' 20

'Where were you?' 21

'In my room.' 22

'In your room? You must have been dreaming.' 23

'No, Papa, I was doing my maths homework.' 24

'Dreaming and mathematics don't go together. If you were studying 25
maths, you should have been paying attention. And when one pays
attention, one hears people call. Bring me some whiskey.'

Emilienne mechanically headed towards the cupboard. She was 26
dreaming of boarding school, and envying her friends who were far from
familial discipline. It must be nice to depend only on oneself. Parents!
They think they're acting for our benefit with all their rules. They don't
even see that we're judging them. Oh! The bottle is almost empty.
Emilienne searched in vain on all the shelves of the cupboard.

'How about my whiskey?' 27

'There isn't any more.' 28

'What? There isn't any more? I forbid you to play with your friends 29
for two days.'

'But Papa, it's not my fault.' 30

'You have to learn that when the bottle is only half full, it's time to go 31
and buy another one. Bring me a beer, then.'

He turned on the TV. Myriam Makeba was singing. Usually he 32
enjoyed listening to her, but that evening she got on his nerves. They
were showing the tape of her most recent concert in the city. Ngouakou-
Ngouakou knew it by heart, since it was broadcast at least twice a week.
When the TV producers run out of ideas for shows, they fall back on
something they have on hand, even if the public has already seen it a
hundred times. Ngouakou-Ngouakou was bored. He checked his watch.

'When can we eat?' 33

'In five minutes,' answered his wife from the kitchen. 34

'I'm hungry.' 35

'The rice isn't quite ready yet.' 36

'It's always the same story. Nothing is ever ready at the right time.' 37

Myriam Makeba was singing 'Malaïka'. Ngouakou-Ngouakou let 38
himself be carried away by the music this time. He liked beautiful songs.
Then the South African singer chose one in which she clicked her tongue
and danced, swaying her backside about like a boat on the waves.

'Dinner is ready,' called his wife. 39

Ngouakou-Ngouakou did not answer. 40

'Dinner! It's getting cold.' 41

Ngouakou-Ngouakou curbed his anger. He disliked being inter- 42 rupted when he was listening to music. He sat down at his place, facing the TV. Myriam continued to sing.

43    'Rice and meat with sauce again?'

44    'At this time of year there isn't much choice at the market.

45    'Not much choice? Isn't there any fish?'

46    'That must be the first time I ever heard you offer any suggestions about meals. It's a fine idea to vary the menu, but there are limits. In the morning when I ask you what you want for dinner, you grab your briefcase and dash off to the office.'

47    'That's the last straw! Don't you think I have enough to handle without having to think about meals on top of it all? You don't go off to work in an office. I'm the one who brings in the money.'

48    'I would gladly change places.'

49    'What I do isn't woman's work. I know many women who dream of being in your place, of having a husband who provides the latest model gas stove, a refrigerator, money . . .'

50    'Money? With the money you give me every week I have to rack my brain to feed a large family like ours.'

51    'Obviously you're not the one earning the money!'
The newscaster began presenting the national news.

52    'Shut up all of you so I can hear!'

'Today marked the opening of the conference sponsored by the National Federation of Radical Women. Several speakers were on the day's roster. This is the second conference of the Federation since its inception. Those present included delegations invited from neighbouring African countries and from friendly countries in Europe, America and Asia.'

53    Ngouakou-Ngouakou was furious. 'Tomorrow I'll speak with the Minister of Information about punishing the newscaster. He didn't even mention my speech.' Ngouakou-Ngouakou pushed away his plate.

54    'I'm not hungry anymore.'

55    The newscaster spoke about the war in Nigeria. Ngouakou-Ngouakou lit a cigarette, thinking how they always seemed to repeat the same things about the war.

56    'How about the girls? Can't they help you with the cooking and housework? Marcelline, how about you?'

57    'But Papa, I have a lot of work.'

58    'Don't forget you're a woman. A woman's most important work is to keep house.'

59    'Be a little more understanding,' cautioned her mother. 'You know perfectly well that Marcelline is in her last year at school and is preparing for her exams so she can receive her diploma.'

60    'Do you think a diploma will help her keep her husband at home? Good food will help, yes, and something else too.'

'You could at least be more discrete in what you say.'        61

'Oh Papa,' cried Bouka-Bouka, 'Look!' Featured on the television        62
were young Biafran children. They looked like fat-bellied skeletons. The
whole family fell silent.

'Why are those children so ugly?'        63

'It's not their fault,' corrected his mother.        64

Ngouakou-Ngouakou stood up and went to his room. Whistling, he        65
threw his clothes on to the bed. His wife would tidy up after him. He
pulled up a pair of light grey trousers, and a short, loose-fitting, bright-
coloured shirt decorated with gold braiding on the sleeves, pockets and
collar. He looked at himself in the mirror. He looked younger. He lit a
cigarette and went out into the night, whistling.

* * *

The Peek-a-Boo bar is located on the outskirts of the city, on an unlit        66
street. The bar itself, though, has electricity. This came about because the
owner, Marguerita, is a remarkably beautiful young widow with regular
features, well-formed breasts peeping out from behind her camisole, and
long fawn-like legs that are difficult to ignore when she wears her
tight-fitting dresses and high-heeled shoes. Some mistake her for a
mulatto, but those who have known her since birth say that her skin tint
has lightened considerably since certain American products have been
for sale in the Congo. Marguerita is very popular. And since she is unable
to satisfy everyone at once, she has cousins living with her, cousins
almost as beautiful as she is. Whenever a high-level official brings a
group of visiting dignitaries to the Peek-a-Boo Bar, he flaunts his pro-
wess by arranging for them to dance cheek to cheek with Marguerita. At
about one in the morning he whispers in her ear and goes off to 'make it'
with her while her cousins 'make it' with foreign dignitaries. In exchange
for these favours, Marguerita obtains what she wants. Two months of
constant attention to the Minister of Energy resulted in the installation of
electricity in her bar.

Marie-Therese had taken a taxi to reach that part of the city. She        67
hesitated a moment before entering the bar. The electricity, used mostly
to power the record player, hardly lit the room. The light bulbs were all
painted red so that only red shadows were distinguishable moving about
or seated at the bar. The room was divided into small compartments,
separated by bamboo partitions. People seated in these compartments
were protected from unwelcome glances. Marie-Therese chose one and
sat down on a small, low, willow bench. Marguerita had seen her and
signalled to one of her cousins who went over to the new customer,
shuffling her feet.

'No thank you, nothing for the moment. I'm waiting for someone.'        68

When the cousin returned to the bar, a man who had been seated on        69
a high stool grabbed her around the waist and led her off to dance the
rumba. The cousin immediately lost her indifference. The two, pelvis to

pelvis, moved with large, circular rubbing movements. They have nothing left to hide from each other, thought Marie-Therese. If the lights weren't so dim we would surely see that their eyes are closed. Marie-Therese felt embarrassed by the display.

70    When the dance ended, the man returned to the bar and flirted laughingly with all the cousins. As the next dance began, he approached Marie-Therese. His self-assurance and beautiful eyes seemed to paralyse her.

71    'No thank you.'

72    'Do you find me so unattractive?'

73    '. . .'

74    She turned her head away and just at that moment Ngouakou-Ngouakou entered.

75    'Oh, excuse me, Representative, Sir. Excuse me . . . I didn't know . . .'

76    Ngouakou-Ngouakou said nothing. He turned away, sat down and mumbled to himself: 'It's that little idiot Bwala. He'll find out who he's talking to.'

77    The cousin returned. She joked informally with the esteemed representative for a few minutes. They knew each other well. The Honourable Representative Ngouakou-Ngouakou is one of the humblest men in the world. He is a child of the proletariat and has no fear of renewing his relations with the masses. He ordered drinks. When the waitress returned with the order and the politician started to pay, she told him that it had already been taken care of by the man at the bar.

78    A *pachanga* was playing and Marie-Therese wanted to dance. Since no one else was on the floor, everyone at the bar watched as she danced with Ngouakou-Ngouakou, and they smiled. They smiled to see a young girl show off her youth through every movement of her hips, legs and shoulders as she moved to the music, smiling wholesomely. Were they also smiling tenderly at the fifty-year old man whose baldness and paunch did not inhibit his nimble movement? The man at the bar could not resist remarking:

79    'Yes, sister, that's Africa for you! Our negritude, our blackness. Our's is the civilization of the dance.'

80    But the dancing couple took no notice of their audience at the bar. They were too engrossed in each other.

81    After three dances, Ngouakou-Ngouakou wanted to leave.

82    'Already!' she asked. 'But it's so nice here.'

83    'It'll be nicer somewhere else.' He took her by the arm, helped her up, and disappeared with her into the dark night.

* * *

84    In front of the Hotel Relais, Ngouakou-Ngouakou repeated to Marie-Therese:

85    'I had my secretary reserve a room in the name of Miss Baker. Go to

the reception desk, and ask for the key. Wait for me in the room. I'll join you there in fifteen minutes.'

As she turned out the light, Marie-Therese felt herself engulfed by   86
strong, well-muscled arms. The hair on her arms intermingled with her partner's. He was panting already. It was always like that with him. He didn't caress her, but preferred to enter her immediately. She could not help crying out, from the depths of her throat, as if in pain.

'Am I hurting you?'   87

'No, just the opposite.'   88

Her nails dug into his flesh. She felt his large muzzle move across her   89
face. She could no longer speak, but only pant, 'yes, yes,' and other things she could not make out herself. It always took him a long time, longer than the young men. She liked that. She knew she was damned. But so what. She vibrated, she lived, she was free.

Four times that night she whimpered and cried out, before finally   90
falling asleep. Each time she repeated:

'Oh, it feels so good! You're pitiless to satisfy me like that.'   91

She dreamed that Ngouakou-Ngouakou came to pick her up in a   92
large, fancy American car. Dressed in black, she was elated. He told her that his wife was dead. He had come directly from the funeral to fetch her and take her abroad. She hardly dared believe it. She wanted to pack some *pagnes** and dresses to take along but Ngouakou-Ngouakou warned her not to waste time.

After helping her into the car, Ngouakou-Ngouakou sped to the   93
airport. Along the way she saw many familiar faces in the street. Despite the speed of the car, she distinctly heard them condemning her for taking an old man away from his children and accusing her of having killed Mrs Ngouakou-Ngouakou. Marie-Therese was dripping with sweat by the time they reached the airport. There was no room on the plane so they were put in the cockpit. Ngouakou-Ngouakou took command of the controls and started the engines. The plane moved along the runway but did not manage to get more than ten feet off the ground. It seemed as if the black dog which had been following Marie-Therese would manage to jump into the plane.

Marie-Therese woke up and saw Ngouakou-Ngouakou already   94
dressed.

'I must leave now.'   95

She reached out to him and smiled. He sat on the edge of the bed,   96
kissed her on the forehead and said: 'I have to go.'

'But I have something to tell you.'   97

'You're just looking for a way to keep me here with you.'   98

'No, it's important.' She took the man's hand and placed it on her   99
belly under the sheet.

'I think I'm carrying your child.'   100

*Cloth worn wrapped about the body. The traditional dress of African women.

101     'What? You're joking!'

102     'No, it's true.'

103     'What proof do you have that it's mine?'

104     Marie-Therese turned on her stomach, buried her head in the pillow, bit and bit it, and started to cry. She beat the bed with her fists and kicked her feet.

105     'What's wrong, honey?'

106     'Bastard, you bastard! Get out of here. Bastard, bastard, bastard . . .'

* * *

107     The sun poked its head over the horizon, and climbed slowly in the sky, promising a hot day. Shining through the windows, the daylight awakened Miss Ngouakou-Ngouakou. As was her custom every morning, she turned on the radio to keep herself from falling back to sleep. She listened to the national news.

> 'Yesterday Representative Ngouakou-Ngouakou presented a keynote address at the opening session of the Radical Women's Federation Conference. In his speech he stressed the need to liberate our women, who are not inferior beings but are men's equals.'

## Evaluating the Text

1. What attitude does Representative Ngouakou-Ngouakou's political speech convey toward the underprivileged in general, and women, in particular?
2. How do Ngouakou-Ngouakou's exchanges with his wife and daughters reveal an underlying male chauvinist attitude? For example, despite his public rhetoric, what views does he express in private about the value of education to women? What does he think is the most important quality a woman should have?
3. What does Ngouakou-Ngouakou's initial reaction to discovering that the newscaster didn't report his speech reveal about his character?
4. How does Lopes construct the unfolding action of the story using the principle of ironic juxtaposition? For instance, how are Ngouakou-Ngouakou's activities in the first scene contrasted with the different side of his personality he reveals to his wife and daughters?
5. How does Ngouakou-Ngouakou's relationship with his mistress at the Peek-a-Boo bar illustrate his hypocrisy?
6. How does the revelation that Ngouakou-Ngouakou's mistress has discovered she is pregnant suggest that Ngouakou-Ngouakou's private life will now become public?
7. How does Lopes use the colors red and black to underscore the importance of certain themes?
8. How would you characterize Lopes's literary style? What are the main techniques he relies on, and how effective are they in conveying the story?
9. How do you think Lopes, a former Prime Minister of the Congo, feels about Ngouakou-Ngouakou and the events in "The Esteemed Representative"? What words or phrases suggest his attitude?
10. Why is the final image of the story ironic?

## Exploring Different Perspectives

1. What similarities can you discern between the life of Ngouakou-Ngouakou's wife and that of the married woman described by Simone de Beauvoir ("The Married Woman")?
2. Compare and contrast the relationships in this story with the depiction of comparable relationships in Margaret Atwood's "Happy Endings." What cultural factors are operating in Lopes's account that are missing from Atwood's "choices"?
3. Compare the treatment Nisa receives from her father and from Tashay (in Marjorie Shostak's "Memories of a !Kung Girlhood") with Ngouakou-Ngouakou's treatment of his wife and daughters in this story. What conclusions can you draw about the treatment of women in tribal versus urban cultures, keeping in mind that both take place in African states?

## Extending Viewpoints through Writing

1. Describe the most blatant example of hypocrisy you have ever encountered. Give details that illuminate the difference between what was thought to be the case and what was really the case.
2. Create a character sketch of a male chauvinist. Do you know anyone who might serve as an example? If so, describe him.
3. Lopes's use of a limited range of colors including red and black in his descriptions influences the reader's perception of the scenes in his story. Describe a place where you hang out, only using two or three colors to describe everything you see. How does limiting yourself to only these colors change the scene?

# David K. Shipler

# *The Sin of Love*

---

*David K. Shipler was born in Orange, New Jersey, in 1942, educated
at Dartmouth, and has been with the* New York Times *since 1966,
reporting from Saigon and Moscow before serving as Jerusalem Bureau
Chief from 1979 to 1984. In 1982, he was the co-recipient of the
George Polk Award for his coverage of the war in Vietnam. His books
include* Russia: Broken Idols, Solemn Dreams *(1983) and* Arab and
Jew: Wounded Spirits in a Promised Land, *for which he received
the 1986 Pulitzer Prize. "The Sin of Love" is taken from this incisive
analysis of relationships between Arabs and Jews in Israel and surrounding territories. In 1987, he became the Chief Diplomatic Correspondent for the* New York Times.

*Israel is a republic in the Middle East, previously part of Palestine,
a historic region on the eastern shore of the Mediterranean sea, made
up of parts of modern Israel, Jordan, and Egypt. Palestine is also
known as the Holy Land because it encompasses areas that are sacred
for Jews, Christians, and Muslims. In November 1947, the United
Nations divided Palestine, then under British mandate, into Jewish
and Arab states. After the British withdrew six months later, the State
of Israel was proclaimed on May 14, 1948. Lebanon, Jordan, Egypt,
and Iraq rejected the partition of Palestine and the existence of Israel
and began the first of a series of wars, including the 1956 Sinai
campaign, the 1967 Six Day War, and the 1973 Yom Kipper War, from
which Israel emerged victorious with additional territories. After a
peace treaty between Israel and Egypt was signed in 1978, Israel
returned the Sinai peninsula to Egypt. Thus far, the fate of the Gaza
strip and the West Bank of Jordan have remained unresolved. Both the
Israelis and the Arabs claim land in Palestine as theirs by ancestral
rights. Israel's sporadic yet violent conflicts with the Palestine Liberation Organization (PLO)—which, under Yasir Arafat, is committed to
establishing a Palestinian state by reclaiming land now occupied by
Israel—led to an Israeli invasion of Lebanon in 1982. In 1987, a
Palestinian uprising (intifada), protesting Israel's occupation of the
West Bank, focused the world's attention on a conflict that shows no
signs of abating. Since late 1990, the unprecedented immigration of
nearly a million Soviet Jews has strained the resources of this small
country of 4.4 million to the breaking point. Settlement of these new
immigrants in the Occupied Territories (the West Bank and Gaza) has*

*made it even more difficult to resolve the conflict between Jews and Palestinian Arabs.*

In October 1983, Israel Radio broadcast a remarkable interview with    1
a twenty-eight-year-old Arab woman who had lived with a right-wing Jew. Her love and misery came spilling out in a bitter torrent of grief and anger. She did not give her name as she spoke in Hebrew, but the agony in her voice, the fury of her words, sketched a sharp portrait of despair.

He was "an ardent Likudnik," a supporter of Begin's rightist Likud    2
Bloc, who "talked about slaughtering the Arabs," she said. "I was for a Palestinian state; he was against." During competing demonstrations at Hebrew University, he dragged her from the lawn by the hair. "Later, he saw me a few times in the student lounge, and he started to get interested. . . . So, he started to run after me for political discussions, right? Not really romantic dates. And after that he started to come over, to drink coffee, coffee with cardamom — son of a Polish family — and he started to tell me what hurt him, why he hated Arabs, because he simply hated. Why did he hate? His brother was killed in a war. I said, 'I'm very sorry about that, but it wasn't I, it wasn't I who started the war. I, I am just I,'" and she laughed. "And fine, dates here, dates there. As in everything, nature did its work — we fell in love." She sighed. "He fell in love with the Palestinian whom he yelled against in demonstrations, and I with the ardent Likudnik who appropriates lands. And it developed and it was great. We lived together and got along wonderfully. We didn't discuss politics. We always tried to ignore it; that's why we didn't have a television in the house either, so as not to watch the news and start to fight.

"My fellow Palestinian students ostracized me. They called me a    3
whore because I socialized with Jews and probably thought I was sleeping with most of them. One day his friends organized with a bunch of Arab students — first time they had the same opinions, for a change — and they simply decided to get tough with the boy. The blows came down on him, and they knocked out his teeth. And he suffered, there's no doubt. And I suffered. His parents, I would go visit them a lot; they really loved me; they accepted me even though they knew I was an Arab. And it hurt them, the picture of his brother sitting there in the room. I understand them, right? True, I wasn't the one who killed him, they know, but they didn't want their son to marry a Palestinian. After his parents kicked us out of the house, we decided to go to the other side, to return to the [occupied] territories. My parents went through the shock of their lives. They knew I had such a boyfriend. They had seen him a few times. He was very nice, they said; he was very nice but too bad he was Jewish. He came from a very rich family, enlightened, a great guy, the kind you don't see every day. He was also very handsome, blue eyes. And my parents, he came to them and said, 'Cards on the table. Listen, I want her.' My father got stubborn, my mother got stubborn: 'No way,

no. Our daughter isn't marrying you.' So he started up with all kinds of ideas. We'll run away, we'll go. I had to be the realistic one. What will we live on? What will we do? Where will we go?" Again she sighed a long, deep sigh.

4        "We decided to end the story. We tried, it didn't work. We tried again, it didn't work. We both really tried to fight our feelings. My parents saw I was having a hard time. It hurt them a lot. But they simply told me, 'That's it. Leave him.'"

5        She began to have such psychological problems that she went into a mental hospital for six months. "For half a year they didn't let me see him. He would come, but they wouldn't let me see him, and apparently it worked. It sounds cruel, but it worked. And he, he ended up nowhere else but a yeshiva in Jerusalem; he became a *baal teshuvah*," a secular Jew who finds extreme orthodoxy, like a born-again Christian. "I run into him once in a while in the city. He doesn't speak to me because he's religious and I'm a woman, and when he looks at me I see the tears in his eyes. And he says to me, 'You haven't forgotten?' And I say, 'No, it's impossible.' He hasn't married yet, and every time I see him I'm torn apart again for a week. It sounds a little like an Arab movie on Friday or a soap opera, but that's what was. It still hurts. It's impossible to forget two years like that. And even now it's hard to find a fitting husband. He was the man I would have liked to dedicate my whole life to. And I lost him. Why? I don't know. Whom to blame? I don't know. I'm one big question mark, and I think I'll be left with this question mark until the grave. There's nothing to do. It is the state of Israel, it is the Middle East, it is all the problems between the Jews and the Arabs. There's nothing to do about it. It begins in politics and ends there. When it reaches the personal level, there, too, it's impossible to disconnect the politics. He, the boy I loved, his brother was killed in the war, his picture is on the wall, and there's nothing to do about it. I remember that at one point I used to wash his reserve uniforms so that he could wear them to some Sabra and Shatila out there. If he had taken part in what was done there, I wouldn't have been able to live with it, I wouldn't have been able to look him in the face, I wouldn't have been able to bear his children and cook him food when he was hungry. I wouldn't have been able to live with it. Despite everything, I am Palestinian. Despite everything, he is a Jew.

6        "I don't know if it would have been good," she went on. "I don't know. But with an Arab boy it definitely won't work. Now I'm twenty-eight. I know that for an Arab boy, my stock has gone down. He can be crazy for me; his family won't go along with it. I understand why Jewish society acts as it does; I understand why the Arab mentality is as it is. I understand why my parents are as they are. I even understand why *I* am as I am. But where do I end up in all this story? I get lost."

## Evaluating the Text

1. What differences in political beliefs and ideologies separate the couple? What would be some of the issues on which they would disagree?

2. How did the couple's relationship require them to try to block out the rest of the world, to stay together?
3. How do you explain the difference in the way the girl was treated by her friends and family on one hand and by her boyfriend's family and friends, on the other?
4. What insight does Shipler provide as to why their two-year relationship became threatening to their families and friends?
5. What cultural assumptions did their relationship challenge? Why was it preferable for them to break up than to reexamine these assumptions? How could the stress of being rejected lead the girl to suffer a mental breakdown?
6. Why do you suppose Shipler chose to report on what happened to this one particular couple? Discuss how they might be considered a symbol of the dilemma facing all Arabs and Israelis.
7. Why do you think the Israeli man, after he and the girl broke up, became an Orthodox Jew—which he was not before he met her?
8. How does the reference to the attack of the Israeli army on Palestinians at Sabra and Shatila dramatize the kind of situation that would have made it impossible for them to get married and live together all their lives?
9. Why has the girl's "stock" gone down as a result of this relationship to the point where she is no longer accepted by the Arab community and now cannot hope to find an Arab husband?

## Exploring Different Perspectives

1. How does Shipler's account illustrate Marilyn French's assertion (in "Gender Roles") that societal structures are built on abstract principles of "restriction, intolerance and hatred," whereas personal relationships are built on connections?
2. How does the political realm impinge on personal relationships in this account and in Henri Lopes's story ("The Esteemed Representative")? Compare the attitudes of Shipler and Lopes toward the pressure of politics on people's lives and relationships.

## Extending Viewpoints through Writing

1. Have you ever been romantically involved with someone from a completely different ethnic, racial, religious, or political background? Describe your experiences, and discuss the kinds of pressures from family and friends to which you were subjected. What was the eventual outcome of this relationship?
2. Discuss how one can love another person while hating the group to which that person belongs. What psychological processes make this possible?

# Margaret Atwood

# *Happy Endings*

---

*Margaret Atwood was born in Ottawa, Canada, in 1939. She received her B.A. from Victoria College in 1961, the year in which she was also awarded the E. J. Cratt Medal for Poetry for* Double Persephone. *She is the author of more than twenty acclaimed volumes of poetry and fiction, including* Surfacing *(1972),* Bodily Harm *(1982), and* The Handmaid's Tale *(1986), a much discussed work that won the Los Angeles Times Book Award and was subsequently made into a 1989 movie. Her most recent novel is the best seller* Cat's Eye *(1989). "Happy Endings," a gleeful dissection of narrative mutations, first appeared in* Ms. *magazine, February 1983.*

*Canada is the world's largest country, after the Soviet Union. It is bordered by the Atlantic, Pacific, and Arctic Oceans and meets the United States to the south at what is the longest unguarded border in the world. The French were the first Europeans to explore Canada, giving the country its name (from* kanata, *the Huron-Iroquois word for settlement) and established Quebec City and Montreal in the 1600s. Commercial interests in North America prompted Britain to gain control of Nova Scotia, Newfoundland, and the Hudson Bay region in the early 1700s. Although control of French Canada was won by the British, French residents were granted rights to their own language, religion, and civil law under the Quebec Act of 1774. The British North America Act of 1867 created a self-governing Dominion of Canada comprising various British colonies, which gradually attained autonomy within the British Empire. In 1982, Canada gained complete legislative independence. Concurrently, a growing French Separatist Movement has sought independence or sovereignty for the province of Quebec. Recently, the United States' relationship with Canada has been strained by conflicts over how to control acid rain pollution of the forests, lakes, and wildlife in both countries.*

1    John and Mary meet.
2    What happens next?
3    If you want a happy ending, try A.

   A.   John and Mary fall in love and get married. They both have
        worthwhile and remunerative jobs which they find stimulating
        and challenging. They buy a charming house. Real estate values

go up. Eventually, when they can afford live-in help, they have two children, to whom they are devoted. The children turn out well. John and Mary have a stimulating and challenging sex life and worthwhile friends. They go on fun vacations together. They retire. They both have hobbies which they find stimulating and challenging. Eventually they die. This is the end of the story.

B. Mary falls in love with John but John doesn't fall in love with Mary. He merely uses her body for selfish pleasure and ego gratification of a tepid kind. He comes to her apartment twice a week and she cooks him dinner, you'll notice that he doesn't even consider her worth the price of a dinner out, and after he's eaten the dinner he fucks her and after that he falls asleep, while she does the dishes so he won't think she's untidy, having all those dirty dishes lying around, and puts on fresh lipstick so she'll look good when he wakes up, but when he wakes up he doesn't even notice, he puts on his socks and his shorts and his pants and his shirt and his tie and his shoes, the reverse order from the one in which he took them off. He doesn't take off Mary's clothes, she takes them off herself, she acts as if she's dying for it every time, not because she likes sex exactly, she doesn't, but she wants John to think she does because if they do it often enough surely he'll get used to her, he'll come to depend on her and they will get married, but John goes out the door with hardly so much as a good-night and three days later he turns up at six o'clock and they do the whole thing over again.

Mary gets run-down. Crying is bad for your face, everyone knows that and so does Mary but she can't stop. People at work notice. Her friends tell her John is a rat, a pig, a dog, he isn't good enough for her, but she can't believe it. Inside John, she thinks, is another John, who is much nicer. This other John will emerge like a butterfly from a cocoon, a Jack from a box, a pit from a prune, if the first John is only squeezed enough.

One evening John complains about the food. He has never complained about the food before. Mary is hurt.

Her friends tell her they've seen him in a restaurant with another woman, whose name is Madge. It's not even Madge that finally gets to Mary: it's the restaurant. John has never taken Mary to a restaurant. Mary collects all the sleeping pills and aspirins she can find, and takes them and a half a bottle of sherry. You can see what kind of a woman she is by the fact that it's not even whiskey. She leaves a note for John. She hopes he'll discover her and get her to the hospital in time and repent and then they can get married, but this fails to happen and she dies.

John marries Madge and everything continues as in A.

C. John, who is an older man, falls in love with Mary, and Mary, who is only twenty-two, feels sorry for him because he's worried about his hair falling out. She sleeps with him even though she's not in love with him. She met him at work. She's in love with someone called James, who is twenty-two also and not yet ready to settle down.

John on the contrary settled down long ago: this is what is bothering him. John has a steady, respectable job and is getting ahead in his field, but Mary isn't impressed by him, she's impressed by James, who has a motorcycle and a fabulous record collection. But James is often away on his motorcycle, being free. Freedom isn't the same for girls, so in the meantime Mary spends Thursday evenings with John. Thursdays are the only days John can get away.

John is married to a woman called Madge and they have two children, a charming house which they bought just before the real estate values went up, and hobbies which they find stimulating and challenging, when they have the time. John tells Mary how important she is to him, but of course he can't leave his wife because a commitment is a commitment. He goes on about this more than is necessary and Mary finds it boring, but older men can keep it up longer so on the whole she has a fairly good time.

One day James breezes in on his motorcycle with some top-grade California hybrid and James and Mary get higher than you'd believe possible and they climb into bed. Everything becomes very underwater, but along comes John, who has a key to Mary's apartment. He finds them stoned and entwined. He's hardly in any position to be jealous, considering Madge, but nevertheless he's overcome with despair. Finally he's middle-aged, in two years he'll be bald as an egg and he can't stand it. He purchases a handgun, saying he needs it for target practice —this is the thin part of the plot, but it can be dealt with later — and shoots the two of them and himself.

Madge, after a suitable period of mourning, marries an understanding man called Fred and everything continues as in A, but under different names.

D.   Fred and Madge have no problems. They get along exceptionally well and are good at working out any little difficulties that may arise. But their charming house is by the seashore and one day a giant tidal wave approaches. Real estate values go down. The rest of the story is about what caused the tidal wave and how they escape from it. They do, though thousands drown, but Fred and Madge are virtuous and lucky. Finally on high ground they clasp each other, wet and dripping and grateful, and continue as in A.

E.   Yes, but Fred has a bad heart. The rest of the story is about how kind and understanding they both are until Fred dies. Then Madge devotes herself to charity work until the end of A. If you like, it can be "Madge," "cancer," "guilty and confused," and "bird watching."

F.  If you think this is all too bourgeois, make John a revolutionary and Mary a counterespionage agent and see how far that gets you. Remember, this is Canada. You'll still end up with A, though in between you may get a lustful brawling saga of passionate involvement, a chronicle of our times, sort of.

You'll have to face it, the endings are the same however you slice it. Don't be deluded by any other endings, they're all fake, either deliberately fake, with malicious intent to deceive, or just motivated by excessive optimism if not by downright sentimentality.

The only authentic ending is the one provided here:                    4

*John and Mary die. John and Mary die. John and Mary die.*

So much for endings. Beginnings are always more fun. True connoisseurs, however, are known to favor the stretch in between, since it's the hardest to do anything with.

That's about all that can be said for plots, which anyway are just one       5
thing after another, a what and a what and a what.

Now try How and Why.                                                6

## Evaluating the Text

1.  In what way does choice A illustrate the conventional happy ending? How does the use of the same superficial phrase ("stimulating and challenging") to describe their sex life and their hobbies call into question the extent to which they really are leading a satisfying life?

2.  How does choice B illustrate an entirely different kind of relationship in which Mary's low self-esteem leads her to bet her life? How is she wrong about what kind of a person John is and how he really feels about her?

3.  How does the language describing choice B differ from the euphemistic language used in choice A? What does Mary's choice of sherry versus whiskey tell you about her? In your opinion, why doesn't Madge let John get away with the kind of abuse that Mary lets him get away with? How is John's behavior in each case directly related to each woman's view of herself?

4.  How is the Mary described in choice C different from the Mary described in choice B? In what way does the John of choice C need Mary and depend on her in the same way that Mary of choice B needs John? How is the response of John in choice C similar to Mary's response in choice B?

5.  How is the tone Atwood uses in describing Fred and Madge in choice D different from the tone she adopts in Choice A? What explains this difference in tone?

6.  What ironic conclusions do you draw about life in Canada from Atwood's comments about the kinds of books (lustful, brawling sagas) that are usually written about it? How does Atwood suggest that life in Canada is really quite boring, staid, and conventional (choice A, as Atwood says)?

7.  In what way is showing the "why" and "how" of a story much more

difficult for a writer than simply stating "what" happens? How do the preceding scenarios illustrate this point?

8. How does each of the scenarios Atwood presents rely on the assumption that in fiction as in life, people make choices based on a balance between security that quickly becomes predictable and boring and excitement that can easily become dangerous?

## Exploring Different Perspectives

1. Analyze either Henri Lopes's "The Esteemed Representative" or Talat Abbasi's "Facing the Light" according to the narrative expectations described by Atwood.
2. Which choices of Atwood's seem to reflect the gender stereotyping of roles discussed by Marilyn French in "Gender Roles"?
3. Which of the choices in "Happy Endings" describe most closely the situation in David K. Shipler's "The Sin of Love"? Where does the conflict come from, and how is it resolved?

## Extending Viewpoints through Writing

1. Describe your own expectations about what constitutes a good story. To what extent do you want a story that will surprise you with different plot developments while at the same time provide a certain predictability? What are some of your favorite works of fiction, and how do they illustrate the characteristic pattern of rising conflicts leading to resolution that Atwood describes?
2. Have you ever been involved in a turbulent relationship? Compare this to a relationship you had that was more stable but not as exciting. Which kind do you prefer for the long-term and why?
3. How are the competing needs people have for security (which can become boring) and surprise (which can become dangerous) reflected in the personal ads singles write to attract other people into their lives? Analyze the wording of some of these ads to show which phrases are keyed to stability and which are keyed to excitement. How might each of these ads be considered the basis for a miniature scenario? Take any one of them and write out a "choice" or two, showing what happens to the writer of the ad and the respondent. You might also wish to write your own personal ad.

# CONNECTING CULTURES

## Marilyn French, "Gender Roles"

1. How does French's discussion of "manliness" illuminate the learned nature of the male sex role as reflected in Henry Allen's description of Marine boot camp in "The Corps" (Chapter 2)?
2. How do Western gender expectations described by French differ from those depicted in Maasai society as described by Tepilit Ole Saitoti ("The Initiation of a Maasai Warrior," Chapter 2)?
3. In what way does Beryl Markham's ("West with the Night," Chapter 4) achievement deviate from traditional gender expectations described by French?
4. To what extent does John Burgess's picture of the Japanese "salaryman" ("A Day in the Life of 'Salaryman'," Chapter 4) confirm French's portrayal of male societal roles?
5. In what way does Bruce Dollar's discussion ("Child Care in China," Chapter 1) of the role of "multiple mothering" in China support French's thesis about the lack of evidence for an innate instinct of mothering? How does the case in China reveal a culturally defined idea of motherhood different from that of the West?

## Clifford Geertz, "Of Cocks and Men"

6. Compare Geertz's analysis with Pico Iyer's commentary in "Perfect Strangers" (Chapter 8) to discover how the games in each society reflect each culture's values, respectively.

## Talat Abbasi, "Facing the Light"

7. Compare and contrast the relationship between the wife and husband in Abbasi's story with the couple Krishnan Varma describes in "The Grass-Eaters" (Chapter 5). What factors might explain why the couple in Varma's story, although they have so little, stay together?
8. What might you infer about the status of women in Pakistan from Abbasi's story that is similar to the predicament of women in Middle Eastern societies described by Nawal El Saadawi ("Circumcision of Girls," Chapter 2)?

## Marjorie Shostak, "Memories of a !Kung Girlhood"

9. How are the courtship experiences of Tepilit Ole Saitoti ("The Initiation of a Maasai Warrior," Chapter 2) in Kenya and Nisa in Botswana strikingly similar to the experiences of their American counterparts?
10. How do Nisa's experiences and those of Tepilit Ole Saitoti ("The Initiation

of a Maasai Warrior," Chapter 2) give you insight into the role initiation rituals play within each culture as rites of passage into womanhood and manhood, respectively?

11. Compare Shostak's report with Bessie Head's story "Looking for a Rain God" (Chapter 8). How does each work illuminate the other by showing a range of reactions to the same condition—drought—in Botswana?

## Simone de Beauvoir, "The Married Woman"

12. Compare Andrew Cherlin and Frank F. Furstenberg, Jr's., analysis ("The American Family in the Year 2000," Chapter 1) of the ways in which family life is changing with the description that de Beauvoir gives of the traditional tasks of the married woman. To what extent have the conditions de Beauvoir observed already changed?

13. To what extent do the households described by William Trevor in "Teresa's Wedding" (Chapter 1) conform to de Beauvoir's characterization of "the married woman"?

14. How does Raymonde Carroll's ("Minor Accidents," Chapter 8) discussion of the kinds of problems facing modern French women suggest the enormous changes in the lives of women in France between 1949 when de Beauvoir published *The Second Sex* and the present?

15. To what extent does de Beauvoir's description of the constraints limiting women in France more than forty years ago reveal restrictions on women's lives similar to those explored by Kyōko Hayashi ("The Empty Can," Chapter 9) in contemporary Japan?

## Henri Lopes, "The Esteemed Representative"

16. Discuss male chauvinism in this story and in William Trevor's "Teresa's Wedding" (Chapter 1) and Francine du Plessix Gray's account ("Sex and Birth," Chapter 1). How do the cultural values of each society (the People's Republic of the Congo, rural Ireland, and the U.S.S.R.) produce distinct brands of male chauvinism?

17. Discuss similarities and differences in the techniques used by Lopes and Kate Wilhelm ("The Village," Chapter 9) to provide readers with insight into how a situation appears from different perspectives.

## David K. Shipler, "The Sin of Love"

18. Compare Toi Derricotte's account (from "The Black Notebooks," Chapter 5) illustrating how racial antagonism from the community can disrupt a marriage with Shipler's examination of how religious divisions can destroy a personal relationship.

19. How is the lack of a common meeting ground illustrated in both Jan Rabie's story "Drought" (Chapter 6) and Shipler's account? Does Rabie's definition of the problem in terms of a parable or allegory add a level of understanding missing from Shipler's report?

# Margaret Atwood, "Happy Endings"

20. Drawing on Atwood's analysis of how stories must meet readers'
expectations in providing a sense of stability, punctuated by excitement,
analyze any of the following stories identifying (1) the initial situation, (2)
how a conflict threatening stability develops, (3) the crisis after which
things could never be the same, and (4) the resolution describing the
aftermath: "Teresa's Wedding" (Chapter 1, William Trevor), "Jing-Mei
Woo: Two Kinds" (Chapter 1, Amy Tan), "Famous All Over Town"
(Chapter 2, Danny Santiago), "A Handful of Dates" (Chapter 2, Tayeb
Salih), "Facing the Light" (Chapter 3, Talat Abbasi), "Paper" (Chapter 4,
Catherine Lim), and "The Falling Girl" (Chapter 5, Dino Buzzati). If you
wish, you might analyze a nonfiction work, such as that of Rigoberta
Menchu ("Birth Ceremonies," Chapter 1); Henry Allen ("The Corps,"
Chapter 2); Douchan Gersi ("Initiated into an Iban Tribe of Headhunters,"
Chapter 2); Christy Brown ("The Letter 'A'," Chapter 2); Tepilit Ole
Saitoti, ("The Initiation of a Maasai Warrior," Chapter 2); or Marjorie
Shostak ("Memories of a !Kung Girlhood," Chapter 3) and discuss the
extent to which nonfiction can embody expectations (of a situation in
which a conflict develops and is resolved) usually associated with fiction.

# 4

# *How Work Creates Identity*

The way we identify ourselves in terms of the work we do is far-reaching. Frequently, the first question we ask when we meet someone for the first time is "What do you do"? It is through work that we define ourselves and others. Yet cultural values also play a part in influencing how we feel about the work we do.

Gene Logsdon provides a fascinating glimpse into the communal approach to farming taken by the Amish in Ohio in "A Lesson for the Modern World: Amish Economics." By contrast, Catherine Lim's story "Paper" probes the consequence of individualism and greed against the backdrop of the turbulence of the Singapore stock exchange. A Korean immigrant, Cha Ok Kim, in "The Peddler," describes how his successful import–export business grew from years of peddling wigs on street corners. The British aviator, Beryl Markham, defines herself through her occupation, in this account, taken from her book, *West with the Night*, of how she became the first person to fly solo across the Atlantic from England to Nova Scotia. In Japan, the daily regimen of the prototypical office worker known as "salaryman" forms the basis of this interesting look behind the scenes by John Burgess (in "A Day in the Life of 'Salaryman'"). An American teacher in China, Mark Salzman, relates (in "Lessons") the unusual bargain he struck with the renowned martial arts master, Pan Qingfu, to exchange English lessons for instruction in the Chinese martial arts. A world away, in France, Daniel Boulanger creates an arresting tale ("The Shoe Breaker"), with overtones of social criticism, of a most unusual occupation.

# Gene Logsdon

# *Amish Economics*

*Gene Logsdon has been farming for over thirty years and raises corn, oats, wheat, hay, chickens, and sheep in Upper Sandusky, Ohio. He writes on a wide range of issues and provides unequalled insight into how the underlying values of Amish culture result in increased productivity, financial solvency, and a better way of life than that enjoyed by other farmers.*

*The Amish are a group of Protestants who, under the leadership of Jacob Ammann, broke away from the main body of Mennonites (who for a time were called the Swiss Brethren) in Europe during the seventeenth century. The Amish live with great simplicity, wear plain clothing, shun modern education, reject conveniences such as automobiles and radios, and refuse to hold public office or serve in the military. There are numerous Amish communities in Pennsylvania and Ohio. In Logsdon's account, we can observe some of the advantages of living in a close Amish community, farming for a living, and making do without modern conveniences such as telephones and tractor-drawn plows.*

The Amish have become a great embarrassment to American agriculture. Many "English" farmers, as the Amish call the rest of us, are in desperate financial straits these days and relatively few are making money. As a result it is fashionable among writers, the clergy, politicians, farm machinery dealers and troubled farm banks to depict the family farmer as a dying breed and to weep great globs of crocodile tears over the coming funeral. All of them seem to forget those small, conservatively-financed family farms that are doing quite well, thank you, of which the premium example is the Amish.

Amish farmers are still making money in these hard times despite (or rather because of) their supposedly outmoded, horse-farming ways. If one of them does get into financial jeopardy, it is most often from listening to the promises of modern agribusiness instead of traditional wisdom. His brethren will usually bail him out. More revealing, the Amish continue to farm profitably not only with an innocent disregard for get-big-or-get-out modern technology, but without participation in direct government subsidies other than those built into market prices, which they can't avoid.

I first learned about the startlingly effective economy of Amish life

211

when I was invited to a barn raising near Wooster, Ohio. A tornado had leveled four barns and acres of prime Amish timber. In just three weeks the downed trees were sawn into girders, posts, and beams and the four barns rebuilt and filled with livestock donated by neighbors to replace those killed by the storm. Three weeks. Nor were the barns the usual modern, one-story metal boxes hung on poles. They were huge buildings, three and four stories high, post-and-beam framed, and held together with hand-hewn mortises and tenons. I watched the raising of the last barn in open-mouthed awe. Some 400 Amish men and boys, acting and reacting like a hive of bees in absolute harmony of cooperation, started at sunrise with only a foundation and floor and by noon, *by noon,* had the huge edifice far enough along that you could put hay in it.

4          A contractor who was watching said it would have taken him and a beefed-up crew all summer to build the barn if, indeed, he could find anyone skilled enough at mortising to do it. He estimated the cost at $100,000. I asked the Amish farmer how much cash he would have in the barn. "About $30,000," he said. And some of that paid out by the Amish church's own insurance arrangements. "We give each other our labor," he explained. "We look forward to raisings. There are so many helping, no one has to work too hard. We get in a good visit." Not the biggest piece of the Rock imaginable carries that kind of insurance.

5          Not long afterwards, I gave a speech to an organization of farmers concerned with alternative methods of agriculture in which I commiserated at length with the plight of financially depressed farmers. When my talk was over, two Amish men approached me, offering mild criticism. "We have just finished one of our most financially successful years," one of them said. "It is only those farmers who have ignored common sense and tradition who are in trouble." What made his remarks more significant is that he went on to explain that he belonged to a group of Amish that had, as an experiment, temporarily allowed its members to use tractors in the field. He also was making payments on land that he had recently purchased. In other words, he was staring at the same economic gun that's pointed at English farmers and he was still coming out ahead. "But," he said, "I'm going back to horses. They're more profitable."

6          From then on, I resolved to start cultivating the Amish as assiduously as they cultivated their fields. I had always taken our sorghum to Joe Bontragger's press in the Kenton, Ohio area not far from our farm. We bought bulk foods and angelfood cake at the Peterscheims', and sought advice about operating a wood-working shop at Troyers', but now I expanded my horizons to include eastern Ohio, center of the largest Amish community in the world. When I helped a neighbor haul hay to that area, I received another lesson in Amish economics. If they need to buy extra feed for their livestock, they almost always choose to buy hay and raise the grain rather than vice versa. The price of the hay is partially regained as manure after it passes through the livestock since it allows them to cut down on the amount of fertilizer they need to buy. The

greater mass of hay generates a greater mass of manure, adding organic matter to the soil. That is valuable beyond computer calculation. Grain farmers in my area who sold their straw and hay to the Amish were trading their soil fertility for cash of flitting value.

Whenever I got to know an Amish farmer well enough, I asked about    7
farm profits. Always the answer was the same, spoken with careful modesty. Not as good as in the '70s, but still okay. I heard that in 1983, '84, and even '85, when finally the agribusiness magazines admitted that agriculture faced a fullblown crisis.

Eventually, or perhaps inevitably, I took my softball team to Holmes    8
County for a cow-pasture doubleheader with neighborhood Amish players organized by David Kline, Abe Troyer and Dennis Weaver, among others. It was a grand day. We were perhaps a run better than the Amish, but they were twice as adept at dodging piles of manure. Our collected "womenfolk" cheered from the shade. The Amish bishop watched from his buggy behind home plate, sorely tempted, I was told, to join the game but afraid it might seem a bit demeaning to some of his congregation. The games themselves taught two lessons in economy. First, our uniforms of blue and gold cost me more money than I care to talk about. The Amish players, with their traditional denims, broadcloth shirts and straw hats, are always in uniform. Second, some of our player/farmers could not take time off from their high-tech machines to play in the game. The Amish, with their slow, centuries-old methods, had plenty of time.

The games became prelude for discussions about Amish farm econ-    9
omy, since some of our players were farmers also. But long before these post-game discussions took place, Henry Hershberger taught me the deeper truth and wisdom of Amish economy. Hershberger is a bishop in the Schwartzentruber branch of the Amish, the strictest of the many sects. I went to visit Hershberger in 1983 because he had just gotten out of jail, which seemed to me a very curious place for an Amish bishop to be. Hershberger had been in jail because he would not apply for a building permit for his new house. Actually, he told me (in his new house), it was not the permit or building code regulations that got him in trouble with the law. He groped for the unfamiliar English words that would make the meaning clear. Most Amish can't meet certain requirements of the code because of religious convictions. But there is an understanding. The Amish buy the permit, then proceed to violate its rules on details, of lighting and plumbing or whatever, that their religion disallows. The authorities look the other way.

Hershberger had given that practice considerable thought. Not only    10
did it smack of dishonesty but, he realized with the wisdom of 400 years of Amish history that had survived more than one case of creeping totalitarianism, at any time the authorities could decide to enforce the letter of the law. This was particularly worrisome because it would mean greatly increased costs of construction, if indeed some way to get around

the religious problem were found. But more importantly, it could mean, with the way the permit business is being handled, that authorities might someday stop Amish from building more houses on their farms. So Hershberger refused to play the game. The bureaucracy was ready to accommodate Hershberger's religion since it is common knowledge that the Amish build excellent houses for themselves — they would be fools not to, of course — but for Hershberger not to offer token obeisance to bureaucracy was unforgivable. That might lead, heaven forbid, to other people questioning the sanctity of the law.

11     Taken to court, Hershberger was found guilty and given 30 days to pay up and get his permit. He refused. The judge, underestimating the resolve of a Schwartzentruber bishop, fined him $5,000. Hershberger refused to pay. The judge sent him to jail to work off his debt at $20 a day. A great public hue and cry arose. In two weeks Hershberger was set free, still owing the court $4,720. The sheriff was ordered to seize enough property to satisfy the debt. But local auctioneers said they would not cry the sale. No one would haul the livestock. The judge resigned (for other reasons, I was told). Henry Hershberger lives in his new house, at peace, at least for now.

12     The flood of letters in the Wooster paper over the event became a community examination of conscience. At first the debate centered on the question of "the law is the law" versus freedom of religion. But slowly the argument got down to the real issue of the permit law: Where does it lead? Who in fact is being protected? Henry Hershberger's contention that building permits can be used to keep housing out of certain areas if the powers on high want it that way is common knowledge: you just make the soil percolation requirement more rigid or start enforcing those already on the books. Nor do building codes guarantee good buildings, as every honest builder will tell you. Codes establish minimum standards which then become ceilings on quality, enabling minimum-standard builders to underbid high-standard builders, encouraging the latter to follow the minimum standards, too. Furthermore, building regulations are rather easily out-maneuvered, glossed over, and bribed away, if the rewards are high enough. Often building codes prevent people from building their own homes for lack of proper certification or a supposedly proper design. Building codes protect not the buyer but the builders, the suppliers of the approved materials, and an army of career regulators. The Amish understand all this. When a culture gives up the knowledge, ability and legality to build its own houses, the people pay. And pay.

13     But there are even more practical reasons why the Amish economy wants to retain control over its housing. First of all, the Amish home doubles as an Amish church. How many millions of dollars this saves the Amish would be hard to calculate. Amish belief wisely provides for the appointment of ministers by lot. No hierarchy can evolve in Amishland. A minister works his farm like everyone else. That is mainly why the

religion so effectively protects the Amish culture of agriculture. Its bishops do not sit in exceedingly well-insulated houses in far-off cities uttering pious pronouncements about the end of family farming.

Secondly, the Amish home doubles as the Amish retirement village    14
and nursing home, thereby saving incalculably more millions of dollars, not to mention the self-respect of the elderly. The Amish do not pay Social Security, nor do they accept it. They know and practice a much better security that requires neither pension nor lifelong savings.

There is an old Amish quiltmaker who lives near Pffeifer's Station, a    15
crossroads store and village I often frequent. Her immediate family is long gone and she lives now with somewhat distant relatives who, being nearest of kin, are pledged to care for her. Her quarters are a wee bit of a house connected to the main house by a covered walkway. I make up excuses to visit, pretending to be interested in quilts. I have no idea how old she is, other than ancient.

Around her I feel the kind of otherworldly peace I used to feel around    16
nuns before they decided to dress up and hustle about like the rest of us. Her bedroom is just big enough for a bed and quilting frame; her kitchen equally tiny. The boys of the family keep the walkway stacked with firewood for her stove. She has her own little garden. Children play on her doorstep.

She has her privacy but surrounded by living love, not the dutiful    17
professionalism of the old folks' home. And she still earns her way. Quilt buyers come, adding to her waiting list more quilts than her fingers, now slowed by arthritis, can ever catch up with. But when she puts down her Bible to dicker over price, she is as canny a businesswoman as any.

I love that scene. She still lives in the real world. If she were not    18
Amish, she would have languished in some nursing home and no doubt be dead by now—from sheer boredom if nothing else.

Between the ballgames, sorghum pressings and barnraisings, I have    19
had the chance to observe several Amish households enough to know that there are few generalities. The Herschbergers of the Schwartzentruber Amish, the Bontraggers and all who live near Kenton, Ohio, and the Holmes County neighborhood where we played softball, all represent different economic levels. I do not wish to say that one is financially better off than another, because I do not know. But compared to a middle-class English household, the Hershbergers have the fewest amenities—not even a soft chair, although there is a beautiful, century-old pendulum clock on the wall. The nearby Kenton community is more "advanced" compared to the Herschbergers'. The Holmes County houses are quite like our own except for the lack of electricity. These latter houses sport gas appliances, modern bathrooms, Maytag wringer washers with Honda gasoline motors (the Amish housewives say Hondas start easier than Briggs & Stratton). Though I saw none in the homes I visited, some Old Order Amish are allowed to use battery-operated kitchen mixers and the like—even battery-operated electric type-

writers! Though there is something of a lack of interior decoration as we would call it (unless you go in for the country-look craze), any middle-class American could move into one of these Holmes County homes and not feel materially deprived until habit called for television, radio, or record player.

20     There are no telephones in the homes, but the Amish use the telephone booths that dot the roadsides. An Amishman views a telephone wire into the home, like an electric line, as an umbilical cord tying it to dangerous worldly influences. You will not talk so long or so often at a pay booth down the road.

21     Whatever one's view of such fence-straddling religious convictions, they obviously reveal tremendous economizing. In a 1972 study of Illinois Old Order Amish similar to the Holmes County Amish, conducted by the Center for the Biology of Natural Systems at Washington University in Saint Louis, Amish housewives said they spent $10 to $15 a week on food and non-food groceries. They reported household living expenses from $1,379 for a small, young family up to $4,700 for a large, better-financed one. My own Amish informants thought that today, that figure might top out at $8,000 for a large family, including transportation by buggy and occasionally renting a car or riding a bus. A horse and new buggy cost about $2,000 and last a good bit longer than a $12,000 car. Throughout Amish country in eastern Ohio, a vigorous small business has grown up taxiing Amish around in vans, successfully competing with older private bus lines that perform the same service at a higher price. Clothing is a low budget item for the Amish as they use long-wearing fabrics and often sew the clothes themselves. Styles do not change.

22     Another surprising element in the Amish economy is the busy social life they lead within a day's ride by buggy or bicycle. We could scarcely schedule a softball game because there was always a wedding, a raising, a sale, a quilting, or church and school doings to attend! I can assure the world that the Amish have just as much fun as anyone, at far less than the cost of weekends made for Michelob.

23     Medical costs are the only expenses the Amish cannot control by their sub-economy. Religion forbids education beyond the early teens so they cannot generate their own doctors and medical facilities, and must pay the same ridiculous rates as the rest of us.

24     It is in agriculture that the Amish raise economy to a high art. After the ballgames, when talk got around to the hard times in farming today, the Amish said a *good* farmer could still make a good living with a herd of 20 to 25 cows. One of our players countered with mock seriousness: "Don't you know that you need at least 70 cows to make a living these days? Ohio State says so." "Oh my," an Amish dairyman replied, not entirely in jest, "If I could milk 70 cows, I'd be a millionaire." The Amish farmers all agreed that with 20 cows, a farmer could gross $50,000 in a good-weather year, of which "about half" would be net after paying farm expenses including taxes and interest on land debt if any. Deduct-

ing $8,000 for family living expenses still leaves a nice nest egg for emergencies, bad years and savings to help offspring get started in farming. Beginning farmers with higher interest payments than normal often work as carpenters or at other jobs on the side. These income estimates agree closely with those in the Washington University study mentioned above and those Wendell Berry reports in *The Gift of Good Land* (WER #33, p. 46), a book that demonstrates the sound fiscal foundation of small-scale, traditional farming, even — or especially — in a modern world.

Because my softball players shook their heads in disbelief at these figures, I asked one of the Amish farmers to compare his costs for producing a corn crop of 150 bushels per acre (his excellent yield in '84 and '85) with the 1984 Ohio State budget estimates as published each year by the state extension service. He returned the budget to me by mail with his figures. The first column of figures represents OSU's estimated typical cash grain farmer's cost per acre; the second, the Amish farmer's. I have added footnotes.

| Item | 1 | 2 |
|------|------|------|
| *Variable Costs:* | | |
| Seed | $ 24.00 | $18.66 |
| Chemical fertilizer | 63.00 | 9.10 |
| Lime | 8.00 | 5.06 |
| Pesticides/herbicides | 28.00[1] | 2.50 |
| Fuel, grease, oil | 19.00 | 3.00* |
| Corn drying, fuel, electric | 23.00 | 0.00 |
| Trucking, fuel only | 3.00 | 0.00 |
| Repairs | 13.00 | .25* |
| Misc. supplies, utilities, soil tests, small tools, crop insurance, etc. | 13.00 | .50* |
| Interest on operating capital | 12.00 | .00 |
| *Fixed Costs:* | | |
| Labor | 9.00 | 0.00[2] |
| Machinery charge | 50.00 | 5.00[3] |
| Land rental charge | 110.00 | 0.00[4] |
| Management charge | 18.00 | 0.00[5] |
| Total | $393.00 | $44.07 |

*estimated.

1. Herbicide cost can be twice that or more if an application has to be repeated. Dennis Weaver, one of the Amish ballplayers, told me his herbicide cost was $14. "An acre?" I asked. "No," he replied. "Altogether."

2.   The Amish farmer explains that he hires no labor and considers his own as part of the profit, not of the cost.

3.   The Amish farmer said he didn't know exactly how to figure this because his machinery was so old it was "actually gaining in value now." His estimate is probably high. An Amish corn harvester, pulled by horses and powered by a Wisconsin 16HP motor, might cost $3,000 but likely half that. A typical agribusiness corn harvester costs over $100,000.

4.   If you don't rent land, this item is called cost of ownership. The Amishmen say owning the land is a reward, not a cost.

5.   "What does this mean?" the Amishman wrote. "Is this time spent asking experts how to farm?" Again he figures this as part of his salary, not a cost.

26      According to Ohio State experts, with the price of corn reckoned at $2.40 a bushel (lower now) a non-Amish farmer would gross $360 per acre against $393 in operating expenses for a net loss of $33 per acre, leading one farmer to comment, "It's a damn good thing I don't have a bigger farm." Meanwhile the Amish would realize a net profit of about $315 per acre. Even if you allow fixed costs in English accounting, Amish farming is better than expert farming by about $150 an acre. Just as important, the Amish seldom sell grain, but feed it to livestock and sell milk, meat, eggs, etc., thus retaining an even greater share of their profit dollar.

27      I told my Amish source he needed to add the cost of cultivating weeds out of the corn rows. He thought another dollar or two per acre would cover that, with horse cultivating. And, I added, he needed to add the cost of hauling all that manure to the fields. His response was a classic lesson in biological economy. "When I'm hauling manure, should I charge that to cleaning out the barn which keeps the cows healthy, or to fertilizing the field which reduces the fertilizer bill and adds organic matter to the soil, which in turn helps it to use soil nutrients more efficiently and soak up rain better to reduce erosion? How much do you charge for that in your computer? Or maybe I should charge manure hauling to training the young colt in the harness or giving winter exercise to the older horses. Or maybe deduct manure from machinery wear because the ground gets mellower with manure and is easier to work. I don't know how to calculate all that *accurately* on a farm."

28      The most amazing part of the Amish economy to me is that, contrary to notions cherished by old farm magazine editors who escaped grim childhoods on 1930s farms for softer lives behind desks, the Amish do not work as hard, physically, as I did when my father and I were milking 100 cows with all the modern conveniences in the 1960s. English farmers like to make fun of the Amish for their hair-splitting ways with technology—allowing tractors or engines for stationary power tools but not in the fields. But in addition to keeping the Amish way of life intact,

such compromises bring tremendous economy to their farming while lightening the workload. A motor-powered baler or corn harvester, pulled by horses ahead of a forecart, may seem ridiculous to a modern agribusinessman, but it saves thousands of dollars over buying tractors for this work. The reason tractors aren't allowed in the fields is that they would then tempt an Amishman to expand acreage, going into steep debt to do so, and in the process drive other Amish off the land—which is exactly why and how American agriculture got into the trouble engulfing it today.

To satisfy religious restrictions, the Amish have developed many    29
other ingenious ideas to use modern technology in economizing ways. Other farmers should be studying, not belittling, them. When Grade A milk regulations forced electric cooling tanks on dairymen, the Amish adopted diesel motors to generate their own electricity for the milk room, cooler and milk machines. They say it's cheaper than buying electricity and keeps them secure from power outages. Similarly, they operate commercial woodworking and other shops with diesel-powered hydraulic pumps rather than individual electric motors for each tool. Their small woodworking shops, like their printing and publishing houses and a lot of other enterprises, make money where others so often fail.

Where Amish are active, countryside and town are full of hustling    30
shops and small businesses, neat homes, solid schools and churches, and scores of roadside stands and cheese factories. East central Ohio even has a small woolen mill, one of the few remaining in the country. Compare this region with the decaying towns and empty farmsteads of the land dominated by large-scale agribusiness. The Amish economy spills out to affect the whole local economy. Some farmers, like Lancie Cleppinger near Mount Vernon, have the great good sense to farm like the Amish, even though they don't live like them. They enjoy profits too. When discussing the problems agribusiness farmers have brought on themselves, Cleppinger just keeps shaking his head and repeating, "What in the world are they thinking?" The Amish sum it up in a sentence. "Don't spend more than you make and life will be good to you." Uncle Deficit should be so wise.

## Evaluating the Text

1. What can you infer about the underlying cultural assumptions of the Amish from the fact that they avoid technology?
2. How does the vantage point from which this account is narrated and Logsdon's own background enhance the credibility of the conclusions he reaches?
3. Why was the question as to who should exercise control over building permits such a crucial one for the Amish? How are these issues involved in the case of Henry Hershberger? Why did he go to jail?
4. What surprised Logsdon about the extent to which the Amish have fun

and enjoy themselves? Compare their ways of having fun to those of the general population.

5. What contrasts between U.S. and Amish farming expenses emerged from the comparative analysis conducted by Ohio State University? How are the underlying values of Amish culture revealed in their attitude toward the cost of their own labor and their views regarding owning land?

6. To what extent does the closely knit culture of the Amish make it possible for them to farm in ways that the general farmer would find very difficult to copy? Locate specific values, techniques, approaches, and relationships that would not transfer to the general U.S. farmer. Are the Amish really a good model, as Logsdon claims, for other U.S. farmers to emulate? If not, why?

## Exploring Different Perspectives

1. Compare Logsdon's analysis of Amish economics with John Burgess's report on the economic profile of the Japanese "salaryman" (see "A Day in the Life of 'Salaryman'"). What role does subordination of the individual to the group play in both cultures? How are important differences determined by different cultural values? What are these differences?

2. How does the Amish view of their own effort shed light on the concept of "exchange value of labor" in both this account and that of Mark Salzman in "Lessons"?

3. In your opinion, how might the Amish view Pinceloup in "The Shoe Breaker," Daniel Boulanger's story?

4. Compare Logsdon's essay with Catherine Lim's story, "Paper." What great differences in underlying economic philosophy can you observe that distinguish Amish culture from the speculators at the Singapore Stock Exchange?

## Extending Viewpoints through Writing

1. Were you surprised to discover that the Amish lead less physically strenuous lives than their American counterparts and do not have to work as hard as do other farmers? How does Logsdon account for this?

2. How did this article affect your perception of what goes on in Amish culture? What misconceptions did this account correct?

3. Discuss the economic principles that the Amish apply in their centuries-old farming methods. For example, why is is significant that Amish economics are not driven by market competition, that neighbors assist each other financially, that cultural ties make the entire community a family? How do the different expectations the Amish have reduce machinery costs; cut costs on fertilizer, fuel, trucking, repairs, and crop insurance; eliminate interest on capital, labor, land rental, and management charges; and produce very few electric bills?

# Catherine Lim

# *Paper*

Catherine Lim is one of Singapore's foremost writers, whose works include Little Ironies — Stories of Singapore (1978), from which "Paper" is taken; Or Else, The Lightning God and Other Stories (1980); and The Shadow of a Shadow of a Dream — Love Stories of Singapore (1981). "Paper" dramatically explores how the lure of easy money leads a man and his wife to tragic consequences.

The city of Singapore (in Malay, "City of Lions") and about sixty islets make up the Republic of Singapore at the southern tip of the Malay peninsula. The British East India Company purchased it in 1819 through the efforts of Sir T. S. Raffles. After occupation by the Japanese in World War II, Singapore became a British colony in 1946 and an independent self-governing state in 1959. Three of the major Asian cultures — Chinese, Malay, and Indian — are all represented in the great diversity of peoples in Singapore. In a country's whose population density is over 11,800 persons per square mile, making it one of the most densely populated countries in the world, Singapore has achieved an admirable harmony among many religions. Buddhist and Hindu temples are next to Muslim mosques, Christian churches, and Jewish synogogues. Singapore is now a major financial, industrial, and commercial center as well as one of the world's largest shipping ports. Although the smallest country in southeast Asia, Singapore has the highest standard of living in east Asia after Japan. The Singapore stock exchange (SES All-Singapore), which serves as the backdrop for Lim's story, is one of the world's most volatile.

He wanted it, he dreamed of it, he hankered after it, as an addict after 1 his opiate. Once the notion of a big beautiful house had lodged itself in his imagination, Tay Soon nurtured it until it became the consuming passion of his life. A house. A dream house such as he had seen on his drives with his wife and children along the roads bordering the prestigious housing estates on the island, and in the glossy pages of *Homes* and *Modern Living*. Or rather, it was a house which was an amalgam of the best, the most beautiful aspects of the houses he had seen. He knew every detail of his dream house already, from the aluminium sliding doors to the actual shade of the dining room carpet to the shape of the swimming pool. Kidney. He rather liked the shape. He was not ashamed of the enthusiasm with which he spoke of the dream house, an enthusi-

221

asm that belonged to women only, he was told. Indeed, his enthusiasm was so great that it had infected his wife and even his children, small though they were. Soon his wife Yee Lian was describing to her sister Yee Yeng, the dream house in all its perfection of shape and decor, and the children were telling their cousins and friends, "My daddy says that when our house is ready . . ."

2    They talked of the dream house endlessly. It had become a reality stronger than the reality of the small terrace house which they were sharing with Tay Soon's mother, to whom it belonged. Tay Soon's mother, whose little business of selling bottled curries and vegetable preserves which she made herself, left her little time for dreams, clucked her tongue and shook her head and made sarcastic remarks about the ambitiousness of young people nowadays.

3    "What's wrong with this house we're staying in?" she asked petulantly. "Aren't we all comfortable in it?"

4    Not as long as you have your horrid ancestral altars all over the place, and your grotesque sense of colour — imagine painting the kitchen wall bright pink. But Yee Lian was tactful enough to keep the remarks to herself, or to make them only to her sister Yee Yeng, otherwise they were sure to reach the old lady, and there would be no end to her sharp tongue.

5    The house — the dream house — it would be a far cry from the little terrace house in which they were all staying now, and Tay Soon and Yee Lian talked endlessly about it, and it grew magnificently in their imaginations, this dream house of theirs with its timbered ceiling and panelled walls and sunken circular sitting room which was to be carpeted in rich amber. It was no empty dream, for there was much money in the bank already. Forty thousand dollars had been saved. The house would cost many times that, but Tay Soon and Yee Lian with their good salaries would be able to manage very well. Once they took care of the down payment, they would be able to pay back monthly over a period of ten years — fifteen, twenty — what did it matter how long it took as long as the dream house was theirs? It had become the symbol of the peak of earthly achievement, and all of Tay Soon's energies and devotion were directed towards its realisation. His mother said, "You're a show-off; what's so grand about marble flooring and a swimming pool? Why don't you put your money to better use?" But the forty thousand grew steadily, and after Tay Soon and Yee Lian had put in every cent of their annual bonuses, it grew to forty eight thousand, and husband and wife smiled at the smooth way their plans were going.

6    It was a time of growing interest in the stock market. The quotations for stocks and shares were climbing the charts, and the crowds in the rooms of the broking houses were growing perceptibly. Might we not do something about this? Yee Lian said to her husband. Do you know that Dr. Soo bought Rustan Banking for four dollars and today the shares are worth seven dollars each? The temptation was great. The rewards were

almost immediate. Thirty thousand dollars' worth of NBE became fifty-five thousand almost overnight. Tay Soon and Yee Lian whooped. They put their remaining eighteen thousand in Far East Mart. Three days later the shares were worth twice that much. It was not to be imagined that things could stop here. Tay Soon secured a loan from his bank and put twenty thousand in OHTE. This was a particularly lucky share; it shot up to four times its value in three days.

"Oh, this is too much, too much," cried Yee Lian in her ecstasy, and she sat down with pencil and paper, and found after a few minutes' calculation that they had made a cool one hundred thousand in a matter of days. 7

And now there was to be no stopping. The newspapers were full of it, everybody was talking about it, it was in the very air. There was plenty of money to be made in the stock exchange by those who had guts — money to be made by the hour, by the minute, for the prices of stocks and shares were rising faster than anyone could keep track of them! Dr. Soo was said — he laughingly dismissed it as a silly rumour — Dr. Soo was said to have made two million dollars already. If he sold all his shares now, he would be a millionaire twice over. And Yee Yeng, Yee Lian's sister, who had been urged with sisterly goodwill to come join the others make money, laughed happily to find that the shares she had bought for four twenty on Tuesday had risen to seven ninety-five on Friday — she laughed and thanked Yee Lian who advised her not to sell yet, it was going further, it would hit the ten dollar mark by next week. And Tay Soon both laughed and cursed — cursed that he had failed to buy a share at nine dollars which a few days later had hit seventeen dollars! Yee Lian said reproachfully, "I thought I told you to buy it, darling," and Tay Soon had beaten his forehead in despair and said, "I know, I know, why didn't I! Big fool that I am!" And he had another reason to curse himself — he sold five thousand West Parkes at sixteen twenty-three per share, and saw, to his horror, West Parkes climb to eighteen ninety the very next day! 8

"I'll never sell now," he vowed. "I'll hold on. I won't be so foolish." And the frenzy continued. Husband and wife couldn't talk or think of anything else. They thought fondly of their shares — going to be worth a million altogether soon. A million! In the peak of good humour, Yee Lian went to her mother-in-law, forgetting the past insults, and advised her to join the others by buying some shares; she would get her broker to buy them immediately for her, there was sure money in it. The old lady refused curtly, and to her son later, she showed great annoyance, scolding him for being so foolish as to put all his money in those worthless shares. "Worthless!" exploded Tay Soon. "Do you know, Mother, if I sold all my shares today, I would have the money to buy fifty terrace houses like the one you have?" 9

His wife said, "Oh, we'll just leave her alone. I was kind enough to offer to help her make money. But since she's so nasty and ungrateful, 10 we'll leave her alone." The comforting, triumphant thought was that soon, very soon, they would be able to purchase their dream house; it would be even more magnificent than the one they had dreamt of, since they had made almost a — Yee Lian preferred not to say the sum. There was the old superstitious fear of losing something when it is too often or too directly referred to, and Yee Lian had cautioned her husband not to make mention of their gains.

11    "Not to worry, not to worry," he said jovially, not superstitious like his wife, "After all, it's just paper gains so far."

12    The downward slide, or the bursting of the bubble as the newspapers dramatically called it, did not initially cause much alarm, for the speculators all expected the shares to bounce back to their original strength and thence continue the phenomenal growth. But that did not happen. The slide continued.

13    Tay Soon said nervously, "Shall we sell? Do you think we should sell?" but Yee Lian said stoutly, "There is talk that this decline is a technical thing only — it will be over soon, and then the rise will continue. After all, see what is happening in Hong Kong and London and New York. Things are as good as ever."

14    "We're still making, so not to worry," said Yee Lian after a few days. Their gains were pared by half. A few days later, their gains were pared to marginal.

15    "There is talk of a recovery," insisted Yee Lian. "Do you know, Tay Soon, Dr. Soo's wife is buying up some OHTE and West Parkes now? She says these two are sure to rise. She has some inside information that these two are going to climb past the forty-dollar mark — "

16    Tay Soon sold all his shares and put the money in OHTE and West Parks. OHTE and West Parkes crashed shortly afterwards. Some began to say the shares were not worth the paper of the certificates.

17    "Oh, I can't believe, I can't believe it," gasped Yee Lian, pale and sick. Tay Soon looked in mute horror at her.

18    "All our money was in OHTE and West Parkes," he said, his lips dry.

19    "That stupid Soo woman!" shrieked Yee Lian. "I think she deliberately led me astray with her advice! She's always been jealous of me — ever since she knew we were going to build a house grander than hers!"

20    "How are we going to get our house now?" asked Tay Soon in deep distress, and for the first time he wept. He wept like a child, for the loss of all his money, for the loss of the dream house that he had never stopped loving and worshipping.

21    The pain bit into his very mind and soul, so that he was like a madman, unable to go to his office to work, unable to do anything but haunt the broking houses, watching with frenzied anxiety for OHTE and West Parkes to show him hope. But there was no hope. The decline continued with gleeful rapidity. His broker advised him to sell, before it was too late, but he shrieked angrily, "What! Sell at a fraction at which I bought them! How can this be tolerated!"

And he went on hoping against hope.                                      22

He began to have wild dreams in which he sometimes laughed and      23
sometimes screamed. His wife Yee Lian was afraid and she ran sobbing
to her sister who never failed to remind her curtly that all her savings
were gone, simply because when she had wanted to sell, Yee Lian had
advised her not to.

"But what is your sorrow compared to mine," wept Yee Lian, "see      24
what's happening to my husband. He's cracking up! He talks to himself,
he doesn't eat, he has nightmares, he beats the children. Oh, he's
finished!"

Her mother-in-law took charge of the situation, while Yee Lian,      25
wide-eyed in mute horror at the terrible change that had come over her
husband, shrank away and looked to her two small children for comfort.
Tight-lipped and grim, the elderly woman made herbal medicines for
Tay Soon, brewing and straining for hours, and got a Chinese medicine
man to come to have a look at him.

"There is a devil in him," said the medicine man, and he proceeded to      26
make him a drink which he mixed with the ashes of a piece of prayer
paper. But Tay Soon grew worse. He lay in bed, white, haggard and
delirious, seeming to be beyond the touch of healing. In the end, Yee
Lian, on the advice of her sister and friends, put him in hospital.

"I have money left for the funeral," whimpered the frightened Yee      27
Lian only a week later, but her mother-in-law sharply retorted, "You
leave everything to me! I have the money for his funeral, and I shall give
him the best! He wanted a beautiful house all his life; I shall give him a
beautiful house now!"

She went to the man who was well-known on the island for his      28
beautiful houses, and she ordered the best. It would come to nearly a
thousand dollars, said the man, a thin, wizened fellow whose funereal
gauntness and pallor seemed to be a concession to his calling.

"That doesn't matter," she said, "I want the best. The house is to be      29
made of superior paper," she instructed, and he was to make it to her
specifications. She recollected that he, Tay Soon, had often spoken of
marble flooring, a timbered ceiling and a kidney-shaped swimming pool.
Could he simulate all these in paper?

The thin, wizened man said, "I've never done anything like that      30
before. All my paper houses for the dead have been the usual kind — I
can put in paper furniture and paper cars, paper utensils for the kitchen
and paper servants, all that the dead will need in the other world. But I
shall try to put in what you've asked for. Only it will cost more."

The house when it was ready, was most beautiful to see. It stood      31
seven feet tall, a delicate framework of wire and thin bamboo strips
covered with finely worked paper of a myriad colours. Little silver
flowers, scattered liberally throughout the entire structure, gave a carni-
val atmosphere. There was a paper swimming pool (round, as the man
had not understood 'kidney') which had to be fitted inside the house

itself, as there was no provision for a garden or surrounding grounds. Inside the house were paper figures; there were at least four servants to attend to the needs of the master who was posed beside two cars, one distinctly a Chevrolet and the other a Mercedes.

32     At the appointed time, the paper house was brought to Tay Soon's grave and set on fire there. It burned brilliantly, and in three minutes was a heap of ashes on the grave.

## Evaluating the Text

1. To what extent are Tay Soon and his wife and children caught up in the idea of buying a magnificent dream house? How does the elaborate nature of the house Tay Soon wishes to own symbolize the peak of achievement?
2. How does Lim establish that Tay Soon's mother (with whom Tay Soon and his wife live) is indifferent to and even critical of their dream house? How would you characterize the difference in values of Tay Soon and his wife as compared with those of his mother?
3. What is Lim's attitude toward the events she describes in her story? How do you think she feels toward her characters—Tay Soon, Yee Lian, and Tay Soon's mother?
4. Why doesn't Tay Soon sell his shares and capitalize on his first remarkable gains instead of staying in the market in hopes of being able to build an even more magnificent house? What in Tay Soon's nature makes him his own worst enemy?
5. What role does Tay Soon's wife, Yee Lian, play in contributing to the entire disaster? You might examine her actions both at the beginning of the story and later when the disastrous outcome might still have been averted.
6. How does the recurrent mention of the word *paper* (paper profits, certificates of paper, prayer paper, a paper house, and shares not worth the paper they are printed on) focus the reader's attention on one of the story's central themes?
7. Analyze the structure of the story, and follow its development through the four separate scenes of ever-rising tension and final resolution. How would you describe the action in each of these scenes?
8. How does the miniature paper house that Tay Soon's mother has constructed for him after his death contrast ironically to the magnificent dream house Tay Soon had envisioned? How does the contrast of these two houses (the miniature paper version of his dream house) dramatize the story's central theme?

## Exploring Different Perspectives

1. Contrast the get-rich-quick philosophy of Tay Soon and Yee Lian with the attitude toward material wealth displayed by the Amish (see Gene Logsdon's "Amish Economics"). To what extent do the great differences in these value systems reflect culturally based differences?
2. To what extent do material goods described by John Burgess in "A Day in the Life of 'Salaryman'" symbolize aspirations in the way the house does in "Paper"? For example, what value does the Japanese "salaryman"

attach to the purchase of golf clubs despite the fact there is not enough space in Tokyo to really play golf?

## Extending Viewpoints through Writing

1. If you have ever been involved in a gambling venture in which the psychological dynamics of greed and fear were operating, describe the experiences.
2. What is your attitude toward deferring material gratification? Did you find yourself valuing the fantasies you had about a vacation, car, clothes, jewelry, or whatever, in ways comparable to the feelings of Tay Soon?
3. To discover what you really value, consider the following hypothetical situation: a raging fire has started where you live. You can only save one item other than another person or a pet. What item would you save? How does the value of this item (material, sentimental, or both) imply what is really important to you? Discuss your reactions.

# Cha Ok Kim

# *The Peddler*

---

*Cha Ok Kim was born near Kwangju, South Korea. Orphaned during the Korean War, he kept from starving by selling cigarettes in the streets of Kwangju. In 1971, fresh out of school and newly married, he landed in New York with the dream of becoming an international statesman. Three years later, he and his wife were living in a hotel for transients with three hungry babies. He invested his savings in a bag of ladies' wigs and began peddling door to door in Harlem. Today, Kim's import–export company is doing $4–$5 million annually. Although more dramatic because of his great success, Kim's narrative shows how thousands of Korean immigrants who own small and middle-size businesses have, despite language barriers, helped revitalize New York City's economy. Kim's story is told in Al Santoli's* New Americans: An Oral History, Immigrants and Refugees in the U.S. Today *(1988).*

*Korea is a six-hundred-mile-long peninsula off northeastern China separating the Yellow Sea from the Sea of Japan. Founded in 2333 B.C., Korea came under Chinese control in the thirteenth century, during which time Confucianism was established as the official state doctrine. The Japanese invaded Korea in 1894, formally annexed the country in 1910, and ruled it as a colony until 1945. At the end of World War II, Korea was divided at the thirty-eighth parallel of north latitude into two zones with Soviet troops in the north and U.S. troops in the south. By 1948, two separate governments were established, the Republic of Korea in the south and the Democratic People's Republic under Communist rule in the north. The Korean War (1950–1953) began when North Korean forces invaded South Korea, and the United Nations authorized member nations to aid South Korea. Although tensions remained high between the two nations after the cease fire in 1953, a period of improved relations began in 1990, which may ultimately lead to the reunification of the two nations. Kim and his wife left Korea for American in 1971, during the period (1961–1979) when South Korea was under the authoritarian rule of General Park Chung Hee.*

1  We arrived in the United States in September 1971. Our first home was in Camden, New Jersey, outside of Philadelphia. My wife had a good friend there. Before we left Korea, I looked at a map and thought,

228

"Camden is a good location. Not far from both New York and Philadelphia. I can work during the days and at night go to New York to attend university classes." In reality, Camden is two hours by train from New York.

I began looking for work the first day we arrived in the United States. 2
The next day I found a job at the Amalgamated Textile factory in Philadelphia. Everyone there was stronger and much bigger than I. My legs were too short to work the machines. But after a while I built up big muscles in my legs.

Min Cha had no idea that she was pregnant when we left Korea. 3
Because of this, she was unable to take the job at the hospital pharmacy. She tried working in a factory. Eight hours on her feet . . . she would have to take a half-hour break in the ladies' room during the middle stages of her pregnancy. In Korea, she had never worked at a hard physical job. Before the baby was born, she had to stop working.

My pay was $2 an hour. I only brought home between $65 and $70 a 4
week. In April 1972, my son, John, was born. After six months of working, I had only saved $300. I realized that, after taxes and carfare, I was only earning $1.50 an hour. There was no way that I would be able to take care of my family and save for my graduate studies, which cost at least $700 a semester. I thought, "We have to go to New York, it's better there."

In March 1973, after my second child, Julie, was born, we moved to 5
New York City. We lived on West 95th Street, in a residential hotel. The neighborhood was not great, but rent was only $100 a month.

I was able to find another job in an Amalgamated Textile factory in 6
midtown Manhattan, making men's clothing. The pay was a little higher
—$3 an hour. But living expenses were also higher, so there was no change in our financial situation.

In December 1974, my wife gave birth to our third child, Joon. It was 7
a very difficult period for us, living in one room in the hotel with three small children. The baby was crying. My wife and I only got five hours of sleep each night.

I inquired about my education and found that it was very hard to get 8
accepted into graduate school. First I had to pass the English-language test. Though my English was proficient enough in Korea, here people couldn't understand my accent and I needed a larger vocabulary. So, while I worked days at the cutting machine at the factory, I studied an English dictionary that I kept beside me.

My supervisor would yell at me when he saw me studying, "You are 9
being paid to work." So I kept the dictionary hidden under the machine table. When the supervisor wasn't looking in my direction, I would peek at it to try to learn a new word while I kept the textile machine running. I wouldn't recommend this as the best way to study. But I had to spend eight to ten hours a day on the job, so I had no other choice.

I developed a study system. At night I would study part of the 10 dictionary at home. I wrote down definitions of words on a piece of paper. In the morning I folded the paper and put it in my shirt pocket. Then, while I ran the cutting machine all day, I would sneak looks at the paper to memorize new words.

11      Around thirty Korean families lived in the Monteri Hotel. Most of them had decent educations in Korea. Now some less educated Koreans are allowed into the United States for family reunification. But fifteen years ago, only higher-educated and professional people were allowed to immigrate. All of the men at the hotel had finished college, as had my wife. There were medical doctors, pharmacists, engineers. But here we were starting from the bottom, looking for any kind of work to support ourselves. We would get together to try to determine how we could study and take care of our families at the same time. Because of our language problems, we couldn't find good jobs in offices or banks.

12      Tuition is very high for foreign students at New York University, which was where I wanted to study. I determined that going into my own business would be better than factory work. At the time, ladies' wigs were very popular. My idea was to get ladies' wigs and take them around to make money. This is where my childhood experience as a peddler was very helpful.

13      My wife went to various wholesale stores during the days, while I worked at the factory. We were able to buy wigs for $3 apiece in bulk orders. On weekends I would go into the streets and sell them. I started out peddling in Harlem.

14      I put fifty wigs in a cloth bag that I carried over my shoulder. I would walk into any place—restaurants, bars, hospitals, and door to door. I learned to stand in a visible place on the sidewalk. I'd pull a wig out of the bag and start combing it. Ladies would come up and ask what I was doing. I would pull a few wigs out of the bag to show them the different styles. I'd say, "Do you like red? Okay, here's red." That wasn't so dangerous, because I dealt with ladies only. But sometimes men followed me, looking for a chance to rob me.

15      In one day of selling wigs I could make as much money as one week in the factory. So I left the textile job and expanded my selling trips to Newark and Philadelphia. Then I found out where the black neighborhoods, where people appreciated our low-cost merchandise, were in Boston, Cleveland, and Detroit.

16      I saved enough money to begin graduate school in NYU in September 1974. On weekends and during vacations, I went on the road with friends, selling wigs throughout the Eastern United States. We would take a bus to Buffalo, Detroit, Miami. Sometimes five of us would pile into a friend's car and go together. We'd carry an almanac with us. I'd study the demographics of each neighborhood of the city we were approaching. I'd say, "This neighborhood is dangerous; we have to be careful. This area is more high-class, middle-class." After we visited an area, we had established customers, who would recognize us or be waiting for us to come back again.

We'd go to Albany, Syracuse, and Buffalo. Then we'd swing across to    17
Cleveland, Toledo, then Indiana and Detroit. We would just follow the
road maps and the almanac. I had a Korean friend who was a professor
in Miami. He lived there for fifteen years. But after one or two short
peddling trips, I knew Miami better than him.

I would walk down a street and see someone having a party in their    18
backyard. They'd say, "We don't want to buy any wigs." I'd say, "Okay.
I'll just rest here for a minute." I'd look around and choose the most
beautiful lady. I'd go up to her and start to talk: "Whether you want to
buy one or not, I'd like for you to try this new style one time." I'd take
out a wig that was very beautiful. She'd shout, "Oh! That's beautiful."
And all the people would come around and buy. [Laughs]

Sometimes men would buy for their wife or mother. Older people    19
saw us working all day, came to us, and said, "Why don't you come to
my home and marry my daughter?" [Laughs] They saw how hard we
worked and thought we'd make good husbands.

In the mornings I would go from store to store, from 9:00 A.M. until    20
mid-afternoon, collecting wholesale orders from merchants. I would
telephone my wife in New York and tell her where to ship the orders.
Then, around 4:00 P.M., I would peddle on the streets. I'd look for a good
spot to sit and display my wigs. I'd earn $50 to $100. After sundown, my
friends and I got into our car and drove to the next city.

Around 1:00 A.M., we'd stop at a roadside rest area to get a few hours'    21
sleep. We'd try to be in the next town by 9:00 A.M. Fridays, Saturdays,
and Sundays were our best days. We'd be so busy that we couldn't talk
or take time to eat. We saved a lot of money this way.

On a weekday, we might be on the highway between Toledo and    22
Columbus. I'd look in the almanac and see that we were approaching a
big cigar factory. We'd pull into the factory parking lot at 5:00 P.M., when
people were getting out of work, stand outside with our bags, and sell.
Black ladies liked the wigs, because they don't have long straight hair.
Most couldn't afford to buy a $300 or $400 human-hair wig. My wigs
looked like human hair but only cost $10. They were made from a nylon
material. The colors were black, red, all shades of brown. And older
women liked mixed gray. Some women bought a few different colors to
match their dresses.

In Indianapolis, we'd stand in front of a big hospital. Sometimes we'd    23
go right into the lobby and sell. A nurse would come by and say, "Okay,
I want to buy a wig." They would go get their money and forget about
their patients. Police would come by and check us. They said, "You can't
work here. The nurses will get distracted, and their patients will all die."

One time we were standing on a sidewalk and people came by in a    24
long black car, going to a funeral. They stopped at a red light and came
over to buy wigs.

When a policeman would check me out, I would show my New York    25
sales license. Sometimes that would be legal. But other times I had to
purchase a permit at the local city hall. The prices varied from $3 to $60.

26     Sometimes we tried our luck in restricted areas. The police would come by to warn us. The next time, angry, he'd say, "One more time and I'll send you all to jail." I'd say, "Officer, I'm a student. I don't have tuition. That's why I sell here." He'd look at me and say quietly, "Well, then, that's okay. You're a student. You can stay here except from ten until twelve." Sometimes the police helped us like that.

27     For us, time was money. And we had orders to fill. I would send the money we earned to my wife with new order forms. She purchased the requested number and sent me two to three hundred wigs by UPS to a city where we were going to be in a few days. We asked her for as much merchandise as we could carry in our peddling bags. All the money we made, we reinvested to keep our business growing.

28     After a few months on the road, my business was established. A group of Korean graduate students came to me in New York and asked me to teach them how to do business. They said, "You purchase the wigs wholesale, and we will buy from you for ourselves to sell." That's business, right? I named my company Dong Jin, "Going East," because I imported from Asia.

29     The students branched out to different cities. They'd go their separate ways all over the United States. Each was responsible for their own peddling business. My wife and I only supplied them with merchandise. I was like the organizer of a group of businessmen. Now some are professors back in Korea, some are presidents of large companies, others work in the Korean government. And some are American citizens and doing quite well.

30     At first, my wife and I used our apartments as our warehouse and office. When we began to import wigs, business was brisk. Within four months, I found a small office at 1261 Broadway, in the midtown business district. I would go out on the road selling while my wife ran the warehouse.

31     Min Cha had to bring our three small children with her to the warehouse. We didn't have anyone to babysit, but it was important to keep the business going. She would walk up and down Broadway comparing prices in different import and wholesale shops to find the best deal. We knew some Korean importers and factories in the area. We could buy a wig for 50¢ and sell it at a fair price for our friends to peddle.

32     Our children were only one, two, and three years old. Oh! my wife had to take them everywhere with her! [Laughs] The babies would go into the stores and play with everything.

33     Once we got our business going, we moved to Flushing, in Queens, in 1976. Shortly after we moved, my wife's parents arrived from Korea. Now, there are almost forty thousand Koreans living in Queens. Back then the neighborhood was mostly Jewish. We found a nice apartment with enough room for the kids, who were becoming pretty active. When my wife's parents moved in with us, her mother helped with the kids. That made things a lot easier.

Our home in Flushing was very near the subway to Manhattan. I read    34
newspapers and studied while riding to school. We didn't buy a car until
1979. So, on wig-selling trips to different cities, I continued to use the
Greyhound bus, the Amtrak, or my friend's car. I had a lot of interesting
experiences while peddling. One time I was able to learn a lot about
politics in this country.

Worcester, Massachusetts, was the home of Senator Edward Brooke,    35
who was the only black U.S. senator since the post–Civil War period. He
was on the Foreign Relations Committee. I went to his election campaign
headquarters to ask questions about U.S.–Korea relations and to see how
they ran a campaign. About twenty or thirty women who worked there
told me that they wanted to buy wigs. I said, "No, I came to see Senator
Brooke." I spoke with some of the Senator's aides about political situations. They liked me and said, "While you're doing your wig selling, why
don't you campaign for Brooke?" I said, "Okay." And went house to
house for Brooke. Thirty or forty people bought my wigs. [Laughs]

I asked Brooke's aides many questions about how they handled the    36
Senator's re-election. Twenty or thirty campaigners for Brooke went into
a neighborhood to shake hands with people. I told the lady campaigners,
"How about wearing a red wig? You'll look very beautiful." The staff
bought wigs so they would look nice. And they taught me how to do a
political campaign.

In some cities I would walk into the neighborhood bar. There would    37
be many people drinking, many ladies. I'd say, "Hello, ladies. Wigs for
sale. I am a student trying to pay for my schooling." The owners of
the bars were always black people. Sometimes people would say to me,
"You go back to your own country." I said to them, "You go to your
country. This is my country." They'd say, "You're Chinese. Why do you
say this is your country?" I'd say, "Because I am an Indian. You're from
Africa. This is my country. I'm not Chinese, I am American Indian."
[Laughs]

I make a joke. But it's true that some American Indians came from    38
Manchuria and Korea centuries ago. They came across the Bering Strait
into Alaska, then down the Canadian mountains into the United States.
Look at Indian facial structures. They are very Oriental. Same eyes, same
bone structure. Eskimos in Alaska, and Apache Indians and Koreans
have some similar customs.

Once I met a man and said hello to him in Korean. He didn't under-    39
stand. I said to him, "You are not Korean?" He said, "No," I said, "Are
you Chinese?" "No." "Japanese?" "No." "What are you?" He said,
"American Indian."

One time I was in Detroit. My friend went into a bar to sell, and I    40
went into an apartment building. A man called, "Hey, Chinese." And he
started going toward my friend with a gun. I saw him and said, "I know
you want to rob my friend. We know kung fu. The Oriental custom is not
to report to the police. If you try to rob us one more time, I will attack
you."

41      In the Korean army we learned self-defense called "tae kwan do."
One or two robbers we could fight off. But if there were more than three
with an ax or gun, no way. I was robbed many times—seven or eight
times. In New York Harlem, dangerous areas of Detroit, Cleveland,
Toledo, Richmond, Atlanta—people would come up to me with a gun
and pull off my bag.

42      One time the robbers jumped into a car. It wouldn't start up for them.
I asked local residents if I could use their phone to call the police. The
police wouldn't come. They were afraid of that neighborhood.

43      My first ten years in the United States, I never rested. I worked seven
days a week and studied, too. My teachers assigned us to read three to
five hundred pages every week. It was very hard to keep up with my
studies.

44      I finished graduate school at New York University in 1977. I was
forty-two years old and had no money saved: I spent everything on my
education and taking care of my children. My wife was still developing
the wholesale wig business, which was just successful enough to support
my education. Because she put so much time into the business and caring
for the children, she never re-entered her pharmacist profession.

45      I was very sad. Even though I finished my second master's degree,
after six years in the United States I still didn't have any money. I said,
"All right, a master's degree is enough for me. Now I will establish
myself." So I picked up the bag full of wigs and again began going door
to door. In one or two days I made $200 or $300. My plan was for my
wife and me to help ourselves by expanding our business. We could
create very good jobs for students by peddling in their spare time.

46      I began to teach the students: "When you come into our wholesale
shop, we'll give you enough credit to sell for the week." Twenty or thirty
students asked us, "Mr. Kim, if you import the products from Korea, we
will buy at wholesale prices from you."

47      The plan began to work, and we were able to save and expand. In
1979, we moved our Dong Jin Trading Company into our current business building, on the corner of Broadway and West 29th Street. I didn't
have the $10,000 necessary to put down on my store, so a friend co-
signed for a bank loan. The space is a thousand square feet. With a
twenty-foot ceiling, we were able to build a loft to use as our business
office. And we have five hundred square feet in the basement for
storage. There were four of us on our staff—my wife, her father, one
employee, and me.

48      We would open in the mornings, at 8:00 A.M. At 7:00 P.M., we would
close the doors and begin packing the out-of-town orders until 1:00 A.M.
or 3:00 A.M. We slept right in the store. Woke up at 6:00 A.M. and got back
to work. After six months, we were making enough money to hire two
more employees, including my wife's brother, who arrived from Korea.

49      We set up a small machine to make ladies' belts for wholesale. There
was a customer demand, and when we ordered belts from the factory,
sometimes they couldn't deliver. So I said to my wife's father and

brother, "Let's try to make our own belts downstairs. We can cut the cloth with scissors and sew on metal buckles."

The two of them worked all day long, producing around three dozen belts each. We made around $1 on each belt. My brother-in-law became frustrated. He told me: "Working like this, we'll never make any money. I'm going to buy a cutting machine. This way we can produce ten dozen belts per person each day."

When we earned back the money we spent on the machine, we bought another. Soon we had three, four, five machines. The next step was to rent another small space, in a building on West 31st Street, a few blocks from our store, to be our factory. I went to the bank at least twenty times trying to get a loan to improve the business. But they always refused. I said, "Okay, I must work harder."

Other Korean friends had the same experience with the banks, so we decided to form our own credit union or investment corporation. We each put $500 into one account, creating a seed fund of $8,000. Each month we contributed to the fund. The account can be used to help finance projects of our membership or to make small loans to other people who would like to start their own business. As they continually paid back the fund, the account continued to grow.

Enough Korean businesses were established that we developed associations to help each other and introduce newcomers to the American system. For example, I had two managers who worked at my shop for four years. They were very faithful to me. I cosigned a bank loan so that they could each have their own store. I've also helped four or five other people find empty stores to buy in Brooklyn, Harlem, or the Bronx. I enjoyed helping these people to become independent.

Rent is serious problem for any businesses in Manhattan. In Korea, rents go up at most ten percent in a year. But in New York City, a store owner can lose his business because of skyrocketing increasing. Some rents in this area have jumped from $1,000 a month to more than $10,000 in just five years.

Around sixty-five percent of Koreans in New York work in Korean-owned small or middle-size businesses, either as the owner or employees. On both sides of Broadway, between 25th and 34th Streets, more than half the stores are owned by Koreans.

In the building where our store is housed, we are still renting. But some friends and I pooled our money and bought another building in this neighborhood. One of my friends manages that building, where five or six companies rent offices. Step by step, I've learned to invest our money and still have enough to manage the import–export business efficiently.

The products we sell come in large quantity from Korea, Taiwan, China, Japan. Large shipments come into the warehouse every week. We use a small computer to make our orders and determine how much we need. My wife handles most of the day-to-day management.

In the factory we have stacks and stacks of materials that we cut into belts: cloth, leather, plastics. We use different machines in an assembly line: cutting, stamping holes, inserting buckles. We've hired a dozen people now to make belts and do the stock work. Some are Vietnamese, some are Chinese. They work only one shift, from 8:00 A.M. until 4:00 P.M. My father manages the factory and watches over the warehouse. We have ten thousand square feet full of merchandise. You can see three hundred different types of items piled to the ceiling. Long boxes from Japan contain scarves. Stacks of square boxes are full of gloves from Taipei. Hats from Korea . . . We need to expand into a larger warehouse.

59    I go on business trips throughout Asia to establish contacts with the trade agencies who ship products to my store. My customers tell me the types of items and volumes they need, then I place the orders. Many of my customers have small retail shops in poor neighborhoods, so we make sure the items we import can be sold inexpensively. Rhinestone costume jewelry we carry can be sold retail for $2 or $3. Sunglasses, gloves, baseball caps are all under $5 or $10. During Christmas, we sell a lot of small toys.

60    We ship orders to many states. I have good contacts throughout the East Coast and Midwest from when I was a peddler in all those cities. And some of our orders go to South America, Canada, even to Africa. We ship mostly by airplane, but you'd be surprised — people come in from as far away as Canada to buy in large quantities.

61    During the course of a year, we are doing around $4 – 5 million worth of transactions. We make a five- to six-percent net profit on that amount. We have to pay the overhead on our store, taxes, salaries for our workers, and other expenses.

62    A number of our clients in Manhattan are West Indian merchants and Africans who peddle on the streets, as well as Korean shopowners. We have to open early, because some clients like to come in before they open their shops. Others like to come in after they close shop. So we seldom leave the store before 7:00 or 8:00 P.M., and we still get up for work at 5:30 A.M.

63    In 1982, we moved to Paramus, New Jersey, a suburban area. After ten years of always working, studying, and take care of the family, my business had become more successful. I thought that I could finally start to get a little more rest on weekends. At that time, my son, John, was in the fifth grade. He wanted to take a job delivering newspapers to save money for his education. I said, "Okay, good idea." Then he said to me, "Sunday is a very big day for newspapers. Father, you must help me by driving the car." [Laughs]

64    I've come full circle. When I was in middle school in Korea, I began delivering papers. And thirty-five years later, I am delivering newspapers again [laughs] with my boy.

65    For three or four years, John has kept the paper route and has saved a lot of money. He is very stingy; he never spends it. He appreciates that it

is hard to make money. He has around $2,500 saved in the bank under his name. Sometimes, when he has too much homework, he subcontracts his paper route to another boy. He says, "I am the newspaper delivery president." His own business.

At first the family bankbook was only in my name. But one day John 66 walked right into the bank and asked for his own account. [Laughs] And they gave him a bank book.

He came home and showed the bank book to me. He said, "Father, 67 it's not your money. I told the bank I wanted my account under 'John Kim' only." Some Korean kids aren't like my son. He's a real individualist, a real American. [Laughs]

In the Oriental tradition, the father works and provides money to the 68 other members of the family, and children believe that their parents' house is their house. But my son says that he is just living in my house, and eventually one day he will buy his own.

## Evaluating the Text

1. What can you infer about Kim's personality from the way in which he solves problems (such as not knowing the language well, discovering he has moved to the wrong city, etc.) he encounters?
2. What details tell you that education is an all-important value for Kim?
3. How did Kim get into the wig-peddling business initially?
4. How does Kim take advantage of existing opportunities and create new ones? For example, look at his use of the almanac, how he markets his wigs.
5. How does Kim's success generate opportunities for many other people to also become successful?
6. How would you characterize the relationship between Kim and his wife and children? To what extent do they contribute to his success?
7. How does Kim's decision of when to buy a car differ from what most Americans would do under the same circumstances? What does this difference reveal about American cultural values as contrasted to those of most Korean immigrants?
8. How does the episode with Edward Brooke's campaign for the Senate from Massachusetts illustrate Kim's unrelenting devotion to selling wigs in whatever circumstances he finds himself?
9. What might you infer about Korean cultural values from the importance Kim attaches to bringing family members and others from Korea and helping them become established in America?
10. What does it tell you about credit availability to immigrants that Kim and other Koreans had to form their own credit union?
11. What does it tell you about Kim that although extraordinarily successful, he still puts in the same hours as he did when he was just starting out?
12. What details suggest that Kim has passed along his values to his son?

## Exploring Different Perspectives

1. What common elements can you discover between Kim's success and the practices that have made the Amish prosper (see Gene Logsdon's, "Amish

Economics")? How does the Amish attitude toward assimilating into American culture differ from Kim's?

2. Read Catharine Lim's "Paper." How do Kim's expectations and the methods he uses to achieve his goal differ from those of Tay Soon?

3. Compare Kim's motive for learning English and the methods he uses with those of Pan in Mark Salzman's "Lessons."

## Extending Viewpoints through Writing

1. What differentiates Kim from most people that helps explain his extraordinary success? Would most people in his situation have, for example, thought of sleeping at rest stops instead of motels?

2. Describe a period in your life that might enable you to understand what Kim was going through.

3. As a research project, investigate the basis for the theory Kim discusses about a land bridge between Russia and Alaska across the Bering Strait, which might have permitted migration of Mongolian people, who were the ancestors of Native Americans.

4. Have you ever known anyone who is like Kim, that is, someone who is very frugal, only gets what they need when they need it, can put off rewards, and is willing to subordinate everything to achieve success? If so, describe this person.

# Beryl Markham

# *West with the Night*

---

*Beryl Markham was born in England in 1902 and was taken by her father to East Africa in 1906. From 1931 to 1936, Markham carried mail, passengers, and supplies in her small plane to the remote corners of the Sudan, Tanganyika, Kenya, and Rhodesia. In September 1936, she became the first person to fly solo across the Atlantic from East to West—taking off in England and crash-landing in Nova Scotia twenty-one hours and twenty-five minutes later. After reading* West with the Night *(1942), Markham's memoir, Hemingway said, "She can write rings around all of us who consider ourselves as writers." In the selection that follows (the last chapter of her book), Markham describes the harrowing circumstances of her flight.*

I have seldom dreamed a dream worth dreaming again, or at least none worth recording. Mine are not enigmatic dreams; they are peopled with characters who are plausible and who do plausible things, and I am the most plausible amongst them. All the characters in my dreams have quiet voices like the voice of the man who telephoned me at Elstree one morning in September of nineteen-thirty-six and told me that there was rain and strong head winds over the west of England and over the Irish Sea, and that there were variable winds and clear skies in mid-Atlantic and fog off the coast of Newfoundland.

'If you are still determined to fly the Atlantic this late in the year,' the voice said, 'the Air Ministry suggests that the weather it is able to forecast for tonight, and for tomorrow morning, will be about the best you can expect.'

The voice had a few other things to say, but not many, and then it was gone, and I lay in bed half-suspecting that the telephone call and the man who made it were only parts of the mediocre dream I had been dreaming. I felt that if I closed my eyes the unreal quality of the message would be re-established, and that, when I opened them again, this would be another ordinary day with its usual beginning and its usual routine.

But of course I could not close my eyes, nor my mind, nor my memory. I could lie there for a few moments—remembering how it had begun, and telling myself, with senseless repetition, that by tomorrow morning I should either have flown the Atlantic to America—or I should not have flown it. In either case this was the day I would try.

5    I could stare up at the ceiling of my bedroom in Aldenham House, which was a ceiling undistinguished as ceilings go, and feel less resolute than anxious, much less brave than foolhardy. I could say to myself, 'You needn't do it, of course,' knowing at the same time that nothing is so inexorable as a promise to your pride.

6    I could ask, 'Why risk it?' as I have been asked since, and I could answer, 'Each to his element.' By his nature a sailor must sail, by his nature a flyer must fly. I could compute that I had flown a quarter of a million miles; and I could foresee that, so long as I had a plane and the sky was there, I should go on flying more miles.

7    There was nothing extraordinary in this. I had learned a craft and had worked hard learning it. My hands had been taught to seek the controls of a plane. Usage had taught them. They were at ease clinging to a stick, as a cobbler's fingers are in repose grasping an awl. No human pursuit achieves dignity until it can be called work, and when you can experience a physical loneliness for the tools of your trade, you see that the other things — the experiments, the irrelevant vocations, the vanities you used to hold — were false to you.

8    Record flights had actually never interested me very much for myself. There were people who thought that such flights were done for admiration and publicity, and worse. But of all the records — from Louis Blériot's first crossing of the English Channel in nineteen hundred and nine, through and beyond Kingsford Smith's flight from San Francisco to Sydney, Australia — none had been made by amateurs, nor by novices, nor by men or women less than hardened to failure, or less than masters of their trade. None of these was false. They were a company that simple respect and simple ambition made it worth more than an effort to follow.

9    The Carberrys (of Seramai) were in London and I could remember everything about their dinner party — even the menu. I could remember June Carberry and all her guests, and the man named McCarthy, who lived in Zanzibar, leaning across the table and saying, 'J. C., why don't you finance Beryl for a record flight?'

10    I could lie there staring lazily at the ceiling and recall J. C.'s dry answer: 'A number of pilots have flown the North Atlantic, west to east. Only Jim Mollison has done it alone the other way — from Ireland. Nobody has done it alone from England — man or woman. I'd be interested in that, but nothing else. If you want to try it, Burl, I'll back you. I think Edgar Percival could build a plane that would do it, provided you can fly it. Want to chance it?'

11    'Yes.'

12    I could remember saying that better than I could remember anything —except J. C.'s almost ghoulish grin, and her remark that sealed the agreement: 'It's a deal, Burl. I'll furnish the plane and you fly the Atlantic — but, gee, I wouldn't tackle it for a million. Think of all that black water! Think how cold it is!'

13    And I had thought of both.

I had thought of both for a while, and then there had been other 14
things to think about. I had moved to Elstree, half-hour's flight from the
Percival Aircraft Works at Gravesend, and almost daily for three months
now I had flown down to the factory in a hired plane and watched the
Vega Gull they were making for me. I had watched her birth and
watched her growth. I had watched her wings take shape, and seen
wood and fabric moulded to her ribs to form her long, sleek belly, and I
had seen her engine cradled into her frame, and made fast.

The Gull had a turquoise-blue body and silver wings. Edgar Percival 15
had made her with care, with skill, and with worry—the care of a
veteran flyer, the skill of a master designer, and the worry of a friend.
Actually the plane was a standard sport model with a range of only six
hundred and sixty miles. But she had a special undercarriage built to
carry the weight of her extra oil and petrol tanks. The tanks were fixed
into the wings, into the centre section, and into the cabin itself. In the
cabin they formed a wall around my seat, and each tank had a petcock of
its own. The petcocks were important.

'If you open one,' said Percival, 'without shutting the other first, you 16
may get an airlock. You know the tanks in the cabin have no gauges, so it
may be best to let one run completely dry before opening the next. Your
motor might go dead in the interval—but she'll start again. She's a De
Havilland Gipsy—and Gipsys never stop.'

I had talked to Tom. We had spent hours going over the Atlantic 17
chart, and I had realized that the tinker of Molo, now one of England's
great pilots, had traded his dreams and had got in return a better thing.
Tom had grown older too; he had jettisoned a deadweight of irrelevant
hopes and wonders, and had left himself a realistic code that had no
room for temporizing or easy sentiment.

'I'm glad you're going to do it, Beryl. It won't be simple. If you can get 18
off the ground in the first place, with such an immense load of fuel,
you'll be alone in that plane about a night and a day—mostly night.
Doing it east to west, the wind's against you. In September, so is the
weather. You won't have a radio. If you misjudge your course only a few
degrees, you'll end up in Labrador or in the sea—so don't misjudge
anything.'

Tom could still grin. He had grinned; he had said: 'Anyway, it ought 19
to amuse you to think that your financial backer lives on a farm called
"Place of Death" and your plane is being built at "Gravesend." If you
were consistent, you'd christen the Gull "The Flying Tombstone."'

I hadn't been that consistent. I had watched the building of the plane 20
and I had trained for the flight like an athlete. And now, as I lay in bed,
fully awake, I could still hear the quiet voice of the man from the Air
Ministry intoning, like the voice of a dispassionate court clerk: '. . . the
weather for tonight and tomorrow . . . will be about the best you can
expect.' I should have liked to discuss the flight once more with Tom
before I took off, but he was on a special job up north. I got out of bed

and bathed and put on my flying clothes and took some cold chicken packed in a cardboard box and flew over to the military field at Abingdon, where the Vega Gull waited for me under the care of the R.A.F. I remember that the weather was clear and still.

21    Jim Mollison lent me his watch. He said: 'This is not a gift. I wouldn't part with it for anything. It got me across the North Atlantic and the South Atlantic too. Don't lose it—and, for God's sake, don't get it wet. Salt water would ruin the works.'

22    Brian Lewis gave me a life-saving jacket. Brian owned the plane I had been using between Elstree and Gravesend, and he had thought a long time about a farewell gift. What could be more practical than a pneumatic jacket that could be inflated through a rubber tube?

23    'You could float around in it for days,' said Brian. But I had to decide between the life-saver and warm clothes. I couldn't have both, because of their bulk, and I hate the cold, so I left the jacket.

24    And Jock Cameron, Brian's mechanic, gave me a sprig of heather. If it had been a whole bush of heather, complete with roots growing in an earthen jar, I think I should have taken it, bulky or not. The blessing of Scotland, bestowed by a Scotsman, is not to be dismissed. Nor is the well-wishing of a ground mechanic to be taken lightly, for these men are the pilot's contact with reality.

25    It is too much that with all those pedestrian centuries behind us we should, in a few decades, have learned to fly; it is too heady a thought, too proud a boast. Only the dirt on a mechanic's hands, the straining vise, the splintered bolt of steel underfoot on the hanger floor—only these and such anxiety as the face of a Jock Cameron can hold for a pilot and his plane before a flight, serve to remind us that, not unlike the heather, we too are earthbound. We fly, but we have not 'conquered' the air. Nature presides in all her dignity, permitting us the study and the use of such of her forces as we may understand. It is when we presume to intimacy, having been granted only tolerance, that the harsh stick falls across our impudent knuckles and we rub the pain, staring upward, startled by our ignorance.

26    'Here is a sprig of heather,' said Jock, and I took it and pinned it into a pocket of my flying jacket.

27    There were press cars parked outside the field at Abingdon, and several press planes and photographers, but the R.A.F. kept everyone away from the grounds except technicians and a few of my friends.

28    The Carberrys had sailed for New York a month ago to wait for me there. Tom was still out of reach with no knowledge of my decision to leave, but that didn't matter so much, I thought. It didn't matter because Tom was unchanging—neither a fairweather pilot nor a fairweather friend. If for a month, or a year, or two years we sometimes had not seen each other, it still hadn't mattered. Nor did this. Tom would never say, 'You should have let me know.' He assumed that I had learned all that

he had tried to teach me, and for my part, I thought of him, even then, as the merest student must think of his mentor. I could sit in a cabin overcrowded with petrol tanks and set my course for North America, but the knowledge of my hands on the controls would be Tom's knowledge. His words of caution and words of guidance, spoken so long ago, so many times, on bright mornings over the veldt or over a forest, or with a far mountain visible at the tip of our wing, would be spoken again, if I asked.

So it didn't matter, I thought. It was silly to think about.    29

You can live a lifetime and, at the end of it, know more about other    30
people than you know about yourself. You learn to watch other people, but you never watch yourself because you strive against loneliness. If you read a book, or shuffle a deck of cards, or care for a dog, you are avoiding yourself. The abhorrence of loneliness is as natural as wanting to live at all. If it were otherwise, men would never have bothered to make an alphabet, nor to have fashioned words out of what were only animal sounds, nor to have crossed continents — each man to see what the other looked like.

Being alone in an aeroplane for even so short a time as a night and a    31
day, irrevocably alone, with nothing to observe but your instruments and your own hands in semi-darkness, nothing to contemplate but the size of your small courage, nothing to wonder about but the beliefs, the faces, and the hopes rooted in your mind — such an experience can be as startling as the first awareness of a stranger walking by your side at night. You are the stranger.

It is dark already and I am over the south of Ireland. There are the    32
lights of Cork and the lights are wet; they are drenched in Irish rain, and I am above them and dry. I am above them and the plane roars in a sobbing world, but it imparts no sadness to me. I feel the security of solitude, the exhilaration of escape. So long as I can see the lights and imagine the people walking under them, I feel selfishly triumphant, as if I have eluded care and left even the small sorrow of rain in other hands.

It is a little over an hour now since I left Abingdon. England, Wales,    33
and the Irish Sea are behind me like so much time used up. On a long flight distance and time are the same. But there had been a moment when Time stopped — and Distance too. It was the moment I lifted the blue-and-silver Gull from the aerodrome, the moment the photographers aimed their cameras, the moment I felt the craft refuse its burden and strain toward the earth in sullen rebellion, only to listen at last to the persuasion of stick and elevators, the dogmatic argument of blueprints that said she *had* to fly because the figures proved it.

So she had flown, and once airborne, once she had yielded to the    34
sophistry of a draughtsman's board, she had said, 'There: I have lifted the weight. Now, where are we bound?' — and the question had frightened me.

35    We are bound for a place thirty-six hundred miles from here—two thousand miles of it unbroken ocean. Most of the way it will be night. We are flying west with the night.'

36    So there behind me is Cork; and ahead of me is Berehaven Lighthouse. It is the last light, standing on the last land. I watch it, counting the frequency of its flashes—so many to the minute. Then I pass it and fly out to sea.

37    The fear is gone now—not overcome nor reasoned away. It is gone because something else has taken its place; the confidence and the trust, the inherent belief in the security of land underfoot—now this faith is transferred to my plane, because the land has vanished and there is no other tangible thing to fix faith upon. Flight is but momentary escape from the eternal custody of earth.

38    Rain continues to fall, and outside the cabin it is totally dark. My altimeter says that the Atlantic is two thousand feet below me, my Sperry Artificial Horizon says that I am flying level. I judge my drift at three degrees more than my weather chart suggests, and fly accordingly. I am flying blind. A beam to follow would help. So would a radio—but then, so would clear weather. The voice of the man at the Air Ministry had not promised storm.

39    I feel the wind rising and the rain falls hard. The smell of petrol in the cabin is so strong and the roar of the plane so loud that my senses are almost deadened. Gradually it becomes unthinkable that existence was ever otherwise.

40    At ten o'clock P.M. I am flying along the Great Circle Course for Harbour Grace, Newfoundland, into a forty-mile headwind at a speed of one hundred and thirty miles an hour. Because of the weather, I cannot be sure of how many more hours I have to fly, but I think it must be between sixteen and eighteen.

41    At ten-thirty I am still flying on the large cabin tank of petrol, hoping to use it up and put an end to the liquid swirl that has rocked the plane since my take-off. The tank has no gauge, but written on its side is the assurance: 'This tank is good for four hours.'

42    There is nothing ambiguous about such a guaranty. I believe it, but at twenty-five minutes to eleven, my motor coughs and dies, and the Gull is powerless above the sea.

43    I realize that the heavy drone of the plane has been, until this moment, complete and comforting silence. It is the actual silence following the last splutter of the engine that stuns me. I can't feel any fear; I can't feel anything. I can only observe with a kind of stupid disinterest that my hands are violently active and know that, while they move, I am being hypnotized by the needle of my altimeter.

44    I suppose that the denial of natural impulse is what is meant by 'keeping calm,' but impulse has reason in it. If it is night and you are sitting in an aeroplane with a stalled motor, and there are two thousand feet between you and the sea, nothing can be more reasonable than the

impulse to pull back your stick in the hope of adding to that two thousand, if only by a little. The thought, the knowledge, the law that tells you that your hope lies not in this, but in a contrary act—the act of directing your impotent craft toward the water—seems a terrifying abandonment, not only of reason, but of sanity. Your mind and your heart reject it. It is your hands—your stranger's hands—that follow with unfeeling precision the letter of the law.

I sit there and watch my hands push forward on the stick and feel the     45
Gull respond and begin its dive to the sea. Of course it is a simple thing; surely the cabin tank has run dry too soon. I need only to turn another petcock . . .

But it is dark in the cabin. It is easy to see the luminous dial of the     46
altimeter and to note that my height is now eleven hundred feet, but it is not easy to see a petcock that is somewhere near the floor of the plane. A hand gropes and reappears with an electric torch, and fingers, moving with agonizing composure, find the petcock and turn it; and I wait.

At three hundred feet the motor is still dead, and I am conscious that     47
the needle of my altimeter seems to whirl like the spoke of a spindle winding up the remaining distance between the plane and the water. There is some lightning, but the quick flash only serves to emphasize the darkness. How high can waves reach—twenty feet, perhaps? Thirty?

It is impossible to avoid the thought that this is the end of my flight,     48
but my reactions are not orthodox; the various incidents of my entire life do not run through my mind like a motion-picture film gone mad. I only feel that all this has happened before—and it has. It has all happened a hundred times in my mind, in my sleep, so that now I am not really caught in terror; I recognize a familiar scene, a familiar story with its climax dulled by too much telling.

I do not know how close to the waves I am when the motor explodes     49
to life again. But the sound is almost meaningless. I see my hand easing back on the stick, and I feel the Gull climb up into the storm, and I see the altimeter whirl like a spindle again, paying out the distance between myself and the sea.

The storm is strong. It is comforting. It is like a friend shaking me and     50
saying, 'Wake up! You were only dreaming.'

But soon I am thinking. By simple calculation I find that my motor     51
had been silent for perhaps an instant more than thirty seconds.

I ought to thank God—and I do, though indirectly. I thank Geoffrey     52
De Havilland who designed the indomitable Gipsy, and who, after all, must have been designed by God in the first place.

A lighted ship—the daybreak—some steep cliffs standing in the sea.     53
The meaning of these will never change for pilots. If one day an ocean can be flown within an hour, if men can build a plane that so masters time, the sight of land will be no less welcome to the steersman of that fantastic craft. He will have cheated laws that the cunning of science has

taught him how to cheat, and he will feel his guilt and be eager for the sanctuary of the soil.

54   I saw the ship and the daybreak, and then I saw the cliffs of New-foundland wound in ribbons of fog. I felt the elation I had so long imagined, and I felt the happy guilt of having circumvented the stern authority of the weather and the sea. But mine was a minor triumph; my swift Gull was not so swift as to have escaped unnoticed. The night and the storm had caught her and we had flown blind for nineteen hours.

55   I was tired now, and cold. Ice began to film the glass of the cabin windows and the fog played a magician's game with the land. But the land was there. I could not see it, but I had seen it. I could not afford to believe that it was any land but the land I wanted. I could not afford to believe that my navigation was at fault, because there was no time for doubt.

56   South to Cape Race, west to Sydney on Cape Breton Island. With my protractor, my map, and my compass, I set my new course, humming the ditty that Tom had taught me: 'Variation West—magnetic best. Varia-tion East—magnetic least.' A silly rhyme, but it served to placate, for the moment, two warring poles—the magnetic and the true. I flew south and found the lighthouse of Cape Race protruding from the fog like a warning finger. I circled twice and went on over the Gulf of Saint Lawrence.

57   After a while there would be New Brunswick, and then Maine—and then New York. I could anticipate. I could almost say, 'Well, if you stay awake, you'll find it's only a matter of time now'—but there was no question of staying awake. I was tired and I had not moved an inch since that uncertain moment at Abingdon when the Gull had elected to rise with her load and fly, but I could not have closed my eyes. I could sit there in the cabin, walled in glass and petrol tanks, and be grateful for the sun and the light, and the fact that I could see the water under me. They were almost the last waves I had to pass. Four hundred miles of water, but then the land again—Cape Breton. I would stop at Sydney to refuel and go on. It was easy now. It would be like stopping at Kisumu and going on.

58   Success breeds confidence. But who has a right to confidence except the Gods? I had a following wind, my last tank of petrol was more than three-quarters full, and the world was as bright to me as if it were a new world, never touched. If I had been wiser, I might have known that such moments are, like innocence, short-lived. My engine began to shudder before I saw the land. It died, it spluttered, it started again and limped along. It coughed and spat black exhaust toward the sea.

59   There are words for everything. There was a word for this—airlock, I thought. This had to be an airlock because there was petrol enough. I thought I might clear it by turning on and turning off all the empty tanks, and so I did that. The handles of the petcocks were sharp little pins of metal, and when I had opened and closed them a dozen times, I saw that

my hands were bleeding and that the blood was dropping on my maps and on my clothes, but the effort wasn't any good. I coasted along on a sick and halting engine. The oil pressure and the oil temperature gauges were normal, the magnetos working, and yet I lost altitude slowly while the realization of failure seeped into my heart. If I made the land, I should have been the first to fly the North Atlantic from England, but from my point of view, from a pilot's point of view, a forced landing was failure because New York was my goal. If only I could land and then take off, I would make it still . . . if only, if only . . .

The engine cuts again, and then catches, and each time it spurts to life I climb as high as I can get, and then it splutters and stops and I glide once more toward the water, to rise again and descend again, like a hunting sea bird. 60

I find the land. Visibility is perfect now and I see land forty or fifty miles ahead. If I am on my course, that will be Cape Breton. Minute after minute goes by. The minutes almost materialize; they pass before my eyes like links in a long slow-moving chain, and each time the engine cuts, I see a broken link in the chain and catch my breath until it passes. 61

The land is under me. I snatch my map and stare at it to confirm my whereabouts. I am, even at my present crippled speed, only twelve minutes from Sydney Airport, where I can land for repairs and then go on. 62

The engine cuts once more and I begin to glide, but now I am not worried; she will start again, as she has done, and I will gain altitude and fly into Sydney. 63

But she doesn't start. This time she's dead as death; the Gull settles earthward and it isn't any earth I know. It is black earth stuck with boulders and I hang above it, on hope and on a motionless propeller. Only I cannot hang above it long. The earth hurries to meet me, I bank, turn, and side-slip to dodge the boulders, my wheels touch, and I feel them submerge. The nose of the plane is engulfed in mud, and I go forward striking my head on the glass of the cabin front, hearing it shatter, feeling blood pour over my face. 64

I stumble out of the plane and sink to my knees in muck and stand there foolishly staring, not at the lifeless land, but at my watch. 65

Twenty-one hours and twenty-five minutes. 66

Atlantic flight, Abingdon, England, to a nameless swamp—nonstop. 67

A Cape Breton Islander found me—a fisherman trudging over the bog saw the Gull with her tail in the air and her nose buried, and then he saw me floundering in the embracing soil of his native land. I had been wandering for an hour and the black mud had got up to my waist and the blood from the cut in my head had met the mud halfway. 68

From a distance, the fisherman directed me with his arms and with shouts toward the firm places in the bog, and for another hour I walked on them and came toward him like a citizen of Hades blinded by the sun, but it wasn't the sun; I hadn't slept for forty hours. 69

70      He took me to his hut on the edge of the coast and I found that built upon the rocks there was a little cubicle that housed an ancient telephone — put there in case of shipwrecks.

71      I telephoned to Sydney Airport to say that I was safe and to prevent a needless search being made. On the following morning I did step out of a plane at Floyd Bennett Field and there was a crowd of people still waiting there to greet me, but the plane I stepped from was not the Gull, and for days while I was in New York I kept thinking about that and wishing over and over again that it had been the Gull, until the wish lost its significance, and time moved on, overcoming many things it met on the way.

## *Evaluating the Text*

1. What does being a pilot mean to Markham? Why is this form of work so important to her? How does the reader know that she thinks of herself as a rather ordinary person while, at the same time, she expects a great deal from herself?
2. Why is Markham careful to mention that the flight is not intended as a stunt but rather as a test of her abilities as a pilot?
3. To what extent does Markham downplay the fact that she is a woman? How important is it to her to be accepted by other pilots as just one of them?
4. How does the title ("West with the Night") of Markham's memoir suggest the distinctive nature of her achievement?
5. What is the relationship between Markham's drive to succeed and her perfectionism? At what points is it obvious she is not egotistical and, if anything, lacks self-esteem? How is this evident in the voice she uses to relate the events?
6. How does Markham construct the narrative so that it goes full circle? How does this method of organization contribute to the effectiveness of her account?
7. How would you characterize the humor displayed by Markham and her fellow pilots, especially when it deals with the very real possibility of dying?
8. Based on conversations between Markham and Tom, what kind of a relationship would you say they had?
9. What specific details most effectively convey the perilous nature of the mission?
10. Explain the psychological process at work in Markham's need to believe the motor of the Gull would always start again. Do you think she would have been able to undertake the flight if she thought there was even a slight possibility that it would stall? In view of the fact that it did stall, why is it significant that Markham does not blame the De Havilland manufacturers even years after the incident took place?
11. How does the reader know that Markham holds herself to a higher standard than anyone else does? For example, why is it significant that she views her flight as a failure because she only flew from Abingdon, England, to Nova Scotia rather than to New York as she had intended?

## Exploring Different Perspectives

1. How does Markham's self-esteem depend on being a successful pilot according to her own standards? What similarities can you discover between her values and those of the Amish (see Gene Logsdon's "Amish Economics")?
2. To what extent do Markham and Min Cha, Cha Ok Kim's wife in "The Peddler" deviate from the traditional roles of women in their respective societies?

## Extending Viewpoints through Writing

1. Just as Markham seems to have more insight into Tom's personality than into her own, is there anyone you feel you know better than you know yourself? Write a character sketch of this person.
2. At crucial moments during her flight, Markham had to perform actions that went against what she would have done instinctively out of fear. If you have ever been in a comparable situation, describe it and how any training you received enabled you to respond constructively.
3. Read the following definition of a workaholic (according to Marilyn Machlowitz in "What is Workaholism?" from *Workaholics*, Reading, MA: Addison-Wesley, 1980):

> What truly distinguishes workaholics from other hard workers is that others work only to please a boss, earn a promotion, or meet a deadline. . . . I will use the word "workaholic" to describe those whose desire to work long and hard is intrinsic and whose work habits almost always exceed the prescriptions of the job they do and the expectations of the people with whom or for whom they work.

To what extent would you consider Markham a workaholic according to this definition? Have you ever thought of yourself as a workaholic? Explain your answer.

# John Burgess

# *A Day in the Life of*
# *"Salaryman"*

---

*John Burgess spent the years 1984 through 1987 as Northeast Asia correspondent for the* Washington Post. *A prolific writer, Burgess is responsible for over 600 articles on business and politics in Japan, Korea, China, Vietnam, Thailand, Laos, and Cambodia. "A Day in the Life of 'Salaryman'" (August 1987) provides insight into how Japanese cultural values shape attitudes toward work in this detailed account of a day in the life of "salaryman," the average Japanese white-color worker.*

*Although Japan's population at 124 million is half that of the United States, the habitable areas in Japan amount to less than 5% of the land area of the United States. As a result, Japan is one of the most densely populated countries in the world. Most of the people live in urban areas, and Tokyo, the capital, now has 8⅓ million inhabitants. An efficient mass transportation system including "bullet" trains allows workers to commute from great distances to their jobs in the major cities. The annual GNP (gross national product) per person in U.S. dollars is $23,000. Japan's growth into an economic superpower since the 1960s has produced foreign trade imbalances that have strained Japan's relations with the United States and the Common Market countries.*

1    TOKYO — He is hailed here as an "industrial warrior," the driving force behind Japan's economic success. He is also ridiculed in cartoons and commercials as a wimp who lives in terror of the boss' glower and chews antacids by the case.

2    He is as much a part of the Japanese cityscape as neon and sushi bars. He is found in dark suit, imported necktie, short hair parted on the left. No beards or moustaches. Accessories are standard, too — pocket calculator, leather briefcase, commuting pass, business cards, pornographic comic book for long subway rides.

3    Most of all, he is mass-produced. The "salaryman," as the male white-collar worker is called in Japan, is what most of the 280,000 young men who graduate from universities each year quickly become.

4    The good salaryman devotes himself body and soul to the company.

*(For additional background on Japan, see pp. 35 and 632.)

If the company thrives, so will he. He loves his wife and children, but in a pinch he can be counted on to put the office first.

In few countries do such stereotypes hit so close to the truth. The 5 Japanese joke endlessly about the salaryman, but not much is happening to replace him as an important bearer of the national standard. Some commentators predict that the new generation of young people, more devoted, it is said, to family and self-expression, will undermine the salaryman lifestyle. But for now, a good job at a good company is what the average young man aspires to and the salaryman lifestyle generally goes with that territory.

What follows is a day in the life of a prototypical salaryman, a 6 portrait based on interviews, observations and reading over a three-year period of reporting in Japan. Salaryman represents no specific person and his company is no specific company. But when the Japanese think salaryman, someone like him comes to mind automatically, perhaps the guy living next door.

We join Salaryman as he rises from bed in the cramped master 7 bedroom of his house, a thin-walled, heavily mortgaged affair deep in Tokyo's teeming suburban expanses. . . .

Salaryman's wife of 12 years has already been up more than an hour 8 and gotten the two children off to school. Our man was too late getting home the previous night to see them. On Sunday, he is planning to take his wife and children to an amusement park a half hour's drive from the house — it's been a while since the family had a decent outing together.

After a wash, shave and quick dressing, Salaryman lights the first 9 "Mild Seven" of the day, the brand that he and a third of all Japanese smokers favor. He wanders down the narrow stairs to the breakfast table, where his wife has laid out eggs, thick toast and coffee. He digs in and they talk about the new car they are planning to buy. "You're still against the Crown?" Salaryman asks. His wife doesn't answer. The Crown is a type of Toyota that she feels is not only too expensive but too flashy for someone of his rank at the company.

Salaryman opens his newspaper and sees another article about sky- 10 rocketing land prices. Good thing we bought when we did, he thinks. We could never afford this house now.

His wife drives him 10 minutes to the train station, where he slips 11 into a throng of other salarymen embarking on the 70-minute journey to central Tokyo, site of the company where he has been employed since he graduated from college 15 years ago. The train that stops before Salary-man is packed, as it always is.

He pushes his way in and, after staking out a strap, pulls from a 12 pocket a book on computer science. Salaryman is 37, a shade too old to have grown up with computers. He is now determined to catch up and stop feeling the fool on this subject around the youngsters at the office. Thirty minutes later, a seat opens up and he drops into it. He is soon dozing, the book forgotten.

13      There are two kinds of salarymen, the elite and the run-of-the mill. Salaryman counts himself among the former, the men heading for the top. But he is starting to slip. When he should be at home boning up on some new commercial skill or at a special night course, he is more likely to be out drinking with office buddies.

14      At 9:10, he steps into his real home, the sales division, on the 11th floor of the glass-skinned headquarters of his company. There are 40 cluttered desks in this room, and no partitions. Salaryman's is at the head of a bank of eight desks pushed head-to-head with four on each side. It is his little empire within the company. He fires up another Mild Seven and gets down to work.

15      There is no privacy in a Japanese office. Every phone call, every coffee break, is communal knowledge. A certain amount of slacking-off is permissible, but everyone does his or her best to look busy. No one, after all, wants a reputation for letting the section down.

16      Salaryman has risen to the rank of kacho, or section manager. His job consists largely of analyzing sales data sent up from field offices and processed by his own subordinates before being passed his way. This morning, he must assemble material for a contract the company is after. Finishing right on time, he runs into a 10:30 meeting.

17      The meeting lasts more than an hour and helps members inch toward a strategy for grabbing the sale. "Let's give our all to this contract," the dour-faced department manager tells the group as it breaks up after an hour. Perhaps the Sunday outing with the family could be squeezed into the morning, leaving the afternoon for the office.

18      Salaryman is 10 years younger than his manager and part of his batsu, or faction. The manager has done well, rising ahead of his due according to seniority. He has carried Salaryman along with him much of the way since Salaryman first worked for him in a provincial branch of the company years ago. Salaryman defers to his manager in the elevator, seeks advice on personal problems, and even volunteered for some heavy lifting one weekend when the manager was moving house. It meant cancelling the baseball game with his son, but what could he do?

19      Lunch today is noodles, grabbed in a shop in the building's basement. Salaryman eats with a fellow member of his "class" at the company, the group of 140 young men who were ceremonially inducted into its ranks 15 years before, singing for the first time the company song. Salaryman, like most of his type, can never converse with a co-worker without marking unconsciously whether he is ahead or behind in seniority.

20      With this colleague, though, things are more relaxed. The two men have become fast friends. Over the noodles, they talk of their passion, golf. Neither has the money, or the time, to join a golf club. But both have bought complete sets of clubs and imported clothes and shoes. At lunch, Salaryman sometimes manages to stop into a driving range on the roof of a building near his company, where under a pro's direction he whacks balls into a net eight yards away. His own clubs are used maybe

one weekend a month on a larger range near his house, where the ball can actually fly 80 yards before being arrested by the net.

Soon talk turns to his colleague's interest in leaving his job in procurement for one in Salaryman's department. There is an opening, but it wouldn't do to apply for the job outright. He might not get it, after all, and the shame would be public. And the manager might be put off by a man who places his personal preferences ahead of what the company needs.

Salaryman promises to help, but his mind right now is more on his own future. Few people ever reach the rank of department manager and Salaryman is beginning to have doubts about his own chances. Salaryman knows of others from his class who are already assistant department managers, the next rung on the ladder. Salaryman thinks he will make assistant department manager but after that, who knows? He may hold steady at that grade until his mid-50s and then be farmed out as a senior executive to one of the smaller of the company's many subsidiaries.

Neither Salaryman or his friend would consider doing what one classmate did. This man quit the company two years ago to set up his own consulting business. He has prospered, but in Salaryman's mind lacks the most satisfying element of professional life, membership in a large and respected organization.

Waiting for the elevator, Salaryman decides to sprint up the stairs instead. By the third floor, he is breathless and cursing. Last year, he actually bought a membership in a sports center near the office, then used it only twice, wasting a wad of money. But how could he exercise when his colleagues remained behind to work?

Back at his desk, Salaryman groans. A new batch of sales orders has appeared during lunch to be analyzed. Ganbatte (Fight!), he thinks to himself, and hunkers down. Work is interrupted at 4 p.m. for another meeting, to which he has nothing to contribute but which he must attend to appear part of the team. It ends at just before 6.

By now most of the secretaries and tea-pouring women have gone home. By 7, Salaryman has finished his compiling. But he does not leave—in fact, the thought never occurs to him. None of the other men has. Besides, he has been included in a 7:30 dinner at a nearby restaurant, where the department is entertaining some people from the buying department of a client company.

There business cards are exchanged and the men, numbering four from each side, sit down in a private room. The restaurant is in a basement, but false paper windows and the gurgle of an artificial spring give the feeling of a feudal-era teahouse. Beer is poured, and on cue, everyone raises a glass and the dinner is officially underway.

It runs two hours, through course after course of raw fish and vegetable and rice. Women in kimonos glide in discreetly to fuss over the men, flirt a bit and top off their beer glasses. Talk touches on the price of golf clubs, the fight for the Japan Central League Pennant, the weather. Everything, in fact, except the equipment sale that has brought them together.

29      They get up to leave. With drinks, the bill comes to about $1,600, which the restaurant will add to the company's tab and forward at the end of the month. Salaryman's manager is pleased with how the dinner has gone. "They seemed really to enjoy your story about the ski trip," he whispers as he walks out.

30      Now the manager is going on with two of the client company men to a pricey hostess bar. He rolls in to the drinking spot they have decided on at about 10, two hours after things have gotten underway. Three other friends arrive from a parlor where they have been playing mahjong, and the gathering gets a second wind. Soon, people are yelling at Salaryman to sing. He struggles to his feet and stumbles through his standard number in such a situation, a teary ballad called "At the End of a Journey." One of these days I've got to get new material, he thinks, as he drops back down, feeling a bit boozed. Another Mild Seven is lit, the 45th of the day.

31      As 11 p.m. rolls around, several friends are talking—it is unclear how seriously—about going to a sopurando (soapland), a type of bath- house where young women suds up clients and offer sexual services. "Just call your wife and tell her the boss is making you work overnight," says one.

32      Salaryman has been to such places since his marriage. For a while, he had a thing going with a young woman from the audit department. But he broke it off when he felt she was making too many demands. Lately, he has lost interest in such diversions—they're too expensive, he tells himself. "No thanks," Salaryman tells them, and steps outside to flag a taxi for the ride to the station.

33      As the train races into the suburbs, Salaryman pulls an adult comic book from his briefcase and for 30 minutes gets caught up in sex-laced detective and samurai dramas. After scanning a sports paper that some- one has left behind (his baseball team, the Yomiuri Giants, has won again, he notes with satisfaction) he dozes the rest of the way. By some near uncanny ability this and other nights, he rouses himself promptly as the train reaches his station.

34      After waiting 20 minutes for a cab, Salaryman rides toward his home. In the early days of his marriage, there was always a ride waiting for him—his wife, whom he would telephone on the way from a transfer station. In the car, he would rest his eyes and listen half-way to her talk of the day's happenings, how their girl's piano lessons were going, how their son was still crazy over those robot models.

35      About two years ago, that began tapering off. Salaryman's wife developed interests of her own, got involved in pottery courses and became less willing to tailor her life to his. Now, if he telephones from a

station, he is likely to wake her up and get little sympathy for the late-night shortage of taxis.

At home, he lets himself in the door, quietly. On the table his wife    36
has left ochazuke, a rice, pickle and fish concoction over which hot tea is poured. With the remote control, Salaryman zaps on the color TV, keeping it at its lowest volume. He takes in a late-night talk show while slurping down the final food of the day. Ten minutes later, after opening his children's door for a sentimental gaze at them as they sleep, he scrubs himself down and eases into a hot bath.

Sunday, Sunday, he thinks. If we're back here by 1, I could be on the    37
train by 1:30. The job shouldn't take so long. I know it by heart.

## Evaluating the Text

1. What attitude toward work, in Japan, does the name "salaryman" imply? How does the fact that Burgess compiled data for this article over a three-year period suggest that "salaryman" is representative of Japanese white-collar workers?
2. What is "salaryman's" job, and why do you think Burgess chose this type of career to represent Japanese middle-management workers? What is the function of each of the articles that make up "salaryman's " work outfit and tools of his trade?
3. How is salaryman's life based on trading off time with his family for office duties or work-related activities?
4. How does "salaryman's" conversation with his wife about the kind of car they should get reveal the importance of not being out of step in Japanese culture? How does this attitude differ from those of an American faced with the same choice? What difference in cultural values between the United States and Japan does this reveal?
5. How does "salaryman's" decision to stay in the same company for all his working life promote attitudes toward his career that are very different from those of his American counterpart?
6. What is the significance of the time "salaryman" spends outside his job improving work skills and attending training programs?
7. What does the fact that no women are mentioned as holding any middle- or upper-level executive positions tell you about Japanese society? What kinds of jobs do women have in Japanese corporations?
8. What insight does Burgess's discussion of "salaryman's" "golf game" give you about the availability of space in any major city in Japan and the symbolic importance golf has assumed?
9. Based on how success is achieved by moving up the ranks of very large corporations, what inferences can you draw about the importance of group membership in conferring identity in Japanese culture?
10. How does the competitive ethic reflected in the phrase Ganbatte (Fight!) reveal how Japanese society views workers as soldiers in the trenches of economic warfare? How does this connect to Japan's past militaristic ethic of nationalism?
11. How are the methods of carrying on business conferences different from those in the United States? What can you infer about values in Japanese

culture from these differences? For example, why is it important for a Japanese executive to spend a great deal of time establishing common ground before negotiating a particular deal?

## Exploring Different Perspectives

1. To what extent does the concept of "shame" or "losing face" play an important role in both Japanese and Chinese cultures? What part does this idea play in both Burgess's report and in Mark Salzman's account in "Lessons" of how his martial arts teacher, Pan, was afraid he would "shame" Salzman by not being a good enough pupil of English?
2. In what ways do Burgess's article and Cha Ok Kim's account ("The Peddler") illustrate the important differences between working for a large corporation and being self-employed? Keep in mind, both workers put in tremendously long hours and devote much effort to their jobs.

## Extending Viewpoints through Writing

1. Write an essay exploring the difficulties a young woman would face in attempting to pursue a career such as the kind "salaryman" has. How would traditional Japanese society view a career woman who stayed out half the night in business-related entertaining, left her children, and slept over in the city? How might traditional expectations produce the kinds of dissatisfactions with a stay-at-home life of the kind described by Simone de Beauvoir in "A Married Woman" (Chapter 3)?
2. What insight does Burgess's report give you on how individuals in Japanese culture derive their sense of self-esteem and identity from belonging to a corporation? Compare this with the value Americans place on owning their own businesses.
3. Compare the advantages and disadvantages of the indirect approach Japanese take in negotiating business deals with the direct approach taken by American business people.
4. How do you react to the idea of having a job like that of "salaryman's"? If you get a bit queasy, what conclusions can you draw about the importance Americans attach to having personal freedom in choosing how to spend their time (versus adapting yourself to choices made for you by your corporation)?
5. Create a point-by-point comparison of an American white-collar worker with his or her counterpart, "salaryman," in a typical workday, taking into account each of the following aspects: (a) commuting; (b) valuing work over family; (c) privacy in allotted work space; (d) being one's own boss versus working for someone else; (e) what kind of car one can buy; (f) allocation of time between the office, home, and leisure; and (g) pressure to conform in terms of the clothes one wears.
6. After reading the following excerpt from "They Get by with a Lot of Help from their Kyoiku Mamas" by Carol Simons (*Smithsonian*, March 1987), write a short essay discussing the extent to which competition permeates even the home life of "salaryman's" family. Were you ever subjected to this kind of pressure to succeed academically? Describe your experiences.

No one doubts that behind every high-scoring Japanese student—and they are among the highest scoring in the world—there stands a mother, supportive, aggressive and completely involved in her child's education. She studies, she packs lunches, she waits for hours in lines to register her child for exams and waits again in the hallways for hours while he takes them. She denies herself TV so her child can study in quiet and she stirs noodles at 11 P.M. for the scholar's snack. She shuttles youngsters from exercise class to rhythm class to calligraphy and piano, to swimming and martial arts. She helps every day with homework, hires tutors and works part-time to pay for *juku* [cram school]. Sometimes she enrolls in "mother's class" so she can help with the drills at home.

So accepted is this role that it has spawned its own label, *kyoiku mama* (education mother). This title is not worn openly. Many Japanese mothers are embarrassed, or modest, and simply say, "I do my best." But that best is a lot, because to Japanese women, motherhood is a profession, demanding and prestigious, with education of the child the number-one responsibility. Cutthroat competition in postwar Japan has made her job harder than ever. And while many critics tend to play down the idea of the perpetually pushy mother, there are those who say that a good proportion of the credit for Japan's economic miracle can be laid at her feet.

# Mark Salzman

# *Lessons*

---

*Mark Salzman graduated Phi Beta Kappa, summa cum laude from Yale in 1982 with a degree in Chinese language and literature. From 1982 to 1984, he lived in Chang-sha, Hunan, in the People's Republic of China, where he taught English at Hunan Medical College. There he studied under Pan Qingfu, one of China's greatest traditional boxers and martial arts masters. In October 1985, he was invited back to China to participate in the National Martial Arts Competition and Conference in Tianjin.* Iron and Silk *(1986) recounts his adventures and provides a fascinating behind-the-scenes glimpse into the workings of Chinese society. His experiences also formed the basis for a 1991 film of the same name starring the author. "Lessons," from this book, describes the extraordinary opportunity that studying martial arts with Pan Qingfu offered, along with the comic misunderstandings produced by their being from such different cultures.*

*The period when Salzman was in China coincided with liberal developments within the society, under the leadership of Zhan Ziyang as prime minister, and a more conciliatory relationship with the United States. President Reagan visited China in April 1984 and signed an agreement on nuclear cooperation in nonmilitary areas. In September 1984, China and Britain signed accords designed to facilitate the return of Hong Kong (a British Crown Colony leased in 1898 for 99 years) to Chinese control in 1998.*

1    I was to meet Pan at the training hall four nights a week, to receive private instruction after the athletes finished their evening workout. Waving and wishing me good night, they politely filed out and closed the wooden doors, leaving Pan and me alone in the room. First he explained that I must start from scratch. He meant it, too, for beginning that night, and for many nights thereafter, I learned how to stand at attention. He stood inches away from me and screamed, "Stand straight!" then bored into me with his terrifying gaze. He insisted that I maintain eye contact for as long as he stood in front of me, and that I meet his gaze with one of equal intensity. After as long as a minute of this silent torture, he would shout "At ease!" and I could relax a bit, but

*(For more background on China, see pp. 60 and 70.)

not smile or take my eyes away from his. We repeated this exercise countless times, and I was expected to practice it four to six hours a day. At the time, I wondered what those staring contests had to do with wushu, but I came to realize that everything he was to teach me later was really contained in those first few weeks when we stared at each other. His art drew strength from his eyes; this was his way of passing it on.

After several weeks I came to enjoy staring at him. I would break into a sweat and feel a kind of heat rushing up through the floor into my legs and up into my brain. He told me that when standing like that, I must at all times be prepared to duel, that at any moment he might attack, and I should be ready to defend myself. It exhilarated me to face off with him, to feel his power and taste the fear and anticipation of the blow. Days and weeks passed, but the blow did not come.

One night he broke the lesson off early, telling me that tonight was special. I followed him out of the training hall, and we bicycled a short distance to his apartment. He lived with his wife and two sons on the fifth floor of a large, anonymous cement building. Like all the urban housing going up in China today, the building was indistinguishable from its neighbors, mercilessly practical and depressing in appearance. Pan's apartment had three rooms and a small kitchen. A private bathroom and painted, as opposed to raw, cement walls in all the rooms identified it as the home of an important family. The only decoration in the apartment consisted of some silk banners, awards and photographs from Pan's years as the national wushu champion and from the set of *Shaolin Temple*. Pan's wife, a doctor, greeted me with all sorts of home-made snacks and sat me down at a table set for two. Pan sat across from me and poured two glasses of baijiu. He called to his sons, both in their teens, and they appeared from the bedroom instantly. They stood in complete silence until Pan asked them to greet me, which they did, very politely, but so softly I could barely hear them. They were handsome boys, and the elder, at about fourteen, was taller than me and had a moustache. I tried asking them questions to put them at ease, but they answered only by nodding. They apparently had no idea how to behave toward something like me and did not want to make any mistakes in front of their father. Pan told them to say good night, and they, along with his wife, disappeared into the bedroom. Pan raised his glass and proposed that the evening begin.

He told me stories that made my hair stand on end, with such gusto that I thought the building would shake apart. When he came to the parts where he vanquished his enemies, be brought his terrible hand down on the table or against the wall with a crash, sending our snacks jumping out of their serving bowls. His imitations of cowards and bullies were so funny I could hardly breathe for laughing. He had me spell-bound for three solid hours; then his wife came in to see if we needed any more food or baijiu. I took the opportunity to ask her if she had ever been afraid for her husband's safety when, for example, he went off alone to bust up a gang of hoodlums in Shenyang. She laughed and touched his right hand. "Sometimes I figured he'd be late for dinner." A look of tremendous satisfaction came over Pan's face, and he got up to use the bathroom. She sat down in his chair and looked at me. "Every day he receives tens of letters from all over China, all from people asking to become his student. Since he made the movie, it's been almost impossible for him to go out during the day." She refilled our cups, then looked at me again. "He has trained professionals for more than twenty-five years now, but in all that time he has accepted only one private student." After a long pause, she gestured at me with her chin. "You." Just then Pan came back into the room, returned to his seat and started a new story. This one was about a spear:

5     While still a young man training for the national wushu competition, Pan overheard a debate among some of his fellow athletes about the credibility of an old story. The story described a famous warrior as being able to execute a thousand spear-thrusts without stopping to rest. Some of the athletes felt this to be impossible: after fifty, one's shoulders ache, and by one hundred the skin on the left hand, which guides the spear as the right hand thrusts, twists and returns it, begins to blister. Pan had argued that surely this particular warrior would not have been intimidated by aching shoulders and blisters, and soon a challenge was raised. The next day Pan went out into a field with a spear, and as the other athletes watched, executed one thousand and seven thrusts without stopping to rest. Certain details of the story as Pan told it—that the bones of his left hand were exposed, and so forth—might be called into question, but the number of thrusts I am sure is accurate, and the scar tissue on his left palm indicates that it was not easy for him.

6     One evening later in the year, when I felt discouraged with my progress in a form of Northern Shaolin boxing called "Changquan," or "Long Fist," I asked Pan if he thought I should discontinue the training. He frowned, the only time he ever seemed genuinely angry with me, and said quietly, "When I say I will do something, I do it, exactly as I said I would. In my whole life, I have never started something without finishing it. I said that in the time we have, I would make your wushu better than you could imagine, and I will. Your only responsibility to me is to practice and to learn. My responsibility to you is much greater! Every time you think your task is great, think how much greater mine is. Just keep this in mind: if you fail"—here he paused to make sure I understood—"I will lose face."

7     Though my responsibility to him was merely to practice and to learn, he had one request that he vigorously encouraged me to fulfill—to teach him English. I felt relieved to have something to offer him, so I quickly prepared some beginning materials and rode over to his house for the first lesson. When I got there, he had a tape recorder set up on a small table, along with a pile of oversized paper and a few felt-tip pens from a coloring set. He showed no interest at all in my books, but sat me down

next to the recorder and pointed at the pile of paper. On each sheet he had written out in Chinese dozens of phrases, such as "We'll need a spotlight over there," "These mats aren't springy enough," and "Don't worry — it's just a shoulder dislocation." He asked me to write down the English translation next to each phrase, which took a little over two and a half hours. When I was finished, I asked him if he could read my handwriting, and he smiled, saying that he was sure my handwriting was fine. After a series of delicate questions, I determined that he was as yet unfamiliar with the alphabet, so I encouraged him to have a look at my beginning materials. "That's too slow for me," he said. He asked me to repeat each of the phrases I'd written down five times into the recorder, leaving enough time after each repetition for him to say it aloud after me. "The first time should be very slow — one word at a time, with a pause after each word so I can repeat it. The second time should be the same. The third time you should pause after every other word. The fourth time read it through slowly. The fifth time you can read it fast." I looked at the pile of phrase sheets, calculated how much time this would take, and asked if we could do half today and half tomorrow, as dinner was only three hours away. "Don't worry!" he said, beaming. "I've prepared some food for you here. Just tell me when you get hungry." He sat next to me, turned on the machine, then turned it off again. "How do you say, 'And now, Mark will teach me English'?" I told him how and he repeated it, at first slowly, then more quickly, twenty or twenty-one times. He turned the machine on. "And now, Mark will teach me English." I read the first phrase, five times as he had requested, and he pushed a little note across the table. "Better read it six times," it read, "and a little slower."

After several weeks during which we nearly exhausted the phrasal [8] possibilities of our two languages, Pan announced that the time had come to do something new. "Now I want to learn routines." I didn't understand. "Routines?" "Yes. Everything, including language, is like wushu. First you learn the basic moves, or words, then you string them together into routines." He produced from his bedroom a huge sheet of paper made up of smaller pieces taped together. He wanted me to write a story on it. The story he had in mind was a famous Chinese folk tale, "How Yu Gong Moved the Mountain." The story tells of an old man who realized that, if he only had fields where a mountain stood instead, he would have enough arable land to support his family comfortably. So he went out to the mountain with a shovel and a bucket and started to take the mountain down. All his neighbors made fun of him, calling it an impossible task, but Yu Gong disagreed: it would just take a long time, and after several tens of generations had passed, the mountain would at last become a field and his family would live comfortably. Pan had me write this story in big letters, so that he could paste it up on his bedroom wall, listen to the tape I was to make and read along as he lay in bed.

Not only did I repeat this story into the tape recorder several dozen [9] times — at first one word at a time, and so on — but Pan invited Bill, Bob and Marcy over for dinner one night and had them read it a few times for variety. After they had finished, Pan said that he would like to recite a few phrases for them to evaluate and correct. He chose some of his favorite sentences and repeated each seven or eight times without a pause. He belted them out with such fierce concentration we were all afraid to move lest it disturb him. At last he finished and looked at me, asking quietly if it was all right. I nodded and he seemed overcome with relief. He smiled, pointed at me and said to my friends, "I was very nervous just then. I didn't want him to lose face."

10    While Pan struggled to recite English routines from memory, he began teaching me how to use traditional weapons. He would teach me a single move, then have me practice it in front of him until I could do it ten times in a row without a mistake. He always stood about five feet away from me, with his arms folded, grinding his teeth, and the only time he took his eyes off me was to blink. One night in the late spring I was having a particularly hard time learning a move with the staff. I was sweating heavily and my right hand was bleeding, so the staff had become slippery and hard to control. Several of the athletes stayed on after their workout to watch and to enjoy the breeze that sometimes passed through the training hall. Pan stopped me and indicated that I wasn't working hard enough. "Imagine," he said, "that you are participating in the national competition, and those athletes are your competitors. Look as if you know what you are doing! Frighten them with your strength and confidence." I mustered all the confidence I could, under the circumstances, and flung myself into the move. I lost control of the staff, and it whirled straight into my forehead. As if in a dream, the floor raised up several feet to support my behind, and I sat staring up at Pan while blood ran down across my nose and a fleshy knob grew between my eyebrows. The athletes sprang forward to help me up. They seemed nervous, never having had a foreigner knock himself out in their training hall before, but Pan, after asking if I felt all right, seemed positively inspired. "Sweating and bleeding. Good."

* * *

11    Every once in a while, Pan felt it necessary to give his students something to think about, to spur them on to greater efforts. During one morning workout two women practiced a combat routine, one armed with a spear, the other with a *dadao*, or halberd. The dadao stands about six feet high and consists of a broadsword attached to a thick wooden pole, with an angry-looking spike at the far end. It is heavy and difficult to wield even for a strong man, so it surprised me to see this young woman, who could not weigh more than one hundred pounds, using it so effectively. At one point in their battle the woman with the dadao swept it toward the other woman's feet, as if to cut them off, but the other woman jumped up in time to avoid the blow. The first woman,

without letting the blade of the dadao stop, brought it around in another sweep, as if to cut the other woman in half at the waist. The other woman, without an instant to spare, bent straight from the hips so that the dadao slashed over her back and head, barely an inch away. This combination was to be repeated three times in rapid succession before moving on to the next exchange. The women practiced this move several times, none of which satisfied Pan. "Too slow, and the weapon is too far away from her. It should graze her back as it goes by." They tried again, but still Pan growled angrily. Suddenly he got up and took the dadao from the first woman. The entire training hall went silent and still. Without warming up at all, Pan ordered the woman with the spear to get ready, and to move fast when the time came. His body looked as though electricity had suddenly passed through it, and the huge blade flashed toward her. Once, twice the dadao flew beneath her feet, then swung around in a terrible arc and rode her back with flawless precision. The third time he added a little twist at the end, so that the blade grazed up her neck and sent a little decoration stuck in her pigtails flying across the room.

I had to sit down for a moment to ponder the difficulty of sending an object roughly the shape of an oversized shovel, only heavier, across a girl's back and through her pigtails, without guide ropes or even a safety helmet. Not long before, I had spoken with a former troupe member who, when practicing with this instrument, had suddenly found himself on his knees. The blade, unsharpened, had twirled a bit too close to him and passed through his Achilles' tendon without a sound. Pan handed the dadao back to the woman and walked over to me. "What if you had made a mistake?" I asked. "I never make mistakes," he said, without looking at me.

## *Evaluating the Text*

1. Why is the standing-at-attention exercise so important in learning *wushu* (Kung Fu)? What abilities does this exercise develop?
2. What is the relevance of the Chinese folk tale, "How Yu Gong Moved the Mountain" to Salzman's apprenticeship?
3. What evidence can you cite to show that Pan applies the same standard (based on fear of "losing face") to Mark as he does to himself? What part does the concept of "losing face" play in Chinese culture, and what values are expressed through this term?
4. What similarities can you discover between Pan's approach to learning English and his methods of teaching Chinese martial arts?
5. What factors do you believe might explain why Pan chooses Mark to be the only private student he has ever had? Why is this especially significant because Mark is an American and Pan has never taken one private student within China in twenty-five years?
6. To what extent was Pan's choice of Mark an expression of Pan's personality in terms of always taking on the hardest challenge possible? In view of

this, what would have been involved for Pan if he were to "lose face" if Mark were to perform his martial arts routine poorly?

7. What conclusions can you draw about the standard of living in China, from the way in which Pan and his family live? Keep in mind that being a champion in martial arts is comparable to being an outstanding baseball, football, or basketball player and that Pan's wife is a physician.

8. Why is Pan's performance with a heavy spear, without any warm-up, so impressive? How does the placement of this episode at the end of the chapter serve as an appropriate and dramatic conclusion?

## Exploring Different Perspectives

1. Compare and contrast the impression you get of Beryl Markham (in "West with the Night") with that of Pan. What common features can you discover in terms of the goals they set for themselves and how they go about reaching these goals? In what respects are they different from one another?

2. What common elements can you discover between the self-imposed discipline of Cha Ok Kim in "The Peddler" and of Pan in "Lessons"? How do the values of the two cultures shape the way their individualism expresses itself?

## Extending Viewpoints through Writing

1. Describe an experience, including martial arts instruction, that you have had that gave you an insight into Salzman's experiences.

2. If you could master anything you wished, what would it be, and who would you want to be your teacher? Would you want to learn from someone like Pan?

# Daniel Boulanger

# *The Shoe Breaker*

---

*Daniel Boulanger was born in Compiègne, France, in 1922. An enormously prolific writer, he has written novels, short stories, children's stories, and film scripts. In 1973, he won the prestigious "Goncourt de la nouvelle" for his short fiction, and ten years later he was elected to the Academy Goncourt. American audiences may recognize him as an actor who has played the part of the gangster in* Shoot the Piano Player *(1960, directed by François Truffaut), the German general in* King of Hearts *(1966, directed by Philippe de Broca), and the cop who kills Jean Paul Belmondo in* Breathless *(1960, directed by Jean-Luc Godard). "The Shoe Breaker" from* Les Noces du Merle *(1963), translated by Penny Million Pucelik and Maryjo Despréaux Schneider in 1989, reveals the extent to which French society is still based on class distinctions, in this unforgettable portrait of a most unique occupation.*

*Traditionally an ally of the United States, France was a world power and cultural center in Europe during the reign of Louis XIV (1653–1715). The French absolute monarchy was brought to an end during the French Revolution, a tumultuous period that set the stage for Napoleon's rise to power during the late eighteenth century. France emerged from the Napoleonic Wars as a modern bureaucratic state dominated by the bourgeoise (middle class), a social structure that endures to the present. In the twentieth century, France has endured two world wars fought on its territory and has been involved in colonial wars in Indochina and Algeria. The difficulty of governing a people so exasperating and stimulating was perhaps best stated by Charles de Gaulle (president from 1959 to 1969), who returned France to a position of prestige in world affairs: "How can you be expected to govern a country that has 246 kinds of cheese?" Since 1981, Francois Mitterrand, a socialist, has been president of the republic. In "The Shoe Breaker," Boulanger vividly examines how class distinctions are still an integral part of French society.*

"Where is Pinceloup?"    1

"I don't know, sir," replied the clerk.    2

"Baron," the owner said, as he turned to speak to the client who had    3
just come in, "my staff and I saw him leave early this morning on your
behalf."

4    "What I see," retorted the other, "is that I was counting on my shoes being ready at four o'clock. You assured me they would be. It is now six o'clock and the dinner is at eight. I don't intend to stand here cooling my heels."

5    "But, sir . . . "

6    "Don't tell me you're sorry. It is I, my dear man, who am sorry. You can't depend on anyone nowadays."

7    The baron looked down at his feet and wiggled his toes under the worn calfskin. He'd have to go to the dinner party in his old shoes, bulging from his bunions and bubbled by his corns. Obviously he was comfortable in them, but aren't we always anxious to try out our latest purchase? The pair of dress shoes that he had bought the day before that tortured him so when he first put them on were still walking the streets of Paris, being broken in by a fellow named Pinceloup.

8    "May I make a suggestion?" ventured the owner. "I know the man well. I have used him for more than thirty years, Sir. He has broken in over twelve thousand pairs of shoes for me, following the customers' directives. He figures a morning per pair for normal feet, but an entire afternoon should there be any deformity. Our exceptional patrons . . . "

9    The baron didn't readily count himself among the latter.

10   " . . . I mean those whom it was nature's whim to deform, and God knows I pity them, will sometimes cost Pinceloup an entire day."

11   With the tip of his cane, the baron maliciously applied pressure to the corn crowning the big toe of his right foot, swollen by gout.

12   "Pinceloup is, moreover, a great judge of physiognomy and I shall miss him. He knows at a glance whether to walk pigeon-toed or duck-footed, or to stuff a wad of cotton in the shoe at just the right place, that is to say at the place that . . . Baron, sir?"

13   "Yes?"

14   "People like Pinceloup will be hard to come by in the future. Love for one's work is a thing of the past. Love for art is disappearing. But please sit down, he should be here any time now."

15   "Art?" cried out the baron. "Indeed I shall sit down."

16   "Pinceloup," the owner continued, "belonged to my father before I took over the business."

17   This sort of talk the baron savored, and time wore on. The salesmen, meanwhile, were coming and going, carrying piles of boxes, kneeling, wielding their shoehorns, here lacing up an Oxford, there vaunting the quality of the alligator and, over in the women's section, assuming feminine poses as they side-saddled their fitting stools, clamping their knees together like women in bathing suits, not hesitating to look away should gaping thighs offer them the forbidden view. The owner kept a watchful eye on his people without diverting his attention from the baron who, though not a particularly good customer, was a man of great

renown. The Petit–Chablis clan, lest one forget, still owned half of the country's railroads, and that is indeed what drew a good part of the clientele.

"Honestly, I can't understand what's keeping him."  18

"And it's getting dark," the baron sighed.  19

They were about to give up when the door opened and Pinceloup  20
appeared, green around the gills and dragging at the heels.

"Ah! There you are."  21

The baron looked at his dress shoes now gracing the shoe breaker's  22
feet. They no longer bore a resemblance to the ones the Baron had purchased, but rather to the good old pair he now wore. His eyes wandered from the one to the other.

"My dear fellow," he exclaimed, putting his hand on Pinceloup's  23
shoulder, "did everything go well?"

"Everything, Baron, sir. There might still be a hint of stiffness in the  24
reinforcement of the outer left heel. I apologize for that."

Am I getting old, Pinceloup wondered. Is the leather less supple due  25
to the new fangled methods of tanning and splicing? Or might the stitching or the lining be too heavy?

"Unshoe him," the owner told a clerk.  26

"I'd appreciate it," Pinceloup uttered feebly.  27

"Are you otherwise satisfied?" Baron Petit–Chablis inquired.  28

With the tip of his cane, he pointed to the already bloated shoes, now  29
emptied of Pinceloup's feet, as well as of the scraps of cardboard, cotton balls, strips of cork, rubber disks and the like.

"They've put in eighteen kilometers," Pinceloup declared. "I advise  30
you to put them on right away while they're still warm. We'll obtain a more generous contact. Talcum powder . . . "

"The talc," shouted the owner.  31

The talcum powder will save the day, mused Pinceloup.  32

The baron had himself shod, laced up and helped to his feet. He  33
shook hands with the owner. At the same time, he extended his left hand which held his cane, trying discreetly to offer Pinceloup a coin. He nearly blinded the poor devil in the process.

The breaker watched the baron as he left with short and hesitant  34
steps.

Seeing him stop in the middle of the street for relief, Pinceloup felt  35
the pain and even a twinge of shame.

"Monsieur," he said to the owner, "I just can't do it any more."  36

"What's that?"  37

"I've lost my touch. Look!" They could see the baron limping off.  38

"I did what I could," Pinceloup muttered as he examined his lacer-  39
ated feet. His socks were embedded in his flesh and darkened in spots with blood stains.

40    "Come on now, don't give up for heaven's sake. You're the best breaker in all of Paris, Pinceloup. The main thing in life is to be tops at something. Remember . . . "

41    "And tomorrow?" interrupted Pinceloup, his sense of honor reviving.

42    "You'll do two pairs for me. They'll be a snap."

43    "But I didn't see them on the customers' feet." The owner went to his file and pulled two sheets of vellum.

44    "Here." He knows that Pinceloup can't read and Pinceloup knows that he knows. If the boss is being mean again, it's because he esteems him, needs him, and can boast that no one else in all of Paris can break in shoes as well as Pinceloup.

45    "See you tomorrow," Pinceloup murmured.

46    Since his feet hurt him so, he put on his espadrilles, which he saved for the bad evenings. The boss, despite the fact that it was closing time, asked him to leave through the back service door.

*Translated by Penny Million Pucelik*
*and Marijo Despréaux Schneider*

## Evaluating the Text

1. What does being a "shoe breaker" actually entail?
2. How does the phrase "I have used him for more than thirty years" suggest a gulf between social classes in France? How is Pinceloup viewed by his employer and the employer's father before him? How old would you say Pinceloup is, and how long has he been a "shoe breaker"?
3. When Pinceloup arrives, is he what you expected, or is he different in some way from the picture painted by his employer and the Baron? How do the Baron's remarks about Pinceloup reveal his distrust of those in lower social positions?
4. What means does the employer use to persuade Pinceloup into staying? How does the form his flattery takes suggest a weak spot in Pinceloup's nature the owner can appeal to? How is Pinceloup's perverse pride in doing what no one else can do the very means by which he can be manipulated?
5. What is the significance of the Baron's offer of a small coin to Pinceloup, in view of what Pinceloup suffers to produce comfortable shoes for the Baron?
6. Why is it significant that Pinceloup is asked to leave by the rear entrance, even though it is late and he has had an especially difficult day?

## Exploring Different Perspectives

1. How do the "shoe breaker" and the "salaryman" (see John Burgess's "A Day in the Life of 'Salaryman'") both bend themselves out of shape (one physically, the other in terms of time and energy) to suit the requirements of their jobs? What significant differences in the cultural value of

perfectionism can you observe between France and Japan from these two works?

2. To what extent does Beryl Markham ("West with the Night") exhibit the same personality traits as does Pinceloup in terms of needing to succeed at a very difficult task to have higher self-esteem?

## Extending Viewpoints through Writing

1. To what extent can this story be considered a parable of class exploitation in French society? What might you infer about the values of the French in terms of attitudes toward employees by employers, the importance of social titles, and the continuing prestige of the aristocracy?
2. Have you ever worked at a store where some customers were valued more than others, especially if that value was not strictly economic but took a social form as well, such as that dramatized in Boulanger's story?
3. Have you ever known anyone who worked at a job they complained about constantly while never taking any steps to correct the situation or to leave? At what point did you realize that despite their complaints the job satisfied real needs for them?
4. Try your hand at writing a parable similar to Boulanger's story based on another occupation, real or imagined, that expresses larger societal issues through the circumstances of an employee performing a particular job.
5. Describe an experience when you became aware that the person who was waiting on you in a restaurant or store had a "real" life aside from their role at work. For example, you might have seen one of your teachers at a shopping mall, supermarket, or movie. Describe how you felt when you saw someone out of their "context."

# CONNECTING CULTURES

## Gene Logsdon, "Amish Economics"

1. How does the Amish family structure differ from the principal types discussed by Andrew Cherlin and Frank F. Furstenberg, Jr., in "The American Family in the Year 2000" (Chapter 1)? In your opinion, what are the advantages and drawbacks of Amish life?
2. In what sense do the Amish view the land in ways similar to ways in which land is viewed by the Quiché Indians in Guatemala described by Rigoberta Menchu in "Birth Ceremonies" (Chapter 1)?
3. How does Chinese culture, as explored by Bruce Dollar ("Child Care in China" Chapter 1) depend on the subordination of the individual to the community in ways that are similar to those characteristic of Amish society? In what ways to they differ?
4. Read Jo Goodwin Parker's "What Is Poverty?" (Chapter 5) and contrast her predicament with the means the Amish have evolved for dealing with many of the problems she faces such as health care, welfare, and other social services.
5. After reading Joan Didion's "Miami: The Cuban Presence" (Chapter 7), discuss the elements that both the Cuban community and the Amish share that might explain why both of these subcultures have been successful without assimilating into the mainstream of American society.
6. Drawing on Raymonde Carroll's analysis ("Minor Accidents," Chapter 8), discuss how the concept of cultural misunderstanding might operate in terms of the Amish and the surrounding "English" farmers. In what kinds of situations might "English" and Amish farmers misunderstand each other's behavior?

## Catherine Lim, "Paper"

7. Compare and contrast the funeral rites described by Lim with the birth ceremonies described by Rigoberta Menchu ("Birth Ceremonies," Chapter 1). How do these rituals reflect the values of each culture?
8. How do both Lim's story and Dino Buzzati's "The Falling Girl" (Chapter 5) develop as an inexorable set of consequences brought on initially by the lure of material possessions, power, and social status?
9. Contrast Lim's treatment of the effects of individualistic greed in a capitalist society with Octavio Paz's exposition ("The Day of the Dead," Chapter 8) of the religious premise that great sacrifices during fiestas are rewarded, so that villages spend their accumulated wealth in one grand celebration.

## Cha Ok Kim, "The Peddler"

10. To what extent does Kim's narrative contradict Gloria Steinem's thesis ("The Time Factor," Chapter 5) that poverty undercuts the ability to plan for the future?

11. What similarities can you discover between Kim's narrative and Joan Didion's report ("Miami: The Cuban Presence," Chapter 7) that might explain why Koreans and Cubans have become successful after emigrating to the United States? Be sure to consider questions of education, support of family and community, language barriers, and the degree to which each of these two groups have or have not assimilated into American mainstream culture.

12. To what extent does Kim's account confirm or contradict Edward Said's ("Reflections on Exile," Chapter 7) analysis of the personality profile of the displaced person in terms of adaptation to a new environment?

## Beryl Markham, "West with the Night"

13. To what extent are Markham's expectations for herself as extreme in their own way as those of Jing-Mei Woo's mother toward her daughter (Amy Tan, "Jing-Mei Woo: Two Kinds," Chapter 1)? How do these two selections shed light on the psychology of overachievement?

14. How do both Markham's account and that of Douchan Gersi ("Initiated into an Iban Tribe of Headhunters," Chapter 2) provide insight into the psychology of the explorer? In what respects do Markham's motives and purposes differ from Gersi's?

15. Compare and contrast the personal narrative of Markham and Claude Eatherly's responses during the interview with Maurizio Chierici ("The Man from Hiroshima," Chapter 9) as they reveal the internal and external pressures on pilots and the psychological consequences for each of successfully completing their missions.

## John Burgess, "A Day in the Life of 'Salaryman'"

16. After reading Kyōko Hayashi's story, "The Empty Can" (Chapter 9), explore connections between her picture of the extent to which Japanese society is male dominated and Burgess's report on the absence of women holding middle- or upper-level executive positions in contemporary Japan.

17. What insight does Natsume Soseki's chapter (from the novel I Am a Cat, Chapter 1) provide about Japan at the turn of the century when compared with Burgess's account of contemporary Japan? What important changes can you discover in the quality of Japanese life from then until now?

## Mark Salzman, "Lessons"

18. How does the Chinese cultural concept of "losing face" play an important role in both Salzman's account and in "The Big Fish" by Chen Jo-hsi (Chapter 6)?

19. After reading Gretel Ehrlich's "To Live in Two Worlds" (Chapter 8), compare her response to being allowed to witness the sun dance with Saltzman's reaction as Pan's only martial arts private student. In what respects are the two situations comparable?

## Daniel Boulanger, "The Shoe Breaker"

20. How do Ivan Karp's analysis ("Good Marx for the Anthropologist," Chapter 5) and "The Grass-Eaters" by Krishnan Varma (Chapter 5) explore conflicts between upper and lower social classes? How are these expositions of this theme both similar to and different from Boulanger's story?

21. After reading Jan Rabie's story, "Drought" (Chapter 6), discuss the extent to which Boulanger's story may be seen as a parable exploring the interdependence of social classes in France.

# 5
# *Class Conflicts*

Every society is capable of being characterized in terms of social class. Although principles by which class is identified vary widely from culture to culture — from the amount of money you earn in the United States to what kind of accent you speak with in England to what religious caste you are born into in India — class serves to set boundaries around individuals in terms of opportunities and possibilities. Conflicts based on inequalities of social class are often intertwined with those of race because minorities usually receive the least amount of education, have less political clout, earn the least income, and find work in occupations considered menial without the possibility of advancement. Class conditions our entire lives by setting limitations that determine, more than we might like to admit, who we can be friends with, what our goals are, and even who we can marry.

The writers in this chapter explore many of the less obvious connections between social class and the control people exercise over their lives. Gloria Steinem, in "The Time Factor," discusses how the class we belong to shapes our ability to plan for the future. In "What Is Poverty?" Jo Goodwin Parker brings home the day-to-day consequences of being poverty stricken in the southern United States. On the opposite side of the world, in India, Krishnan Varma tells a story ("The Grass-Eaters") of survival and adaptation of a family to the shocking conditions of homelessness in modern-day Calcutta. An extraordinary glimpse into how the Ku Klux Klan exploits class conflicts is provided by C. P. Ellis (in "Why I Quit the Klan"), a former president of the Durham, North Carolina, KKK, whose experiences transformed him into an activist in the civil rights movement. Racism of a more subtle kind is the subject of Toi Derricotte's diary entries recounting her family's experiences in being excluded from membership in their neighborhood's swim club in "The Black Notebooks."

An entirely different perspective on race and class relationships is explored in "An Insolvable Problem of Genetics," Josef Škvorecký's amusing story of a Czechoslovakian family's response to the prospect of their son's forthcoming marriage. In "Good Marx for the Anthropologist," Ivan Karp explains how many of the classic Marx Brothers movies such as *Duck Soup* enlisted audience sympathies on the side of immigrants rebelling against the tyranny of upper-class values. In Italy, Dino Buzzati creates an intriguing parable exploring the irresistible attraction of social status and wealth in "The Falling Girl."

# Gloria Steinem

# *The Time Factor*

---

*Gloria Steinem, born in 1934, is perhaps best known as the founder and editor of* Ms. *magazine. She has played a crucial role as a writer, speaker, and political activist in promoting women's rights. Steinem's columns for* Ms. *were collected and published under the title* Outrageous Acts and Everyday Rebellions *(1983). "The Time Factor," which originally appeared in* Ms. *in 1980, analyzes how lack of social power, whether due to economic deprivation, gender, or race, impairs the ability to plan for the future.*

1   Planning ahead is a measure of class. The rich and even the middle class plan for future generations, but the poor can plan ahead only a few weeks or days.

2   I remember finding this calm insight in some sociological text and feeling instant recognition. Yes, of course, our sense of time was partly a function of power, or the lack of it. It rang true even in the entirely economic sense the writer had in mind. "The guys who own the factories hand them down to their sons and great-grandsons," I remember a boy in my high school saying bitterly. "On this side of town, we just plan for Saturday night."

3   But it also seemed equally true of most of the women I knew — including myself — regardless of the class we supposedly belonged to. Though I had left my factory-working neighborhood, gone to college, become a journalist, and thus was middle class, I still felt that I couldn't plan ahead. I had to be flexible — first, so that I could be ready to get on a plane for any writing assignment (even though the male writers I knew launched into books and other long-term projects on their own), and then so that I could adapt to the career and priorities of an eventual husband and children (even though I was leading a rewarding life without either). Among the results of this uncertainty were a stunning lack of career planning and such smaller penalties as no savings, no insurance, and an apartment that lacked basic pieces of furniture.

4   On the other hand, I had friends who were married to men whose longer-term career plans were compatible with their own, yet they still lived their lives in day-to-day response to any possible needs of their husbands and children. Moreover, the one male colleague who shared or even understood this sense of powerlessness was a successful black journalist and literary critic who admitted that even after twenty years he

planned only one assignment at a time. He couldn't forget his dependence on the approval of white editors.

Clearly there is more to this fear of the future than a conventional definition of class could explain. There is also caste: the unchangeable marks of sex and race that bring a whole constellation of cultural injunctions against power, even the limited power of controlling one's own life.

We haven't yet examined time-sense and future planning as functions of discrimination, but we have begun to struggle with them, consciously or not. As a movement, women have become painfully conscious of too much reaction and living from one emergency to the next, with too little initiative and planned action of our own; hence many of our losses to a much smaller but more entrenched and consistent right wing.

Though the cultural habit of living in the present and glazing over the future goes deep, we've begun to challenge the cultural punishment awaiting the "pushy" and "selfish" women (and the "uppity" minority men) who try to break through it and control their own lives.

Even so, feminist writers and theorists tend to avoid the future by lavishing all our analytical abilities on what's wrong with the present, or on revisions of history and critiques of the influential male thinkers of the past. The big, original, and certainly courageous books of this wave of feminism have been more diagnostic than prescriptive. We need pragmatic planners and visionary futurists, but can we think of even one feminist five-year-plan? Perhaps the closest we have come is visionary architecture or feminist science fiction, but they generally avoid the practical steps of how to get from here to there.

Obviously, many of us need to extend our time-sense—to have the courage to plan for the future, even while most of us are struggling to keep our heads above water in the present. But this does not mean a flat-out imitation of the culturally masculine habit of planning ahead, living in the future, and thus living a deferred life. It doesn't mean the traditional sacrifice of spontaneous action, or a sensitive awareness of the present, that comes from long years of career education with little intrusion of reality, from corporate pressure to work now for the sake of a reward after retirement, or, least logical of all, from patriarchal religions that expect obedience now in return for a reward after death.

In fact, the ability to live in the present, to tolerate uncertainty, and to remain open, spontaneous, and flexible are all culturally female qualities that many men need and have been denied. As usual, both halves of the polarized masculine-feminine division need to learn from each other's experiences. If men spent more time raising small children, for instance, they would be forced to develop more patience and flexibility. If women had more power in the planning of natural resources and other long-term processes—or even in the planning of our own careers and reproductive lives—we would have to develop more sense of the future and of cause and effect.

11    An obsession with reacting to the present, feminine-style, or on controlling and living in the future, masculine-style, are both wasteful of time.

12    And time is all there is.

## Evaluating the Text

1. How do you interpret Steinem's thesis that "our sense of time [is] partly a function of power, or the lack of it"?
2. Of the examples Steinem presents to support her claim that lack of power, whether due to economic deprivation, gender, or race, impairs the ability to plan, which do you find the most persuasive? Discuss your reasons. Do these examples seem to be true to life? Do the conclusions she draws from them seem to be warranted?
3. What do you understand the difference to be between the terms *class* and *caste*? Give a few examples that would clearly illustrate the differences between these terms.
4. Evaluate Steinem's assertion that those who are poor, female, or a member of a minority group are at a disadvantage in planning for the future and tend to react to rather than act on their environments. Explain how these conditions are related. Why would being female, poor, or a member of a minority group tend to focus one's energies more in the present to the exclusion of planning for the future?
5. How does Steinem differentiate the kind of future planning she thinks is valuable from the traditional "culturally masculine habit of planning ahead, living in the future, and . . . living a deferred life"? How would she want women to plan for the future in a way that differs from the way men plan for the future?
6. How does Steinem structure her article so as to convert or transform what she initially treats as a liability—living in the present—to a strength that she suggests men might usefully incorporate into their own lives?

## Exploring Different Perspectives

1. What kinds of connections can you discover between Steinem's observations about the relationship between poverty and the inability to plan and Jo Goodwin Parker's graphic account ("What Is Poverty?") of her situation?
2. To what extent is Steinem's thesis confirmed by the events depicted in Krishnan Varma's story, "The Grass-Eaters"?

## Extending Viewpoints through Writing

1. Examine any situation in which you had to plan for the future, and analyze how much of your decision was a reaction to circumstances and how much of it was an attempt to consciously set a long-term plan.
2. Compare a situation when you had to buy something you needed immediately with the purchase of a similar item when you were not under any pressure. Compare the quality of the decisions you made to determine whether Steinem is correct.

# Jo Goodwin Parker

# *What is Poverty?*

---

*Jo Goodwin Parker's poignant and realistic account of the shame, humiliation, and outrage of being poor was first given as a speech in Deland, Florida, on December 27, 1965, and was published in* America's Other Children: Public Schools Outside Suburbia, *edited by George Henderson (1971). Parker reveals in graphic detail the hard choices she was forced to make in an ever-losing battle to preserve the health of her three children.*

You ask me what is poverty? Listen to me. Here I am, dirty, smelly, and with no "proper" underwear on and with the stench of my rotting teeth near you. I will tell you. Listen to me. Listen without pity. I cannot use your pity. Listen with understanding. Put yourself in my dirty, worn out, ill-fitting shoes, and hear me. 1

Poverty is getting up every morning from a dirt- and illness-stained mattress. The sheets have long since been used for diapers. Poverty is living in a smell that never leaves. This is a smell of urine, sour milk, and spoiling food sometimes joined with the strong smell of long-cooked onions. Onions are cheap. If you have smelled this smell, you did not know how it came. It is the smell of the outdoor privy. It is the smell of young children who cannot walk the long dark way in the night. It is the smell of the mattresses where years of "accidents" have happened. It is the smell of the milk which has gone sour because the refrigerator long has not worked, and it costs money to get it fixed. It is the smell of rotting garbage. I could bury it, but where is the shovel? Shovels cost money. 2

Poverty is being tired. I have always been tired. They told me at the hospital when the last baby came that I had chronic anemia caused from poor diet, a bad case of worms, and that I needed a corrective operation. I listened politely—the poor are always polite. The poor always listen. They don't say that there is no money for iron pills, or better food, or worm medicine. The idea of an operation is frightening and costs so much that, if I had dared, I would have laughed. Who takes care of my children? Recovery from an operation takes a long time. I have three children. When I left them with "Granny" the last time I had a job, I came home to find the baby covered with fly specks, and a diaper that had not been changed since I left. When the dried diaper came off, bits of my baby's flesh came with it. My other child was playing with a sharp bit of broken glass, and my oldest was playing alone at the edge of a lake. I 3

277

made twenty-two dollars a week, and a good nursery school costs twenty dollars a week for three children. I quit my job.

4 Poverty is dirt. You say in your clean clothes coming from your clean house, "Anybody can be clean." Let me explain about housekeeping with no money. For breakfast I give my children grits with no oleo or cornbread without eggs and oleo. This does not use up many dishes. What dishes there are, I wash in cold water and with no soap. Even the cheapest soap has to be saved for the baby's diapers. Look at my hands, so cracked and red. Once I saved for two months to buy a jar of Vaseline for my hands and the baby's diaper rash. When I had saved enough, I went to buy it and the price had gone up two cents. The baby and I suffered on. I have to decide every day if I can bear to put my cracked, sore hands into the cold water and strong soap. But you ask, why not hot water? Fuel costs money. If you have a wood fire it costs money. If you burn electricity, it costs money. Hot water is a luxury. I do not have luxuries. I know you will be surprised when I tell you how young I am. I look so much older. My back has been bent over the wash tubs every day for so long, I cannot remember when I ever did anything else. Every night I wash every stitch my school age child has on and just hope her clothes will be dry by morning.

5 Poverty is staying up all night on cold nights to watch the fire, knowing one spark on the newspaper covering the walls means your sleeping children die in flames. In summer poverty is watching gnats and flies devour your baby's tears when he cries. The screens are torn and you pay so little rent you know they will never be fixed. Poverty means insects in your food, in your nose, in your eyes, and crawling over you when you sleep. Poverty is hoping it never rains because diapers won't dry when it rains and soon you are using newspapers. Poverty is seeing your children forever with runny noses. Paper handkerchiefs cost money and all your rags you need for other things. Even more costly are antihistamines. Poverty is cooking without food and cleaning without soap.

6 Poverty is asking for help. Have you ever had to ask for help, knowing your children will suffer unless you get it? Think about asking for a loan from a relative, if this is the only way you can imagine asking for help. I will tell you how it feels. You find out where the office is that you are supposed to visit. You circle that block four or five times. Thinking of your children, you go in. Everyone is very busy. Finally, someone comes out and you tell her that you need help. That never is the person you need to see. You go see another person, and after spilling the whole shame of your poverty all over the desk between you, you find that this isn't the right office after all—you must repeat the whole process, and it never is any easier at the next place.

7 You have asked for help, and after all it has a cost. You are again told to wait. You are told why, but you don't really hear because of the red cloud of shame and the rising black cloud of despair.

8 Poverty is remembering. It is remembering quitting school in junior

high because "nice" children had been so cruel about my clothes and my smell. The attendance officer came. My mother told him I was pregnant. I wasn't, but she thought that I could get a job and help out. I had jobs off and on, but never long enough to learn anything. Mostly I remember being married. I was so young then. I am still young. For a time, we had all the things you have. There was a little house in another town, with hot water and everything. Then my husband lost his job. There was unemployment insurance for a while and what few jobs I could get. Soon, all our nice things were repossessed and we moved back here. I was pregnant then. This house didn't look so bad when we first moved in. Every week it gets worse. Nothing is ever fixed. We now had no money. There were a few odd jobs for my husband, but everything went for food then, as it does now. I don't know how we lived through three years and three babies, but we did. I'll tell you something, after the last baby I destroyed my marriage. It had been a good one, but could you keep on bringing children in this dirt? Did you ever think how much it costs for any kind of birth control? I knew my husband was leaving the day he left, but there were no good-bys between us. I hope he has been able to climb out of this mess somewhere. He never could hope with us to drag him down.

That's when I asked for help. When I got it, you know how much it 9 was? It was, and is, seventy-eight dollars a month for the four of us; that is all I ever can get. Now you know why there is no soap, no needles and thread, no hot water, no aspirin, no worm medicine, no hand cream, no shampoo. None of these things forever and ever and ever. So that you can see clearly, I pay twenty dollars a month rent, and most of the rest goes for food. For grits and cornmeal, and rice and milk and beans. I try my best to use only the minimum electricity. If I use more, there is that much less for food.

Poverty is looking into a black future. Your children won't play with 10 my boys. They will turn to other boys who steal to get what they want. I can already see them behind the bars of their prison instead of behind the bars of my poverty. Or they will turn to the freedom of alcohol or drugs, and find themselves enslaved. And my daughter? At best, there is for her a life like mine.

But you say to me, there are schools. Yes, there are schools. My 11 children have no extra books, no magazines, no extra pencils, or crayons, or paper and the most important of all, they do not have health. They have worms, they have infections, they have pink-eye all summer. They do not sleep well on the floor, or with me in my one bed. They do not suffer from hunger, my seventy-eight dollars keeps us alive, but they do suffer from malnutrition. Oh yes, I do remember what I was taught about health in school. It doesn't do much good. In some places there is a surplus commodities program. Not here. The county said it cost too much. There is a school lunch program. But I have two children who will already be damaged by the time they get to school.

But, you say to me, there are health clinics. Yes, there are health 12 clinics and they are in the towns. I live out here eight miles from town. I can walk that far (even if it is sixteen miles both ways), but can my little children? My neighbor will take me when he goes; but he expects to get paid, *one way or another.* I bet you know my neighbor. He is that large man who spends his time at the gas station, the barbershop, and the corner store complaining about the government spending money on the immoral mothers of illegitimate children.

13    Poverty is an acid that drips on pride until all pride is worn away. Poverty is a chisel that chips on honor until honor is worn away. Some of you say that you would do *something* in my situation, and maybe you would, for the first week or the first month, but for year after year after year?

14    Even the poor can dream. A dream of a time when there is money. Money for the right kinds of food, for worm medicine, for iron pills, for toothbrushes, for hand cream, for a hammer and nails and a bit of screening, for a shovel, for a bit of paint, for some sheeting, for needles and thread. Money to pay *in money* for a trip to town. And, oh, money for hot water and money for soap. A dream of when asking for help does not eat away the last bit of pride. When the office you visit is as nice as the offices of other governmental agencies, when there are enough workers to help you quickly, when workers do not quit in defeat and despair. When you have to tell your story to only one person, and that person can send you for other help and you don't have to prove your poverty over and over and over again.

15    I have come out of my despair to tell you this. Remember I did not come from another place or another time. Others like me are all around you. Look at us with an angry heart, anger that will help you help me. Anger that will let you tell of me. The poor are always silent. Can you be silent too?

## *Evaluating the Text*

1. Of the many details mentioned by Parker, which made the greatest impression on you about what being poor actually means on a daily basis?
2. In creating this uniquely real and graphic account, how does Parker appeal to the reader's senses? For example, is there such a thing as a smell of poverty? If so, what is it, according to Parker?
3. What are the hard choices that confront Parker when she tries to decide whether she should work and send her three children to nursery school or leave them with her mother?
4. What are the obstacles Parker faces in simply trying to keep her three children clean and fed? What are the trade-offs she is constantly forced to consider because of not having enough money?
5. How do environmental conditions, whether it is cold, or raining, have a direct physical impact on everyday life when you are poor?
6. Explain why being poor and knowing your children will suffer if you do not get help from state or government agencies is a source of shame and

humiliation. What does Parker mean when she says the poor are very polite and good listeners? Why is this so?

7. What sequence of events led to Parker's present situation?

8. How does Parker answer critics who suggest how she might improve her situation? For example, what does she reveal about the amount of money she receives from public relief, what it will buy, the opportunities offered by public schools, food give-away programs, school-lunch programs, and health clinics? How, in each case, does she answer the objections that well-meaning people might raise?

9. What damaging consequences for her children does Parker foresee because of her inability to help them in the present?

10. What evidence does Parker offer to illustrate that being poor and a woman means that you are in constant danger of being exploited by men?

11. What features of this account by Parker suggest that it was originally given as a speech? How might her account change her audience's assumptions about what it means to be poor?

## Exploring Different Perspectives

1. Compare the circumstances Parker is in with those of the husband and wife in Krishnan Varma's "The Grass-Eaters." How are their circumstances very similiar but their reactions quite different? What would Ajit and Swapna think of Parker's situation? What insight does this give you as to what being poor means in America and what being poor means in India in terms of ability to purchase food, indoor plumbing, help from the government, and so on?

2. How does Parker's account confirm Steinem's thesis about how being poor not only deprives you of self-esteem but also of the ability to make plans for the future?

## Extending Viewpoints through Writing

1. How did reading this article change preconceptions you may have had about the poor?

2. If you or anyone you know ever had to rely on public assistance such as welfare, unemployment compensation, or disability compensation, were the experiences similar to or different from those described by Parker? Are there any details that Parker does not mention that you could add?

3. Did you ever have to get by on very little? What trade-offs did you make, as Parker did, when she had to choose between food and soap? How did you make one thing serve another purpose, such as using soap for dishes and baths and as shampoo?

# Krishnan Varma

# *The Grass-Eaters*

---

*Krishnan Varma was born in Kerala, a southwestern state of India. Varma's stories, in both English and Malayalam (an Indian language), have been published in India, the United States, and Canada. "The Grass-Eaters" was first published in* Wascana Review *in 1985. In this shocking depiction of the homelessness of a teacher and his wife in modern-day Calcutta, Varma challenges our assumptions about survival by showing us people in India who eventually come to accept the unthinkable.*

*India is a republic in southern Asia whose 800 million people make it the second most populous country in the world, after China. Although Indian civilization dates back more than five thousand years, European traders only discovered it in the sixteenth century. By 1757, Britain had gained control of India from the Maharajas (ruling princes). In 1919, Mohandas "Mahatma" (great souled) Gandhi, a lawyer who had worked for Indians in South Africa, launched the movement for India's independence from Britain using techniques of passive resistance and civil disobedience. His dream was realized in 1947 with the dissolution of the British Raj. India was then partitioned into India and Pakistan with hopes of ending the civil war between Hindu and Muslim communities. Gandhi was assassinated the following year. In 1984, Prime Minister Indira Gandhi (no relation to Mohandas) was assassinated by Sikh members of her own body guard. She was succeeded by her son, Rajiv Gandhi, who resigned in 1989, and was assassinated himself less than two years later, during a bid for re-election.*

*Calcutta, the site of Varma's story, is located in the eastern part of the country and is one of the largest cities in India. The extreme poverty, overcrowding, and high unemployment experienced by the 3.3 million inhabitants of Calcutta are an integral part of the visceral impact of "The Grass-Eaters."*

1   For some time several years ago I was tutor to a spherical boy (now a spherical youth). One day his ovoid father, Ramaniklal Misrilal, asked me where I lived. I told him.

*(For more background on the conflict between Hindus and Sikhs, see p. 497.)

Misrilal looked exceedingly distressed. "A pipe, Ajit Babu? Did you 2
say—*a pipe*, Ajit Babu?"

His cuboid wife was near to tears. "A *pipe*, Ajit Babu? How can you 3
live in a pipe?"

It was true: at that time I was living in a pipe with my wife, Swapna. 4
It was long and three or four feet across. With a piece of sack cloth hung
at either end, we had found it far more comfortable than any of our
previous homes.

The first was a footpath of Chittaranjan Avenue. We had just arrived 5
in Calcutta from East Bengal where Hindus and Muslims were killing
one another. The footpath was so crowded with residents, refugees like
us and locals, that if you got up at night to relieve yourself you could not
be sure of finding your place again. One cold morning I woke to find that
the woman beside me was not Swapna at all but a bag of bones instead.
And about fifty or sixty or seventy years old. I had one leg over her too. I
paid bitterly for my mistake. The woman very nearly scratched out my
eyes. Then came Swapna, fangs bared, claws out . . . I survived, but
minus one ear. Next came the woman's husband, a hill of a man,
whirling a tree over his head, roaring. That was my impression, anyway.
I fled.

Later in the day Swapna and I moved into an abandoned-looking 6
freight wagon at the railway terminus. A whole wagon to ourselves—a
place with doors which could be opened and shut—we did nothing but
open and shut them for a full hour—all the privacy a man and wife
could want—no fear of waking up with a complete stranger in your
arms . . . it was heaven. I felt I was God.

Then one night we woke to find that the world was running away 7
from us: we had been coupled to a freight train. There was nothing for it
but to wait for the train to stop. When it did, miles from Calcutta, we got
off, took a passenger train back, and occupied another unwanted-look-
ing wagon. That was not the only time we went to bed in Calcutta and
woke up in another place. I found it an intensely thrilling experience, but
not Swapna.

She wanted a stationary home; she insisted on it. But she would not 8
say why. If I persisted in questioning her she snivelled. If I tried to
persuade her to change her mind, pointing out all the advantages of
living in a wagon—four walls, a roof and door absolutely free of charge,
and complete freedom to make love day or night—she still snivelled. If I
ignored her nagging, meals got delayed, the rice undercooked, the curry
over-salted. In the end I gave in. We would move, I said, even if we had
to occupy a house by force, but couldn't she tell me the reason, however
irrelevant, why she did not like the wagon?

For the first time in weeks Swapna smiled, a very vague smile. Then, 9
slowly, she drew the edge of her sari over her head, cast her eyes down,
turned her face from me, and said in a tremulous, barely audible whisper
that she (short pause) did (long pause) not want (very long pause) her (at

jet speed) baby-to-be-born-in-a-running-train. And she buried her face in her hands. Our fourth child. One died of diphtheria back home (no longer our home) in Dacca; two, from fatigue, on our long trek on foot to Calcutta. Would the baby be a boy? I felt no doubt about it; it would be. Someone to look after us in our old age, to do our funeral rites when we died. I suddenly kissed Swapna, since her face was hidden in her hands, on her elbow, and was roundly chided. Kissing, she holds, is a western practice, unclean also, since it amounts to licking, and should be eschewed by all good Hindus.

10    I lost no time in looking for a suitable place for her confinement. She firmly rejected all my suggestions: the railway station platform (too many residents); a little-used overbridge (she was not a kite to live so high above the ground); a water tank that had fallen down and was empty (Did I think that she was a frog?). I thought of suggesting the municipal primary school where I was teaching at the time, but felt very reluctant. Not that the headmaster would have objected if we had occupied one end of the back veranda: a kindly man, father of eleven, all girls, he never disturbed the cat that regularly kittened in his in-tray. My fear was: suppose Swapna came running into my class, saying, "Hold the baby for a moment, will you? I'm going to the l-a-t-r-i-n-e." Anyway, we set out to the school. On the way, near the Sealdah railway station, we came upon a cement concrete pipe left over from long-ago repairs to underground mains. Unbelievably, it was not occupied and, with no prompting from me, she crept into it. That was how we came to live in a pipe.

11    "It is not proper," said Misrilal, "not at all, for a school master to live in a pipe." He sighed deeply. "Why don't you move into one of my buildings, Ajit Babu?"

12    The house I might occupy, if I cared to, he explained, was in Entally, not far from where the pipe lay; I should have no difficulty in locating it; it was an old building and there were a number of old empty coal tar drums on the roof; I could live on the roof if I stacked the drums in two rows and put a tarpaulin over them.

13    We have lived on that roof ever since. It is not as bad as it sounds. The roof is flat, not gabled, and it is made of cement concrete, not corrugated iron sheets. The rent is far less than that of other tenants below us — Bijoy Babu, Akhanda Chatterjee and Sagar Sen. We have far more light and ventilation than they. We don't get nibbled by rats and mice and rodents as often as they do. And our son, Prodeep, has far more room to play than the children below.

14    Prodeep is not with us now; he is in the Naxalite underground. We miss him, terribly. But there is some compensation, small though it is. Had he been with us, we would have had to wear clothes. Now, we don't. Not much, that is. I make do with a loin cloth and Swapna with a piece slightly wider to save our few threadbare clothes from further wear and tear. I can spare little from my pension for new clothes. Swapna

finds it very embarrassing to be in my presence in broad daylight so meagerly clad and so contrives to keep her back turned to me. Like a chimp in the sulks. I am fed up with seeing her backside and tell her that she has nothing that I have not seen. But she is adamant; she will not turn around. After nightfall, however, she relents: we are both night-blind.

When we go out—to the communal lavatory, to pick up pieces of coal from the railway track, to gather grass—we do wear clothes. Grass is our staple food now: a mound of green grass boiled with green peppers and salt, and a few ladles of very thin rice gruel. We took to eating it when the price of rice started soaring. I had a good mind to do as Bijoy Babu below us is believed to be doing. He has a theory that if you reduce your consumption of food by five grams each day, you will not only not notice that you are eating less but after some time you can do without any food at all. One day I happened to notice that he was not very steady on his feet. That gave me pause. He can get around, however badly he totters, because he has two legs; but I have only one. I lost the other after a fall from the roof of a tram. In Calcutta the trams are always crowded and if you can't get into a carriage you may get up on its roof. The conductor will not stop you. If he tries to, the passengers beat him up, set fire to the tram and any other vehicles parked in the vicinity, loot nearby shops, break street lamps, take out a procession, hold a protest meeting, denounce British imperialism, American neo-colonialism, the central government, capitalism and socialism, and set off crackers. I don't mind my handicap at all; I need wear only one sandal and thereby save on footwear. 15

So, on the whole, our life together has been very eventful. The events, of course, were not always pleasant. But, does it matter? We have survived them. And now, we have no fears or anxieties. We have a home made of coal tar drums. We eat two square meals of grass every day. We don't need to wear clothes. We have a son to do our funeral rites when we die. We live very quietly, content to look at the passing scene: a tram burning, a man stabbing another man, a woman dropping her baby in a garbage bin. 16

## Evaluating the Text

1. What details in the story reveal how the dehumanizing conditions and sheer density of human population in Calcutta make it almost impossible to maintain personal relationships?
2. How does the contrast of full and empty geometrical forms convey the theme of the story? For instance, how does Varma associate spherical, ovoid, and cuboid forms with those who are well-fed, while using a hollowed-out pipe to symbolize the home of those who have little or nothing to eat and no place in which to live?
3. Why do you think Varma relies on surrealism (for example, the description of how Ajit loses an ear) to communicate an all-too-real situation?

4. How is the story structured as a series of flashbacks composed of all the places Ajit and Swapna have lived before their present home? What problems did they encounter in their first home, "a footpath on Chittaranjan Avenue"? What experiences in their second home, "an abandoned-looking freight wagon," led them to consider the chance to live in a pipe as a piece of good luck?

5. How does Varma dramatize the importance of privacy as a theme in the story?

6. How do the circumstances in which Swapna's three previous children died make it so important to her to have a home in which her forthcoming child can be born?

7. What evidence can you cite that being a teacher is important to Ajit in maintaining his self-esteem? How is this need related to his anxiety about approaching his headmaster to let him live on the veranda of the school?

8. How is the way the student's father, Misrilal, is depicted suggest that he is the object of satire? Consider the fact that he owns buildings but is only willing to let Ajit and Swapna live on the roof of one of his buildings if they pay him rent.

9. To what extent do you discern an antifemale bias in the teacher's reference to the fact that his boss, the headmaster, has eleven children, who are all girls? How might this be related to an underlying cultural value in India?

10. How do Swapna's responses show you that, for her, modesty is an attempt to preserve the last vestige of humanity under inhuman conditions?

11. How is the story structured to gradually make the reader see that in an environment like that in Calcutta, people get used to, and even are proud of, adapting to circumstances that would be unthinkable in the West? How do apparently grotesque details such as the narrator, Ajit, only having one leg, saving "on footwear," and eating two meals of grass a day contribute to this idea of acceptance?

12. From Ajit's point of view, why is his life a success? Be sure to consider that his son is still alive although he is living elsewhere and Ajit Babu and his wife, Swapna (whose name means "dream" or "aspiration" in Hindi) do have a place to live, albeit a roof?

13. How is the worsening condition of life for Ajit and Swapna representative of deteriorating conditions (the rising cost of rice, increasing civil violence, and an influx of refugees) to which the poor are subjected throughout the country?

## Exploring Different Perspectives

1. How is the depiction of homelessness and poverty in Calcutta both similar to and different from Jo Goodwin Parker's account (in "What Is Poverty?") of poverty in the United States? How do both Parker and Ajit communicate the indignities suffered by the poor in Calcutta and in the southern United States?

2. How is being unable to plan for the future a central theme in both Steinem's account and in Varma's story? How do Ajit and Swapna try to make provisions for their future in any small ways that they can?

# Extending Viewpoint through Writing

1. Are you aware of homeless people in your town or city whose conditions might not be comparable to those of Ajit and Swapna, but whose lives are just as desperate? Discuss your response to the issue of homelessness.

2. To what extent do you find Ajit (whose name means "one who prevails" in Hindi) to be a perennial optimist who always finds something to be happy about in the most horrible situation? How might his attitude represent the profound acceptance of one's fate that is characteristic of the Hindu belief in karma? Discuss the concept of karma and how it relates to the philosophy of fatalism. Do you feel Varma is critical of this philosophy?

# C. P. Ellis

# *Why I Quit the Klan*

---

*"Why I Quit the Klan" is an interview conducted by Studs Terkel with C. P. Ellis, who had been president (Exalted Cyclops) of the Durham, North Carolina, chapter of the Ku Klux Klan, before his experience of class exploitation changed him into a civil rights activist. Eliciting unique insights through thought-provoking interviews has character-ized the work of Studs (Lewis) Terkel, who received a law degree from the University of Chicago in 1932. Terkel's interviews with ordinary people in everyday settings are extraordinarily revealing of the deep, rarely expressed, or recorded concerns that people have about them-selves, their lives, and society. Terkel's "interview books" include* Working: People Talk About What They Do All Day and How They Feel About What They Do *(1974) and* American Dreams: Lost and Found *(1980), in which Ellis's interview first appeared.*

1 All my life, I had work, never a day without work, worked all the overtime I could get and still could not survive financially. I began to see there's something wrong with this country. I worked my butt off and just never seemed to break even. I had some real great ideas about this nation. They say to abide by the law, go to church, do right and live for the Lord, and everything'll work out. But it didn't work out. It just kept gettin worse and worse. . . .

2 Tryin to come out of that hole, I just couldn't do it. I really began to get bitter. I didn't know who to blame. I tried to find somebody. Hatin America is hard to do because you can't see it to hate it. You gotta have somethin to look at to hate. The natural person for me to hate would be black people, because my father before me was a member of the Klan. . . .

3 So I began to admire the Klan. . . . To be part of somethin. . . . The first night I went with the fellas . . . I was led into a large meeting room, and this was the time of my life! It was thrilling. Here's a guy who's worked all his life and struggled all his life to be something, and here's the moment to be something. I will never forget it. Four robed Klansmen led me into the hall. The lights were dim and the only thing you could see was an illuminated cross. . . . After I had taken my oath, there was loud applause goin throughout the buildin, musta been at least four hundred people. For this one little ol person. It was a thrilling moment for C. P. Ellis. . . .

The majority of [the Klansmen] are low-income whites, people who   4
really don't have a part in something. They have been shut out as well as
blacks. Some are not very well educated either. Just like myself. We had
a lot of support from doctors and lawyers and police officers.

Maybe they've had bitter experiences in this life and they had to hate   5
somebody. So the natural person to hate would be the black person. He's
beginnin to come up, he's beginnin to . . . start votin and run for
political office. Here are white people who are supposed to be superior to
them, and we're shut out. . . . Shut out. Deep down inside, we want
to be part of this great society. Nobody listens, so we join these
groups. . . .

We would go to the city council meetings, and the blacks would be   6
there and we'd be there. It was a confrontation every time. . . . We
began to make some inroads with the city councilmen and county com-
missioners. They began to call us friend. Call us at night on the telephone: "C. P., glad you came to that meeting last night." They didn't
want integration either, but they did it secretively, in order to get elected.
They couldn't stand up openly and say it, but they were glad somebody
was sayin it. We visited some of the city leaders in their homes and
talked to em privately. It wasn't long before councilmen would call me
up: "The blacks are comin up tonight and makin outrageous demands.
How about some of you people showin up and have a little balance?" . . .

We'd load up our cars and we'd fill up half the council chambers, and   7
the blacks the other half. During these times, I carried weapons to the
meetings, outside my belt. We'd go there armed. We would wind up just
hollerin and fussin at each other. What happened? As a result of our
fightin one another, the city council still had their way. They didn't want
to give up control to the blacks nor the Klan. They were usin us.

I began to realize this later down the road. One day I was walkin   8
downtown and a certain city council member saw me comin. I expected
him to shake my hand because he was talkin to me at night on the
telephone. I had been in his home and visited with him. He crossed the
street [to avoid me]. . . . I began to think, somethin's wrong here. Most
of em are merchants or maybe an attorney, an insurance agent, people
like that. As long as they kept low-income whites and low-income blacks
fightin, they're gonna maintain control. I began to get that feelin after I
was ignored in public. I thought: . . . you're not gonna use me any
more. That's when I began to do some real serious thinkin.

The same thing is happening in this country today. People are being   9
used by those in control, those who have all the wealth. I'm not espousing communism. We got the greatest system of government in the world.
But those who have it simply don't want those who don't have it to have
any part of it. Black and white. When it comes to money, the green, the
other colors make no difference.

I spent a lot of sleepless nights. I still didn't like blacks. I didn't want   10 to associate with them. Blacks, Jews or Catholics. My father said: "Don't have anything to do with em." I didn't until I met a black person and talked with him, eyeball to eyeball, and met a Jewish person and talked to him, eyeball to eyeball. I found they're people just like me. They cried, they cussed, they prayed, they had desires. Just like myself. Thank God, I got to the point where I can look past labels. But at that time, my mind was closed.

11      I remember one Monday night Klan meeting. I said something was wrong. Our city fathers were using us. And I didn't like to be used. The reactions of the others were not too pleasant: "Let's just keep fightin them niggers."

12      I'd go home at night and I'd have to wrestle with myself. I'd look at a black person walkin down the street, and the guy'd have ragged shoes or his clothes would be worn. That began to do something to me inside. I went through this for about six months. I felt I just had to get out of the Klan. But I wouldn't get out. . . .

13      [Ellis was invited, as a Klansman, to join a committee of people from all walks of life to make recommendations on how to solve racial problems in the school system. He very reluctantly accepted. After a few stormy meetings, he was elected co-chair of the committee, along with Ann Atwater, a black woman who for years had been leading local efforts for civil rights.]

14      A Klansman and a militant black woman, co-chairmen of the school committee. It was impossible. How could I work with her? But it was in our hands. We had to make it a success. This give me another sense of belongin, a sense of pride. This helped the inferiority feeling I had. A man who has stood up publicly and said he despised black people, all of a sudden he was willin to work with em. Here's a chance for a low-income white man to be somethin. In spite of all my hatred for blacks and Jews and liberals, I accepted the job. Her and I began to reluctantly work together. She had as many problems workin with me as I had workin with her.

15      One night, I called her: "Ann, you and I should have a lot of differences and we got em now. But there's something laid out here before us, and if it's gonna be a success, you and I are gonna have to make it one. Can we lay aside some of these feelins?" She said: "I'm willing if you are." I said: "Let's do it.'"

16      My old friends would call me at night: "C. P., what the hell is wrong with you? You're sellin out the white race." This begin to make me have guilt feelins. Am I doin right? Am I doin wrong? Here I am all of a sudden makin an about-face and tryin to deal with my feelins, my heart. My mind was beginnin to open up. I was beginnin to see what was right and what was wrong. I don't want the kids to fight forever. . . .

17      One day, Ann and I went back to the school and we sat down. We began to talk and just reflect. . . . I begin to see, here we are, two people from the far ends of the fence, havin identical problems, except hers bein

black and me bein white. . . . The amazing thing about it, her and I, up to that point, has cussed each other, bawled each other, we hated each other. Up to that point, we didn't know each other. We didn't know we had things in common. . . .

The whole world was openin up, and I was learning new truths that I 18 had never learned before. I was beginning to look at a black person, shake hands with him, and see him as a human bein. I hadn't got rid of all this stuff. I've still got a little bit of it. But somethin was happenin to me. . . .

I come to work one mornin and some guys says: "We need a union." 19 At this time I wasn't pro-union. My daddy was anti-labor too. We're not gettin paid much, we're havin to work seven days in a row. We're all starvin to death. . . . I didn't know nothin about organizin unions, but I knew how to organize people, stir people up. That's how I got to be business agent for the union.

When I began to organize, I began to see far deeper. I begin to see 20 people again bein used. Blacks against whites. . . . There are two things management wants to keep: all the money and all the say-so. They don't want none of these poor workin folks to have none of that. I begin to see management fightin me with everythin they had. Hire anti-union law firms, badmouth unions. The people were makin $1.95 an hour, barely able to get through weekends. . . .

It makes you feel good to go into a plant and . . . see black people 21 and white people join hands to defeat the racist issues [union-busters] use against people. . . .

I tell people there's a tremendous possibility in this country to stop 22 wars, the battles, the struggles, the fights between people. People say: "That's an impossible dream. You sound like Martin Luther King." An ex-Klansman who sounds like Martin Luther King. I don't think it's an impossible dream. It's happened in my life. It's happened in other people's lives in America. . . .

. . . They say the older you get, the harder it is for you to change. 23 That's not necessarily true. Since I changed, I've set down and listened to tapes of Martin Luther King. I listen to it and tears come to my eyes cause I know what he's sayin now. I know what's happenin."

## Evaluating the Text

1. What set of circumstances led Ellis to become a member of the Ku Klux Klan? What is there about these circumstances that lets you understand what the Klan psychologically would provide for Ellis? For example, you might look at his motivations in terms of lack of financial security, his father's attitude toward blacks, and how important it was for Ellis to feel a sense of his own self-worth by belonging to a group. How much of the Klan's appeal is because it scapegoats another group for hardships and inequities?

2. How does the picture Ellis paints reveal that local politicians use Klan members to perpetuate divisions of class as well as race? For example, how does the city council set groups of low-income blacks against groups of low-income whites to ensure their own power? Why is it important for the Klan to make it impossible for these two groups to get together and see that they have similar problems caused by the council?

3. What experience made Ellis see that the city council did not really share the beliefs of the Klan but were using the KKK for their own purposes?

4. What anticipated objection does Ellis hope to counter by mentioning the fact that doctors, lawyers, and police officers also support the Klan?

5. In what way does Ellis view his experiences with the city council member as a microcosm of how people across the country are controlled by those with money and power? Why is he quick to mention he is not espousing communism?

6. How is Ellis's decision to become a union organizer related to his earlier insight that the city council members were using him and the Klan to maintain their own power? In what way does the union management consolidate their control by pitting blacks and whites against each other?

7. What kind of conflict did Ellis have to overcome in terms of hostile remarks by his friends that he "was selling out the white race"? What does this reveal about his strength of character in going against people with whom he had close relationships all his life?

8. How did the problems faced by Ann Atwater in accepting Ellis mirror Ellis's own earlier struggle to overcome his stereotyped impressions?

9. How does Ellis's statement that he felt about groups the way his father told him to feel shed light on the process by which people adopt beliefs for which they do not have personal experience?

10. How did Ellis's change of mind depend on his ability to enter into the condition of another person, in this case, to empathize with a black person with "ragged shoes" and "worn clothes?"

11. What does Ellis's reaction to listening to tapes of Dr. Martin Luther King, Jr., tell you about the great distance, intellectually and emotionally, he has come from being the Exalted Cyclops, or president, of the Durham chapter of the Ku Klux Klan?

## Exploring Different Perspectives

1. What common elements can you discover in the situations of Ellis and Jo Goodwin Parker ("What Is Poverty?")? How do the psychologically damaging effects of poverty help explain why Ellis was ripe for conversion by the KKK?

2. In your opinion, why was Ellis able to change his lifelong attitude toward blacks, whereas Toi Derricotte ("The Black Notebooks") could not change her attitude toward whites?

## Extending Viewpoints through Writing

1. From this interview with Ellis, what can you tell about Studs Terkel as an interviewer? What can you infer about Terkel's attitude toward the subject, the relationship he has established with Ellis? What kind of shape has

Terkel given to the interview? What values or dominant impression emerge during the interview? What cues alert you to how Terkel has edited and formatted the results of his interview, compressing an original that was much longer?

2. Do you agree or disagree with Ellis's conclusion that people with wealth and power foment and exploit racism as a means to maintain their own political power?

3. Reconstruct a conversation you have had with another person about why he or she no longer holds a belief. For example, have you ever known anyone who became a vegetarian or changed his or her attitude toward wearing fur coats? How does being able to see a situation from a completely different perspective create circumstances in which change can occur?

4. Discuss a belief that you once held that you no longer hold. Mention the evidence that led you to hold the original belief. Was it based on something you were told, something you read, or on personal experience? What new experiences raised doubts about this initial belief? How did you revise your attitude in response to these new experiences? Try to capture the essence of the critical thinking process, what Ellis refers to as "wrestlin with himself." What actions have you taken (that you would not have taken previously) that reflect this changed attitude?

# Josef Škvorecký

# *An Insolvable Problem of Genetics*

---

*Josef Škvorecký was born in 1924 in Nachod, Bohemia, Czechoslovakia, educated in Prague, and has worked as a publisher's editor, a magazine editor, and as a free-lance writer. His novels,* The End of the Nylon Age *(1956) and* The Cowards *(1958), were banned after they were published. In 1968, after the Russian occupation of Czechoslovakia, he immigrated to Canada and has taught American literature at the University of Toronto. His work emphasizes the importance of expressing humanity within totalitarian bureaucracies. Škvorecký's other works include the novels* The Bass Saxophone *(1985) and* Dvořk in Love: A Lighthearted Dream *(1987); a collection of detective stories,* The Mournful Demeanor of Lieutenant Boruvka *(1987); and* Talkin' Moscow Blues *(1990). In "An Insolvable Problem of Genetics" (translated by Michal Schonberg, 1983), Škvorecký weaves a hilarious tale, based, as he says, not on "my imagination but [on] something that actually happened to my friend Jan Bich," of racism and hypocrisy in a family that ostensibly champions egalitarian ideals.*

*Bordered by Germany and Poland to the north, the Soviet Union to the east, and Austria and Hungary to the south, Czechoslovakia emerged in 1918 from the collapse of the Austro-Hungarian monarchy as an independent republic. After being liberated from German control by American and Soviet forces as the end of World War II, Czechoslovakia was ruled continuously as a Soviet Satellite (despite the abortive 1968 "Prague Spring" movement led by Alexander Dubček) until late 1989, when millions of people took to the streets to protest communist party domination and demand free elections. In "An Insolvable Problem of Genetics," Škvorecký captures the paranoia and hypocrisy of life under Soviet domination.*

[From the secret diary of Vasil Krátký, a third-grade student at the Leonid Brezhnev High School in K.]

---

*(For further information on Czechoslovakia, see p. 360.)

294

While offering a brotherly hand to many nations, our fatherland also ₁
harbours a certain number of dark-skinned African students; some of
these undergo preparatory courses in the Czech language in our town.
Later they laud the good name of our nation far beyond the borders of
our country, but my brother Adolf lost his lifelong happiness because of
their overly friendly attitude toward the population.

This is how it happened: for two long years Adolf was secretly in love ₂
with the movie star Jana Brejchová and wrote her more than two
hundred letters during this time. The interest shown by the film celebrity
was not in the least comparable to my brother's effort, and so Adolf
began to pursue Freddie Mourek, whose skinny figure and seemly features resembled somewhat those of the aforementioned actress.

The parents welcomed his decision because Freddie, as the illegiti- ₃
mate daughter of the Secretary of the Party cell at the Lentex linen
factory in K., came from a family with an excellent class profile. Nothing
but a single flaw disturbed the great impression made by Adolf's girl
friend on our family, and that was her given name. One day while at our
house, Freddie, to the accompaniment of Adolf's bass guitar, sang a
certain loud song in a foreign language. To my father's uneasy inquiry
concerning the origins of the song she answered that it was a black
American song, whose lyrics protested against discrimination. Father
applauded, then extolled briefly the black struggle for equality; then he
quite suddenly became very angry, and turning dark red, he began to
curse the South African racists. Mother also became angry, and in the
resulting friendly atmosphere Father asked Freddie why a girl as thoroughly progressive and an activist of the Young Communist League,
would call herself by a name apparently of English origin.

At that Freddie blushed and said that she could now reveal to them ₄
the secret of her name because she had just agreed with Adolf to enter
into wedlock in a civil ceremony prior to the final matriculation examinations. Father was very heartened by the news as he happens to favour
early nuptials for youths finding themselves in their reproductive years,
since these are called for by the appropriate authorities in an attempt to
prevent population decrease. He then encouraged Freddie to reveal her
secret without delay. "My name," she said, "I inherited from my father.
He was a certain Frederick Positive Wasserman Brown, a migrant worker
from South Carolina, who as a member of General Georgie Patton's
Third U.S. Army seduced my mummy in Pilsen, and then had himself
transferred to the Far East." "An American?" Father recoiled and turned
gloomy. Then he partially recovered: "A migrant worker?" and Freddie,
attempting to aid the complete recovery of my father who had earlier
lauded so eagerly the heroic struggle of the coloured people, quickly
added: "Yes. And besides my father was black." Against all expectations
Father's gloom became permanent.

In the following days he began to bring home from the People's ₅
Municipal Library books of a certain Lysenko; unable to find in them a

satisfactory answer to what he was looking for, he borrowed a volume of the friar Mendel with pictures of various types of peas, white, gray, and black ones. He studied those very diligently, and later when Freddie again sang at our house negro songs in a foreign language, he asked: "Listen, girl, that father of yours, was he a very black black or was he of a lighter hue?" "Very black," said Freddie, who herself is very white, but has eyes which are very black, large and very beautiful. "So black that during the war they used him in reconnaissance, when, completely naked he would in the darkest night penetrate through the German lines, since he was completely invisible." And Father turned once again gloomy and said no more.

6      However, that evening he advised Adolf to break off without delay his relationship with the black man's daughter. Adolf resisted: "I'm not a racist!" "Neither am I," replied Father. "If Freddie were a dark-skinned girl I would welcome her as a daughter-in-law, because the union with an obvious member of an elsewhere persecuted race would doubtless even further enhance the class profile of our family. But she is white. There arises the danger, that on the basis of the reactionary laws determined by the friar Mendel, she will bear you a black child, and there will be a scandal!" "What scandal? Black or white, it's all the same," Adolf rejoindered, and Father explained: "Nobody will believe that this black child is really yours. Everybody will think that it is the result of the efforts of our guests, the African students, and in that sense they will also slander your wife." And he concluded: "Which is why you will break off the relationship before it is too late."

7      Adolf turned crimson and ponderous. Then he said: "It is already too late. It is impossible to break off the relationship." A deadly silence prevailed, interrupted only by Mother's moaning and Father's fidgeting. From that day on, Adolf also started to carefully study the writings of the friar Mendel.

8      No doubt it was too late; it was, I imagine, because Adolf loved Freddie much more than he had ever loved Jana Brejchová, although he almost never sent her any letters. Freddie's mother, the textile worker and Party Secretary, was invited to our house, and I, hidden behind the large portrait of the Statesman, which conceals the hole where Grandfather's wall safe used to stand, overheard Mother emphasizing the terribly tender age of both the children and asking the esteemed Secretary's consent to apply to some sort of a committee in the matter of an absorption (or something that sounded like that). I really could not understand why the Comrade Mother (Mrs. Mourek) got upset to the point of refusing to co-operate with the committee, slammed the door and left, when on other occasions, as a class-conscious woman, she had always shown full confidence in committees, councils, and organs of all kinds.

9      It did not end there: the Comrade Secretary of the Party Cell at the Lentex linen factory in K. provided us with a further unexpected surprise. Soon after, when Father, Mother, my older sister Margaret, and

even Adolf himself began spreading all around town that the father of
Freddie was the migrant black Frederick Positive Wasserman Brown, and
at the same time introducing the people to the laws of heredity according
to which a completely white person can give birth to a black child thanks
to the genes of its progenitor (in order to preventively protect the reputation of Freddie in case of a child with other than Czech colouring),
Comrade Mourek appeared again, and her squealing voice could be
heard from the parlour, expressing herself to the effect that Father,
Mother, Margaret, and Adolf were giving the girl (meaning Freddie) a
bad name around town and causing trouble, of which she (Comrade
Mourek) had had more than her fill throughout her life, the result of
some youthful transgression. And although Father, having alertly declared himself the enemy of bourgeois morality, began to explain to her
his intentions, he failed nonetheless.

As concerns Adolf, he deteriorated visibly, until finally he spoke       10
about nothing else but the friar Mendel. This aroused the suspicion of
the principal of the high school, Comrade Pavel Běhavka, who for
several Sundays carefully observed, from his table at the Café Beránek,
the entrance to the Catholic church in the town square (adding to his
surveillance later on also the chapel of the Czech Protestants, and that of
the Czech Evangelical Brethen), to find out whether Adolf, as a result of
being converted to the obscurantist faith of the friars, visited the services.
He did not, but being psychologically uprooted, he would acquaint
everyone at any occasion, even completely strange comrades, with the
secret of the background of his fiancée Freddie, as well as with the laws
of genetics. Finally, after a large number of arguments, fights, and confrontations, Freddie one day broke up with him. To the accompaniment
of his bass guitar they sang together for the last time the protest song
"Get Me a New Dolly, Molly!" and then she declared (I overheard it
secretly, hidden behind the portrait of the Statesman): "Your indiscretion
is getting on my nerves, and I don't intend to put up with it any longer.
Also, I would like you to know that I haven't told you everything: for
your information, the mother of my father Frederick Positive Wasserman
Brown was Japanese, his grandfather, who was brought over from Africa
as a slave in chains, was a Pygmy, which, combined with the fact that
my mother is one third a Jewish gypsy, leaves me with a very good
chance of giving birth to a green dwarf, which your father will not be
able to explain to the comrades with or without his Mendel. And it's
good-bye forever, my little imbecile!"

Having said that, she left forever; and so my brother, deprived of his      11
life-long happiness by the presence of the African students, did not
become a father.

Somewhat later Freddie gave birth to twins: one is a boy and the      12
other a girl, and both are completely pink. However, about that phenomenon, Mendel says nothing at all.

*Translated by Michal Schonberg*

# *Evaluating the Text*

1. Why is it significant that the events described in the story are told from the point of view of Adolf's brother, a "third-grade student"? How does Škvorecký get across that these events are to be taken ironically, despite the naive sympathy the narrator expresses for his older brother's plight? For example, what word does Vasil misunderstand as "absorption"? What were his parents really saying?

2. How does the phrase "a brotherly hand" mock, albeit unintentionally, the communist rhetoric propagated by the government? What other phrases (such as "Comrade mother") are in this category?

3. How does the fact that Adolf starts dating Freddie because she reminds him of the movie star Jana Brejchová emphasize the idea that people are not valued for themselves, but rather for their ability to enhance one's social status? Why is coming from a family "with an excellent class profile" an example of this theme?

4. Discuss the significance of each of the characteristics of Freddie's father in relationship to the value system Škvorecký is satirizing. Why are some features perceived of as capable of enhancing social status while others would make Adolf's family politically suspect? For example, in your opinion, might "Frederick" be a reference to Frederick Douglass (1817– 1895), a slave who taught himself how to read and write, escaped to the North, and rose to prominence as ambassador to several foreign countries?

5. What might be the significance of "Positive Wasserman" in light of the fact that Freddie is pregnant?

6. How is the family's hypocrisy illustrated in the changing attitudes of Adolf's father when he discovers Freddie's father was (1) an American, (2) a migrant worker, and (3) black?

7. In your opinion, why is Freddie making all this up? What does it tell you about her and how she might really feel about marrying into this family? How is her story used as a vehicle to satirize the underlying racism and bourgeois values of the supposedly liberated egalitarian society of communist Czechoslovakia?

8. How do we know that Freddie's mother, despite being the Secretary of the Party Cell, has essentially the same values as does the family?

9. What is the father really trying to discover by reading the works of the geneticists, Lysenko and Mendel? The theories of Lysenko, a Russian biologist and agronomist, long since discredited, stated that heredity is not based on chromosomes and genes. His theories were used to justify social engineering on the grounds that environmental benefits could produce direct biological improvements that could be passed on genetically. How does this relate to the title "An Insolvable Problem of Genetics"?

10. What does the reference to the wall-safe and the peep-hole through the portrait imply about how much money the family had before the "revolution" and their values?

11. What does the family's change of position on whether Adolf and Freddie are or are not too young to get married reveal about them?

12. How do Adolph's efforts to diffuse possible negative effects lead to his being suspected of secret religiosity?

13. How does Škvorecký succeed in taking what some people might find to

be a touchy issue and making it into a source of humor? To what extent does this depend on Škvorecký giving readers the choice of either (1) laughing at the story and distancing themselves from racism, pomposity, and bigotry or (2) getting upset and being identified with the humorless hypocritical members of the family?

## *Exploring Different Perspectives*

1. How do the issues of racial prejudice and class enter into both Škvorecký's story and C. P. Ellis's ("Why I Quit the Clan") interview? How does Ellis act on the basis of beliefs as a union organizer, contrasted with the professed beliefs of solidarity with the workers by the family in the Škvorecký story?
2. How does Freddie in this story mock the class values of the family in ways that have similar comic consequences to the Marx Brothers' mockery of upper-class values, in Ivan Karp's article ("Good Marx for the Anthropologist")?

## *Extending Viewpoints through Writing*

1. Have you ever made up a story just to get people's reactions? What story did you invent, and how did the reactions it elicited reveal everyone's true character?
2. How is Freddie's reaction to Adolf's parents a typical, although extreme, example of the generation gap that college students often experience? Can you identify with Freddie? If so, describe your experiences and feelings.
3. If you didn't initially realize Freddie was making everything up just to ridicule Adolf's parents, at what point in the story did you suspect this might be the case? For example, how did you react to the disclosure that Freddie's father was used by the allies to "penetrate through German lines, since he was completely invisible"? How might this be a reference to Ralph Ellison's famous 1947 novel about the black experience, *Invisible Man*?
4. Did you ever "put someone on," as Freddie does to Adolf's family, because their attitude toward you was erroneous and unfair? Did you "put them on" to confirm their worst fears as Freddie does? Did you later reveal your purpose in doing this? Describe your experience.

# Toi Derricotte

# *The Black Notebooks*

---

*Toi Derricotte was born in 1941 in Detroit, Michigan. Her poetry on the black female experience has been widely acclaimed. Her work includes* The Empress of the Death House *(1978) and* Natural Birth *(1983), about which Adrienne Rich says, "Her words touch the reader as life has touched her, soul and body. This is a strong, sensuous, original, courageous book." Her newest collection of poems,* Captivity *(1990), displays her characteristic interweaving of personal history, invention, and reportage. She is a recipient of the Lucille Medwick Memorial Award from the Poetry Society of America (1985) and the Folger Shakespeare Library Poetry Committee Book Award (1990). She is currently the Commonwealth Professor of English at George Mason University and lives in Maryland with her husband, Bruce. "The Black Notebooks" is from* Ariadne's Thread *(1982), in the preface to which Derricotte states, "I write about our family's experiences as one of the first black families in Upper Montclair [New Jersey], of my problems being unrecognized because of my light complexion, and my love and rage towards my neighbors."*

## July 1977

1   Yesterday I put my car in the shop. The neighborhood shop. When I went to pick it up I held a conversation with the man who worked on it. I told him I had been afraid to leave the car there at night with the keys in it. "Don't worry," he said. "You don't have to worry about stealing in Upper Montclair as long as the niggers don't move in." I couldn't believe it. I hoped I had heard him wrong. "What did you say?" I asked. He repeated the same thing without hesitation.

2   In the past my anger would have swelled quickly. I would have blurted out something, hotly demanded he take my car down off the rack immediately though he had not finished working on it, and taken off in a blaze. I love that reaction. The only feeling of power one can possibly have in a situation in which there is such a sudden feeling of powerlessness is to "do" something, handle the situation. When you "do" something, everything is clear. But for some reason yesterday, I, who have been more concerned lately with understanding my feelings than in reacting, repressed my anger. Instead of reacting, I leaned back in myself, dizzy with pain, fear, sadness, and confused.

300

I go home and sit with myself for an hour, trying to grasp the ³
feeling—the odor of self-hatred, the biting stench of shame.


## December 1977

About a month ago we had the guy next door over for dinner. He's about ⁴
twenty-six. The son of a banker. He lived in a camper truck for a year
and came home recently with his dog to "get himself together."

After dinner we got into a conversation about the Hartford Tennis ⁵
Club, where he is the swimming instructor. I asked him, hesitantly, but
unwilling not to get his firsthand information, if blacks were allowed to
join. (Everybody on our block belongs to Hartford, were told about "the
club" and asked to join as soon as they moved in. We were never told
about it or asked to join.) Unemotionally, he said, "No. The man who
owns the club won't let blacks in." I said, "You mean the people on this
block who have had us over to dinner and who I have invited to my
home for dinner, the people I have lived next door to for three years,
these same people are ones I can't swim in a pool with?" "That's the
rule," he said, as if he were stating a fact with mathematical veracity and
as if I would have no feelings. He told us about one girl, the daughter of
the president of a bank, who worked on the desk at the Hartford Club.
When they told her black people couldn't join, she quit her job. I looked
at him. He is the swimming instructor at the club.

My husband and I are in marriage counseling with a white therapist. ⁶
The therapist sees us separately. When I came in upset about that
conversation, he said he didn't believe people were like this anymore. He
said I would have to try to join the club to tell whether in fact this was
true.

Four days ago, the woman down the street called me, asking if my ⁷
son could baby-sit for her. I like this woman, I don't know why. She is
Dutch and has that ruddy coloring, red hair, out of a Rubens painting.
Easy to talk to. She and her husband are members of the club and I
couldn't resist telling her the story of the guy next door to get her
reaction. She said, "Oh, Toi, two years ago, John and I wanted to have
you and Bruce be our guests at a dinner party at the club. I was just
picking up the phone to call and ask you when Holly called [a woman
who lives across the street] and said, 'Do you think that's a good idea?
You better check with the Fullers [old members of the club] first before
you call Bruce and Toi.' I called Steve and he called a meeting of the
executive committee. We met together for four hours. Several of us said
we would turn in our resignations unless you could come. But the
majority of people felt that it wouldn't be a good idea because you would
see all the good things about the club and want to join. And since you
couldn't join, it would just hurt you and be frustrating. John and I
wanted to quit. I feel very ashamed of myself, but the next summer,

when I was stuck in the house with the kids with nothing to do, we joined again."

## *May 1978*

8  I had a dinner party last week. Saturday night, the first dinner party in over a year. The house was dim & green with plants & flowers, light & orange like a fresh fruit tart, openings of color in darkness, shining, the glass in the dark heart of the house opening out.

9      & i made sangria with white wine adding strawberries & apples & oranges & limes & lemon slices & fresh squeezed juice in an ice clear pitcher with cubes like glass lighting the taste with sound & color.

10      & the table was abundant.

11      & they came. one man was a brilliant conversationalist & his wife was happy to offer to help in the kitchen & one woman was quiet & seemed rigid as a fortress & black & stark as night, a wall falling quickly, her brow, that swarthy drop without her, that steep incline away . . . & her husband was a doctor & introduced himself as "dr." & i said "charmed. contessa toinette."

12      & we were black & white together, we were middle class & we had "been to europe" & the doctors were black & the businessmen were white & the doctors were white & the businessmen were black & the bankers were there too.

13      & the black people sat on this side of the room & the white people sat on that & they ate cherried chocolates with dainty fingers & told stories.

14      & soon i found that one couple belonged to the Hartford Club & my heart closed like my eyes narrowing on that corner of the room on that conversation like a beam of light & they said "it isn't our fault. it's the man who owns it." & i was angry & i said it is your fault for you belong & no one made you & suddenly i wanted to belong i wanted them to let me in or die & wanted to go to court to battle to let crosses burn on my lawn let anything happen they will i will go to hell i will break your goddamned club apart don't give me shit anymore.

15      bruce said it is illegal & if we wanted to we could get in no matter what the man at the top did & everyone is blaming it on that one ugly man & behind him they hide their own ugliness & behind his big fat ass they hide their puny hopes & don't want to be seen so god will pass over their lives & not touch, hide their little house & little dishwasher, hide like the egyptians hid their children from the face of god, hide their soaked brown evil smelling odor dripping ass. and they were saying don't blame me please throwing up their hands begging not to be seen, but i see them, my eye like a cat seeing into x-ray the bird's blood-brain: i will not pass, like god i will not pass over their evil.

16      the next day bruce & i talk about it. he still doesn't want to pay 200 dollars to belong. he says it's not worth it to fight about, he doesn't want to fight to belong to something stupid, would rather save his energy to fight for something important.

important.                                                                                17
what is important to me?                                                                  18
    no large goal like integrating a university. just living here on this                 19
cruddy street, taking the street in my heart like an arrow.

## Evaluating the Text

1. Why does Derricotte react to the racist comments of the garage mechanic with paralysis rather than anger? How does the fact that she just moved into an all-white upper-class neighborhood inhibit her from showing her anger?
2. What double standard is revealed in the Hartford swimming "club's" decision to restrict blacks?
3. Why is the white therapist's reaction so upsetting to Derricotte? How much of the stress Derricotte and her husband are experiencing is due to their being the only black couple living in an all-white suburb? If they didn't care what the community thought of them, would the internal conflicts in their relationship be as great?
4. Discuss the reaction of Derricotte's neighbor down the street. What do you think you would have done in Derricotte's situation? What part does convenience play in the neighbor's decision to stay in the club even though she and Derricotte are friends and the club will not allow Derricotte and her husband to become members because they are black?
5. Why is it important to Derricotte to know how each of her neighbors with whom she has had a relationship reacted to her and her husband's not being able to join the club?
6. In what way do stylistic changes between early and late diary entries mirror changes in Derricotte's attitude toward her neighbors?
7. How plausible do you find her hypothesis that everyone on the block is simply "hiding" behind the owner's decision to restrict black members from the club?
8. Discuss the reasons behind Bruce's belief that you cannot use your energy by fighting every battle and must pick those that mean the most to you. Why doesn't Bruce care about being allowed to join the club? Because Derricotte sees his view as an evasion, discuss how these differences might create dissension in their marriage. Evaluate her reasons for believing that joining the club is as important as integrating a university. Who do you agree with, Bruce or Toi? Explain your answer.

## Exploring Different Perspectives

1. When Toi visits the homes of her white neighbors, many of them issue defensive denials regarding the Hartford Club, deny any responsibility, and blame the owner. The more they do this, the more she sees them as guilty. How does the issue of hypocrisy in racial matters also enter into Josef Škvorecký's "An Insolvable Problem of Genetics"?
2. Compare the appearance and expressions of racism in Derricotte's account with those cited by C. P. Ellis ("Why I Quit the Klan"). Which would you find harder to take, an overt racism or the more subtle expression, accompanied by hypocrisy, that Derricotte encounters?

# *Extending Viewpoints through Writing*

1. Have you ever found yourself in a situation where another person, unaware of your particular ethnic or racial background, referred to your group in a disparaging way? What did you do? Describe your emotions and relate them to what Derricotte experienced.

2. Derricotte's diary reveals the psychological and emotional stresses experienced by blacks light enough to "pass" in our society. Analyze the different factors at work in this situation, and speculate on what you would have done if you were in the same situation. You may wish to bring in related experiences if they apply.

3. Have you ever wanted to know more about the reasons for people's behavior, as Derricotte does, even though you suspected it would be painful to find out? Did you still pursue the matter even though there might be nothing you could do to correct it?

4. Have you ever kept a diary? Look back on some of your entries, and see if you dealt with a moment when you found out that a friend you trusted had betrayed you or that someone was keeping something from you. Did you confront them and try to discover the truth even though you knew it would hurt you? Did the style of your diary entries change to become more emotional in ways that were comparable to changes in Derricotte's style?

# Ivan Karp

# *Good Marx for the Anthropologist*

*Ivan Karp is a social anthropologist who has investigated the function of rituals in social organizations. "Good Marx for the Anthropologist" was a paper originally presented at the 1974 annual meeting of the American Anthropological Association and subsequently published in* The American Dimension: Cultural Myths and Social Realities, *second edition, edited by W. Arens and Susan P. Montague (1981). Karp presently is Curator of African Ethnology in the Department of Anthropology, National Museum of Natural History, Smithsonian Institution, Washington, D.C. Among his many books are* Creativity of Power *(1989),* Personhood and Agency *(1990), and* Exhibiting Cultures: The Poetics and Politics of Museum Display *(1990). In the following section from his essay, Karp examines the Marx Brothers' movie* Duck Soup *(1933) and shows how Groucho (as Rufus T. Firefly), Chico, Harpo, and Zeppo, carry out rituals of rebellion, by which the lowly immigrants turn the tables on high society.*

The pivot of most of the Marx Brothers' movies is the relationship   1
between Groucho and those he victimizes. They are, by and large,
persons in social positions that demand respect and deference, and are
naturally offended when they receive less than what they require as their
social due. Ambassador Trentino of *Duck Soup*, or Herman Gottlieb, the
pompous and self-satisfied manager of the New York Opera from *A
Night at the Opera*, are good examples of this type, but the ubiquitous
Margaret Dumont, the archetype of the dowager matron, provides us
with the purest representative of the kind. There is nothing especially
mean or malicious or even particularly self-seeking about Mrs. Teasdale
and the other dowagers that Margaret Dumont usually plays. She is
merely a pompous woman (often a widow) who either represents or
wants to represent the pinnacle of social prestige. She is always wealthy
and willing to use her wealth for philanthropic purposes — as she understands them. Groucho, on the other hand, is willing to use her. She is
destined to be Groucho's foil. His intention is to flatter her, seduce her,
and marry her in order to enjoy her wealth. His exchanges with her start
out with Groucho expressing admiration for her beauty, figure, intelligence, culture, or whatever else comes to mind. Groucho's trouble is that

he can't keep *his* mind on the job at hand. His distaste for Dumont always gets the better of him, and he winds up expressing his genuine and very funny opinion of her. In *Duck Soup* he impugns her honor, insults her figure, portrays her as overcome by uncontrollable sexual desire, and implies that she drove her husband to his death. Otherwise they get on fine.

2      We might conclude that Groucho is not polite to her. And that is precisely what strikes us as particularly funny about their relationship. Proper behavior in a given situation is very important to the characters that Margaret Dumont plays. She stresses both for herself and the people around her proper dress, proper demeanor, and proper etiquette. The formal garden party and the inaugural ball are her milieu in *Duck Soup*. Even in her boudoir she presents us with a formally and impeccably well dressed presence. Her major concern appears to be that the social forms are maintained; and she directs a sense of outrage at persons who do not defer to and recognize the importance of such socially eminent persons as ambassadors and cabinet ministers. She is the type of character who remains a stock figure in satires, from Gilbert and Sullivan's *The Mikado* (which has a good deal in common with *Duck Soup*) on to the present.

3      Because of her emphasis on the structural (i.e., public) character-istics of individuals rather than on their personal qualities, she is a stifl-ing and constraining presence. The very existence of Groucho (not to mention what he says and does to her) liberates the audience from Margaret Dumont. In classical structuralist fashion the differences be-tween Rufus T. Firefly as portrayed by Groucho and Mrs. Teasdale as portrayed by Margaret Dumont can be represented through a series of oppositions.

4      Where Teasdale is always impeccably tailored, Firefly is always dressed in an ill-fitting outfit. Both Mrs. Teasdale and Firefly are aware of the rules of etiquette but while she is concerned with upholding the rules of conventional morality, Firefly pokes fun at the people who live by the rules and respond emotionally to their violations. Thus, the net effect of the Groucho-Dumont opposition or the Firefly-Teasdale oppo-sition (they amount to the same thing) is to provide the audience with a spectacular and ongoing relationship of continual status reversal. By victimizing her on the basis of publicly displaying her disconcerting (for her) personal characteristics, her claims to superiority are turned to a position of social inferiority. The relationship is based on Mrs. Teasdale's claims about her superior status vis-a-vis the rest of the world (including Firefly). Firefly exploits those claims by providing information and atti-tudes that poke fun, often cruel fun, at the pretensions of Teasdale and most of the people he is surrounded by. The audience participates in what becomes the disruption of claims to deference on public occasions. The audience is able, in fact willing, to participate because these claims are based on the assumption that the norms of social behavior express differences of quality between the actors. Firefly expresses what many of

the audience will have felt many times but had been forced to repress—that their definition of the situation does not merit the assumption of inequality, which they see themselves as forced to acknowledge and legitimize on public occasions.

Firefly and Teasdale represent an important starting point for this analysis. Other dimensions are to be found in the characters played by Chico and Harpo. Chico's character is called, with startling originality, Chicolini while Harpo's character has no name, or at least it is not revealed to the audience.

Chicolini is, as with all the characters Chico plays, an immigrant. He wears funny clothes, talks with an accent, and works at what are almost archetypically immigrant occupations. In *Duck Soup* he runs a combination peanut and hotdog stand and supplements his income with a little espionage on the side. If he were an organ grinder and had a monkey on a string, I don't think we would be surprised. But this is no immigrant made for poking fun at. Although he represents the image of the green-horn so dear to vaudeville and later burlesque comedians, he is not the one who is taken in and fleeced. The fleecing, with an appropriately mixed metaphor, is on the other foot. Chico's main contribution to the Marx Brothers' movies in general, and *Duck Soup* in particular, is through a series of outrageous puns. His wit makes no more linear sense than Groucho's or Harpo's. The major difference is that, while Groucho's humor is aimed at deflating pomposity, Chico's humor is aimed at taking advantage of his victim's image of Chico as ignorant and gullible. In *Duck Soup* Chicolini plays with that image by perpetrating on us a series of puns and by taking advantage of the same people that Firefly mocks. Consider the following dialogue:

*The Shadow*

**Trentino:** Oh! Now, Chicolini, I want a full detailed report of your investigation.

**Chico:** All right, I tell you. Monday we watch-a Firefly's house, but he no come out. He wasn't home. Tuesday we go to the ball game, but he fool us. He no show up. Wednesday he go to the ball game, and we fool him. *We* no show up. Thursday was a doubleheader. Nobody show up. Friday it rained all day. There was no ball game, so we stayed home and we listened to it over the radio.

**Trentino:** Then you didn't shadow Firefly?

**Chico:** Oh, sure we shadow Firefly. We shadow him all day.

**Trentino:** But what day was that?

**Chico:** Shadowday! Hahaha. Atsa some joke, eh, Boss?

*(Adamson, 1973: 227)*

or again when Chicolini is on trial for espionage:

*The Trial*

**Groucho:** Chicolini, give me a number from one to ten.
**Chico:** Eleven.
**Groucho:** Right.
**Chico:** Now I ask you one. What is it has a trunk, but no key, weighs 2,000 pounds, and lives in the circus?
**Prosecutor:** That's irrelevant.
**Chico:** A relephant! Hey, that's the answer! There's a whole lotter elephants in the circus.
**Minister:** That sort of testimony we can eliminate.
**Chico:** Atsa fine. I'll take some.
**Minister:** You'll take *what?*
**Chico:** Eliminate. A nice cool glass eliminate.

\* \* \* \* \* \*

**Minister of Finance:** Something must be done! War would mean a prohibitive increase in our taxes.
**Chico:** Hey, I got an uncle lives in Taxes.
**Minister of Finance:** No, I'm talking about taxes—money, dollars.
**Chico:** Dollas! That's-a where my uncle lives. Dollas, Taxes!
**Minister of Finance:** Aww!

*(Adamson, 1973: 242–243)*

7    If Groucho inverts the norms and values of the social reality that is accepted by the Teasdales and Trentinos of his world, we may say that Chico has a *tangential* relationship to that same reality. He approaches reality from an oblique angle. Chico, however, does not usually act alone. He is accompanied by Harpo, who presents us with a persona entirely different from Chico and Groucho. *Duck Soup* is Harpo's finest hour. All the innate anarchy and formlessness of his character is expressed in this film. Perhaps his finest scene is during his and Chico's conference with Ambassador Trentino. His voluminous clothes produce an assortment of tools from scissors to a blowtorch used for lighting cigars. He consistently, persistently, and absolutely destroys every premise on which social action can be based until the scene can continue no longer. There is no way that the everyday rationality of the Trentino character can deal with the phenomenon of Harpo.

8    Even Harpo's appearance and manner deny the categories of everyday life. He is more than just a stock vaudeville clown figure as he is sometimes interpreted. Immediately, one recognizes that his appearance conveys a remarkable kind of sexual ambiguity. His hair, figure, and face cannot be placed in either of the two sexual categories. Perhaps this is because of his childlike manner. His systematic inarticulateness, his lack of social knowledge, his naivete and polymorphous sexuality (in *Duck Soup* he winds up in bed with a horse after chasing a voluptuous blonde)[1] are all reminiscent of the condition of infancy, or at least the Freudian version of infancy.

For whatever the reason, Harpo is not easily placed into basic and perhaps even universal categories of the social world such as man-woman and child-adult. I suggest that this is because Harpo expresses an attitude to the world that is, to quote Turner, "betwixt and between" the world of structure. Harpo is preeminently a *liminal* figure and as such contradicts the most basic values and distinctions of his and our society. Thus, the figure of Harpo represents for the audience the inversion and obliteration of structure in its most elementary forms.

We have in the Marx Brothers' personae three stock figures from drama and comedy, the flimflammer or con man, the immigrant, and the clown. None is admirable by the standards of our society; they are all marginal to the central concerns of anyone trying to get on in life. What these characters have in common, and what the audience responds to, is that they say *NO* to the application of constraints on behavior to which the rest of their world unthinkingly acquiesces. Of course, their very marginality makes them less liable to the imposition of sanctions. They aren't likely to receive the rewards that everyone else is striving so hard to get. Therefore, they are not obliged to accept the discrepancy between the personal perception of a situation and the acknowledgement of a social norm that is part of the audience's experience of the social world. In the case of Harpo, the audience is given an example of freedom from the constraints imposed on action as a result of being placed by other people into basic social categories such as man-woman or child-adult. With Groucho and Chico, the audience is given an example of freedom from constraints (such as being "nice" or "polite" or "paying attention") that are the necessary baggage that accompanies the achievement of social goals through other people.

In fact, I think this is a major aspect of the appeal of the Marx Brothers. Their characters *express* attitudes to the social world that are coterminous with unexpressed attitudes experienced by large portions of the audiences that have appreciated *Duck Soup* and other Marx Brothers films over the years. This is why so many of the Marx Brothers' best scenes are concerned with public occasions such as balls, parties, trials, and operas. On these occasions the presentation of self is limited to the expression of social rather than personal attributes to a far greater degree than on more intimate occasions. In the Marx Brothers films this ritual separation of persons is stood on its head and the brothers and their audience form an unstructured community united through laughter at the structure. Communitas is to be found in the interaction between the audience and the Marx Brothers. In this sense, anyone who attends a performance of *Duck Soup* is engaging in an action akin to taking part in a ritual. How the person responds is, of course, a matter of personal history and temperament. I cannot help but think, however, that the continuing popularity of this movie is based on its ability to strike deep and responsive chords in the experience of the audience.[2]

I have tried, through the use of the concept of anti-structure, to discover within *Duck Soup* elements that correspond to the experiences of the audience that enable it to respond to the movie. I have tried to show that the social world of the Marx Brothers has structural features in common with that of the audience. Instead of viewing *Duck Soup* as an entity in itself, I have stressed a relationship between what is expressed in the film and the social experience of the actors. This relationship demonstrates that anti-structure is not chaotic and formless: it derives its form and meaning from structure.[3] In the case, for example, of Groucho and Margaret Dumont the form of anti-structure is derived from an antithetical relationship of deference expressed in the etiquette of heirarchy. In this sense, anti-structure is like Monica Wilson's (1951) definition of witchcraft as "standardized nightmares" that derive their meaning from tensions found in social relationships (Middleton and Winter, 1963). The difference is that in witchcraft beliefs, the uncertainities that are elements in social action are developed into a moral theory of causation. In Marx Brothers' films the irritants that accompany social action are expressed.

13      But what happens as a result of the expression of these irritants? Surely, the audience's interpretation of similar experiences has been altered after seeing *Duck Soup*, just as it would have been altered after seeing any movie—no matter how banal. Since this paper has treated *Duck Soup* as a ritual it should conclude with at least some comments on the consequences for the actors of participation in the affair. Although rituals obviously serve to ease social tensions, in each society a ritual must be examined anew before such general conclusions can be reaffirmed. In the case of *Duck Soup* it would be easy but incorrect to suggest that after having seen this movie the audience can rest easier in the face of social inequities. If I did suggest that, the analysis would be dialectical in the sense that Turner uses the notion of dialectics. Instead, I wish to suggest that I find it difficult to imagine how anyone can take *Duck Soup* seriously, in the sense of laughing at what it laughs at, and return to the world of structure and accept with reverence and equanimity the received wisdom of public occasions. The consequence of joining with the Marx Brothers in laughing at structure is to formulate and verify for the moviegoer his private and inchoate experience of the structure, and thus to make that experience an objective, social fact.

14      In this sense the title of the paper plays on the historical accident of the identicalness of the surnames of Karl Marx and the Marx Brothers. The young Karl Marx called for *"a ruthless criticism of everything existing . . . ruthless in two senses: The criticism must not be afraid of its own conclusions, nor of conflict with the powers that be"* (Tucker, 1972:9, emphasis in original). The Marx Brothers similarly ask us to take nothing for granted, nor to be afraid of our conclusions. Remember Chico's famous line in *Duck Soup*. Groucho has just left Mrs. Teasdale's boudoir. Chico, dressed as Groucho, crawls out from under the bed. Mrs. Teasdale says, "Why, I can't believe my own eyes." "Lady," replies Chico, "Who you gonna believe? Me or your own eyes?"

## NOTES

1. Is this the same horse whose picture he carried next to his heart in *Animal Crackers?*

2. Here again we confront the problem of assertion about the audience. One reader suggested, for example, that an audience composed largely of college students (as seems to be the case for Marx Brothers fans currently) cannot be analyzed in the same fashion as the earlier, predominantly lower-class audiences of *Duck Soup.* I suggest that the continuing popularity of the Marx Brothers can be analyzed in terms of continuities in the experience of the audiences. One such continuity might be the marginal relationship to sources of power in our society of both contemporary college students and the 1930s audiences of the Marx Brothers.

3. It only *seems* chaotic and formless to the participants. Anti-structure derives its form through inverting and contravening the structure.

## BIBLIOGRAPHY

Adamson, Joe, 1973, *Groucho, Harpo, Chico and Sometimes Zeppo.* New York: Simon & Schuster.

Evans-Prichard, E. E., 1965, *Theories of Primitive Religion.* London: Oxford University Press.

Gluckman, Max, 1962, *Essays on the Ritual of Social Relations.* Manchester: Manchester University Press.

Goffman, Erving 1959, *Presentation of Self in Everyday Life.* New York: Anchor.

Harris, Grace, 1957, "Possession 'Hysteria' in a Kenya Tribe." *American Anthropologist* 59: 1046-1066.

Leach, E. R., 1954, *Political Systems of Highland Burma.* London: Oxford University Press.

Luckmann, Thomas, 1967, *The Invisible Religion.* New York: Macmillan.

Middleton, J. and E. H. Winter, eds., 1963, *Witchcraft and Sorcery in East Africa.* London; Routledge & Kegan Paul.

Tucker, R. C., 1972, *The Marx-Engels Reader.* New York: Norton.

Turner, V. W., 1967, *The Forest of Symbols.* Ithaca: Cornell University Press.

—1968, *The Drums of Affliction.* London: Oxford University Press.

—1969, *The Ritual Process.* Chicago: Aldine.

—1974, *Dramas, Fields, and Metaphors.* Ithaca: Cornell University Press.

Van Gennep, A., 1960, *The Rites of Passage.* London: Routledge & Kegan Paul.

Wilson, Monica, 1951, "Witch Beliefs and Social Structure." *American Journal of Sociology* 56: 307-313.

Zimmerman, Paul and Burt Goldblatt, 1968, *The Marx Brothers at the Movies.* New York: New American Library.

## *Evaluating the Text*

1. How are class relationships a subject of the Marx Brothers' movies? In what way do their movies permit immigrants with relatively little power in

society to turn the tables on those with power? How might audiences identify with the Marx Brothers? In what way does comedy of this kind function as a release for the audience?

2. In what way is the humor of the Marx Brothers a form of thinly disguised aggression toward authority? What evidence can you cite to support this?

3. Discuss the way the Marx Brothers use a range of linguistic techniques such as puns, double meaning, and free association, to mock language used by high-class society and to mock the authority of grammar itself. How does much of their verbal humor turn the tables on those in power by making them feel as helpless as immigrants do in not being able to understand what people are saying?

4. How is the relationship between Groucho and Mrs. Teasdale meant to represent the relationship between immigrants and the power structure of established society?

5. Discuss the verbal means Chico uses to mock the status quo.

6. What is Harpo's particular contribution to the turning of the tables against the power structure? How does his method differ from Chicho's and Groucho's?

7. How does Karp use the results of studies by anthropologists and other expert testimony to support his claim? Evaluate the effectiveness of these diverse sources in making his conclusions credible.

## Exploring Different Perspectives

1. How do both C. P. Ellis ("Why I Quit the Klan") and the Marx Brothers rebel against the power structure? Compare their respective methods. How do both Ellis and Karp offer insights into how class operates in American society?

2. How do each of the Marx Brothers say NO to the application of constraints on behavior to which the rest of their world unthinkingly acquiesces? Compare this freedom to say NO with the constraints on Derricotte's freedom to act on her anger.

## Extending Viewpoints through Writing

1. Applying conclusions reached in Karp's analysis, take a close look at the story line and characters of another of the Marx Brothers' films. To what extent is Karp's analysis supported by Marx Brothers' movies other than Duck Soup?

2. Discuss any contemporary movie, such as Do the Right Thing by Spike Lee, that expresses social criticism in satiric form. Discuss the similarities and differences between these new movies and those of the Marx Brothers in terms of subject matter, characters, and language.

3. Discuss the work of any new comedian whose humor reflects his or her experiences as a member of a recently immigrated ethnic minority.

4. Write a paper analyzing the class-based appeal of a television show (e.g., The Simpsons, Dallas); film (e.g., Cinema Paradisio, My Beautiful Laundrette, Goodfellas); or comic strip (e.g., "Doonesbury") for a particular kind of audience. What features of the work reveal this class-based appeal?

# Dino Buzzati

# *The Falling Girl*

*Dino Buzzati (1906–1972) spent most of his working life in Milan as an editor and correspondent for* Corriere della Sera. *A prolific writer, Buzzati is the author of poems, librettos, a children's book, hundreds of short stories in collections such as* Catastrophe *(1966) and* The Siren *(1984), and novels, including the internationally acclaimed* The Tartar Steppe *(1940). His innovative play,* A Clinical Case *(1955), was translated into French by Albert Camus and performed on stages throughout the world. "The Falling Girl" from his short story collection* Restless Nights *(1983) is a typical Buzzatian mixture of surrealism, journalistic coverage of a human-interest story, and social commentary on the effects of the economic boom in post-World War II Italy.*

*Italy is a republic in southern Europe, extending into the Mediterranean sea as a boot-shaped peninsula, bordered to the northwest by France, to the north by Switzerland and Austria, and to the northeast by Yugoslavia. From the fourth century* B.C. *to the fifth century* A.D., *the history of Italy is for the most part that of the Roman Empire. The Italian Renaissance, in the fourteenth century, awakened Europe from the Middle Ages and bequeathed countless great works of art and culture to the world. Reacting to Austria's domination in the mid-1800s, Italian nationalism (Risorgimento, or "resurgance") ultimately united different political elements under a parliament and a king. In 1922, Italy came under the fascist leadership of Benito Mussolini, who later joined Germany and Japan (as the Axis Powers) in World War II until Fascism was overthrown in 1943. In 1946, Italy became a republic and joined NATO (North Atlantic Treaty Organization) in 1949. The post-war era has been a turbulent one politically with a succession of short-lived coalition governments. The issues of class consciousness and social aspiration dramatized in Buzzati's story reflects Italy's rapid industrialization and the emergence of an upwardly striving middle class since the early 1950s. Recent huge budget deficits have curtailed economic growth and forced the government to cut spending in health and education, moves that have resulted in strikes and social unrest.*

Marta was nineteen. She looked out over the roof of the skyscraper, 1
and seeing the city below shining in the dusk, she was overcome with
dizziness.

313

2      The skyscraper was silver, supreme and fortunate in that most beautiful and pure evening, as here and there the wind stirred a few fine filaments of cloud against an absolutely incredible blue background. It was in fact the hour when the city is seized by inspiration and whoever is not blind is swept away by it. From that airy height the girl saw the streets and the masses of buildings writhing in the long spasm of sunset, and at the point where the white of the houses ended, the blue of the sea began. Seen from above, the sea looked as if it were rising. And since the veils of the night were advancing from the east, the city became a sweet abyss burning with pulsating lights. Within it were powerful men, and women who were even more powerful, furs and violins, cars glossy as onyx, the neon signs of nightclubs, the entrance halls of darkened mansions, fountains, diamonds, old silent gardens, parties, desires, affairs, and, above all, that consuming sorcery of the evening which provokes dreams of greatness and glory.

3      Seeing these things, Marta hopelessly leaned out over the railing and let herself go. She felt as if she were hovering in the air, but she was falling. Given the extraordinary height of the skyscraper, the streets and squares down at the bottom were very far away. Who knows how long it would take her to get there. Yet the girl was falling.

4      At that hour the terraces and balconies of the top floors were filled with rich and elegant people who were having cocktails and making silly conversation. They were scattered in crowds, and their talk muffled the music. Marta passed before them and several people looked out to watch her.

5      Flights of that kind (mostly by girls, in fact) were not rare in the skyscraper and they constituted an interesting diversion for the tenants; this was also the reason why the price of those apartments was very high.

The sun had not yet completely set and it did its best to illuminate Marta's simple clothing. She wore a modest, inexpensive spring dress bought off the rack. Yet the lyrical light of the sunset exalted it somewhat, making it chic.

6      From the millionaires' balconies, gallant hands were stretched out toward her, offering flowers and cocktails. "Miss, would you like a drink? . . . Gentle butterfly, why not stop a minute with us?"

7      She laughed, hovering, happy (but meanwhile she was falling): "No, thanks, friends. I can't. I'm in a hurry."

8      "Where are you headed?" they asked her.

9      "Ah, don't make me say," Marta answered, waving her hands in a friendly good-bye.

10      A young man, tall, dark, very distinguished, extended an arm to snatch her. She liked him. And yet Marta quickly defended herself: "How dare you, sir?" and she had time to give him a little tap on the nose.

The beautiful people, then, were interested in her and that filled her    11
with satisfaction. She felt fascinating, stylish. On the flower-filled terraces, amid the bustle of waiters in white and the bursts of exotic songs,
there was talk for a few minutes, perhaps less, of the young woman who
was passing by (from top to bottom, on a vertical course). Some thought
her pretty, others thought her so-so, everyone found her interesting.

"You have your entire life before you," they told her, "why are you    12
in such a hurry? You still have time to rush around and busy yourself.
Stop with us for a little while, it's only a modest little party among
friends, really, you'll have a good time."

She made an attempt to answer but the force of gravity had already    13
quickly carried her to the floor below, then two, three, four floors below;
in fact, exactly as you gaily rush around when you are just nineteen years
old.

Of course, the distance that separated her from the bottom, that is,    14
from street level, was immense. It is true that she began falling just a
little while ago, but the street always seemed very far away.

In the meantime, however, the sun had plunged into the sea; one    15
could see it disappear, transformed into a shimmering reddish mush-
room. As a result, it no longer emitted its vivifying rays to light up the
girl's dress and make her a seductive comet. It was a good thing that the
windows and terraces of the skyscraper were almost all illuminated and
the bright reflections completely gilded her as she gradually passed by.

Now Marta no longer saw just groups of carefree people inside the
apartments; at times there were even some businesses where the employees, in black or blue aprons, were sitting at desks in long rows.
Several of them were young people as old as or older than she, and
weary of the day by now, every once in a while they raised their eyes
from their duties and from typewriters. In this way they too saw her, and
a few ran to the windows. "Where are you going? Why so fast? Who are
you?" they shouted to her. One could divine something akin to envy in
their words.

"They're waiting for me down there," she answered. "I can't stop.    16
Forgive me." And again she laughed, wavering on her headlong fall, but
it wasn't like her previous laughter anymore. The night had craftily
fallen and Marta started to feel cold.

Meanwhile, looking downward, she saw a bright halo of lights at the    17
entrance of a building. Here long black cars were stopping (from the
great distance they looked as small as ants), and men and women were
getting out, anxious to go inside. She seemed to make out the sparkling
of jewels in that swarm. Above the entrance flags were flying.

They were obviously giving a large party, exactly the kind that Marta    18
dreamed of ever since she was a child. Heaven help her if she missed it.
Down there opportunity was waiting for her, fate, romance, the true
inauguration of her life. Would she arrive in time?

19    She spitefully noticed that another girl was falling about thirty meters above her. She was decidedly prettier than Marta and she wore a rather classy evening gown. For some unknown reason she came down much faster than Marta, so that in a few moments she passed by her and disappeared below, even though Marta was calling her. Without doubt she would get to the party before Marta; perhaps she had a plan all worked out to supplant her.

20    Then she realized that they weren't alone. Along the sides of the skyscraper many other young women were plunging downward, their faces taut with the excitement of the flight, their hands cheerfully waving as if to say: look at us, here we are, entertain us, is not the world ours?

21    It was a contest, then. And she only had a shabby little dress while those other girls were dressed smartly like high-fashion models and some even wrapped luxurious mink stoles tightly around their bare shoulders. So self-assured when she began the leap, Marta now felt a tremor growing inside her; perhaps it was just the cold; but it may have been fear too, the fear of having made an error without remedy.

22    It seemed to be late at night now. The windows were darkened one after another, the echoes of music became more rare, the offices were empty, young men no longer leaned out from the windowsills extending their hands. What time was it? At the entrance to the building down below — which in the meantime had grown larger, and one could now distinguish all the architectural details — the lights were still burning, but the bustle of cars had stopped. Every now and then, in fact, small groups of people came out of the main floor wearily drawing away. Then the lights of the entrance were also turned off.

23    Marta felt her heart tightening. Alas, she wouldn't reach the ball in time. Glancing upwards, she saw the pinnacle of the skyscraper in all its cruel power. It was almost completely dark. On the top floors a few windows here and there were still lit. And above the top the first glimmer of dawn was spreading.

24    In a dining recess of the twenty-eighth floor a man about forty years old was having his morning coffee and reading his newspaper while his wife tidied up the room. A clock on the sideboard indicated 8:45. A shadow suddenly passed before the window.

25    "Alberto!" the wife shouted. "Did you see that? A woman passed by."

26    "Who was it?" he said without raising his eyes from the newspaper.

27    "An old woman," the wife answered. "A decrepit old woman. She looked frightened."

28    "It's always like that," the man muttered. "At these low floors only falling old women pass by. You can see beautiful girls from the hundred-and-fiftieth floor up. Those apartments don't cost so much for nothing."

29    "At least down here there's the advantage," observed the wife, "that you can hear the thud when they touch the ground."

"This time not even that," he said, shaking his head, after he stood ³⁰ listening for a few minutes. Then he had another sip of coffee.

*Translated by Lawrence Venuti*

## Evaluating the Text

1. How does Buzzati use the figurative meaning of falling (as in "falling in love" or as "falling from grace") as a literal premise to suggest how Marta is drawn to the sophistication, excitement, and luxury of the city, seen from the top of a skyscraper?
2. How does the phrase "silly conversation" suggest that the author does not share Marta's naive enthusiasm and may be criticizing the social striving in Italian society?
3. The name *Marta* sounds like *martyr*. What are the other details in the story that suggest she is sacrificing herself to a dream that will "consume" her?
4. How does the phrase "flights of that kind" suggest Buzzati is describing a class phenomenon that is characteristic of a whole generation of young girls, not just Marta personally?
5. In what respects does Buzzati's story communicate the feeling of being nineteen years old? What particular traits and qualities does Marta exhibit that are typical of this age in terms of energy, idealism, and a belief that choices will always be available?
6. Describe the change that takes place in Marta as she falls. In what sense does her psychological state seem to deteriorate; that is, how do her initial reactions of optimism and idealism give way to envy, fear, competition, and possibly even despair?
7. What might be the significance of the fact that her "fall" takes place between sundown and sunrise?
8. In what way do the different levels of the skyscraper give you Buzzati's view of the class structure of Italian society? How are fewer choices available to Marta the further she falls?
9. What do you make of the fact that the couple do not hear a "thud"? Do you interpret the lack of this sound as having positive or negative significance? Does this mean Marta has landed lightly and simply walked away, that she has not made an "impact" on society, or that she continues to fall?

## Exploring Different Perspectives

1. When you compare Buzzati's use of surrealism to tell a human-interest story with Krishnan Varma's use of surrealism in "The Grass-Eaters," which do you find more effective and why?
2. How do both this story and Toi Derricotte's account ("The Black Notebooks") dramatize the situation of an outsider looking in? How do both selections reveal the impact of social class on individuals?

# *Extending Viewpoints through Writing*

1. Have you known anyone who was prepared to sacrifice everyday pleasures to achieve a goal? How did his or her experiences compare to those of Marta in Buzzati's story?
2. How does "The Falling Girl" capture the experience of being nineteen?
3. In an essay, discuss the way in which you might make sense of this story. For example, you might see it as a parable of life, youth and old age, birth and death, social striving, psychological change in someone consumed by ambition, a parable of an idealist who has a martyr (Marta) complex, or a critical depiction of the class structure of Italian society.
4. From whose point of view do Buzzati, Krishnan Varma ("The Grass-Eaters"), and Josef Škvorecký ("An Insolvable Problem of Genetics"), tell their stories? How does the point of view from which Buzzati, Varma, and Škvorecký tell their stories affect the reader's perception of the characters? Which characters in each story are the most and least sympathetic and why?
5. In "The Falling Girl," the innocence of the main character is a central issue. The same might be said of "A Handful of Dates" (Tayeb Salih, Chapter 2), "Famous All Over Town" (Danny Santiago, Chapter 2), "Teresa's Wedding" (William Trevor, Chapter 1), and "An Insolvable Problem of Genetics" (Josef Škvorecký). In an essay, compare and contrast any two of these works exploring each author's attitude toward their character's naiveté.

# CONNECTING CULTURES

## Gloria Steinem, "The Time Factor"

1. Drawing on Steinem's article, analyze Robert Levine and Ellen Wolff's explanation of "social time" ("Social Time: The Heartbeat of Culture," Chapter 8) to discover how the significance of time varies not only within a culture, but between cultures as well. What appear to be the key factors determining the process by which time is given different values in different cultures?

2. What insight does Steinem's article provide into Francine du Plessix Gray's discussion ("Sex and Birth," Chapter 1) of how much of Russian life is constructed around waiting in line for the necessities?

3. How does Steinem's discussion of the relationship between poverty and an inability to plan for the future shed light on the function fiestas play in Mexico as described by Octavio Paz ("The Day of the Dead," Chapter 8)? How do fiestas serve the purpose of a a ritual that stops time for the poor and lets them enjoy themselves?

4. How does John Burgess's article ("A Day in the Life of 'Salaryman'," Chapter 4) illustrate the extent to which salarymen in Japanese society are controlled by rigid schedules? How does this exemplify the liabilities of overplanning in contrast to the inability to plan at all, discussed by Steinem?

5. How do both the accounts by Armando Valladares ("A Nazi Prison in the Caribbean," Chapter 6) and Alicia Partnoy ("Introduction" and "A Conversation under the Rain," Chapter 6) illustrate that one of the most disorienting things about being a prisoner is how the power to control time is in the hands of others? How do their experiences reveal a different perspective on Steinem's thesis?

## Jo Goodwin Parker, "What Is Poverty?"

6. How would many of the problems faced by Parker be handled in the context of Chinese society as described by Bruce Dollar ("Child Care in China," Chapter 1)?

7. How do the everyday stresses faced by Parker in taking care of her children resemble those confronted by Graciela in Nicholasa Mohr's "A Very Special Pet" (Chapter 7)? What insight do both of these selections provide into the difficulties those on the fringe of mainstream society face?

## Krishnan Varma, "The Grass-Eaters"

8. How do both Varma's story and "Teresa's Wedding" by William Trevor (Chapter 1) explore the lives of people who cannot afford to have illusions and often must settle for much less than they would have wanted?

9. In what way do both Varma and Francine du Plessix Gray ("Sex and Birth," Chapter 1) explore social conditions of material deprivation? What

cultural and religious differences might explain the different responses to deprivation in India and Russia?

10. To what extent does Bruce Dollar's account ("Child Care in China," Chapter 1) suggest why China—with approximately the same population as India—is managing to feed and provide shelter for their one billion people, while India has been less successful? What political, cultural, and social values might explain this difference?

11. How do both Varma's story and "The Management of Grief" by Bharati Mukherjee (Chapter 7) give you insight into the extent to which fatalism grounded in Hindu religion plays a crucial role in determining responses to disaster and tragedy in Indian culture?

## C. P. Ellis, "Why I Quit the Klan"

12. After reading Everett C. Hughes's "Good People and Dirty Work" (Chapter 9), compare the process by which both the SS and the KKK enlist recruits to perform the "dirty work"? How do both Ellis and Hughes suggest the "good people" of both societies, those in Nazi Germany and in the South, are implicated in the "dirty work," despite their attempts to distance themselves from the commission of the crimes?

13. Evaluate Studs Terkel's interview with Ellis in comparison with Maurizio Chierici's interview with Claude Eatherly ("The Man from Hiroshima," Chapter 9). What can you discover about the relationship between each interviewer and the subject, and the attitude of each interviewer *toward* the subject? What inferences can you draw about the way each interviewer has edited and formatted the interviews? What dominant impression and recurring motifs are evident in each interview?

## Josef Škvorecký, "An Insolvable Problem of Genetics"

14. Drawing on Marilyn French's ("Gender Roles, Chapter 3) analysis of the extent to which culture conditions gender expectations, explore Škvorecký's portrayal of how political expectations can shape sex role behavior.

15. After reading Slawomir Mrozěk's "The Elephant" (Chapter 6), discuss how both Mrozěk and Škvorecký use similar satiric techniques to poke fun at the absurdities of Eastern-bloc communist bureaucracies.

16. Compare William Trevor's ("Teresa's Wedding," Chapter 1) and Škvorecký's treatment of two young couples (Teresa and Artie, Freddie and Adolf) about to be married. How are differences in style and tone between the two stories related to each author's purpose? How do these stories acquaint the reader with life in rural Ireland and in Czechoslovakia (during the Russian occupation)?

17. How do both Škvorecký's story and Francine du Plessix Gray's account in "Sex and Birth" (Chapter 1) illustrate how governmental bureaucracies influence the life of the average citizen? How effective do you find short fiction compared with an interview in communicating these insights?

18. After reading Amy Tan's "Jing-Mei Woo: Two Kinds" (chapter 1), discuss

how the narrative structures of Tan's story and Škvorecký's tale are shaped by the respective points of view of an adult looking back on her childhood and a child naively commenting on events that happened in his household.

## Toi Derricotte, "The Black Notebooks"

19. To what extent are the members of the country club mentioned in Derricotte's account permitting the owner to do the "dirty work" for them in excluding Derricotte's family in ways that are comparable, on a lesser scale, to the way in which "good" Germans delegated "dirty work" to the SS? (See Everett C. Hughes, "Good People and Dirty Work," Chapter 6.)
20. How does Derricotte's account provide insight into how racial prejudice can undermine a marriage in ways that are similar to the effects of political pressures dramatized by Chen Jo-hsi ("The Big Fish" Chapter 6)?

## Ivan Karp, "Good Marx for the Anthropologist"

21. What can you infer are basic techniques of satire from reading both Karp's article and Slawomir Mrożek's story, "The Elephant" (Chapter 6)?
22. How is the proper use of language an issue in both Danny Santiago's story ("Famous All Over Town, Chapter 2) and in Karp's analysis of the Marx Brothers' movie, Duck Soup? Why are questions of language invariably connected to questions of social class?
23. After reading Salman Rushdie's "A Pen Against the Sword" (Chapter 7), discuss why, in your opinion, Rushdie's satire was greeted with such animosity, while Duck Soup was seen as funny and harmless.
24. How does the effect of Jamaica Kincaid's "A Small Place" (Chapter 7) depend on the satiric tone she employs in her diatribe against wealthy tourists who visit Antigua? How are Kincaid's purposes different from those of the Marx Brothers in making fun of the upper class in Duck Soup?

## Dino Buzzati "The Falling Girl"

25. Contrast Buzzati's use of surrealism with the realistic style William Trevor (Chapter 1) adopts in telling the story of "Teresa's Wedding" (Chapter 1). How is each style suited to the subject of each story?
26. Compare the extent to which self-delusion enters into Buzzati's story and into "Jing-Mei Woo: Two Kinds" by Amy Tan (Chapter 1).
27. How do issues of class play an important role in the view the protagonists have of themselves in both Buzzati's story and in Talat Abbasi's "Facing the Light" (Chapter 3)?

# 6

# *The State and the Individual*

In no area are the conflicts between different points of view more dramatic than those between individual citizens and the nation-states to whom they relinquish a certain degree of freedom to gain benefits that can be achieved only through the collective political and social institutions (the military, the legal system, health care, education). The allegiance individuals owe their governments, and the protection of individual rights citizens expect in return, has been the subject of intense analysis through the ages by such figures as Socrates in Plato's *Apology* and *Crito*, Henry David Thoreau in *Civil Disobedience*, and Martin Luther King, Jr., in "A Letter From Birmingham Jail." The readings that follow continue this debate by providing accounts drawn from many different societies revealing assumptions and expectations very different, in many cases, from our own democratic form of government.

In Cuba, Armando Valladares in "A Nazi Prison in the Caribbean" gives us a devastating inside account of what life is like for Castro's political opponents. In China, Chen Jo-hsi's story, "The Big Fish," provides a poignant account of how personal and family values take second place to the demands of Mao's Cultural Revolution. Then Shen Tong, a student leader of the pro-democracy movement, gives a first-hand account of the massacre in Beijing that took place on June 3, 1989, in "Bloody Sunday in Tiananmen Square." In "The Elephant" by Slawomir Mrożek, one of Poland's most acerbic political satirists creates an ironic fable to point out the absurdities of communist bureaucracy. In "The Velvet Hangover," Václav Havel, the president of Czechoslovakia, looks at the unexpected consequences of his country's successful revolution against Soviet domination. Someth May, a survivor of the Khmer Rouge occupation of Cambodia, describes the experiences that led to his political "re-education" in "The Field Behind the Village." From Argentina, one of the "disappeared," Alicia Partnoy, whose testimony on human rights violations helped bring about the conviction of four generals, tells the shocking story of her arrest and imprisonment, in "Introduction" and "A Conversation Under the Rain," from *The Little School: Tales of Disappearance and Survival in Argentina.* Iraq's Saddam Hussein's calculated use of fear to maintain power is the subject of the revealing inside account, "Authority," by Samir Al-Khalil. Speaking from a post-colonial perspective in Kenya, Ngũgĩ wa Thiong'o analyzes, in "Decolonising the Mind," the damaging psychological consequences of having been forbidden by the British rulers to write or speak his native language while in school. In South Africa, the devastating consequences of apartheid for both blacks and whites are illuminated by Jan Rabie's thought-provoking parable, "Drought."

# Armando Valladares

# *A Nazi Prison in the Caribbean*

*Armando Valladares was arrested at the age of twenty-three for op-*
*posing communism in Cuba. He was imprisoned for over two decades*
*until he was released as a result of an international campaign of*
*protest. This chapter, "A Nazi Prison in the Caribbean," from his book*
Against All Hope *(translated by Andrew Hurley, 1986), is an elo-*
*quent account of his struggle to retain his humanity amid the horrors*
*he witnessed and endured during his confinement in Boniato prison.*

*Cuba, the largest island in the West Indies, is located in the*
*Caribbean Sea at the entrance of the Gulf of Mexico. Christopher*
*Columbus discovered the island in 1492, and Spain colonized it from*
*1511, using it as a staging point for its New World exploration. In*
*1898, the Spanish American War resulted in the establishment of*
*Cuba as a republic. Promising agrarian reform, Fidel Castro took over*
*control of the Cuban government in 1959, and Cuba became the only*
*communist state in Latin America and a firm ally of the Soviet Union.*
*In 1961 (the first year of Valladares's twenty-two-year political im-*
*prisonment), American-trained Cuban exiles were defeated by Castro's*
*forces during the unsuccessful Bay of Pigs invasion. This was followed*
*in 1962 by the Cuban missile crisis, brought about by Soviet introduc-*
*tion of nuclear weapons onto the island that were capable of striking*
*targets in the United States. By 1980, Cuban refugees to the United*
*States numbered at least 700,000 (for information on Cuban exiles, see*
*Joan Didion's "Miami: The Cuban Presence" p. 446). In 1989, Castro*
*marked the thirtieth anniversary of the Cuban revolution by denounc-*
*ing the Soviet government's reform policies of* perestroika *and* glasnost *under Mikhail Gorbachev. In February of that year, the United*
*Nations officially condemned Cuba for continued human rights viola-*
*tions of the kind so graphically described by Armando Valladares.*

1    Of all the prisons and concentration camps in Cuba, the most repressive was Boniato Prison, on the extreme eastern end of the island.
Perhaps in the past it had not been so bad for other prisoners, but it has
been and will always be for political prisoners. Even today, when prison
authorities want to put a group of prisoners through the worst imaginable experiences, when they want to perform biological or psychological
experiments on them, when they want to hold prisoners completely

incommunicado, to beat and torture them, the jail at Boniato is the installation of choice.

Built at the lowest point in a valley, surrounded by military encamp-     2
ments, far away from towns and highways, it is the ideal location for their plans. The cries of tortured men and the bursts of machine-gun fire are heard by no one; they fade away into the solitude of the place, are lost in the hills and valleys. Relatives are often as far as seven hundred miles away, so they're very seldom standing at the prison entrance asking for news. And if after a long exhausting pilgrimage they manage to arrive at the outskirts of the prison installation, the guards send them back home. The isolation of a jail may be one of its main advantages, and the jail at Boniato is the most isolated of all the prisons in Cuba.

Our trip to Boniato was the worst we had ever made. The police van     3
held twenty-two prisoners uncomfortably, but the authorities crammed twenty-six of us inside.

I was in a cage with three other men. Since we couldn't all sit down at     4
once, I crawled under the wooden seat and curled up. I knocked contin-
ually against the other men's legs. I fell asleep with the rocking and rolling of the vehicle and slept until Piloto, nauseated by the smell of gasoline and the rocking of the truck, began to vomit. The only thing to hold the vomit was my aluminum drinking cup, so I gave it to him. About two hundred miles farther on, in the city of Santa Clara, they gave each cage a can to urinate into. I got under the seat again. Urine kept splashing out of the can and wetting my legs from the rough braking and the potholes in the road. Piloto was still very motion-sick, but we didn't have anything to give him to control his nausea. One of the prison vans broke down as we were coming into Camagüey. The trip took more than twenty-five hours.

At last the caravan stopped at the entrance of Boniato Prison. When     5
the door opened, I saw a great billboard saying "CUBA — FIRST FREE TERRI-
TORY IN AMERICA."

They took us out of the trucks and led us to Building 5, Section C.     6
Taking advantage of the tumult of prisoners and guards, I managed to hand a package I was carrying to Enrique Díaz Correa, who had arrived previously and was already inside. Had I not given him the package with the penpoint, a tiny photo of Martha, some small sheets of onion-skin, and a jar of ink made in the prison, I would have lost it all in the search, since they stripped us and even looked under our testicles.

A circle of hostile faces and fixed bayonets surrounded us, but there     7
were no beatings. The food that afternoon was served in tins that had contained Russian beef. It was three spoonfuls of boiled macaroni and a piece of bread. That was February 11, 1970.

That day saw the beginning of a plan for biological and psychological     8
experimentation more inhuman, brutal, and merciless than anything the western world had known with the exception of the Nazis' activities. Boniato and its blackout cells will always be an accusation. If all the other

human-rights violations had not occurred, what happened at Boniato would be enough in itself to condemn the Cuban regime as the most cruel and degrading ever known in the Americas.

9     We were locked up in forty separate cells. To go to the latrine you had to call the soldiers. I thought it was strange that we had not been counted at dusk as was usual in the jails. My cell had a burlap cot, but it sagged like a hammock.

10     At sunrise the garrison flooded the hallway. They came in shouting and cursing. It was the same as always; they had to get all heated up to come in. They beat on the walls and the bars with the weapons they were carrying—rubber-hose-covered iron bars (so they wouldn't break the skin), thick clubs and woven electrical cables, chains wrapped around their hands, and bayonets. There was no justification, no pretext. They just opened the cells, one by one, and beat the prisoners inside. The first cell they opened was Martin Pérez'. I remember his big husky voice cursing the Communists, but without saying a single dirty word. I got close to the bars to try to look out, and a chain blow made me jump back. I was lucky it hadn't hit me in the face.

11     They opened cell number 3, number 4, number 5. As they approached my cell, I trembled inside. My muscles contracted spasmodically. My breathing came with difficulty and I felt the fear and rage that always possessed me.

12     Some men, their psychological resistance wasted away already, couldn't contain themselves, and before the soldiers even entered their cells they began to shriek and wail hysterically. Those shrieks multiplied the horror. The soldier that opened the bars to our cell was armed with a bayonet. Behind him were three more, blocking the entrance. I saw only that one of the guards was carrying a chain. They pushed us to the back of the cell so they'd have room to swing their weapons. We tried not to get separated, because we knew that was the most dangerous thing you could do. That was when they would kick you and knee you in the groin. They knocked me to the floor, and one of them kicked me in the face and split my lower lip. When I recovered consciousness my head was lying in a pool of blood. My cellmate was bleeding through the nose and his hand was fractured near his wrist.

13     Several men were seriously injured. One of the Graiño brothers had his cheekbone fractured by Sergeant "Good Guy"; he spit out broken teeth. He'd been beaten so brutally his face looked like one huge black eye. Pechuguita, a peaceable little campesino from Pinar del Rio, had his head split open; the wound was so large it took twenty stitches to close it. Every man, without exception, was beaten. The guards went about it systematically, cell by cell.

14     After the beating the officers and a military doctor passed through to examine us. They took wounded men out of the cells, but right there on the spot a medic with a little first-aid cart sewed up and bandaged the wounds. When they finished bandaging us they said, "Don't say we

didn't give you medical treatment!" and put us back into the cells, where we waited for our next beating.

I was bruised all over. My face was swollen and bloody. I could [15] hardly stand up for the pain all over my body. They had given me the worst beating of my life. But what had affected me most was waiting for them to come to my cell and beat me. That did more damage to me than the blows themselves. A thousand times I wished I had been in the first cell. That way they would come in, beat me, and go back out again. I wanted it over with once and for all so I wouldn't have to go through that torture of waiting and dreading. My nerves were destroyed by it.

The guards came back in the afternoon, almost at nightfall, and the [16] nightmare of the morning was repeated—beatings, cell by cell, with more wounded men the result. We could communicate with the other sections of the building by shouting back and forth, so we traded the names of the most gravely wounded men.

Odilo Alonso woke up the next morning with his head monstrously [17] swollen; I would never have imagined that anyone could have looked so grotesquely deformed. His ears were so swollen he looked as though he were wearing a helmet. After three days of those two-a-day beatings, many men could no longer stand. Martín Pérez was urinating blood, as was de Vera, and other men's eyes were so blackened and swollen shut by the blows that they could hardly see. But that didn't matter to the soldiers—they beat men again and again.

Sergeant Good Guy, whose real name was Ismael, belonged to the [18] Communist Party. He had a big Pancho Villa moustache. Whenever the garrison came in to beat us, he cried *"Viva Communism!"* madly, over and over. It was his war cry. He would tell the other soldiers to beat the wounded on top of their bandages, so that nobody could say that the soldiers had beaten them more than once. Another sergeant did exactly the opposite—he would beat the wounded men on their bare skin and say with a sneer, "I wanna see 'em sew you up again."

Odilo was getting worse and worse. The blows to his head had [19] affected him horribly. His ears were leaking pus and bloody liquid, and his face was monstrously inflamed. Finally he could no longer stand erect. It was only then that they took him to the prison hospital.

They gave not so much as an aspirin to even the most seriously [20] wounded men. They didn't take any prisoner out of the section unless he was in danger of death. They didn't try to kill us quickly; that would have been too generous a gesture to have hoped for from those sadists. Their object was to force us, by means of terror and torture, into the Political Rehabilitation Program. To do that, they were slowly and inexorably destroying us. They would take us to the very brink of death and keep us there, without letting us cross it. We had even been vaccinated against tetanus, so they could bayonet us, wound us with machetes and iron bars, and break our skulls, sure that at least we wouldn't contract tetanus.

21    The attitude maintained by our group was discussed in the magazine *Moncada*, the official organ of the Ministry of the Interior, in an article written by the head of Jails and Prisons, Medardo Lemus. He wrote that our resistance was a major block to the plans the government had for enlisting all prisoners in the Political Rehabilitation Program, and that our rebelliousness and especially our refusal to conform with prison discipline was a bad example for the other prisoners. The authorities therefore saw themselves obliged to separate us from the rest of the penal population.

22    But men could not stand up forever to the daily beatings, the terror, the psychological tortures, and some took on the uniform. Those desertions caused us great pain. It was as though the authorities were pulling off pieces of our own bodies. I felt diminished every time one of our men left; years of terror, misery, and the dream of freedom had united us.

23    The capacity to stand up to something like that is very difficult to gauge. Men who had stood up to the Castro dictatorship in all-out combat in the mountains or in the cities, who had gone in and out of Cuba clandestinely on missions of war, who were full of bravery and heroism, could not, unarmed, confront the terror, the lack of communication, the solitary confinement for very long, and they finally gave in. But that might have been better in one sense, because that way our position solidified. Our bodies grew thinner day by day, our strength slipped away, our legs were beginning to look like toothpicks, but inside, the foundations of our spirits, our faith and determination, grew stronger and stronger with every blow of a bayonet, with every ignominy, with every harassment, with every beating.

24    Every afternoon at dusk the thundering voice of the Brother of the Faith, as we called Gerardo, the Protestant preacher, echoed through those passages, calling out to the prayer meeting. They tried to keep us from our religious practices, to interrupt, silence the prayers, and that cost us extra quotas of blows. The first time this happened the guards unleashed a beating in the midst of the prayer meeting, cell by cell, but as soon as they left the beaten men continued singing, and the other prisoners followed their lead. The guards moved back and forth and handed out blows in what seemed to be a different dimension from the one in which we were praying and singing hymns to God. In the cell in front of mine, I watched guards kicking two prisoners lying on the floor. Those prisoners also began to sing and pray as soon as the guards had left. Now those men over there, who had been singing before, were being beaten. And so the surreal scene went on. Above the shouting and tumult, the voice of the Brother of the Faith was singing "Glory, glory Hallelujah!"

25    In Building 4 they were renovating the cells, making them even more inhumane and repressive than they had ever been before. Only the drawer cells in the concentration camps of Tres Macíos and San Ramón were comparable to these.

We watched with horror day by day as the construction progressed. 26
We suffered those cells in anticipation. We tried never to mention them.
We would look at them in despair, but not a word was spoken about
them.

On January 6 we were taken from Block 5 to the blackout cells, as 27
though it were a sinister Three Kings Day present—although by now
that day of joy for children had been abolished in Cuba. Almost the
whole population of the prison watched the parade of our starving
bodies. Our bones stuck out like scarecrows' frames. Some men dragged
their legs, others could walk only with help. Men who pushed the
wheelchairs of the invalids had to lean on them to stand up. We were
human ruins by now, and in a way the torment had hardly begun. But
I think all our eyes still glowed with vigorous life; there was a flame,
a keenness and zeal in us—our jailers had not been able to uproot
that.

The blackout-cell hallway looked like a crypt, with twenty niches on 28
each side. The cells were about ten feet long by four and a half feet wide.
In one corner there was a hole for a latrine, and above it, almost at the
ceiling, a piece of bent tubing, the shower. The guard posted at the bars
could open or close all the showers on one or the other side of the
passageway from the outside, with two master faucets.

The leaders of prisons were delighted with the results of their con- 29
struction. Concentration-camp directors from the province and from
other jails came to Boniato. They laughed and smiled with the same
pride that philanthropists, men of goodwill, do when they inaugurate a
hospital or a school. There was a tone of mockery and sarcastic pleasure
in their voices, as though they were savoring beforehand the triumph
they had so long awaited. At last the creation of the blackout cells was a
reality, for all the Russians', Czechs', Hungarians', and East Germans'
combined experience in torture and psychological annihilation was
brought to the creation of the blackout cells. Doctors and psychologists
from Communist countries, including Cuba, had lent their scientific
expertise to the questions of diet, calories, the creation of disorienting
situations, the manipulation of wasting diseases, and so forth. When the
authorities finished the blackout cells at Boniato Prison, they decided to
try out their effectiveness on the common prisoners, so they put in them
the toughest, the most ferocious men, the biggest troublemakers they
could find, the prisoners who had spent years going from one jail to
another. And these men would slice their wrists, swallow nails and
pieces of spoons and razor blades, trying to get the authorities to take
them out of the cells. The prisoners would rather have their stomachs
operated on than stay in the blackout cells. Three months was the
longest anyone lasted.

When we were inside the cells, some officers told us about the 30
common prisoners, and they said within six months we'd be begging to
be released. The crunching of the heavy metal doors that closed behind
us was followed by the sound of locks and chains. We did not know how

long we would be there, but we knew some men would not come out alive.

31      (Now as I write these memoirs, I cannot keep from thinking about the hundreds of my friends and comrades who are still there, now in still worse conditions. Two years ago, to isolate them even more, the authorities erected a wall at each end of the building higher than the roof. Then they strung a fence between the two walls so that the block is now inside a cage. Closed-circuit television is trained on all the passageways.)

32      Mornings the sun heated up the iron sheets across my window, which faced the east, and the cell became an oven. I sweated torrents of water, and it exhausted me. The sweat and grease pouring out of my body took on a peculiar odor in that closed space and in the darkness— the smell of rotten fish. In the afternoon, the metal sheets on the front of the cell heated up as the sun set. We spent whole weeks without bathing. At their whim or as they were ordered, the guards at the front gate would open the showers from their desk. The water might come at any hour of the day or night. In the summertime they turned on the water when the metal sheets were too hot to touch; in the wintertime they would do it in the early morning. They would come into the long passageway and shout that we had five minutes to bathe, and then when they figured we were soaped up, they turned off the water, and that produced a hellish racket from the prisoners. But the guards would tranquilly go back to the kitchen to chat with the guards from the other buildings. The soap dried on us and made our sticky skin feel stretched and tight, matted our hair. Not only did this new filthiness upset us, the cries for water became yet another torture. That whole inferno, in fact, little by little upset the equilibrium of our minds. That, of course, was precisely our jailers' objective.

33      We were not allowed any container for water except one, a quarter-liter jar. The latrine hole of my cell stopped up within a few days. Around it the cement depression soon filled with urine and excrement. When it finally overflowed, the entire floor of the cell was covered with that filth. Pepín and I did all we could to unstop the latrine. We stuck our arms into the hole, we used our spoons, but all our efforts were futile. We applied to the authorities to unstop the latrine, but there was no response. When they turned on the water for the showers, we had to stand there in the latrine where there were already maggots. The shower fell directly into the center of the pool of urine and splashed all over the walls. We lived inside a toilet bowl. The stench was unbearable. Our nostrils were encrusted with filth, as if our noses were constantly stopped up with shit. When the food came we would take the little can in the palm of our hands, as we always did in situations like this, and try as best we could not to touch the food. We didn't even use our spoons; we would pour the food directly into our mouths, as though it were liquid. It was always the same—boiled macaroni, maybe a little spaghetti, bread; bread, spaghetti, a little boiled macaroni.

One night the guards took out four of us and put us into other cells,   34
and in the empty cells they put two prisoners brought in from outside.
When the noise of locks and bolts had subsided and the guards went
away, we tried to identify the men who had just come in. The men in the
cells next to theirs called out to them, but the new men didn't respond.
We spoke to them in English and French, thinking they might be foreigners. Nothing. Silence. So we lay down to sleep. The next day we
would try to find out who the new men were. They might have been
afraid, or have been just a short time in prison.

A horrible scream shook us awake. It echoed down the passageway,   35
which was like an echo chamber. The second was deafening, and then
came howls of laughter, shouts, and incoherent gabble. They had put
two madmen into those cells.

Often we'd be violently wakened in the mornings by the raving of   36
those poor wretches. The two common prisoners, lost in the shadows of
their own minds, were another ingredient in a plan to unhinge *our*
minds. We spent whole nights unable to sleep. The madmen slept during
the day and at night wouldn't let the rest of us sleep.

Every two or three days, the guards came in and searched us. The   37
only purpose of those searches was to keep the pressure on, just like the
surveillance to remind us that we were watched, so that we would
constantly feel the repression. One thing about the searches was almost
good — the guards opened several cells at once, so this was an opportunity to see our comrades in the neighboring cells. The guards searched
the cells, then they would physically search us, and then we went back
inside the cells again.

They always compared the control identification card with our faces.   38
Every hallway or section had a file with our photos, personal data, and
the cell number. We had all been photographed before we went into the
blackout cells. There was one comrade of ours, a very dynamic, rebel-
lious young man named Alfredo Fernández Gámez, who refused to be
photographed. They took him out and beat him unmercifully, and, of
course, then photographed him. With these cards they could keep permanent control over us. If the guard was spying on the cell, he knew
who he was spying on.

Months passed, and one day a captain from the Political Police   39
visited us. They were amazed at our resistance, and not a little bewildered. So he had been sent to us with a threat. We were standing naked
for a search, with our backs to the wall next to the door, when the soldier
entered. His face was completely inexpressive, and he didn't walk, he
marched, as though he were doing infantry drills. He stopped about
halfway down the hallway, his hands behind his back, and he announced to us that the Revolution could not tolerate this irritating attitude of ours any longer. If we did not relent, they would have to be
"energetic" with us. He went on talking, saying the Revolution offered
us a way out, that we need not fear vengeance being taken against us,

but that if we didn't accept their terms there were new plans from the high command of the Ministry of the Interior to be put into effect. They had been very tolerant up to now, but their patience was running out.

40    "The Revolution does not want to have to exercise all its severity against you, but if you force us, you will never be men again. We are not going to kill you, but we will make you eunuchs. Don't forget what I've told you," he said just as he was leaving. And his words were more than simple threats.

## Evaluating the Text

1. How does Valladares's opening paragraph create a context in which the reader can properly understand the significance of the events he is going to describe?
2. How does the sight of the message on the billboard greeting the newly arrived prisoners serve as an ironic counterpoint to their situation?
3. What do each of the elements in the package given for safe-keeping by Valladares to his friend, Correa, signify about what was important in enabling him to bear the psychological and physical pressures of Boniato Prison?
4. Why was it so important for the prisoners to continue their prayer meetings even though holding these meetings would mean they would receive additional beatings?
5. How was the disruption of the water supply intended to upset the equilibrium of the prisoners' minds?
6. Why, in your opinion, does Valladares place such importance on giving complete details about what was happening to his fellow prisoners? How does the fact that he does not simply dwell on his own predicament suggest that this account is intended to serve an evidentiary or historical function?
7. How does Valladares's description of the way in which the blackout cells differ from the prisoners' usual confinement allow the reader to enter into his experience and understand why confinement there would be so terrible? How does the description of the cells substantiate his claim that this prison was used for experimental purposes? To what extent do both the prisoners and officials share the common assumption that if these political prisoners could be broken, anyone could be broken? How does Valladares communicate to the reader this idea that both the prisoners and the guards understand exactly what is at stake?
8. What details reveal the range of techniques and special skills perfected in other concentration camps that had been brought to bear against this group of prisoners in Boniato Prison? Specifically, what details relating to water, diet, cell size, lighting, temperature, and surveillance does Valladares mention to support his claim?
9. How does Valladares's statement that the guards had to get "heated up" give you insight into the kind of psychological changes the guards had to undergo before they could, as a matter of routine, simply walk in and savagely beat the prisoners? To what extent was Valladares able to get into the psyche of his tormenters and understand what drove them to commit such atrocities?

10. How does the idea of accountability before the outside world enter into this report and play a significant role both in the statements of the guards and in Valladares's own broad and detailed coverage of the events? For example, why would the prison officials even go through the motions of providing medical care and state "don't say we didn't give you medical treatment?"

11. What insight does the article written by Medardo Lemus provide into why it was important for prison officials to break the will of the political prisoners? Why was it more important to convert these prisoners than to simply kill them?

12. Can you explain why for some men, who had already proven their bravery as soldiers, the circumstances of isolation, beatings, and lack of communication proved intolerable?

13. Explain how the placement of the two mentally deranged men into neighboring cells was designed to disorient and demoralize the prisoners. What assumptions about human nature does this plan imply?

14. How is the captain's use of understatement when referring to the supposedly "tolerant" attitude of the Cuban government toward the prisoners intended to further threaten them? How does the visit of the captain from the Political Police tell you about how important the recantation of the prisoners must have been to Castro's regime?

## Exploring Different Perspectives

1. To what extent are both Valladares and Alicia Partnoy in "Introduction" and "A Conversation Under the Rain" compelled to think of ways to affirm human values within dehumanizing prison environments in Cuba and Argentina, respectively? Compare and contrast how each meets this challenge.

2. How is the challenge Valladares faces in maintaining his humanity similar to that faced by K'uai Shih-fu in the communist China of Mao-Tse tung, in Chen Jo-hsi's "The Big Fish"?

## Extending Viewpoints through Writing

1. Explain why the anticipation of the beating was worse for Valladares than the actual beating itself. Relate this concept to any circumstance where the dread of a situation was worse than the actual experience, however terrible.

2. Why was Valladares's ability to gain an even momentary glimpse of other prisoners so important to him? How would the knowledge that others are in the same situation you are in enable you to tolerate what you otherwise might not?

3. Why is it important for political regimes to obtain confessions and recantations of those who oppose their administrations? How could these confessions be used to blackmail prisoners or as propaganda for the outside world?

# Chen Jo-hsi

# *The Big Fish*

---

*Chen Jo-hsi was born in Taiwan in 1938 into a proletarian family—
her father and grandfather were carpenters. She and her husband lived
through the entire "Cultural Revolution" in the People's Republic of
China. She is the only Chinese creative writer of major stature to
provide us with literary testimony on what life was like for common
people under Mao's regime.* The Big Fish *is taken from* The Execution
of Mayor Yin and Other Stories from the Great Proletarian Cultural Revolution *(1979), translated from the Chinese by Nancy Ing
and Howard Goldblatt. This story simply and eloquently expresses the
plight of an old man who wishes to buy a fish to make soup for his sick
wife.*

    *The Cultural Revolution of 1966–1969 was a massive campaign
begun by Mao Tse-tung to renew the nation's revolutionary spirit by
purging society of its liberal elements. Revolutionary Red Guards
comprised of young men and women acted with the Army to attack
so-called bourgeoise elements in the government and in the culture at
large. Mao's wife, Jing Quing, played an active role and was caught in
the backlash to this violent and oppressive movement when Mao died
in 1976.*

1    K'uai Shih-fu came home early one February day. He popped his
head inside the door and asked his wife, who was lying in bed, "How are
you feeling? Any better?"

2    Mama K'uai had turned her head at the sound of the door opening,
and now her face lit up at the unexpected pleasure of seeing her husband. She didn't wish to worry him so she answered evasively, "Seems
better. Doesn't hurt so much."

3    The windows and doors were tightly shut against the bitter cold, with
wads of newspaper stuffed into the cracks. The odor of Chinese herbal
medicine permeated the room.

4    "Have you taken your medicine?" K'uai Shih-fu asked as he glanced
at the earthen pot on the small round table beside the bed.

5    "Yes, Chang Sao prepared it. She even cooked lunch for me."

6    Mama K'uai's voice was filled with gratitude, even though the person

*(For further information on China, see pp. 60, 70, and 344.)

who had done all these favors was not present. Her old backaches had recurred, and for the past few days she had spent most of her time in bed. Without their neighbors' help, K'uai Shih-fu wouldn't have been able to go to work.

"Why are you home so early?" asked Mama K'uai, looking at the old clock on the wall near the foot of the bed. It was only three o'clock.   7

K'uai Shih-fu worked at the dockyards, some distance away. His work and his meetings usually kept him busy from morning to night, and since he had to change buses to get from the Yangtze River Bridge to Cock Crow Temple, he never got home before dark.   8

"This afternoon we were supposed to have political study, but they said some American newspapermen were coming to Nanking, so at the last minute it was changed to a general clean-up. Those two apprentices of mine are really very thoughtful. They know you're sick and they wouldn't let me do anything. They practically forced me to go home."   9

As he talked, the old man took off his gloves and poured himself a glass of hot water from the thermos bottle on top of the chest of drawers. He cupped his hands around the glass for warmth.   10

Mama K'uai smiled. "Those two young fellows seem to be all right. Let's just hope they won't turn out like the last one, who cursed you as though you weren't worth a cent as soon as the Cultural Revolution began!"   11

The old man grinned as he sat down by the small round table. He blew on the glass of hot water before taking a tentative sip; he found that it was not too hot and gulped it all down.   12

"What else could he have done under the circumstances?" he asked without resentment. "The campaign was in full swing and he had to take a radical stand if he didn't want to get in trouble himself. He felt sorry about it afterward, and he used to come when no one was around to apologize for what he did. At the time he thought about nothing but the revolution, so he neglected his work entirely. Now whenever he is in difficulty, doesn't he always come running to me?"   13

"That's because you're so good-hearted!" Mama K'uai laughed. She was able to accept the incident now, but two years earlier, when she had learned that the old man's apprentice had attacked him in wall posters, she had been very upset. Especially disturbing was the fiasco of inviting the apprentice over for dinner one New Year's eve. It was entirely her idea, but the apprentice accused the old man of having ulterior motives, of going the way of the "imperialists," trying to "cultivate" and "corrupt" young workers. When the old man was subsequently forced onto the stage for "confession and criticism," the old woman seethed with anger.   14

"Speaking of my apprentices, I almost forgot!" the old man exclaimed. "They said that during the welcome for the American newspapermen, for the next couple of days the markets will be better stocked than usual, especially the one on Tung Jen Street. They said you can get   15 anything you want, so tell me what you feel like eating and I'll go out and get it for you."

16 The old woman closed her eyes and thought it over. Since she had not been to market for over a week, her husband had had to pick up what he could on his way home from work, and they had eaten nothing but frozen cabbage for some time. It had been cabbage with soy sauce one day and cabbage with salt pork the next. The old woman was bothered by a bad stomach to begin with, and the monotony of the diet had robbed her of what little appetite she had left.

17 "I could go for a taste of fish soup," she said, her eyes brightening at the prospect. "It would be nice if you could get a fish. Just think how delicious it would be, cooked with a few slices of ginger and some scallions. We could add a little bit of rice wine just before we eat it!"

18 That was enough to make the old man's mouth water. "You want to eat fish? All right, you shall have it!"

19 He stood up and straightened his cotton-padded cap, which he had not even removed after entering the house. Then he patted the pocket of his quilted jacket to make sure his money was there.

20 "I'll go to the Tung Jen Street market right away. My apprentices said they've got everything there!"

21 He went into the kitchen, took a look at the stove, and was pleased to see a circle of blue flame underneath. He opened the bottom door a slit wider to get a little more ventilation, and picked up the market basket.

22 K'uai Shih-fu considered the distance between Cock Crow Temple and Tung Jen Street and decided to go by bicycle. It took him some time to get his bicycle out from under the bed, where it was stored. The tires were flat, of course, so he had to find the pump and inflate them. After all this effort the old man was breathing hard, but the thought of the fish he was going to bring home made him jubilant. His wife was every bit as elated as he as she watched him bustling about.

23 "I'm leaving," he called as he pushed the bicycle out the door.

24 "Hurry back," she said. "If you can manage to buy a fish, that'll be just grand."

25 K'uai Shih-fu turned out of the small lane onto Cock Crow Temple Road, which led all the way to the south gate of People's Park and was always crowded. Accustomed as he was to lining up for the bus before daybreak, K'uai Shih-fu rode his bicycle with a great feeling of freedom and exhilaration. As he wove in and out among the pedestrians, the hoarse sound of the bell was music to his ears. When he turned onto the wider and more congested Peking Avenue, trucks began whizzing past him one after another as they sped toward Drum Tower Circle. The old man had always dreaded traffic at the circle, so he took a short cut through a small alley and quickly reached Tung Jen Street.

26 It had been a long time since his last visit to the market. In fact, it had been over a year, when his son came home on leave from the Northeast, and K'uai Shih-fu had gotten up very early one morning to buy a chicken.

The market on Tung Jen Street and the Central Market on New 27
Market Square were both well known. The Municipal Revolutionary
Committee looked upon them as places of importance, so they were
excellently managed and always well stocked with a wide assortment of
fish, meat, and vegetables. Although a good many people came from far
away to shop there, the K'uais were not among them. Most of the people
who patronized these two markets were Liberation Army personnel and
the servants of families of high-level Party members who lived in the
area. They spent their money freely, and Mama K'uai, who had always
lived a frugal life, disapproved of their ways.

The first thing K'uai Shih-fu noticed was that the entire street had 28
been renovated since his last visit. The grounds had been swept clean
and the walls had been washed; and the newly posted political slogans
were particularly attractive. Whether they were selling soy sauce, pickled
vegetables, groceries, brooms, or toilet paper, the shops on both sides of
the street looked as though they had all been carefully rearranged. The
windows shone, and even the door fronts had been scrubbed until the
bricks were bright red.

K'uai Shih-fu parked his bicycle at the entrance to the marketplace 29
and walked in with his basket. The spotless cement floor had obviously
just been washed, so that as he walked K'uai Shih-fu looked back guiltily
at the footprints his large cotton-padded shoes had made. There weren't
many customers in the market, but there were enough so that every stall
had some business. All the stall keepers were wearing freshly washed
and starched white knee-length aprons, while those selling meat and fish
even had white cotton caps on their heads.

Of all the places in the market, K'uai Shih-fu liked the fish stall the 30
best. The shiny tile counter made the various kinds of fish on display
particularly attractive. From a distance, he could see the ribbon-fish and
bream that covered the stand. But he could also see that there was a line
of people waiting. Just as he was about to get in line, he spotted some
other fish on the counter. He stepped forward and saw several large
*ch'ing* fish,* all shiny and fresh-looking, laid out in a row.

"Why buy bream when there is *ch'ing* fish?" he thought. Bream has a 31
muddy taste that no amount of seasoning can get rid of.

He saw a stall keeper busily weighing fish, calling out the weights as 32
his free hand clicked the abacus. Another man was squatting in a corner
sorting fish from a big wooden box, throwing the large ones into one
basket and the small ones into another. K'uai Shih-fu tried to catch the
second man's attention. He called out, "Are these *ch'ing* fish for sale?"

The man looked up, frowning at him for some time before answering, 33
"They're out on the stand, so of course they're for sale."

"Then weigh me half a fish!" As he spoke he placed his basket beside 34
the stand, trying to make up his mind which half of the fish he should
buy. Mama K'uai had said she wanted some fish soup, and the fish head

*A flat gray freshwater fish, popular in central China for making soup.

would make a tastier soup than a chicken! So he had better buy the top half.

35    "Give me the top half, with the head."

36    "Can't sell half a fish," the stall keeper answered, shaking his head as he went back to his sorting. "If you want it, you'll have to take the whole fish!"

37    The old man hesitated. Buy the whole fish? He looked at the price — sixty-five cents a catty. A whole fish would come to two or three dollars.* His hand instinctively moved up to the pocket of his quilted jacket.

38    "Well?" the man asked, raising his head again. Seeing the look of indecision on K'uai's face, he added coldly, "Each one weighs about four or five catties."

39    The stall keeper's attitude annoyed K'uai. He patted the top part of his jacket where his month's pay, which he had just received, lay hidden in his inner pocket.

40    "Okay, go ahead and weigh the whole fish!" he answered briskly.

41    This caught the man by surprise. Giving K'uai a hard look, he got up slowly and, without saying a word, picked up a large fish and put it on the hook of the steelyard.

42    "Oh, I'd like that one," K'uai Shih-fu hastily pointed to a smaller fish.

43    "What's the matter?" The stall keeper pretended not to understand. Lifting the steelyard higher, he swung the dangling fish in front of his customer's face so that the tail nearly brushed against K'uai's chin.

44    The old man took a step backward and waved his hand in a conciliatory gesture. "Go ahead and weigh it." He'd better not make a fuss, he decided. He consoled himself with the thought that it was a rare opportunity to get such good fish, even though it meant that he and his wife would have to eat fish for the next three days. Luckily the weather was cold, and the fish would not spoil.

45    "Sixty-five cents . . . four catties and a half . . . that comes to $2.93." The stall keeper blinked his eyes and announced the price without bothering to use his abacus.

46    K'uai quickly took a five dollar bill from his inner pocket. The man gave him his change and carefully placed the fish in the basket. After another curious look at K'uai Shih-fu, he went back to sorting fish.

47    The old man let out a deep sigh, but he picked up his market basket and left the fish stall with a feeling of satisfaction. Those young fellows were right, he thought. This Tung Jen Street market was quite a place; a person could actually buy a large *ch'ing* fish here. He was sure his wife wouldn't believe her eyes when she saw the size of the fish. Absorbed in his own sense of accomplishment and grinning happily, he did not notice the curious looks the other customers were giving him. Some of them were even pointing at his basket.

*Here "dollars" refers to "renminbi" or "people currency." One dollar renminbi equals a little more than half a U.S. dollar.

As he passed a vegetable stand, K'uai Shih-fu's eyes lit up. At the end 48
of February produce was always scarce, and he would never have
thought that there could be so many kinds of vegetables on display. In
addition to the turnips, carrots, and frozen cabbages that were usually
available, there were also tomatoes and cucumbers—things he had not
seen for a long time. These delicacies were attractively displayed in
separate little baskets placed at the most conspicuous spots in the stand.
He looked at the price of the tomatoes—fifty cents a catty. He shook his
head. They were intentionally priced out of the common people's reach,
he thought. In the summer they were only five cents a catty. There was
no price on the cucumbers, but since his wife had always been fond of
them, he decided to get one, whatever the cost, just so she could eat
some fresh vegetables. After being ill for several days, she would enjoy
the taste of something different.

"How much are the cucumbers?" he asked a woman vendor.          49

"The cucumbers are not for sale!" she answered bluntly, her eyes 50
fixed on the fish in his basket.

The old man was disappointed, but since there was nothing he could 51
do, he looked around to see what he could get to cook with the fish head.

"Hurry! Hurry! There are people in line behind you!" The woman 52
gestured impatiently with the steelyard, sending the lead weight and
bronze plate clanging against each other.

Under this pressure, K'uai Shih-fu lost his composure and couldn't 53
make up his mind. All of a sudden he remembered that they might be
out of ginger at home. "Give me a half a catty of tender ginger." Then he
spotted a small basket of bamboo shoots in a corner. He knew that
bamboo shoots were very expensive, but they would be delicious cooked
with the fish head. He thought of how frugal his wife had been through
the years, and decided that she deserved at least one good meal now that
she was ill. Bamboo shoots cooked with the fish head—he had not
indulged in such luxury in years. "Give me two bamboo shoots." This
time he did not even bother to ask the price.

"Sixty-five cents a catty," the woman announced. She emptied the 54
ginger into his basket and went over to weigh the bamboo shoots.

After paying for the vegetables, K'uai Shih-fu picked up the market 55
basket. Feeling its weight, he decided not to buy anything else, but to go
straight home and cook the fish. Countless varieties of dishes were
displayed in the glass showcases on the prepared food counter, but he
gave them only a cursory glance as he hurried toward the main entrance.

More people were coming to shop now. Housewives, laborers coming 56
from work, cadremen, and soldiers in neat uniforms were pouring into
the market. He walked over to the place where he had parked his bicycle,
which was now just one among many.

"Comrade, is there any more of that fish left?" A man who brushed 57
by him turned back to ask anxiously.

"Yes!" he assured the man enthusiastically. "Hurry, there are still 58 several . . ." Before he had finished speaking, a housewife carrying a basket hurried up to him and broke in, "Comrade, how much is this fish selling for? Is there a long line?"

59     "No need to stand in line. It's sixty-five cents a catty."

60     After all the attention his market basket had attracted, K'uai Shih-fu took another look at the large *ch'ing* fish. With its clear bulging eyes and bright scales, it was very impressive looking indeed. The old man's heart was filled with joy.

61     He carefully hung the market basket on the handlebar of his bicycle. Because of the crowd, he had to push the bicycle out to Tung Jen Street. But when he was about to get on his bicycle, someone tapped him on the shoulder.

62     "Hey, comrade, take that fish back."

63     The old man lowered his right leg to the ground and turned to see a middle-aged man with small protruding eyes. From his manner and dress, the old man could tell he was a cadre member.

64     "What did you say?" He thought the man had mistaken him for someone else.

65     "That fish isn't for sale," the man said in a low voice, trying to be patient. "Take it back to the cashier's office immediately, and they'll refund you what you paid for it."

66     "What?" K'uai raised his voice. "Not for sale? Damn it! Then why the hell didn't they say so in the first place? Now you want to snatch it away when it's about to be dropped in the pot!"

67     At the old man's curses the cadreman's face hardened and he glared at K'uai.

68     "If they're all sold out, what'll be left to show the foreign visitors when they arrive?"

69     K'uai Shih-fu wanted to say something more to give vent to his grievance, but when he heard the words "foreign visitors" he stopped short. The issue was closed. He gulped, then blinked his eyes in stony silence.

70     The cadreman, seeing that K'uai was not responding, demanded, "What unit do you belong to?"

71     His insolent tone of voice angered K'uai Shih-fu, who blurted out, "Nanking Dockyard, ironworker for thirty years!" To save himself from further questioning, he gave his type of work and the length of time he had served.

72     The cadreman softened when he heard that K'uai was an old worker. "Never mind," he said, nodding his head. "You didn't know. Just take the fish back, and the cashier's office will . . ."

73     "If you want the fish," the old man broke in, "you take it! I'm not going to!"

74     He recalled the hard looks the man at the fish stall had given him. Now if he were to take the fish back, not only the stall keeper but all the people in the market would stare at him.

A crowd had gathered by this time, looking curiously at the two men.     75
The cadreman was afraid the matter might get out of hand, so he backed
down. "I'll take it back for you," he said, "Wait here. I'll bring the money
back right away."

Without waiting for an answer, he thrust his hand into the basket and     76
grabbed the fish. With everyone's eyes riveted on him, he walked into
the market, holding the fish by the gills.

K'uai Shih-fu looked on helplessly as the fish, its huge tail swinging     77
back and forth, disappeared into the distance. He looked into the basket
again. It was empty except for a few pieces of ginger root and two
withered bamboo shoots. He could go back and try to buy a bream, but it
would probably be all sold out by now. Then as he thought of the long
lines, his legs felt weak.

What would he say to Mama K'uai when he got home? That was the     78
most difficult part. She would be even more disappointed if she found
out just how close she had come to feasting on that fish. It would
probably be best to tell her a lie. In all their years of marriage, K'uai had
never lied to his wife.

As he stood there, dazed, a bystander came up and said to him, "You     79
don't seem to know the ropes, do you? Before the foreign visitors have
come to look, they won't sell any of the good things. We're all waiting
until the foreigners have come and gone before we try to buy any of the
specials."

"You can buy them before the foreign visitors arrive," someone said     80
sarcastically with a knowing air. "The only trouble is that you have to
take them back. Last time, when Prince Sihanouk came to Nanking, they
even brought in turkeys from somewhere. One of my neighbors, who
had never seen a turkey, bought one out of curiosity. But he only got it as
far as the rear gate before it was sent back. They said they started with
five turkeys, and after two days of brisk sales, there were still five
turkeys left!"

K'uai Shih-fu couldn't bear to listen any longer. He turned abruptly,     81
and with a backward kick of his right leg, mounted his bicycle.

"Comrade, he hasn't given you back your money!"     82

"Tell him to give it to the foreign visitors!"     83

## Evaluating the Text

1. How would you characterize the relationship between K'uai Shih-fu and
   his wife? How old do they seem to be? How long do you think they have
   been married?
2. From Mama K'uai's comments about the behavior of previous apprentices
   toward her husband, what can you infer about the nature of the Cultural
   Revolution and its effect on workers like K'uai Shih-fu?
3. What do details like paper wedged in the cracks to keep out the cold and
   the fact that all there is to drink is a thermos of hot water tell you about
   the standard of life customary for workers?

4. What clues tell you that the old man does not see life in political terms, but rather in human terms?

5. Why is it significant in light of what later happens that the reader knows that K'uai Shih-fu and his wife were not accustomed to shopping at Tung Jen Street market? Who actually did shop there and what can you infer about the social structure from this?

6. What thoughts do you think passed through K'uai's mind when he was considering whether or not to buy a whole fish when he had planned to buy a half? Be sure to relate the amount he would have to pay to the amount he earns.

7. In light of what later happens, why is it significant that the stall keeper in the fish market pressures K'uai Shih-fu into buying a larger fish than he wanted to. How does the shopkeeper's expression give the reader a clue as to his intentions toward K'uai Shih-fu? How might events have turned out if K'uai Shih-fu had been allowed to buy the smaller fish?

8. Why is it significant that K'uai Shih-fu doesn't think through the implications of there being such highly priced tomatoes and cucumbers displayed, but not for sale? Why do you think K'uai Shih-fu cannot afford to perceive what is really going on in the market?

9. What does being able to bring home a big fish, bamboo shoots, and ginger mean to K'uai Shih-fu in terms of his feelings toward his wife?

10. How do you know that impressing "foreign visitors" has become so important that everything in Chinese life must be subordinated to this objective?

11. What evidence is there that the cadreman standing guard at the market sympathizes with K'uai's plight and makes allowances for his mistake?

12. How does K'uai Shih-fu's fear of being embarrassed illustrate how powerful the controlling force of shame and fear of "losing face" is in Chinese culture?

13. How does the political atmosphere invade and contaminate even the most hitherto private areas of K'uai's life? How would his relationship with his wife be altered were he to either tell her the truth or lie to her about the fish?

14. What is the significance of K'uai's final comment when he doesn't wait to get his money back?

## Exploring Different Perspectives

1. How do both this story and the account of Someth May in Cambodia (in "The Field behind the Village") illustrate that in a society where everything is politicized, affirming human values becomes extremely difficult?

2. How do governmental expectations as to what is meant by being a "good Chinese" citizen enter into both this story and Shen Tong's firsthand account ("Bloody Sunday in Tiananmen Square") of the June 1989 massacre of pro-democracy demonstrators in Bejing?

## Extending Viewpoints through Writing

1. Describe a situation when you counted on something as being a sure thing that never materialized or that was taken away from you, even after you

had it "in your hands." The something can be a material object, a trip, an event, a relationship, or anything else that seems to fit. In what way is counting on something that never materialized or was taken away from you more dispiriting than never having believed this event was possible at all? How did this experience enhance your understanding of K'uai's feelings?

# Shen Tong

# *Bloody Sunday in*
# *Tiananmen Square*

---

*Shen Tong was born on July 30, 1968, in Zhangjiakou, a small town northwest of Beijing, China. His involvement with political demonstrations began in the mid-1980s. In 1989 he established the Olympic Institute in Beijing, an independent student organization that served as the nucleus for the pro-democracy movement. As one of the prominent leaders, Tong put together the Dialogue Delegation, which negotiated with government officials and ran the student news center from a wing of his dormitory at Beijing University. The following account based on his firsthand experience in Tiananmen Square on the night of June 3 is drawn from his autobiography* Almost a Revolution *(1990), translated by Marianne Yen. Tong's account tells how his hopes and dreams of a new China ended with the horrifying events of the Tiananmen Square massacre. Tong was one of the few student leaders to escape capture and is now attending Brandeis University in Massachusetts.*

*In early 1989, massive demonstrations in favor of democratic reforms, initiated by university students, but soon joined by millions of workers throughout China, embarrassed the government during a May visit to Beijing by Soviet leader Mikhail Gorbachev, aimed at normalizing thirty years of strained relations between the U.S.S.R. and China. The students had peacefully occupied the center of the city, Tiananmen Square. When students and workers initially prevailed in preventing local Army troops from clearing the square, Army units from outside the city, who had violently suppressed demonstrations in Tibet the year before, were sent in on June 3. The massacre that followed claimed the lives of thousands and precipitated widespread foreign outrage. The Chinese government has subsequently instituted tighter controls over the universities to prevent any recurrence of the pro-democracy movement.*

## June 3, Saturday

1     The French journalists called me at school in the morning to tell me that troops had driven into the downtown area the night before and had

*(For further background on China, see p. 334.)

left five trucks on Changan Avenue near Xinhuamen after they were stopped by citizens. This concerned me, because I knew that at this point the troops couldn't be so easily stopped, nor would they abandon their trucks unless it was part of a plan, a kind of trick. The reporters urged me to leave my dorm and come back to the area around the square. Something could happen very quickly now.

After arriving at the French journalists' hotel and checking to see 2 whether they had any more information, I called Andrea to ask whether she had heard any news from CBC. She said that the abandoned trucks were loaded with weapons, including butcher knives, chains, and clubs. Apparently the government was trying to goad the students into taking these weapons, so it would be able to call us violent counterrevolutionaries and use this to justify a crackdown.

As we watched CNN in the hotel room, the news report showed tear 3 gas being used near the square. I was pretty sure the footage was taken at a spot called Liubukou, on Changan Avenue near Xidan. A reporter from *Paris Match* decided to take a taxi to the square, so I rode with him. When he got out, I continued on toward the corner of Xidan. Crowds of people were running in the street. Abandoning the taxi when it could go no farther, I walked toward the place where I thought the tear gas was being used. As I got closer to Xidan, I could see the fumes rising from the street. I also saw that some of the people had blood on their faces.

My house was only a few blocks away, so I rushed home. My mother 4 and Nainai said that they had heard loud explosions, apparently the sound of the tear gas canisters going off, and that a lot of people had run into our courtyard to wash the fumes from their eyes. All the neighbors gathered in front of our house and talked about how powerful the Chinese-made tear gas was.

Many people had also been wounded. "I was standing on Liubukou 5 when the police charged the crowd," one person said. "A tear gas canister exploded and blew off a small boy's legs. I saw it with my own eyes. The boy's mother was holding him and crying. She just stood on the avenue not knowing what to do. She was too hysterical to take him to the hospital."

When they heard this story, the neighborhood women were so 6 shocked that they put their hands over their mouths. Another neighbor said he had seen a man whose eye had been destroyed by a tear gas canister.

While we were talking, a few of my sister's friends who were medical 7 interns at a nearby hospital came over. They told us that they had seen hundreds of armed police run out of the Zhongnanhai compound and use billy clubs to beat the hunger strikers, who were still holding their sit-in. The police had also started firing tear gas. When a few children were hurt by the exploding canisters, some who saw this ran to a nearby construction site and got bricks and rocks to throw at the armed police.

"I'm going to see what's going on," I said. 8

9     I was heading for the street when one of my sister's friends pulled me aside. "We need to talk to you," he said. He was standing very still, and I could tell that he had something important to tell me. "Your father has leukemia."

10    I just looked at him blankly. It didn't quite sink in at first. I was preoccupied with what was happening outside, so I couldn't fully comprehend what he had said. At the time I thought this meant my father had only a few years to live, not that the situation was critical then. I didn't do anything or say anything. I was trying to decide whether I should go to Beida [student organization] or to the square, with no regard for my parents. I was incredibly insensitive.

11    My sister's friend had told me because it was so obvious that I didn't know my father was so ill. "We are doing everything we can to take care of him," he said now. "But we can't take care of his son. You should stay home and be with your mother."

12    My mother had already left for the hospital, so I didn't pay any attention. Instead I went out. As I walked down Changan Avenue, I kept hearing the words in my mind: "Your father has leukemia." The truth slowly began to come to me.

13    Soon I was overwhelmed by guilt. I hated myself for not seeing what had been happening in my own family. To do something for my father, I used the money I still had from the federation and bought two large shopping bags full of food, which I carried home. I asked my sister to take them to the hospital, and left the house again at around 7 p.m.

14    I walked east about a third of the way to Tiananmen Square. Truckloads of soldiers were parked on Changan Avenue, where they had been stopped by the people the night before. A warning was being broadcast over the Beijing public address system, telling everyone to stay off the street tonight or suffer grave consequences. That same warning was being broadcast repeatedly on the radio and on television.

15    I wanted to call the news center at Beida to tell them what was happening in this area, so I waited in a long line that had formed at the public telephone. When I was next to use the phone, I heard the man in front of me say into the receiver, "What is going on over there?" He then turned and handed it to me. "Listen," he said nervously, "they're firing over at Muxidi."

16    I put the receiver to my ear and heard the sound of gunshots in the background. Muxidi was a congested downtown intersection five kilometers west of Tiananmen Square. I decided not to make my call but to start walking back home.

17    At this point I saw one of the student marshals racing toward the square. Blood and sweat were running down his forehead.

18    "What's happening?" I asked him.

19    "The troops are coming from the northwest corner of Second Ring Road and are already at Muxidi. They're firing real bullets, and the people are burning their trucks," he said, hardly taking a breath between

sentences. "I just came from Muxidi. One of the students I was with died—I'm covered with his blood. I've got to run to the square and warn the others."

I let go of his arm and he continued running. 20

I ran in the opposite direction, toward my house, to tell everyone that 21 the troops were shooting. As I entered our courtyard, I caught sight of my mother.

"I thought you were at the hospital with Dad," I said to her. 22

"Qing is there," she replied. "Your father sent me home to watch 23 you. He said, knowing you, that you'd probably go to the square tonight and wait to die. He sent me back here to keep you at home."

I told my mother that I wouldn't go out, and I really meant it. The 24 news about my father's illness was still fresh in my mind, and I wanted to do everything I could to cooperate with my parents because I felt it was important to my father.

It was just after ten o'clock. For the next hour I tried to block out what 25 was happening nearby, but around eleven the noise became too loud for me to ignore any longer and I went into our courtyard. The neighbors were coming by to tell us that armed police were driving people off the streets, but the people were fighting back, getting into pushing and shouting matches with the police. The gunshots sounded closer and closer every minute. When the people from our neighborhood began to build a barricade on the street, I couldn't stand it any longer.

"Yuan Yuan, don't go," my mother said, grabbing my shirt as I tried 26 to go out the door. Nainai[1] came to help pull me back, and my uncles, who had just walked in, joined the effort.

As I gave up struggling, we heard more shots, and my uncles went 27 out to see where they had come from. Nainai stood in the doorway while my mother, who was outside, held her arm across the frame to keep her from leaving. I was the only one still inside. The gunfire became more rapid, and tear gas canisters seemed to be exploding all over. Every few minutes someone staggered into our alley, covering his eyes with his hands, and my mother and Nainai took basins of water into the court-yard so these people could wash the tear gas out of their eyes. Puddles collected in the courtyard as people wildly splashed water on their stinging faces.

In the middle of all this chaos, I sneaked out of the house. On 28 Changan Avenue, people were dousing the abandoned army trucks with gasoline and setting them on fire. I wanted to get a group of students together to try and persuade people to go back to their homes, because with more troops only a few blocks away, we didn't have much chance of stopping them, and I didn't want to see anyone else killed. But I looked all around and couldn't find any other students, and everything was so crazy that it would have been impossible to organize anything.

---

[1]Shen Tong's grandmother [editor].

29     While I was standing on Changan Avenue, my uncles found me and dragged me home. On the way I saw a graduate student who had been on the first Beida Preparatory Committee with me. He was walking his bicycle calmly toward the square.

30     "What are you doing here?" I asked him.

31     "I want to be in the square," he said. "I can't stay at school any longer."

32     "Are many from Beida going there?"

33     "I don't know," he answered. "I had a hard time getting past the barriers the people put up, just to get this far."

34     "See if you can recruit some students to help calm this crowd down," I said.

35     "I'll try," he replied calmly.

36     As he walked on, I watched him, admiring his quiet courage. After he left the Beida Preparatory Committee, he had become a hunger striker. His commitment had never waned, even after he lost his leadership role.

37     My uncles urged me to get going, so we headed toward my house. By now there were dead and wounded people all over the sidewalks and under the trees along Changan Avenue, and the alleys off the avenue could no longer hold all the wounded. When we got to our courtyard, I noticed that one of my uncles was lagging behind, dragging a man who was screaming in agonizing pain. This man had been wounded in his leg, and blood was shooting out of a main artery. There was no way we could get him to a hospital on this night. He bled to death in front of our door.

38     My uncles dragged some of the others who had been wounded into our courtyard to make more room in the alley. While they and my mother were busy taking care of these people, I sneaked out again. As soon as I was in the alley, I heard a low rumbling noise and felt the ground quake beneath me.

39     "The tanks are coming!" someone shouted.

40     *It can't be,* I thought. *How can they drive tanks into the downtown area?*

41     A crowd had gathered at the corner of Xidan, and when I got there a seemingly endless line of headlights stretched as far as I could see down Changan Avenue to the west. I couldn't believe my eyes. It was so bright I almost couldn't see. There were maybe twenty army tanks, but it seemed like many more, and they were headed right for us. The people around me were throwing stones at them and at the foot soldiers walking beside them, and in response the soldiers started spraying gunfire at our feet.

42     "Rubber bullets!" I shouted as people began to scream with fear. "Stop throwing things—there's no way to stop them!"

43     I fought my way through the crowd, trying to get onto the avenue, but I stopped when one of the soldiers fired rapidly at my feet. I wasn't hurt, so I tried to look for the shells, to see whether the bullets were real. Hundreds of people rushed into the avenue to put up barricades, but as soon as they reached the middle of the street, a spray of machine-gun

fire scattered them. People who had been hit fell to the ground and lay still. *Those people are dead,* I thought to myself. *The bullets are real.* I couldn't believe it. It was as if this were all happening in a dream.

Everyone around me was still throwing things at the tanks, and it was odd to see people picking up anything, even a little pebble, and throwing it at the metal monsters coming toward us. It was totally useless. I grabbed a young man by the collar just as he was about to lob a small rock and screamed at him, "If you throw one more thing, I'll strangle you!" 44

The people near me were taken aback. I looked at the crowd and said, "When the troops come, just stand here and be still. Otherwise, go home. If you run, you're almost asking them to shoot you. If you throw things, you're asking them to shoot you. Just stand your ground." 45

Just then three soldiers jumped from an armored car and shot into the crowd. A flash of bright orange light went up a few meters away; two buses had been set on fire by the people. I walked toward the wreckage and stood behind a tree, watching the flames, which actually looked beautiful against the night sky. More shots were fired at my feet. When I looked in the direction of the gunfire, I found myself staring at a soldier's face. His eyes were popping, bloodshot, and dazed, as if he were on drugs. 46

Two tanks rolled forward and pushed aside the burning buses. Once the line of tanks began to pass, the soldiers stopped shooting and moved ahead. Some of them had large wooden clubs covered with metal on one end, and they were also armed with pistols and machine guns. Wearing leather shoes instead of canvas-and-rubber army boots, they looked ready for hand-to-hand combat with the civilians. They fired occasional shots into the air and shouted warnings through megaphones, saying that we should get off the streets. 47

Some people ran into the middle of the avenue to pick up the bullet casings, taking them back to the sidewalks to show the others. I don't know why we all felt so little fear. After living under marital law for so many days, and after so many nights of expecting the oncoming troops, we seemed to feel that violence could no longer defeat us. I know now that this was a triumph of our spirit. 48

I counted forty-six tanks and armored personnel carriers advancing steadily toward Tiananmen Square. In addition to the military vehicles there were propaganda trucks carrying public address equipment. Their loudspeakers were blaring slogans like "The People's Liberation Army loves the capital" and "We love the people of Beijing. Soldiers and people are one" as civilians were gunned down in the streets. These lies so infuriated us that people hurled anything they could find with even more hatred than before. 49

Two young men near me took the bloody shirt off a corpse on the ground and walked toward one of the personnel carriers to show the soldiers what their comrades had done. The military vehicles suddenly 50 stopped. I followed the two men, and as we approached the carrier, the soldiers looked at each other, not knowing what to do. It was clear that we were unarmed and weren't throwing stones. By the time we got up to the truck, a middle-aged woman and a young girl were with us. The woman spoke up first.

51    "You soldiers, how can you do this?" she said.

52    They didn't answer. Shocked and hurt and still not quite sure that I believed what I was seeing, I wanted to reason with them. I realized that I had to control myself and speak civilly.

53    "What regiment are you from?" I asked.

54    They didn't answer.

55    "Do you know where you are? Do you know that you are in Beijing?"

56    One of the soldiers, who looked very young, shook his head.

57    "You don't know you're in Beijing?" I shouted in disbelief. "You are on Changan Avenue. Do you know the history of Changan Avenue? In 1949, when the People's Liberation Army liberated the city from the Guomindang, no shots were fired on Changan Avenue. When the foreign armies invaded Beijing, no one was killed on Changan Avenue. You are the People's Liberation Army and you're shooting your own people. We are students peacefully petitioning the government. We are against violence."

58    I was talking nonstop, desperately trying to get them to understand. The other people around me were at a loss for words. The two young men held up the bloodstained shirt and cried, but no words came out of their open mouths.

59    "Talk to me! You heard what I said—say something!" I pleaded. "Tell the other soldiers they cannot shoot anymore."

60    An officer got up, took out his pistol, and pointed it at me. I was still talking and didn't pay any attention to what he was doing, but one of my uncles came up to me, tugged at me, and said frantically, "Come on, Yuan Yuan, let's go home."

61    All of a sudden someone pulled me backward. Then a shot rang out, and everyone started screaming. I turned around to see the girl who had been standing next to me fall straight back to the ground. I hadn't even noticed her standing there, and now her face was completely gone; there was nothing but a bloody hole.

62    As the people who had gathered around ran away, my uncle and some men who recognized me as a student leader tried to get me away from the personnel carrier. "Take him home, they're going to kill him," I heard someone say. We stepped over a concrete divider separating the street from the pedestrian walkway. As they were dragging me away, I looked at the girl again, then fought their tugging and forced my way a few steps toward her. Four men had run to where her body lay. The screaming and the gunfire melded together into white noise. All I remember of this time is four men, like pallbearers, taking the girl's body

away in slow motion, unaware of the chaos around them. They paused and looked back at the personnel carrier a number of times. Then they were gone.

When I looked up, I saw a group of young men running and trying to 63 jump over a fence across the avenue. Several soldiers leaped down from another personnel carrier and went after them. One of the young men fell as he tried to get over to safety, and crouched with his back against the fence and his hands clutching the rails. I will never forget how he looked around quickly, with no fear on his face, as the soldiers surrounded him. All at once they fired shots at his head. His skull must have shattered, because pieces of his head went flying and splattered on the white fence. As his body slowly slid to the ground, a piece of his skull landed on the gold metal ball on top of the railing.

The trucks started moving again, but I was completely numb. "Come 64 with me, I'll take you away from here," I heard my uncle say. He took my arm and led me home. I looked down and saw that his trousers were covered with blood from the man he had dragged into our courtyard.

The moment we walked into the house, my mother came right up to 65 us. "You can't wait any longer," she said to my uncle. "Take Yuan Yuan away quickly." Neither Nainai nor she tried to speak to me; they could see that I was in a trance. "I'm putting my son's life in your hands," my mother said.

My uncle took me into the courtyard, where he put me on the back of 66 his bicycle. We rode down the alley, turned onto Changan Avenue, and headed west. As soon as I saw the scene before me, I became alert again. All the way across the six lanes, thousands of Beijing residents were jamming the avenue, following the army to the square. The soldiers on the last personnel carrier were firing at the feet of the first row of people, and their shots were hitting the legs and feet of a few of those in the front, who knelt down in pain. But the people behind them kept coming. The crowd stepped over the wounded and the dead and continued to follow the trucks.

My uncle's bicycle was now flying down Changan Avenue. "The 67 people of Beijing are so brave," I said, uttering the first words out of my mouth since the girl next to me was killed. I looked at my watch. It was 4 a.m.

To avoid the soldiers, my uncle began taking the side streets. We 68 passed the temple where Rong Dong and I had played. Smoldering army vehicles were everywhere, and I could smell the fumes of the burning rubber and paint.

When we entered one alley, we saw a man in an official-looking 69 green uniform being chased by an angry mob of Beijing residents, who caught up with him at a construction site and picked up pieces of brick to hit him with. The man didn't make a sound. I jumped off the bicycle, almost knocking over my uncle, and ran toward them. Pushing the people aside, I saw him lying face down, with blood pouring out of his nostrils as he exhaled rapidly. He looked about eighteen years old.

70     "Stop hitting him!" I pleaded with the crowd.

71     "It's none of your business," a man said, shoving me away.

72     "Please stop it," I begged. "We have to take him to the hospital, we have to find him an ambulance."

73     My uncle pulled me away from the mob. "Forget it, Yuan Yuan. He's almost dead — there's no use."

74     He put me back on his bicycle and rode off quickly.

75     "The soldiers are killing the people, the people are killing the soldiers, right in the middle of the capital," I mumbled.

76     Eventually my uncle and I arrived at an empty apartment building that had recently been constructed. This was to be my hiding place.

77     "Don't use the elevator and don't let anyone see you here," my uncle warned. "Don't leave. We'll come and bring you food and clothes. You must not leave here."

78     He waited until I had started climbing the stairs before he left. The building had fourteen floors, and I walked to the ninth floor, to the apartment he had told me to stay in. It was almost dawn. I had seen too much to feel anything anymore. I fell asleep as the sun was coming up.

## *Evaluating the Text*

1. How does the description of the abandoned truckload of weapons provide insight into the way the Chinese government was planning to create a justification for a real crackdown by the army?

2. What can you infer about the role Tong had played as a student leader before June 3 from the fact that he was contacted by reporters from the French news service?

3. How do Tong's reactions and those of his mother and aunts reveal how reluctant Chinese citizens were to believe that the government would actually send soldiers and tanks into the heart of Beijing to shoot the demonstrators?

4. Discuss why Tong's family chose this particular moment to tell him about how ill his father was.

5. How would you characterize the competing set of values involved in Tong's decision as to whether or not he should go to Tiananmen Square?

6. What details suggest the extent to which opposition to the government came from people in the community, not just pro-democracy student demonstrators?

7. What is the significance of Tong's comment that even during past revolutions and military uprisings, tanks had never been sent into the heart of the city?

8. How would you characterize Tong's encounters with the soldiers? If the officer had not intervened and shot the girl, what do you think the soldiers would have done?

9. After being retrieved by his uncles, why was it important that Tong be hidden from the authorities?

10. How do Tong's reactions toward the soldiers and toward the citizens who surrounded the army official show the reader that he was truly nonviolent?

## Exploring Different Perspectives

1. What conclusions can you draw about the changes in the nature of Chinese society that resulted in such a massive rejection by young people of precisely the form of government an earlier generation, during Mao Tse-tung's Cultural Revolution, had so wholeheartedly supported? Explore this contrast after reading Chen Jo-hsi's "The Big Fish" and Tong's account. How do both Tong and Chen Jo-hsi explore the conflicts between personal and political allegiances?
2. Why do you suppose that regimes in Communist China and in Cuba do not simply kill their enemies but seem to have a great investment in converting them? Discuss the role of propaganda in Tong's narrative; in Armando Valladares's account ("A Nazi Prison in the Caribbean"); and in Slawomir Mrożek's story ("The Elephant").

## Extending Viewpoints through Writing

1. If you have seen television broadcasts of the events described by Shen Tong, discuss how Tong's account differs from the way these events were presented in the media. What additional insights did this "inside" account give you?
2. Have you ever been in a situation where the emotions you experienced were similar to Tong's in that you had to choose between a cause that meant a great deal to you and personal obligations to your family? Describe the situation and what you decided to do and why.
3. George Bush's administration was criticized because it did not aggressively protest or take any punitive action against the Chinese government for the Tiananmen Square "incident." In your opinion, was the U.S. government's reaction the correct one? Explain your answer.
4. Read the following paragraph written by John Simpson, foreign affairs editor for the BBC, from his article "Tiananmen Square," which describes events on the evening of June 3 (*Granta*, Autumn 1989, pp. 11–24). What impression do you get from Simpson's description when you compare it to Shen Tong's narrative? What cultural differences might explain their different perspectives on the same events?

The screaming around me rose even louder: the handle of the door at the rear of the vehicle had turned a little, and the door began to open. A soldier pushed the barrel of a gun out, but it was snatched from his hands, and then everyone started grabbing his arms, pulling and wrenching until finally he came free, and then he was gone: I saw the arms of the mob, flailing, raised above their heads as they fought to get their blows in. He was dead within seconds, and his body was dragged away in triumph. A second soldier showed his head through the door and was then immediately pulled out by his hair and ears and the skin on his face. This soldier I could see: his eyes were rolling, and his mouth was open, and he was covered with blood where the skin had been ripped off. Only his eyes remained—white and clear—but then someone was trying to get them as well, and someone else began beating his skull until the skull came apart, and there was blood all over the ground, and his brains, and still they kept on beating and beating what was left.

# Slawomir Mrożek

# *The Elephant*

---

*Slawomir Mrożek, born in 1930 in Poland, has come to be known as
that country's foremost political satirist and playwright. His plays
include* Tango *(1964) and* The Police *(1958) and two volumes of short
stories,* The Elephant *(1962) and* The Ugupu Bird *(1968). In 1968,
Mrożek's work was banned in Poland, and he made his home in Paris.
Since then, political developments have permitted his works to be
performed and published in Poland. The story "The Elephant" (translated by Konrad Syrop) wryly dramatizes the absurdities of life under
the communistic bureaucracy.*

*The invasion of Poland by Germany in 1939 precipitated World
War II, during which six million Poles, including three million Jews,
died from starvation, disease, massacres, and executions in concentra-
tion camps such as Auschwitz and Treblinka. After the war, Poland
was taken over by the Soviet Union, and in 1952 became a People's
Republic ruled without the overt repression seen in Hungary and
Romania. Mrożek's fable captures the flavor of life in Poland when
Soviet control even extended to the allocation of zoo animals. Diminishing antagonism between the Communist Party and the Roman
Catholic Church during the 1970s paved the way for Pope John Paul
II's 1979 visit to his homeland. An independent labor union known as
Solidarity, led by Lech Walesa, emerged in the 1980s, demanding
greater worker control in Polish industry. After a long struggle—
during which Solidarity was banned, marshal law imposed, and its
members arrested—the deteriorating Polish economy, and Gorbachev's hands-off attitude, compelled the government to end marshal
law in 1984, lift the ban on Solidarity in 1986, and announce, in 1989,
the first semi-democratic elections in Poland's history. The overwhelming victory of Solidarity candidates led to the appointment of
Tadeusz Mazowiecki, a close associate of Walesa's, as premier, and
marked the end of forty years of Communist Party domination in
Poland. The struggle for a stable economy continues as Walesa, now
premier, calls for Western investment in Poland during this period of
transition.*

The director of the Zoological Gardens had shown himself to be an   1
upstart. He regarded his animals simply as stepping stones on the road of
his own career. He was indifferent to the educational importance of

his establishment. In his zoo the giraffe had a short neck, the badger had no burrow and the whistlers, having lost all interest, whistled rarely and with some reluctance. These shortcomings should not have been allowed, especially as the zoo was often visited by parties of schoolchildren.

2    The zoo was in a provincial town, and it was short of some of the most important animals, among them the elephant. Three thousand rabbits were a poor substitute for the noble giant. However, as our country developed, the gaps were being filled in a well-planned manner. On the occasion of the anniversary of the liberation, on 22nd July, the zoo was notified that it had at long last been allocated an elephant. All the staff, who were devoted to their work, rejoiced at this news. All the greater was their surprise when they learned that the director had sent a letter to Warsaw, renouncing the allocation and putting forward a plan for obtaining an elephant by more economic means.

3    "I, and all the staff," he had written, "are fully aware how heavy a burden falls upon the shoulders of Polish miners and foundry men because of the elephant. Desirous of reducing our costs, I suggest that the elephant mentioned in your communication should be replaced by one of our own procurement. We can make an elephant out of rubber, of the correct size, fill it with air and place it behind railings. It will be carefully painted the correct color and even on close inspection will be indistinguishable from the real animal. It is well known that the elephant is a sluggish animal and it does not run and jump about. In the notice on the railings we can state that this particular elephant is particularly sluggish. The money saved in this way can be turned to the purchase of a jet plane or the conversation of some church monument.

4    "Kindly note that both the idea and its execution are my modest contribution to the common task and struggle.

5    "I am, etc."

6    This communication must have reached a soulless official, who regarded his duties in a purely bureaucratic manner and did not examine the heart of the matter but, following only the directive about reduction of expenditure, accepted the director's plan. On hearing the Ministry's approval, the director issued instructions for the making of the rubber elephant.

7    The carcass was to have been filled with air by two keepers blowing into it from opposite ends. To keep the operation secret the work was to be completed during the night because the people of the town, having heard that an elephant was joining the zoo, were anxious to see it. The director insisted on haste also because he expected a bonus, should his idea turn out to be a success.

8    The two keepers locked themselves in a shed normally housing a workshop, and began to blow. After two hours of hard blowing they discovered that the rubber skin had risen only a few inches above the floor and its bulge in no way resembled an elephant. The night pro-

gressed. Outside, human voices were stilled and only the cry of the jackass interrupted the silence. Exhausted, the keepers stopped blowing and made sure that the air already inside the elephant should not escape. They were not young and were unaccustomed to this kind of work.

"If we go on at this rate," said one of them, "we shan't finish by morning. And what am I to tell my missus? She'll never believe me if I say that I spent the night blowing up an elephant."                    9

"Quite right," agreed the second keeper. "Blowing up an elephant is not an everyday job. And it's all because our director is a leftist."                    10

They resumed their blowing, but after another half-hour they felt too tired to continue. The bulge on the floor was larger but still nothing like the shape of an elephant.                    11

"It's getting harder all the time," said the first keeper.                    12

"It's an uphill job, all right," agreed the second. "Let's have a little rest."                    13

While they were resting, one of them noticed a gas pipe ending in a valve. Could they not fill the elephant with gas? He suggested it to his mate.                    14

They decided to try. They connected the elephant to the gas pipe, turned the valve, and to their joy in a few minutes there was a full-sized beast standing in the shed. It looked real: the enormous body, legs like columns, huge ears and the inevitable trunk. Driven by ambition the director had made sure of having in his zoo a very large elephant indeed.                    15

"First class," declared the keeper who had the idea of using gas. "Now we can go home."                    16

In the morning the elephant was moved to a special run in a central position, next to the monkey cage. Placed in front of a large real rock it looked fierce and magnificent. A big notice proclaimed: "Particularly sluggish. Hardly moves."                    17

Among the first visitors that morning was a party of children from the local school. The teacher in charge of them was planning to give them an object-lesson about the elephant. He halted the group in front of the animal and began:                    18

"The elephant is a herbivorous mammal. By means of its trunk it pulls out young trees and eats their leaves."                    19

The children were looking at the elephant with enraptured admiration. They were waiting for it to pull out a young tree, but the beast stood still behind its railings.                    20

". . . The elephant is a direct descendant of the now-extinct mammoth. It's not surprising, therefore, that it's the largest living land animal."                    21

The more conscientious pupils were making notes.                    22

". . . Only the whale is heavier than the elephant, but then the whale lives in the sea. We can safely say that on land the elephant reigns supreme."                    23

A slight breeze moved the branches of the trees in the zoo.                    24

25     ". . . The weight of a fully grown elephant is between nine and thirteen thousand pounds."

26     At that moment the elephant shuddered and rose in the air. For a few seconds it swayed just above the ground, but a gust of wind blew it upward until its mighty silhouette was against the sky. For a short while people on the ground could see the four circles of its feet, its bulging belly and the trunk, but soon, propelled by the wind, the elephant sailed above the fence and disappeared above the treetops. Astonished monkeys in the cage continued staring into the sky.

27     They found the elephant in the neighboring botanical gardens. It had landed on a cactus and punctured its rubber hide.

28     The schoolchildren who had witnessed the scene in the zoo soon started neglecting their studies and turned into hooligans. It is reported that they drink liquor and break windows. And they no longer believe in elephants.

*Translated by Konrad Syrop*

## Evaluating the Text

1. What is the relationship between the character of the zoo director, the condition of the animals he chooses to exhibit, and the decision he makes regarding the elephant?
2. What significance do you discern in the contrast between the three thousand rabbits and the noble giant — the elephant?
3. How does the way the elephant will be constructed, what it will be filled with, and how it will be labeled satirize the governmental bureaucracy in Poland?
4. At what point in Mrożek's story did you begin to suspect he was being ironic rather than serious? What were these clues? What other features contribute to the story's total effect?
5. How are all the director's suggestions and proposals forms of self-promotion disguised as sincere concern for the common good?
6. What details in the account of the schoolchildren's visit to see the elephant and their subsequent disillusionment suggest Mrożek's subject is what really happens when citizens question the political rhetoric, propaganda, and party-line indoctrinations intended to mold them into good citizens?

## Exploring Different Perspectives

1. How do this story and Chen Jo-hsi's "The Big Fish" explore the role propaganda and political indoctrination play in totalitarian bureaucracies?
2. Compare "The Elephant" with Jan Rabie's "Drought," and discuss why writers whose subject is the relationship of the state and the individual might wish to use such unusual literary forms as the parable or allegory.

# Extending Viewpoints through Writing

1. Discuss the relationship between political rhetoric used to disguise reality
   (e.g., the sign setting expectations that states "particularly sluggish" and
   "hardly moves") and what George Orwell called "doublespeak" in *1984*
   (Harcourt, Brace Jovanovich, 1949). You might wish to read William Lutz's
   *Doublespeak* (Harper & Row, 1989) and then look for examples of
   bureaucratic "doublespeak" in any institutional sphere. How is
   "doublespeak" the equivalent in language of the rubber elephant?

2. Discuss any recent incident that seems to you to express the conflict
   between appearance and reality, as does Mrożek's political allegory. For
   example, under Mayor Koch, New York City officials proposed painting
   fake windows with curtains on the devastated buildings in the South Bronx
   to give the impression people were living there. Or, you might consider the
   instant renovations that precede the visit of an important high-ranking
   personage where roads are suddenly paved or cleaned. (See Jamaica
   Kincaid's "A Small Place," Chapter 7, for a satiric account of road
   improvements that preceded Queen Elizabeth's visit to Antigua.)

3. Discuss some of the ways Mrożek's fable functions as a political allegory.
   For example, why might it be significant that the zoo is a kind of prison?
   What might the elephant, the schoolchildren, the workers who attempt to
   blow up the elephant, the kinds of animals on display and the condition
   they are in, and the "soulless" bureaucrat who approves the idea represent?
   What is the significance of describing disillusioned schoolchildren as
   "hooligans" (a term of political condemnation used, e.g., by government
   officials to characterize the pro-democracy demonstrators in Tiananmen
   Square)?

# Václav Havel

# *The Velvet Hangover*

---

*Václav Havel, born in Prague in 1936, is Czechoslovakia's foremost playwright, who since 1969 had been imprisoned several times by the country's communist regime. Among his many plays are* Temptation *(1989),* Largo Desolato *(1990), and* The Memorandum *(1990). His nonfiction works include* Living in Truth *(1989),* Disturbing the Peace *(1990), and a volume of letters written to his wife while he was in prison,* Letters to Olga: June 1979–September 1982 *(1990). As reform spread through Eastern Europe in 1989, it would have been difficult to predict the speed with which the communist system fell in Czechoslovakia. A series of mass demonstrations following brutal police attacks on student demonstrators, on November 17, 1989, led to the resignation of the conservative Communist party's leadership and the formation of the country's first noncommunist government in forty-one years. The "velvet revolution," as this event was called because of its bloodless and surprisingly smooth transition from communism, led to the free election a month later of Havel, a long-time human rights activist, as President of the Republic. The desire by Slovakians for greater recognition has led the government to change the official name of the country to the Czech and Slovak Federal Republic. "The Velvet Hangover" (translated by K. P. Henley) is a speech that Havel gave in July 1990 at the opening of the Salzburg Festival in Austria. In it, Havel explores how fear of an unknown future now that Czechoslovakia is free has replaced the old known fears of totalitarian rule.*

1    This June our country held its first free elections in many long decades. On July 5 a freely elected parliament reelected me president of Czechoslovakia. These events marked the culmination of one of the most dramatic periods of our modern history: the shattering of the totalitarian system. It was a time of excitement, swift decisions, and countless improvisations; an utterly thrilling, even adventurous time. It was a little like a mildly bewildering but essentially wonderful dream. It was, in a way, a fairy tale. There were so many things that could have gone wrong! We were traveling on totally unknown terrain, and none of us had any reason to believe that it wouldn't collapse under our feet.

*(For further information on Czechoslovakia, see p. 294.)

It didn't, though. And now the time has come when there is indeed 2 reason to rejoice. The revolution, with all its perils, is behind us, and the prospect of building a democratic state, in peace, is before us. Could there be a happier moment in the life of a land that has suffered so long under totalitarianism?

And yet precisely as that splendid historical moment dawned, a 3 peculiar thing happened to me: When I arrived at work on the day after the election, I found I was depressed. I was in some sort of profoundly subdued state. I felt strangely paralyzed, empty inside. I suddenly seemed to have lost all my ideas and goals, my skills, hope, and resolve. I felt deflated, spent, lacking in imagination. Even though just a few days earlier I had been terribly busy, I suddenly had no idea what I was supposed to be doing.

The pressure of exhilarating events, which until then had aroused in 4 me a surprising level of energy, abruptly vanished, and I found myself standing bewildered, lacking the inner motivation for anything at all, feeling exhausted, almost irrelevant. It was an extremely odd sensation, comparable to a bad hangover after some wild binge, to awakening from a pleasant dream to the ugly reality of cold daylight, to the shock of a man in love discovering his sweetheart's treachery.

I wasn't the only one with these strange feelings; many of my col- 5 leagues at Prague Castle felt the very same way. We realized that the poetry was over and the prose was beginning; that the county fair had ended and everyday reality was back. It was only then that we realized how challenging and in many ways unrewarding was the work that lay ahead of us, how heavy a burden we had shouldered. It was as if up to that moment the wild torrent of events had not allowed us to step back and consider whether we were up to the tasks we had undertaken. We had simply been tossed into the current and forced to swim.

It seemed to us that only now could we begin to appreciate fully the 6 weight of the destiny we had chosen. That realization brought with it a sudden, and under the circumstances entirely groundless, sense of hopelessness.

Somewhere in the depths of this feeling lay fear: fear that we had 7 taken on too much, fear that we wouldn't be up to the job, fear of our own inadequacy; in short, fear of our very selves.

At the very deepest core of this feeling there was, ultimately, a 8 sensation of the absurd: what Sisyphus might have felt if one fine day his boulder stopped, rested on the hilltop, and failed to roll back down. It was the sensation of a Sisyphus mentally unprepared for the possibility that his efforts might succeed, a Sisyphus whose life had lost its old purpose and hadn't yet developed a new one.

About a year ago, when I was asked to launch this august festival 9 with a brief lecture, I never considered that I might be able to attend in person. Still, I was pleased to accept the offer and planned to submit my contribution in writing. During the tranquil Christmas season I would calmly compose a little essay on the theme of fear and the sense of danger in Central European literature. But history got in my way, robbing me of both time and concentration. So I decided to complete the task after the elections; in fact, I was truly looking forward to it, since it would allow me to enjoy a brief return to my original profession as a writer and because I planned to use the occasion as a dividing mark between the first, revolutionary, stage of my political commitment and the second stage, a calmer one, which involved building up rather than tearing down.

10     I did, in fact, find the time to write. But the time I found was the period of my peculiar hangover. First history got in my way; now I was getting in my *own* way: I was simply unable to write anything; I was depleted, paralyzed, powerless.

11     What a paradox: I had wanted to write about fear, and here it was fear that was incapacitating me in my writing. Fear of my subject matter, fear of the act of writing itself, fear of my own inadequacy, fear of myself.

12     All I could do about this paradox was try to approach the topic paradoxically: by describing the situation that led to my inability to approach it. There is nothing new in that. In fact, part of why most writers write is to divert their despair into their work and thus overcome it. Perhaps this explains why I am talking so much about myself here. It isn't out of any complacent egocentrism but because, simply, I have no other options.

13     No inventory of the various characteristics specific to Central European culture and literature would be complete without one particularly important one: an increased perception of danger, a heightened sensitivity to the phenomenon of fear. It makes perfect sense: In a place where history has always been so intricately tangled; in a place with such complex cultural, ethnic, social, and political structures; in a place that saw the origins of the most varied of European catastrophes, fear and danger are the very dimensions of human experience that must be felt and analyzed most intensely.

14     I believe that even the kind of fear that I experienced is typical of the Central European spiritual world, or at least is understandable against its background. Certainly it would be hard to imagine that in England, France, or the United States a person could be depressed by his political victory. In Central Europe, on the other hand, it seems perfectly natural.

15     For that matter, the experience of the hangover-type void is certainly not unique to me, nor is that odd sense of fear. I have observed variations of that fear and emptiness quite often, not only in Czechoslovakia but also in other countries of Central and Eastern Europe that have shaken off totalitarianism.

16     It was with a great deal of effort that people in these lands attained

the freedom they yearned for. The moment they gained that freedom, however, it was as if they had been ambushed by it. Unaccustomed to freedom, they now, suddenly, don't know what to do with it; they are afraid of it; they don't know what to fill it with. Their Sisyphean struggle for freedom has left a vacuum; life seems to have lost its purpose.

Similarly, in this part of the world we observe symptoms of a new 17 fear of the future. Unlike totalitarian times, when the future, though wretched, was certain, today it is very unclear. The single (if ubiquitous) familiar danger represented by totalitarian oppression seems to have been replaced by an entire spectrum of new and unfamiliar — or long-forgotten — dangers: from the danger of national conflicts to the danger of losing social-welfare protections to the danger of the new totalitarianism of consumption, commerce, and money.

We were very good at being persecuted and at losing. That may be 18 why we are so flustered by our victories and so disconcerted that no one is persecuting us. Now and then I even encounter indications of nostalgia for the time when life flowed between banks that, true, were very narrow but that were unchanging and apparent to everyone. Today we don't know where the banks lie, and it makes us a little uncomfortable.

I repeat the existential situation I illustrated for you on my own 19 person, and which I have also observed in various forms in my fellow citizens, is, in my opinion, a particularly Central European one. Our literature contains innumerable examples of it in our not too distant past, in the atmosphere following both World War I and World War II.

In short, it seems that fate has ordained that we, more frequently 20 than others, and often in unexpected situations, shall be afraid.

For us, fear of history is not just fear of the future but also fear of the 21 past. I might even say that these two fears are conditional one on the other: A person who is afraid of what is yet to come is generally also reluctant to look in the face of what has been. And a person afraid to look at his own past must fear what is to come.

All too often in this part of the world, fear of one lie gives birth to 22 another lie, in the foolish hope that by protecting ourselves from the first lie we will be protected from lies in general. But a lie can never protect us from a lie. Those who falsify history do not protect the freedom of a nation but rather constitute a threat to it.

The idea that a person can rewrite his autobiography is one of the 23 traditional self-deceptions of Central Europe. Trying to do that means hurting oneself and one's fellow countrymen. When a truth is not given complete freedom, freedom is not complete.

One way or another, many of us are guilty. But we cannot be for- 24 given, nor can there be peace in our souls, until we confess our guilt.

I have many reasons for believing that the truth purges one from fear. 25 Many of us who, in recent years, strove to speak the truth in spite of everything were able to maintain an inner perspective, a willingness to endure, a sense of proportion, an ability to understand and forgive our neighbors, and a light heart only because we were speaking the truth. Otherwise, we might have perished from despair.

26    Our specific Central European fear has led to many a misfortune. It could be shown that in it lies the primal origin of not only countless local conflicts but also some global ones. Here, the fear that possesses petty souls has often led to violence, brutality, and fanatical hatred.

27    But fear is not only a destructive condition. Fear of our own incompetence can evoke new competency; fear of God or of our own conscience can evoke courage; fear of defeat can make us prevail. Fear of freedom can be the very thing that will ultimately teach us to create a freedom of real value. And fear of the future could be exactly what we need to bring about a better future.

28    The more sensitive a person is to all the dangers that threaten him the better able he is to defend against them. For that matter, I have always thought that feeling empty and losing touch with the meaning of life are in essence only a challenge to seek new things to fill one's life, a new meaning for one's existence. Isn't it the moment of most profound doubt that gives birth to new certainties? Perhaps hopelessness is the very soil that nourishes human hope; perhaps one could never find sense in life without first experiencing its absurdity.

29    In spite of having spoken in such an unstatesmanlike manner about my moments of hopelessness, I will conclude on a constructive note.

30    Let us finally endeavor, in this sorely tried place, to get rid of our fear of lies and also of our fear of truth. Let us finally take a direct, calm, and unwavering look into our own countenances: our past, our present, and our future. Let us try to delve into the core of our doubts, our fears, and our despair to come up with the seeds of a new European self-confidence — the self-confidence of those who are not afraid of looking beyond the horizon of their personal and community interests, beyond the horizon of this moment.

## Evaluating the Text

1. What is the significance of the title in relationship to the so-called "velvet revolution," that is, an unexpectedly smooth, bloodless transition from communist domination?
2. What evidence is there that Havel's experience is not isolated but is shared by other new political leaders of Czechoslovakia as well? What is the significance of Havel's statement that "the poetry was over and the prose was beginning"?
3. How does Havel use the image of Sisyphus to illustrate new anxieties that he and others were experiencing, paradoxically, after having succeeded in winning freedom for their country?
4. What features of shared history in Central Europe might explain why fear of one kind or another plays such an important role in the political life of the countries in this region? How does the fear Havel describes differ from that experienced under communist domination?

5. Discuss the three dangers Havel identifies, and explain why each has come into existence at this particular time.
6. What stylistic and organizational features of this essay let you know that it was originally delivered as a speech? What might you infer about the audience before whom Havel delivered "The Velvet Hangover"?
7. How has speaking the truth been a source of strength to Havel in the past, and why does he believe that it is more important than ever to confront fear directly?

## Exploring Different Perspectives

1. How is the concept of *fear* explored by Havel similar to or different from the meaning of *fear* developed by Samir al-Khalil in "Authority," his analysis of Iraqi society?
2. After reading "The Elephant" by Slawomir Mrożek, discuss how both this story and Havel's speech criticize public "lying." What insight do both these works give you about the quality of life in Central European countries during and after Soviet domination?

## Extending Viewpoints through Writing

1. Have you ever had an experience similar emotionally to what Havel describes in which initial happiness over having achieved a goal gave way to unanticipated depression and fear? How do you react to unexpected feelings?
2. Discuss any work of Central European literature that deals with themes related to existential freedom or persecution by the state. You might wish to read any of the works of Czechoslovakian writers such as Franz Kafka's "The Metamorphosis" (1968), *The Trial* (1968), *The Castle* (1954), and *Amerika* (1962); Milan Kundera's *The Book of Laughter and Forgetting* (translated in 1980) and *The Unbearable Lightness of Being* (translated in 1984); or Josef Škvorecký's *Dvořák in Love: A Lighthearted Dream* (1987) and *Talkin' Moscow Blues* (1990).
3. Drawing on information in (and the introductions to) works by Havel, Josef Škvorecký ("An Insolvable Problem of Genetics," Chapter 5), and Mrożek, write an expository essay about the recent history of communism in transition in Russia, Czechoslovakia, Poland, or Germany. How do the changes that have taken place illustrate the new political forces at work? You might wish to construct your essay as a comparison between any of these countries and the hard-line communist states of Cuba, China, Cambodia, and Vietnam illustrated in the works of Armando Valladares ("A Nazi Prison in the Caribbean"); Shen Tong ("Bloody Sunday in Tiananmen Square"); Someth May ("The Field behind the Village"); and Le Ly Hayslip ("Sisters and Brothers," Chapter 7).

# Someth May

# *The Field behind the Village*

---

*Someth May was born in Phnom Penh and was studying medicine when he and his family were forced to flee when the Khmer Rouge came to power in 1975. He eventually escaped to a refugee camp on the Thai–Cambodian border. Only four of his family of fourteen survived. Subsequently, he journeyed to England and then to America. "The Field behind the Village" is from his 1986 autobiography,* Cambodian Witness.

*Cambodia (also known as* Kampuchea) *is a nation in Southeast Asia bordered by Laos to the north, Vietnam to the east, the Gulf of Siam to the south, and Thailand to the west and north. Granted full independence in 1953 after nearly a century of French rule, Cambodia became in 1970 a major battlefield of the Vietnam war. The country was plunged into civil war when the Chinese-backed Khmer Rouge succeeded in overthrowing the government and installing Pol Pot as leader in 1975. The massive drive toward collectivization in which urban populations were uprooted and forced to work in the country-side produced conditions reflected in Someth May's narrative. Between 1975 and 1978, it is estimated that half the country's population of six million were killed in "fields behind the village" under the Khmer Rouge's genocidal reign of terror. Nearly every Cambodian lost a family member during the Pol Pot regime. Border conflicts with Vietnam led to the Vietnamese invasion in 1978–1979 and a protracted guerrilla war between the Vietnamese-installed government and the Khmer Rouge. By 1989, after losing 60,000 men, Vietnam withdrew its soldiers, leaving a Cambodian government consisting of a three-part coalition (including the Khmer Rouge).*

1    The unit meetings were held once every three days, normally at seven in the evening, after we had eaten. A meeting was usually a series of speeches made by the unit leader, the company leader and the group leader, in which we were told to 'attack' our work, to lose our feelings of possessiveness and to give everything to the Angkar. The speeches were endlessly repetitive, meandering, wandering backwards and forwards as the leaders tried to think of another way of saying the same thing. They were punctuated by long pauses, and it was not unusual for members of

*(For additional information on Cambodian refugees, see p. 466.)

the audience to keel over into sleep: they would be woken up and warned. At the end, the leaders opened the meeting to the people, but nobody dared ask any questions. A year before, one man had asked for the meaning of the word *Angkar* to be explained — but although he had survived, nobody else had thought of copying him.

Then one day, Comrade Chhith, a boy of about seventeen — a quiet   2
character who seldom chatted to anybody and always sat by himself — suddenly put his hand up and asked whether the unit leader would answer some questions about the revolution and explain a few points which Chhith had not understood so far. His request was granted and he rose to speak.

'Friends and Comrades, it is a great opportunity for me,' said   3
Comrade Chhith, 'that the meeting has allowed me to ask some questions about the revolution. In every meeting, thousands of them so far, I have been told that the people in the revolutionary territory are equal and that equality has been achieved everywhere. Could you please tell me, Comrade,' said the boy, looking straight into the eyes of the unit leader, 'what is the meaning of the word equality?'

The unit leader, Comrade Khann, stood up to reply.   4

'Equality,' he said, 'means the *same*. In other words, it means that the   5
people in the revolution are the same. . . .' And he paused as if stumped by the boy's question. 'That is, there is no supervision in the revolution. Everyone is the same.'

The boy stood up again. 'You've just said that everybody is the same   6
and that there is no supervision in the revolution,' he said, and I noticed that he was becoming excited and that his voice was trembling. 'Then why am I always told or ordered to *do this* or *do that*?' And he sat down again.

'Well, that is a very good question indeed,' said the unit leader   7
sarcastically. He was beginning to get annoyed. 'If you are not told what you're supposed to do, none of the work that our Angkar wants will get done.'

Now Comrade Chhith sprang to his feet and came straight back into   8
the argument. 'I see. Now let me return to the word equality. From what you have said, the people in the revolution are equal. But why doesn't equality exist in every unit of the co-operative?' he asked. You could see anger and excitement mounting in him.

'How do you mean — equality does not exist in the units?' asked the   9
unit leader, his tone hardening.

The unit leader was not a Khmer Rouge soldier. He was a peasant   10
who, until 1975, had been working under the Khmer Rouge. It was only with the arrival of the New People that he would have been put in charge of a unit. He was not a well-educated man. He had the handwriting of a child.

Comrade Chhith, who now returned to his feet, was (I later gathered)   11
the son of an officer in Lon Nol's army. He was obviously well-educated,

and he had thought out his argument a long time before beginning it. Now he reached the crux.

12     'Well, let me explain. Take, for instance, our own unit. Why do you all, who call yourselves the Old People, have enough food to eat, when we don't? This is the main question I want you to answer.'

13     Heads shot up when this question was put, but Comrade Chhith had not finished. Indeed he had lost his self-control: 'As far I can tell, from listening to the songs that were broadcast every evening at Wat Chass labour field, I can't see *equality* in our unit. We have two meals a day—quite often none. *You* and your *Old People* always eat more than three times. Please, Comrade. Tell me more about the word *equality.*'

14     'Comrade,' the unit leader's voice was more menacing, 'you should think very, very carefully before you open your mouth again to ask more questions. We Old People have been fighting very hard over the last few years to achieve equality and freedom for all of you here. We suffered all kinds of miseries while you were in luxury villas in the capital, doing nothing but enjoying yourselves in the decadent culture of the East and West. Do you think what *you* did was fair to *us*? What right do *you* have to complain about the food you have eaten? Come on, tell me more about the way we Old People have behaved.'

15     The boy was really brave and seemed to have recovered his control a little. He stood up again and said: 'What I want to know from you Old People is—is there any *equality* in our unit, and, if so, what sort of equality is it?'

16     The unit leader was calmer in turn: 'I admit that there doesn't seem to be equality in our unit. But if we Old People didn't have enough to eat, we would be starving like you. Leaders have to eat more in order to have enough energy to lead you the way our Angkar wants. As I told you a few minutes ago—you have to be told, otherwise none of the work would get done. Any more questions?'

17     'No, I think the answers are very good,' said Comrade Chhith, stressing each word. 'Thank you. They are very understandable.'

18     The meeting broke up at one in the morning. We went off to our sleeping-quarters with much to think about. I was pleased by the boy's questions, and worried for his safety.

19     About once a week, the unit and company leaders had a fourth meal around midnight. On one such night, they sat by the fire cooking the rice, and the New People watched, as usual, from their sleeping-places. As they began to eat, Comrade Chhith got up from his mosquito-net and went straight to the fire, sat down and without a word began eating with them. Conversation around the fire stopped immediately, but nobody prevented Chhith from eating. Then, one by one, the leaders got up and left him alone with his meal. When they had gone, several boys from the unit came over and started to join in. During the whole incident nobody said a word.

Some time during the next week, the unit's rations were stopped 20
without explanation. After working a day without food, I could think
only of finding some way of filling my stomach. I thought of the potato-
field next to the village. If I was careful, I might go there in the night.
Most of the people in the unit were asleep by midnight, except for three
groups huddled around camp-fires, roasting the small creatures which
they had caught during the day. The clouds were thick. It would rain
soon, and I thought that this was a good opportunity.

As the rain began to fall, I wandered over to one of the fires and 21
chatted a little with one of the men. When it seemed a good moment, I
slipped away in the direction of the potato-field. It took about twenty
minutes to cross the open ground, and I stopped and hid for ten minutes,
listening for voices. Then I tried to pull up a potato stem, but I was too
weak for the task.

I should explain that this form of potato grows like a small tree, about 22
the height of a sunflower but with a strong woody stem. The part you eat
is the tuber, which can grow to the size of your forearm. Most flour used
in Southeast Asia is made from this potato. It is also boiled as a
vegetable.

Normally I could have pulled up the plant without any difficulty, but 23
now I had to dig out the tubers with my hands. I ate as much as I could,
raw, and then dug up some more to take with me. When I got back to the
camp-fire everyone had gone to sleep. The rain had just stopped and the
fire was nearly out. I put the potatoes among the coals—covering them
with wet dead leaves—and blew gently.

I heard a voice calling my name. The voice came nearer and nearer 24
and I recognized it as Comrade Khann's, the unit leader. I called out: 'I'm
over here, Comrade.'

'Hey, Comrade Meth, what are you doing here?' asked Comrade 25
Khann, joining me at the fireside, squatting and warming his hands.

'I couldn't sleep,' I replied. 'I want to warm myself. It's too cold over 26
there.'

'Come on, go back to sleep. You have to get up early to work.' 27

'Okay, Comrade, I'll go in a minute after I've warmed myself,' I 28
replied, glancing at the potatoes in the fire to see if they were well
covered.

'Come along, now. It's not right to sit out in the middle of the night 29
like this. Come on!' He slapped me on the shoulder, but in a friendly way
he was ordering me to leave. I was sorry to lose the potatoes. It was
months since I had eaten a properly cooked potato.

'Please, Comrade,' I said, 'I can't sleep over there. It's too cold.' 30

'No problem,' said the unit leader, 'I'll lend you my blanket. Come 31
on, let's go now.'

Lend me his blanket! I'd never had that kind of generous offer before. 32
He must be 'chasing a footprint,' as we say in Cambodian. I got up and

followed him reluctantly to the sleeping-quarters, where he gave me his blanket and saw me to my mosquito-net.

33      That night the raw potato I had eaten attacked my stomach and I couldn't sleep at all.

34      The next night I went off to the potato-field again. Nothing happened. By the third night, I'd got into the swing of it. I went off again, and while digging for the potatoes — this time with a piece of dead wood instead of my bare hands — I heard a group of people coming towards me.

35      As they approached I wondered whether to run or stay still. If I ran, and if they happened to have a gun among them, I might get shot. I hesitated. They moved closer. I lay stock still on the ground and tried to stop breathing. They paused about sixty feet from me, and I could see by the moonlight that there were four men. Each wore a black uniform and carried a long parang. I knew from this that they were the reconnaissance team, drawn from the most senior of the Old People. We called them *Kang Chhlob*. When we had first come to this place they patrolled the sleeping-quarters at night, and if they heard anyone say something wrong, that person would be called away by the Angkar the next day, and would not reappear. Once they called you, you were never seen again.

36      They were speaking among themselves. One of them said, 'It's my turn. If I catch someone, I want to show what I can do.'

37      His friend was irritated. 'Enough. Do whatever you want. But don't do it here. It's not allowed.'

38      I closed my eyes and tried to stop shivering. Hunger disappeared. I could think only of what I would do if I was caught.

39      They stopped and stood still for about five minutes, watching the field and trying to catch the slightest noise. I held my breath. Eventually they moved on. I thought: I'm alive again! I swore never to come back here at night, however hungry I was.

40      As soon as they had gone, I got up and tried to work out how to get back to my quarters. I had been lying on a nest of red ants and was bitten all over. I was nervous and did not know which way to go. Very slowly I edged in what I thought was the right direction, but ten minutes later I found myself at the wrong end of the potato-field. I retraced my steps towards the village. As soon as I was out of the field there was a noise behind me.

41      'You there, stop and put your hands up. You're the one we're looking for.'

42      I stopped and turned around. It was the four men I had just seen, the members of the reconnaissance team. Although I had seen them often around the village, I never knew their names and I had never even looked into their faces. Whenever they passed, we simply stared at the ground and continued our work.

43      'What are you doing?' said another of them. 'We've been watching you and we know that you were in the potato-field.'

'No, Comrade . . .' I stuttered, 'I'm going for a walk because I   44
couldn't sleep.'

'Going for a walk? Come here. Walk slowly and keep your hands up.'   45

I did as I was told and as I came closer I noticed their wristwatches in   46
the moonlight. One of them stepped towards me, grabbed my hands,
twisting them behind my back. I looked at the ground.

'You're a liar. Tell us the truth. How many times have you done this?'   47

'What have I done, Comrade? I don't understand what you're talking   48
about.'

'You've been stealing potatoes from the commune field.'   49

'No, I'm going for a walk.' By now I was trembling violently and my   50
voice was out of control.

The man in front rolled up his sleeves and placed his hands on his   51
hips. I noticed a great scar on his forearm.

'Scum, I said tell us the truth before you get hurt.'   52

I couldn't answer. I could only, with great difficulty, raise my eyes   53
from the ground and look in his face, which I then saw for the first time.
It was the face and weirdly cruel expression of a man who had spent a
long time on the battlefield. His eyes were bloodshot and bulging and
the lines in his brow were deep with anger. His hair was greying and his
skin was dark.

My mind seemed to drift. I do not know what I was thinking when I   54
felt a terrible blow to my mouth. His fist had knocked out one of my
teeth, and my mouth and tongue started to bleed. My eyes were filled
with tears and the pain spread immediately through my skull. The man
on my right pulled a piece of parachute cord from his pocket and went
behind me. As he tied my arms together at the elbows he kicked me in
the back several times.

The man tying me up asked: 'What are we going to do? The field   55
behind the village?'

'I don't know,' said another, after a short pause, 'I've no idea.'   56

'Let's take him to the field behind the village,' said another.   57

That phrase 'the field behind the village' meant the killing ground. I'd   58
never been to it, but I'd heard about it when I was company leader.
There were in fact, for our village, two main killing grounds. The bigger
one was near the re-education centre, the former pagoda. When people
were taken to the re-education centre, and afterwards killed, their deaths
were reported to the regional Angkar Loeu. But if for some reason they
wanted to kill one of us without reporting it, they took the victim to the
field behind the village.

The field was about two miles away, a patch of open ground with a   59
small wood at one end. When we went to work, we passed it and could
see from a distance three large open pits from which came the most
horrific smell. We could have gone there if we'd wanted to, since they
were intended to keep us in terror. But nobody I knew ever went. There
was always a flock of crows around.

(There was a separate graveyard nearby for victims of famine and   60 disease, and for those who didn't survive the hospital. Formerly in Cambodia we always cremated our dead, but the Khmer Rouge believed that corpses fertilized the ground. Only once during their regime did I witness a cremation. That was in the bamboo jungle, and the ashes were used afterwards for growing vegetables, which we then ate.)

61 As I listened to the conversation of my captors, all sense seemed to drain from me. I couldn't understand anything. Blood flowed from my gum where my tooth was broken. I tried to swallow as much of it as I could, thinking that this would conserve my energy. I spat out the broken tooth.

62 One of them said 'We've no right. We can't take him there. We need permission from his unit leader. Otherwise we'll be in trouble.'

63 'Nobody will know about it, except the four of us, unless someone talks,' said the one behind me.

64 'But the Angkar is smart. Sooner or later someone will talk.'

65 'Stop arguing. Take him to his leader,' said the one holding my arms. He was irritated and he pushed me forward.

66 They continued hitting me with their fists on the way back to the village. A few people were awake in the sleeping-quarters. They were shocked at the state I was in and roused their neighbours, pointing at me and wondering what it was I had done. One of the reconnaissance team went to the unit leader and spoke to him. Then he and his companions left.

67 It was about two in the morning. I was thrown on the ground with my arms still tied, and Comrade Khann began to ask me what I had done. I told him that I was caught while walking near the potato-field, but he did not believe me and began searching my pockets. He found a small piece of potato.

68 He kicked me in the ribs. Instinctively I rolled with the blow, but I was too weak to avoid the impact altogether. He came at me again and aimed another kick in the same place. This time I took the full force and fell, immediately unconscious.

69 I was woken by a cold breeze. My mouth and ribs were still hurting, and I tried to move my hands and feet in order to curl up and keep warm. My right foot felt heavy. Opening my eyes with great pain, I discovered that my foot had been chained to a tree.

70 The sky was clear, showing all the stars and a half moon. From its position I reckoned it was around four in the morning. I was outside the unit camp. I was shivering. My shirt had been removed, I didn't know when. I was wearing only a pair of shorts. I closed my eyes and tried to sleep, but I was too cold. The pain in my mouth and ribs was excruciating. I began to recall the conversation of the four men. I assumed they were waiting till daylight to take me to the field behind the village. I tried to resist the pain. I was scared.

71 The sky began to glow in the east. I began thinking about my sisters.

Did they know what had happened to me? And, if I was killed, what would happen to them? One of my sisters had already been executed for criticizing the revolution. Now that I was found out, perhaps they would decide to destroy my whole family. And then I thought of Comrade Khann, and how he had been turned down by Comrade Ran, and how she had subsequently asked to marry me. Comrade Khann had every reason for taking his revenge. I was at his mercy.

As it started to grow light, Comrade Khann came towards me with three other men. He was armed with a parang, and another man was carrying a spade. I was going to be killed.

It was still not yet light when we set out across the fields. At this time of day, everyone would be getting ready for the regular morning check-up, and so we did not meet anyone on our way. I was limping in front, dragging my chain. There was no conversation, just a series of orders barked out in my direction: hurry up, left, right, get a move on. The sun had not yet dispersed the mist, and I could only just make out the small patch of woodland which marked the mass graves.

We walked about a mile.

I knew something of the pleasure they took in killing people. When we were working on the Ream Kun dam, the men from the reconnaissance team used to come and sit near us, and we could not help overhearing their conversation. They would boast about how somebody screamed and cried for mercy before he died. They said that after people had had their livers cut out they could do nothing — they couldn't talk, only blink their eyes. They said that fat people had small livers and thin people had big livers. They would sit there laughing together as they exchanged these details. I once heard one of them say that when you put human liver in the frying pan it jumps.

When we were within a mile of the open pits, they suddenly told me to stop, and walked away to talk. I couldn't hear their conversation, which lasted about five minutes. When they returned, they told me to start walking again, to the right. We were not going to the open pits after all.

A quarter of an hour later we came to a field I did not know. There were several grave mounds, some of them new, some old. Comrade Khann tied my chain to a small tree, took the spade from one of his companions and threw it down in front of me.

'Here is your pen!' he said. 'Go ahead and dig the ground.'

I understood and I began digging my own grave — began immediately to avoid being hurt. Two of the men left, and Comrade Khann and the fourth man sat on the low dike at the edge of the field, chatting and laughing together just out of earshot. At around noon, when I had finished digging a grave about a foot and a half deep, Comrade Khann came up to me and told me to lie in it. He asked me whether I felt comfortable or not. I made no reply. It was slightly small for me. He told me to make it a bit wider. When I had done that, by about three o'clock, I was told to rest. I sat on the edge of the grave, looking into it. A piece of cooked potato was given to me. I was not hungry.

80    'Why don't you eat?' asked the leader. 'Is it because you've had too many potatoes in the last few days?' He was smiling and he slapped my back.

81    'No, Comrade . . . I'm very hungry indeed.' I started eating the potato and continued staring into the grave. I used to like potatoes. This one tasted like rotten wood.

82    In the distance I saw the two other men returning, with three others. They were carrying something which looked like a log, wrapped in a piece of old matting. I thought it must be a corpse. They dropped it on the ground near the grave, and one of them said with a smile: 'You won't be lonely here. We've found a friend for you.'

83    He unwrapped the matting. There lay the body of Comrade Chhith, the boy who had asked the meaning of the word equality. I closed my eyes.

84    'Come on,' they said, 'look at your friend.' They weren't smiling now.

85    They rolled the body into the grave with their feet.

86    The unit leader walked towards me with his parang in his hand and ordered me to fill in the grave. I started shovelling, but the whole time I had an intense feeling that something was about to hit the back of my neck, and that I would fall into the grave. Dusk was falling as I finished. I was taken back to the unit camp, my right foot still chained. I was tethered to the support of the barn and given a small bowl of rice soup.

87    That night the unit meeting took place as usual, and after the regular, long speech, the leader, Comrade Khann, came to my case. A fourteen-year-old boy from the reconnaissance team was sent to fetch me. He told me to crawl to the meeting. I went before the comrades on all fours. Comrade Khann said: 'This person is a thief of the Angkar. He has broken the rules of the commune by stealing potatoes from the field. However, I am very glad to say that the co-operative leader told us not to put him away. He will have to work very hard in the next few days.' He paused a moment and then turned to me: 'Now, Comrade Meth, come and address the meeting and tell us what you want us to do if you are caught again, or if you do something else to destroy the discipline of the Angkar.'

88    I stood: 'Friends and Comrades, this is a very great opportunity for me to re-educate myself in the way our Angkar requires. If I do anything wrong again, please banish me from the Angkar's territory. Friends and Comrades, do not emulate my behaviour.'

89    At the end of the meeting I was allowed back to the sleeping-quarters. As I lay down and closed my eyes, the body of Comrade Chhith reappeared before me with a horrible vividness. I realized that he had been beaten to death. The back of his neck was bruised and his skull was smashed in. I lay there for about an hour thinking about him.

Suddenly two boys crept in under the mosquito-net.          90

'We're hungry,' one said. 'Take us to the potato-field.' I was irritated          91
and told them to leave. But they were insistent.

'Nobody will know. You need not be involved. You can watch. We'll          92
dig.' I threatened to tell the leader. They left.

The next day the company leader spoke to me. 'You are lucky. If you          93
had followed the two boys last night, you wouldn't be here today.'

The immediate effect of my experiences was to make me ashamed in          94
front of my friends and to withdraw from all company. I don't know
why I should have felt so ashamed. Before I was exposed as a thief, I
used to be held up as an example of hard work and revolutionary
potential by my company and unit leaders. Now I worked hard to
recover my lost position. Try as they might, the Khmer Rouge could spot
no fault in my labour. I worked in continual terror, and as I toiled away I
often wondered why I had not been killed. Was it because I had previously been a good worker? Or had Comrade Ran's mother intervened
with the co-operative leader on my behalf? And if she had done so, why
had she not also intervened to save my sister Mealea's life? These are
questions I still ask myself.

## Evaluating the Text

1. What is Meth's (an abbreviation of Someth) position within the unit?
2. What is the basis for the distinction between the "Old People" and the
   others? What insight does this give you into the principles underlying the
   Khmer Rouge's reorganization of Cambodian society?
3. Why is the issue of "equality" such a sore point from the perspective of
   the unit leader?
4. How does comrade Chhith's background differ from that of the unit
   leader? Why is his background held against him by those now in power?
5. In your opinion, would comrade Khann, the unit leader, have been
   willing to let the matter rest if Chhith had not insisted on sitting down to
   eat with the "Old People," as a demonstration of his speech about
   "equality"? Explain your answer.
6. Why is the whole issue of "equality" such a touchy point, especially in
   view of the clear differences in food allotments, and power to give orders,
   that the higher-ups enjoy? Why must everyone continue to maintain the
   pretense that the revolution has brought about a "classless society" in
   Cambodia?
7. Compare Khann's attitude toward Meth when he doesn't know about the
   potatoes and his later treatment of Meth after he has been apprehended.
   Although Meth thinks Khann has always had it in for him because of
   jealousy, what different conclusions might you draw?
8. How do you know that the reconnaisance team were answerable for their
   actions to higher-ups, known collectively as the Angkar?
9. What is the significance of the title "The Field behind the Village"?
10. In your opinion, why did the Khmer Rouge leadership choose to kill
    comrade Chhith but only to scare and humiliate Meth? Why did the kind

of opposition Chhith represented pose more of a threat than Meth's crime of stealing potatoes? To answer this question, you might look at the immediate effect of Chhith's speeches on "equality" on other members of the unit.

11. Why was it more important to have Meth remain as a living example of the possibilities of "reeducation" rather than simply killing him? To what extent was the leadership's assessment of Meth's character correct? From the leadership's point of view, why is it significant that Meth never held a political stance, unlike Chhith, but simply wanted something to eat?

## Exploring Different Perspectives

1. In comparing the accounts of Someth May in Cambodia and Armando Valladares in Cuba (in "A Nazi Prison in the Caribbean"), analyze why in one case, attempts at political "reeducation" succeeded in achieving the desired change of attitude, while in the other, Valladares held to his beliefs. In your analysis, be sure to consider the relevant psychological, political, or social forces that may have made the difference in how each prisoner reacted?

2. Contrast how the "big fish" at the center of Chen Jo-hsi's story comes to signify inequities in the entire political and social structure of rural China during Mao's Cultural Revolution, while the potato in May's account remains merely a potato. Which of the two works did you find more believable, despite the fact that one is fiction and the other is a firsthand account based on May's personal experiences?

3. Drawing on Samir al-Khalil's account, "Authority," of how Saddam Hussein maintains power, discuss the role fear plays in restraining people from speaking out in Iraq and in Cambodia as described by May. How has fear become an integral, officially sanctioned part of both societies?

## Extending Viewpoints through Writing

1. Are you familiar with the history of other revolutions that were fought to achieve "equality"? Did the outcome in any of these produce "inequality" of the kind May dramatizes?

2. In your opinion, would it be desirable to live in a completely "classless" society? Why or why not?

3. How have the Khmer Rouge's inclusion in a three-part coalition government representing Cambodia in the United Nations reactivated many of the concerns May describes?

Alicia Partnoy

# The Little School: Tales of Disappearance and Survival in Argentina

*Alicia Partnoy, born in Argentina in 1955, was arrested with her husband, and was detained as a political prisoner along with the thirty thousand other "disappeared" citizens until international pressure compelled the military junta to release her. Her testimony on human rights violations in Argentina has been presented to the United Nations, the Organization of American States, and Amnesty International, and helped bring about the conviction of four of the junta generals in Buenos Aires when the dictatorship collapsed after 1983. During her years as a political prisoner, her stories and poems were smuggled out of prison and published anonymously. The following selection includes both the introduction and a chapter, "Conversation under the Rain," from her book* The Little School: Tales of Disappearance and Survival in Argentina *(1986).*

*Argentina, the second largest nation in South America after Brazil, won independence from Spain in 1819 and quickly became a favored destination for European immigrants, who today make up a sizable majority of the population. Repeated coups and military dictatorships have marked Argentina's history in the twentieth century. General Juan Perón came to power in 1944, established a dictatorship, and ruled with the aid of his wife Eva Perón ("Evita"), until he was overthrown by a coup in 1955. He returned to power in 1973, died in 1974, and was succeeded by his third wife, Isabel, who was overthrown by a military coup in March 1976. The junta made up of commanders of the military was led by General Jorge Videla. Under his rule, tens of thousands of political opponents who had supported Perón were seized, often never to be seen again. Partnoy's narrative recounts her experience as one of these "disappeared" (the* Desaparecidos*) citizens. In 1982, Argentina's unsuccessful war against Great Britain over the Falkland Islands (Islas Malvinas) led to the fall of General Leopoldo Galtieri, who had replaced Videla the year before, and to democratic elections in 1983, which returned the country to civilian rule. In 1989, a Peronist, Carlos Raúl Menem, was elected* *president as Argentina faced devastating inflation and a deteriorating economy.*

1        In the summer of 1984, after four and a half years in exile, I returned to my homeland to mourn my friends who had disappeared or were killed by the military, to mourn the members of my family who had died during my ordeal of seven years in prison and banishment, and to suffer at the sight of my country ruined after years of dictatorship.

2        Almost 30,000 Argentines "disappeared" between 1976 and 1979, the most oppressive years of the military rule.

3        Military coups have not been rare events in the history of my country. In fact, I was born in 1955, the year of the coup that overthrew Juan Peron. A succession of military and short-lived civilian governments followed. It was not until I turned seventeen that Peronists were permitted to participate in Argentina's political life. The Peronist party won the elections. How could a teenager who had never heard anything positive about Peronism from teachers or from the censored media get strongly involved in the movement? My "conversion," as well as that of thousands of youth who had not come from Peronist families, was a gradual process. I grew up loving my country and its people and hating injustice. I did not have many doubts left when I learned that Peronism had given power to the workers by organizing them in strong unions; had improved the living conditions of people through fair wages, retirement plans, vacations, and a good public health system; and had granted women the right to vote. I also learned about the work of Evita, Peron's wife, who was responsible for many of these gains. I knew that Peronism was a very broad movement and that under the umbrella of economic independence, political sovereignty and social justice, there was room for all ideologies. However, like most of the younger generation, I thought that the movement bore the seeds of change to socialism.

4        At my home town university in Bahía Blanca, I began to get involved. Our main goal was to change the concept of universities as "islands" for scholars who were not concerned with the country's reality. As a student, I worked with others to create programs that would meet what we perceived to be the needs of the Argentine people. I was elected student government representative and was active in the Peronist Youth Movement *(Juventud Universitaria Peronista)*. One of my closest friends, Zulma "Vasca" Izurieta, who like myself majored in Literature, worked in a literacy campaign in one of the city's shanty towns. Some of my best friends were Christians who advocated Liberation Theology. The names of most of them are on lists of those who disappeared at the Little School.

5        By 1975, Peron had died, and Isabel, his third wife and Vice President, was left in charge. Unlike Evita, Isabel did not truly represent the interests of the workers. Furthermore, she handed over control of the repressive apparatus to the military. The youth movement was attacked

as a threat to our country's security. Paramilitary groups kidnapped and killed political activists with the support of the police. At the same time the Montoneros, an urban guerrilla movement within Peronism, targeted members of the Armed Forces and big factory owners who were not complying with their workers' demands. The Revolutionary People's Party (ERP), the second largest guerrilla movement, aimed at the same targets.

Finally, in March 1976, the military — along with the national oligarchy and backed by multinational corporations — launched a coup. The new junta heavily censored the media and annulled the constitution. They felt that this was the only way to control not only the youth but also the workers, whose demands for better wages and whose continuous strikes were getting out of hand.  6

Attending school became hazardous. I had to pass between two soldiers who were sitting with machine guns at the entrance of the building. A highly ranked officer would request my I.D., check it against a list of "wanted" activists and search my belongings. I did not know when my name was going to appear on that list. I stopped going to classes. But the coup triggered my rage, and I decided to become more militant. That decision meant risking my life. My daughter, Ruth, was nine months old. My answer to my own fears was that I had to work for a better society for the sake of my child's future. For almost a year I did so. I clandestinely reproduced and distributed information on the economic situation, the workers' strikes, and the repression.  7

I learned about "disappearance": the kidnapping of an individual followed by torture and secret detention, which meant that the military denied the fact that the prisoner was in their hands. I did not know that very soon I would become a disappeared person.  8

On January 12, 1977, at noon, I was detained by uniformed Army personnel at my home, Canadá Street 240, Apt. 2, Bahía Blanca; minutes later the same military personnel detained my husband at his place of work. I was taken to the headquarters of the 5th Army Corps and from there to a concentration camp, which the military ironically named the Little School (La Escuelita). We had no knowledge of the fate of Ruth, our daughter. From that moment on, for the next five months, my husband and I became two more names on the endless list of disappeared people.  9

The old house of the Little School was located behind the headquarters of the 5th Army Corps, fifteen blocks from the You and I Motel (Tü y Yo) on Carrindanga Road, a beltway. The house was near a railroad; one could hear trains, the shots fired at the army command's firing range, and the mooing of cows. I stepped off the Army truck, handcuffed and blindfolded, and by tilting my head, was able to read on the face of the house the letters A.A.A., which stood for Alianza Anticomunista Argentina, the name of the parapolice group with whom the military has since denied any relation.  10

In the Little School there were two rooms where an average of fifteen  11 prisoners remained prone, our hands bound. The floors were wood, the walls yellowing with high windows and dark green shutters and Colonial wrought iron bars. Separating these rooms was a tiled hall where the presence of a guard insured that we neither moved nor spoke. At the end of the hall were the guards' room, a kitchen and a bathroom. A door opened on the patio, where the "torture room," latrine and water tank were located. There was also a trailer where the guards slept; and later they added one or two trailers for more "disappeared" people.

12      When it rained, the water streamed into the rooms and soaked us. When the temperature fell below zero, we were covered with only dirty blankets; when the heat was unbearable, we were obligated to blanket even our heads. We were forced to remain silent and prone, often immobile or face down for many hours, our eyes blindfolded and our wrists tightly bound.

13      Lunch was at 1:00 P.M. and dinner at 7:00 P.M.; we went without food for eighteen consecutive hours daily. We were constantly hungry. I lost 20 pounds, going down to 95 pounds (I am 5 ft. 5 in.). Added to the meager food, the lack of sugar or fruits, was the constant state of stress that made our bodies consume calories rapidly. We ate our meals blindfolded, sitting on the bed, plate in lap. When we had soup or watery stew, the blows were constant because the guards insisted that we keep our plates straight. When we were thirsty, we asked for water, receiving only threats or blows in response. For talking, we were punished with blows from a billy jack, punches, or removal of our mattresses. The atmosphere of violence was constant. The guards put guns to our heads or mouths and pretended to pull the trigger.

14      On April 25, after three and a half months, the guards told me they were taking me "to see how the radishes grow"—a euphemism for death and burial. Instead, I was transferred from the Little School to another place where I remained disappeared for fifty-two more days. The living conditions were better: no blindfold, no blows, better food, a clean cell, daily showers. The isolation was complete and the risk of being killed the same. By June, 1977, my family was informed of my whereabouts. I "re-appeared" but remained a political prisoner for two and a half more years. I could see my daughter, and I knew that my husband had also survived.

15      I never discovered why the military had spared my life. My parents, who knocked at every door looking for me, might have knocked at the correct door. Yet it is also true that some of the most influential people in the country were not able to rescue their own children. My degree of involvement was not the reason for my luck either. People who participated less in politics did not survive. We were hostages and, as such, our lives were disposed of according to the needs of our captors.

16      While I was imprisoned, no charges were brought against me. Like the majority of the 7,000 political prisoners, I was held indefinitely and considered to be a threat to national security. It is estimated that over

30,000 people "disappeared" to detention centers like the Little School. Among them were over 400 children who were either kidnapped with their parents or — like Graciela's baby — born in captivity. All but a few of the disappeared still remain unaccounted for.

Human rights groups launched an international campaign denounc- 17 ing the repression in Argentina. One of these was the Mothers of Plaza de Mayo movement, an organization of mothers of disappeared people that demanded answers from the government on the whereabouts of their children. These women soon became targets of repression, and several members disappeared.

Domestic and international pressure forced the junta to free a number 18 of political prisoners. In 1979, after the Organization of American States sent a fact finding mission to Argentina, I was released and forced to leave the country. President Carter's human rights policy had also helped. Since some of us were granted U.S. visas and refugee status, the junta knew the United States wanted the release of prisoners.

By Christmas, 1979, I was taken directly from jail to the airport, 19 where I was reunited with my daughter. Some hours later we flew to the United States. My husband had come two months before.

A short time after my arrival, I started to work on behalf of the 20 remaining prisoners and the disappeared ones. I soon learned more about the widespread use of disappearance as a tool for repression in Latin America. As a survivor, I felt my duty was to help those suffering injustice.

By the middle of 1983 the dictatorship collapsed. The junta could not 21 withstand the impact of strikes, demonstrations, international pressure, a chaotic economy, and fights within the military after their defeat in the Malvinas/Falklands war. In December a democratically elected president was inaugurated.

When I went back to Argentina in the summer of 1984, lawsuits had 22 been filed against those who had taken part in the bloody repression. Hundreds of unidentified corpses were being exhumed, most of them with signs of torture. The Little School had been leveled, but the site was identified through information provided by several survivors, including myself. I testified before the judge temporarily assigned to the case of the Little School. I also testified before the Commission (CONADEP)[1] appointed to investigate disappearance. Despite overwhelming evidence, one year later only two military leaders, General Jorge Videla and Admiral Emilio Massera, have been given life sentences for their part in the disappearance of almost 30,000 people. Only three others have been convicted, and four military leaders were acquitted of all charges. The rest of the criminals enjoy freedom. It is true that a very important trial has taken place against the generals who presided over the country, the men responsible for the massive assassinations. But it is also true that not

[1]Argentine Commission for the Investigation of Disappearances

until justice is brought in cases like that of the Little School will there be a safeguard against the recurrence of these crimes in the future.

23    This past summer I met Adrianita, the daughter of Graciela and Raul. When her grandparents visited the authorites to request information about their children, this girl, then four years old, furiously pounded the table and demanded: "Sir, give me back my parents and my little brother!" Adrianita calls me Aunt. I was reunited with Vasca and Graciela's mother, who told me that even though she does not have any daughters left, she still has me. The voices of my friends at the Little School grew stronger in my memory. By publishing these stories I feel those voices will not pass unheard. I asked my mother, who is an artist, to illustrate this book. Her suffering during the years of repression has given her the tools to show this terrible reality in her powerful drawings.

24    Today, while sharing this part of my experience, I pay tribute to a generation of Argentines lost in an attempt to bring social change and justice. I also pay tribute to the victims of repression in Latin America. I knew just one Little School, but throughout our continent there are many "schools" whose professors use the lessons of torture and humiliation to teach us to lose the memories of ourselves. Beware: in little schools the boundaries between story and history are so subtle that even I can hardly find them.

*Washington D.C.*
*December, 1985*

## A Conversation under the Rain

25    This day had been different: the rain had made it different. Shortly after lunch it had begun to rain. The smell of damp earth made her come to grips with the fact that she was still alive. She inhaled deeply and a rare memory of freedom tickled her cheekbones. The open window let some rain in . . . A drop fell on her forehead, just above the blindfold, and slowly began to make its way to her heart. Her heart, hard as stone, after having shrunk to dodge anguish, finally softened. Like day-old bread soaking in water, her heart was swelling and dissolving, slowly but unavoidably . . . When she thought she was about to cry, she heard her window close.

26    The Little School was full of roof leaks; she had confirmed this while she was still in the other room, when it rained cats and dogs in January. On that day, water had fallen in buckets on the bunk beds; it had been cold. This time, on the contrary, rain was just beginning to fall. When almost as many drops had fallen as the days she had spent there, they placed cans under the leaks. The first four cans were making the sweetest music she had heard in a very long time. For a while she concentrated on figuring out the frequency of the drops: *clink . . . clonk . . . plunkplunk*

*. . . clink . . . clonkpluck . . . plunk . . . clink . . . clonk . . . plop . . .
plop . . .* Can number one was near the back window, the one that had
been boarded up. The second can was by Vasca's bed, the third was right
in the center of the room, and the fourth was probably by the door
frame. Suddenly she heard: *drip . . . drip . . . drip . . .* She stretched
out her hand and the drops found a place in her palm. She treasured five
of them in the hollow of her hand, five little pools of freshness and life
among all that dirtiness . . . She washed her hands. That contact with
water, the first in more than twenty days, made her feel as if she was also
washing away some of the bitterness that—mixed with filth—was
clinging to her skin. She used the next few drops to wet her lips.

She slept a while, lulled by the sound of the rain, dreaming of *mate*[1]      27
and *tortas fritas*[2] and windows framing gray skies that could be seen
without a blindfold on her eyes. It must have been about 6 P.M. when she
decided to wake up. They had placed a can under the leak near her bed;
she could count about eight cans but it was hard to figure out where the
new ones were. She was afraid that her blindfold was loose and thought
she'd better have it changed before the next shift. She began calling the
guard. Shortly before supper (her blindfold replaced) she cupped her
hand under the leak one more time. She remained in that position for a
long time, feeling the water slip through the lines of life and death
etched in her palm. She couldn't resist temptation:

"María Elena," she called out.                                                 28

"Yes . . ." the answer came back in a whisper.                                 29

"I own a leak."                                                                30

"Me, too."                                                                     31

The leaks had multiplied after supper.                                         32

First, they moved María Elena's bed toward hers; after a while—                33
leaks pelted her bed on all sides—they also had to move her bed. When
the guard left, she called María Elena again. Happiness filled her body
when she heard María Elena's voice only four feet from her head.

"We're very close."                                                            34

For the first time in more than two months the guards had placed her          35
next to someone else's bed. Both women's heads were facing in the same
direction. The guard had forgotten to make them lie with their heads in
opposite directions . . . perhaps it had been an intentional omission.

"Where is he?"                                                                 36

"I don't hear him."                                                            37

"I heard him leave."                                                           38

"Could we talk?"                                                               39

"I guess so, we're really close, he can't hear us."                            40

"The sound of water helps to conceal our voices . . ."                         41

"It feels like we're paying each other a social visit."                        42

---

[1]*mate:* a bitter Argentine tea.
[2]*tortas fritas:* fried pastries usually made when it rains.

43    They silently laughed, feeling comfortable in their bunk beds, and ready to enjoy some chatting. They sighed at the same time, relaxing. They laughed again. She had not been able to talk to María Elena for two days; the last time, in a rush, she had given María Elena some ideas about yoga.

44    "Could you sleep?"

45    "Yes! It was fantastic. I breathed rhythmically as you'd told me, then I was so busy noticing the muscles of my body, relaxing them and feeling them heavily sink into the mattress that for a while I even forgot where I was."

46    "What about the other problem?"

47    "I haven't menstruated yet. I'm worried. I think I'm pregnant."

48    "Don't worry, wait some more. Remember that none of us are menstruating. Vasca, for example, hasn't for five months . . . but she isn't pregnant. I don't menstruate either, and also María Angélica . . . I don't know, it's as if our bodies were protecting themselves . . ."

49    "I told the 'doctor' yesterday. He said that he'll give us all injections so we become regular, but that he'll do it the day we're sent to prison."

50    "Did he say that? Maybe they'll send us all to prison, then. Did he say anything about Benja?"

51    "Pato told me that if I wanted he would bring Benja over so I can go to bed with him."

52    "But . . . what does the guard ask for in return?"

53    "Nothing, nothing."

54    "Who else is on that shift? Bruja?"

55    "Yes, and Loro, but they don't ask for anything either . . . it's 'entertainment' they want. They'll masturbate looking at us, even if we don't do anything."

56    "So . . . what do you think?"

57    "I don't know . . . I get furious when I think that those . . . but I love Benja so much! If only we were left alone . . . Last time they brought him I didn't know what to tell him."

58    "Well, at least you could see he was doing okay . . . this time you'll have to plan what to tell him and how. You don't have to think they're watching you . . . It'll be good for him to feel you close . . . at least for five minutes. Besides, there isn't any way those jerks' filth could stain us. Our bodies might stink, but we are clean inside."

59    María Elena smiled. "You're right . . . It won't stop raining; those cans . . . so noisy! I guess this one is already filled, the drops are splashing me."

60    "I think I heard they were taking the guys outside, to bathe them under the rain . . . and with the hoses . . ."

61    "Poor boys! It's cold out there. I guess I'm going to ask them to bring Benja, so I can tell him I'm probably pregnant."

62    "It's possible that they'll bring him tomorrow, isn't it?"

63    Silence.

64    "Did you hear me?"

Silence. "María Elena?" She heard María Elena clear her throat and 65
look for her shoes under the bed. Then she knew it. She held her breath
and froze, waiting. She felt a hand like a hook on her shoulder. "Get up!
Put your slippers on."

Peine took her to the kitchen. He didn't say a word. It might have 66
been eleven at night, and it was silent at the Little School. They walked
through the iron grate and the wooden door. When they got there, Peine
ordered the other guard: "Untie her hands."

She summoned all her defenses, blocking out any speculation about 67
her fate. She did not indulge in self-pity. The hatred she felt for them
shielded her. She waited.

"Take off your clothes." 68

She stood in her underwear, her head up. She waited. 69

"All clothes off, I told you." 70

She took off the rest of her clothes. She felt as if the guards did not 71
exist, as if they were just repulsive worms that she could erase from her
mind by thinking of pleasant things . . . like rain falling inside the cans,
her conversation with María Elena. She thought the conversation had
been worth it, despite the beatings that could come, despite humiliation.
They tied her hands behind her back.

One by one, the drops on her skull were telling her a ridiculous story, 72
a story that made her laugh just because she was not allowed to laugh.
Those two killers had been glancing through the pages of an encyclopedia. On the Chinese history page, they had seen a drawing of the
Chinese torture method "the drop of water"; puzzled to see that there
still existed tortures that they had not used, they wanted to try this one to
see how it worked.

Chinese torture under a roof leak! . . . Black humor made her shield 73
thicker and more protective. Drops of water sliding down her hair damp-
ened the blindfold on her eyes. Threats and insults sliding down her
shield shattered into pieces on the kitchen floor.

She thought of little María Elena. When they first met, María Elena 74
was only fifteen. Five years older and carrying a baby in her womb, she
had become motherly with the teenagers in her theatre classes. Two
years later she was still feeling the need to protect María Elena, the girl
who had dreamt of knitting socks for the baby and had found sweet
names for it. She did not know that María Elena was involved in politics.
However, she had some hints: her way of debating in class discussions,
the kind of controversies that María Elena helped to stimulate. Her
intuition proved correct the time they had run into each other in the
street. It had been a coincidence; both of them had excuses, obviously, to
take off in a hurry for their meetings.

Underneath the roof leak she was thinking of María Elena, her brand 75
new seventeen years, her flight towards a future caught in that cage of
death. Half an hour later they untied her hands.

"Put your clothes on." 76

77     She dressed very fast, as if she had suddenly become aware of her nakedness. In the corridor that led to the iron grate, Peine kicked her roughly several times. She thought he was mad because she had neither cried nor pleaded for mercy, because she had not even trembled. She thought he was upset because in spite of the blows and restraints, in spite of the filth and torture, both women had had that long and warm conversation under the rain.

# Evaluating the Text

## "INTRODUCTION"

1. How is the introduction organized as a retrospective analysis of Partnoy's experiences?
2. Based on her account, what factors proved most influential in changing her from an apolitical teenager into an activist? What role did Perónism play in her transformation? How did the treatment to which she was subjected as a university student change her outlook?
3. Why is the unusual phrase "disappeared" invariably used to refer to political prisoners in Argentina? How does this label accurately describe the circumstances Partnoy herself encountered?
4. What details in Partnoy's description of her confinement did you find the most significant (e.g., the physical environment, being blindfolded all the time, the kinds of food the prisoners received, how often and for what offenses the prisoners were beaten) in terms of how you yourself would have reacted if you were in her position?
5. What insight did you gain as to why Partnoy was ultimately released? Which of the possibilities she mentions appears to you to have been the most likely reason?
6. How does Partnoy's dissatisfaction with the outcome of her testimony before the Argentine Commission for the Investigation of Disappearances explain why she wrote *The Little School?*

## "A CONVERSATION UNDER THE RAIN"

7. How does Partnoy let the reader hear the "voices" of those who, in many cases, did not survive to tell their stories? How effective do you find "A Conversation under the Rain" in serving to document the kinds of abuses that occurred under the dictatorship of the Argentine generals?
8. What specific details of her imprisonment described in the "Introduction" are evident in "A Conversation under the Rain"? How does the different perspective from which they are seen change how Partnoy presents them? Select one or two of these details (e.g., "in the Little School there were two rooms where an average of 15 prisoners remained prone, our hands bound"), and compare how they reemerge, altered by the narrator's restricted circumstances.
9. What factors contribute to the feeling of fear and paranoia that the narrator experiences? For example, for what kinds of things can a prisoner be beaten? Why are prisoners responsible for notifying the guards if their blindfolds become loose?

10. What details tell you how important the ability to communicate with fellow prisoners becomes after months of being blindfolded and savagely punished for speaking?
11. How is everything the guards do designed to dehumanize the prisoners? For example, what is their attitude toward letting a husband and wife sleep together?
12. What conclusions does the narrator reach about the mental capacity of her guards when they decide to employ the Chinese water torture? How does the feeling she has about them enable her to create a protective mental barrier between herself and the guards, so that being forced to strip off all her clothes, or being beaten, does not crush her spririt?
13. Why is it so important that the narrator is able to remember her past relationship with María Elena?
14. Discuss different possible meanings suggested by the title "A Conversation under the Rain." For example, consider the different kinds of "conversations" she has (with María Elena, with her captors) and the different ways "rain" is perceived by guards and prisoners.

## Exploring Different Perspectives

1. A comparison of Partnoy's account with that of Armando Valladares in "A Nazi Prison in the Caribbean" reveals striking similarities and a number of differences. Compare these two accounts with respect to how the prisoners were treated, the relative sophistication of their respective inquisitors, the respective goals of each regime with regard to political prisoners (keeping in mind that one is fascist and the other is communist), and the extent to which each regime wished to reveal or conceal what was going on from the public and humanitarian organizations like the International Red Cross and Amnesty International. Why is so much of what goes on in both prisons designed to isolate the prisoners from each other?
2. What insight does Partnoy's account provide in illustrating the difference between punishment for political beliefs and punishment designed to achieve "reeducation," when compared with the accounts of Someth May in Cambodia ("The Field Behind the Village") and Valladares in Cuba ("A Nazi Prison in the Caribbean")?

## Extending Viewpoints through Writing

1. What is the effect of Partnoy telling her story in the third person as if she were speaking about an unnamed "she"? Might this way of relating the experiences have allowed her to be more objective about events that otherwise would have been too traumatic to relive? To understand how telling her story in the first person would produce a different effect on the reader, rewrite one paragraph in the first person (substituting "I" for "she"). What differences result from this change in point of view? Which version do you find more effective?
2. If you have ever been politically active on your campus, discuss how the way you were treated (by teachers, fellow students, or members of the administration) changed, if at all, as a result.

3. As a research project, you might investigate the role Amnesty International has played in securing the release of political prisoners all over the world. You might also wish to research the activities of the Mothers of Plaza de Mayo (an organization consisting of mothers of children who "disappeared") in Argentina.
4. If you have seen the film *The Official Story* (1985), how did Partnoy's account clarify aspects of the film about which you might have had some questions?

# Samir al-Khalil

# *Authority*

---

Samir Al-Khali *is a pseudonym adopted to protect the writer's family against reprisals. "Authority" originally appeared in* Republic of Fear *(1989), an insider's view of the nightmare of living in Iraq under the savage dictatorship of Saddam Hussein.*

*Modern-day Iraq is located where the first great civilization, Mesopotamia, appeared after 4000 B.C. in the region between the Tigris and Euphrates rivers. Before the Arab conquest in the seventh century A.D., this was the site of many flourishing civilizations, including the Sumerians, Assyrians, and Babylonians. After the British invaded Iraq in World War I, the country became a League of Nations mandate under British administration and was governed as a kingdom under the monarchy of Faisal I. After the termination of the British mandate in 1932, Iraq became an independent state and joined the Arab League. The domestic politics of Iraq have been turbulent as the country experienced a score of military coups between 1936 and 1958, when the monarchy was overthrown by General Abdul Kassem, who was later himself overthrown and executed in 1963. Iraq's domestic situation was aggravated by Kurdish demands for an autonomous region in northern Iraq. The Nationalist Ba'ath Party came to power in Iraq in the wake of the Arab defeat in the Six Day War against Israel in 1967. Saddam Hussein rose to power in 1979 as the leader of the Ba'ath Party and the head of state. Iraq's continuing dispute with Iran over the strategic Shatt Al-'Arab waterway erupted in 1980 into a full-scale war that was to last for eight years and claim over one million lives from both sides. On August 3, 1990, Iraqi troops invaded Kuwait and took over the country, a move that prompted the United States and other countries, including several Arab states, to impose economic sanctions and send one-half million troops into neighboring Saudi Arabia, to forestall any Iraqi expansion into that country. When the deadline (January 15, 1991) set by the United Nations for an unconditional Iraqi withdrawal from Kuwait passed, allied forces launched Operation Desert Storm. Less than six weeks later, Kuwait was liberated from Iraqi occupation.*

---

*(For more information on the War in Iraq, see pp. 676–681.)

# The Leader Syndrome

1　Portraits of leaders signify power in the Middle East. But these are rarely as big and varied as in Ba'thist Iraq. A large painted cutout figure of Saddam Husain[1] towers over the entrance of every Iraqi village; often at night it emits a lurid fluorescent glow. A thirty-foot high version can be seen near Baghdad city center. Photographs adorn every shop, school, police station, army barracks, and public building, and can be seen in people's offices and living rooms and overhanging the streets from the parapets of houses. No official will appear before a camera without a picture of the president in the background, and his name is evoked in every public address.

2　Saddam is president of the republic, chairman of the Council of Ministers, commander in chief of the armed forces, chairman of the RCC, general secretary of the Regional Command of the ABSP, chairman of the Supreme Planning Council, chairman of the Committee on Agreements, chairman of the Supreme Agricultural Council, and chairman of the Supreme Council for the Compulsory Eradication of Illiteracy, among other things. In addition to these party and state functions, an impressive array of honorific titles and forms of address include the leader-president, the leader-struggler, the standard bearer, the Arab leader, the knight of the Arab nation, the hero of national liberation, the father leader (previously held by al-Bakr), and the daring and aggressive knight (al-faris al-mighwar).

3　On radio, in a typical political broadcast, his name is mentioned thirty to fifty times an hour, along with reams of titles suited to the occasion.[2] News broadcasts shower him with congratulatory telegrams and grovelling speeches. The streets of Baghdad grind to a halt whenever he leaves the presidential palace; sirens go off, soldiers line the route, and busy people rush to the public squares to see him pass. School children memorize verses in his honour, praising his qualities. Slogans attributed to him are visible everywhere. School notebooks carry his portrait on the front and his latest sayings on the back. Iraqi teenagers wear Saddam Husain T-shirts, and the real enthusiast can buy a gold wristwatch with Saddam Husain peering through the dials.[3]

4　Following a coup in the Middle East, the pictures disappear as instantly as the reality behind the shift in power. By the late 1970s this could no longer be said of Ba'thist Iraq, where the imagery is so much more orchestrated. The concern now is with making a completely different statement about power. When Ahmad Hasan al-Bakr was purged in

---

[1] A variant spelling of Hussein [Editor's note].
[2] This count was done by A. Hottinger, "Personality Cult and Party in Iraq," *Swiss Review of World Affairs* (June 1984): 12.
[3] On T-shirts, see *Christian Science Monitor*, July 20, 1984. A blow-up of a Saddam wristwatch is displayed in the pictorial, "The New Face of Baghdad," *National Geographic* 167, no. 1 (January 1985).

1979, his photographs were slowly phased out, while Saddam's were gradually built up. Al-Bakr's photographs in a handful of standard poses used to appear by themselves in the first years of the second Ba'thi regime; around the mid-1970s they hung alongside those of Saddam Husain. By the summer of 1982 they were withdrawn completely from circulation. No painted thirty-foot cutouts were ever made of al-Bakr, much less a statue in every village. When Iraqis saw the pictures of al-Bakr after 1979, and heard that he was still being referred to as "a father to Saddam Husain," they knew the son had been true to his 1977 speech; he had informed on his "father" but with all the proper deference and respect.[4]

In this way Iraqis learned to become more afraid of Saddam Husain 5 as they looked at the picture of Ahmad Hasan al-Bakr and reflected on their loss of authority over their children. The political reality behind all the photographs and appearances is the power of fear. Very soon the same people were "choosing" to surround themselves with pictures of Saddam Husain in their homes and offices, hoping in this way to "ward off evil." This is how it looks at first sight, on the surface. Once people stop saying things in front of their children, and even encourage them in their spoon-fed enthusiasm for the Great Leader, things become less clear. Raw power lording it over civil society has been turned into a new kind of authority, one that rules inside each soul. No longer merely signified, this authority is expressed as so omniscient and absolute that it intended the humiliation of everyone: making them do, say, and begin to believe things are other than what they really are.

The new Leader heaps contempt and disdain even upon those who 6 surround him. In conferences and public assemblies attended by Saddam Husain, the most powerful men of the country can usually be seen with folded hands, peering down at the ground, or applauding him harder than anyone else. Ministers do not turn their backs on Saddam when leaving the room; they shuffle out sideways, inconspicuously. In a party-political videotape, made after the start of the Iraq-Iran war, a scene is shown of Saddam Husain humiliating a group of sheepish-looking ministers and party bureaucrats. They are being hauled over the coals for not having enthusiastically volunteered for the front trenches, an omission they hastily proceeded to rectify. The tape was given a limited release to pep up party loyalists on Ba'thi egalitarianism in warfare. But it had to be quickly withdrawn after it began circulating in the Gulf and the Ba'th realized they had made a terrible mistake. The mistake is as revealing as the tape, because the moral is that in the fictional world of Ba'thism, an emperor who has no clothes can forget his condition when he ventures outside.

[4]Saddam Husain maintained that Ahmad Hasan al-Bakr was like a father to him. In the summer of 1981, RCC member Taha Yasin Ramadhan was still referring to Saddam as being a son to Bakr. See the interview with Christine Moss Helms, *Iraq: Eastern Flank of the Arab World* (Washington, D.C.: The Brookings Institution, 1984), 95.

7        All the pictures, big cutouts, and film clips work for a reason; when not present, ridicule takes over from fear. The problem is to understand this reason. Ideology as mythmaking exists at the heart of Ba'thism, both as a movement and in power. Fictional goals and ideals about the future are axiomatic in the present and self-defining to every militant. Normally these are screened by rituals of membership and a hierarchy of degrees of commitment through sympathizers to the mass organizations and finally to the remains of a less organized population within whom can be found degrees of subservience, neutrality, and opposition to Ba'thism. In such a mediated and graduated environment, the inner sanctum of total fiction is rarely perceived as such, being buffered by layers of people whose location in the hierarchy generates confidence in the layers below and provides a small window on reality to those above. Ba'thism grew in this way as an opposition movement and set out to organize society along the same lines once it took power.[5]

8        Larger-than-life leadership originates in sweeping social control administered by the party political organization. The party is only superficially at variance with its Leader for having been supplanted in its vanguard role. As soon as the party ceases to compete in the political arena because all opposition has been consumed by it (the outcome of how sweeping its social control really is), the two functions previously housed within — generation of ideology and the organization of members — tend towards separate identities. The whole of society is in principle being routinely organized by the party; the vision that led an individual into the party when competing world views were at stake has its charisma threatened by routinism, drudgery, administration patronage, and personal incompetence.

9        The tendency for the original vision to become the substance of politics is matched, therefore, by a countervailing tendency for it to preserve itself by receding away from the mass of party members in the direction of ever more removed and secretive bodies. The mark of the emerging separation is that the original vision, along with its interpretation (politics), is now the domain of the secret police. That most dreaded of all institutions judges everybody and everything in relation to this vision and, in the absence of opposition, administers and monitors the masses' conformity with it. The relationship of the secret police to the person of the Leader is absolutely crucial to a regime like the Ba'th; not only do these agencies always report directly to him, but his rise invariably originates in them.

10       The Leader at this point appears to be taking over from the party political organization; in fact, a new division of labour is emerging between them, which artificially replicates the distinction between civil society and the state. The vision whose original purity was bound to be

[5]Hannah Arendt has analysed this phenomenon with striking brilliance in *The Origins of Totalitarianism* (New York: Harcourt Brace and Jovanovich, 1973), 364–88.

tainted by the spread of the party's elephantine organization is now swaddled up in the terrifying aura of omniscient "presence" associated with the secret police. The separation reinforces the social weight of the party and its overall bureaucratic efficiency, making it more "rational." All political charisma can now be located in the person of the Leader. One's colleague or boss can be criticized for insufficient loyalty to the party when he shows up late for work because such criticism (like all public forms of "self"-criticism) no longer introduces wrinkles into the world of the party line, and what the Leader said or did not say. Before the separation it was harder to ask such questions because these instantly took on a "political" character, threatening the fictional core of the party and jeopardizing the organization.

To be such a Leader, the part must be well acted out. Authority is not 11 in the form of "pure" Weberian charisma, rooted in personal attributes like extraordinary heroism or revelatory powers; it is rehearsed, staged, and elaborately organized. Charisma is indissolubly bound up with bureaucratic organization. The Leader's image must be at least as ubiquitous as his secret police, but in contrast to the hidden presence of agents and informers, it must be visible, solid, and overpowering.

In October 1983 new images of Saddam Husain disappeared from 12 the media. Sources within the Iraqi government confirmed that an attempted coup had taken place, led by the head of Intelligence, Saddam's half-brother, Barazan al-Takriti. Months later Arab diplomats dismissed the initial reports, claiming there had been a family quarrel between the two men over Saddam's daughter's choice of fiancé. The president himself appeared to confirm this new interpretation in a news interview around the same time when he said his ousted half-brother was "not a plotter" and "no conspirator."[6] What was going on?

No one apart from Saddam Husain himself knew in 1983, or knows 13 today, what if anything actually happened. More important, no one could find out even if they were foolish enough to try. This precondition makes the affair serve Saddam's absolutism, as opposed to undermining it. The signal to the masses that something was going on, or that they were supposed to start thinking that something was going on, was the disappearance of fresh images of the Leader from the news media. This was all the "proof" needed for whatever story Saddam Husain wished to concoct. Earlier conspiracies, the reader will remember, required a considerably larger dosage of "proofs" to achieve the same politically stabilizing effect. By 1983 Iraqis had become more gullible — that is, less political — than they were in 1969 – 70. It is quite wrong to think that "all of this can have happened only under pressure from high-ranking military officers."[7] Even perceptive and highly critical commentators fail to

[6] For the first interpretation that a coup attempt had been foiled, see the report in *The Times*, October 27, 1983. For the new interpretation of a year later, see the *Christian Science Monitor*, July 20, 1984.
[7] This is Hottinger's interpretation of the incident ("Personality Cult," 15).

appreciate just how bizarre is the form of government that has arisen in Iraq.

14    Saddam's appearances on television lasting several hours a day in various guises are masterpieces of calculated duplicity. Only when we impose the criteria of the outside do we fail to see the deadening impact on the mind of this continuous flow of images. The propaganda is so "bad" that even some Iraqis will pretend to dismiss it; yet they bring their children up to applaud it. Imagine endlessly varied film clips of Saddam Husain in local Arab attire one day and Kurdish dress the next. Picture him crouching around trenches in camouflage fatigues, standing erect in full parade uniform, embracing foreign dignitaries at the airport in the latest Pierre Cardin suit, handling machinery, reading the Qur'an, meeting Shi'ite religious notables, opening new buildings, giving lectures on architecture and the environment, looking grim, smiling, berating officials, sucking Cuban cigars, fondling babies, dropping in on "unsuspecting" citizens for breakfast, as a family man, and reviewing the latest captured military hardware. Saddam Husain had his family tree issued to the public; it traced his roots to 'Ali, the fourth caliph and patron imam of Shi'ism.[8] 'Ali was related to the prophet of course, but the tree does not make this last link in order to underline the political point of the whole exercise, and leave a little something to the imagination. This gesture was not made in weakness, or as an attempt by Saddam to ingratiate himself with Shi'is at a time of their regional activism. On the contrary it signified total contempt for the populace, large numbers of whom he knew would accept this proof of ancestry, largely because there was no longer a soul in the length and breadth of the country who could be heard if they were prepared to deny it.

15    Subjection to Ba'thist propaganda and organization over an extended period left the populace as cynical as it had become gullible. Politics in a country like Iraq is invariably associated with cheating and lying. This union of cynicism and gullibility begins to appear everywhere in society. No one has expressed it better than Arendt:

> In an ever-changing, incomprehensible world the masses had reached the point where they would, at the same time, believe everything and nothing, think that everything was possible and that nothing was true. . . . Mass propaganda discovered that its audience was ready at all times to believe the worst, no matter how absurd, and did not particularly object to being deceived because it held every statement to be a lie anyhow. The totalitarian mass leaders based their propaganda on the correct psychological assumption that, under such conditions, one could make people believe the most fantastic statements one day, and trust

[8] The tree is reproduced in his semiofficial biography. See Amir Iskander, *Saddam Husain: Munadhilan, wa Mufakiran wa Insanan* (Paris: Hachette, 1981), 21.

that if the next day they were given irrefutable proof of their falsehood, they would take refuge in cynicism; instead of deserting the leaders who had lied to them, they would protest that they had known all along that the statement was a lie and would admire the leaders for their superior tactical cleverness.[9]

Like infallibility, which is continually tested and reaffirmed through the pervasive recycling of lies, the Leader's omnipotence is acted out dramatically, as though performed on a stage. Favours are bestowed on people in such a way as to break the very rules the Leader's state enforces; he opens a hot line to the citizens at a fixed hour in order to listen to complaints, and follows this up by releasing someone's husband or son from a life sentence that his police had originally imposed; he hands out television sets and wads of freshly minted notes while touring villages in the south; and he drops in on apparently unsuspecting humble citizens to have breakfast and listen to their complaints. In all of this his freedom to act, even to break his own rules, is intentionally pitted against everyone else's profound unfreedom. The effect, however, is not to highlight the latter, but to confound it with the former. [16]

The combination of all-pervasive organization and a closed ideological system, in which reasons for everything "float" magically in relation to the objectivity of the world, produces not only a stable polity (while the Leader is alive) but also citizens who feel extremely fragile. Doomed to teeter on the edge of a precipice, they are possessed by the need for a safety line of some sort. Hero worship of the Great Leader variety presents itself as such a safeguard. The heroes that do not exist in reality have to be clutched at in the imagination. This has now become possible (even necessary) because an individual's freedom has become so totally fused with the nation's sovereignty, which is only real because of the Leader's absolute freedom. Just as sovereignty is indivisible and singular, so too must personal freedom conform to the nation's dictate and adopt these attributes. The notion of freedom as a political condition that only exists because of the capacity of human beings to be different, to be in a minority, and not have to think the same deathly "free" thoughts is absent in Iraqi society. When it arose in the modern era, it was snuffed out, first by the growing ideological hegemony of pan-Arabism and later by the social organization of the second Ba'thi regime. The absence not only of freedom, but also of the very *idea* of this kind of freedom, makes Saddam Husain's role-playing so effective. [17]

The separation between organization and the generation of ideology taking place in the emergence of the Leader corresponds to a growing loss of identity on the part of the public. The original distinction in reality and definitionally between any public and those who rule over it was being erased in Iraq. Pervasive fear and insecurity resulted in a collapse [18]

[9] Arendt, *The Origins*, 382.

of self-confidence. To the extent that society was successfully organized along Ba'thist lines (and only to that extent), this fundamental boundary between ruler and ruled was torn down, and the Iraqi public lost its most important safeguard against the vagaries of authority. The masses' need for a leader correspondingly intensified as it took the form of a longing for that which they had allowed to be taken away from them.

19      The outcome can actually be seen in the physical appearance of a large number of Iraqi men, in their mannerisms, dress, mustache styles, and even some of their acquired character traits. The greater the pervasiveness of this manufactured aura of leadership, the more it is surrounded by fear and awe and the more it gets identified with the original vision of the party, not as this manifests itself in party platforms, but as the vision is now crystallized in the dreams of one man. Saddam Husain can now say anything with impunity. He can expostulate on the virtues of 'Ali, pray like a Shi'ite, and even espouse a new-found Iraqi patriotism. Unlike outsiders, the mass of Iraqis have not been duped into this stance; they have arrived at it by coming to believe in their own utter political worthlessness after having also experienced the same. Now the very phenomenon of Saddam Husain has about it the air of an "iron necessity" if the fragmentation and backwardness of the past is to be overcome.

20      As constitutions, laws, government departments, and routine procedures come and go, and as edicts continuously shower down from those on high with the most improbable and unpredictable implications on daily and personal affairs, the reality of the political edifice continuously slips out of the public's reach. Even in dealing with government departments or one's colleagues, things are never what they seem; the janitor may command more real power than the boss. A new directive does not have to have reasons for existing in the public mind, and reflecting on what they might be, even to oneself, would only distract from accepting the directive for what it is: an emanation of the will of the Leader, that one irreducible and solid fact from which the ephemerality of all the rest can be organized in the imagination. From all of this springs the oneness of identity between the public and its Leader created by *total* organization and the impossibility of achieving the same through populism or mere military dictatorship, no matter how brutal.

21      Even the most popular Third World leaders never commanded such a death-grip on their image and status as leaders. Thus, whereas Nasser's leadership was greatly tarnished by the magnitude of the 1967 defeat, the Egyptian public remained intact, demonstrating this to itself and to those who had defeated it by tossing back into office this ghost of the hero that once had been. Soon, this same self-assured public made the impossible—a peace treaty with Israel—possible, and even desirable as shown by the hundreds of thousands that came to greet Sadat upon his return from Jerusalem. It is simply unimaginable that an Iraqi defeat in the Iraq-Iran war would have remotely comparable consequences.

Unlike Nasser, the phenomenon of Saddam Husain does not arise       22
from personal accomplishments; it originates in his relation to the party.
Saddam emerged as Leader while lacking some of Nasser's greatest
assets: his personal magnetism, powers of oratory, sense of diplomacy
and political timing, and most important "his" Suez.[10] Nonetheless, it
takes a very special kind of person to become Saddam Husain's kind of
Leader.

Ironically, the Suez watershed in Arab politics first brought the       23
young Saddam into the Iraqi branch of the Ba'th party while still a
teenage secondary-school student. Shortly after joining, Saddam ("the
one who confronts") made his mark by assassinating a prominent Qassem supporter in his hometown of Takrit. The party leadership subsequently selected him as a member of the hit team that tried to assassinate
Qassem in 1959. The myth and the man merge in this episode. His
biography — and Iraqi television, which stages the story ad nauseam —
tells of his familiarity with guns from the age of ten; his fearlessness and
loyalty to the party during the 1959 operation; his bravery in saving his
comrades by commandeering a car at gunpoint; the bullet that was
gouged out of his flesh under his direction in hiding; the iron discipline
that led him to draw a gun on weaker comrades who would have
dropped off a seriously wounded member of the hit team at a hospital;
the calculating shrewdness that helped him save himself minutes before the police broke in leaving his wounded comrades behind; and
finally the long trek of a wounded man from house to house, from city to
town, across the desert to refuge in Syria.[11]

Saddam Husain, the quintessential professional militant, had no per-       24
sonal or working life outside the party. Even his years in secondary
school and college were immersed in political activity. His lack of military training sets him apart from so many other militant youth of his
generation (although his political vocabulary is permeated with military
metaphors). The pent-up violence in the man's personal makeup was
always controlled and directed by a political sense of judgement. The
Ba'thi traditions in which he was immersed were originally applied to the
new problems of consolidation, elimination of opponents, and organiza-

---

[10] Saddam Husain understood that his relation to the party was the basis of the differences
between himself and Nasser. In December 1978 he had this conversation with Castro:

   *Castro*: Time works in favor of Iraq, because you are developing the country as a
   whole, you are mobilizing the masses. This was not done in Egypt.
   *Saddam*: There was no revolutionary party in Egypt; there was only 'Abd al-
   Nasir. He was a revolutionary, but his conditions differed from yours [i.e., Cuba's].
   You created revolutionaries before you came to power; this 'Abd al-Nasir did not
   do. In Iraq, we created revolutionaries before taking power . . . the party gave
   sacrifices and martyrs and suffered imprisonment and torture. All of this was
   indispensable in order to forge revolutionaries who know how to hold on to the
   revolution." From Iskander, *Saddam Husain*, 214.

[11] The lurid details are in ibid, chap. 3–7.

tion of a new Iraqi social order. Saddam Husain, unlike Idi Amin or Papa Doc, is marked by this calculated, disciplined, and above all effortless resort to violence genuinely conceived to be in the service of more exalted aims. His language is therefore a reflection of his personality — as opposed to professional training — in which violence and vision, through party organization, got distilled into a volatile mixture.

25      Such men are feared, not loved; above all they command enormous respect in a populace to whom strength of character is invariably associated with the ability to both sustain and inflict pain. The madness inherent in the elevation of raw violence to such a status in the affairs of human beings appears as such only from the outside; from within respect, no matter how grudgingly bestowed, eventually gives way to awe. Promoted by the organizational omnipotence of the party and the preeminence of fear in people's daily lives, such awe accentuates individual feelings of utter helplessness and worthlessness. The size of the gap between awe and worthlessness is a measure of the Leader's infallibility in the eyes of his followers, a perception that follows from their loss of identity and defencelessness brought on by the dissolution of all moral norms that are not those of the Ba'th. The public's ability to judge what is right or wrong about its affairs, what is real as opposed to mere illusion, has broken down completely.

26      The rise of Saddam Husain signifies the fulfillment of a logic in Ba'thism that had almost been choked off by the party's long-standing love-hate relationship with the military. Ideologically the Ba'th were inimically hostile to military rule, but the founding leaders had toyed with using the military to gain power. In view of the attraction that pan-Arabism has always exerted among officer elites, the combination (which overwhelmed the Syrian branch) had on several occasions threatened the entire existence of the party in its original form. The legacy of Saddam Husain is that he kept alive that original purist content in Ba'thism by realizing it in one country. He held the military at bay while cutting away at their power base, and eventually he transformed them into creatures of the party that had nurtured him and that had been the obsession of his entire mature life.

27      This rise took place at the expense of other leaders in the RCC. The July 1979 purge was a blow against the political authority of the party only in the sense that it completed the transfer of its ideology-generating, politics-making, and charismatic functions into his person; the rest of the party's organizing function remained intact. It therefore clarified an ambiguity that existed in the formal status of the RCC as the highest decision-making authority in the land, despite the fact that Saddam Husain had actually been in control of all real power for many years now. This ambiguity tainted Ba'thism as much as the party's organization of society tended to do, because just as no two people can tell a lie or keep a secret as well as one, so too no plurality of men can ever be as good an embodiment of a fictional essence — or a sovereign "general

will" — as one man. With this last impediment out of the way, the stage was set for the will of the Leader to be ipso facto that of the party leadership, the party organization, and society as a whole. The freedom of all was now completely coincident with the absolutely unfettered freedom of Saddam Husain. At this crucial point it became possible for Ba'thi violence, hitherto contained within Iraqi confines, to spill over into a great war with the least chance of a split in the party's own ranks and hence in the loyalties of the masses.

Saddam Husain as a phenomenon goes beyond the Ba'th party and the extent of its organization of Iraqi society. He has become the personification of what that same public perceives to be its own "Iraqi" character. [28]

# Evaluating the Text

1. What is the significance of the many pictures of Saddam Hussein (ranging from notebook-sized to 30-foot-high billboard-sized cutouts) that are omnipresent throughout Iraq?
2. How do citizens in Iraq come to depend on the appearance or disappearance of public figures in these pictures as a way of discovering who is gaining or losing power at any given moment? That is, how do these pictures act as a type of code communicating political messages to citizens?
3. Explain the distinction that al-Khalil draws between external brainwashing and the internalization of these beliefs. How does this help explain Saddam Hussein's rise to power through fear?
4. What can you infer about Hussein's control of Iraqi society even down through the family level from the reference to a son informing on the "father"?
5. How has Hussein managed to create a nation of citizens who have so little confidence in their ability to rule their own lives that they must of necessity depend on him for everything? What role has fear played in creating this state?
6. What connection exists between the fact that Hussein rose to power through a secular B'ath movement and the fact that all other Arab nations are ruled by royal families or are religious states? How is the secular nature of the Iraqi government related to the psychological needs Hussein fills for the Iraqi people? How might these same needs be met by other Arab governments?
7. How does the omission of the last link in Hussein's family tree illustrate the power he has to redefine reality? In what way is this related to al-Khalil's point that Iraqi life is based on the assumption that Hussein's absolute freedom is predicated on the profound lack of freedom of every Iraqi citizen?
8. Why is it significant that a large number of Iraqi men affect the same mannerisms, dress, and moustache styles as Hussein?
9. How does Hussein differ from Gamal Abdul Nassar in terms of the emotions each elicited from those they ruled?

10. *Samir al-Khalil* is a pseudonym used by an Iraqi writer who fears reprisals were he to write under his own name. What can you infer about him from reading "Authority" in terms of his background, level of education, political ideology, and so on, and what can you infer about his audience?

11. In al-Khalil's view, how does the hierarchical structure of the B'ath party insulate those at the top from reality?

12. Why is the 1959 episode significant, and how has Hussein used it to promote his larger-than-life image?

## Exploring Different Perspectives

1. Compare and contrast the regimes of Saddam Hussein and Fidel Castro after reading Armando Valladares's account ("A Nazi Prison in the Caribbean"). How are political crimes defined in both societies, and how do both regimes depend on larger-than-life images of the leader? Would Hussein's regime attach the same importance as Castro's to reforming political dissidents? Why or why not? How does the way the B'ath party came to power differ from Castro's Communist revolution? How might this difference explain the role of fear versus love in creating allegiance among followers?

2. How do both al-Khalil's account and Slawomir Mrożek's story, "The Elephant," illustrate differences in regimes that manipulate reality? How might you explain the difference in tone between the two readings and the different attitudes of the authors toward their subjects?

3. Compare al-Khalil's analysis with Chen Jo-hsi's story, "The Big Fish." What insight do you gain into the way totalitarian regimes permeate every sphere of society and even politicize personal relationships at the level of the family?

4. Discuss how fear is used to control citizens, as described in both this account and in Someth May's account ("The Field behind the Village") of living under the Communist Khmer Rouge regime in Cambodia.

## Extending Viewpoints through Writing

1. Can you think of other examples of a charismatic leader who seems to embody the hopes and dreams of the state? How has Hussein, according to al-Khalil, achieved the authority that goes with this condition without having those personal virtues that would seem to be the precondition for being viewed in this way?

2. Discuss any current development in the news concerning Iraq, drawing on the insights you have gained from reading al-Khalil's analysis. In what way did "Authority" enhance your understanding of anything reported about Saddam Hussein in the news?

3. If you have read George Orwell's *1984* (1949), in what respects do Hussein's rise to power and methods of control resemble those used by "Big Brother" in Orwell's novel?

4. Al-Khalil, Armando Valladares ("A Nazi Prison in the Caribbean"); Shen Tong ("Bloody Sunday in Tiananmen Square"); Someth May ("The Field behind the Village"); and Alicia Partnoy ("The Little School: Tales of

Disappearance and Survival in Argentina'') all show people who have withstood years of imprisonment, fear, and even physical torture and who are willing to die for their beliefs. Is there an idea or belief that is so important to you that you would be prepared to undergo any of these experiences to defend it? Put yourself in any of the situations the writers describe, and discuss as honestly as you can if you think you could endure the pressures brought to bear against you.

5. How does the following account of Dr. Yihya Mohamad Ahmad, a physician working in a hospital in Kuwait that was occupied by invading Iraqi troops (reported in Jean P. Sasson's *The Rape of Kuwait*, 1991), confirm al-Khalil's observations as to the psychological role Saddam Hussein's photos play in maintaining a mood of fear in areas under his control, which at this point included Kuwait:

Yihya came close to death over the photo of Saddam Hussein. The first day, the Iraqi soldiers had ripped the photos of the Emir and the Crown Prince of Kuwait off the walls and replaced them with the photo of Saddam Hussein. Yihya smiles when he recalls the writings under the photo of Saddam: "Saddam Hussein, Hero of War and Peace and Extraordinary Leader." Yihya and his colleagues tried to ignore the obnoxious photo. Apparently they succeeded, for they did not even notice when the photo was removed by some unknown Kuwaiti patriot. The Iraqis noticed. They rushed into the physicians' lounge and held Yihya and his colleagues at gunpoint, threatening to kill them all if they did not point out the guilty party. Innocent of the knowledge the Iraqis were seeking, the doctors barely managed to convince the soldiers that they were telling the truth. Finally, the Iraqis lowered their guns, but told the doctors in no uncertain terms that they would all die should Hussein's photo be removed again. From that moment the hospital staff tried to keep a close watch on Hussein's photo; they knew the Iraqis would keep their word.

# Ngũgĩ wa Thiong'o

# *Decolonising the Mind*

---

*Ngũgĩ wa Thiong'o is regarded as one of the most important contemporary writers on the African continent. He wrote his first novels,* Weep Not, Child *(1964) and* The River Between *(1965), in English, and* Caitaani Mũtharava-Ini *(translated as* Devil on the Cross, *1982) in his native language, Gĩkũyũ. He was chairman of the department of literature at the University of Nairobi, until his detention without trial by the Kenyan authorities in 1977, an account of which appeared under the title* Detained: A Writer's Prison Diary *(1981). The international outcry over his imprisonment eventually produced his release. This selection is drawn from* Decolonising the Mind: The Politics of Language in African Literature *(1986), a work that constitutes, says Ngũgĩ, "my farewell to English as a vehicle for any of my writings." Subsequently, he has written novels and plays in Gĩkũyũ.*

*Kenya is a republic in East Africa. Discoveries by anthropologists and archaeologists in the Great Rift Valley in Kenya have unearthed remains of what may be the earliest known humans, believed to be some two million years old. German missionaries were the first Europeans to make their way into Kenya in 1844, making contact with the then-ruling Maasai (for more background on the Maasai, see p. 115) and Kĩkũyũ tribes. The Imperial British East Africa Company wrested political control from Germany, and Kenya became a British protectorate in 1890 and a Crown Colony in 1920. Increasingly violent confrontations between European settlers and the Kĩkũyũs reached a crisis in the 1950s during the terror campaign of the Mau Mau rebellion. In response, the British declared a state of emergency, which was not lifted until 1960.*

*Originally a leader of the Mau Mau uprising, Jomo Kenyatta became Kenya's first president in 1964, on the first anniversary of Kenya's independence, and served until his death in 1978. Continuing opposition and unrest prompted Kenyatta's government to imprison political dissidents, including Ngũgĩ wa Thiong'o.*

*Black Africans of forty different ethnic groups make up 97 percent of the population. The official languages are Swahili and English. The situation described by Thiong'o has changed to the extent that children are now taught in their native languages for the first three years of school, after which instruction is exclusively in English.*

I was born into a large peasant family: father, four wives and about twenty-eight children. I also belonged, as we all did in those days, to a wider extended family and to the community as a whole.

We spoke Gĩkũyũ as we worked in the fields. We spoke Gĩkũyũ in and outside the home. I can vividly recall those evenings of story-telling around the fireside. It was mostly the grown-ups telling the children but everybody was interested and involved. We children would re-tell the stories the following day to other children who worked in the fields picking the pyrethrum flowers, tea-leaves or coffee beans of our European and African landlords.

The stories, with mostly animals as the main characters, were all told in Gĩkũyũ. Hare, being small, weak but full of innovative wit and cunning, was our hero. We identified with him as he struggled against the brutes of prey like lion, leopard, hyena. His victories were our victories and we learnt that the apparently weak can outwit the strong. We followed the animals in their struggle against hostile nature — drought, rain, sun, wind — a confrontation often forcing them to search for forms of co-operation. But we were also interested in their struggles amongst themselves, and particularly between the beasts and the victims of prey. These twin struggles, against nature and other animals, reflected real-life struggles in the human world.

Not that we neglected stories with human beings as the main characters. There were two types of characters in such human-centred narratives: the species of truly human beings with qualities of courage, kindness, mercy, hatred of evil, concern for others; and a man-eat-man two-mouthed species with qualities of greed, selfishness, individualism and hatred of what was good for the larger co-operative community. Co-operation as the ultimate good in a community was a constant theme. It could unite human beings with animals against ogres and beasts of prey, as in the story of how dove, after being fed with castor-oil seeds, was sent to fetch a smith working far away from home and whose pregnant wife was being threatened by these man-eating two-mouthed ogres.

There were good and bad story-tellers. A good one could tell the same story over and over again, and it would always be fresh to us, the listeners. He or she could tell a story told by someone else and make it more alive and dramatic. The differences really were in the use of words and images and the inflexion of voices to effect different tones.

6     We therefore learnt to value words for their meaning and nuances. Language was not a mere string of words. It had a suggestive power well beyond the immediate and lexical meaning. Our appreciation of the suggestive magical power of language was reinforced by the games we played with words through riddles, proverbs, transpositions of syllables, or through nonsensical but musically arranged words.[1] So we learnt the music of our language on top of the content. The language, through images and symbols, gave us a view of the world, but it had a beauty of its own. The home and the field were then our pre-primary school but what is important, for this discussion, is that the language of our evening teach-ins, and the language of our immediate and wider community, and the language of our work in the fields were one.

7     And then I went to school, a colonial school, and this harmony was broken. The language of my education was no longer the language of my culture. I first went to Kamaandura, missionary run, and then to another called Maanguuũ run by nationalists grouped around the Gĩkũyũ Independent and Karinga Schools Association. Our language of education was still Gĩkũyũ. The very first time I was ever given an ovation for my writing was over a composition in Gĩkũyũ. So for my first four years there was still harmony between the language of my formal education and that of the Limuru peasant community.

8     It was after the declaration of a state of emergency over Kenya in 1952 that all the schools run by patriotic nationalists were taken over by the colonial regime and were placed under District Education Boards chaired by Englishmen. English became the language of my formal education. In Kenya, English became more than a language: it was *the* language, and all the others had to bow before it in deference.

9     Thus one of the most humiliating experiences was to be caught speaking Gĩkũyũ in the vicinity of the school. The culprit was given corporal punishment — three to five strokes of the cane on bare buttocks — or was made to carry a metal plate around the neck with inscriptions such as I AM STUPID or I AM A DONKEY. Sometimes the culprits were fined money they could hardly afford. And how did the teachers catch the culprits? A button was initially given to one pupil who was supposed to hand it over to whoever was caught speaking his mother tongue. Whoever had the button at the end of the day would sing who had given it to him and the ensuing process would bring out all the culprits of the day. Thus children were turned into witch-hunters and in the process were being taught the lucrative value of being a traitor to one's immediate community.

[1] Example from a tongue twister: 'Kaana ka Nikoora koona koora koora: na ko koora koona kaana ka Nikoora koora koora.' I'm indebted to Wangui wa Goro for this example. "Nichola's child saw a baby frog and ran away: and when the baby frog saw Nichola's child it also ran away.' A Gĩkũyũ speaking child has to get the correct tone and length of vowel and pauses to get it right. Otherwise it becomes a jumble of k's and r's and na's [author's note].

The attitude to English was the exact opposite: any achievement in    10
spoken or written English was highly rewarded; prizes, prestige, applause; the ticket to higher realms. English became the measure of
intelligence and ability in the arts, the sciences, and all the other
branches of learning. English became *the* main determinant of a child's
progress up the ladder of formal education.

As you may know, the colonial system of education in addition to its    11
apartheid racial demarcation had the structure of a pyramid: a broad
primary base, a narrowing secondary middle, and an even narrower
university apex. Selections from primary into secondary were through an
examination, in my time called Kenya African Preliminary Examination,
in which one had to pass six subjects ranging from Maths to Nature
Study and Kiswahili. All the papers were written in English. Nobody
could pass the exam who failed the English language paper no matter
how brilliantly he had done in the other subjects. I remember one boy in
my class off 1954 who had distinctions in all subjects except English,
which he had failed. He was made to fail the entire exam. He went on to
become a turn boy in a bus company. I who had only passes but a credit
in English got a place at the Alliance High School, one of the most elitist
institutions for Africans in colonial Kenya. The requirements for a place
at the University, Makerere University College, were broadly the same:
nobody could go on to wear the undergraduate red gown, no matter how
brilliantly they had performed in all the other subjects unless they had a
credit — not even a simple pass! — in English. Thus the most coveted
place in the pyramid and in the system was only available to the holder
of an English language credit card. English was the official vehicle and
the magic formula to colonial elitedom.

Literary education was now determined by the dominant language    12
while also reinforcing that dominance. Orature (oral literature) in Kenyan languages stopped. In primary school I now read simplified Dickens
and Stevenson alongside Rider Haggard. Jim Hawkins, Oliver Twist,
Tom Brown — not Hare, Leopard and Lion — were now my daily companions in the world of imagination. In secondary school, Scott and G. B.
Shaw vied with more Rider Haggard, John Buchan, Alan Paton, Captain
W. E. Johns. At Makerere I read English: from Chaucer to T. S. Eliot with
a touch of Graham Greene.

Thus language and literature were taking us further and further from    13
ourselves to other selves, from our world to other worlds.

What was the colonial system doing to us Kenyan children? What    14
were the consequences of, on the one hand, this systematic suppression
of our languages and the literature they carried, and on the other the
elevation of English and the literature it carried? To answer those questions, let me first examine the relationship of language to human experience, human culture, and the human perception of reality.

Language, any language, has a dual character: it is both a means of    15
communication and a carrier of culture. Take English. It is spoken in

Britain and in Sweden and Denmark. But for Swedish and Danish people English is only a means of communication with non-Scandinavians. It is not a carrier of their culture. For the British, and particularly the English, it is additionally, and inseparably from its use as a tool of communication, a carrier of their culture and history. Or take Swahili in East and Central Africa. It is widely used as a means of communication across many nationalities. But it is not the carrier of a culture and history of many of those nationalities. However in parts of Kenya and Tanzania, and particularly in Zanzibar, Swahili is inseparably both a means of communication and a carrier of the culture of those people to whom it is a mother-tongue.

. . .

16     Culture transmits or imparts those images of the world and reality through the spoken and the written language, that is through a specific language. In other words, the capacity to speak, the capacity to order sounds in a manner that makes for mutual comprehension between human beings is universal. This is the universality of language, a quality specific to human beings. It corresponds to the universality of the struggle against nature and that between human beings. But the particularity of the sounds, the words, the word order into phrases and sentences, and the specific manner, or laws, of their ordering is what distinguishes one language from another. Thus a specific culture is not transmitted through language in its universality but in its particularity as the language of a specific community with a specific history. Written literature and orature are the main means by which a particular language transmits the images of the world contained in the culture it carries.

17     Language as communication and as culture are then products of each other. Communication creates culture: culture is a means of communication. Language carries culture, and culture carries, particularly through orature and literature, the entire body of values by which we come to perceive ourselves and our place in the world. How people perceive themselves affects how they look at their culture, at their politics and at the social production of wealth, at their entire relationship to nature and to other beings. Language is thus inseparable from ourselves as a community of human beings with a specific form and character, a specific history, a specific relationship to the world.

18     So what was the colonialist imposition of a foreign language doing to us children?

19     The real aim of colonialism was to control the people's wealth: what they produced, how they produced it, and how it was distributed; to control, in other words, the entire realm of the language of real life. Colonialism imposed its control of the social production of wealth through military conquest and subsequent political dictatorship. But its most important area of domination was the mental universe of the colonised, the control, through culture, of how people perceived them-

selves and their relationship to the world. Economic and political control can never be complete or effective without mental control. To control a people's culture is to control their tools of self-definition in relationship to others.

For colonialism this involved two aspects of the same process: the destruction or the deliberate undervaluing of a people's culture, their art, dances, religions, history, geography, education, orature and literature, and the conscious elevation of the language of the coloniser. The domination of a people's language by the languages of the colonising nations was crucial to the domination of the mental universe of the colonised.

Take language as communication. Imposing a foreign language, and suppressing the native languages as spoken and written, were already breaking the harmony previously existing between the African child and the three aspects of language. Since the new language as a means of communication was a product of and was reflecting the 'real language of life' elsewhere, it could never as spoken or written properly reflect or imitate the real life of that community. This may in part explain why technology always appears to us as slightly external, *their* product and not *ours*. The word 'missile' used to hold an alien far-away sound until I recently learnt its equivalent in Gĩkũyũ, *ngurukuhĩ*, and it made me apprehend it differently. Learning, for a colonial child, became a cerebral activity and not an emotionally felt experience.

But since the new, imposed languages could never completely break the native languages as spoken, their most effective area of domination was the third aspect of language as communication, the written. The language of an African child's formal education was foreign. The language of the books he read was foreign. The language of his conceptualisation was foreign. Thought, in him, took the visible form of a foreign language. So the written language of a child's upbringing in the school (even his spoken language within the school compound) became divorced from his spoken language at home. There was often not the slightest relationship between the child's written world, which was also the language of his schooling, and the world of his immediate environment in the family and the community. For a colonial child, the harmony existing between the three aspects of language as communication was irrevocably broken. This resulted in the disassociation of the sensibility of that child from his natural and social environment, what we might call colonial alienation. The alienation became reinforced in the teaching of history, geography, music, where bourgeois Europe was always the centre of the universe.

This disassociation, divorce, or alienation from the immediate environment becomes clearer when you look at colonial language as a carrier of culture.

Since culture is a product of the history of a people which it in turn reflects, the child was now being exposed exclusively to a culture that was a product of a world external to himself. He was being made to stand outside himself to look at himself. *Catching Them Young* is the title of a book on racism, class, sex, and politics in children's literature by Bob Dixon. 'Catching them young' as an aim was even more true of a colonial child. The images of this world and his place in it implanted in a child take years to eradicate, if they ever can be.

25    Since culture does not just reflect the world in images but actually, through those very images, conditions a child to see that world in a certain way, the colonial child was made to see the world and where he stands in it as seen and defined by or reflected in the culture of the language of imposition.

26    And since those images are mostly passed on through orature and literature it meant the child would now only see the world as seen in the literature of his language of adoption. From the point of view of alienation, that is of seeing oneself from outside oneself as if one was another self, it does not matter that the imported literature carried the great humanist tradition of the best in Shakespeare, Goethe, Balzac, Tolstoy, Gorky, Brecht, Sholokhov, Dickens. The location of this great mirror of imagination was necessarily Europe and its history and culture and the rest of the universe was seen from that centre.

27    But obviously it was worse when the colonial child was exposed to images of his world as mirrored in the written languages of his coloniser. Where his own native languages were associated in his impressionable mind with low status, humiliation, corporal punishment, slow-footed intelligence and ability or downright stupidity, non-intelligibility and barbarism, this was reinforced by the world he met in the works of such geniuses of racism as a Rider Haggard or a Nicholas Monsarrat; not to mention the pronouncement of some of the giants of western intellectual and political establishment, such as Hume ('. . . the negro is naturally inferior to the whites . . .'),[2] Thomas Jefferson ('. . . the blacks . . . are inferior to the whites on the endowments of both body and mind . . .'),[3] or Hegel with his Africa comparable to a land of childhood still enveloped in the dark mantle of the night as far as the development of self-conscious history was concerned. Hegel's statement that there was nothing harmonious with humanity to be found in the African character is representative of the racist images of Africans and Africa such a colonial child was bound to encounter in the literature of the colonial languages.[4] The results could be disastrous.

[2] Quoted in Eric Williams *A History of the People of Trinidad and Tobago*, London 1964, p. 32 [Author's note].
[3] Eric Williams, ibid, p. 31 [Author's note].
[4] In references to Africa in the introduction to his lectures in *The Philosophy of History*, Hegel gives historical, philosophical, rational expression and legitimacy to every conceivable European racist myth about Africa. Africa is even denied her own geography where it does not correspond to the myth. Thus Egypt is not part of Africa; and North Africa is part of Europe. Africa proper is the especial home of ravenous beasts, snakes of all kinds. The African is not part of humanity. Only slavery to Europe can raise him, possibly, to the lower ranks of humanity. Slavery is good for the African. 'Slavery is in and for itself *injustice*, for the essence of humanity is *freedom*; but for this man must be matured. The gradual abolition of slavery is therefore wiser and more equitable than its sudden removal.' (Hegel *The Philosophy of History*, Dover edition, New York: 1956, pp. 91–9.) Hegel clearly reveals himself as the nineteenth-century Hitler of the intellect [Author's note].

In her paper read to the conference on the teaching of African literature in schools held in Nairobi in 1973, entitled 'Written Literature and Black Images',[5] the Kenyan writer and scholar Professor Mĩcere Mũgo related how a reading of the description of Gagool as an old African woman in Rider Haggard's *King Solomon's Mines* had for a long time made her feel mortal terror whenever she encountered old African women. In his autobiography *This Life* Sydney Poitier describes how, as a result of the literature he had read, he had come to associate Africa with snakes. So on arrival in Africa and being put up in a modern hotel in a modern city, he could not sleep because he kept on looking for snakes everywhere, even under the bed. These two have been able to pinpoint the origins of their fears. But for most others the negative image becomes internalised and it affects their cultural and even political choices in ordinary living.

## *Evaluating the Text*

1. From Thiong'o's description in the first paragraph, what picture do you get of the role Gĩkũyũ played in tribal, village, and family life in Kenya?

2. In what way would stories involving animals as heroes be especially important to the children to whom they were told? How might the nature of the conflicts in the animal stories better prepare children to deal with conflicts in real life? To what extent do these stories transmit cultural values by stressing the importance of resourcefulness, high self-esteem, a connection to the past, and a pride in one's culture?

3. What unique set of values does Thiong'o believe are expressed in stories told to children featuring human characters? How do these stories stress the kind of cooperation that a child would need to value in order to grow up within the extended family structure that Thiong'o describes (in his case, growing up in a family of twenty-eight children)?

4. In addition to transmitting cultural values, how did hearing these stories, along with riddles and proverbs, imbue the children with a love of the language of Gĩkũyũ and enhance their responsiveness to and their skill with features of narrative, imagery, inflection, and tone? How did hearing different people tell the same stories contribute to their development of critical abilities in distinguishing whether a given story was told well or poorly?

5. Describe the disruption Thiong'o experienced when he first attended a colonial school where he was forbidden to speak the language of the community from which he came. How do the kinds of punishments meted out for speaking Gĩkũyũ give you some insight into how psychologically damaging such an experience could be for a child? Why is Thiong'o especially bitter about the ingenious method of button passing that was used to identify speakers of Gĩkũyũ in the school?

6. Which of the examples Thiong'o gives, in your opinion, most clearly reveals the extent to which speaking English was rewarded? In what way

---

[5] The paper is now in Akivaga and Gachukiah's *The Teaching of African Literature in Schools*, published by Kenya Literature Bureau [Author's note].

was knowledge of English the single most important determinant of advancement?

7. How does language, in Thiong'o's view, serve as a vehicle for the values of the culture? How does his earlier example of childhood stories told in Gĩkũyũ substantiate this claim?

8. Explain Thiong'o's assertion that economic and political control can never be complete without mental control of the colonized by the colonizer. How does mental control determine how people see themselves, the value they place on their activities, the assumptions they form as to what is right and wrong, and the conclusions they draw as to what are approved or prohibited forms of behavior?

9. Explain how the British, as colonizers of Kenya, sought to achieve dominance by (1) devaluing native speech, dance, art, and traditions and (2) promoting the worth of everything British, including the speaking of English.

10. How does changing the language a people are allowed to speak change the way they perceive themselves and their relationship to those around them? Why did the British try to make it impossible for Kenyans to draw on the cultural values and traditions embodied in their language, Gĩkũyũ? Why was it also in the British interest to encourage and even compel Kenyans to look at themselves only through a British perspective? How was this view reinforced by teaching Kenyans British literature?

11. Why would exposing children to "images of his world as mirrored in the written languages of his coloniser" be especially damaging in the cases of the literature of Rider Haggard, Nicholas Monsarrat, and the opinions of Hume, Jefferson, and Hegel? How does Thiong'o's account of the damaging impact of these writers and thinkers give you an entirely different perspective?

## Exploring Different Perspectives

1. Compare and contrast the methods used to demean Ngũgĩ, discourage him and other Kenyan students from speaking Gĩkũyũ, and "reprogram" him into being a good British subject under the colonial system of education with the experiences of Someth May in Cambodia (in "The Field behind the Village") and Armando Valladares in Cuba (in "A Nazi Prison in the Caribbean").

2. In what way did the methods employed by the British rulers of Kenya encourage the same kind of diminished self-esteem in blacks, coupled with an inflated false view of white superiority, as does apartheid (see Jan Rabie's "Drought")? How do both these selections illustrate, in diverse ways, the importance of cultural programming in reinforcing low self-esteem coupled with an overevaluation of those in power? In what way is Thiong'o's reaction to this state of affairs, occurring in Kenya, very different from the black man in Rabie's fable, set in South Africa? Keep in mind that Rabie wrote "Drought" in the 1960s and that Thiong'o's account was written in the 1980s.

## Extending Viewpoints through Writing

1. For a research project, you might compare Thiong'o's discussion of the stories he heard as a child with Bruno Bettleheim's study, *The Uses of*

*Enchantment: The Meaning and Importance of Fairy Tales* (1976). Bettleheim suggests that these traditional forms of storytelling help children build inner strength by acknowledging that real evil exists and can be dangerous while offering hope that those who are resourceful can overcome the evil.

2. Discuss the extent to which Thiong'o's argument expresses a rationale similar to that advanced by proponents of bilingualism. You might also wish to consider the similarities and differences in political terms between the situation Thiong'o describes and that facing a Hispanic or Chinese child in the United States.

3. If you come from a culture where English was not your first language, to what extent did your experiences match Thiong'o's when you entered a school where English was the required language?

4. Some writers are more persuasive than others. How do Thiong'o; Alicia Partnoy ("Little School: Tales of Disappearance and Survival in Argentina"); Someth May ("The Field behind the Village"); Shen Tong ("Bloody Sunday in Tiananmen Square"); and Armando Valladares ("A Nazi Prison in the Caribbean") convey a sense of authority that makes their works believable and persuasive?

# Jan Rabie

# *Drought*

---

*Jan Rabie was born in the Cape in 1920. He is best known as a short story writer and novelist. In 1969, he wrote the novel* A Man Apart, *a historical work dealing with racial issues. "Drought" is a compelling parable that addresses the relationship of the races in South Africa.*

*The Republic of South Africa occupies the southern tip of Africa at the Cape of Good Hope, where the Atlantic meets the Indian Ocean. Blacks of Bantu descent constitute about 70 percent of the population of thirty-nine million, which also includes 17 percent Afrikaners (Boers or whites descended from the Dutch settlers); 3 percent Asians, who are mostly from India; and 9 percent Coloreds (of mixed Khoisan and white descent). Bantu-speaking black Africans moved into the region from East Central Africa about 1500 and joined the native Khoisan tribes (also known as Bushmen) before Dutch settlers arrived in the seventeenth century. British occupation of the Cape of Good Hope in 1806 and anger at the British abolition of slavery in 1833 led many Dutch Boers (Dutch for farmers) to abandon the Cape and move north to found two new republics, the Transvaal and the Orange Free State. Continued tensions between the British and the Dutch culminated in the Boer War (1899–1902), in which the British defeated the Afrikaners. Although the Boers lost the war, peace negotiations in 1902 guaranteed their rights as white men over all blacks. In 1961, the Union of South Africa became a republic and severed ties with the British Commonwealth. In 1989, reformist F. W. de Klerk replaced conservative P. W. Bota as President and has since taken steps (including desegregating hospitals and other public facilities, and the release of the African National Congress leader, Nelson Mandela) to end apartheid without being toppled by a right-wing backlash. In response to these and other reforms, the United States lifted economic sanctions against South Africa on July 11, 1991. Ironically, even as progress is being made against apartheid, an upsurge in tribal-linked murderous violence between Zulus (known as the Inkatha) and young ANC (African National Congress) militants threatens to plunge the country into chaos.*

1    Whirling pillars of dust walk the brown floor of the earth. Trembling, the roots of the withered grass await the rain; thirsty for green love the

vast and arid plain treks endlessly out to its horizon. One straight ruler-laid railway track shoots from under the midday sun's glare towards where a night will be velvet-cool with stars. The landscape is that of drought. Tiny as two grains of sand, a white man and a black man build a wall. Four walls. Then a roof. A house.

The black man carries blocks of stone and the white man lays them in place. The white man stands inside the walls where there is some shade. He says: 'You must work outside. You have a black skin, you can stand the sun better than I can.' 2

The black man laughs at his muscles glistening in the sun. A hundred years ago his ancestors reaped dark harvests with their assegais, and threshed out the fever of the black sun in their limbs with the Ngoma-dance. Now the black man laughs while he begins to frown. 3

'Why do you always talk of my black skin?' he asks. 4

'You are cursed,' the white man says. 'Long ago my God cursed you with darkness.' 5

'Your God is white,' the black man angrily replies. 'Your God lies! I love the sun and I fear the dark.' 6

The white man speaks dreamily on: 'Long ago my forefathers came across the sea. Far they came, in white ships tall as trees, and on the land they built them waggons and covered them with the sails of their ships. Far they travelled and spread their campfire ashes over this vast barbaric land. But now their children are tired, we want to build houses and teach you blacks how to live in peace with us. It is time, even if your skins will always be black . . .' 7

Proudly the black man counters: 'And my ancestors dipped their assegais in the blood of your forefathers and saw that it was red as blood. Red as the blood of the impala that our young men run to catch between the two red suns of the hills!' 8

'It's time you forgot the damned past,' the white man sadly says. 'Come, you must learn to work with me. We must build this house.' 9

'You come to teach me that God is white. That I should build a house for the white man.' The black man stands with folded arms. 10

'Kaffir!' the white man shouts, 'will you never understand anything at all! Do what I tell you!' 11

'Yes, Baas,' the black man mutters. 12

The black man carries blocks of stone and the white man lays them in place. He makes the walls strong. The sun glares down with its terrible eye. Far, as the only tree in the parched land, a pillar of dust walks the trembling horizon. 13

'This damned heat!' the white man mutters, 'if only it would rain.' 14

Irritably he wipes the sweat from his forehead before he says: 'Your ancestors are dead. It's time you forgot them.' 15

Silently the black man looks at him with eyes that answer: Your ancestors, too, are dead. We are alone here. 16

Alone in the dry and empty plain the white man and the black man 17 build a house. They do not speak to each other. They build the four walls and then the roof. The black man works outside in the sun and the white man inside in the shade. Now the black man can only see the white man's head. They lay the roof.

18     'Baas,' the black man asks at last, 'why has your house no windows and no doors?'

19     The white man has become very sad. 'That, too, you cannot under-stand,' he says. 'Long ago in another country my forefathers built walls to keep out the sea. Thick, watertight walls. That's why my house, too, has no windows and no doors.'

20     'But there's no big water here!' the black man exclaims, 'the sand is dry as a skull!'

21     You're the sea, the white man thinks, but is too sad to explain.

22     They lay the roof. They nail the last plank, the last corrugated iron sheet, the black man outside and the white man inside. Then the black man can see the white man no more.

23     'Baas!' he calls, but hears no answer.

24     The Inkoos cannot get out, he thinks with fright, he cannot see the sky or know when it is day or night. The Inkoos will die inside his house!

25     The black man hammers with his fists on the house and calls: 'But Baas, no big water will ever come here! Here it will never rain for forty days and forty nights as the Book of your white God says!'

26     He hears no answer and he shouts: 'Come out, Baas!'

27     He hears no answer.

28     With his fists still raised as if to knock again, the black man raises his eyes bewilderedly to the sky empty of a single cloud, and stares around him at the horizon where red-hot pillars of dust dance the fearful Ngoma of the drought.

29     Alone and afraid, the black man stammers: 'Come out, Baas . . . Come out to me . . .'

*Translated from the Afrikaans by the Author*

## *Evaluating the Text*

1. What particular word and phrases do you find most effectively create the impression of a vast, dry, and sweltering landscape in the midst of which exist two infinitesimal beings, "a white man and a black man"? What might the landscape parched for rain suggest? What might the comparison of the two men to grains of sand suggest? Why is it significant that they are building "a wall"? What might the wall represent?

2. Why is it significant that, in building the wall, the black man is the laborer, carrying "blocks of stone," while the white man takes on the role of supervisor?

3. What kinds of justification does the white man invoke to rationalize the disproportionate allocation of labor between himself and the black man?

4. How does the black man's response reveal the self-serving nature of the white man's theology? How are these religious assumptions alien to the black man's cultural traditions?

5. How does the next phase of the parable take the form of a debate in which the white man further justifies his actions by suggesting that before his arrival Africa was a "vast barbaric land," civilized only through the white man's intervention? How does the black man's response refute this claim by referring to the history of his African ancestors, their nobility, their right to the land, and their right to equality and justice?

6. Why does the black man resent the white man's attempt to justify all his actions on the assumptions that God is white and has supposedly cursed the black man? What lines in the parable most forcefully express the black man's rejection of this rationale and its conclusion that he should always accept a subservient role? In your opinion, why does the black man, at this point, continue to build the house for the white man?

7. At what point did you begin to sense that the peculiar architecture of the house, having no windows and no doors, might suggest the nature of the predicament the white man has created in South Africa? Without limiting the interpretation of this parable to any particular set of meanings, how might the windowless, doorless house suggest the isolating nature of apartheid, enclosing those who engineered its construction in a system that makes it impossible to see anything outside of its narrow realm? How does Rabie suggest the impossibility of communication between blacks and whites across this barrier?

8. How does Rabie suggest that the house being constructed will ultimately become the white man's tomb?

9. How does the equation of the black man to the sea ("you're the sea") give you an insight into the white man's attitude toward the black man, which might explain why, from the white man's point of view, it was necessary to build such a house?

10. To what extent does the conclusion of the parable suggest that Rabie sees the solution of the racial problem in South Africa as possible only through mutual interdependence, where neither is the "boss"? What other interpretations might the ending of the parable suggest?

11. Taking into consideration your responses to the previous questions, evaluate the title as a metaphor by which to express the predicament of both races in South Africa.

## Exploring Different Perspectives

1. To what extent does Rabie's parable about the relationship between the races in South Africa express a point of view that is similar in some respects to Thiong'o's criticism of the effects of white colonial rule in Kenya? In what important ways do Rabie's views differ from those of Thiong'o's?

2. Contrast the methods used by the repressive regime of Saddam Hussein in Iraq (see Samir al-Khalil, "Authority") and the white South African government to consolidate and maintain power. To what extent do both regimes depend on psychological manipulation through propaganda as well as on the threat of force or force itself to maintain power?

## Extending Viewpoints through Writing

1. You might wish to examine the passages in the Old Testament (Genesis 9: 18–25—the episode of Noah's drunkenness; the behavior of his three sons, Shem, Ham, and Japheth; and the judgment on Ham) that the white man in this parable is probably referring to when he says "you are cursed . . . long ago my God cursed you with darkness," and analyze these lines to see whether they support the interpretation given to them by the white man.
2. What insight did "Drought" give you into the network of psychological interdependency between the races in South Africa? In what sense did the parable formulate both a history and a criticism of the system of apartheid?
3. To what extent have current events in South Africa changed the situation in Jan Rabie's story? If you were rewriting the end of the parable now, to more closely fit reality, how would you change the conclusion?

# CONNECTING CULTURES

## Armando Valladares, "A Nazi Prison in the Caribbean"

1. How does Everett C. Hughes's article ("Good People and Dirty Work," Chapter 9) provide insight into the process by which Valladares's jailers were recruited? In what way did at least one of Valladares's jailers display unexpected compassion?
2. What are the different faces of communism you see from Valladares's account as compared with that of George Orwell ("Homage to Catalonia," Chapter 9)?
3. How does Valladares's picture of Cuba under Fidel Castro provide an insight into the circumstances responsible for so many Cubans deciding to move to Miami? How does his account dramatize the very different fates of Cubans who stayed and those who left (see Joan Didion, "Miami: The Cuban Presence," Chapter 7)?

## Chen Jo-hsi, "The Big Fish"

4. How are the issues of conscience and authority dramatized in both "The Big Fish" and in Panos Ioannides's story, "Gregory" (Chapter 9)?
5. How does David K. Shipler's report ("The Sin of Love," Chapter 3), dramatizing the disruptive effects on personal relationships of a political ideology, explore consequences similar to those dramatized by Chen Jo-hsi?

## Shen Tong, "Bloody Sunday in Tiananmen Square"

6. Analyze Tong's account in relationship to Bruce Dollar's discussion ("Child Care in China," Chapter 1) of how Chinese children are imbued with societal expectations of cooperation and sharing. In your opinion, were the pro-democracy demonstrators idealistic and naive in their belief that they could reform the government? To what extent did they believe they could succeed because of the way they were raised?
7. How were the events in Tiananmen Square similar to the events dramatized in Kate Wilhelm's story, "The Village" (Chapter 9)? In your opinion, why would this particular generation of Chinese have not anticipated that soldiers of their own government would shoot them down in cold blood?
8. How does Everett C. Hughes' discussion ("Good People and Dirty Work," Chapter 9) of the methods by which the SS were trained to do the "dirty work" shed light on Tong's narrative, especially on the fact that an officer had to take charge when his men seemed unwilling to shoot the demonstrators?

## Sławom·ːᵛ Mrożek, "The Elephant"

9. Compare Francine du Plessix Gray's account ("Sex and Birth," Chapter 1) revealing the ineptitude of Soviet bureaucracy in delivering health care with Mrożek's satire. In light of what Francine du Plessix Gray reveals, is Mrożek's fable really all that exaggerated?

10. Compare Mrożek's story to that of Natsume Soseki's chapter from *I Am a Cat* (Chapter 1) in terms of how effectively both works offer serious social criticism disguised as amusing satires.

11. To what extent do Bharati Mukherjee's ("The Management of Grief," Chapter 7) portrayal of Canadian bureaucracy and Jo Goodwin Parker's ("What Is Poverty?" Chapter 5) involvement with the welfare system illustrate Mrożek's criticism of all bureaucracies?

## Václav Havel, "The Velvet Hangover"

12. How do Josef Škvorecký's story "An Insolvable Problem of Genetics" (Chapter 5) and Havel's speech offer views of life in Czechoslovakia during and after Soviet domination?

13. In what way is Havel's morning-after reaction to the successful overthrow of the communist regime similar to Douchan Gersi's ("Initiated into an Iban Tribe of Headhunters," Chapter 2) reaction to having survived the tests of the Iban?

## Someth May, "The Field behind the Village"

14. How is the political ideology of the Khmer Rouge a military application of the communist Chinese system one can see at work in a benign form in Bruce Dollar's article "Child Care in China" (Chapter 1)?

15. How do both May's account and Kate Wilhelm's story, "The Village," (Chapter 9) present different perspectives on the dehumanizing effects of war?

16. Compare May's account with that of George Orwell ("Homage to Catalonia," Chapter 9) to discover differences in the way two armies, both adhering to communist ideology, were run. In particular, consider whether officers ate the same food and wore the same uniforms as did the men under their command and the reasons for any inequalities you discover.

## Alicia Partnoy, "The Little School: Tales of Disappearance and Survival in Argentina"

17. What similarities and differences can you discover between Partnoy's account of her imprisonment and Panos Ioannides's story, "Gregory" (Chapter 9)? How do differences in the points of view from which each story is told affect your response to the events described? Keep in mind that Partnoy speaks as a victim, while the narrator in "Gregory" is a soldier under orders.

18. How are both Partnoy's account and that of Kyōko Hayashi in "The

Empty Can" (Chapter 9) presented as the personal memories of survivors, albeit in a thinly fictional form?

## Samir al-Khalil, "Authority"

19. Compare the extent to which life under Saddam Hussein in Iraq resembles life under Hitler in Nazi Germany (see Everett C. Hughes, "Good People and Dirty Work," Chapter 9) in terms of a citizenry manipulated to project all their hopes onto a mythic leader, the role of propaganda, and the role of the secret police. What distinguishes the two regimes?
20. In what way does Hussein's politicization of everyday Iraqi life even at the level of the family produce a situation like that described by Le Ly Hayslip in "Sisters and Brothers" (Chapter 7)?

## Ngũgĩ wa Thiong'o, "Decolonising the Mind"

21. How do Thiong'o's analysis and Marjorie Shostak's report "Memories of a !Kung Girlhood" (Chapter 3) illuminate the extraordinarily vital role played by village life in African cultures?
22. How do both Thiong'o and V. S. Naipaul ("Prologue in an Autobiography," Chapter 7) draw on the events of their childhoods to explain the path each has taken as a writer?

## Jan Rabie, "Drought"

23. How does Toi Derricotte's portrayal ("The Black Notebooks," Chapter 5) of the dynamics and consequences of racism differ from that of Rabie? Why is the form into which Rabie projects the problem more appropriate for giving a clear picture of a society that has officially condoned the policy of apartheid?
24. In what respects is the picture Jamaica Kincaid ("A Small Place," Chapter 7) presents of tourism from the perspective of Antiguans similar to Rabie's depiction of the isolation and mutual dependency of blacks and whites on each other in South Africa?
25. How does the process C. P. Ellis ("Why I Quit the Klan," Chapter 5) went through in which he was able to see things from the opposite point of view suggest a solution to the problem portrayed in Rabie's story?

# 7

# *Strangers in a Strange Land*

In some ways, our age—the age of the refugee, of the displaced person, and of mass immigration—is defined by the condition of exile. The jarring, intense, and often painful emotional experience of having to redefine oneself in a strange land, of trying to reconcile conflicting cultural values, forces exiles to surrender all ideas of safety, the comfort of familiar surroundings, and a common language. Ironically, the condition of *not* belonging, of being caught between two cultures, at home in neither, gives the exile the chance to develop a tolerance for conflicting messages and the ability to see things from outside the controlling frame of reference of a single culture.

Edward Said in "Reflections on Exile" explores how the psychological characteristics of exile—isolation, loneliness, persecution, and the re-creation of a lost homeland—play a central role in the works of James Joyce and other twentieth-century writers. Born in Trinidad and educated at Oxford, V. S. Naipaul describes, in "A Prologue to an Autobiography," how becoming a writer required him to come to terms with a past he had rejected. Nicholasa Mohr writes an amusing and touching story, "A Very Special Pet," about a family in the South Bronx trying to make a new life far from the home they had left in Puerto Rico.

In "Miami: The Cuban Presence," Joan Didion reports on the phenomenal success story of the Cuban immigrants in Dade County, Florida, and the resistance they encounter from the Anglo community. Born in Vietnam, emigrating to America, and returning to Vietnam after thirty years, Le Ly Hayslip, in "Sisters and Brothers," describes the difficulty of overcoming political ideology when she is reunited with her brother, now a North Vietnamese communist official. In "Trouble for America's 'Model' Minority," David Whitman documents the challenges faced by the 640,000 Indo-Chinese war refugees who have come to the United States since 1978. How tourists' perceptions of Antigua differ from those of native Antiguans is the subject of the eye-opening account, "A Small Place," by Jamaica Kincaid. The question of where to draw the line between an individual's freedom of speech and the sensitivities of millions of devout Muslims is explored by Salman Rushdie in "A Pen against the Sword," as he defends his controversial book, *The Satanic Verses*, the work that forced him into hiding. Bharatj Mukherjee, in "The Management of Grief," creates a poignant story of conflicting cultural values as an Indian widow encounters Canadian bureaucracy in the aftermath of the bombing of an Air India flight on which her husband and children were killed.

# Edward Said

# *Reflections on Exile*

*Edward Said (born in 1935) is a Palestinian who was educated in Palestine and Egypt when those countries were under British jurisdiction. Said is Parr Professor of English and Comparative Literature at Columbia University. Said is best known for his critical works, in-cluding* Orientalism *(1978), a lively analysis of how the West has created certain cultural stereotypes about the East;* The World, Text, and the Critic *(1983); and (with Christopher Hitchens)* Blaming the Victims: Spurious Scholarship and the Palestinian Question *(1987). "Reflections on Exile," which first appeared in* Granta *(Autumn 1984), offers a penetrating analysis of the plight of the exiled and the role this condition has played in literature of the twentieth century.*

1      Exile is strangely compelling to think about but terrible to experience. It is the unhealable rift forced between a human being and a native place, between the self and its true home: its essential sadness can never be surmounted. And while it is true that literature and history contain heroic, romantic, glorious, even triumphant episodes in an exile's life, these are no more than efforts meant to overcome the crippling sorrow of estrangement. The achievements of exile are permanently undermined by the loss of something left behind for ever.

2      Exiles look at non-exiles with resentment. *They* belong in their surroundings, you feel, whereas an exile is always out of place. What is it like to be born in a place, to stay and live there, to know that you are of it, more or less for ever?

3      Although it is true that anyone prevented from returning home is an exile, some distinctions can be made between exiles, refugees, expatriates and émigrés. Exile originated in the age-old practice of banishment. Once banished, the exile lives an anomalous and miserable life, with the stigma of being an outsider. Refugees, on the other hand, are a creation of the twentieth-century state. The word 'refugee' has become a political one, suggesting large herds of innocent and bewildered people requiring urgent international assistance, whereas 'exile' carries with it, I think, a touch of solitude and spirituality.

4      Expatriates voluntarily live in an alien country, usually for personal or social reasons. Hemingway and Fitzgerald were not forced to live in France. Expatriates may share in the solitude and estrangement of exile,

but they do not suffer under its rigid proscriptions. Émigrés enjoy an ambiguous status. Technically, an émigré is anyone who emigrates to a new country. Choice in the matter is certainly a possibility. Colonial officials, missionaries, technical experts, mercenaries and military advisers on loan may in a sense live in exile, but they have not been banished. White settlers in Africa, parts of Asia and Australia may once have been exiles, but as pioneers and nation-builders the label 'exile' dropped away from them.

Much of the exile's life is taken up with compensating for disorienting loss by creating a new world to rule. It is not surprising that so many exiles seem to be novelists, chess players, political activists, and intellectuals. Each of these occupations requires a minimal investment in objects and places a great premium on mobility and skill. The exile's new world, logically enough, is unnatural and its unreality resembles fiction. Georg Lukács, in *Theory of the Novel*, argued with compelling force that the novel, a literary form created out of the unreality of ambition and fantasy, is *the* form of 'transcendental homelessness'. Classical epics, Lukács wrote, emanate from settled cultures in which values are clear, identities stable, life unchanging. The European novel is grounded in precisely the opposite experience, that of a changing society in which an itinerant and disinherited middle-class hero or heroine seeks to construct a new world that somewhat resembles an old one left behind for ever. In the epic there is no *other* world, only the finality of *this* one. Odysseus returns to Ithaca after years of wandering; Achilles will die because he cannot escape his fate. The novel, however, exists because other worlds *may* exist, alternatives for bourgeois speculators, wanderers, exiles.

No matter how well they may do, exiles are always eccentrics who *feel* their difference (even as they frequently exploit it) as a kind of orphanhood. Anyone who is really homeless regards the habit of seeing estrangement in everything modern as an affectation, a display of modish attitudes. Clutching difference like a weapon to be used with stiffened will, the exile jealously insists on his or her right to refuse to belong.

This usually translates into an intransigence that is not easily ignored. Wilfulness, exaggeration, overstatement: these are characteristic styles of being an exile, methods for compelling the world to accept your vision —which you make more unacceptable because you are in fact unwilling to have it accepted. It is yours, after all. Composure and serenity are the last things associated with the work of exiles. Artists in exile are decidedly unpleasant, and their stubbornness insinuates itself into even their exalted works. Dante's vision in *The Divine Comedy* is tremendously powerful in its universality and detail, but even the beatific peace achieved in the *Paradiso* bears traces of the vindictiveness and severity of judgement embodied in the *Inferno*. Who but an exile like Dante, banished from Florence, would use eternity as a place for settling old scores?

James Joyce *chose* to be in exile: to give force to his artistic vocation. In an uncannily effective way—as Richard Ellmann has shown in his biography—Joyce picked a quarrel with Ireland and kept it alive so as to sustain the strictest opposition to what was familiar. Ellmann says that 'whenever his relations with his native land were in danger of improving, [Joyce] was to find a new incident to solidify his intransigence and to reaffirm the rightness of his voluntary absence.' Joyce's fiction concerns what in a letter he once described as the state of being 'alone and friendless'. And although it is rare to pick banishment as a way of life, Joyce perfectly understood its trials.

9      But Joyce's success as an exile stresses the question lodged at its very heart: is exile so extreme and private that any instrumental use of it is ultimately a trivialization? How is it that the literature of exile has taken its place as a *topos* of human experience alongside the literature of adventure, education or discovery? Is this the *same* exile that quite literally kills Yanko Goorall and has bred the expensive, often dehumanizing relationship between twentieth-century exile and nationalism? Or is it some more benign variety?

10      Much of the contemporary interest in exile can be traced to the somewhat pallid notion that non-exiles can share in the benefits of exile as a redemptive motif. There is, admittedly, a certain plausibility and truth to this idea. Like medieval itinerant scholars or learned Greek slaves in the Roman Empire, exiles—the exceptional ones among them—do leaven their environments. And naturally 'we' concentrate on that enlightening aspect of 'their' presence among us, not on their misery or their demands. But looked at from the bleak political perspective of modern mass dislocations, individual exiles force us to recognize the tragic fate of homelessness in a necessarily heartless world.

11      A generation ago, Simone Weil posed the dilemma of exile as concisely as it has ever been expressed. 'To be rooted,' she said, 'is perhaps the most important and least recognized need of the human soul.' Yet Weil also saw that most remedies for uprootedness in this era of world wars, deportations and mass exterminations are almost as dangerous as what they purportedly remedy. Of these, the state—or, more accurately, statism—is one of the most insidious, since worship of the state tends to supplant all other human bonds.

12      Weil exposes us anew to that whole complex of pressures and constraints that lie at the centre of the exile's predicament, which, as I have suggested, is as close as we come in the modern era to tragedy. There is the sheer fact of isolation and displacement, which produces the kind of narcissistic masochism that resists all efforts at amelioration, acculturation and community. At this extreme the exile can make a fetish of exile, a practice that distances him or her from all connections and commitments. To live as if everything around you were temporary and perhaps trivial is to fall prey to petulant cynicism as well as to querulous lovelessness. More common is the pressure on the exile to join—parties, national movements, the state. The exile is offered a new set of affiliations and

develops new loyalties. But there is also a loss — of critical perspective, of intellectual reserve, of moral courage.

It must also be recognized that the defensive nationalism of exiles 13 often fosters self-awareness as much as it does the less attractive forms of self-assertion. Such reconstitutive projects as assembling a nation out of exile (and this is true in this century for Jews and Palestinians) involve constructing a national history, reviving an ancient language, founding national institutions like libraries and universities. And these, while they sometimes promote strident ethnocentrism, also give rise to investigations of self that inevitably go far beyond such simple and positive facts as 'ethnicity'. For example, there is the self-consciousness of an individual trying to understand why the histories of the Palestinians and the Jews have certain patterns to them, why in spite of oppression and the threat of extinction a particular ethos remains alive in exile.

Necessarily, then, I speak of exile not as a privilege, but as an *alterna-* 14 *tive* to the mass institutions that dominate modern life. Exile is not, after all, a matter of choice: you are born into it, or it happens to you. But, provided that the exile refuses to sit on the sidelines nursing a wound, there are things to be learned: he or she must cultivate a scrupulous (not indulgent or sulky) subjectivity.

Perhaps the most rigorous example of such subjectivity is to be found 15 in the writing of Theodor Adorno, the German-Jewish philosopher and critic. Adorno's masterwork, *Minima Moralia*, is an autobiography written while in exile; it is subtitled *Reflexionen aus dem beschädigten Leben (Reflections from a Mutilated Life)*. Ruthlessly opposed to what he called the 'administered' world, Adorno saw all life as pressed into ready-made forms, prefabricated 'homes'. He argued that everything that one says or thinks, as well as every object one possesses, is ultimately a mere commodity. Language is jargon, objects are for sale. To refuse this state of affairs is the exile's intellectual mission.

Adorno's reflections are informed by the belief that the only home 16 truly available now, though fragile and vulnerable, is in writing. Elsewhere, 'the house is past. The bombings of European cities, as well as the labour and concentration camps, merely precede as executors, with what the immanent development of technology had long decided was to be the fate of houses. These are now good only to be thrown away like old food cans.' In short, Adorno says with a grave irony, 'it is part of morality not to be at home in one's home.'

To follow Adorno is to stand away from 'home' in order to look at it 17 with the exile's detachment. For there is considerable merit in the practice of noting the discrepancies between various concepts and ideas and what they actually produce. We take home and language for granted; they become nature, and their underlying assumptions recede into dogma and orthodoxy.

The exile knows that in a secular and contingent world, homes are 18 always provisional. Borders and barriers, which enclose us within the safety of familiar territory, can also become prisons, and are often defended beyond reason or necessity. Exiles cross borders, break barriers of thought and experience.

19    Hugo of St Victor, a twelfth-century monk from Saxony, wrote these hauntingly beautiful lines:

> It is, therefore, a source of great virtue for the practised mind to learn, bit by bit, first to change about invisible and transitory things, so that afterwards it may be able to leave them behind altogether. The man who finds his homeland sweet is still a tender beginner; he to whom every soil is as his native one is already strong; but he is perfect to whom the entire world is as a foreign land. The tender soul has fixed his love on one spot in the world; the strong man has extended his love to all places; the perfect man has extinguished his.

Erich Auerbach, the great twentieth-century literary scholar who spent the war years as an exile in Turkey, has cited this passage as a model for anyone wishing to transcend national or provincial limits. Only by embracing this attitude can a historian begin to grasp human experience and its written records in their diversity and particularity; otherwise he or she will remain committed more to the exclusions and reactions of prejudice than to the freedom that accompanies knowledge. But note that Hugo twice makes it clear that the 'strong' or 'perfect' man achieves independence and detachment by *working through* attachments, not by rejecting them. Exile is predicated on the existence of, love for, and bond with, one's native place; what is true of all exile is not that home and love of home are lost, but that loss is inherent in the very existence of both.

20    Regard experiences as if they were about to disappear. What is it that anchors them in reality? What would you save of them? What would you give up? Only someone who has achieved independence and detachment, someone whose homeland is 'sweet' but whose circumstances makes it impossible to recapture that sweetness, can answer those questions. (Such a person would also find it impossible to derive satisfaction from substitutes furnished by illusion or dogma.)

21    This may seem like a prescription for an unrelieved grimness of outlook and, with it, a permanently sullen disapproval of all enthusiasm or buoyancy of spirit. Not necessarily. While it perhaps seems peculiar to speak of the pleasures of exile, there are some positive things to be said for a few of its conditions. Seeing 'the entire world as a foreign land' makes possible originality of vision. Most people are principally aware of one culture, one setting, one home; exiles are aware of at least two, and this plurality of vision gives rise to an awareness of simultaneous dimensions, an awareness that—to borrow a phrase from music—is *contrapuntal*.

22    For an exile, habits of life, expression or activity in the new environ-

ment inevitably occur against the memory of these things in another environment. Thus both the new and the old environments are vivid, actual, occurring together contrapuntally. There is a unique pleasure in this sort of apprehension, especially if the exile is conscious of other contrapuntal juxtapositions that diminish orthodox judgement and elevate appreciative sympathy. There is also a particular sense of achievement in acting as if one were at home wherever one happens to be.

This remains risky, however: the habit of dissimulation is both wearying and nerve-racking. Exile is never the state of being satisfied, placid, or secure. Exile, in the words of Wallace Stevens, is 'a mind of winter' in which the pathos of summer and autumn as much as the potential of spring are nearby but unobtainable. Perhaps this is another way of saying that a life of exile moves according to a different calendar, and is less seasonal and settled than life at home. Exile is life led outside habitual order. It is nomadic, decentred, contrapuntal; but no sooner does one get accustomed to it than its unsettling force erupts anew. 23

## Evaluating the Text

1. In what way does all sense of exile stem from a feeling of separation between the self and its true home? Would the opposite be an identification of self with place, a feeling that one is in the right place and has found a home? Why, in your opinion, is exile accompanied by feelings of sadness and estrangement?

2. How does someone born in a place knowing he or she will be there forever experience that place differently from someone who has recently arrived? How is the experience of exile connected with not being able to put down roots? Why would it be difficult for an exile to settle into a new place if she or he always had to be ready to return to the homeland?

3. What is the distinction Said draws between an exile (i.e., anyone prevented from returning home) and the circumstances of being a refugee, an expatriate or an émigré? How is being an exile an isolating psychological condition, whereas being a refugee is a communal experience that connects one with all other refugees?

4. Why are so many exiles chess players, novelists, and intellectuals? How is much of the exile's life "taken up with compensating for disorienting loss by creating a new world to rule"?

5. In Said's view, how does the idea on which the modern European novel is based differ from classic literary epics? How is one an imaginative compensation for lost reality while the other is an exploration and return to a known world? In what way are the great fictional works of Dante and Joyce a projection into an imaginative form of the psychological characteristics of exile—isolation, loneliness, persecution, and imaginative compensation for a lost reality?

6. How, in Said's view, can the uniquely detached perspective produced by the state of exile be a liberating force in everyday life? How could the exile's detachment become a positive refusal to become overly attached to objects and institutions?

7. How might the attitude of detachment Said describes be characterized as a religious attitude, similar to that fostered by Eastern religions? Specifically, how is this attitude similar to the value placed on objectivity in Buddhism, nonattachment in Hindu philosophy, and the spiritual, rather than material focus, of the New Testament?
8. How does the exile's simultaneous awareness of the culture left behind and the culture presently inhabited give rise to a dual perspective that could be beneficial? Why would it be valuable to be able to see the customs of the country you are living in from an outside perspective? How might this give you freedom to choose or reject these customs as you wish?

## Exploring Different Perspectives

1. Explore the differences between the condition of exile described by Said and the situation of the Cubans in Miami in Joan Didion's account ("Miami: The Cuban Presence"). To what extent has the Cuban community adjusted to being in exile? What role does the premise of someday returning to Cuba play?
2. How is Le Ly Hayslip's situation ("Sisters and Brothers") complicated by the fact she is exiled twice, as it were, once from Vietnam and a second time from her immediate family to whom she has become politically suspect (because of having lived in America)?
3. What insight do you gain from V. S. Naipaul's account ("Prologue to an Autobiography") of how important it was for him to be able to repossess the childhood he left behind as a way of coming to terms with his exile from Trinidad?
4. What evidence is there in Nicholasa Mohr's story ("A Very Special Pet") that the Puerto Rican family she describes is unwilling to let go of the past?
5. How does Jamaica Kincaid's discussion ("A Small Place") of tourists from a native Antiguan's point of view illuminate differences between the artificially created sense of being in a different place with the true experience of exile?
6. Read Salman Rushdie's article, "A Pen against the Sword," and discuss the extent to which Rushdie's predicament as someone forced to hide because of political and religious persecution illustrates Said's analysis.
7. In what way does Bharati Mukherjee's story ("The Management of Grief") relate the experience of exile from many perspectives? How do the visions experienced by Shaila suggest a form of imaginative compensation for lost reality that offset her experience of estrangement, isolation, and loneliness?

## Extending Viewpoints through Writing

1. What personal experience have you had living in or visiting places other than where you grew up? What insights into different cultural perspectives did you gain from your experiences?
2. Have you or any members of your family experienced any of the psychological problems associated with a forced or voluntary dislocation?

To what extent do your experiences confirm Said's observations of both the negative and positive results associated with exile? Do you think it is really possible to develop detachment and flexibility and to not identify with property and material goods in the way Said describes? Keep in mind that exile can be both a literal experience and the psychological feeling of not belonging.

3. What recent world development has highlighted the problem of refugees, displaced persons, or immigrants?

4. How is Said's rhetorical strategy based on challenging the popular definition of "exile"? How do works by Simone de Beauvoir ("The Married Woman," Chapter 3); Jo Goodwin Parker ("What Is Poverty?", Chapter 5); and Paul Fussell ("Taking It All Off in the Balkans," Chapter 8) also challenge popular definitions of "the married woman," "poverty," and "nudism"? Write an essay arguing for a redefinition of any term you choose, stating why you think it should be changed.

# V. S. Naipaul

# *Prologue to an Autobiography*

---

*V. S. Naipaul was born in 1932 in Trinidad to descendants of Hindu immigrants from northern India. In 1950, at the age of eighteen, he immigrated to England to study at Oxford University on a government scholarship. Three years later, he became a broadcaster for the Caribbean Service of the British Broadcasting Company (BBC). Naipaul has lived in India, Africa, South America, and the Middle East as well as England. His many books exploring the plight of the displaced have earned him recognition as a major figure in world literature, and many awards including England's Booker Prize. His works include* Miguel Street *(1959), a collection of stories based on his childhood experiences in Trinidad;* A House for Mr. Biswas *(1961); and* The Enigma of Arrival *(1987). "Prologue to an Autobiography" is drawn from* Finding the Center: Two Narratives *(1984) and describes how he had to come to terms with his state of exile in order to write his first story, "Bogart."*

*In July of 1498, Christopher Columbus became the first European to visit the two islands now known as Trinidad and Tobago, off the northern coast of Venezuela. In 1532, the islands were declared part of Spanish territory until they were seized by the British in 1797. The abolition of slavery in 1838 paved the way for a large migration of foreign workers, mostly Indians, who now make up 40 percent of the population. Trinidad and Tobago were united as a British Crown Colony in 1888, a situation that remained unchanged until Trinidad gained its independence in 1962 and became a republic with a parliamentary system of government in 1976. The population of Trinidad is particularly heterogeneous, comprising black African, Indian, Chinese, European, and Middle-Eastern settlers. Unemployment has always been high, and the deteriorating economy led the government to dismiss 25,000 of 60,000 employees in 1988.*

1    It is now nearly thirty years since, in a BBC room in London, on an old BBC typewriter, and on smooth, "non-rustle" BBC script paper, I wrote the first sentence of my first publishable book. I was some three months short of my twenty-third birthday. I had left Oxford ten months before, and was living in London, trying to keep afloat and, in between, hoping to alleviate my anxiety but always only adding to it, trying to get started as a writer.

At Oxford I had been supported by a Trinidad government scholarship. In London I was on my own. The only money I got—eight guineas a week, less "deductions"—came from the BBC Caribbean Service. My only piece of luck in the past year, and even in the past two years, had been to get a part-time job editing and presenting a weekly literary program for the Caribbean.

The Caribbean Service was on the second floor of what had been the Langham Hotel, opposite Broadcasting House. On this floor the BBC had set aside a room for people like me, "freelances"—to me then not a word suggesting freedom and valor, but suggesting only people on the fringe of a mighty enterprise, a depressed and suppliant class: I would have given a lot to be "staff."

The freelances' room didn't encourage thoughts of radio glory; it was strictly for the production of little scripts. Something of the hotel atmosphere remained: in the great Victorian-Edwardian days of the Langham Hotel (it was mentioned in at least one Sherlock Holmes story), the freelances' room might have been a pantry. It was at the back of the heavy brick building, and gloomy when the ceiling lights were turned off. It wasn't cheerful when the lights were on: ocher walls with a pea-green dado, the gloss paint tarnished; a radiator below the window, with grit on the sill; two or three chairs, a telephone, two tables, and two old standard typewriters.

It was in that Victorian-Edwardian gloom, and at one of those typewriters, that late one afternoon, without having any idea where I was going, and not perhaps intending to type to the end of the page, I wrote: *Every morning when he got up Hat would sit on the banister of his back verandah and shout across, "What happening there, Bogart?"*

That was a Port of Spain memory. It seemed to come from far back, but it was only eleven or twelve years old. It came from the time when we—various branches of my mother's family—were living in Port of Spain, in a house that belonged to my mother's mother. We were country people, Indians, culturally still Hindus, and this move to Port of Spain was in the nature of a migration: from the Hindu and Indian countryside to the white-negro-mulatto town. (At that time in Trinidad *black*, used by a non-black, was a word of insult; *negro* was—and remains—a polite word.)

Hat was our neighbor on the street. He wasn't negro or mulatto. But we thought of him as halfway there. He was a Port of Spain Indian. The Port of Spain Indians—there were pockets of them—had no country roots, were individuals, hardly a community, and were separate from us for an additional reason: many of them were Madrassis, descendants of South Indians, not Hindi-speaking, and not people of caste. We didn't see in them any of our own formalities or restrictions; and though we lived raggedly ourselves (and were far too numerous for the house), we thought of the other Indians in the street only as street people.

That shout of "Bogart!" was in more than one way a shout from the street. And, to add to the incongruity, it was addressed to someone in our yard: a young man, very quiet, yet another person connected in some way with my mother's family. He had come not long before from the country and was living in the separate one-room building at the back of our yard.

9        We called this room the servant room. Port of Spain houses, up to the 1930s, were built with these separate servant rooms — verandah-less little boxes, probably descended in style from the ancillary "negro houses" of slave times. I suppose that in one or two houses in our street servants of the house actually lived in the servant room. But generally it wasn't so. Servant rooms, because of the privacy they offered, were in demand, and not by servants.

10        It was wartime. The migration of my own family into the town had become part of a more general movement. People of all conditions were coming into Port of Spain to work at the two American bases. One of those bases had been built on recently reclaimed land just at the end of our street — eight houses down. Twice a day we heard the bugles; Americans, formal in their uniforms, with their khaki ties tucked into their shirts, were another part of the life of our street. The street was busy; the yards were crowded. Our yard was more crowded than most. No servant ever lodged in our servant room. Instead, the room sheltered a succession of favored transients, on their way to better things. Before the big family rush, some of these transients had been outsiders; but now they were mostly relations or people close to the family, like Bogart.

11        The connection of Bogart with my mother's family was unusual. At the turn of the century Bogart's father and my mother's father had traveled out together from India as indentured immigrants. At some time during the long and frightening journey they had sworn a bond of brotherhood; that was the bond that was being honored by their descendants.

12        Bogart's people were from the Punjab, and handsome. The two brothers we had got to know were ambitious men, rising in white-collar jobs. One was a teacher; the other (who had passed through the servant room) was a weekend sportsman who, in the cricket season, regularly got his name in the paper. Bogart didn't have the education or the ambition of his brothers; it wasn't clear what he did for a living. He was placid, without any pronounced character, detached, and in that crowded yard oddly solitary.

13        Once he went away. When he came back, some weeks or months later, it was said that he had been "working on a ship." Port of Spain was a colonial port, and we thought of sailors as very rough, the dregs. So this business of working on a ship — though it suggested money as well as luck, for the jobs were not easy to come by — also held suggestions of danger. It was something for the reckless and the bohemian. But it must have suited Bogart, because after a time he went away — disappeared — again.

There was a story this time that he had gone to Venezuela. He came 14
back; but I had no memory of his return. His adventures—if he had had
any—remained unknown to me. I believe I was told that the first time
he had gone away, to work on the ship, he had worked as a cook. But
that might have been a story I made up myself. All that I knew of Bogart
while he lived in the servant room was what, as a child, I saw from a
distance. He and his comings and goings were part of the confusion and
haphazardness and crowd of that time.

I saw a little more of him four or five years later. The war was over. 15
The American base at the end of the street was closed. The buildings
were pulled down, and the local contractor, who knew someone in our
family, gave us the run of the place for a few days, to pick up what
timber we wanted. My mother's extended family was breaking up into its
component parts; we were all leaving my grandmother's house. My
father had bought a house of his own; I used timber from the old
American base to make a new front gate. Soon I had got the Trinidad
government scholarship that was to take me to Oxford.

Bogart was still reportedly a traveler. And in Trinidad now he was 16
able to do what perhaps he had always wanted to do: to put as much
distance as possible between himself and people close to him. He was
living in Carenage, a seaside village five miles or so west of Port of Spain.
Carenage was a negro-mulatto place, with a Spanish flavor ('pagnol, in
the local French patois). There were few Indians in Carenage; that would
have suited Bogart.

With nothing to do, waiting to go away, I was restless, and I some- 17
times cycled out to Carenage. It was pleasant after the hot ride to splash
about in the rocky sea, and pleasant after that to go and have a Coca-
Cola at Bogart's. He lived in a side street, a wandering lane, with yards
that were half bush, half built-up. He was a tailor now, apparently with
customers; and he sat at his machine in his open shop, welcoming but
undemonstrative, as placid, as without conversation, and as solitary as
ever. But he was willing to play with me. He was happy to let me paint a
signboard for his shop. The idea was mine, and he took it seriously. He
had a carpenter build a board of new wood; and on this, over some days,
after priming and painting, I did the sign. He put it up over his shop
door, and I thought it looked genuine, a real sign. I was amazed; it was
the first signboard I had ever done.

The time then came for me to go to England. I left Bogart in Caren- 18
age. And that was where he had continued to live in my memory, faintly,
never a figure in the foreground: the man who had worked on a ship,
then gone to Venezuela, sitting placidly ever after at his sewing machine,
below my sign, in his little concrete house-and-shop.

That was Bogart's story, as I knew it. And—after all our migrations 19
within Trinidad, after my own trip to England and my time at Oxford—
that was all the story I had in mind when—after two failed attempts at
novels—I sat at the typewriter in the freelances' room in the Langham

Hotel, to try once more to be a writer. And luck was with me that afternoon. *Every morning when he got up Hat would sit on the banister of his back verandah and shout across, "What happening there, Bogart?"* Luck was with me, because that first sentence was so direct, so uncluttered, so without complications, that it provoked the sentence that was to follow. *Bogart would turn in his bed and mumble softly, so that no one heard, "What happening there, Hat?"*

20    The first sentence was true. The second was invention. But together —to me, the writer—they had done something extraordinary. Though they had left out everything—the setting, the historical time, the racial and social complexities of the people concerned—they had suggested it all; they had created the world of the street. And together, as sentences, words, they had set up a rhythm, a speed, which dictated all that was to follow.

21    The story developed a first-person narrator. And for the sake of speed, to avoid complications, to match the rhythm of what had gone before, this narrator could not be myself. My narrator lived alone with his mother in a house on the street. He had no father; he had no other family. So, very simply, all the crowd of my mother's extended family, as cumbersome in real life as it would have been to a writer, was abolished; and, again out of my wish to simplify, I had a narrator more in tune with the life of the street than I had been.

22    Bogart's tailoring business, with the signboard I had done for him, I transferred from the Carenage side street to the Port of Spain servant room, and with it there came some hint of the silent companionableness I had found in Bogart at that period. The servant room and the street— the houses, the pavements, the open yards, the American base at the end of the street—became like a stage set. Anyone might walk down the street; anyone might turn up in the servant room. It was enough—given the rhythm of the narrative and its accumulating suggestions of street life—for the narrator to say so. So Bogart could come and go, without fuss. When, in the story, he left the servant room for the first time, it took little—just the dropping of a few names—to establish the idea of the street as a kind of club.

23    So that afternoon in the Langham Hotel, Port of Spain memories, disregarded until then, were simplified and transformed. The speed of the narrative—that was the speed of the writer. And everything that was later to look like considered literary devices came only from the anxiety of the writer. I wanted above all to take the story to the end. I feared that if I stopped too long anywhere I might lose faith in what I was doing, give up once more, and be left with nothing.

24    Speed dictated the solution of the mystery of Bogart. He wished to be free (of Hindu family conventions, but this wasn't stated in the story). He was without ambition, and had no skill; in spite of the signboard, he was hardly a tailor. He was an unremarkable man, a man from the country, to whom mystery and the name of Bogart had been given by the street,

which had its own city sense of drama. If Bogart spent whole afternoons in his servant room playing Patience, it was because he had no other way of passing the time. If, until he fell into the character of the film Bogart, he had no conversation, it was because he had little to say. The street saw him as sensual, lazy, cool. He was in fact passive. The emotional entanglements that called him away from the street were less than heroic. With women, Bogart—unlike most men of the street—had taken the easy way out. He was that flabby, emasculated thing, a bigamist. So, looking only for freedom, the Bogart of my story had ended up as a man on the run. It was only in the solitude of his servant room that he could be himself, at peace. It was only with the men and boys of the street that he could be a man.

The story was short, three thousand words, two fools-cap sheets and a bit. I had—a conscious piece of magic that afternoon—set the typewriter at single space, to get as much as possible on the first sheet and also to create the effect of the printed page. 25

## Evaluating the Text

1. To what extent does Naipaul imaginatively reconstruct his childhood in Trinidad?
2. How was Naipaul employed? What efforts had he made in the past to be a writer, and with what success or lack of it? What might explain why he was able to succeed at this particular point in his life?
3. What did you learn about Naipaul's life in Trinidad before he left for Oxford? What kinds of difficulties do you feel he had to face in adapting to his new environment in England?
4. How does Naipaul differ from the narrator he created? What is significant about the differences?
5. Naipaul mentions the presence of U.S. troops in Trinidad. What impressions did you get of the impact Americans had on Trinidadian life during that period of time?
6. How would you characterize Bogart? After the town gives him the name "Bogart," after American film star Humphrey Bogart, how does his behavior change?
7. How does Naipaul's account reveal the way writers invent a reality by selecting and transposing details from a real environment onto a fictional one? Give some specific examples of this process at work in this account.
8. Naipaul characterizes Bogart as being uneducated, unambitious, and without a steady job; coming and going whenever he wants to; and disappearing only to return a month later, saying he has been working on a boat. Why do you think a character like this appealed to Naipaul?

## Exploring Different Perspectives

1. How does Naipaul's account reflect the experience of being an exile in ways similar to those described by Said?

2. How does Naipaul's reconstruction of his lost childhood in Trinidad confirm Said's observations about how other twentieth-century writers, such as James Joyce, were able to transcend exile through imaginative creations?

## Extending Viewpoints through Writing

1. If you have moved from the street where you lived as a child, try your hand at writing a short account of someone living on the block who was important or interesting to you then. Recreate the setting as accurately as possible, and describe an incident that would reveal to the reader why this person captured your imagination.
2. If you selected a nickname for yourself, what would it be? Explain your choice and the character traits the nickname would imply.
3. In a short essay, discuss how this narrative by Naipaul illustrates the process by which one can become a writer. You might touch on his growing up in Trinidad and the choice he made of writing in a simple and direct manner, telling stories he knew from childhood, populated with characters based on people who were important to him.
4. Naipaul and Boris Yeltsin ("Childhood in Russia," Chapter 1) both describe places they lived in childhood that they left behind. In an essay, describe a place you lived in during your childhood. Can you recapture how it looked and felt at the time, describe what was important or significant about it, or discover something you didn't see as important then, but do now?
5. Works by Naipaul, Margaret Atwood ("Happy Ending," Chapter 3); Toi Derricotte ("The Black Notebooks," Chapter 5); Alicia Partnoy ("The Little School: Tales of Disappearance and Survival in Argentina," Chapter 6); Václav Havel ("The Velvet Hangover," Chapter 6); and Ngũgĩ wa Thiong'o ("Decolonising the Mind," Chapter 6) emphasize the role writing plays in their lives. Create an imaginary dialogue between any two of these authors in which they explain why writing is important to them.

# Nicholasa Mohr

# *A Very Special Pet*

*Nicholasa Mohr grew up in an inner-city barrio of New York City in the South Bronx. Her uncommon sensitivity in depicting life among immigrants was recognized with the publication of her first novel, Nilda (1973). Mohr's second book, El Bronx Remembered: A Novella and Stories (1975), from which "A Very Special Pet" was taken, was nominated for a National Book Award. This story displays great compassion for inner-city families trying to adapt to a new culture while pining for the beautiful island they have left behind.*

*Puerto Rico is a Commonwealth, that is, a self-governing entity in association with the United States, located in the Caribbean Sea south of Florida. As members of a Commonwealth, citizens of Puerto Rico are American citizens but do not vote in federal elections or pay federal taxes on local earnings. The debate over the island's status is split three ways between those who advocate statehood, those who support continued commonwealth status, and those who are nationalist advocates of independence from the United States. Economic problems and population growth have spurred emigration, and one-third of all Puerto Ricans now live in the United States, often in circumstances similar to those described by Mohr in this story.*

The Fernández family kept two pets in their small five-room apart- 1
ment. One was a large female alley cat who was a good mouser when she wasn't in heat. She was very large and had a rich coat of grey fur with black stripes and a long bushy tail. Her eyes were yellow and she had long white whiskers. Her name was Maríalu.

If they would listen carefully to what Maríalu said, Mrs. Fernández 2
assured the children, they would hear her calling her husband Raúl.

"Raúl . . . Raúl . . . this is Maríalu . . . Raúl . . . Raúl . . . 3
this is Maríalu," the children would sing loudly. They all felt sorry for Maríalu, because no matter how long and hard she howled, or how many times she ran off, she could never find her real husband, Raúl.

The second pet was not really supposed to be a pet at all. She was a 4
small, skinny white hen with a red crest and a yellow beak. Graciela and Eugenio Fernández had bought her two years ago, to provide them with their eight children with good fresh eggs.

Her name was Joncrofo, after Graciela Fernández's favorite Holly- 5

437

wood movie star, Joan Crawford. People would repeat the hen's name as she pronounced it, "Joncrofo la gallina."

6  Joncrofo la gallina lived in the kitchen. She had one foot tied with a very long piece of twine to one of the legs of the kitchen sink. The twine was long enough for Joncrofo to wander all over the kitchen and even to hop onto the large window with the fire escape. Under the sink Mrs. Fernández kept clean newspapers, water, and cornmeal for the hen, and a wooden box lined with some soft flannel cloth and packing straw. It was there that they hoped Joncrofo would lay her eggs. The little hen slept and rested there, but perhaps because she was nervous, she had never once laid an egg.

7  Graciela and Eugenio Fernández had come to the Bronx six years ago and moved into the small apartment. Except for a trip once before to the seaport city of Mayagüez in Puerto Rico, they had never left their tiny village in the mountains. To finance their voyage to New York, Mr. and Mrs. Fernández had sold their small plot of land, the little livestock they had, and their wooden cabin. The sale had provided the fare and expenses for them and their five children. Since then, three more children had been born. City life was foreign to them, and they had to learn everything, even how to get on a subway and travel. Graciela Fernández had been terribly frightened at first of the underground trains, traffic, and large crowds of people. Although she finally adjusted, she still confined herself to the apartment and seldom went out.

8  She would never complain; she would pray at the small altar she had set up in the kitchen, light her candles, and murmur that God would provide and not forget her and her family. She was proud of the fact that they did not have to ask for welfare or home relief, as so many other families did.

9  "Papi provides for us. We are lucky and we have to thank Jesus Christ," she would say, making the sign of the cross.

10  Eugenio Fernández had found a job as a porter in one of the large buildings in the garment center in Manhattan. He still held the same job, but he hoped to be promoted someday to freight-elevator operator. In the meantime, he sold newspapers and coffee on the side, ran errands for people in the building, and was always available for extra work. Still, the money he brought home was barely enough to support ten people.

11  "Someday I'm gonna get that job. I got my eye on it, and Mr. Friedlander, he likes me . . . so we gotta be patient. Besides the increase in salary, my God!—I could do a million things on the side, and we could make a lotta money. Why I could . . . " Mr. Fernández would tell his family this story several times a week.

12  "Oh, wow! Papi, we are gonna be rich when you get that job!" the children would shriek.

13  "Can we get a television when we get rich, Papi?" Pablito, the oldest boy, would ask. Nellie, Carmen, and Linda wanted a telephone.

"Everybody on the block got a telephone but us." Nellie, the oldest 14
girl, would speak for them.

The younger children, William, Olgita, and Freddie, would request 15
lots of toys and treats. Baby Nancy would smile and babble happily with
everybody.

"We gonna get everything and we gonna leave El Bronx," Mr. Fer- 16
nández would assure them. "We even gonna save enough to buy our
farm in Puerto Rico—a big one! With lots of land, maybe a hundred
acres, and a chicken house, pigs, goats, even a cow. We can plant coffee
and some sugar, and have all the fruit trees—make a lotta money. Why I
could . . . " Mr. Fernández would pause and tell the children all about
the wonderful food they could eat back in his village. "All you need to
get the farm is a good start."

"We gonna take Joncrofo, right?" the kids would ask. "And Maríalu? 17
Her too?"

"Sure," Mr. Fernández would say good-naturedly, "even Raúl, her 18
husband, when she finds him, eh?" He would wink, laughing. "And
Joncrofo don't have to be tied up like a prisoner no more—she could run
loose."

It was the dream of Graciela and Eugenio Fernández to go back to 19
their village as owners of their own farm, with the faith that the land
would provide for them.

This morning Mrs. Fernández sat in her kitchen, thinking that things 20
were just not going well. Now that the holidays were coming and
Christmas would soon be here, money was scarcer than ever and prices
were higher than ever. Things had been hard for Eugenio Fernández; he
was still working as a porter and lately had been sick with a bad throat.
They had not saved one cent toward their farm. In fact, they still owed
the dry-goods salesman for the kitchen curtains and two bedspreads;
even insurance payments were long overdue. She wanted to find a job
and help out, but there were still three small preschool children at home
to care for. Lately, she had begun to worry; it was hard to put meat on
the table.

Graciela Fernández sighed, looking about her small, clean kitchen, 21
and caught sight of Joncrofo running frantically after a stray cockroach.
The hen quickly jerked her neck and snapped up the insect with her
beak. In spite of all the fumigation and daily scrubbing, it seemed there
was always a cockroach or two in sight. Joncrofo was always searching
for a tasty morsel—spiders, ants, even houseflies. She was quick and
usually got her victim.

The little white hen had a wicked temper and would snap at anyone 22
she felt was annoying her. Even Maríalu knew better; she had a permanent scar on her right ear as a result of Joncrofo's sharp yellow beak.
Now the cat carefully kept her distance.

In spite of Joncrofo's cantankerous ways, the children loved her. 23

They were proud of her because no one else on the block had such a pet. Whenever other children teased them about not having a television, the Fernández children would remind them that Joncrofo was a very special pet. Even Baby Nancy would laugh and clap when she saw Joncrofo rushing toward one of her tiny victims.

24     For some time now, Mrs. Fernández had given up any hope of Joncrofo producing eggs and had also accepted her as a house pet. She had tried everything: warm milk, fresh grass from the park, relining the wooden box. She had even consulted the spiritualist and followed the instructions faithfully, giving the little hen certain herbs to eat and reciting the prayers; and yet nothing ever worked. She had even tried to fatten her up, but the more Joncrofo ate, it seemed, the less she gained.

25     After thinking about it for several days, this morning Graciela Fernández reached her decision. Tonight, her husband would have good fresh chicken broth for his cold, and her children a full plate of rice with chicken. This silly hen was really no use alive to anyone, she concluded.

26     It had been six long years since Mrs. Fernández had killed a chicken, but she still remembered how. She was grateful that the older children were in school, and somehow she would find a way to keep the three younger ones at the other end of the apartment.

27     Very slowly she got up and found the kitchen cleaver. Feeling it with her thumb, she decided it should be sharper, and taking a flat stone, she carefully sharpened the edge as she planned the best way to finish off the hen.

28     It was still quite early. If she worked things right, she could be through by noontime and have supper ready before her husband got home. She would tell the children that Joncrofo flew away. Someone had untied the twine on her foot and when she opened the window to the fire escape to bring in the mop, Joncrofo flew out and disappeared. That's it, she said to herself, satisfied.

29     The cleaver was sharp enough and the small chopping block was set up on the kitchen sink. Mrs. Fernández bent down and looked Joncrofo right in the eye. The hen stared back without any fear or much interest. Good, thought Mrs. Fernández, and she walked back into the apartment where Olgita, Freddie, and Baby Nancy were playing.

30     "I'm going to clean the kitchen, and I don't want you to come inside. Understand?" The children looked at her and nodded. "I mean it — you stay here. If I catch you coming to the kitchen where I am cleaning, you get it with this," she said, holding out her hand with an open palm, gesturing as if she were spanking them. "Now, I'm going to put the chair across the kitchen entrance so that Baby Nancy can't come in. O.K.?" The childen nodded again. Their mother very often put one of the kitchen chairs across the kitchen entrance so the baby could not come inside. "Now," she said, "you listen and you stay here!" The children began to play, interested only in their game.

31     Mrs. Fernández returned to the kitchen, smoothed down her hair,

readjusted her apron, and rolled up her sleeves. She put one of the chairs across the threshold to block the entrance, then found a couple of extra rags and old newspapers.

"Joncrofo," she whispered and walked over to the hen. To her surprise, the hen ran under the sink and sat in her box. Mrs. Fernández bent down, but before she could grab her, Joncrofo jumped out of her box and slid behind one of the legs of the kitchen sink. She extended her hand and felt the hen's sharp beak nip one of her fingers. "Ave Maria!" she said, pulling away and putting the injured finger in her mouth. "O.K., you wanna play games. You dumb hen!"    32

She decided to untie the twine that was tied to the leg of the sink and then pull the hen toward her. Taking a large rag, she draped it over one hand and then, bending down once more, untied the twine and began to pull. Joncrofo resisted, and Mrs. Fernández pulled. Harder and harder she tugged and pulled, at the same time making sure she held the rag securely, so that she could protect herself against Joncrofo's sharp beak. Quickly she pulled, and with one fast jerk of the twine, the hen was up in the air. Quickly, Mrs. Fernández draped the rag over the hen. Frantically, Joncrofo began to cackle and jump, flapping her wings and snapping her beak. Mrs. Fernández found herself spinning as she struggled to hold on to Joncrofo, who kept wriggling and jumping. With great effort, Joncrofo got her head loose and sank her beak into Mrs. Fernández's arm. In an instant she released the hen.    33

Joncrofo ran around the kitchen cackling loudly, flapping her wings and ruffling her feathers. The hen kept an eye on Mrs. Fernández, who also watched her as she held on to her injured arm. White feathers were all over the kitchen; some still floated softly in the air.    34

Each time Mrs. Fernández went toward Joncrofo, she fled swiftly, cackling even louder and snapping wildly with her beak.    35

Mrs. Fernández remained still for a moment, then went over to the far end of the kitchen and grabbed a broom. Using the handle, she began to hit the hen, swatting her back and forth like a tennis ball. Joncrofo kept running and trying to dodge the blows, but Mrs. Fernández kept landing the broom each time. The hen began to lose her footing, and Mrs. Fernández vigorously swung the broom, hitting the small white hen until her cackles became softer and softer. Not able to stand any longer, Joncrofo wobbled, moving with slow jerky movements, and dropped to the floor. Mrs. Fernández let go of the broom and rushed over to the hen. Grabbing her by the neck, she lifted her into the air and spun her around a few times, dropping her on the floor. Near exhaustion, Mrs. Fernández could hear her own heavy breathing.    36

"Mami . . . Mamita. What are you doing to Joncrofo?" Turning, she saw Olgita, Freddie, and Baby Nancy staring at her wide-eyed. "Ma . . . Mami . . . what are you doing to Joncrofo?" they shouted and began to cry. In her excitement, Mrs. Fernández had forgotten completely about the children and the noise the hen had made.    37

38    "Oooo . . . is she dead?" Olgita cried, pointing. "Is she dead?" She began to whine.

39    "You killed Joncrofo, Mami! You killed her. She's dead." Freddie joined his sister, sobbing loudly. Baby Nancy watched her brother and sister and began to cry too. Shrieking, she threw herself on the floor in a tantrum.

40    "You killed her! You're bad, Mami. You're bad," screamed Olgita.

41    "Joncrofo . . . I want Joncrofo. . . ." Freddie sobbed. "I'm gonna tell Papi," he screamed, choking with tears.

42    "Me too! I'm gonna tell too," cried Olgita. "I'm telling Nellie, and she'll tell her teacher on you," she yelled.

43    Mrs. Fernández watched her children as they stood looking in at her, barricaded by the chair. Then she looked down at the floor where Joncrofo lay, perfectly still. Walking over to the chair, she removed it from the entrance and before she could say anything, the children ran to the back of the apartment, still yelling and crying.

44    "Joncrofo. . . . We want Joncrofo. . . . You're bad . . . you're bad. . . ."

45    Mrs. Fernández felt completely helpless as she looked about her kitchen. What a mess! she thought. Things were overturned, and there were white feathers everywhere. Feeling the tears coming to her eyes, she sat down and began to cry quietly. What's the use now? She sighed and thought, I should have taken her to the butcher. He would have done it for a small fee. Oh, this life, she said to herself, wiping her eyes. Now my children hate me. She remembered that when she was just about Olgita's age she was already helping her mother kill chickens and never thought much about slaughtering animals for food.

46    Graciela Fernández took a deep breath and began to wonder what she would do with Joncrofo now that she was dead. No use cooking her. They won't eat her, she thought, shaking her head. As she contemplated what was to be done, she heard a low grunt. Joncrofo was still alive!

47    Mrs. Fernández reached under the sink and pulled out the wooden box. She put the large rag into the box and placed the hen inside. Quickly she went over to a cabinet and took out an eyedropper, filling it with water. Then she forced open Joncrofo's beak and dropped some water inside. She put a washcloth into lukewarm water and washed down the hen, smoothing her feathers.

48    "Joncrofo," she cooed softly, "cro . . . cro . . . Joncrofita," and stroked the hen gently. The hen was still breathing, but her eyes were closed. Mrs. Fernández went over to the cupboard and pulled out a small bottle of rum that Mr. Fernández saved only for special occasions and for guests. She gave some to Joncrofo. The hen opened her eyes and shook her head, emitting a croaking sound.

49    "What a good little hen," said Mrs. Fernández. "That's right, come on . . . come, wake up, and I'll give you something special. How about if I get you some nice dried corn? . . . Come on." She continued

to pet the hen and talk sweetly to her. Slowly, Joncrofo opened her beak and tried to cackle, and again she made a croaking sound. Blinking her eyes, she sat up in her box, ruffled her feathers, and managed a low soft cackle.

"Is she gonna live, Mami?" Mrs. Fernández turned and saw Olgita, Freddie, and Baby Nancy standing beside her. 50

"Of course she's going to live. What did you think I did, kill her? Tsk, tsk . . . did you really think that? You are all very silly children," she said, and shook her finger at them. They stared back at her with bewilderment, not speaking. "All that screaming at me was not nice." She went on, "I was only trying to save her. Joncrofo got very sick, and see?" She held up the eyedropper. "I had to help her get well. I had to catch her in order to cure her. Understand?" 51

Olgita and Freddie looked at each other and then at their mother. 52

"When I saw that she was getting sick, I had to catch her. She was running all around, jumping and going crazy. Yes." Mrs. Fernández opened her eyes and pointed to her head, making a circular movement with her right index finger. "She went cuckoo! If I didn't stop her, Joncrofo would have really killed herself," she said earnestly. "So I gave her some medicine—and now. . . ." 53

"Is that why you got her drunk, Mami?" interrupted Olgita. 54

"What?" asked Mrs. Fernández. 55

"You gave her Papi's rum . . . in the eyedropper. We seen you," Freddie said. Olgita nodded. 56

"Well," Mrs. Fernández said, "that don't make her drunk. It . . . it . . . ah . . . just calms her down. Sometimes it's used like a medicine." 57

"And makes her happy again?" Olgita asked. "Like Papi? He always gets happy when he drink some." 58

"Yes, that's right. You're right. To make Joncrofo happy again," Mrs. Fernández said. 59

"Why did she get sick, Mami, and go crazy?" asked Freddie. 60

"I don't know why. Those things just happen," Mrs. Fernández responded. 61

"Do them things happen on the farm in Puerto Rico?" 62

"That's right," she said. "Now let me be. I gotta finish cleaning here. Go on, go to the back of the house; take Baby Nancy . . . go on." 63

The children left the kitchen, and Mrs. Fernández barricaded the entrance once more. She picked up the box with Joncrofo, who sat quietly blinking, and shoved it under the sink. Then she put the cleaver and the chopping board away. Picking up the broom, she began to sweep the feathers and torn newspapers that were strewn all about the kitchen. 64

In the back of the apartment, where the children played, they could hear their mother singing a familiar song. It was about a beautiful island where the tall green palm trees swayed under a golden sky and the flowers were always in bloom. 65

# Evaluating the Text

1. How long has the family lived in their apartment in the Bronx? How have they made an irrevocable decision by moving to the United States?
2. What hints can you discover about what Graciela plans to do with Joncrofo? How is this decision related to her acceptance of the fact that Joncrofo will never lay eggs despite everything she has tried to get her to do so?
3. How does the title illustrate the importance the children attach to their pet hen, especially because they do not have things other children have, such as a television set?
4. To what extent does the hen symbolize the family's predicament? Consider the possible equation of the husband, Eugenio, who will never make enough money to allow them to return to Puerto Rico, whose health she will try to restore with "chicken" soup, with Joncrofo (who will never lay eggs and whose health is restored with Eugenio's rum).
5. What precautions does Graciela take to prevent the children from knowing what she plans to do?
6. What prevents her from going through with her plan to kill Joncrofo to make chicken soup for Eugenio and to feed the family?
7. How does Mohr suggest correspondences between Graciela and Joncrofo?
8. In view of Graciela and Eugenio's dream of making lots of money, going back to Puerto Rico, and owning their own farm, how does Joncrofo symbolize the connection to Puerto Rico and to the idea of keeping this dream alive?
9. In what sense is the decision to kill the hen equivalent to accepting the reality that they will never return to Puerto Rico? How is not killing the hen and Graciela's song about a "beautiful island" equivalent to returning to the fantasy?

# Exploring Different Perspectives

1. How does the predicament of the family in Mohr's story express the dilemma of living between cultures, as exiles, described by Edward Said ("Reflections on Exile")?
2. How does nostalgia for the lost homeland play a key role in Mohr's story and in V. S. Naipaul's account (in "Prologue to an Autobiography") of Trinidad.
3. In what way do both Mohr and Bharati Mukherjee ("The Management of Grief") illuminate the kinds of difficulties mothers face in trying to raise their families far from their native countries?

# Extending Viewpoints through Writing

1. If you or your children were starving, would you ever consider killing your pet for food? Why or why not?
2. Do you know a family that has moved to America to have a better life? How do their experiences compare to those of the family Mohr describes?
3. Do you know of any family in which a pet has been perceived to have

taken on qualities of someone in the household? Describe the family and their "very special pet."

4. Nicholasa Mohr, Joan Didion ("Miami: The Cuban Presence"); V. S. Naipaul ("Prologue to an Autobiography"); and Le Ly Hayslip ("Sisters and Brothers") all describe the experience of living somewhere else and having to decide whether to remain there or return home. Did you ever have a comparable experience? What circumstances led you to live away from home?

# Joan Didion

# *Miami: The Cuban Presence*

---

*Joan Didion was born in 1934 in Sacramento, a sixth-generation Californian. After graduating from the University of California at Berkeley, she worked as a feature editor at* Vogue *magazine. Her published work includes novels such as* Play It as It Lays *(1971);* A Book of Common Prayer *(1977), and* Democracy *(1984); two collections of essays,* Slouching Towards Bethlehem *(1968) and* The White Album *(1979); and a book-length account of her experiences as a reporter, entitled* Salvador *(1983). "Miami: The Cuban Presence" originally appeared in the* New York Review of Books *for May 28, 1987, and evolved into her book* Miami *(1987). This enlightening essay challenges views of longtime Dade County residents with facts and statistics that reveal the vital part that Cuban immigrants have played in the rebirth of Miami.*

1      On the 150th anniversary of the founding of Dade County, in February of 1986, the Miami *Herald* asked four prominent amateurs of local history to name "the ten people and the ten events that had the most impact on the county's history." Each of the four submitted his or her own list of "The Most Influential People in Dade's History," and among the names mentioned were Julia Tuttle ("pioneer businesswoman"), Henry Flagler ("brought the Florida East Coast Railway to Miami"), Alexander Orr, Jr. ("started the research that saved Miami's drinking water from salt"), Everest George Sewell ("publicized the city and fostered its deepwater seaport"). . . . There was Dr. James M. Jackson, an early Miami physician. There was Napoleon Bonaparte Broward, the governor of Florida who initiated the draining of the Everglades. There appeared on three of the four lists the name of the developer of Coral Gables, George Merrick. There appeared on one of the four lists the name of the coach of the Miami Dolphins, Don Shula.

2      On none of these lists of "The Most Influential People in Dade's History" did the name Fidel Castro appear, nor for that matter did the name of any Cuban, although the presence of Cubans in Dade County did not go entirely unnoted by the *Herald* panel. When it came to naming the Ten Most Important "Events," as opposed to "People," all four panelists mentioned the arrival of the Cubans, but at slightly off angles

---

*(For more background on Cuba, see p. 324.)

446

("Mariel Boatlift of 1980" was the way one panelist saw it), and as if the arrival had been just another of those isolated disasters or innovations which deflect the course of any growing community, on an approximate par with the other events mentioned, for example the Freeze of 1895, the Hurricane of 1926, the opening of the Dixie Highway, the establishment of Miami International Airport, and the adoption, in 1957, of the metropolitan form of government, "enabling the Dade County Commission to provide urban services to the increasingly populous unincorporated area."

This set of mind, in which the local Cuban community was seen as a civic challenge determinedly met, was not uncommon among Anglos to whom I talked in Miami, many of whom persisted in the related illusions that the city was small, manageable, prosperous in a predictable broad-based way, southern in a progressive Sunbelt way, American, and belonged to them. In fact 43 percent of the population of Dade County was by that time "Hispanic," which meant mostly Cuban. Fifty-six percent of the population of Miami itself was Hispanic. The most visible new buildings on the Miami skyline, the Arquitectonica buildings along Brickell Avenue, were by a firm with a Cuban founder. There were Cubans in the board rooms of the major banks, Cubans in clubs that did not admit Jews or blacks, and four Cubans in the most recent mayoralty campaign, two of whom, Raul Masvidal and Xavier Suarez, had beaten out the incumbent and all other candidates to meet in a runoff, and one of whom, Xavier Suarez, a thirty-six-year-old lawyer who had been brought from Cuba to the United States as a child, was by then mayor of Miami.

The entire tone of the city, the way people looked and talked and met one another, was Cuban. The very image the city had begun presenting of itself, what was then its newfound glamour, its "hotness" (hot colors, hot vice, shady dealings under the palm trees), was that of prerevolutionary Havana, as perceived by Americans. There was even in the way women dressed in Miami a definable Havana look, a more distinct emphasis on the hips and décolletage, more black, more veiling, a generalized flirtatiousness of style not then current in American cities. In the shoe departments at Burdine's and Jordan Marsh there were more platform soles than there might have been in another American city, and fewer displays of the running shoe ethic. I recall being struck, during an afternoon spent at La Liga Contra el Cancer, a prominent exile charity which raises money to help cancer patients, by the appearance of the volunteers who had met that day to stuff envelopes for a benefit. Their hair was sleek, of a slightly other period, immaculate pageboys and French twists. They wore Bruno Magli pumps, and silk and linen dresses of considerable expense. There seemed to be a preference for strictest gray or black, but the effect remained lush, tropical, like a room full of perfectly groomed mangoes.

5    This was not, in other words, an invisible 56 percent of the population. Even the social notes in *Diario Las Americas* and in *El Herald*, the
daily Spanish edition of the *Herald* written and edited for *el exilio*,
suggested a dominant culture, one with money to spend and a notable
willingness to spend it in public. La Liga Contra el Cancer alone sponsored, in a single year, two benefit dinner dances, one benefit ball, a
benefit children's fashion show, a benefit telethon, a benefit exhibition
of jewelry, a benefit presentation of Miss Universe contestants, and a
benefit showing, with Saks Fifth Avenue and chicken *vol-au-vent*, of the
Adolfo (as it happened, a Cuban) fall collection.

6    One morning *El Herald* would bring news of the gala at the Pavillon
of the Amigos Latinamericanos del Museo de Ciencia y Planetarium;
another morning, of an upcoming event at the Big Five Club, a Miami
club founded by former members of five fashionable clubs in prerevolutionary Havana: a *coctel*, or cocktail party, at which tables would be
assigned for yet another gala, the annual "Baile Imperial de las Rosas" of
the American Cancer Society, Hispanic Ladies Auxiliary. Some members
of the community were honoring Miss America Latina with dinner dancing at the Doral. Some were being honored themselves, at the Spirit of
Excellence Awards Dinner at the Omni. Some were said to be enjoying
the skiing at Vail; others to prefer Bariloche, in Argentina. Some were
reported unable to attend (but sending checks for) the gala at the Pavillon of the Amigos Latinamericanos del Museo de Ciencia y Planetarium
because of a scheduling conflict, with *el coctel de* Paula Hawkins.

7    Fete followed fete, all high visibility. Almost any day it was possible
to drive past the limestone arches and fountains which marked the
boundaries of Coral Gables and see little girls being photographed in the
tiaras and ruffled hoop skirts and maribou-trimmed illusion capes they
would wear at their *quinces*, the elaborate fifteenth-birthday parties at
which the community's female children come of official age. The favored
facial expression for a *quince* photograph was a classic smolder. The
favored backdrop was one suggesting Castilian grandeur, which was
how the Coral Gables arches happened to figure. Since the idealization
of the virgin implicit in the *quince* could exist only in the presence of its
natural foil, *machismo*, there was often a brother around, or a boyfriend.
There was also a mother, in dark glasses, not only to protect the symbolic
virgin but to point out the better angle, the more aristocratic location. The
*quinceanera* would pick up her hoop skirts and move as directed, often
revealing the scuffed Jellies she had worn that day to school. A few
weeks later there she would be, transformed in *Diario Las Americas*, one
of the morning battalion of smoldering fifteen-year-olds, each with her
arch, her fountain, her borrowed scenery, the gift if not exactly the
intention of the late George Merrick, who built the arches when he
developed Coral Gables.

8    Neither the photographs of the Cuban *quinceaneras* nor the notes
about the *coctel* at the Big Five were apt to appear in the newspapers read
by Miami Anglos, nor, for that matter, was much information at all about

the daily life of the Cuban majority. When, in the fall of 1986, Florida International University offered an evening course called "Cuban Miami: A Guide for Non-Cubans," the *Herald* sent a staff writer, who covered the classes as if from a distant beat. "Already I have begun to make some sense out of a culture, that, while it totally surrounds us, has remained inaccessible and alien to me," the *Herald* writer was reporting by the end of the first meeting, and, by the end of the fourth:

> What I see day to day in Miami, moving through mostly Anglo corridors of the community, are just small bits and pieces of that other world, the tip of something much larger than I'd imagined. . . . We may frequent the restaurants here, or wander into the occasional festival. But mostly we try to ignore Cuban Miami, even as we rub up against this teeming, incomprehensible presence.

Only thirteen people, including the *Herald* writer, turned up for the 9 first meeting of "Cuban Miami: A Guide for Non-Cubans" (two more appeared at the second meeting, along with a security guard, because of telephone threats prompted by what the *Herald* writer called "somebody's twisted sense of national pride"), an enrollment which suggested a certain willingness among non-Cubans to let Cuban Miami remain just that, Cuban, the "incomprehensible presence." In fact there had come to exist in South Florida two parallel cultures, separate but not exactly equal, a key distinction being that only one of the two, the Cuban, exhibited even a remote interest in the activities of the other. "The American community is not really aware of what is happening in the Cuban community," an exiled banker named Luis Botifoll said in a 1983 *Herald* Sunday magazine piece about ten prominent local Cubans. "We are clannish, but at least we know who is whom in the American establishment. They do not." About another of the ten Cubans featured in this piece, Jorge Mas Canosa, the *Herald* had this to say:

> He is an advisor to US Senators, a confidant of federal bureaucrats, a lobbyist for anti-Castro US policies, a near unknown in Miami. When his political group sponsored a luncheon speech in Miami by Secretary of Defense Caspar Weinberger, almost none of the American business leaders attending had ever heard of their Cuban host.

The general direction of this piece, which appeared under the cover 10 line "THE CUBANS: *They're ten of the most powerful men in Miami. Half the population doesn't know it*," was, as the *Herald* put it,

> to challenge the widespread presumption that Miami's Cubans are not really Americans, that they are a foreign presence here, an exile community that is trying to turn South Florida into North

Cuba. . . . The top ten are not separatists; they have achieved success in the most traditional ways. They are the solid, bedrock citizens, hard-working humanitarians who are role models for a community that seems determined to assimilate itself into American society.

11    This was interesting. It was written by one of the few Cubans then on the *Herald* staff, and yet it described, however unwittingly, the precise angle at which Miami Anglos and Miami Cubans were failing to connect: Miami Anglos were in fact interested in Cubans only to the extent that they could cast them as aspiring immigrants, "determined to assimilate," a "hard-working" minority not different in kind from other groups of resident aliens. (But had I met any Haitians, a number of Anglos asked when I said that I had been talking to Cubans.) Anglos (who were, significantly, referred to within the Cuban community as "Americans") spoke of cross-culturalization, and of what they believed to be a meaningful second-generation preference for hamburgers, and rock-and-roll. They spoke of "diversity," and of Miami's "Hispanic flavor," an approach in which 56 percent of the population was seen as decorative, like the Coral Gables arches.

12    Fixed as they were on this image of the melting pot, of immigrants fleeing a disruptive revolution to find a place in the American sun, Anglos did not on the whole understand that assimilation would be considered by most Cubans a doubtful goal at best. Nor did many Anglos understand that living in Florida was still at the deepest level construed by Cubans as a temporary condition, an accepted political option shaped by the continuing dream, if no longer the immediate expectation, of a vindicatory return. *El exilio* was for Cubans a ritual, a respected tradition. *La revolución* was also a ritual, a trope fixed in Cuban political rhetoric at least since José Martí, a concept broadly interpreted to mean reform, or progress, or even just change. Ramón Grau San Martín, the president of Cuba during the autumn of 1933 and from 1944 until 1948, had presented himself as a revolutionary, as had his 1948 successor, Carlos Prío. Even Fulgencio Batista had entered Havana life calling for *la revolución*, and had later been accused of betraying it, even as Fidel Castro was now.

13    This was a process Cuban Miami understood, but Anglo Miami did not, remaining as it did arrestingly innocent of even the most general information about Cuba and Cubans. Miami Anglos for example still had trouble with Cuban names, and Cuban food. When the Cuban novelist Guillermo Cabrera Infante came from London to lecture at Miami-Dade Community College, he was referred to by several Anglo faculty members to whom I spoke as "Infante." Cuban food was widely seen not as a minute variation on that eaten throughout both the Caribbean and the Mediterranean but as "exotic," and full of garlic. A typical Thursday food section of the *Herald* included recipes for Broiled Lemon-Curry

Cornish Game Hens, Chicken Tetrazzini, King Cake, Pimiento Cheese, Raisin Sauce for Ham, Sauteed Spiced Peaches, Shrimp Scampi, Easy Beefy Stir-Fry, and four ways to used dried beans ("Those cheap, humble beans that have long sustained the world's poor have become the trendy set's new pet"), none of them Cuban.

This was all consistent, and proceeded from the original construction, 14 that of the exile as an immigration. There was no reason to be curious about Cuban food, because Cuban teenagers preferred hamburgers. There was no reason to get Cuban names right, because they were complicated, and would be simplified by the second generation, or even by the first, "Jorge L. Mas" was the way Jorge Mas Canosa's business card read. "Raul Masvidal" was the way Raul Masvidal y Jury ran for mayor of Miami. There was no reason to know about Cuban history, because history was what immigrants were fleeing.

Even the revolution, the reason for the immigration, could be covered 15 in a few broad strokes: "Batista," "Castro," "26 Julio," this last being the particular broad stroke that inspired the Miami Springs Holiday Inn, on July 26, 1985, the thirty-second anniversary of the day Fidel Castro attacked the Moncada Barracks and so launched his six-year struggle for power in Cuba, to run a bar special on Cuba Libres, thinking to attract local Cubans by commemorating their holiday. "It was a mistake," the manager said, besieged by outraged exiles. "The gentleman who did it is from Minnesota."

There was in fact no reason, in Miami as well as in Minnesota, to 16 know anything at all about Cubans, since Miami Cubans were now, if not Americans, at least aspiring Americans, and worthy of Anglo attention to the exact extent that they were proving themselves, in the *Herald's* words, "role models for a community that seems determined to assimilate itself into American society"; or, as George Bush put it in a 1986 Miami address to the Cuban American National Foundation, "the most eloquent testimony I know to the basic strength and success of America, as well as to the basic weakness and failure of Communism and Fidel Castro."

The use of this special lens, through which the exiles were seen as a 17 tribute to the American system, a point scored in the battle of the ideologies, tended to be encouraged by those outside observers who dropped down from the northeast corridor for a look and a column or two. George Will, in *Newsweek*, saw Miami as "a new installment in the saga of America's absorptive capacity," and Southwest Eighth Street as the place where "these exemplary Americans," the seven Cubans who had been gotten together to brief him, "initiated a columnist to fried bananas and black-bean soup and other Cuban contributions to the tanginess of American life." George Gilder, in *The Wilson Quarterly*, drew pretty much the same lesson from Southwest Eighth Street, finding it "more effervescently thriving than its crushed prototype," by which he seemed to mean Havana. In fact Eighth Street was for George Gilder a street that seemed to "percolate with the forbidden commerce of the dying island to the south . . . the Refrescos Cawy, the Competidora and El Cuño cigarettes, the *guayaberas*, the Latin music pulsing from the storefronts, the pyramids of mangoes and tubers, gourds and plantains, the iced coconuts served with a straw, the new theaters showing the latest anti-Castro comedies."

18    There was nothing on this list, with the possible exception of the "anti-Castro comedies," that could not most days be found on South-west Eighth Street, but the list was also a fantasy, and a particularly *gringo* fantasy, one in which Miami Cubans, who came from a culture which had represented western civilization in this hemisphere since before there was a United States of America, appeared exclusively as vendors of plantains, their native music "pulsing" behind them. There was in any such view of Miami Cubans an extraordinary element of condescension, and it was the very condescension shared by Miami Anglos, who were inclined to reduce the particular liveliness and sophis-tication of local Cuban life to a matter of shrines on the lawn and love potions in the *botanicas*, the primitive exotica of the tourist's Caribbean.

19    Cubans were perceived as most satisfactory when they appeared most fully to share the aspirations and manners of middle-class Ameri-cans, at the same time adding "color" to the city on appropriate occa-sions, for example at their *quinces* (the *quinces* were one aspect of Cuban life almost invariably mentioned by Anglos, who tended to present them as evidence of Cuban extravagance, i.e., Cuban irresponsibility, or child-ishness), or on the day of the annual Calle Ocho Festival, when they could, according to the *Herald*, "samba" in the streets and stir up a paella for two thousand (ten cooks, two thousand mussels, two hundred and twenty pounds of lobster, and four hundred and forty pounds of rice), using rowboat oars as spoons. Cubans were perceived as least satisfac-tory when they "acted clannish," "kept to themselves," "had their own ways," and, two frequent flash points, "spoke Spanish when they didn't need to" and "got political"; complaints, each of them, which suggested an Anglo view of what Cubans should be at significant odds with what Cubans were.

20    This question of language was curious. The sound of spoken Spanish was common in Miami, but it was also common in Los Angeles, and Houston, and even in the cities of the Northeast. What was unusual about Spanish in Miami was not that it was so often spoken, but that it was so often heard: In, say, Los Angeles, Spanish remained a language only barely registered by the Anglo population, part of the ambient noise, the language spoken by the people who worked in the car wash and came to trim the trees and cleared the tables in restaurants. In Miami Spanish was spoken by the people who ate in the restaurants, the people who owned the cars and the trees, which made, on the socio-auditory

scale, a considerable difference. Exiles who felt isolated or declassed by language in New York or Los Angeles thrived in Miami. An entrepreneur who spoke no English could still, in Miami, buy, sell, negotiate, leverage assets, float bonds, and, if he were so inclined, attend galas twice a week, in black tie. "I have been after the *Herald* ten times to do a story about millionaires in Miami who do not speak more than two words in English," one prominent exile told me. "'Yes' and 'no.' Those are the two words. They come here with five dollars in their pockets and without speaking another word of English they are millionaires."

The truculence a millionaire who spoke only two words of English 21 might provoke among the less resourceful native citizens of a nominally American city was predictable, and manifested itself rather directly. In 1980, the year of Mariel, Dade County voters had approved a referendum requiring that county business be conducted exclusively in English. Notwithstanding the fact that this legislation was necessarily amended to exclude emergency medical and certain other services, and notwithstanding even the fact that many local meetings continued to be conducted in that unbroken alternation of Spanish and English which had become the local patois ("I will be in Boston on Sunday and *desafortunadamente yo tengo un compromiso en* Boston *qu no puedo romper y yo no podre estar con Vds.*," read the minutes of a 1984 Miami City Commission meeting I had occasion to look up. *"En espiritu, estaré, pero* the other members of the commission I am sure are invited . . ."),[1] the very existence of this referendum, was seen by many as ground regained, a point made. By 1985 a St. Petersburg optometrist named Robert Melby was launching his third attempt in four years to have English declared the official language of the state of Florida, as it would be in 1986 of California. "I don't know why our legislators here are so, how should I put it? — spineless," Robert Melby complained about those South Florida politicians who knew how to count. "No one down here seems to want to run with the issue."

Even among those Anglos who distanced themselves from such ef- 22 forts, Anglos who did not perceive themselves as economically or socially threatened by Cubans, there remained considerable uneasiness on the matter of language, perhaps because the inability or the disinclination to speak English tended to undermine their conviction that assimilation was an ideal universally shared by those who were to be assimilated. This uneasiness had for example shown up repeatedly during the 1985 mayoralty campaign, surfacing at odd but apparently irrepressible angles. The winner of that contest, Xavier Suarez, who was born in Cuba but educated in the United States, a graduate of Harvard Law, was

---

[1] "I will be in Boston on Sunday and unfortunately I have an appointment in Boston that I can't break and I won't be able to be with you. In spirit, I will be, but the other members of the commission I am sure are invited. . . ."

reported in a wire service story to speak, an apparently unexpected accomplishment, "flawless English."

23        A less prominent Cuban candidate for mayor that year had unsettled reporters at a televised "meet the candidates" forum by answering in Spanish the questions they asked in English. "For all I or my dumbstruck colleagues knew," the *Herald* political editor complained in print after the event, "he was reciting his high school's alma mater or the ten Commandments over and over again. The only thing I understood was the occasional *Cubanos vota Cubano* he tossed in." It was noted by another *Herald* columnist that of the leading candidates, only one, Raul Masvidal, had a listed telephone number, but: ". . . if you call Masvidal's 661-0259 number on Kiaora Street in Coconut Grove—during the day, anyway—you'd better speak Spanish. I spoke to two women there, and neither spoke enough English to answer the question of whether it was the candidate's number."

24        On the morning this last item came to my attention in the *Herald* I studied it for some time. Raul Masvidal was at that time the chairman of the board of the Miami Savings Bank and the Miami Savings Corporation. He was a former chairman of the Biscayne Bank, and a minority stockholder in the M Bank, of which he had been a founder. He was a member of the Board of Regents for the state university system of Florida. He had paid $600,000 for the house on Kiaora Street in Coconut Grove, buying it specifically because he needed to be a Miami resident (Coconut Grove is part of the city of Miami) in order to run for mayor, and he had sold his previous house, in the incorporated city of Coral Gables, for $1,100,000.

25        The Spanish words required to find out whether the number listed for the house on Kiaora Street was in fact the candidate's number would have been roughly these: "*¿Es la casa de Raul Masvidal?*" The answer might have been "*Sí*," or the answer might have been "*No*." It seemed to me that there must be very few people working on daily newspapers along the southern borders of the United States who would consider this exchange entirely out of reach, and fewer still who would not accept it as a commonplace of American domestic life that daytime telephone calls to middle-class urban households will frequently be answered by women who speak Spanish.

26        Something else was at work in this item, a real resistance, a balkiness, a coded version of the same message Dade County voters had sent when they decreed that their business be done only in English: WILL THE LAST AMERICAN TO LEAVE MIAMI PLEASE BRING THE FLAG, the famous bumper stickers had read the year of Mariel. "It was the last American stronghold in Dade County," the owner of the Gator Kicks Longneck Saloon, out where Southwest Eighth Street runs into the Everglades, had said after he closed the place for good the night of Super Bowl Sunday, 1986. "Fortunately or unfortunately, I'm not alone in my inability," a *Herald* columnist named Charles Whited had written a week or so later, in a

column about not speaking Spanish. "A good many Americans have left Miami because they want to live someplace where everybody speaks one language: theirs." In this context the call to the house on Kiaora Street in Coconut Grove which did or did not belong to Raul Masvidal appeared not as a statement of literal fact but as shorthand, a glove thrown down, a stand, a cry from the heart of a beleaguered raj.

## Evaluating the Text

1. How do the results of the poll taken by the *Miami Herald* with which Didion begins her essay reveal the extent to which the Cuban influx has been misperceived by the Miami Anglo community? How does her article attempt to correct these misperceptions?
2. How does Didion use striking examples and news items to establish the impact of the 56 percent of Miami's population that is Cuban and the extent to which Cubans are an integral part of the political and social structure of the city?
3. What evidence does Didion provide to show that the Cuban majority is more powerful politically and economically than most Anglos would care to admit?
4. How does Didion develop her essay to show that Cubans have succeeded without conforming to the American cultural idea of assimilation?
5. Explain why Anglos would wish to perceive Miami as being essentially the same as any other southern city despite its strikingly foreign character? the same as any other southern city despite its strikingly foreign character?
6. Why is it significant that the *Miami Herald* did not have a Cuban on the staff reporting on cultural events in the Cuban community when they comprise 56 percent of Dade County's population? What other evidence does Didion offer to show that Anglos living side by side with Cubans in Miami are unaware of activities taking place in their community?
7. To what extent is the unwillingness of Cubans to assimilate into mainstream American culture a result of the widespread belief that they are in the United States temporarily and that they will return to Cuba after Castro is no longer in power?
8. What are *quinces* and how are they perceived very differently by Anglos and by the Cuban community? How does the difference in perception of *quinces* underscore Didion's thesis?
9. Why is it significant that Dade County business is conducted in both English and Spanish? How is the history of resistance to using Spanish for county business a reflection of the political struggle of Cubans in Dade County?

## Exploring Different Perspectives

1. What factors might explain the difference between Cuban success in Dade County and the failure of the Puerto Rican family in Nicholasa Mohr's story ("A Very Special Pet")?
2. In what significant ways do Cubans differ from Edward Said's ("Reflections on Exile") characterization of exiles? What factors are responsible for these differences?

3. In what way does Didion's use of the word *raj* suggest that the Anglos in Miami are similar to the British in India, behaving as though they are still dominant? How is the attitude of the British toward Antiguan natives, as described by Jamaica Kincaid ("A Small Place") similar to the Anglo attitude toward Cubans in Miami?

## Extending Viewpoints through Writing

1. What series of historical events resulted in the Cuban exodus after Fidel Castro's rise to power? What would you infer about their situation in Cuba at the time Castro took over? How do the Cubans who came to Miami differ from most groups of immigrants that come to America?

2. Write a brief essay describing the role played by a particular ethnic group in a town or city with which you are familiar. Highlight the contributions of this group in real and specific ways to the spirit and culture of the city.

3. How is the issue of language connected to refugees and immigrants moving to an area in the United States? Discuss this idea in relationship to proposals that English should be the official state language in Florida, California, and in other states that have large immigrant populations. What is your view on whether English should be declared the official language in your state?

4. Evaluate Didion's assessment that Anglos only become resentful when Spanish is spoken by those who are their social and economic equals and do not mind when Spanish is spoken by people considered to belong to a lower social class. To what extent do you think hostility may be due to jealousy on the part of Anglos toward immigrants who have succeeded in the United States?

5. Didion said of the book that evolved from this essay, "*Miami* [1987], its title not withstanding, is mainly about what I think is wrong in Washington" (quoted by James Chase in the *New York Times Book Review*, October 25, 1987). How does Didion's characterization of politicians in Washington point out a reluctance to come to terms with the enormously influential role Hispanics now play and will continue to play in American culture?

# Le Ly Hayslip

# *Sisters and Brothers*

---

*Le Ly Hayslip, the youngest of six children in a close-knit Buddhist family, was twelve years old when U.S. helicopters landed in Ky La, in central Vietnam. Before she was sixteen, Le Ly experienced near starvation, imprisonment, torture, rape, and the deaths of family members. After a courageous escape to America, she settled in Los Angeles with her three sons, where she started the East Meets West Foundation, a charitable relief organization. The following account is from her eloquent memoir,* When Heaven and Earth Changed Places *(with Jay Wurts, 1989), which details her return to Vietnam after thirty years. Hayslip discusses the difficulties she faced in trying to overcome her brother's lingering political suspicions when she was reunited with the family she had left behind in Vietnam.*

*Bordered by Cambodia and Laos to the west, China to the north, and the South China Sea to the east and south, Vietnam was first visited by European traders in the early sixteenth century. After the French captured Saigon in 1859, Vietnam was under the control of France until World War II, when the Viet Minh, a coalition of nationalists and communists, established a republic headed by Ho Chi Minh. France's attempts to reassert control resulted in the French Indochina War (1946–1954), in which the French were defeated. In the Geneva Conference of 1954, Vietnam was divided, pending nationwide free elections, into North Vietnam, controlled by communists, and South Vietnam, controlled by nationalists. Ngo Dinh Diem's refusal to hold these elections, out of fear of a communist victory, precipitated the Vietnam War of 1954–1975, in which South Vietnam, aided by the United States, fought communist insurgents, who were supported by North Vietnam. United States troops were withdrawn in 1973, after a cease fire, and in 1975 the communists overran the south. The country was reunified as the Socialist Republic of Vietnam in 1976. In 1978, Vietnam invaded Cambodia, deposed the genocidal Pol Pot regime, and installed a government that remained until the Vietnamese withdrew in 1989. Hayslip's narrative offers insight into the lives of great numbers of Vietnamese who fled the country during and after the war.*

*(For more information on Vietnamese refugees, known as "boat people," see p. 466; for additional information on the Vietnam war, see p. 659; for more information on Cambodia, see p. 366.)

EVENING, APRIL 7, 1986:
TINH'S HOUSE, DANANG

1    We sit around Tinh's table and she serves *ca thu* fish and shrimp she bought at the market, salty *mon man* pork to clear the palate, followed by a main course of *xoa*, or chow mein vegetables.

2    While we eat, I expect to learn what will happen when and if I meet my brother Bon Nghe. Sadly, my four companions seem to have grave doubts that such a meeting should take place at all.

3    Tinh says to her mother, Hai (who was against the idea from the start), "Bon Nghe will faint when he see Bay Ly. He never believed she would be allowed to come home. He called me a dreamer for even suggesting it. I say: Let him see her for himself."

4    "Oh." Hai turns pale and shakes her head. "He'll think she's a spy or saboteur! Maybe even a party agent assigned to ferret out defectors!"

5    "Bon Nghe can't believe Bay Ly even *wants* to return," Anh says. "Why would an American come back to Vietnam? People pay pirates and profiteers to take them out and the orderly departure program has been logjammed for years. It just doesn't make sense to him."

6    Logical or not, it makes perfect sense to me. I have not seen my older brother — keeper of my father's and my family's name — for over thirty-two years. When he left, I was a worshipful sister of five. As a teenager, Bon Nghe was more like another father than a brother. Where Sau Ban had my father's easygoing nature, Bon Nghe was more like my mother: serious, filled with duty, less partial to the spiritual world than to the world of day and night, a person singled out in youth to show courage and independence. From what little I know about Communists, I'm sure he makes a good one — and is probably better than most, since it's unlikely his Phung nature has been soiled by abuse of power.

7    Hai looks at me while she picks through her mint salad, served by Tinh as a final treat.

8    "Besides, Bay Ly," she says, "Bon Nghe's a different man from the boy you kissed good-bye back in 1954. He's a dedicated party man. He studied accounting as well as war in Hanoi. Uncle Ho's government trusted him to deliver payrolls to the south for many years — and they don't trust Southerners easily. If you really want to see him, you must be willing to risk disappointment."

9    "I haven't come this far to back out now," I reply. "And Bon Nghe is not the only person who's changed. Maybe we'll both be pleased by what we see."

10    Bien leaves for Bon's house on Anh's motorbike and I help Tinh wash the dishes. He's gone a long time — over an hour — and I begin to feel nervous. Perhaps Bon's out of town and I'll miss him altogether. Or worse, perhaps he's home but doesn't want to see me, despite Bien's pleading. Gradually, I notice Anh and Hai sitting like baby-sitters on either side of me. I laugh and take their hands and they take mine, and so we sit and wait.

Around eight we hear the Honda sputter outside and the kickstand 11
snap into place. Male voices speak but I can't make out a thing, although
I grasp for clues. Is the other voice Bon Nghe's? If it is, does it sound
happy, sad, or cross?

"Well—it's about time!" Tinh says, and all of us get up. Our eyes are 12
riveted on the space on the door where we know Bon Nghe's face will
appear. An instant later, a boy-man who looks exactly like the dog-eared
photo I have carried from America comes in. Bon's chestnut face is better
preserved than Hai's, although care lines crease the mouth and eyes and
the boyish mop of hair shows streaks of gray. He shakes hands cordially
with Anh, bowing slightly in the manner of close-but-not-too-close
relations, then turns toward me. Like Hai's, his initial expression is one of
shock, not pleasure.

"Co Bay!" (Miss Number-Six "Aunt"!) He uses the ceremonial form of 13
greeting—one reserved for distant relatives—rather than the familiar
*em bay* for number-six sister. It almost breaks my heart. Before this
greeting, I thought about throwing myself in his arms. Now I know that
although the gulf between us has been narrowed greatly, these last few
feet may be the hardest of all to cross.

"How did you get here?" His voice is barely a whisper. 14

Obviously, he thinks I landed with a CIA parachute or bribed my 15
way past Vietnam's stolid watchmen. Had I been wearing designer jeans,
high heels, and a Disneyland sweatshirt, I could not have felt more
conspicuously American.

"Like any other tourist," I answer with a smile, longing to hug him, 16
"on an airplane at the airport. You look wonderful, Bon Nghe!"

"Airport? You mean Ton San Nhut—Ho Chi Minh City? Or Hanoi?" 17

These are a policeman's, not a brother's, questions and I feel tears 18
come again to my eyes. Bien, now inside the door, also senses the tension
and hovers close to Bon, perhaps to restrain him if he becomes enraged.
Yet it is essential that I keep my composure. East is meeting West.
Despite my warmest feelings, an epoch of war and politics has come
between us. I must play the game on dear Bon's terms until he feels
comfortable enough to play on mine.

"Tan Son Nhut," I answer, "with lots of other people—UN workers, 19
some French and Russians—lots of people. But you took so long getting
here. I hope my visit didn't take you away from important business."

Bon Nghe relaxes a little and Bien laughs. 20

"As a matter of fact," Bien says, "Bon Nghe wasn't home when I 21
called. I sent his son looking for him with a message: 'You must come to
Tinh's at once,' and he thought something had happened to his mother.
So when he rushed home and learned it was you, Bay Ly, who wanted to
see him, he was relieved and shocked at the same time. You should have
seen his face!"

Bon steps closer, but his manner is still guarded. "So, you're here on 22
an American passport and everything's okay?"

He is still worried that I sneaked into the country! *How can I convince* 23 *you, brother Bon!* "Yes," I laugh as carelessly as I am able. "Everything's okay! My passport is safe at my hotel. But I have a *Ban Viet Kieu* travel card and a letter from the Vietnamese mission at the United Nations, if you'd like to see those—"

24    I begin to fish in my purse and Bon Nghe, perhaps feeling a little sheepish for doubting me, reaches out to stop me. The Phung male hand on my arm almost turns me to butter, but I hang tough.

25    "Oh no, that's not necessary," he says, then withdraws the hand quickly. "So—how are you getting along in the United States?" At least he tries to smile. "How's your family? Do they get enough to eat?"

26    "I'm doing okay," I say firmly, genuinely touched by his concern. "We're doing just fine. And your family? Can you provide for them okay?"

27    I sense that Bon's waiting for me to ask him about his politics—is he really a Communist or not? Perhaps he's waiting for me to ask him for a favor, as most bureaucrats expect—especially from relatives. I had learned already that most Vietnamese officials feel defensive about their poverty-stricken country. Instead, we talk about our families, and I hear in his voice an earnest desire to push governments and politics aside. The problem is—after all those years of discipline and training—he doesn't quite know how.

28    Tinh invites us to tea and the last of the New Year's cookies. Anh and Hai and Bien try to break the tension by crowding in their own light questions: *Wasn't today a scorcher? Bon Nghe—how's that new accountant working out at the office? Do you think they'll end rice rationing soon? You should've seen all the snails Hai sold today!* But Bon Nghe and I just sit there looking at each other, and after everyone has had enough cookies and tea to be polite, Anh and Bien go outside and Tinh and Hai play busy in the kitchen. I am left alone with my brother to talk.

29    "You know, Bon Nghe," I begin, "I had this terrible fear you would despise me."

30    "Oh no—!" He tosses the idea off politely.

31    "Well, you know, I married one of your enemies—an American civilian worker—and left the country while you were still fighting. That doesn't bother you now?"

32    "Well, it's been so many years—" Bon's voice trails away and he changes the topic. "I just can't believe you're really here. You just got your visa and flew in?"

33    "No," I smile, "I had to write some letters first. And boy, did I talk to a lot of people! Some said go and some said stay, so I finally had to follow my heart. But if my earlier gifts could make the journey, why not me?"

34    "I wouldn't know about those," Bon Nghe says quickly. "I never touched them. Not that I didn't appreciate your thoughtfulness, *Co Bay,* but it wouldn't have been right. I am a member of the party, after all. But for Tinh and Ba and the others—that's all right. They needed all the help they could get. Things have been very hard for them."

"And for you?" 35

Bon smiles his *old soldier* smile—almost every veteran has one. 36
"Well, I had been through the war, you know? For us, it was a seven-days-a-week, twenty-four-hour-a-day job. We used our own excrement to grow vegetables, eh? Rice was a luxury. I ate enough *cu san cu mi*—coarse yams—to last a lifetime! And of course, we never had a full night's sleep. Half my life in those years was spent underground—to walk around on a sunny day was high holiday, I'll tell you! Once, I was wounded by a fragment from a mortar round. I woke up in a coffin and escaped being buried only by pounding on the lid! I tell you, *Co Bay*, our life was so lousy, all we had to hold onto was the future. And because we knew that future wouldn't arrive unless we won, we kept fighting no matter what. It wasn't so much because we were brave but because we just didn't have the option of quitting."

"Like the Americans?" 37

"Yes, like the Americans. If the situation had been reversed, I'd have 38
quit too—wouldn't you, Bay Ly?"

My familiar name on my brother's lips is music to my ears. I wriggle 39
closer to him in my chair.

"But you missed out on so much!" I say, touching his arm for empha- 40
sis. "You never knew about Sau Ban or Father, or how Lan and I went to America, until after the war!"

"I never heard anything from anyone. You know, in 1971, I was 41
trapped on a mountainside by an enemy bombardment. In the foxhole next to me was another Regular—but from a different unit. We started talking to pass the time and I noticed he had a Central accent. 'What village are you from?' I asked. He answered, 'From Ky La.' I couldn't believe it! So I asked, 'What's your father's name?' And you know what? He was Aunt Lien's son—my own cousin! So we sort of hung around together after that. He didn't know much about the village, except that it had suffered a lot of damage. I didn't know about you and Lan until much later. Nineteen seventy-five was a bad year for us, despite libera-tion. In some ways, for those of us who fought for the North, it was worse than the war. When we came south on furlough to find our families or to take posts with the new government, we saw that every-thing was different from what we had been told. We believed the South was poor—but look at the wealth of Saigon! We thought Southerners would welcome us as liberators, but everyone was suspicious. Our mother was even afraid to tell me that you and Lan had gone to America until she was certain there would be no retribution. She just said some-thing must have happened to you in the city—can you believe it? So for a couple of years, I thought more than half my family was dead! I even asked her for a recent picture so I could look for you, but she refused—worried that someone who knew you would tell me the truth. When your letters and presents started coming, of course, she couldn't deny you were alive in America."

"What did you think when you found out?" 42

43    Bon Nghe laughed, "I couldn't believe it! At first I was offended —
that any relative of mine could live with the enemy. Then, I didn't care so
much, as long as my sisters were alive. *Cuc mau cat lam doi*, eh? — How
can you divide a pool of blood? I thought you must be living in prison or
in a reeducation camp. I couldn't believe Vietnamese could just walk into
the United States and start a new life."

44    "What did you think of my letters?" I asked.

45    Bon Nghe looked down at the table. "Somehow it didn't seem right
to read them. We were still brother and sister — we shared the same
mother — but we have different hearts and minds. I respect you for
coming back, Bay Ly — for taking the risks, whatever they were. But I
must ask you now to do something else."

46    "What's that?"

47    "Leave Mama *Du* alone. Don't go to the village, whatever you do. If
she wants to come and visit, she will — but let her do it in her own way."

48    For an instant I think Bon Nghe is telling me that my mother no
longer loves me and tears fill my eyes. Certainly, she had a chance to
come and see me this afternoon, but sent little Cu back to Tinh's with the
flimsy story that she had to stay and feed the chickens. "I don't
understand —"

49    "You must understand, Bay Ly: the war is still going on for us. We
can't turn trust on and off like a light switch —"

50    "I have come here only to make my heart and soul happy, Bon
Nghe," I sob. "I don't want to harm anyone. I don't want to open any
wounds. You see, I waited all those years in America, just like you waited
in the jungle, to see my family again. That's what kept me going. I came
back to see you and Mother and everyone else — to see if I still had a
family."

51    "Good. Then don't spoil things for them. If the officials think your
mother is receiving money from the capitalists, she may lose her pension.
And there are still certain villagers — you know the ones I mean — who
haven't forgotten the war: the things our mother was accused of. She
must still be very careful. *You* must be very careful."

52    I take out a handkerchief and blow my nose. Tinh and Hai take it as a
signal to come to my rescue with happy talk. As I put my hankie back in
my purse, I notice I still have an American-made chocolate left over from
the flight from the United States. Having nothing else with me to offer,
and being unsure that I will ever see Bon Nghe again after tonight, I take
the candy out and hold it up as a pathetic gift.

53    "*Moi Anh an?*" (Would you like a candy?) I smile through my tears as I
did when I was five years old offering my brother sweet rice on the day
he left for Hanoi. "They're pretty good!"

54    Bon Nghe refuses to take it — to even touch the wrapper. "No, no
thanks," he says, holding up his hands.

55    "Oh, come on! When's the last time you ate good chocolate?"

56    "I couldn't really. You see, a lot of the American food was booby-

trapped after liberation. Even the grocers didn't know about it. I wouldn't feel right, honestly—"

Honestly, my brother thinks I might—just *might*—offer him food tainted on purpose in America! A weight so heavy I can't breathe pushes me into my seat. I turn immediately to Tinh. 57

"Tinh—may I give some candy to your son?" The oldest boy was still awake and doing homework in the other room. 58

She answers yes and the ten-year-old is beside me before I can call his name. He unwraps the candy the way a groom unveils his bride and slips it into his mouth, intent, apparently, on making it last the whole night. Before he leaves, Tinh barks another order. 59

"Oh no, you don't, young man!" She snaps her finger at the fire under the stove. "The wrapper—into the fire with it! Right now, before you forget!" 60

I sag deeper into my chair. Even Tinh must be careful not to let so dangerous a thing as a capitalist candy wrapper incriminate her family! All evidence must be eaten or burned! The long day and the weight of the war and all the years in between bear down on me like the planet itself. My feelings must have shown on my face. 61

"Look, it's getting late," Bon Nghe says. He reaches into his shirt pocket and brings out a piece of paper and pencil. "I want you to meet my family, Bay Ly—and I don't want to have to lie to my superiors to arrange it. Please write down what I tell you, eh? Go ahead—'I, Phung Thi Le Ly Hayslip, ask permission to visit with my brother, Phung Nghe, and his wife and son, at two o'clock on April 9, at—' Where are you staying?" 62

"At the old Pacific Hotel—" 63

"Oh, that's a nice place—kept up well for important visitors! '. . . at the Pacific Hotel, Danang City.' Now sign your name—right there below it—and I'll take it to the office. This first visit, the one tonight—we'll agree didn't happen, okay? It's just for you and me. For the record, we'll meet for the first time on Wednesday. I hope that's okay?" 64

I tell him I would be happy to see him again anyway I could, and would love to meet his pretty wife and fine son. I again resist the urge to give him a hug and kiss—it would not be proper and even if it was, he would likely worry that I was wearing poisoned lipstick, compliments of the CIA! 65

I say good night to Tinh and her son and after Bien runs Bon Nghe back to his house, Anh takes me to the hotel on his Honda. Despite the barriers between us, I cannot say that I have ever loved my older brother more than I do right now. No matter how many men you love, or how many men love you, no bond is thicker than the blood which passes through the umbilicus to brothers and sisters—*Mau dam hon nuoc la*, blood *is* thicker than water—and Bon and I, through our poor old mother, can never lose that connection. 66

I get off at the hotel's front entrance and before leaving for his sister's 67 house—Anh's residence in Danang—he says over the noise of the motor, "Don't worry, Bay Ly. Bon Nghe knows why you came back. He admires you very much, though it will be difficult for him to say so. He even knows you're writing a book. He told me he wants to write one too, when he retires. It's true! He's very proud of you for telling your family's story, even to the Americans."

68    "Maybe our relatives should read it too, eh?" I pat Anh's shoulder. "Then maybe everyone can stop refighting the war!"

69    "Don't hold your breath, Bay Ly," Anh smiles bravely, waves, and drives away.

70    In my room, I take a tepid shower (the best my hot-water faucet will do) and am amazed at how kind to me my life has been. Even if my visit ended now, I have at least had the satisfaction of seeing my sister Hai—the next best thing to my mother—and my long-lost brother Bon Nghe, who now heads my father's family. As I pull my fingers through my wet hair, I can feel the tendrils of my life forming a circle before my eyes—but in such colors and such rich textures as I could scarcely have imagined.

71    I climb into bed, rejoicing at the roar of surf. Tomorrow, if fate or luck or god is willing, maybe I'll see my mother and smell the perfume of her leather skin and brittle hair and feel those ancient arms wrap around me and make me, for an instant at least, as contented as the newborn infant they once held.

72    But fate is sometimes fickle; luck is not always good; and god, in his heaven, sometimes turns his face from life. What if my poor old mother still refuses to see me or is destined to breathe her last tonight? There are more than enough things for which I can be punished—and what jungle justice it would be for me to come all this way after all these years just to walk in my mother's funeral!

73    *Bay Ly, Bay Ly,* the whispering ocean says, *My little peach blossom . . .!*

## Evaluating the Text

1. Describe Bay Ly's feelings at seeing an older brother whom she had not seen for over thirty years. Why might Bon Nghe fear that he would become politically suspect if he visited with her?

2. What do Bon Nghe's initial reactions show about his personality and character? What evidence is there that he has difficulty in getting past a "being-at-war" mentality toward Americans?

3. Why is it significant that Bon Nghe's questions to his sister about her life in America are phrased in terms of whether she and her family get enough to eat? What does this tell you about life in Vietnam?

4. What is the significance of Bon Nghe's comment that although it was all right for his sisters to take the gifts sent from America, he could not?

5. How is the issue of trust involved in Bon Nghe's advice to Bay Ly not to see their mother? How has Bon Nghe himself been lied to about economic conditions in South Vietnam?

6. To what extent have Bon Nghe and his family had to endure the political consequences caused by Bay Ly's actions in marrying an American? How does the episode involving the candy reveal the political atmosphere in which her family still must live?

## Exploring Different Perspectives

1. How does Bay Ly's situation reflect the predicament of being an exile described by Edward Said ("Reflections on Exile")? How are the conflicts she experiences, produced by being between two cultures, similar to those all exiles experience?
2. What connections can you discover between Bay Ly's situation in Vietnam and that of Shaila in Canada (Bharati Mukherjee, "The Management of Grief")? How do political and/or religious barriers create conflicts for Shaila and Bay Ly?

## Extending Viewpoints through Writing

1. Have you ever been reunited with a relative, in this country or abroad, whom you had not seen for some time? Were you afraid that the intervening years had changed things so much that it might be difficult to reestablish the relationship? What happened?
2. Have you ever had an experience similar to Bay Ly's, where a personal relationship was overshadowed by differences in political ideology? What happened?

# David Whitman

# Trouble for America's "Model" Minority

---

*David Whitman is an associate editor of* U.S. News and World
Report. *Whitman refutes the impression created by the media that
recent Indochinese refugees are flourishing in America. His in-depth
report uses interviews and case histories to document the enormous
obstacles confronting the second wave of 640,000 Indochinese war
refugees who came to the United States from Vietnam, Laos, and
Cambodia since 1978. "Trouble for America's 'Model' Minority" was
first published in the February 23, 1987, issue of* U.S. News and
World Report.

*The first wave of people attempting to escape oppression in Indo-
china were from Vietnam, after the communist victory in 1975. In
1978 and 1979, Vietnam invaded Cambodia, overthrowing the regime
of the Khmer Rouge under Pol Pot and provoking a brief invasion by
China. The political and social upheaval in this area prompted the
flight of great numbers of refugee "boat people" who attempted to
escape the conditions in their countries by taking to the South China
sea in makeshift boats, often dying in the attempt. After ten years, by
1989, the last Vietnamese troops sent into Cambodia were withdrawn,
a move many fear will permit a return to power of the Khmer Rouge, a
regime responsible for the wholesale slaughter of millions of
Cambodians.*

1    When 12-year-old Hue Cao shyly read her prize-winning essay at
last year's nationally televised Statue of Liberty centennial celebration,
she seemed the very model of a thriving Indochinese boat person. Only
six years before, Hue, her mother, four brothers and two sisters fled
Vietnam in a fishing boat, and now she was the center of national
attention, having bested 2,000 other children in a highly competitive
essay contest. "This nation has given my family a brand-new life," Hue
recited proudly as tens of millions of equally proud Americans looked
on.

2    Unfortunately, however, what they saw on their TV screens was

---

*(For additional information on Cambodia and the Khmer Rouge, see p. 366.)

something of a sham. Far from flourishing in the U.S., the Cao family turned out to be on welfare, unable even to accept the contest prize—a new automobile—because it would have meant surrendering their public-assistance benefits. "The girl's mother was in tears," recalls Reg Schwenke of the Aloha Liberty Foundation, sponsor of the essay contest. "She was both anxious and ashamed."

The problems of Hue Cao and her family illustrate a major but    3 long-hidden difference in social backgrounds between the two groups that make up the more than 800,000 Indochinese who sought refuge in the U.S. in the past 11 years. The first wave of 130,000 refugees—those who arrived in the immediate aftermath of the fall of Saigon in 1975— was largely an elite group. They were officials of the deposed South Vietnamese government, employees of the American military, dependents of U.S. servicemen and upper-echelon staffers of multinational corporations. Given their experience and contacts, these refugees made a relatively easy transition to life in the U.S. and created a near mythic image of the Indochinese as brilliant students, flourishing entrepreneurs and altogether successful symbols of the American dream. After only four years in the U.S., the first wave of Indochinese refugees earned 18 percent more than the average American.

## Behind the Myth

The story, however, is far different for the second wave, the 640,000    4 who arrived in the U.S. following Vietnam's invasion of Cambodia in 1978. For many of them, life in America has been far less satisfying and considerably more precarious. In contrast to those who preceded them, the second wave of refugees had little education and few skills to bolster them in their new homes. Instead of sophisticated city dwellers, they were mostly rural people—farmers, fishers, small merchants and mountain tribespeople—many unable to speak English and illiterate in their own language. Half came from Laos and Cambodia, nations considerably poorer and socially less developed than Vietnam. And unlike the earlier refugees, those in the second wave often suffered brutal physical and psychological traumas before arriving in the United States. Many had been imprisoned in Vietnamese re-education camps, nearly starved and tortured in Pol Pot's Cambodia, or raped, beaten and robbed by the Thai pirates who preyed on the boat people in the Gulf of Thailand.

"This was the largest nonwhite, non-Western, non–English-speaking    5 group of people ever to enter the country at one time," said Peter Rose, a Smith College professor who has written widely on the refugees. "The public assumed they succeeded just because the first wave did." Adds Ruben Rumbaut, director of the Indochinese Health and Adaptation Research Project at San Diego State University: "The Southeast Asian success stories play well in Peoria. Those of the losers don't."

6    Even when compared with depressed minorities in the U.S., "second wave" Indochinese fare poorly. A staggering 64 percent of the Indochinese households headed by refugees who arrived after 1980 are on public assistance — three times the rate of American blacks and four times that of Hispanics. And among refugee groups as a whole, the newly arrived Indochinese are by far the most dependent upon the dole.

7    *"In our old country, whatever we had was made or brought in by our hands," said Chong Sao Yang, 62, a former farmer and soldier who moved to San Diego from Laos. Yang and three family members have been on welfare for seven years. 'We are not born on earth to have somebody give us food. Here, I'm sure we're going to starve, because since our arrival there is no penny I can get that is money I earn from work. I've been trying very hard to learn English, and at the same time look for a job. But no matter what kind of job — even a job to clean peoples's toilets — still people don't trust you or offer you such work. I'm not even worth as much as a dog's stool. Talking about this, I want to die right here so I won't see my future."*

8    Many in the newer wave of refugees grew up in Laos and Cambodia without electricity, running water, clocks or stoves — much less banks, savings accounts and credit cards. And Hmong tribesmen like Yang from the highlands of Laos feel even more isolated because of their illiteracy and traditional beliefs in witchcraft and shamans. "What we have here are 16th-century people suddenly thrust into 20th-century life," says Ernest Velasquez of the welfare department in Fresno, Calif., home for an estimated 18,000 Hmong. . . .

9    *Nao Chai Her was the respected head of a Hmong village of more than 500 people in Laos. Here, he is on welfare and shares a cramped three-bedroom apartment with 20 relatives. 'We are just like the baby birds," says Nao, 61, "who stay in the nest opening their mouths, waiting only for the mother bird to bring the worms. When the government doesn't send the cash on time, we even fear we'll starve. I used to be a real man like any other man, but not any longer. The work I used to do, I can't do here. I feel like a thing which drops in the fire but won't burn and drops in the river but won't flow."*

10   Many Indochinese experience similar sieges of depression but manage to carefully disguise the condition behind a mask of hard work and traditional courtesy. In one standardized psychological test given in San Diego, 45 percent of the adult refugees showed distress symptoms serious enough to require clinical treatment, four times the proportion among the population at large. Cambodian women, many left husbandless by Pol Pot's genocide, are especially troubled. Lay Plok, 34, of Arlington, Va., lost her husband in 1977 when they fled the famine in Cambodia. "I'm down," she says quietly, "and yet I don't know what would make life feel better."

11   Like U.S. veterans with painful memories of Vietnam, some Indochinese refugees suffer repeated nightmares and evidence a variety of stress-related disorders. Indeed, emotional trauma among the new arrivals is so extensive and little understood that Dr. Richard Mollica and

social worker James Lavelle of St. Elizabeth's Hospital set up the Indo-chinese Psychiatry Clinic in 1981 in Boston just to assist refugees. One woman treated at the clinic wandered from city to city in the U.S., fearful that her Communist jailers were out to recapture her. She told clinic doctors a harrowing but not atypical story of having been repeatedly raped, tortured and given mind-altering drugs while imprisoned.

For all their problems, however, the newer refugees don't fully fit the     12 underclass stereotype. Most cherish hard work and stress the value of family and education. Divorce and out-of-wedlock pregnancy are still taboo. Drug and alcohol abuse is minimal. Studies of the refugee children, including those with illiterate Hmong parents, indicate they do quite well in school. And even where most of the family gets public-assistance payments, at least one member has a paying job, sometimes off the books. "The refugees make exemplary use of the welfare system," argues Nathan Caplan of the University of Michigan, an expert on the second wave of refugees. "They tend to have large families, so they pool resources to finance education and training. And they rely on welfare less as time goes by."

In the end, however, whatever their cultural liabilities, the refugees'     13 greatest asset may be simply that they are survivors. Puthnear Mom, 22, also of Arlington, lost her husband while crossing the Cambodian border to Thailand. She can't read or write, and has been unemployed for two years. "I'm unhappy to receive welfare," she says through a translator, "but life is better now than in Cambodia or the refugee camp. I can learn anything here I want. Freedom does matter."

## Evaluating the Text

1. How does Whitman use the case of Hue Cao to illustrate the gap between public perception of the success of Indo-Chinese immigrants and the reality of their situation?
2. How did the first wave of Indochinese immigrants differ from the second in terms of skills, familiarity with urban culture, and the ease or difficulty with which they adapted to living in the United States?
3. In what sense are the 18,000 Hmong "16th-century people suddenly thrust into 20th-century life"? How does the cultural background of the Hmong tribespeople create an enormous barrier to their adjusting to life in the United States?
4. What are some of the causes of the unusually high percentage of adult refugees who display stress-related disorders requiring clinical treatment?
5. How do the strong family bonds among the Indochinese refugees enable them to make effective use of the welfare system? How do they work together to pool their resources?
6. How does the testimony of Chong Sao Yang and Nao Chai Her illustrate Whitman's thesis?
7. What do you think Nao Chai Her means when he says "I feel like a

thing which drops in the fire but won't burn and drops in the river but won't flow"? What does this tell you about his situation?

8. Evaluate the range of sources and the kinds of examples Whitman uses to support his view that "for all their problems . . . the newer refugees don't fully fit the underclass stereotype."

## Exploring Different Perspectives

1. How does the media's need to manipulate the case of Hue Cao to fit the stereotype of the successful Asian immigrant compare with how Cuban success in Miami is downplayed by the media (see Joan Didion "Miami: The Cuban Presence")? Why would one group of immigrants be assigned the role of carrying out the "American dream" while another group actually doing so is not recognized at all?

2. Compare Whitman's account of difficulties faced by the second wave of Indochinese immigrants with the experiences of the Puerto Rican family in Nicholasa Mohr's story ("A Very Special Pet"). What similarities can you discover in terms of the role played by a language barrier, rural background, and the lack of money, education, or marketable skills?

3. In what sense might Bay Ly be considered a typical first-wave Indochinese refugee (see Le Ly Hayslip, "Sisters and Brothers")? How does her situation compare with those second-wave Indochinese refugees described by Whitman?

## Extending Viewpoints through Writing

1. Describe an experience you have had that allows you to relate to the difficulties faced by people who arrive with little money in a place where they do not know the language or customs.

2. For a research project, investigate the political events that caused so many Indochinese refugees to flee to America. You might consult Someth May's account, "The Field behind the Village" (Chapter 6), or Hearts of Sorrow: Vietnamese-American Lives, edited by James M. Freeman (1989).

3. Interview an Indochinese refugee on your campus with a view toward discovering interesting contrasts between aspects of your own culture (family life, education, religion, marriage customs, holidays, etc.) and Indochinese culture.

4. If you were able to imaginatively become "a 16th-century person suddenly thrust into 20th-century life," describe what aspects of your life, society, and environment would appear the strangest to you. How would your town or city look to a person arriving in the country, not knowing the language, without marketable skills, with little prospect for employment and completely different customs?

# Jamaica Kincaid

# *A Small Place*

---

*Jamaica Kincaid was born in St. John's, Antigua, in 1949 and educated there at the Princess Margaret School. She is a staff writer for the New Yorker. Her work has appeared in* Rolling Stone *magazine and in* The Paris Review. *She is the author of a highly praised collection of stories,* At the Bottom of the River *(1984), which won the Morton Dauwen Zabel Award of the American Academy and Institute of Arts and Letters, and a book of related stories,* Annie John *(1985), an autobiographical account of a girl's coming of age in the West Indies. Her most recent book, a novel,* Lucy *(1990), is based on her experiences of beginning a new life in the United States. "A Small Place," from the 1988 book of that name, is an impassioned diatribe on the sweeping corruption, dilapidated schools, inadequately staffed hospital, and shameful legacy of Antigua's colonial past, which tourists, absorbed in their self-centered pleasures, fail to recognize.*

*Antigua, a small island in the Antilles, was discovered by Christopher Columbus in 1493, on his second voyage to the Americas. He named the island after the Church of Santa Maria de la Antigua of Seville in Spain. The British occupied and colonized Antigua (and two smaller islands, Barbuda and Redonda) in 1632 and set up sugar plantations, which flourished until the abolition of slavery in 1834. Antigua achieved full independence in 1981 as a member of the Commonwealth, with Queen Elizabeth II as head of state. The tourist industry described by Kincaid (averaging 275,000 visitors each year) brings in approximately $225 million each year, or over half of the island's yearly gross national product.*

If you go to Antigua as a tourist, this is what you will see. If you come 1
by aeroplane, you will land at the V. C. Bird International Airport. Vere
Cornwall (V. C.) Bird is the Prime Minister of Antigua. You may be the
sort of tourist who would wonder why a Prime Minister would want an
airport named after him — why not a school, why not a hospital, why
not some great public monument? You are a tourist and you have not yet
seen a school in Antigua, you have not yet seen the hospital in Antigua,
you have not yet seen a public monument in Antigua. As your plane
descends to land, you might say, What a beautiful island Antigua is —
more beautiful than any of the other islands you have seen, and they
were very beautiful, in their way, but they were much too green, much

too lush with vegetation, which indicated to you, the tourist, that they got quite a bit of rainfall, and rain is the very thing that you, just now, do not want, for you are thinking of the hard and cold and dark and long days you spent working in North America (or, worse, Europe), earning some money so that you could stay in this place (Antigua) where the sun always shines and where the climate is deliciously hot and dry for the four to ten days you are going to be staying there; and since you are on your holiday, since you are a tourist, the thought of what it might be like for someone who had to live day in, day out in a place that suffers constantly from drought, and so has to watch carefully every drop of fresh water used (while at the same time surrounded by a sea and an ocean — the Caribbean Sea on one side, the Atlantic Ocean on the other), must never cross your mind.

2     You disembark from your plane. You go through customs. Since you are a tourist, a North American or European — to be frank, white — and not an Antiguan black returning to Antigua from Europe or North America with cardboard boxes of much needed cheap clothes and food for relatives, you move through customs swiftly, you move through customs with ease. Your bags are not searched. You emerge from customs into the hot, clean air: immediately you feel cleansed, immediately you feel blessed (which is to say special); you feel free. You see a man, a taxi driver; you ask him to take you to your destination; he quotes you a price. You immediately think that the price is in the local currency, for you are a tourist and you are familiar with these things (rates of exchange) and you feel even more free, for things seem so cheap, but then your driver ends by saying, "In U.S. currency." You may say, "Hmmmm, do you have a formal sheet that lists official prices and destinations?" Your driver obeys the law and shows you the sheet, and he apologises for the incredible mistake he has made in quoting you a price off the top of his head which is so vastly different (favouring him) from the one listed. You are driven to your hotel by this taxi driver in his taxi, a brand-new Japanese-made vehicle. The road on which you are travelling is a very bad road, very much in need of repair. You are feeling wonderful, so you say, "Oh, what a marvellous change these bad roads are from the splendid highways I am used to in North America." (Or, worse, Europe.) Your driver is reckless; he is a dangerous man who drives in the middle of the road when he thinks no other cars are coming in the opposite direction, passes other cars on blind curves that run uphill, drives at sixty miles an hour on narrow, curving roads when the road sign, a rusting, beat-up thing left over from colonial days, says 40 MPH. This might frighten you (you are on your holiday; you are a tourist); this might excite you (you are on your holiday; you are a tourist), though if you are from new York and take taxis you are used to this style of driving: most of the taxi drivers in New York are from places in the world like this. You are looking out the window (because you want to get your money's worth); you notice that all the cars you see are brand-new, or

almost brand-new, and that they are all Japanese-made. There are no
American cars in Antigua — no new ones, at any rate; none that were
manufactured in the last ten years. You continue to look at the cars and
you say to yourself, Why, they look brand-new, but they have an awful
sound, like an old car — a very old, dilapidated car. How to account for
that? Well, possibly it's because they use leaded gasoline in these brand-
new cars whose engines were built to use non-leaded gasoline, but you
mustn't ask the person driving the car if this is so, because he or she has
never heard of unleaded gasoline. You look closely at the car; you see
that it's a model of a Japanese car that you might hesitate to buy; it's a
model that's very expensive; it's a model that's quite impractical for a
person who has to work as hard as you do and who watches every penny
you earn so that you can afford this holiday you are on. How do they
afford such a car? And do they live in a luxurious house to match such a
car? Well, no. You will be surprised, then, to see that most likely the
person driving this brand-new car filled with the wrong gas lives in a
house that, in comparison, is far beneath the status of the car; and if you
were to ask why you would be told that the banks are encouraged by the
government to make loans available for cars, but loans for houses not so
easily available; and if you ask again why, you will be told that the two
main car dealerships in Antigua are owned in part or outright by ministers in government. Oh, but you are on holiday and the sight of these
brand-new cars driven by people who may or may not have really
passed their driving test (there was once a scandal about driving licences
for sale) would not really stir up these thoughts in you. You pass a
building sitting in a sea of dust and you think, It's some latrines for
people just passing by, but when you look again you see the building has
written on it PIGOTT'S SCHOOL. You pass the hospital, the Holberton
Hospital, and how wrong you are not to think about this, for though you
are a tourist on your holiday, what if your heart should miss a few beats?
What if a blood vessel in your neck should break? What if one of those
people driving those brand-new cars filled with the wrong gas fails to
pass safely while going uphill on a curve and you are in the car going in
the opposite direction? Will you be comforted to know that the hospital is
staffed with doctors that no actual Antiguan trusts; that Antiguans
always say about the doctors, "I don't want them near me"; that Antiguans refer to them not as doctors but as "the three men" (there are three
of them); that when the Minister of Health himself doesn't feel well he
takes the first plane to New York to see a real doctor; that if any one of
the ministers in government needs medical care he flies to New York to
get it?

   It's a good thing that you brought your own books with you, for you
couldn't just go to the library and borrow some. Antigua used to have a
splendid library, but in The Earthquake (everyone talks about it that
way — The Earthquake; we Antiguans, for I am one, have a great sense
of things, and the more meaningful the thing, the more meaningless we

make it) the library building was damaged. This was in 1974, and soon
after that a sign was placed on the front of the building saying, THIS
BUILDING WAS DAMAGED IN THE EARTHQUAKE OF 1974. REPAIRS ARE PENDING. The
sign hangs there, and hangs there more than a decade later, with its
unfulfilled promise of repair, and you might see this as a sort of quaint-
ness on the part of these islanders, these people descended from slaves
—what a strange, unusual perception of time they have. REPAIRS ARE
PENDING, and here it is many years later, but perhaps in a world that is
twelve miles long and nine miles wide (the size of Antigua) twelve years
and twelve minutes and twelve days are all the same. The library is one
of those splendid old buildings from colonial times, and the sign telling
of the repairs is a splendid old sign from colonial times. Not very long
after The Earthquake Antigua got its independence from Britain, making
Antigua a state in its own right, and Antiguans are so proud of this that
each year, to mark the day, they go to church and thank God, a British
God, for this. But you should not think of the confusion that must lie in
all that and you must not think of the damaged library. You have
brought your own books with you, and among them is one of those new
books about economic history, one of those books explaining how the
West (meaning Europe and North America after its conquest and settlement by Europeans) got rich: the West got rich not from the free (free—
in this case meaning got-for-nothing) and then undervalued labour, for
generations, of the people like me you see walking around you in Antigua but from the ingenuity of small shopkeepers in Sheffield and York-
shire and Lancashire, or wherever; and what a great part the invention of
the wristwatch played in it, for there was nothing noble-minded men
could not do when they discovered they could slap time on their wrists
just like that (isn't that the last straw; for not only did we have to suffer
the unspeakableness of slavery, but the satisfaction to be had from "We
made you bastards rich" is taken away, too), and so you needn't let that
slightly funny feeling you have from time to time about exploitation,
oppression, domination develop into full-fledged unease, discomfort;
you could ruin your holiday. They are not responsible for what you
have; you owe them nothing; in fact, you did them a big favour, and you
can provide one hundred examples. For here you are now, passing by
Government House. And here you are now, passing by the Prime Minister's Office and the Parliament Building, and overlooking these, with a
splendid view of St. John's Harbour, the American Embassy. If it were
not for you, they would not have Government House, and Prime Minister's Office, and Parliament Building and embassy of powerful country.
Now you are passing a mansion, an extraordinary house painted the
colour of old cow dung, with more aerials and antennas attached to it
than you will see even at the American Embassy. The people who live in
this house are a merchant family who came to Antigua from the Middle
East less than twenty years ago. When this family first came to Antigua,
they sold dry goods door to door from suitcases they carried on their

backs. Now they own a lot of Antigua; they regularly lend money to the government, they build enormous (for Antigua), ugly (for Antigua), concrete buildings in Antigua's capital, St. John's, which the government then rents for huge sums of money; a member of their family is the Antiguan Ambassador to Syria; Antiguans hate them. Not far from this mansion is another mansion, the home of a drug smuggler. Everybody knows he's a drug smuggler, and if just as you were driving by he stepped out of his door your driver might point him out to you as the notorious person that he is, for this drug smuggler is so rich people say he buys cars in tens — ten of this one, ten of that one — and that he bought a house (another mansion) near Five Islands, contents included, with cash he carried in a suitcase: three hundred and fifty thousand American dollars, and, to the surprise of the seller of the house, lots of American dollars were left over. Overlooking the drug smuggler's mansion is yet another mansion, and leading up to it is the best paved road in all of Antigua — even better than the road that was paved for the Queen's visit in 1985 (when the Queen came, all the roads that she would travel on were paved anew, so that the Queen might have been left with the impression that riding in a car in Antigua was a pleasant experience). In this mansion lives a woman sophisticated people in Antigua call Evita. She is a notorious woman. She's young and beautiful and the girlfriend of somebody very high up in the government. Evita is notorious because her relationship with this high government official has made her the owner of boutiques and property and given her a say in cabinet meetings, and all sorts of other privileges such a relationship would bring a beautiful young woman.

Oh, but by now you are tired of all this looking, and you want to reach your destination — your hotel, your room. You long to refresh yourself; you long to eat some nice lobster, some nice local food. You take a bath, you brush your teeth. You get dressed again; as you get dressed, you look out the window. That water — have you ever seen anything like it? Far out, to the horizon, the colour of the water is navy-blue; nearer, the water is the colour of the North American sky. From there to the shore, the water is pale, silvery, clear, so clear that you can see its pinkish-white sand bottom. Oh, what beauty! Oh, what beauty! You have never seen anything like this. You are so excited. You breathe shallow. You breathe deep. You see a beautiful boy skimming the water, godlike, on a Windsurfer. You see an incredibly unattractive, fat, pastrylike-fleshed woman enjoying a walk on the beautiful sand, with a man, an incredibly unattractive, fat, pastrylike-fleshed man; you see the pleasure they're taking in their surroundings. Still standing, looking out the window, you see yourself lying on the beach, enjoying the amazing sun (a sun so powerful and yet so beautiful, the way it is always overhead as if on permanent guard, ready to stamp out any cloud that dares to darken and so empty rain on you and ruin your holiday; a sun that is your personal friend). You see yourself taking a walk on that beach, you see yourself meeting new people (only they are new in a very limited way, for they are people just like you). You see yourself eating some delicious, locally grown food. You see yourself, you see yourself . . . You must not wonder what exactly happened to the contents of your lavatory when you flushed it. You must not wonder where your bathwater went when you pulled out the stopper. You must not wonder what happened when you brushed your teeth. Oh, it might all end up in the water you are thinking of taking a swim in; the contents of your lavatory might, just might, graze gently against your ankle as you wade carefree in the water, for you see, in Antigua, there is no proper sewage-disposal system. But the Caribbean Sea is very big and the Atlantic Ocean is even bigger; it would amaze even you to know the number of black slaves this ocean has swallowed up. When you sit down to eat your delicious meal, it's better that you don't know that most of what you are eating came off a plane from Miami. And before it got on a plane in Miami, who knows where it came from? A good guess is that it came from a place like Antigua first, where it was grown dirt-cheap, went to Miami, and came back. There is a world of something in this, but I can't go into it right now.

5    The thing you have always suspected about yourself the minute you become a tourist is true: A tourist is an ugly human being. You are not an ugly person all the time; you are not an ugly person ordinarily; you are not an ugly person day to day. From day to day, you are a nice person. From day to day, all the people who are supposed to love you on the whole do. From day to day, as you walk down a busy street in the large and modern and prosperous city in which you work and live, dismayed, puzzled (a cliché, but only a cliché can explain you) at how alone you feel in this crowd, how awful it is to go unnoticed, how awful it is to go unloved, even as you are surrounded by more people than you could possibly get to know in a lifetime that lasted for millennia, and then out of the corner of your eye you see someone looking at you and absolute pleasure is written all over that person's face, and then you realise that you are not as revolting a presence as you think you are (for that look just told you so). And so, ordinarily, you are a nice person, an attractive person, a person capable of drawing to yourself the affection of other people (people just like you), a person at home in your own skin (sort of; I mean, in a way; I mean, your dismay and puzzlement are natural to you, because people like you just seem to be like that, and so many of the things people like you find admirable about yourselves — the things you think about, the things you think really define you — seem rooted in these feelings): a person at home in your own house (and all its nice house things), with its nice back yard (and its nice back-yard things), at home on your street, your church, in community activities, your job, at home with your family, your relatives, your friends — you are a whole person. But one day, when you are sitting somewhere, alone in that

crowd, and that awful feeling of displacedness comes over you, and really, as an ordinary person you are not well equipped to look too far inward and set yourself aright, because being ordinary is already so taxing, and being ordinary takes all you have out of you, and though the words "I must get away" do not actually pass across your lips, you make a leap from being that nice blob just sitting like a boob in your amniotic sac of the modern experience to being a person visiting heaps of death and ruin and feeling alive and inspired at the sight of it; to being a person lying on some faraway beach, your stilled body stinking and glistening in the sand, looking like something first forgotten, then remembered, then not important enough to go back for; to being a person marvelling at the harmony (ordinarily, what you would say is the backwardness) and the union these other people (and they are other people) have with nature. And you look at the things they can do with a piece of ordinary cloth, the things they fashion out of cheap, vulgarly colored (to you) twine, the way they squat down over a hole they have made in the ground, the hole itself is something to marvel at, and since you are being an ugly person this ugly but joyful thought will swell inside you: their ancestors were not clever in the way yours were and not ruthless in the way yours were, for then would it not be you who would be in harmony with nature and backwards in that charming way? An ugly thing, that is what you are when you become a tourist, an ugly, empty thing, a stupid thing, a piece of rubbish pausing here and there to gaze at this and taste that, and it will never occur to you that the people who inhabit the place in which you have just paused cannot stand you, that behind their closed doors they laugh at your strangeness (you do not look the way they look); the physical sight of you does not please them; you have bad manners (it is their custom to eat their food with their hands; you try eating their way, you look silly; you try eating the way you always eat, you look silly); they do not like the way you speak (you have an accent); they collapse helpless from laughter, mimicking the way they imagine you must look as you carry out some everyday bodily function. They do not like you. *They do not like me!* That thought never actually occurs to you. Still, you feel a little uneasy. Still, you feel a little foolish. Still, you feel a little out of place. But the banality of your own life is very real to you; it drove you to this extreme, spending your days and your nights in the company of people who despise you, people you do not like really, people you would not want to have as your actual neighbour. And so you must devote yourself to puzzling out how much of what you are told is really, really true (Is ground-up bottle glass in peanut sauce really a delicacy around here, or will it do just what you think ground-up bottle glass will do? Is this rare, multicoloured, snout-mouthed fish really an aphrodisiac, or will it cause you to fall asleep permanently?). Oh, the hard work all of this is, and is it any wonder, then, that on your return home you feel the need of a long rest, so that you can recover from your life as a tourist?

That the native does not like the tourist is not hard to explain. For 6 every native of every place is a potential tourist, and every tourist is a native of somewhere. Every native everywhere lives a life of overwhelming and crushing banality and boredom and desperation and depression, and every deed, good and bad, is an attempt to forget this. Every native would like to find a way out, every native would like a rest, every native would like a tour. But some natives — most natives in the world — cannot go anywhere. They are too poor. They are too poor to go anywhere. They are too poor to escape the reality of their lives; and they are too poor to live properly in the place where they live, which is the very place you, the tourist, want to go — so when the natives see you, the tourist, they envy you, they envy your ability to leave your own banality and boredom, they envy your ability to turn their own banality and boredom into a source of pleasure for yourself.

## *Evaluating The Text*

1. How does the example with which Kincaid begins her essay dramatize the very different needs and expectations tourists bring to Antigua from those of native Antiguans?
2. How is what happens to waste water an example of the kinds of consequences tourists are unaware of as they pursue their vacations?
3. How does the fact that tourists do not know that the "local" food is imported from Miami illustrate the artificially created impression of Antigua tourists have?
4. Which phenomena described by Kincaid are desirable features from the tourist's point of view and at the same time hardships to be endured by native Antiguans?
5. How does the different treatment of tourists and Antiguans by customs officials, as well as the different kinds of materials brought in by tourists and returning natives, reveal a vast gap between the everyday life of Antiguans and the people who visit the island?
6. Try outlining Kincaid's essay to discover the extent to which she organizes it as a comparison. How well suited is this form to expressing Kincaid's thesis?
7. How do vacations create an atmosphere in which tourists apply very different standards than they would if the same "exciting" events happened back home? How do their expectations differ from people who must live there all the time?
8. What inferences might you draw about the government's attitude toward tourists (compared with their concern about Antiguans) from the sight of the dilapidated schools and hospital alongside brand-new taxi-cabs and fine governmental buildings?
9. What inferences does Kincaid wish the reader to draw from the fact that tourists perceive the sign stating the library is awaiting repairs as "quaint"? Discuss Kincaid's tone and her attitude toward the subject in this example.
10. Why is it significant, according to Kincaid, that most history books omit the extent to which the wealth of Great Britain was derived from exploiting the labor of natives in their colonial possessions? Why is it ironic that history books credit England's wealth to the ingenuity of British shopkeepers?

11. What inferences does Kincaid suggest the reader might draw about the rise to prominence and power of Syrian families in Antigua?
12. How did the kind of treatment given to the Queen of England (the ultimate "tourist" to Antigua) suggest the local government's double standard?
13. Evaluate Kincaid's argument that nice people are transformed into ugly people when they become tourists. Do you agree that tourists travel to places where they can enjoy a feeling of being priviledged as a way of reaffirming an impaired sense of self-worth? Explain your reasons.

## Exploring Different Perspectives

1. How are both Kincaid's discussion and Le Ly Hayslip's narrative ("Sisters and Brothers") based on differences in perception between how one is viewed by others and how one perceives oneself? Contrast the reasons for the dissonance in both accounts.
2. How does the voluntary displacement characteristic of the tourist encourage perceptions that are very different from those of exiles who are forced to emigrate to a strange land? You may wish to draw on the discussion of Edward Said "Reflections on Exile") and the stories of Nicholasa Mohr ("A Very Special Pet") and Bharati Mukherjee ("The Management of Grief").

## Extending Viewpoints through Writing

1. To what extent was your perception of yourself as a tourist changed by reading Kincaid's account? Describe how you would have appeared from the perspective of any of the people who live where you took your last vacation.
2. Write a counterargument to Kincaid's position from a native Antiguan who believes tourism is beneficial to the island.
3. What strategies for arguing does Kincaid use? How do they differ from those of Nawal El Saadawj ("Circumcision of Girls, Chapter 2); Jo Goodwin Parker ("What Is Poverty?" Chapter 5); and Salman Rushdie ("A Pen against the Sword")?
4. Before traveling to a place, did you ever construct a mental picture of what the place would be like only to discover that it did not match your expectations? In what way were your expectations unrealistic?
5. In an essay, explore contrasting impacts of the culture on business practices and attitudes toward material possessions in the works of Kincaid, Tayeh Salih ("A Handful of Dates," Chapter 2); Gene Logsdon ("Amish Economics," Chapter 4); Catherine Lim ("Paper," Chapter 4); John Burgess ("A Day in the Life of 'Salaryman'," Chapter 4); and Cha Ok Kim ("The Peddler," Chapter 4).

# Salman Rushdie

# *A Pen against the Sword*

*Salman Rushdie is the author of* Midnight's Children *(1981), a work about India's independence and partition that won Britain's prestigious Booker Prize in 1981;* Shame *(1983), a satire set in Pakistan;* The Jaguar's Smile: A Nicaraguan Journey *(1987); and* Haroun and the Sea of Stories *(1990), a fairy-tale exploration of Rushdie's real-life predicament. His novel,* The Satanic Verses, *was first published in the United Kingdom in September 1988. On February 14, 1989, Iran's Ayotolleh Khomeini called for the execution of Rushdie, a death sentence that still stands, as does the $5.2 million bounty Iranians had put as a price on Rushdie's head, despite the Ayotolleh's death in June 1989. The* Satanic Verses *has thus far been translated into fifteen languages, and Rushdie remains in hiding protected by Scotland Yard's Special Branch. "A Pen against the Sword," which first appeared in* Newsweek, *February 12, 1990, speaks directly to the clash between religious sensitivity and freedom to publish created by the release of* The Satanic Verses.*

*Iran, known as Persia until 1935, is an Islamic republic south of the Soviet Union and northeast of Saudi Arabia. Shi'ite Islam has been the state religion since the 1500s. Iran has the largest population of Shi'ite Muslims in the world. The Qur'an (Koran), the scripture of the Muslims, is made up of revelations delivered to Mohammed by the Angel Gabriel and also includes revelations to other prophets (Adam, Noah, Abraham, Isaac, Jacob, Joseph, Moses, and Jesus). The discovery of oil in Iran in the early 1900s made the country the object of British and Russian attempts at domination. Between 1925 and 1979, Iran was ruled by the Shahs (father and son), whose regime was supported by the United States, until Muhammad Reza Shah Pahlevi was ousted by popular opposition and replaced by the aged Muslim leader, Ayatollah Ruhollah Khomeini. Since this time, the clergy (Mullahs) have carried out a conservative and fundamentalist interpretation of Islam. In 1979, Iranian militants seized the U.S. Embassy in Teheran and held the occupants hostage until a negotiated agreement freed them in 1981. Concurrently, a full-scale border war with Iraq began in 1980 and ended eight years later, with casualties estimated at one million. In June 1989, Khomeini died, four months after exorting the Muslim*

---

*(For more information on Iraq, see p. 389.)

*world to assassinate British author Salman Rushdie. Emerging from hiding on Christmas Day 1990, Rushdie, in an attempt to appease the Muslim world, announced that he would prohibit* The Satanic Verses *from being issued in paperback and from being translated into additional languages. In response, Iran's supreme religious leader, Ali Hoseine Khamenei declared that the death sentence against Rushdie could never be lifted.*

It has been a year since I last spoke in defence of my novel "The Satanic Verses." I have remained silent, though silence is against my nature, because I felt that my voice was simply not loud enough to be heard above the clamour of the voices raised against me.

I hoped that others would speak for me, and many have done so eloquently, among them an admittedly small but growing number of Muslim readers, writers and scholars. Others, including bigots and racists, have tried to exploit my case (using my name to taunt Muslim and non-Muslim Asian children and adults, for example) in a manner I have found repulsive, defiling and humiliating.

At the centre of the storm stands a novel, a work of fiction, one that aspires to the condition of literature. It has often seemed to me that people on all sides of the argument have lost sight of this simple fact. "The Satanic Verses" has been described, and treated, as a work of bad history, as an anti-religious pamphlet, as the product of an international capitalist-Jewish conspiracy, as an act of murder ("he has murdered our hearts"), as the product of a person comparable to Hitler and Attila the Hun. It felt impossible, amid such a hubbub, to insist on the fictionality of fiction.

Let me be clear: I am not trying to say that "The Satanic Verses" is "only a novel" and thus need not to be taken seriously, even disputed with the utmost passion. I do not believe that novels are trivial matters. The ones I care most about are those which attempt radical reformulations of language, form, and ideas, those that attempt to do what the word *novel* seems to insist upon: to see the world anew. I am well aware that this can be a hackle-raising, infuriating attempt.

What I have wished to say, however, is that the point of view from which I have, all my life, attempted this process of literary renewal is the result not of the self-hating, deracinated uncle-Tomism of which some have accused me, but precisely of my determination to create a literary language and literary forms in which the experience of formerly-colonized, still-disadvantaged peoples might find full expression. If "The Satanic Verses" is anything, it is a migrant's-eye view of the world. It is written from the very experience of uprooting, disjuncture and metamorphosis (slow or rapid, painful or pleasurable) that is the migrant condition, and from which, I believe, can be derived a metaphor for all humanity.

Standing at the centre of the novel is a group of characters, most of whom are British Muslims, or not-particularly-religious persons of Muslim background, struggling with just the sort of great problems that have arisen to surround the book, problems of hybridisation and ghettoisation, of reconciling the old and the new. Those who oppose the novel most vociferously today are of the opinion that intermingling with a different culture will inevitably weaken and ruin their own. I am of the opposite opinion. "The Satanic Verses" celebrates hybridity, impurity, intermingling, the transformation that comes of new and unexpected combinations of human beings, cultures, ideas, politics, movies, songs. It rejoices in mongrelisation and fears the absolutism of the Pure. Mélange, hotch-potch, a bit of this and a bit of that is *how newness enters the world*. It is the great possibility that mass migration gives the world, and I have tried to embrace it. "The Satanic Verses" is for change-by-fusion, change-by-conjoining. It is a love-song to our mongrel selves.

7    Throughout human history, the apostles of purity, those who have claimed to possess a total explanation, have wrought havoc among mere mixed-up human beings. Like many millions of people, I am a bastard child of history. Perhaps we all are, black and brown and white, leaking into one another, as a character of mine once said, *like flavours when you cook.*

8    The argument between purity and impurity, which is also the argument between primness and impropriety, between the stultifications of excessive respect and the sandals of impropriety, is an old one; I say, let it continue. Human beings understand themselves and shape their futures by arguing and challenging and saying the unsayable; not by bowing the knee, whether to gods or to men.

9    "The Satanic Verses" is, I profoundly hope, a work of radical dissent and questioning and re-imagining. It is not, however, the book it has been made out to be, that book containing "nothing but filth and insults and abuse" that has brought people out on to the streets across the world.

10    That book simply does not exist.

11    This is what I want to say to the great mass of ordinary, decent, fair-minded Muslims, of the sort I have known all my life, and who have provided much of the inspiration for my work: to be rejected and reviled by, so to speak, one's own characters is a shocking and painful experience for any writer. I recognize that many Muslims have felt shocked and pained, too. Perhaps a way forward might be found through the mutual recognition of that mutual pain. Let us attempt to believe in each other's good faith.

12    I am aware that this is asking a good deal. There has been too much name-calling. Muslims have been called savages and barbarians and worse. I, too, have received my share of invective. Yet I still believe—perhaps I must—that understanding remains possible, and can be achieved without the suppression of the principle of free speech.

You see, it's my opinion that if we could only dispose of the "insults 13
and abuse" accusation, then we might be able, at the very least, to agree
to differ about the book's real themes, about the relative value of the
sacred and the profane, about the merits of purity and those of hotch-
potch, and about how human beings really become whole: through the
love of God or through the love of their fellow-men and women.

And to dispose of the argument, we must return for a moment to the 14
actually-existing book, not the book described on the various pamphlets
that have been circulated to the faithful, not the "unreadable" text of
legend, not two chapters dragged out of the whole; not a piece of blubber
but the whole wretched whale.

Let me say this first: I have never seen this controversy as a struggle 15
between Western freedoms and Eastern unfreedom. The freedoms of the
West are rightly vaunted, but many minorities — racial, sexual, political
— also rightly feel excluded from full possession of these liberties; while,
in my lifelong experience of the East, from Turkey and Iran to India and
Pakistan, I have found people to be every bit as passionate for freedom
as any Czech, Rumanian, German, Hungarian, or Pole.

How is freedom gained? It is taken: never given. To be free, you must 16
first assume your right to freedom. In writing "The Satanic Verses," I
wrote from the assumption that I was, and am, a free man.

What is freedom of expression? Without the freedom to offend, it 17
ceases to exist. Without the freedom to challenge, even to satirise all
orthodoxies, including religious orthodoxies, it ceases to exist. "The Satanic Verses" is, in part, a secular man's reckoning with the religious
spirit. It is by no means always hostile to faith. "If we write in such a way
as to pre-judge such belief as in some way deluded or false, then are we
not guilty of elitism, of imposing our world-view on the masses?" asks
one of its Indian characters. Yet the novel does contain doubts, uncertainties, even shocks that may well not be to the liking of the devout.
Such methods have, however, long been a legitimate part even of Islamic
literature.

What does the novel dissent from? Certainly not from people's right 18
to faith, though I have none. It dissents most clearly from imposed
orthodoxies *of all types*, from the view that the world is quite clearly This
and not That. It dissents from the end of debate. Hindu communalist
sectarianism, the kind of Sikh terrorism that blows up planes, the fa-
tuousnesses of Christian creationism are dissented from as well as the
narrower definitions of Islam. But such dissent is a long way from
"insults and abuse." I do not believe that most of the Muslims I know
would have any trouble with it.

What they have trouble with are statements like these: "He calls the 19
Prophet Muhammad a homosexual." "He says the Prophet Muhammad
asked God for permission to fornicate with every woman in the world."
"He says the Prophet's wives are whores." "He calls the Prophet by a
devil's name." "He calls the Companions of the Prophet *scums and*

*bums."* "He says that the whole Quran was the Devil's work." And so
forth.

20      It has been bewildering to watch the proliferation of such statements,
and to watch them acquire the authority of truth by virtue of the power
of repetition. It has been bewildering to learn that people, millions upon
millions of people, have been willing to judge "The Satanic Verses" and
its author, without reading it, without finding out what manner of man
this fellow might be, on the basis of such allegations as these.

21      "The Satanic Verses" is the story of two painfully divided selves. In
the case of one, Saladin Chamcha, the division is secular and societal: he
is torn, to put it plainly, between Bombay and London, between East and
West. In the other, Gibreel Farishta, the division is spiritual, a rift in
the soul. He has lost his faith and is strung out between his immense
need to believe and his new inability to do so. The novel is "about" their
quest for wholeness.

22      Why "Gibreel Farishta" (*Gabriel Angel*)? Not to "insult and abuse"
the "real" Archangel Gabriel. Gibreel is a movie star, and movie stars
hang above us in the darkness, larger than life, halfway to the divine. To
give Gibreel an angel's name was to give him a secular equivalent of
angelic half-divinity. When he loses his faith, however, this name becomes the source of all his torments. His greatest torments have come to
him in the form of dreams. His most painful dreams, the ones at the
centre of the controversy, depict the birth and growth of a religion
something like Islam, in a magical city of sand named Jahilia (that is
"ignorance," the name given by Arabs to the period before Islam).
Almost all the alleged "insults and abuses" are taken from these
sequences.

23      The first thing to be said about these dreams is that they are *agoniz-
ingly painful to the dreamer*. They are "a nocturnal retribution, a punishment" for his loss of faith. This man, desperate to regain belief, is
haunted, possessed, by visions of doubt, visions of scepticism and questions and faith-shaking allegations that grow more and more extreme as
they go on. He tries in vain to escape them, fighting against sleep; but
then the visions cross over the boundary between his waking and sleeping self; they infect his daytimes: that is, they drive him mad. The
dream-city is called "Jahilia" not to "insult and abuse" Mecca Sharif, but
because the dreamer, Gibreel, has been plunged by his broken faith back
into the condition the word describes. The first purpose of these sequences is not to vilify or "disprove" Islam, but to portray a soul in crisis,
to show how the loss of God can destroy a man's life.

24      See the "offensive" chapters through this lens, and many things may
seem clearer. The use of the so-called "incident of the satanic verses,"
the quasi-historical tale of how Muhammad's revelation seemed briefly
to flirt with the possibility of admitting three pagan and female deities
into the pantheon, is, first of all, a key moment of doubt in dreams which

persecute a dreamer by making vivid the doubts he loathes but can no longer escape.

The most extreme passage of doubting in the novel, in which the 25 character "Salman the Persian"—named not to "insult and abuse" Muhammad's companion Salman al-Farisi, but more as an ironic reference to the novel's author—voices his many scepticisms. It is quite true that the language here is forceful, satirical, and strong meat for some tastes, but it must be remembered that the waking Gibreel is a coarse-mouthed fellow, and it would be surprising if the dream-figures he conjures up did not sometimes speak as rough and even obscene a language as their dreamer.

Let me not be disingenuous, however. The rejection of the three 26 goddesses in the novel's dream-version of the "satanic verses" story is also intended to make other points, for example about the religion's attitude to women. "Shall He (God) have daughters while you have sons? That would be an unjust division," read the verses still to be found in the Quran. I thought it was at least worth pointing out that one of the reasons for rejecting these goddesses was that *they were female*. The rejection has implications that are worth thinking about. I suggest that such highlighting is a proper function of literature.

Or, again, when Salman the Persian, Gibreel's dream-figment, ful- 27 minates against the dream-religion's aim of providing "rules for every damn thing," he is not only tormenting the dreamer, but asking the reader to think about the validity of religion's rules. To those who have felt able to justify the most extreme Muslim threats towards me and others by saying I have broken an Islamic rule, I would ask the following question: are all the rules laid down at a religion's origin immutable for ever? How about the penalties for prostitution (stoning to death) or thieving (mutilation)? How about the prohibition of homosexuality? What of the Islamic law of evidence, which makes a woman's testimony worth only half that of a man? Are these, too, to be given unquestioning respect: or may writers and intellectuals ask the awkward questions that are a part of their reason for being what they are?

Let no one suppose that such disputes about rules do not take place 28 daily throughout the Muslim world. Muslim divines may insist that women dress "modestly" according to the Hijab code, covering more of their bodies than men because they possess what one Muslim absurdly described on television as "more adorable parts"; but the Muslim world is full of women who reject such strictures. Islam may teach that women should be confined to the home and to childbearing, but Muslim women everywhere insist on leaving the home to work. If Muslim society questions its own rules daily—and make no mistake, Muslims are as accustomed to satire as anyone else—why must a novel be proscribed for doing the same?

But to return to the text. Certain supposed "insults" need specific 29 rebuttals. For example, the scene in which the Prophet's Companions are called "scum" and "bums" is a depiction of the early persecution of the believers, and the insults quoted are clearly not mine but those hurled at the faithful by the ungodly. How, one wonders, could a book portray persecution without allowing the persecutors to be seen persecuting? (Or again: how could a book portray doubt without allowing the uncertain to articulate their uncertainties?)

30    As to the matter of the Prophet's wives: what happens in Gibreel's dreams is that the whores of a brothel *take the names* of the wives of the Prophet Mahound in order to arouse their customers. The "real" wives are clearly stated to be living "chastely" in their harem. But why introduce so shocking an image? For this reason: throughout the novel, I sought images that crystallized the opposition between the sacred and profane worlds. The harem and the brothel provide such an opposition. Both are places where women are sequestered, in the harem to keep them from all men except their husband and close family members, in the brothel for the use of strange males. Harem and brothel are antithetical worlds, and the presence in the harem of the Prophet, the receiver of a scared text, is likewise contrasted with the presence in the brothel of the clapped-out poet, Baal, the creator of profane texts. The two struggling worlds, pure and impure, chaste and coarse, are juxtaposed by making them echoes of one another; and, finally, the pure eradicates the impure. Whores and writer ("I see no difference here," remarks Mahound) are executed. Whether one finds this a happy or sad conclusion depends on one's point of view.

31    The purpose of the "brothel sequence," then, was not to "insult and abuse" the Prophet's wives, but to dramatize certain ideas about morality; and sexuality, too, because what happens in the brothel is that the men of "Jahilia" are enabled to act out an ancient dream of power and possession, the dream of possessing the queen. That men should be so aroused by the great ladies' whorish counterfeits says something about *them*, not the great ladies, and about the extent to which sexual relations have to do with possession.

32    *I must have known*, my accusers say, that my use of the old devil-name "Mahound," a medieval European demonization of "Muhammad," would cause offence. In fact, this is an instance in which de-contextualization has created a complete reversal of meaning. A part of the relevant context is on page 93 of the novel. "To turn insults into strengths, whigs, tories, Blacks all chose to wear with pride the names they were given in scorn; likewise, our mountain-climbing, prophet-motivated solitary is to be the mediaeval baby-frightener, the Devil's synonym: Mahound." Central to the purposes of "The Satanic Verses" is the process of reclaiming language from one's opponents. *Trotsky* was Trotsky's jailer's name. By taking it for his own, he symbolically conquered his captor and set himself free. Something of the same spirit lay behind my use of the name "Mahound."

The attempt at reclamation goes even further than this. When Saladin    33
Chamcha finds himself transformed into a goatish, horned and hoofy
demon, in a bizarre sanatorium full of other monstrous beings, he is told
that they are all, like him, aliens and migrants, demonized by the "host
culture's" attitude to them. "They have the power of description, and we
succumb to the pictures they construct." So the very title, "The Satanic
Verses," is an aspect of this attempt at reclamation. You call us devils? it
seems to ask. Very well then, here is the devil's version of the world, of
"your" world, the version written *from the experience* of those who have
been demonized by virtue of their otherness. Just as the Asian kids in the
novel wear toy devil-horns proudly, as an assertion of pride in identity,
so the novel proudly wears its demonic title. The purpose is not to
suggest that the Quran is written by the devil; it is to attempt the sort of
act of affirmation that, in the United States, transformed the word Black
from the standard term of racist abuse into a "beautiful" expression of
cultural pride.

The process of hybridization which is the novel's most crucial dy-     34
namic means that its ideas derive from many sources other than Islamic
ones. There is, for example, the pre-Christian belief, expressed in the
Books of Amos and Deutero-Isaiah and quoted in "The Satanic Verses,"
that God and the Devil were one and the same: "it isn't until the Book of
Chronicles, merely fourth century B.C., that the word *Satan* is used to
mean a being, and not only an attribute of God." It should also be said
that the two books that were most influential on the shape this novel
took do not include the Quran. One was William Blake's "The Marriage
of Heaven and Hell," the classic meditation on the interpenetration of
good and evil; and "The Master and Margarita" by Mikhail Bulgakov,
the great Russian lyrical and comical novel in which the Devil descends
upon Moscow and wreaks havoc upon the corrupt, materialist, decadent
inhabitants, and turns out, by the end, not to be such a bad chap at all.
"The Master and Margarita" and its author were persecuted by Soviet
totalitarianism. It is extraordinary to find my novel's life echoing that of
one of its greatest models.

Nor are these the only non-Muslim influences at work. I was born an    35
Indian, and not only an Indian, but a Bombayite — Bombay, most cosmopolitan, most hybrid, most hotch-potch of Indian cities. My writing
and thought has therefore been as deeply influenced by Hindu myths
and attitudes as Muslim ones (and my movie star Gibreel is also a figure
of such inter-religious tolerance, playing Hindu gods without causing
offence, in spite of his Muslim origins). Nor is the West absent from
Bombay. I was already a mongrel self, history's bastard, before London
aggravated the condition.

To be a Bombayite (and afterwards a Londoner) was also to fall in     36
love with the metropolis. The city as a reality and as metaphor is at the
heart of all my work. "The modern city," says a character in "The
Satanic Verses," "is the locus classicus of incompatible realities." Well,

*that* turned out to be true. "As long as they pass in the night, it's not so bad. But if they meet! It's uranium and plutonium, each makes the other decompose, boom." It is hard to express how it feels to have attempted to portray an objective reality and then to become its subject . . .

37        The point is this: Muslim culture has been very important to me, but it is not by any means the only shaping factor. I am a modern, and a modern*ist*, urban man, accepting uncertainty as the only constant, change as the only sure thing. I believe in no god, and have not done so since I was a young adolescent. I have spiritual needs, and my work has, I hope, a moral and spiritual dimension, but I am content to try and satisfy those needs without recourse to any idea of a Prime Mover or ultimate arbiter.

38        To put it simply as possible: *I am not a Muslim.* It feels bizarre, and wholly inappropriate, to be described as some sort of heretic after having lived my life as a secular, pluralist, eclectic man. I am being enveloped in, and described by, a language that does not fit me. I do not accept the charge of blasphemy, because, as somebody says in "The Satanic Verses," "where there is no belief, there is no blasphemy." I do not accept the charge of apostasy, because I have never in my adult life affirmed any belief, and what one has not affirmed one cannot be said to have apostasized from. The Islam I know states clearly that "there can be no coercion in matters of religion." The many Muslims I respect would be horrified by the idea that they belong to their faith *purely by virtue of birth*, and that any person so born who freely chose not to be a Muslim could therefore be put to death.

39        When I am described as an apostate Muslim, I feel as if I have been concealed behind a *false self*, as if a shadow has become substance while I have been relegated to the shadows. Jorge Luis Borges, Graham Greene and other writers have written about their sense of an Other who goes about the world bearing their name. There are moments when I worry that my Other may succeed in obliterating me.

40        During 1989 Britain witnessed a brutalization of public debate that seemed hard to believe. Incitement to murder was tolerated on the nation's streets. (In Europe and the United States, swift government action prevented such incitement at a very early stage.) On TV shows, studio audiences were asked for a show of hands on the question of whether I should live or die. A man's murder (mine) became a legitimate subject for a national opinion poll. And slowly, slowly, a point of view grew up, and was given voice by mountebanks and bishops, fundamentalists and Mr. John le Carré, which held that *I knew exactly what I was doing.* I must have known what would happen; therefore, I did it on purpose, to profit by the notoriety that would result. This accusation is, today, in fairly wide circulation, and so I must defend myself against it, too.

41        I find myself wanting to ask questions: when Osip Mandelstam wrote

his poem against Stalin, did he "know what he was doing" and so deserve his death? When the students filled Tiananmen Square to ask for freedom, where they not also, and knowingly, asking for the murderous repression that resulted? When Terry Waite was taken hostage, hadn't he been "asking for it"? I find myself thinking of Jodie Foster in her Oscar-winning role in "The Accused." Even if I were to concede (and I do not concede it) that what I did in "The Satanic Verses" was the literary equivalent of flaunting oneself shamelessly before the eyes of aroused men, is that really a justification for being, so to speak, gang-banged? Is any provocation a justification for rape?

Threats of violence ought not to coerce us into believing the victims    42
of intimidation to be responsible for the violence threatened. I am aware, however, that rhetoric is an insufficient response. Nor is it enough to point out that nothing on the scale of this controversy has, to my knowledge, ever happened in the history of literature.

It's true that some passages in "The Satanic Verses" have now ac-    43
quired a prophetic quality that alarms even me. "Your blasphemy, Salman, can't be forgiven . . . To set your words against the Word of God." Et cetera. But to write a dream based around events that took place in the seventh century of the Christian era, and to create metaphors of the conflict between different sorts of "author" and different types of "text" — to say that literature and religion, like literature and politics, fight for the same territory — is very different from somehow knowing, in advance, that your dream is about to come true, that the metaphor is about to be made flesh, that the conflict your work seeks to explore is about to engulf it, and its publishers and booksellers; and you.

At least (small comfort) I wasn't wrong.    44

Books choose their authors; the act of creation is not entirely a    45
rational and conscious one. But this, as honestly as I can set it down, is, in respect of the novel's treatment of religion, what "I knew I was doing":

I set out to explore, through the process of fiction, the nature of    46
revelation and the power of faith. The mystical, revelatory experience is quite clearly a genuine one. This statement poses a problem to the non-believer: if we accept that the mystic, the prophet, is sincerely undergoing some sort of transcendent experience, yet we cannot believe in a supernatural world, then *what is going on*? To answer this question, among others, I began work on the story of "Mahound." I was aware that the "satanic verses" incident is much disputed by Muslim theologians; that the life of Muhammad has become the object of a kind of veneration that some would consider un-Islamic, since Muhammad himself always insisted that he was merely a messenger, an ordinary man; and that, therefore, great sensitivities were involved. I genuinely believed that my overt use of fabulation would make it clear to any reader that I was not attempting to falsify history, but to allow a fiction to take off from history. The use of dreams was intended to say: the point is

not whether this is "really" supposed to be Muhammad, or whether the satanic verses incident "really" happened; the point is to examine what such an incident might reveal about what revelation is, about the extent to which the mystic's conscious personality informs and interacts with the mystical event; the point is to try and understand the *human event* of revelation. The use of fiction was a way of creating the sort of distance from actuality that I felt would prevent offence from being taken. I was wrong.

47    Here is more of what I knew: I knew that stories of Muhammad's doubts, uncertainties, errors, fondness for women abound in and around Muslim tradition. To me, they seemed to make him more vivid, more human, and therefore more interesting, even more worthy of admiration. The greatest human beings must struggle against themselves as well as the world. I never doubted Muhammad's greatness, nor, I believe, is the "Mahound" of my own novel belittled by being portrayed as human.

48    *He did it on purpose* is one of the strangest accusations ever levelled at a writer. Of course I did it on purpose. The question is, and it is what I have tried to answer: what is the "it" that I did?

49    What I did not do was conspire against Islam; or write—after years and years of anti-racist work and writing—a text of incitement to racial hatred; or anything of the sort. My golem, my false Other, may be capable of such deeds, but I am not.

50    Would I have written differently if I had known what would happen? Truthfully, I don't know. Would I change any of the text now? I would not. It's too late. As Friedrich Dürrenmatt wrote in "The Physicists": "What has once been thought cannot be unthought."

51    The controversy over "The Satanic Verses" needs to be looked at as a political event, not purely a theological one. In India, where the trouble started, the Muslim fundamentalist MP Shahabuddin used my novel as a stick with which to threaten the wobbling Rajiv Gandhi government. The demand for the book's banning was a power-play to demonstrate the strength of the Muslim vote, on which Congress has traditionally relied and which it could ill-afford to lose. (In spite of the ban, Congress lost the Muslims and the election anyway. Put not your trust in Shahabuddins.)

52    In South Africa, the row over the book served the purposes of the regime by driving a wedge between the Muslim and non-Muslim members of the United Democratic Front. In Pakistan, it was a way for the fundamentalists to try and regain the political initiative after their trouncing in the general election. In Iran, too, the incident could only be properly understood when seen in the context of the country's internal political struggles. And in Britain, where secular and religious leaders had been vying for power in the community for over a decade, the "affair" swung the balance of power back towards the mosques. Small wonder, then, that the various councils of mosques are reluctant to bring the protest to an end, even though many Muslims up and down the

country find it embarrassing, even shameful, to be associated with such illiberalism and violence.

*The responsibility for violence lies with those who perpetrate it.* In the past twelve months, bookshop workers have been manhandled, spat upon, verbally abused; bookshop premises have been threatened, and, on several occasions, actually firebombed. Publishing staff have had to face a campaign of hate mail, menacing phone calls, death threats and bomb scares. Demonstrations have, on occasion, turned violent, too. During the big march in London last summer, peaceful counter-demonstrators on behalf of humanism and secularism were knocked to the ground by marchers, and a counter-demo by the courageous (and largely Muslim) Women Against Fundamentalism group was also threatened and abused.

There is no conceivable reason why such behaviour should be privileged because it is done in the name of an affronted religion. If we are to talk about "insults," "abuse," "offence," then the campaign against "The Satanic Verses" has been, very often, as insulting and abusive and offensive as it's possible to be.

I am not the first writer to be persecuted by Islamic fundamentalism in the modern period; among the greatest names so victimized are the Iranian writer Ahmad Kasravi, assassinated by fanatics, and the Egyptian Nobel laureate Naguib Mahfouz, often threatened but still, happily, with us. I am not the first artist to be accused of blasphemy and apostasy; these are, in fact, probably the most common weapons with which fundamentalism has sought to shackle creativity in the modern age. It is sad, then, that so little attention has been paid to this crucial literary context; and the Western critics like John Berger, who once spoke messianically of the need for new ways of seeing, should now express their willingness to privilege one such way over another, to protect a religion boasting one billion believers from the solitary figure of a single writer brandishing an "unreadable" book.

I would like to say this to the Muslim community: life without God seems to believers to be an idiocy, pointless, beneath contempt. It does not seem so to non-believers. To accept that the world, here, is all there is; to go through it, towards and into death, without the consolations or religion seems, well, at least as courageous and rigorous to us as the espousal of faith seems to you. Secularism and its works deserve your respect, not your contempt.

A great wave of freedom has been washing over the world. Those who resist it — in China, in Rumania — find themselves bathed in blood. I should like to ask Muslims — that great mass of ordinary, decent, fair-minded Muslims to whom I have imagined myself to be speaking for most of this piece — to choose to ride the wave; to renounce blood; not to let Muslim leaders make Muslims seem less tolerant than they are. "The Satanic Verses" is a serious work, written from a non-believer's point of view. Let believers accept that, and let it be.

In the meantime, I am asked, how do I feel?

59    I feel grateful to the British Government for defending me. I hope that such a defence would be made available to any citizen so threatened, but that doesn't lessen my gratitude. I needed it, and it was provided. (I'm still no Tory, but that's democracy.)

60    I feel grateful, too, to my protectors, who have done such a magnificent job, and who have become my friends.

61    I feel grateful to everyone who has offered me support. The one real gain for me in this bad time has been the discovery of being cared for by so many people. The only antidote to hatred is love.

62    Above all, I feel great gratitude towards, solidarity with and pride in all the publishing people and bookstore workers around the world who have held the line against intimidation, and who will, I am sure, continue to do so as long as it remains necessary.

63    I feel as if I have been plunged, like Alice, into the world beyond the looking glass, where nonsense is the only available sense. And I wonder if I'll ever be able to climb back through the mirror.

64    Do I feel regret? Of course I do: regret that such offence has been taken against my work when it was not intended — when dispute was intended, and dissent, and even, at times, satire, and criticism of intolerance, and the like, but not the thing of which I'm most often accused, not "filth," not "insult," not "abuse." I regret that so many people who might have taken pleasure in finding their reality given pride of place in a novel will now not read it because of what they believe it to be, or will come to it with their minds already made up.

65    And I feel sad to be so grievously separated from my community, from India, from everyday life, from the world.

66    Please understand, however: I make no complaint. I am a writer. I do not accept my condition; I will strive to change it; but I inhabit it, I am trying to learn from it.

67    Our lives teach us who we are.

## Evaluating the Text

1. What is the nature of the controversy in which Rushdie finds himself embroiled?

2. Why does Rushdie feel that the support of "an admittedly small but growing number of Muslim readers, writers and scholars" is important enough to warrant mentioning at the beginning of his "defense"?

3. How would it be helpful to his argument if Rushdie could persuade his readers to agree that *The Satanic Verses*, because it is a work of fiction, should be judged by different standards than a historical nonfiction account?

4. What is the relationship between the self-proclaimed theme of all of Rushdie's work — celebrating "hybridity, impurity, intermingling, the transformation that comes of new and unexpected combinations of human beings, cultures, ideas, politics, movies, songs" — and the fact that the most vehement opposition has come from uncompromising Islamic fundamentalists?

5. Discuss the conflicting perspectives with which each side judges the literary techniques Rushdie employs in *The Satanic Verses*. For example, how is it to Rushdie's advantage to characterize his self-proclaimed use of "parody, mockery, scandal and lack of respect" as perfectly legitimate literary techniques, whereas Islamic fundamentalists, from their perspective, see what he does as a blasphemy against Islam?

6. To what extent do details in the text alert you to the nature of the audience whom Rushdie is addressing and hopes to persuade? For example, to whom is Rushdie appealing by stating that freedom isn't something only desired by people in the West?

7. How does Rushdie attempt to establish common ground between himself and those who oppose him? Where does he downplay potential differences between himself and those he is trying to persuade?

8. How does Rushdie use the fact that even Islamic fundamentalist positions regarded as immutable (e.g., the elimination of "stoning to death" for prostitution) have changed to strengthen his case?

9. How does Rushdie's defense of episodes in *The Satanic Verses* that critics found scandalous take the form of examining them within the overall context of where they first appeared? Do these episodes, especially those involving Gibreel, and the dreams of Jahilia, including the infamous "brothel sequence," seem to express religious self-doubt, as Rushdie claims, or should they be seen as blasphemous?

10. How persuasive do you find Rushdie's claim that he is speaking for minorities and for the plight of women by raising the question of the low status of women in Islamic countries?

11. How is Rushdie's citation of "blacks" and "Trotsky" an example of arguing by analogy? How does this phase of his argument depend on the concept of "reclamation of language" from one's opponents?

12. Evaluate the reasons Rushdie offers to defend himself against the charge that he wrote the kind of book he did, knowing the uproar it would produce, purposely to generate sales.

13. How does Rushdie's defense take the form of linking himself with other writers who were persecuted following the publication of their books?

## Exploring Different Perspectives

1. What additional dimension of Rushdie's predicament as a political exile does Edward Said's discussion of exile ("Reflections on Exile") provide?

2. How do both Rushdie's account and Bharati Mukherjee's story ("The Management of Grief") involve the consequences of religious intolerance?

## Extending Viewpoints through Writing

1. Based on what Rushdie tells the reader about himself in "A Pen against the Sword," what similarities can you discern between Rushdie and the protagonist of *The Satanic Verses*?

2. Evaluate Rushdie's justification of the blasphemous parts of *The Satanic Verses* after reading the original chapters from this work. Is Rushdie's argument more or less persuasive when considered in the original context?

3. To what extent does Rushdie's argument rest on the assumption that a work that shows a religious leader, in this case, Mohammed, as more human, is at least as valuable as more traditional works depicting Mohammed as a transcendent figure, a prophet of God, without human failings? Keep in mind that Rushdie says he is not a believer. You might wish to compare the methods used and reactions to *The Satanic Verses* with the re-envisioning of Christ's life and the adverse reactions to it on the part of some Christians with the release of Martin Scorsese's film *The Last Temptation of Christ* (1988), based on the novel by the same name by Nikos Kazantzakis. Explore the similarities and differences in the respective portrayals of Mohammed and Jesus. In your opinion, does the depiction of a divine figure as having human desires enhance or diminish your religious belief?

4. After reading the following statement by S. Nomanul Haq, which first appeared in *The International Herald Tribune,* February 24, 1989, evaluate whether he or Rushdie presents a stronger case. Keep in mind that Haq's response was written after demonstrations against Rushdie in India and Pakistan in which at least five people were killed. Dr. Haq, a historian of Arab-Islamic science, is a research fellow at Harvard's Center for Middle Eastern Studies and a lecturer at Tufts University.

## A MUSLIM TELLS SALMAN RUSHDIE HE DID WRONG
## S. NOMANUL HAQ

Cambridge Massachusetts — Dear Salman Rushdie: a few years ago, when I read your *Midnight's Children,* I was overwhelmed. It was not the exuberance of your narrative and stylistic craft, nor the threads of your rich imagination woven with such effective intellectual control that engulfed me. Rather it was your formidable grasp of history and, through that, of the psyche of a complex culture in all its variations that formed the substratum of your tale.

And yet it is this question of your knowledge of history that I shall raise in connection with your seriously and alarmingly controversial *The Satanic Verses.*

Let me say at once that I do hold you as an artist, not as a historian or a psychologist — nor as a theologian. But at the same time you do make use of what are facts of history and psychology, giving them your own distinct treatment.

No writer, you will agree, writes in a historical vacuum. But then, a responsible artist does not, without powerful grounds, mutilate history, nor, unless there exists a mammoth justification, does he disregard the sensibilities and sensitivities of his own milieu, especially when it forms both the subject matter and the bulk of his or her audience.

Strangely, what I am saying is something that I learned from none other than yourself. You might recall your telling criticism of Sir Richard Attenborough's celebrated film *Gandhi.* You enraged Sir Richard, but in the controversy I remained your passionate supporter.

You censured the film for disregarding or minimizing certain important historical facts. And you said that in a work of an artistic nature, one cannot say everything, that there has to be a choice — but that there has to be a rationale of choice. One selects not to mislead but to make the story more meaningful. Ironically, this has precisely been your lapse in *The Satanic Verses.*

Most of your Western readers are unable to gauge the acuteness of your blow to the very core of the Indian subcontinental culture. They cannot estimate the seriousness of the injury because they do not know the history of the aggrieved.

You do know it and therefore one feels that you foresaw, at least to some extent, the consequences.

There is in your book, for example, the phantasmagoria of your own namesake Salman's corruption of the revealed word by his erroneous rendering of the words of Mahound.

Here the veil is too thin to cover the identity of Mahound: He can be understood in no other way than as a caricature of the Moslem Prophet. You do know that Islam is consistently, acutely and uniquely sensitive to its scripture. Ordinarily, Arabic is written without short vowels, but no copy of the Koran today is vowelless: Moslems insist that it should and can be read only in one way. The Moslem view is that even incorrectly reading the Koran is a cardinal sin. The Koran is neither read nor recited in translation for the very reason that translation might introduce alteration.

This matter is deadly serious, and to make it a subject of insensitive fantasy is equally serious.

There is a further issue that your Western reader does not sense: that your corrupt Salman is the namesake not only of you in your book but of a historical personage who was a Persian companion of the Prophet, a companion who has been accorded a particularly elevated status by the Shiites. Given the militancy of the Shiites, when you made Salman the polluter of the revelation, you knew that you were planting your hand in the cluster of bees!

Your response to the uproar has been wavering and inconsistent, and your defense has the odor of self-righteousness. You say that people who have not read your book have no right to criticize it. But do you really think that reading the book will drastically alter their opinions? Then you talk about freedom of expression. Free speech is a tricky issue and cannot be taken too literally.

What do you think the response of black Americans would be if you were to mock Martin Luther King Jr.? Or the reaction of the Jewish community if you eulogized Hitler? Or the anger of a pious Hindu if you were to present a graphic description of the slaughtering of a cow?

And to say that the Moslem world has demonstrated a total lack of dignity and tolerance is to utter a historical irrelevance. The Moslem nations have not gone through the turmoils of the Enlightenment and they have seen no scientific revolution; their sensibilities are different. Often, a peaceful demonstration is not their way, and we cannot change them overnight. The best thing is to avoid hitting their most sensitive chords. And, Mr Rushdie, you knew that.

As for your waverings, you started out by expressing regret over the fact that you did not write even a more controversial book. You accused the leaders of the angry demonstrations in Islamabad of exploiting a religious slogan for secular and political ends. They may have done so, but what about the innocent and ignorant people who died in the violence? You expressed no sympathy for them. And now you issue a three-sentence statement that, at best, has the semblance of regret. Quite honestly, Mr Rushdie, your heart does not beat in this statement, your expression is glaringly perfunctory.

I am saddened that a bounty has been placed on your head and that a great writer like you, rather than presenting himself to the public, is in hiding. You have elicited the rage of nations. This is a pity. But, Mr Rushdie, you have cut them and they are bleeding: Do something quickly to heal the wound.

# Bharati Mukherjee

# *The Management of Grief*

---

*Bharati Mukherjee, born in 1940 and educated in Calcutta, earned a doctorate at the University of Iowa. She is the author of short stories and three novels,* The Tiger's Daughter *(1972),* Wife *(1975), and* Jasmine *(1989). Her stories have appeared in* Best American Short Stories, *1987 and 1989, and* Editor's Choice. *A recent work,* The Middleman and Other Stories *(1989), from which "The Management of Grief" was taken, received the National Book Critics Circle Award for Fiction. Mukherjee is now a professor in the English Department at the University of California at Berkeley. "The Management of Grief" tells of the horrendous consequences following a real-life event, the destruction by a terrorist's bomb, thought to be planted by a Sikh extremist, of an Air-India Boeing 747 on June 23, 1985, as it flew from Toronto to Delhi. Mukherjee says of this event in which 329 passengers and crew were killed, "I knew a few of the passengers. I might have been a passenger myself."*

*The conflict between Hindus and Sikhs, a religious community of six million inhabitants, mainly in the Punjab region of northern India, is an old one. Sikhs oppose the caste system of four hereditary social divisions (Brahman [priests and scholars], Kshatriya [warriors and rulers], the Vaisya [farmers and merchants], and the Sudra [peasants and laborerers]) that has shaped the class structure of Indian society. The caste system continues to be practiced although it has been constitutionally abolished. Founded in the fifteenth century, Sikhs were united in the seventeenth century by Govind Singh, as a warrior fraternity who adopted the practice of wearing a turban and never cutting the hair. The hostilities between Hindus and Sikh separatists in the Punjab led Prime Minister Indira Gandhi to order the Indian Army to attack Sikh extremists who had taken over the Golden Temple in the city of Amritsar in 1984. Over one thousand people were killed. Indira Gandhi was subsequently assassinated by Sikh members of her own bodyguard.*

A woman I don't know is boiling tea the Indian way in my kitchen. 1
There are a lot of women I don't know in my kitchen, whispering and

---

*(For further information on Canada, see p. 202, and for India, see p. 282.)

moving tactfully. They open doors, rummage through the pantry, and try not to ask me where things are kept. They remind me of when my sons were small, on Mother's Day or when Vikram and I were tired, and they would make big, sloppy omelets. I would lie in bed pretending I didn't hear them.

2      Dr. Sharma, the treasurer of the Indo-Canada Society, pulls me into the hallway. He wants to know if I am worried about money. His wife, who has just come up from the basement with a tray of empty cups and glasses, scolds him. "Don't bother Mrs. Bhave with mundane details." She looks so monstrously pregnant her baby must be days overdue. I tell her she shouldn't be carrying heavy things. "Shaila," she says, smiling, "this is the fifth." Then she grabs a teenager by his shirttails. He slips his Walkman off his head. He has to be one of her four children; they have the same domed and dented foreheads. "What's the official word now?" she demands. The boy slips the headphones back on. "They're acting evasive, Ma. They're saying it could be an accident or a terrorist bomb."

3      All morning, the boys have been muttering, Sikh bomb, Sikh bomb. The men, not using the word, bow their heads in agreement. Mrs. Sharma touches her forehead at such a word. At least they've stopped talking about space debris and Russian lasers.

4      Two radios are going in the dining room. They are tuned to different stations. Someone must have brought the radios down from my boys' bedrooms. I haven't gone into their rooms since Kusum came running across the front lawn in her bathrobe. She looked so funny, I was laughing when I opened the door.

5      The big TV in the den is being whizzed through American networks and cable channels.

6      "Damn!" some man swears bitterly. "How can these preachers carry on like nothing's happened?" I want to tell him we're not that important. You look at the audience, and at the preacher in his blue robe with his beautiful white hair, the potted palm trees under a blue sky, and you know they care about nothing.

7      The phone rings and rings. Dr. Sharma's taken charge. "We're with her," he keeps saying. "Yes, yes, the doctor has given calming pills. Yes, yes, pills are having necessary effect" I wonder if pills alone explain this calm. Not peace, just a deadening quiet. I was always controlled, but never repressed. Sound can reach me, but my body is tensed, ready to scream. I hear their voices all around me. I hear my boys and Vikram cry, "Mommy, Shaila!" and their screams insulate me, like headphones.

8      The woman boiling water tells her story again and again. "I got the news first. My cousin called from Halifax before six A.M., can you imagine? He'd gotten up for prayers and his son was studying for medical exams and he heard on a rock channel that something had happened to a plane. They said first it had disappeared from the radar, like a giant eraser just reached out. His father called me, so I said to him, what do you mean, 'something bad'? You mean a hijacking? And he said, *Behn,*

there is no confirmation of anything yet, but check with your neighbors because a lot of them must be on that plane. So I called poor Kusum straight-away. I knew Kusum's husband and daughter were booked to go yesterday."

Kusum lives across the street from me. She and Satish had moved in less than a month ago. They said they needed a bigger place. All these people, the Sharmas and friends from the Indo-Canada Society, had been there for the housewarming. Satish and Kusum made tandoori on their big gas grill and even the white neighbors piled their plates high with that luridly red, charred, juicy chicken. Their younger daughter had danced, and even our boys had broken away from the Stanley Cup telecast to put in a reluctant appearance. Everyone took pictures for their albums and for the community newspapers—another of our families had made it big in Toronto—and now I wonder how many of those happy faces are gone. "Why does God give us so much if all along He intends to take it away?" Kusum asks me.

I nod. We sit on carpeted stairs, holding hands like children. "I never once told him that I loved him," I say. I was too much the well-brought-up woman. I was so well brought up I never felt comfortable calling my husband by his first name.

"It's all right," Kusum says. "He knew. My husband knew. They felt it. Modern young girls have to say it because what they feel is fake."

Kusum's daughter Pam runs in with an overnight case. Pam's in her McDonald's uniform. "Mummy! You have to get dressed!" Panic makes her cranky. "A reporter's on his way here."

"Why?"

"You want to talk to him in your bathrobe?" She starts to brush her mother's long hair. She's the daughter who's always in trouble. She dates Canadian boys and hangs out in the mall, shopping for tight sweaters. The younger one, the goody-goody one according to Pam, the one with a voice so sweet that when she sang *bhajans* for Ethiopian relief even a frugal man like my husband wrote out a hundred-dollar check, *she* was on that plane. *She* was going to spend July and August with grandparents because Pam wouldn't go. Pam said she'd rather waitress at McDonald's. "If it's a choice between Bombay and Wonderland, I'm picking Wonderland," she'd said.

"Leave me alone," Kusum yells. "You know what I want to do? If I didn't have to look after you now, I'd hang myself."

Pam's young face goes blotchy with pain. "Thanks," she says, "don't let me stop you."

"Hush," pregnant Mrs. Sharma scolds Pam. "Leave your mother alone. Mr. Sharma will tackle the reporters and fill out the forms. He'll say what has to be said."

Pam stands her ground. "You think I don't know what Mummy's thinking? *Why her?* That's what. That's sick! Mummy wishes my little sister were alive and I were dead."

19    Kusum's hand in mine is trembly hot. We continue to sit on the stairs.

20    She calls before she arrives, wondering if there's anything I need. Her name is Judith Templeton and she's an appointee of the provincial government. "Multiculturalism?" I ask, and she says "partially," but that her mandate is bigger. "I've been told you knew many of the people on the flight," she says. "Perhaps if you'd agree to help us reach the others . .. . ?"

21    She gives me time at least to put on tea water and pick up the mess in the front room. I have a few *samosas* from Kusum's housewarming that I could fry up, but then I think, why prolong this visit?

22    Judith Templeton is much younger than she sounded. She wears a blue suit with a white blouse and a polka-dot tie. Her blond hair is cut short, her only jewelry is pearl-drop earrings. Her briefcase is new and expensive looking, a gleaming cordovan leather. She sits with it across her lap. When she looks out the front windows onto the street, her contact lenses seem to float in front of her light blue eyes.

23    "What sort of help do you want from me?" I ask. She has refused the tea, out of politeness, but I insist, along with some slightly stale biscuits.

24    "I have no experience," she admits. "That is, I have an M.S.W. and I've worked in liaison with accident victims, but I mean I have no experience with a tragedy of this scale—"

25    "Who could?" I ask.

26    "—and with the complications of culture, language, and customs. Someone mentioned that Mrs. Bhave is a pillar—because you've taken it more calmly."

27    At this, perhaps, I frown, for she reaches forward, almost to take my hand. "I hope you understand my meaning, Mrs. Bhave. There are hundreds of people in metro directly affected, like you, and some of them speak no English. There are some widows who've never handled money or gone on a bus, and there are old parents who still haven't eaten or gone outside their bedrooms. Some houses and apartments have been looted. Some wives are still hysterical. Some husbands are in shock and profound depression. We want to help, but our hands are tied in so many ways. We have to distribute money to some people, and there are legal documents—these things can be done. We have interpreters, but we don't always have the human touch, or maybe the right human touch. We don't want to make mistakes, Mrs. Bhave, and that's why we'd like to ask you to help us."

28    "More mistakes, you mean," I say.

29    "Police matters are not in my hands," she answers.

30    "Nothing I can do will make any difference," I say. "We must all grieve in our own way."

31    "But you are coping very well. All the people said, Mrs. Bhave is the strongest person of all. Perhaps if the others could see you, talk with you, it would help them."

"By the standards of the people you call hysterical, I am behaving 32
very oddly and very badly, Miss Templeton." I want to say to her, *I wish
I could scream, starve, walk into Lake Ontario, jump from a bridge.* "They
would not see me as a model. I do not see myself as a model."

I am a freak. No one who has ever known me would think of me 33
reacting this way. This terrible calm will not go away.

She asks me if she may call again, after I get back from a long trip that 34
we all must make. "Of course," I say. "Feel free to call, anytime."

Four days later, I find Kusum squatting on a rock overlooking a bay in 35
Ireland. It isn't a big rock, but it juts sharply out over water. This is as
close as we'll ever get to them. June breezes balloon out her sari and
unpin her knee-length hair. She has the bewildered look of a sea creature
whom the tides have stranded.

It's been one hundred hours since Kusum came stumbling and 36
screaming across my lawn. Waiting around the hospital, we've heard
many stories. The police, the diplomats, they tell us things thinking that
we're strong, that knowledge is helpful to the grieving, and maybe it is.
Some, I know, prefer ignorance, or their own versions. The plane broke
into two, they say. Unconsciousness was instantaneous. No one suffered.
My boys must have just finished their breakfasts. They loved eating on
planes, they loved the smallness of plates, knives, and forks. Last year
they saved the airline salt and pepper shakers. Half an hour more and
they would have made it to Heathrow.

Kusum says that we can't escape our fate. She says that all those 37
people—our husbands, my boys, her girl with the nightingale voice, all
those Hindus, Christians, Sikhs, Muslims, Parsis, and atheists on that
plane—were fated to die together off this beautiful bay. She learned this
from a swami in Toronto.

I have my Valium. 38

Six of us "relatives"—two widows and four widowers—chose to 39
spend the day today by the waters instead of sitting in a hospital room
and scanning photographs of the dead. That's what they call us now:
relatives. I've looked through twenty-seven photos in two days. They're
very kind to us, the Irish are very understanding. Sometimes understanding means freeing a tourist bus for this trip to the bay, so we can
pretend to spy our loved ones through the glassiness of waves or in
sun-speckled cloud shapes.

I could die here, too, and be content. 40

"What is that, out there?" She's standing and flapping her hands, 41
and for a moment I see a head shape bobbing in the waves. She's
standing in the water, I on the boulder. The tide is low, and a round,
black, head-sized rock has just risen from the waves. She returns, her
sari end dripping and ruined, and her face is a twisted remnant of hope,
the way mine was a hundred hours ago, still laughing but inwardly
knowing that nothing but the ultimate tragedy could bring two women

together at six o'clock on a Sunday morning. I watch her face sag into blankness.

42    "That water felt warm, Shaila," she says at length.

43    "You can't," I say. "We have to wait for our turn to come."

44    I haven't eaten in four days, haven't brushed my teeth.

45    "I know," she says. "I tell myself I have no right to grieve. They are in a better place than we are. My swami says depression is a sign of our selfishness."

46    Maybe I'm selfish. Selfishly I break away from Kusum and run, sandals slapping against stones, to the water's edge. What if my boys aren't lying pinned under the debris? What if they aren't stuck a mile below that innocent blue chop? What if, given the strong currents . . .

47    Now I've ruined my sari, one of my best. Kusum has joined me, knee deep in water that feels to me like a swimming pool. I could settle in the water, and my husband would take my hand and the boys would slap water in my face just to see me scream.

48    "Do you remember what good swimmers my boys were, Kusum?"

49    "I saw the medals," she says.

50    One of the widowers, Dr. Ranganathan from Montreal, walks out to us, carrying his shoes in one hand. He's an electrical engineer. Someone at the hotel mentioned his work is famous around the world, something about the place where physics and electricity come together. He has lost a huge family, something indescribable. "With some luck," Dr. Ranganathan suggests to me, "a good swimmer could make it safely to some island. It is quite possible that there may be many, many microscopic islets scattered around."

51    "You're not just saying that?" I tell Dr. Ranganathan about Vinod, my elder son. Last year he took diving as well.

52    "It's a parent's duty to hope," he says. "It is foolish to rule out possibilities that have not been tested. I myself have not surrendered hope."

53    Kusum is sobbing once again. "Dear lady," he says, laying his free hand on her arm, and she calms down.

54    "Vinod is how old?" he asks me. He's very careful, as we all are. *Is*, not *was*.

55    "Fourteen. Yesterday he was fourteen. His father and uncle were going to take him down to the Taj and give him a big birthday party. I couldn't go with them because I couldn't get two weeks off from my stupid job in June." I process bills for a travel agent. June is a big travel month.

56    Dr. Ranganathan whips the pockets of his suit jacket inside out. Squashed roses, in darkening shades of pink, float on the water. He tore the roses off creepers in somebody's garden. He didn't ask anyone if he could pluck the roses, but now there's been an article about it in the local papers. When you see an Indian person, it says, please give them flowers.

"A strong youth of fourteen," he says, "can very likely pull to safety 57 a younger one."

My sons, though four years apart, were very close. Vinod wouldn't 58 let Mithun down. *Electrical engineering*, I think, foolishly perhaps: this man knows important secrets of the universe, things closed to me. Relief spins me lightheaded. No wonder my boys' photographs haven't turned up in the gallery of photos of the recovered dead. "Such pretty roses," I say.

"My wife loved pink roses. Every Friday I had to bring a bunch 59 home. I used to say, Why? After twenty-odd years of marriage you're still needing proof positive of my love?" He has identified his wife and three of his children. Then others from Montreal, the lucky ones, intact families with no survivors. He chuckles as he wades back to shore. Then he swings around to ask me a question. "Mrs. Bhave, you are wanting to throw in some roses for your loved ones? I have two big ones left."

But I have other things to float: Vinod's pocket calculator; a half- 60 painted model B-52 for my Mithun. They'd want them on their island. And for my husband? For him I let fall into the calm, glassy waters a poem I wrote in the hospital yesterday. Finally he'll know my feelings for him.

"Don't tumble, the rocks are slippery," Dr. Ranganathan cautions. He 61 holds out a hand for me to grab.

Then it's time to get back on the bus, time to rush back to our waiting 62 posts on hospital benches.

Kusum is one of the lucky ones. The lucky ones flew here, identified 63 in multiplicate their loves ones, then will fly to India with the bodies for proper ceremonies. Satish is one of the few males who surfaced. The photos of faces we saw on the walls in an office at Heathrow and here in the hospital are mostly of women. Women have more body fat, a nun said to me matter-of-factly. They float better.

Today I was stopped by a young sailor on the street. He had loaded 64 bodies, he'd gone into the water when — he checks my face for signs of strength — when the sharks were first spotted. I don't blush, and he breaks down. "It's all right," I say. "Thank you." I heard about the sharks from Dr. Ranganathan. In his orderly mind, science brings understanding, it holds no terror. It is the shark's duty. For every deer there is a hunter, for every fish a fisherman.

The Irish are not shy; they rush to me and give me hugs and some are 65 crying. I cannot imagine reactions like that on the streets of Toronto. Just strangers, and I am touched. Some carry flowers with them and give them to any Indian they see.

After lunch, a policeman I have gotten to know quite well catches 66 hold of me. He says he thinks he has a match for Vinod. I explain what a good swimmer Vinod is.

"You want me with you when you look at photos?" Dr. Ranganathan 67 walks ahead of me into the picture gallery. In these matters, he is a scientist, and I am grateful. It is a new perspective. "They have performed miracles," he says. "We are indebted to them."

68     The first day or two the policemen showed us relatives only one picture at a time; now they're in a hurry, they're eager to lay out the possibles, and even the probables.

69     The face on the photo is of a boy much like Vinod; the same intelligent eyes, the same thick brows dipping into a V. But this boy's features, even his cheeks, are puffier, wider, mushier.

70     "No." My gaze is pulled by other pictures. There are five other boys who look like Vinod.

71     The nun assigned to console me rubs the first picture with a fingertip. "When they've been in the water for a while, love, they look a little heavier." The bones under the skin are broken, they said on the first day — try to adjust your memories. It's important.

72     "It's not him. I'm his mother. I'd know."

73     "I know this one!" Dr. Ranganathan cries out, and suddenly, from the back of the gallery, "And this one!" I think he senses that I don't want to find my boys. "They are the Kutty brothers. They were also from Montreal." I don't mean to be crying. On the contrary, I am ecstatic. My suitcase in the hotel is packed heavy with dry clothes for my boys.

74     The policeman starts to cry. "I am so sorry, I am so sorry, ma'am. I really thought we had a match."

75     With the nun ahead of us and the policeman behind, we, the unlucky ones without our children's bodies, file out of the make-shift gallery.

76     From Ireland most of us go on to India. Kusum and I take the same direct flight to Bombay, so I can help her clear customs quickly. But we have to argue with a man in a uniform. He has large boils on his face. The boils swell and glow with sweat as we argue with him. He wants Kusum to wait in line and he refuses to take authority because his boss is on a tea break. But Kusum won't let her coffins out of sight, and I shan't desert her though I know that my parents, elderly and diabetic, must be waiting in a stuffy car in a scorching lot.

77     "You bastard!" I scream at the man with the popping boils. Other passengers press closer. "You think we're smuggling contraband in those coffins!"

78     Once upon a time we were well-brought-up women; we were dutiful wives who kept our heads veiled, our voices shy and sweet.

79     In India, I become, once again, an only child of rich, ailing parents. Old friends of the family come to pay their respects. Some are Sikh, and inwardly, involuntarily, I cringe. My parents are progressive people; they do not blame communities for a few individuals.

80     In Canada it is a different story now.

81     "Stay longer," my mother pleads. "Canada is a cold place. Why would you want to be by yourself?" I stay.

Three months pass. Then another.          82

"Vikram wouldn't have wanted you to give up things!" they protest.          83
They call my husband by the name he was born with. In Toronto he'd
changed to Vik so the men he worked with at his office would find his
name as easy as Rod or Chris. "You know, the dead aren't cut off from
us!"

My grandmother, the spoiled daughter of a rich zamindar, shaved          84
her head with rusty razor blades when she was widowed at sixteen. My
grandfather died of childhood diabetes when he was nineteen, and she
saw herself as the harbinger of bad luck. My mother grew up without
parents, raised indifferently by an uncle, while her true mother slept in a
hut behind the main estate house and took her food with the servants.
She grew up a rationalist. My parents abhor mindless mortification.

The zamindar's daughter kept stubborn faith in Vedic rituals; my          85
parents rebelled. I am trapped between two modes of knowledge. At
thirty-six, I am too old to start over and too young to give up. Like my
husband's spirit, I flutter between worlds.

Courting aphasia, we travel. We travel with our phalanx of servants          86
and poor relatives. To hill stations and to beach resorts. We play contract
bridge in dusty gymkhana clubs. We ride stubby ponies up crumbly
mountain trails. At tea dances, we let ourselves be twirled twice round
the ballroom. We hit the holy spots we hadn't made time for before. In
Varanasi, Kalighat, Rishikesh, Hardwar, astrologers and palmists seek
me out and for a fee offer me cosmic consolations.

Already the widowers among us are being shown new bride candi-          87
dates. They cannot resist the call of custom, the authority of their parents
and older brothers. They must marry; it is the duty of a man to look after
a wife. The new wives will be young widows with children, destitute but
of good family. They will make loving wives, but the men will shun
them. I've had calls from the men over crackling Indian telephone lines.
"Save me," they say, these substantial, educated, successful men of
forty. "My parents are arranging a marriage for me." In a month they
will have buried one family and returned to Canada with a new bride
and partial family.

I am comparatively lucky. No one here thinks of arranging a husband          88
for an unlucky widow.

Then, on the third day of the sixth month into this odyssey, in an          89
abandoned temple in a tiny Himalayan village, as I make my offering of
flowers and sweetmeats to the god of a tribe of animists, my husband
descends to me. He is squatting next to a scrawny sadhu in moth-eaten
robes. Vikram wears the vanilla suit he wore the last time I hugged him.
The sadhu tosses petals on a butter-fed flame, reciting Sanskrit mantras,
and sweeps his face of flies. My husband takes my hands in his.

*You're beautiful,* he starts. Then, *What are you doing here?*          90

*Shall I stay?* I ask. He only smiles, but already the image is fading. *You*          91
*must finish alone what we started together.* No seaweed wreathes his

mouth. He speaks too fast, just as he used to when we were an envied family in our pink split-level. He is gone.

92    In the windowless altar room, smoky with joss sticks and clarified butter lamps, a sweaty hand gropes for my blouse. I do not shriek. The sadhu arranges his robe. The lamps hiss and sputter out.

93    When we come out of the temple, my mother says, "Did you feel something weird in there?"

94    My mother has no patience with ghosts, prophetic dreams, holy men, and cults.

95    "No," I lie. "Nothing."

96    But she knows that she's lost me. She knows that in days I shall be leaving.

96    Kusum's put up her house for sale. She wants to live in an ashram in Hardwar. Moving to Hardwar was her swami's idea. Her swami runs two ashrams, the one in Hardwar and another here in Toronto.

97    "Don't run away," I tell her.

99    "I'm not running away," she says. "I'm pursuing inner peace. You think you or that Ranganathan fellow are better off?"

100    Pam's left for California. She wants to do some modeling, she says. She says when she comes into her share of the insurance money she'll open a yoga-cum-aerobics studio in Hollywood. She sends me postcards so naughty I daren't leave them on the coffee table. Her mother has withdrawn from her and the world.

101    The rest of us don't lose touch, that's the point. Talk is all we have, says Dr. Ranganathan, who has also resisted his relatives and returned to Montreal and to his job, alone. He says, Whom better to talk with than other relatives? We've been melted down and recast as a new tribe.

102    He calls me twice a week from Montreal. Every Wednesday night and every Saturday afternoon. He is changing jobs, going to Ottawa. But Ottawa is over a hundred miles away, and he is forced to drive two hundred and twenty miles a day from his home in Montreal. He can't bring himself to sell his house. The house is a temple, he says; the king-sized bed in the master bedroom is a shrine. He sleeps on a folding cot. A devotee.

103    There are still some hysterical relatives. Judith Templeton's list of those needing help and those who've "accepted" is in nearly perfect balance. Acceptance means you speak of your family in the past tense and you make active plans for moving ahead with your life. There are courses at Seneca and Ryerson we could be taking. Her gleaming leather briefcase is full of college catalogues and lists of cultural societies that need our help. She has done impressive work, I tell her.

104    "In the textbooks on grief management," she replies—I am her confidante, I realize, one of the few whose grief has not sprung bizarre obsessions—"there are stages to pass through: rejection, depression,

acceptance, reconstruction." She has compiled a chart and finds that six months after the tragedy, none of us still rejects reality, but only a handful are reconstructing. "Depressed acceptance" is the plateau we've reached. Remarriage is a major step in reconstruction (though she's a little surprised, even shocked, over *how* quickly some of the men have taken on new families). Selling one's house and changing jobs and cities is healthy.

How to tell Judith Templeton that my family surrounds me, and that 105 like creatures in epics, they've changed shapes? She sees me as calm and accepting but worries that I have no job, no career. My closest friends are worse off than I. I cannot tell her my days, even my nights, are thrilling.

She asks me to help with families she can't reach at all. An elderly 106 couple in Agincourt whose sons were killed just weeks after they had brought their parents over from a village in Punjab. From their names, I know they are Sikh. Judith Templeton and a translator have visited them twice with offers of money for airfare to Ireland, with bank forms, power-of-attorney forms, but they have refused to sign, or to leave their tiny apartment. Their sons' money is frozen in the bank. Their sons' investment apartments have been trashed by tenants, the furnishings sold off. The parents fear that anything they sign or any money they receive will end the company's or the country's obligations to them. They fear they are selling their sons for two airline tickets to a place they've never seen.

The high-rise apartment is a tower of Indians and West Indians, with 107 a sprinkling of Orientals. The nearest bus-stop kiosk is lined with women in saris. Boys practice cricket in the parking lot. Inside the building, even I wince a bit from the ferocity of onion fumes, the distinctive and immediate Indianness of frying ghee, but Judith Templeton maintains a steady flow of information. These poor old people are in imminent danger of losing their place and all their services.

I say to her, "They are Sikh. They will not open up to a Hindu 108 woman." And what I want to add is, as much as I try not to, I stiffen now at the sight of beards and turbans. I remember a time when we all trusted each other in this new country, it was only the new country we worried about.

The two rooms are dark and stuffy. The lights are off, and an oil lamp 109 sputters on the coffee table. The bent old lady has let us in, and her husband is wrapping a white turban over his oiled, hip-length hair. She immediately goes to the kitchen, and I hear the most familiar sound of an Indian home, tap water hitting and filling a teapot.

They have not paid their utility bills, out of fear and inability to write 110 a check. The telephone is gone; electricity and gas and water are soon to follow. They have told Judith their sons will provide. They are good boys, and they have always earned and looked after their parents.

We converse a bit in Hindi. They do not ask about the crash and I 111 wonder if I should bring it up. If they think I am here merely as a translator, then they may feel insulted. There are thousands of Punjabi speakers, Sikhs, in Toronto to do a better job. And so I say to the old lady, "I too have lost my sons, and my husband, in the crash."

112    Her eyes immediately fill with tears. The man mutters a few words which sound like a blessing. "God provides and God takes away," he says.

113    I want to say, But only men destroy and give back nothing. "My boys and my husband are not coming back," I say. "We have to understand that."

114    Now the old woman responds. "But who is to say? Man alone does not decide these things." To this her husband adds his agreement.

115    Judith asks about the bank papers, the release forms. With a stroke of the pen, they will have a provincial trustee to pay their bills, invest their money, send them a monthly pension.

116    "Do you know this woman?" I ask them.

117    The man raises his hand from the table, turns it over, and seems to regard each finger separately before he answers. "This young lady is always coming here, we make tea for her, and she leaves papers for us to sign." His eyes scan a pile of papers in the corner of the room. "Soon we will be out of tea, then will she go away?"

118    The old lady adds, "I have asked my neighbors and no one else gets *angrezi* visitors. What have we done?"

119    "It's her job," I try to explain. "The government is worried. Soon you will have no place to stay, no lights, no gas, no water."

120    "Government will get its money. Tell her not to worry, we are honorable people."

121    I try to explain the government wishes to give money, not take. He raises his hand. "Let them take," he says. "We are accustomed to that. That is no problem."

122    "We are strong people," says the wife. "Tell her that."

123    "Who needs all this machinery?" demands the husband. "It is unhealthy, the bright lights, the cold air on a hot day, the cold food, the four gas rings. God will provide, not government."

124    "When our boys return," the mother says.

125    Her husband sucks his teeth. "Enough talk," he says.

126    Judith breaks in. "Have you convinced them?" The snaps on her cordovan briefcase go off like firecrackers in that quiet apartment. She lays the sheaf of legal papers on the coffee table. "If they can't write their names, an X will do—I've told them that."

127    Now the old lady has shuffled to the kitchen and soon emerges with a pot of tea and two cups. "I think my bladder will go first on a job like this," Judith says to me, smiling. "If only there was some way of reaching them. Please thank her for the tea. Tell her she's very kind."

128    I nod in Judith's direction and tell them in Hindi, "She thanks you for the tea. She thinks you are being very hospitable but she doesn't have the slightest idea what it means."

I want to say, Humor her. I want to say, My boys and my husband    129
are with me too, more than ever. I look in the old man's eyes and I can
read his stubborn, peasant's message: *I have protected this woman as best I
can. She is the only person I have left. Give to me or take from me what you
will, but I will not sign for it. I will not pretend that I accept.*

In the car, Judith says, "You see what I'm up against? I'm sure they're    130
lovely people, but their stubbornness and ignorance are driving me
crazy. They think signing a paper is signing their sons' death warrants,
don't they?"

I am looking out the window. I want to say, *In our culture, it is a*    131
*parent's duty to hope.*

"Now Shaila, this next woman is a real mess. She cries day and night,    132
and she refuses all medical help. We may have to —"

"Let me out at the subway," I say.    133

"I beg your pardon?" I can feel those blue eyes staring at me.    134

It would not be like her to disobey. She merely disapproves, and    135
slows at a corner to let me out. Her voice is plaintive. "Is there anything I
said? Anything I did?"

I could answer her suddenly in a dozen ways, but I choose not to.    136
"Shaila? Let's talk about it," I hear, then slam the door.

A wife and mother begins her new life in a new country, and that life    137
is cut short. Yet her husband tells her, Complete what we have started.
We, who stayed out of politics and came half-way around the world to
avoid religious and political feuding, have been the first in the New
World to die from it. I no longer know what we started, nor how to
complete it. I write letters to the editors of local papers and to members
of Parliament. Now at least they admit it was a bomb. One MP answers
back, with sympathy, but with a challenge. You want to make a difference? Work on a campaign. Work on mine. Politicize the Indian voter.

My husband's old lawyer helps me set up a trust. Vikram was a saver    138
and a careful investor. He had saved the boys' boarding school and
college fees. I sell the pink house at four times what we paid for it and
take a small apartment downtown. I am looking for a charity to support.

We are deep in the Toronto winter, gray skies, icy pavements. I stay    139
indoors, watching television. I have tried to assess my situation, how best
to live my life, to complete what we began so many years ago. Kusum
has written me from Hardwar that her life is now serene. She has seen
Satish and has heard her daughter sing again. Kusum was on a pilgrimage, passing through a village, when she heard a young girl's voice,
singing one of her daughter's favorite *bhajans*. She followed the music
through the squalor of a Himalayan village, to a hut where a young girl,
an exact replica of her daughter, was fanning coals under the kitchen
fire. When she appeared, the girl cried out, "Ma!" and ran away. What
did I think of that?

I think I can only envy her.    140

141     Pam didn't make it to California, but writes me from Vancouver. She works in a department store, giving makeup hints to Indian and Oriental girls. Dr. Ranganathan has given up his commute, given up his house and job, and accepted an academic position in Texas, where no one knows his story and he has vowed not to tell it. He calls me now once a week.

142     I wait, I listen and I pray, but Vikram has not returned to me. The voices and the shapes and the nights filled with visions ended abruptly several weeks ago.

143     I take it as a sign.

144     One rare, beautiful, sunny day last week, returning from a small errand on Yonge Street, I was walking through the park from the subway to my apartment. I live equidisant from the Ontario Houses of Parliament and the University of Toronto. The day was not cold, but something in the bare trees caught my attention. I looked up from the gravel, into the branches and the clear blue sky beyond. I thought I heard the rustling of larger forms, and I waited a moment for voices. Nothing.

145     "What?" I asked.

146     Then as I stood in the path looking north to Queen's Park and west to the university, I heard the voices of my family one last time. *Your time has come,* they said. *Go, be brave.*

147     I do not know where this voyage I have begun will end. I do not know which direction I will take. I dropped the package on a park bench and started walking.

## *Evaluating the Text*

1. How would you characterize the situation in which Shaila finds herself? What is so unusual about the way Shaila reacts? Why might her reaction lead others to draw the wrong conclusions?

2. What is the advantage of telling the story from Shaila's point of view (first person)? How might a third-person account suggest Shaila was calm and in control when she really was not?

3. What would you conclude about the relationship between Shaila and her husband? Why is it significant that Shaila did not call him by his first name after being married for many years? How does the poem Shaila throws into the water express her real feelings toward her husband?

4. What does the bombing of the plane reveal about underlying religious and cultural conflicts in India? What is Mukherjee's attitude toward these conflicts?

5. How would you characterize Judith Templeton? What is her job? How sensitive is she to the feelings of those she interviews, and what does she want Shaila to do? How does Mukherjee's description of Templeton's background and actions suggest that Templeton is a product of her cultural conditioning in her attitude toward "managing grief"?

6. What might you infer from the fact that Shaila, who seems to accept the situation, has brought dry clothes with her from Toronto for her boys?

How does Shaila's reaction to seeing Kusum wade into the water (ruining her sari) show you how she really feels, although others see her as coping very well?

7. What is at stake in the attempt of officials to get Shaila to identify Vinod's body? Why does she refuse to make the identification?

8. How do you understand the visitation to her of Vikram? Does it appear to be a hallucination, an inner projection, or a real manifestation? How would the way you interpret this event reveal much about your own cultural assumptions toward the supernatural?

9. In what way are Pam's reactions typical of the newer generation of Indians living in the West? How do they differ from the traditional reactions of Kusum; the logical, if hopeful, reactions of Dr. Ranganathan; and those of Shaila? To what extent is Shaila the only one who actually comes to terms with what has happened?

10. What does Templeton's expectation that Shaila can act as an interpreter for the Sikh couple reveal about Templeton's ignorance about issues important to Indians?

11. Why are the Sikhs unwilling to sign papers? In what way does Shaila sympathize with their obligation to keep hope alive? How does Shaila's interaction with the Sikh couple help her to accept what she was unable to come to terms with previously?

12. Why does Shaila ultimately refuse to help Templeton intercede with local Indian families?

13. How do you interpret the line, "Your time has come," and in what way is this phrase ambiguous? What different kinds of things might it mean in the context of the story?

## Exploring Different Perspectives

1. Drawing on Edward Said's characterization of exile ("Reflections on Exile"), discuss Shaila's predicament of being between the two cultures of India and Canada, at home in neither.

2. Discuss how V. S. Naipaul ("Prologue to an Autobiography"), born in Trinidad of an Indian family, who later immigrated to England, is also someone caught between two cultures, as Shaila is. Compare the efforts of both to come to terms with their biculturality.

## Extending Viewpoints through Writing

1. Discuss the culturally based differences in managing grief that emerge from Mukherjee's story. What are these differences, and how are they related to different cultural assumptions as to the meaning of death and what survivors ought to do in the aftermath of such events?

2. What does the reaction of the people in Ireland to Shaila and to other Indians tell you about the Irish culture? How does it seem to differ from Canadian culture?

3. Analyze the cultural assumptions underlying the Western belief that the mourning process is characterized by stages of grief, and analyze the related assumptions that one expresses grief differently in front of one's

immediate family and closest friends than with acquaintances. You might also analyze the different lengths of time Eastern and Western cultures deem appropriate in the grieving process. How are different cultural attitudes toward reincarnation responsible for different expectations as to how one should manage grief?

4. Describe the first experience you had in which you perceived death as an adult might rather than as a child would. What distinguishes the two perceptions from each other? In the situation, did others try to "manage" your grief, and tell you how to express it? To what extent were these ways culturally conditioned?

5. Mukherjee's story illustrates a cultural confrontation between those at the margin of a culture with those at the center. Write an expository essay showing how any of the following authors do not subscribe to the values, beliefs, and rhetoric of the dominant mainstream culture they are in: Francine du Plessix Gray ("Sex and Birth," Chapter 1); Natsume Soseki ("I Am a Cat," Chapter 1); Rigoberta Menchu, ("Birth Ceremonies, Chapter 1); Danny Santiago ("Famous All Over Town," Chapter 2); Nawal El-Saadawi ("Circumsion of Girls," Chapter 2); Simone de Beauvoir ("The Married Woman," Chapter 3); Josef Škvorecký ("An Insolvable Problem of Genetics," Chapter 5); Chen Jo-hsi ("The Big Fish," Chapter 6); Shen Tong ("Bloody Sunday in Tiananmen Square," Chapter 6); Samir al-Khalil ("Authority," Chapter 6); Ngũgĩ wa Thiong'o ("Decolonising the Mind," Chapter 6); or Salman Rushdie ("A Pen against the Sword").

# CONNECTING CULTURES

## Edward Said, "Reflections on Exile"

1. How does David K. Shipler's "The Sin of Love" (Chapter 3) confirm many of Said's observations about the difficulty exiles have in maintaining personal relationships? How are both the Arab woman and Israeli man exiled from the community?
2. To what extent do the narratives of Napoleon A. Chagnon ("Doing Fieldwork among the Yąnomamö," Chapter 8), and Douchan Gersi ("Initiated into an Iban Tribe of Headhunters," Chapter 2) dramatize the "culture shock" of trying to get one's bearings in a completely new environment? What evidence can you find within these works that support Said's observations?
3. To what extent does being compelled to not speak one's native language as described by Ngũgĩ wa Thiong'o ("Decolonising the Mind," Chapter 6) result in cultural alienation similar to that experienced by exiles, according to Said?
4. How are American baseball players on Japanese teams as described by Pico Iyer ("Perfect Strangers," Chapter 8) faced with problems similar to those confronting exiles as described by Said?
5. Can you discover any differences in the reactions of those who, like Mark Salzman ("Lessons," Chapter 4), voluntarily move to new cultures as compared with the kinds of problems faced by refugees, immigrants, and other involuntary exiles, discussed by Said?
6. How do Toi Derricotte's account ("The Black Notebooks," Chapter 5) and Krishnan Varma's story ("The Grass-Eaters," Chapter 5) reveal that one can experience the feelings of being an exile without moving to a new country?

## V. S. Naipaul, "Prologue to an Autobiography"

7. How do Naipaul and Ngũgĩ wa Thiong'o ("Decolonising the Mind," Chapter 6) underscore the importance of the language one learns as a child in conserving cultural traditions? How do these essays emphasize different aspects of this issue?
8. After reading Naipaul's essay, analyze how the experience of alienation provides both him and Toi Derricotte ("The Black Notebooks," Chapter 5) with a subject for their writing. How do their responses to the experience of displacement differ?

## Nicholasa Mohr, "A Very Special Pet"

9. Discuss the experiences of the family in Mohr's story as they compare with those of Cha Ok Kim's family ("The Peddler," Chapter 4). What factors seem to determine whether one adapts successfully to life in a new country?

513

10. What connections can you discover between Simone de Beauvoir's characterization of "The Married Woman" (Chapter 3) and the portrait Mohr creates of Graciela?

## Joan Didion, "Miami: The Cuban Presence"

11. In what respects can the *quinces* depicted in Didion's article be seen as an initiation ceremony much like those described by Tepilit Ole Saitoti ("The Initiation of a Maasai Warrior," Chapter 2)? How do the differences between these two reflect the differences in cultural values between Cubans in Miami and the Maasai in Kenya?
12. What distinctive strengths do the Cuban community in Miami have that enable them to be successful without assimilating into mainstream American culture? For a contrast, you might read Danny Santiago's "Famous All Over Town" (Chapter 2).

## Le Ly Hayslip, "Sisters and Brothers"

13. How do the accounts by Hayslip and David K. Shipler ("The Sin of Love," Chapter 3) dramatize the destructive effects of political ideologies on personal relationships?
14. How does Hayslip provide a perspective on the Vietnam war different from that of Robert Santos ("My Men," Chapter 9)?
15. How are Hayslip's family in Vietnam subject to the same kinds of surveillance by authorities as is Someth May ("The Field behind the Village," Chapter 6) in Cambodia?
16. After reading Kyōko Hayashi's "The Empty Can" (Chapter 9), discuss how both it and Hayslip's account involve coming to terms with traumatic events that happened during wartime.

## David Whitman, "Trouble for America's 'Model' Minority"

17. In what sense does Amy Tan's story ("Jing-Mei Woo: Two Kinds," Chapter 1), exploring the pressure second-generation Asian children are under to succeed, complement Whitman's account of second-wave Indochinese immigrants who find it more difficult to succeed than the first wave of immigrants?
18. How is Whitman's discussion of the archaic sixteenth-century background of Indochinese immigrants substantiated by Someth May's ("The Field behind the Village," Chapter 6) description of work in the fields in Cambodia?
19. We usually think of "culture shock" as Napoleon A. Chagnon ("Doing Fieldwork among the Yąnomamö, Chapter 8) uses the term; that is, to characterize the unexpected primitive conditions that explorers like Douchan Gersi ("Initiated into an Iban Tribe of Headhunters," Chapter 2) and anthropologists encounter. In what sense can one speak of the "culture shock" experienced by second-wave Indochinese immigrants to the United States?

## Jamaica Kincaid, "A Small Place"

20. To what extent do both Chen Jo-hsi's story ("The Big Fish," Chapter 6) and Kincaid's analysis reflect the author's criticism of governments who are more concerned with impressing foreign visitors than with the welfare of their own citizens?

21. How do both Kincaid and Gretel Ehrlich ("To Live in Two Worlds," Chapter 8) explore the theme of acceptance or nonacceptance of outsiders by in-groups?

## Salman Rushdie, "A Pen against the Sword"

22. How do the religious doctrines of the Koran play as important a role in Tayeb Salih's story "A Handful of Dates" (Chapter 2) as they do in Rushdie's account? Contrast Tayeb Salih's attitude toward Islamic beliefs with Rushdie's.

23. What significant differences in tone and in purpose distinguish Rushdie's literary techniques (e.g., externalizing a psychological crisis through allegory) from Jan Rabie's use of parable in "Drought" (Chapter 6)?

24. How do both Rushdie's account and Samir al-Khalil's analysis ("Authority," Chapter 6) illuminate the role of charismatic larger-than-life leaders in focusing the aspirations of their respective societies? Although Ayotellah Khomeini was the head of a religious state (Iran) and Saddam Hussein is the head of a secular nationalistic state (Iraq), what similarities can you discover in terms of the allegiance they command? How do the personalities of the two leaders help explain why the war between Iran and Iraq lasted eight years and cost over one million lives?

## Bharati Mukherjee, "The Management of Grief"

25. Compare the culturally based differences of how grief is expressed in Mukherjee's story with Kyōko Hayashi's treatment of the same theme in "The Empty Can" (Chapter 9).

26. Compare Margaret Atwood's characterization in "Happy Endings" (Chapter 3) of Canadian life (staid, concerned with social propriety and the appearance of things) with Shaila's experience of what it is like to live in Toronto.

27. Which of the conflicts between Shaila and Templeton and between Templeton and the Sikh couple are due to culturally based misunderstandings of the kind discussed by Raymonde Carroll in "Minor Accidents" (Chapter 8)?

28. Compare Pam in Mukherjee's story with the daughter in Amy Tan's "Jing-Mei Woo: Two Kinds" (Chapter 1). What common elements can you discover that connect them as second-generation daughters of immigrants?

29. To what extent do the culturally based "gender roles" discussed by Marilyn French ("Gender Roles," Chapter 3) hold true for the sex roles of Indian husbands and wives as revealed in "The Management of Grief"?

# 8

# *The Role Customs Play in Different Cultures*

In the customs that guide behavior within any particular society, we can see most clearly the hidden cultural logic and unconscious assumptions that people in that society rely on to interpret everything that goes on in their world. Customs and rituals that may seem bizarre or strange to an outsider appear entirely normal and natural to those within the culture. Unfortunately, the potential for conflict exists as soon as people from different cultures whose "natural" ways do not coincide make contact with each other. As communications, immigration, and travel make the world grow smaller, the potential for cross-cultural misunderstandings accelerate. Correspondingly, the need to become aware of the extent to which our and other people's conclusions about the world are guided by different cultural presuppositions grows accordingly. The analysis of customs of cultures other than our own allows us to temporarily put aside our taken-for-granted ways of seeing the world, even if we are unaware of the extent to which we rely on these implicit premises, to understand that the meanings we give to events, actions, and statements, are not their only meanings.

Robert Levine with Ellen Wolff in "Social Time: The Heartbeat of Culture" first broaden our perceptions about something seemingly as indisputable as "clock time" by disclosing how different cultures rely on different assumptions as to what being early, on time, or late means in regulating the pace of life. Pico Iyer in "Perfect Strangers" provides a fascinating glimpse into the cultural presuppositions the Japanese rely on in reshaping America's national pastime, baseball, to make it uniquely Japanese. Iyer illuminates the process by which the Japanese adapt and reconstruct aspects of Western culture. In Napoleon A. Chagnon's account, from "Doing Fieldwork among the Yąnomamö," we can experience the meaning of "culture shock," as Chagnon became aware of the vast difference in values and attitudes that separated him from the people in this Brazilian tribe among whom he lived for forty-one months. Raymonde Carroll, in "Minor Accidents," provides a penetrating analysis of the different cultural "scripts" French and Americans bring to interpreting everyday accidents such as spilling red wine on a friend's light-colored carpet. Carroll reveals that seemingly objective concepts of accountability are in fact culturally conditioned.

In Gretel Ehrlich's "To Live in Two Worlds," we benefit from the opportunity she was granted in being privileged to observe the Kiowa Sun Dance, their most sacred religious ritual. Unlike other cultures, the Kiowa combine the secular and the sacred and do not relegate religious practice to one day a week. Paul Fussell's account, "Taking It All Off in the Balkans," not only describes how he had to "take it all off" during his visit to the nude beaches on the Adriatic coast but how he had to become aware of and revise his own cultural assumptions and value judgments about naturism.

Octavio Paz, in "The Day of the Dead," explores the important role fiestas play in Mexican culture and their relationship to the Mexican national character. Paz reveals how fiestas create their own world, involving enormous expenditures of money, time, and energy, encouraging forms of behavior normally not permitted, in a ritual of yearly regeneration and renewal. We gain additional insight into how customs and rituals ensure a cohesive system of social control in Gino Del Guercio's "The Secrets of Haiti's Living Dead," by discovering that the practice of voodoo, in contrast to its stereotyped image in the popular media, is an integral and constructive force in Haitian society. Del Guercio's report on the pioneering research of Wade Davis reveals how the threat of zombification, itself a provable medical condition produced by potent neurotoxins, ensures social control in deterring crimes against the community. Last, Bessie Head relates a fact-based story that illustrates how one family in drought-plagued Botswana was driven beyond the limits of physical and psychological endurance and resorted to an outlawed tribal ritual of sacrificing their children in exchange for rain in "Looking for a Rain God." The story illuminates the conflict experienced by people who live in countries where Western Christian colonial values have been superimposed on ancient tribal customs and beliefs.

The range and diversity of these selections is meant to encourage you to understand the many ways in which meaning can be produced and received. In the process of responding to the suggestions for discussion and writing, you can not only temporarily replace your own ways of perceiving the world with those of others but become aware, perhaps for the first time, of your own cultural presuppositions, the implicit assumptions that govern your interpretation of the world.

Robert Levine with Ellen Wolff

# Social Time: The Heartbeat of Culture

*Robert Levine is a social psychologist on the faculty at California State University at Fresno. The following study, originally published in* Psychology Today *(March 1985) reveals that to understand society we must learn its sense of time. The authors show how "social time" reflects the culture's attitude toward "clock time" in regulating the pace of life. Levine became aware of the importance of "social time" when he spent a year teaching in Niterói, Brazil, as a Latin American Teaching Fellow. Further observations followed during a year-long trip he made around the world in 1980. He contacted Ellen Wolff, a former student and a free-lance writer, to help him convert his scientific data and technical observations into an article for a general audience. The article explores several ways to measure cultural attitudes toward time and reveals that cultures differ radically from each other in their conceptions of being early, on time, or late. For example, in Japan, public clocks are seldom more than a few seconds off the exact time.*

1    *"If a man does not keep pace with his companions, perhaps it is because he hears a different drummer."* This thought by Thoreau strikes a chord in so many people that it has become part of our language. We use the phrase "the beat of a different drummer" to explain any pace of life unlike our own. Such colorful vagueness reveals how informal our rules of time really are. The world over, children simply "pick up" their society's time concepts as they mature. No dictionary clearly defines the meaning of "early" or "late" for them or for strangers who stumble over the maddening incongruities between the time sense they bring with them and the one they face in a new land.

2    I learned this firsthand, a few years ago, and the resulting culture shock led me halfway around the world to find answers. It seemed clear that time "talks." But what is it telling us?

3    My journey started shortly after I accepted an appointment as visiting

(For background information on Brazil, see p. 536 and for information on Japan, see pp. 35 and 250.)

professor of psychology at the federal university in Niterói, Brazil, a midsized city across the bay from Rio de Janeiro. As I left home for my first day of class, I asked someone the time. It was 9:05 a.m., which allowed me time to relax and look around the campus before my 10 o'clock lecture. After what I judged to be half an hour, I glanced at a clock I was passing. It said 10:20! In panic, I broke for the classroom, followed by gentle calls of "Hola, professor" and "Tudo bem, professor?" from unhurried students, many of whom, I later realized, were my own. I arrived breathless to find an empty room.

Frantically, I asked a passerby the time. "Nine forty-five" was the 4 answer. No, that couldn't be. I asked someone else. "Nine fifty-five." Another said: "Exactly 9:43." The clock in a nearby office read 3:15. I had learned my first lesson about Brazilians: Their timepieces are consistently inaccurate. And nobody minds.

My class was scheduled from 10 until noon. Many students came 5 late, some very late. Several arrived after 10:30. A few showed up closer to 11. Two came after that. All of the latecomers wore the relaxed smiles that I came, later, to enjoy. Each one said hello, and although a few apologized briefly, none seemed terribly concerned about lateness. They assumed that I understood.

The idea of Brazilians arriving late was not a great shock. I had heard 6 about "mãnha," the Portuguese equivalent of "mañana" in Spanish. This term, meaning "tomorrow" or "the morning," stereotypes the Brazilian who puts off the business of today until tomorrow. The real surprise came at noon that first day, when the end of class arrived.

Back home in California, I never need to look at a clock to know 7 when the class hour is ending. The shuffling of books is accompanied by strained expressions that say plaintively, "I'm starving. . . . I've got to go to the bathroom. . . . I'm going to suffocate if you keep us one more second." (The pain usually becomes unbearable at two minutes to the hour in undergraduate classes and five minutes before the close of graduate classes.)

When noon arrived in my first Brazilian class, only a few students left 8 immediately. Others slowly drifted out during the next 15 minutes, and some continued asking me questions long after that. When several remaining students kicked off their shoes at 12:30, I went into my own "starving/bathroom/suffocation" routine.

I could not, in all honesty, attribute their lingering to my superb 9 teaching style. I had just spent two hours lecturing on statistics in halting Portuguese. Apparently, for many of my students, staying late was simply of no more importance than arriving late in the first place. As I observed this casual approach in infinite variations during the year, I learned that the "mãnha" stereotype oversimplified the real Anglo/Brazilian differences in conceptions of time. Research revealed a more complex picture.

With the assistance of colleagues Laurie West and Harry Reis, I 10 compared the time sense of 91 male and female students in Niterói with that of 107 similar students at California State University in Fresno. The universities are similar in academic quality and size, and the cities are both secondary metropolitan centers with populations of about 350,000.

11     We asked students about their perceptions of time in several situations, such as what they would consider late or early for a hypothetical lunch appointment with a friend. The average Brazilian student defined lateness for lunch as 33½ minutes after the scheduled time, compared to only 19 minutes for the Fresno students. But Brazilians also allowed an average of about 54 minutes before they'd consider someone early, while the Fresno students drew the line at 24.

12     Are Brazilians simply more flexible in their concepts of time and punctuality? And how does this relate to the stereotype of the apathetic, fatalistic and irresponsible Latin temperament? When we asked students to give typical reasons for lateness, the Brazilians were less likely to attribute it to a lack of caring than the North Americans were. Instead, they pointed to unforeseen circumstances that the person couldn't control. Because they seemed less inclined to feel personally responsible for being late, they also expressed less regret for their own lateness and blamed others less when they were late.

13     We found similar differences in how students from the two countries characterized people who were late for appointments. Unlike their North American counterparts, the Brazilian students believed that a person who is consistently late is probably more successful than one who is consistently on time. They seemed to accept the idea that someone of status is expected to arrive late. Lack of punctuality is a badge of success.

14     Even within our own country, of course, ideas of time and punctuality vary considerably from place to place. Different regions and even cities have their own distinct rhythms and rules. Seemingly simple words like "now," snapped out by an impatient New Yorker, and "later," said by a relaxed Californian, suggest a world of difference. Despite our familiarity with these homegrown differences in tempo, problems with time present a major stumbling block to Americans abroad. Peace Corps volunteers told researchers James Spradley of Macalester College and Mark Phillips of the University of Washington that their greatest difficulties with other people, after language problems, were the general pace of life and the punctuality of others. Formal "clock time" may be a standard on which the world agrees, but "social time," the heartbeat of society, is something else again.

15     How a country paces its social life is a mystery to most outsiders, one that we're just beginning to unravel. Twenty-six years ago, anthropologist Edward Hall noted in *The Silent Language* that informal patterns of time "are seldom, if ever, made explicit. They exist in the air around us. They are either familiar and comfortable, or unfamiliar and wrong." When we realize we are out of step, we often blame the people around us to make ourselves feel better.

Appreciating cultural differences in time sense becomes increasingly    16
important as modern communications put more and more people in
daily contact. If we are to avoid misreading issues that involve time
perceptions, we need to understand better our own cultural biases and
those of others.

When people of different cultures interact, the potential for misun-    17
derstanding exists on many levels. For example, members of Arab and
Latin cultures usually stand much closer when they are speaking to
people than we usually do in the United States, a fact we frequently
misinterpret as aggression or disrespect. Similarly, we assign personality
traits to groups with a pace of life that is markedly faster or slower than
our own. We build ideas of national character, for example, around the
traditional Swiss and German ability to "make the trains run on time."
Westerners like ourselves define punctuality using precise measures of
time: 5 minutes, 15 minutes, an hour. But according to Hall, in many
Mediterranean Arab cultures there are only three sets of time: no time at
all, now (which is of varying duration) and forever (too long). Because of
this, Americans often find difficulty in getting Arabs to distinguish between waiting a long time and a very long time.

According to historian Will Durant, "No man in a hurry is quite    18
civilized." What do our time judgments say about our attitude toward
life? How can a North American, coming from a land of digital precision,
relate to a North African who may consider a clock "the devil's mill"?

Each language has a vocabulary of time that does not always survive    19
translation. When we translated our questionnaires into Portuguese for
my Brazilian students, we found that English distinctions of time were
not readily articulated in their language. Several of our questions concerned how long the respondent would wait for someone to arrive, as
compared with when they hoped for arrival or actually expected the
person would come. In Portuguese, the verbs "to wait for," "to hope for"
and "to expect" are all translated as "esperar." We had to add further
words of explanation to make the distinction clear to the Brazilian
students.

To avoid these language problems, my Fresno colleague Kathy Bart-    20
lett and I decided to clock the pace of life in other countries by using as
little language as possible. We looked directly at three basic indicators of
time: the accuracy of a country's bank clocks, the speed at which pedestrians walked and the average time it took a postal clerk to sell us a single
stamp. In six countries on three continents, we made observations in
both the nation's largest urban area and a medium-sized city: Japan
(Tokyo and Sendai), Taiwan (Taipei and Tainan), Indonesia (Jakarta and
Solo), Italy (Rome and Florence), England (London and Bristol) and the
United States (New York City and Rochester).

What we wanted to know was: Can we speak of a unitary concept    21
called "pace of life"? What we've learned suggests that we can. There
appears to be a very strong relationship between the accuracy of clock

time, walking speed and postal efficiency across the countries we studied.

22    We checked 15 clocks in each city, selecting them at random in downtown banks and comparing the time they showed with that reported by the local telephone company. In Japan, which leads the way in accuracy, the clocks averaged just over half a minute early or late. Indonesian clocks, the least accurate, were more than three minutes off the mark.

23    I will be interested to see how the digital-information age will affect our perceptions of time. In the United States today, we are reminded of the exact hour of the day more than ever, through little symphonies of beeps emanating from people's digital watches. As they become the norm, I fear our sense of precision may take an absurd twist. The other day, when I asked for the time, a student looked at his watch and replied, "Three twelve and eighteen seconds."

"'Will you walk a little faster?' said a whiting to a snail. 'There's a porpoise close behind us, and he's treading on my tail.'"

24    So goes the rhyme from *Alice in Wonderland,* which also gave us that famous symbol of haste, the White Rabbit. He came to mind often as we measured the walking speeds in our experimental cities. We clocked how long it took pedestrians to walk 100 feet along a main downtown street during business hours on clear days. To eliminate the effects of socializing, we observed only people walking alone, timing at least 100 in each city. We found, once again, that the Japanese led the way, averaging just 20.7 seconds to cover the distance. The English nosed out the Americans for second place — 21.6 to 22.5 seconds — and the Indonesians again trailed the pack, sauntering along at 27.2 seconds. As you might guess, speed was greater in the larger city of each nation than its smaller one.

25    Our final measurement, the average time it took postal clerks to sell one stamp, turned out to be less straightforward than we expected. In each city, including those in the United States, we presented clerks with a note in the native language requesting a common-priced stamp — a 20-center in the United States, for example. They were also handed paper money, the equivalent of a $5 bill. In Indonesia, this procedure led to more than we bargained for.

26    At the large central post office in Jakarta, I asked for the line to buy stamps and was directed to a group of private vendors sitting outside. Each of them hustled for my business: "Hey, good stamps, mister!" "Best stamps here!" In the smaller city of Solo, I found a volleyball game in progress when I arrived at the main post office on Friday afternoon. Business hours, I was told, were over. When I finally did get there during business hours, the clerk was more interested in discussing relatives in America. Would I like to meet his uncle in Cincinnati? Which did I like better: California or the United States? Five people behind me in line

waited patiently. Instead of complaining, they began paying attention to our conversation.

When it came to efficiency of service, however, the Indonesians were    27
not the slowest, although they did place far behind the Japanese postal clerks, who averaged 25 seconds. That distinction went to the Italians, whose infamous postal service took 47 seconds on the average.

*"A man who wastes one hour of time has not discovered the meaning of*    28
*life. . . ."*

That was Charles Darwin's belief, and many share it, perhaps at the    29
cost of their health. My colleagues and I have recently begun studying the relationship between pace of life and well-being. Other researchers have demonstrated that a chronic sense of urgency is a basic component of the Type A, coronary-prone personality. We expect that future research will demonstrate that pace of life is related to rate of heart disease, hypertension, ulcers, suicide, alcoholism, divorce and other indicators of general psychological and physical well-being.

As you envision tomorrow's international society, do you wonder    30
who will set the pace? Americans eye Japan carefully, because the Japanese are obviously "ahead of us" in measurable ways. In both countries, speed is frequently confused with progress. Perhaps looking carefully at the different paces of life around the world will help us distinguish more accurately between the two qualities. Clues are everywhere but sometimes hard to distinguish. You have to listen carefully to hear the beat of even your own drummer.

## Evaluating the Text

1. What alerted Levine that his concept of time was not shared by Brazilians? How did his sense of time differ from theirs? How does "social time" differ from "clock time" according to Levine? What experiences led him to conclude that "social time" was more important than "clock time" to the Brazilian students?
2. What assumptions underlie Brazilian explanations about causes for lateness? How are cultural expectations regarding success, prestige, and personal responsibility revealed through the Brazilian attitude toward being early or late?
4. Why was it necessary to make further additions to the Portuguese verb *esperar* in order to elicit the exact information the researchers were interested in obtaining?
5. What three measures did the researchers use to gauge the meaning of a country's sense of time? Are there additional measures you would have used if you were doing this experiment? Explain the reasons for your suggestions.
6. What general correlations between pace of life and nationality did the researchers find? Had you expected different results from these kinds of experiments? What inferences about the cultures involved do you draw from these results?

7. Although this article was written for a popular audience, it relies on research techniques used by scientists (noticing an anomaly or discrepancy that needs further explanation, formulating a hypothesis to explain it, designing experiments to test a key variable, and drawing conclusions from the data ). How does Levine make these technical features interesting for a nonacademic reader?

## Exploring Different Perspectives

1. Drawing on Levine's research and conclusions, discuss how the experience of time during the fiesta period, described by Octavio Paz in "The Day of the Dead" differs qualitatively from the way time is experienced the rest of the year for people in Mexico.
2. How do the investigations of different cultural phenomenon by Raymonde Carroll ("Minor Accidents") and the authors of "Social Time" reveal that phenomena such as "clock time" and the way people react to "minor accidents" are constructed to mean different things in different cultures? Why would it be useful to know that supposedly unalterable meanings commonly attributed to things are really culturally defined and conditioned?

## Extending Viewpoints through Writing

1. How do your expectations as to when classes are scheduled to begin and end differ from those of the Brazilian students?
2. If you performed the same experiment as Levine did on earliness or lateness of clocks around your town and campus, what conclusions would you draw?
3. What would you consider being "late" or "early" for an appointment with a friend, and to what extent does your answer differ from the average answer given by the Brazilian students queried by Levine's colleagues?
4. How does the concept of being on time in your section of the country differ from a sense of timeliness in other regions of the United States? Have you had the experience of living in small, medium-sized, or large cities in the same culture where you were able to observe time differences in the "pace of life"? Discuss your experiences that illustrate these differences. Have you ever observed differences in the "pace of life" in different cultures? If so, discuss them.
5. Why is it important to understand the unconscious assumptions that different societies apply to concepts of being on time, early, or late? How is being able to understand these different values important in doing business (how might an American misunderstand the meaning of his or her Brazilian counterpart being late for a meeting?), politics, tourism, and other features of everyday life?

# Pico Iyer

# *Perfect Strangers*

*Pico Iyer was born of Indian parents in Oxford, England, and educated at Eton, Oxford, and Harvard. He has written on world affairs for* Time *magazine. The following reading, "Perfect Strangers" is from the Japan chapter of his cross-cultural travelogue* Video Night in Kathmandu: And Other Reports From the Not-So Far East *(1988). Although traditional sports such as judo, kendo (fencing using bamboo poles), and karate continue to be popular, as is sumo wrestling as a spectator sport, baseball has become the national sport. The game was brought to Japan in the 1800s by an American educator and is played on both professional and amateur levels. All Japan follows the progress of the annual National High School playoffs. Sports Day (October 10) is celebrated as a national holiday.*

At the heart of Japan's relations with the outside world, then, stood a paradox as large and implacable as the Sphinx. The Japanese might study and imitate all things Western, but they did not really like Westerners (in much the same way, perhaps, as they had liberally borrowed from the Chinese during the Nara period without ever acknowledging much fondness for the Chinese people). In answer to a 1980 poll, 64 percent of all Japanese had claimed that they did not wish to have anything to do with foreigners. In ancient times, people who committed the crime of being foreign were beheaded; nowadays, they were simply placed before the diminishing eye of the TV camera (entire shows were devoted to portraying the stupidities of *gaijin*). In the Japanese context, imitation was the insincerest form of flattery.

For all that, however, the Japanese were still determined to impress *gaijin*, and they still coveted the foreigners' lifestyles. In the flesh, *gaijin* might strike many Japanese as freakish, foul-smelling and crude; but as symbols — of prosperity and progress — they possessed a glamour to which few Japanese were immune. Thus blue-eyed blondes were still much sought after for commercials and regarded almost as trophies — walking advertisements for the Good Life — to be shown off to the neighbors, even as they were giggled at by schoolgirls and inspected by toddlers with fearful fascination.

(For more background information on Japan, see pp. 35 and 250.)

3    When it came to baseball, of course, this already vexing double standard grew even more vexed. For the Americans, as the creators of the sport, were generally assumed to be its masters; yet the Japanese could not, would not, be content with being number two — they were determined to try harder and try harder and try still harder until they were the best. Unlike, say, the Filipinos, who play baseball, or the Latin Americans, who have taken up baseball, the Japanese refused to accede to Americans the home-team advantage.

4    This insistent desire to escape the shadow of Big Brother had begun to haunt every aspect of the game. During my visit, I heard much lamentation about the eclipse of the traditional *obento* box lunches at baseball games by American fast-food imports — Korakuen, the National Shrine of Baseball, was appointed with a Kentucky Fried Chicken outlet, a Mister Donut store and, of course, the Golden Arches. I read a column in the *Japan Times* that grimly debated whether foreigners should be admitted to the *meikyukai* club, the country's unofficial Hall of Fame, reserved for players with 200 wins or 2,000 hits. The anxiety had even, by now, seeped into the trade war: Washington had persuaded the Japanese to accept U.S.-made aluminum bats, and Japan had accepted, but then had quickly modified its rules so as to make the bats effectively illegal.

5    Yet in typically contradictory fashion, the Japanese had also sought to reverse the supremacy of the American leagues by importing American players. And as I followed the major leagues at home, I noticed, every now and then, that a onetime star, now in his early thirties perhaps, and three or four years away from his last All-Star appearance, would suddenly vanish; he was reborn, I gathered, across the Pacific. By now, Don Newcombe, Frank Howard, Clete Boyer, Joe Pepitone and a hundred other stars had jumped to Japan. And when I attended my first Giants game, I was startled to see a familiar form standing in front of me in center field. I looked a little closer, and saw that it was Warren Cromartie, who, when last I looked, had been leading the Montreal Expos to one near-pennant after another. Old players didn't die; they just went to Japan.

6    American baseball, of course, takes great pride in its role as a model of the melting pot, a happy community of integration. Black-dominated basketball is often shadowed by the prospect of racism, inverted or otherwise; football coaches still tend to give the most cerebral positions to whites, the most athletic to blacks. But baseball ideally presents a rainbow coalition of Hispanics, blacks and All-American boys, integrated as slaphappily as a prime-time platoon. Willie Mays has become as much a part of the pantheon as Mickey Mantle, while the Minnesota Twins boast a pitcher who last went to bat for Anastasio Somoza's National Guard. A single small town in the Dominican Republic, San Pedro de Macorís, is the birthplace of fourteen current major-league players.

7    In Japan, however, the incorporation of foreign players was an alto-

gether trickier proposition. For one thing, Japanese baseball turned all the values of the American game on their head, imposing on every alien an entirely new set of values. Thus the recently arrived American had to learn to be as obedient and well disciplined as a child. He had to agree not to show off his talent, not to seek out flashy statistics, not, in short, to become a star. He had to recall that unity came from unanimity, that his identity lay only with the team. When one player made an error, all his colleagues hit one another so as to share the responsibility. And strategic decisions were reached, not by the pitcher and catcher alone, but by huge consensus (in the first two innings of a 1–0 game, I saw seven different board meetings on the mound, many of them attended by a full quorum of nine). In Japan, players were nothing more than verses in a single poem.

In a system in which everyone was everyone else's peer, moreover,    8 peer pressures were unavoidably intense. Thus *gaijin* had to submit to fifteen-hour days and backbreaking workouts. Sometimes, they had to live with their fellows in a collective dorm and observe an unyielding 10 p.m. curfew. In the off-season, they had to accompany the team as it toured remote areas to play exhibition games for those who would not otherwise be able to see professionals; almost immediately thereafter, they had to report back to training camp in time for the next season. "In my country," writes Oh, "it is impossible to play just for oneself. You play for the team, the country, for others."

The transplant had also to pledge lifelong loyalty to his squad. In    9 Japan, a baseball team does not represent a city, but a company; team spirit is thus indistinguishable from corporate loyalty. Players in Japan, moreover, are good company men; they do not, as a rule, offer their talents to the highest bidder, or negotiate with owners; their reward is simply the support of the corporate clan (while a World Series winner in 1984 received $50,000, a Japan Series winner made only $2,500). Comfort, in fact, is almost regarded as a handicap. ("He has big salary, he has good family," a Japanese colleague of mine once complained about a star. "He has no fighting spirit.") And as with any other Japanese company, the team becomes for its employee family, home and religion (if marriages in Japan often seem like corporate mergers, jobs often resemble surrogate spouses). "I guess [my colleagues] have girlfriends," said Dennis Barfield, the first American to live in a team dorm, "but I don't see them."

Many onetime American stars were little disposed, however, to check   10 in their individualism at customs. They were accustomed to arguing and bartering and basking in the limelight. They talked back to managers and haggled with owners. They led their own lives and battled with their teammates. They even—and this was heresy in the Japanese game— showed emotion. In Japan, a player smiles when he strikes out and does not try to break up double plays. After every one of his home runs, Oh had circled the bases without a trace of emotion, lest, in exulting, he humiliate his opposition. What, then, could the fans of the Yomiuri Giants be expected to make of such imported stars as Clyde Wright, a fallen California Angel? On being taken out of a 1–1 game one day, as Robert Whiting tells it, Wright did not calmly hand the ball to the Giant manager, the revered Nagashima. Instead, he flung it into the stands, stalked into the dugout, tore up his uniform, threw it into the team bath, kicked over a trash can and threatened to leave Japan — all before 25-million stunned citizens on national television! In panic, the Giant front office instantly laid down a formal series of 10 Commandments which every *gaijin* was expected to obey. The list made specific the need for obedience, discretion, tidiness and teamwork. ("Do not severely tease your teammates." "Do not return home during the season." "Take good care of your uniform." "Do not scream or yell in the dugout or destroy objects in the clubhouse.") The only thing the elaborate battery of rules did not address, however, was the most basic problem of all —the reluctance of American players to adhere to rules in the first place.

11      Sometimes, Japanese teams tried to solve the problem by simply jettisoning American players who would not play by Japanese rules, while keeping those who would (the Chunichi Dragons recently got rid of the American who was their leading home-run hitter, while hanging on to a less troublesome *gaijin* who was hitting .190). Yet even that did not get around the most difficult problem of all: that many American imports, however accommodating and acclimatized, were simply too good for the league. Cromartie, for example, had won over many Japanese by graciously giving his newborn child the middle name of "Oh"; yet still the fact remained that every time he came up to the plate, it looked as if he could hit the ball into the next prefecture, almost at will. The first three times I saw him hit, he smashed three solid singles without even appearing to exert himself; over the previous six games, he had hit five home runs. Another American, Boomer Wells, had been virtually pushed out of the Minnesota Twins organization and forced against his will to move to Japan. A failure at home, he had won the Triple Crown in his second season in Japan.

12      In 1985, in embarrassing fact, the list of statistical league leaders was a virtual roll call of American names. Randy Bass, who had distinguished himself with all of seven home runs in his first five years in the United States, made mincemeat of the pitchers in Japan's Central League, hitting a remarkable 54 home runs in a 130-game season, and coasting to the Triple Crown (a feat he repeated the next season too). In the Japan Series, Bass helped the Hanshin Tigers to victory by belting homers in each of the first three games; inevitably, he was voted the Series' Most Valuable Player. The winning pitcher in two of the three Tiger victories was Rich Gale, in his first season away from the Kansas City Royals. And the star of the Tigers' opponents, the Seibu Lions, was a former Chicago Cub by the name of Steve Ontiveros. By 1987, the crisis was becoming

even more acute, as Bob Horner, a superstar still in his prime, came over and clouted four home runs in his first two games.

That the league's few *gaijin* so effortlessly dominated the game was a source of abiding unease for the Japanese. The imported stars could, to be sure, be shown off as adornments of the Japanese game; but they were also unpleasant reminders of the apparent superiority of the American game. Thus the Japanese found themselves painfully divided. On the one hand, they did not like *gaijin;* on the other, they did not like losers (incredibly, almost one fan in every two across the country supports the Yomiuri Giants, the powerhouse that once won nine pennants in a row). 13

In the end, then, the Japanese had tried to unriddle the knot with still more regulations, many of them unwritten. The Giants had long made a point of fielding no foreigners at all. For years, no foreigner appeared on the cover of *Baseball* magazine. And to this day, only two *gaijin* are allowed on every team (even in the All-Star Game, where, by rights, five or six probably deserve to qualify). Sometimes, however, even rules cannot bend Nature, and the Japanese were driven to acts of quiet desperation. At the end of the '85 season, Bass came into Tokyo needing only one more home run to tie the all-time single-season record, set by the legendary Oh in his miracle season of 1964. The American's opponents were the Giants, managed by Oh. The first time Bass came up to the plate, he was intentionally walked. The second time, he was walked again. And the third time too. And yet again the fourth. And four times the next game too. No matter that the play was foul; by taking the bat out of Bass's hands, the Giants successfully ensured that the record remained safely in Oh's thoroughly Japanese hands (that Oh was in fact half-Chinese was a fact usually overlooked). "It's a funny situation when a foreigner is the ace pitcher of the team or the home-run leader," Whiting quotes the League Commissioner as declaring. "Foreigners, at best, should be by-players to bolster Japanese teams." 14

Foreign players, then, were simultaneously given the red carpet and the cold shoulder. The Japanese flocked to see Bass hit, and he was once rewarded for his skills with a year's supply of rice; yet nobody wanted him to beat Oh's record. Within a few days of his arrival, Horner had become a kind of folk hero, and as three TV stations organized "Horner Corner" updates, while a soft drink company asked him to endorse a vegetable drink called "Toughman," many Japanese spoke fretfully of a dangerous "Horner Syndrome." Yet as I looked down on Cromartie doffing his cap in center field, as the Korakuen crowd cheered his every move ("Cro mar tei! Cro mar tei!"), and raising his glove to acknowledge their applause after his catching of a routine fly ball, he struck me as a slightly lonely and bewildered figure. 15

Off the field, many *gaijin* found themselves in even more of a gilded cage. Horner, for example, was paid $1.3 million for one year, more than 20 Japanese players might hope to earn, in addition to a $500,000 bonus just for signing; all his living expenses were paid for him, and he and his 16 family were set up in a three-bedroom "mansion" apartment. Many others were given personal interpreters, and chauffeurs to drive them to each game. But there they had to practice—often for six hours each day—with teammates who could not speak their language and did not share their interests. And though they might be feted—waiters at restaurants would often give them free meals, for example—they were also fated never to be accepted as part of Japan. "You read a lot of books," said Bass in describing his life in Japan. "You can't talk to anyone. You've got nothing to do but sit here and think." In coming to Japan, the typical American had traded in a cozy mediocrity for the most alienating kind of success.

17    The contradictions that haunted Japan's uneasy importing of baseball were very similar, I thought, to those that shadowed all the goods and techniques that it had brought over from the West. For even as the Japanese omnivorously cannibalized the world outside, they never appeared to defer to it, or to worry that Japanese integrity might be compromised by the feverish importation. Their willy-nilly consumption of foreign goods seemed less, in fact, an act of homage than a way of making their own land a composite of all that was best in the world. Again, the logic was flawless: if Japan had everything good from the West, together with all its own homegrown virtues, how could anyone surpass it?

18    And again, I thought, Tokyo Disneyland was eloquent. For though it was based, down to the last detail, upon its American counterpart, its effect was to serve as a shrine to Japan's self-validating beliefs, a monument to the motherland. Thus it fed off borrowed images from the Wild West, but domesticated them with its own urban cowboys. It took what is known in American Disneylands as Main Street, and turned it into the World Bazaar, where all the products and all the possibilities of all the continents in the world are brought together in one synthetic complex that was wholly Japanese. In the Meet the World pavilion—a ride not to be found in American Disneylands—a sagacious crane guides a little boy and his kid sister around what is not only a history of Japan but also a defense of the Japanese way. The bird points out a group of cavemen seated around a campfire. "They have learned," pronounces the Feathered One, "the importance of banding together to survive." Then it goes on to introduce the children to a samurai. "At least," boasts the warrior, "we never became a colony." And in the Magic Journeys ride—again peculiar to Tokyo Disneyland—a whirlwind trip across all five continents culminates, dramatically, in a return to "our beloved Japan, where our heart always remains."

19    Some of that same spirit could be found among Japanese in the United States. When Chinese or Indian or Korean or Vietnamese immigrants move to the Promised Land, they generally lose no time at all in assimilating themselves; they set up shops and set about working, often very hard, in the confident hope that if they work hard enough, they can

create a new life for themselves in the land of opportunity, fashion a fresh American destiny. Many Japanese in America, however, were much less conspicuous, and much less American. One third of the Japanese in New York, according to a poll, never read an American periodical; around a half admitted (or boasted?) that they had no American friends at all.

The Japanese abroad, indeed, whether tourist or expat, often reminded one less of sightseers than of undercover spies, assiduously observing, and even mastering, the ways of an alien land, in order to bring home new assets to the motherland. Instead of mingling with the locals, the Japanese famously traveled in groups (confirming many a Western stereotype, in part perhaps because a stereotype is what they aspire to) and sequestered themselves in specifically Japanese base camps: in Manhattan, they generally forswore the Rainbow Room or the roadside hot-dog stand in favor of transplanted Japanese piano bars, and on their sex tours, salarymen did not hit the streets along with German or Australian or American males, but stayed in special Japanese hotels appointed with Japanese waiters and Japanese-seeming girls. Even their furious clicking away with cameras could sometimes seem a way of capturing a foreign place only in order to take it back home. The Japanese, as John David Morley notes, are unrivaled in their collection of *omiyage*, or souvenirs. Yet as a Japanese friend explains to Morley, "We take something back home less as a reminder of the place where it was bought then as proof we'd been thinking of home at the place we bought it." [20]

In its relations to the world at large, then, Japan reminded me, in the end, of a tribal conqueror who dons the armor, or even eats the heart, of a defeated opponent, so that his enemy's strength will become his own. Oh's spiritual breakthrough had come, I recalled, when his teacher took him to another *sensei* for an explanation of the central Kabuki principle of *ma*, "the space and/or time in between." "Make the opponent yours," declared the sage. "Absorb and incorporate his thinking as your own. Become one with him so you know him perfectly and can be one step ahead of his every movement." The central notion of *ki*, or "spirit power," like the guiding principle of judo, was similarly angled: "Make use of an opponent's strength and yours will be doubled." [21]

In recent years of course, this strategy had met with astonishing success; Japan had made good, to a remarkable degree, on its determination to beat the West at its own game, be it baseball or technology or trade. While mastering nearly every Western technique, the Japanese had overtaken nearly every Western nation. On the day that I left New York for Tokyo, the cover story of *The New York Times Magazine* was a long article by Theodore H. White describing the Japanese surrender in 1945, and discussing the country's almost militaristic drive for success in the intervening forty years. Japan, White implied, had exacted revenge for its defeat in the war by trouncing the West in the trade war. Though [22]

America had invented the radio and the black-and-white TV, he noted, it now imported both products from Japan, together with nearly all its VCRs, calculators, watches and even pianos. "Perhaps we did not win the war," he wrote, with some rancor. "Perhaps the Japanese, unknown even to them, were the winners."

23    A former baseball reporter from Minneapolis made the same point to me, more casually, after attending a game in Koshien. "Jesus!" he marveled. "They've out-Americaned America."

24    Yet still the Japanese seemed as unready to accept victory as defeat, as anxious as ever, and as serene. This came home to me most hauntingly when I went to Hiroshima on the fortieth anniversary of the day the American bomb had dropped from the heavens. I arrived at the Peace Park expecting to find the historic occasion marked by huge crowds, lobby groups, placards and policemen. There was none of that. The moment was observed with quintessential Japanese delicacy: it was a day of resounding quietness.

25    In the great open space of the park, little girls in bonnets were bending down to feed pigeons. Old men in T-shirts that said "Peace" staggered, foot by twisted foot, toward the shrine. In the shade, a schoolgirl sat under her mother's parasol, sketching the outline of the famous dome whose skeleton was all that remained after the bombing. Off to one side, in a quiet grove, an old lady who had survived the attack stood before a circle of hushed listeners, describing all that she had experienced. And everywhere, heaped on the Children's Peace Monument, gathered in boxes, fluttering across the grass, were hundreds upon hundreds of rainbowed banners plaited together in the shape of a many-colored crane. Anyone who tied 1,000 of these streamers together, the Japanese believed, was assured of a long life. The paper that now blanketed the park recalled a little girl who had survived the bombing and managed to tie together 960 colored banners, and then had died.

26    As the day wore on, all the soft moments began to gather weight, and their pathos started to build. Six old women held up sticks of incense before a Buddhist cenotaph, to be joined by a pudgy teenage monk in a steady, mournful keening. And in a golden glade at twilight, in a circle of trees spangled by the sun, thirty anti-nuclear protesters put their arms around each other's shoulders and sang, slowly and with feeling, "We Shall Overcome."

27    That night, hundreds upon hundreds of candlelit paper lanterns — golden and red and green and white — were sent down the Honkawa River, in memory of the departed. Along the riverbank, the faces of children, lit up by the flickering candles, looked hollow and unearthly. Nothing was said as the lanterns continued their silent, leisurely flow. For more than an hour they drifted downriver, with the gentleness of time or reminiscence. Then, in silence, they sailed under a bridge and away into the dark.

Like much else I had seen in Japan, the occasion was graced, almost    28 transfigured, by a beauty that left the heart quite still.

Yet the surfaces that surrounded me were as busy and incongruous as ever. Inside the Peace Museum, rows of stark black-and-white photos chronicled, unblinkingly, the inexpressible horror of the bomb: long, terrible processions of the lame and dying through gutted streets, whole neighborhoods wiped from the earth, ghastly disfigurements tearing skins apart, bodies twisted in the last convulsions of protracted deaths. The Japanese who inspected these harrowing documents wore T-shirts that said "No. 1 American Beer," "Carolina Western Express" and "Cherry ice-cube steak." Others were emblazoned with "Billy Club" and "Carrot Club" and "Baseball Club." One advertised "U.S.A. Soul: Nostalgic Train." 29

By then, I had grown familiar with the willful brightness of Japanese surfaces, the mass-produced optimism of a culture awash in sugary tunes that sold "Sunny California" cars and "Sunshine Heart" coolers, consumed "Sweet Kiss" candies and tuned TV sets to *The Nice Morning Show*. By then too, I knew that the Japanese had followed, to perfection, Arnold's famous maxim that "the pursuit of perfection is the pursuit of sweetness and light." But still I could not reconcile the memory of 200,000 lives destroyed in an instant with T-shirts that said "Fine Day" and "Good Time." The Japanese were not just putting the best face on things, they were putting an ideal face on them, as if to deny themselves, even in the face of their deepest sorrow, a human response, which could only be a flawed response. "Have a nice day," they seemed to sing in unison as they trotted toward Apocalypse. 30

Modern Japan had in a sense been created by the most advanced of all scientific achievements, the Bomb, that monster marvel that revealed, in a terrible flash, how far progress can push us backwards and how much technology may outstrip vision. In that single nightmare moment, the full breadth of human possibility had been suddenly lit up, and it was a prospect that brought as much horror as awe. Begotten in that double-edged instant, modern Japan had now become almost a model of that uplifting and unsettling ambiguity. It had revealed, exhilaratingly, how much humanity can achieve—but it had done so, perhaps, at the expense of humanity. It had shown how close perfection could be, but also how terribly costly. It had extended sophistication to the limit, but also to the breaking point. And whenever I looked at Japan, I could not help but think of the haiku of the Zen poet Issa: "Closer, closer to paradise. How cold!" And I could not help but wonder whether the sticking-out nails that were being so efficiently hammered down were, in fact, being driven into perfect, look-alike coffins. 31

Yet who but a churl would argue with success? 32

In 1985, for the first time ever, not a single American team qualified for the final of baseball's Little League World Series, and, for the fifteenth time in eighteen years, the competition was won by a team from Asia. 33

And at the Los Angeles Olympics in 1984, where the United States, 34 as host, chose to introduce baseball to the world as an exhibition sport, the home team fielded what was said to be the strongest amateur team in history. "The gold is ours," said one American pitcher, speaking for the entire country. "They'll need an army to take it away from us." In the final, however, before 55,235 fans, one of the largest crowds ever to witness a game at Dodger Stadium, the Japanese decisively trounced the Americans at the American national sport, by a score of 6–3.

## Evaluating the Text

1. How does the Japanese incorporation of foreign players into their baseball teams reveal their underlying attitude toward consumption of foreign goods? Discuss the process by which the Japanese redefine what they consider to be the best aspects of Western life and reconstruct them in a way that makes them uniquely Japanese. How does this process differ from simple imitation?
2. What are some of the important differences between American baseball and Japanese baseball in terms of individualism allowed to players, the way decisions are reached, salaries paid to the players, emotions exhibited by the players when they hit well or poorly, fan allegiance to a winning team, and the attitude toward breaking records (e.g., most home runs in a season)? How do the differences in these values affect American players who go over there to play on Japanese baseball teams?
3. What are the implications of the Japanese's choice of the uniquely American sport of baseball as a game to make their own national sport? In your opinion, does it reveal a desire to beat the United States at its own game? Explain your answer.
4. What about the public behavior of the Japanese people strikes Iyer as incongruous when he visited Hiroshima to attend ceremonies on the fortieth anniversary of the bombing of the city?
5. How would you characterize Iyer's attitude toward the Japanese? Do his generalizations about Japanese culture seem to be based on representative experiences of important aspects of Japanese life?

## Exploring Different Perspectives

1. How is the idea of selflessness, of subordination of the individual to the group, an important theme in both Japanese and Kiowa societies (see Gretel Ehrlich's description of the sun dance in "To Live in Two Worlds")?
2. At first glance, Japanese and Mexican cultures seem to be diametrically opposite from each other, yet Iyer's and Octavio Paz's ("Day of the Dead") descriptions disclose many similarities in attitudes, values, and social behavior, such as the masking of private emotion under ordinary circumstances. How do these two cultures compare in terms of their respective attitudes toward the accumulation of wealth, behavior at public ceremonies, and display of emotion in public?

# *Extending Viewpoints through Writing*

1. What other Western cultural phenomena (clothes, dress, music, food) have the Japanese adapted?

2. Discuss the differences between Japanese and American attitudes toward star baseball players. How does the Japanese attitude toward individual achievement differ from American attitudes? How are American baseball stars treated differently in terms of salary and kinds of behavior tolerated on and off the field? What do these differences reveal about the two cultures?

3. What insights did you gain about the Japanese culture from this article? Discuss how these factors are related to the great economic success Japan has experienced since 1945. To what extent is this success, like the Japanese assimilation of baseball, an expression of the desire to surpass the West at its own game of capitalism?

# Napoleon A. Chagnon

# *Doing Fieldwork*
# *Among the Yąnomamö*

---

*Napoleon A. Chagnon is a renowned anthropologist whose research into the social aspects of tribal warfare among the Indians of South America are best represented by* Yąnomamö: The Fierce People *(1968) and* Studying the Yąnomamö *(1974). In addition, he has written and produced more than twenty documentary films about the Yąnomamö, a tribe of roughly ten thousand, living mostly in southern Venezuela and Brazil, for which he was awarded the Grand Prize of the Brussels' Film Festival in 1970.*

*The largest South American country, Brazil occupies almost half of the continent and is the only country in South America whose culture, history, and language were shaped by Portugal, whose first permanent settlement in what is present-day São Paulo occurred in 1532. Since the Europeans landed in 1500, the population of native tribes has been reduced from an estimated six million to 200,000 today. Brazil's population is an amalgam of Indian, black, and European strains. Native Indians of several tribes (including the Yąnomamö studied by Chagnon) live along the Amazon river, which flows across northern Brazil to the Atlantic Ocean. The Yąnomamös have been subject to the steady encroachment of civilization as the Brazilian government, despite international pressure, has permitted wholesale destruction of the rain forest in the Amazon River basin. Despite being the world's largest coffee producer, in 1989 Brazil experienced the devastating combination of 600 percent inflation rates and the largest foreign debt of any developing nation. In 1990, President Collor instituted a program of price freezes, privatization of industry, higher utility rates, and devaluation of the currency (cruzado novo) that brought the rate of inflation down to 10 percent a month.*

(For further information on Brazil, see p. 518.)

The Yąnomamö[1] indians live in southern Venezuela and the adjacent    1
portions of northern Brazil. Some 125 widely scattered villages have
populations ranging from 40 to 250 inhabitants, with 75 to 80 people the
most usual number. In total numbers their population approaches 10,000
people, but this is merely a guess. Many of the villages have not yet been
contacted by outsiders, and nobody knows for sure exactly how many
uncontacted villages there are, or how many people live in them. By
comparison to African or Melanesian tribes, the Yąnomamö population
is small. Still, they are one of the largest unacculturated tribes left in all of
South America.

But they have a significance apart from tribal size and cultural purity:    2
the Yąnomamö are still actively conducting warfare. It is in nature of
man to fight, according to one of their myths, because the blood of
"Moon" spilled on this layer of the cosmos, causing men to become
fierce. I describe the Yąnomamö as "the fierce people" because that is the
most accurate single phrase that describes them. That is how they con-
ceive themselves to be, and that is how they would like others to think of
them.

I spent nineteen months with the Yąnomamö,[2] during which time I    3
acquired some proficiency in their language and, up to a point, sub-
merged myself in their culture and way of life. The thing that impressed
me most was the importance of aggression in their culture. I had the
opportunity to witness a good many incidents that expressed individual
vindictiveness on the one hand and collective bellicosity on the other.
These ranged in seriousness from the ordinary incidents of wife beating
and chest pounding to dueling and organized raiding by parties that set
out with the intention of ambushing and killing men from enemy villages. One of the villages discussed in the chapters that follow was
raided approximately twenty-five times while I conducted the fieldwork,
six times by the group I lived among.

The fact that the Yąnomamö live in a state of chronic warfare is    4
reflected in their mythology, values, settlement pattern, political behavior, and marriage practices. Accordingly, I have organized this case study

---

[1]The word Yąnomamö is nasalized through its entire length, indicated by the diacritical
mark [ą]. When this mark appears on a word, the entire word is nasalized. The terminal
vowel [-ö] represents a sound that does not occur in the English language. It corresponds to
the phone [ɨ] of linguistic orthography. In normal conversation, Yąnomamö is pronounced
like "Yah-no-mama," except that it is nasalized. Finally, the words having the [-ä] vowel
are pronounced as that vowel with the "uh" sound of "duck." Thus, the name Kąobawä
would be pronounced "cow-ba-wuh," again nasalized.

[2]I spent a total of twenty-three months in South America of which nineteen were spent
among the Yąnomamö on three separate field trips. The first trip, November 1964 through
February 1966, was to Venezuela. During this time I spent thirteen months in direct contact
with the Yąnomamö, using my periodic trips back to Caracas to visit my family and to
collate the genealogical data I had collected up to that point. On my second trip, January
through March 1967, I spent two months among Brazilian Yąnomamö and one more
month with the Venezuelan Yąnomamö. Finally, I returned to Venezuela for three more
months among the Yąnomamö, January through April 1968.

in such a way that students can appreciate the effects of warfare on Yąnomamö culture in general and on their social organization and politics in particular.

5     I collected the data under somewhat trying circumstances, some of which I will describe in order to give the student a rough idea of what is generally meant when anthropologists speak of "culture shock" and "fieldwork." It should be borne in mind, however, that each field situation is in many respects unique, so that the problems I encountered do not necessarily exhaust the range of possible problems other anthropologists have confronted in other areas. There are a few problems, however, that seem to be nearly universal among anthropological fieldworkers, particularly those having to do with eating, bathing, sleeping, lack of privacy and loneliness, or discovering that primitive man is not always as noble as you originally thought.

6     This is not to state that primitive man everywhere is unpleasant. By way of contrast, I have also done limited fieldwork among the Yąnomamö's northern neighbors, the Carib-speaking Makiritare Indians. This group was very pleasant and charming, all of them anxious to help me and honor bound to show any visitor the numerous courtesies of their system of etiquette. In short, they approached the image of primitive man that I had conjured up, and it was sheer pleasure to work with them. The recent work by Colin Turnbull (1966) brings out dramatically the contrast in personal characteristics of two African peoples he has studied.

7     Hence, what I say about some of my experiences is probably equally true of the experiences of many other fieldworkers. I write about my own experiences because there is a conspicuous lack of fieldwork descriptions available to potential fieldworkers. I think I could have profited by reading about the private misfortunes of my own teachers; at least I might have been able to avoid some of the more stupid errors I made. In this regard there are a number of recent contributions by fieldworkers describing some of the discomforts and misfortunes they themselves sustained.[3] Students planning to conduct fieldwork are urged to consult them.

8     My first day in the field illustrated to me what my teachers meant when they spoke of "culture shock." I had traveled in a small, aluminum rowboat propelled by a large outboard motor for two and a half days. This took me from the Territorial capital, a small town on the Orinoco River, deep into Yąnomamö country. On the morning of the third day we reached a small mission settlement, the field "headquarters" of a group of Americans who were working in two Yąnomamö villages. The mis-

[3]Maybury-Lewis 1967, "Introduction," and 1965b; Turnbull, 1966; L. Bohannan, 1964. Perhaps the most intimate account of the tribulations of a fieldworker is found in the posthumous diary of Bronislaw Malinowski (1967). Since the diary was not written for publication, it contains many intimate, very personal details about the writers' anxieties and hardships.

sionaries had come out of these villages to hold their annual conference on the progress of their mission work, and were conducting their meetings when I arrived. We picked up a passenger at the mission station, James P. Barker, the first non-Yąnomamö to make a sustained, permanent contact with the tribe (in 1950). He had just returned from a year's furlough in the United States, where I had earlier visited him before leaving for Venezuela. He agreed to accompany me to the village I had selected for my base of operations to introduce me to the Indians. This village was also his own home base, but he had not been there for over a year and did not plan to join me for another three months. Mr. Barker had been living with this particular group about five years.

We arrived at the village, Bisaasi-teri, about 2:00 PM and docked the 9 boat along the muddy bank at the terminus of the path used by the Indians to fetch their drinking water. It was hot and muggy, and my clothing was soaked with perspiration. It clung uncomfortably to my body, as it did thereafter for the remainder of the work. The small, biting gnats were out in astronomical numbers, for it was the beginning of the dry season. My face and hands were swollen from the venom of their numerous stings. In just a few moments I was to meet my first Yąnomamö, my first primitive man. What would it be like? I had visions of entering the village and seeing 125 social facts running about calling each other kinship terms and sharing food, each waiting and anxious to have me collect his genealogy. I would wear them out in turn. Would they like me? This was important to me; I wanted them to be so fond of me that they would adopt me into their kinship system and way of life, because I had heard that successful anthropologists always get adopted by their people. I had learned during my seven years of anthropological training at the University of Michigan that kinship was equivalent to society in primitive tribes and that it was a moral way of life, "moral" being something "good" and "desirable." I was determined to work my way into their moral system of kinship and become a member of their society.

My heart began to pound as we approached the village and heard the 10 buzz of activity within the circular compound. Mr. Barker commented that he was anxious to see if any changes had taken place while he was away and wondered how many of them had died during his absence. I felt into my back pocket to make sure that my notebook was still there and felt personally more secure when I touched it. Otherwise, I would not have known what to do with my hands.

The entrance to the village was covered over with brush and dry 11 palm leaves. We pushed them aside to expose the low opening to the village. The excitement of meeting my first Indians was almost unbearable as I duck-waddled through the low passage into the village clearing.

I looked up and gasped when I saw a dozen burly, naked, filthy, 12 hideous men staring at us down the shafts of their drawn arrows! Immense wads of green tobacco were stuck between their lower teeth and lips making them look even more hideous, and strands of dark-green slime dripped or hung from their noses. We arrived at the village while the men were blowing a hallucinogenic drug up their noses. One of the side effects of the drug is a runny nose. The mucus is always saturated with the green powder and the Indians usually let it run freely from their nostrils. My next discovery was that there were a dozen or so vicious, underfed dogs snapping at my legs, circling me as if I were going to be their next meal. I just stood there holding my notebook, helpless and pathetic. Then the stench of the decaying vegetation and filth struck me and I almost got sick. I was horrified. What sort of a welcome was this for the person who came here to live with you and learn your way of life, to become friends with you? They put their weapons down when they recognized Barker and returned to their chanting, keeping a nervous eye on the village entrances.

13      We had arrived just after a serious fight. Seven women had been abducted the day before by a neighboring group, and the local men and their guests had just that morning recovered five of them in a brutal club fight that nearly ended in a shooting war. The abductors, angry because they lost five of the seven captives, vowed to raid the Bisaasi-teri. When we arrived and entered the village unexpectedly, the Indians feared that we were the raiders. On several occasions during the next two hours the men in the village jumped to their feet, armed themselves, and waited nervously for the noise outside the village to be identified. My enthusiasm for collecting ethnographic curiosities diminished in proportion to the number of times such an alarm was raised. In fact, I was relieved when Mr. Barker suggested that we sleep across the river for the evening. It would be safer over there.

14      As we walked down the path to the boat, I pondered the wisdom of having decided to spend a year and a half with this tribe before I had even seen what they were like. I am not ashamed to admit, either, that had there been a diplomatic way out, I would have ended my fieldwork then and there. I did not look forward to the next day when I would be left alone with the Indians; I did not speak a word of their language, and they were decidedly different from what I had imagined them to be. The whole situation was depressing, and I wondered why I ever decided to switch from civil engineering to anthropology in the first place. I had not eaten all day, I was soaking wet from perspiration, the gnats were biting me, and I was covered with red pigment, the result of a dozen or so complete examinations I had been given by as many burly Indians. These examinations capped an otherwise grim day. The Indians would blow their noses into their hands, flick as much of the mucus off that would separate in a snap of the wrist, wipe the residue into their hair, and then carefully examine my face, arms, legs, hair, and the contents of my pockets. I asked Mr. Barker how to say "Your hands are dirty"; my comments were met by the Indians in the following way: They would "clean" their hands by spitting a quantity of slimy tobacco juice into them, rub them together, and then proceed with the examination.

Mr. Barker and I crossed the river and slung our hammocks. When he      15
pulled his hammock out of a rubber bag, a heavy, disagreeable odor of
mildewed cotton came with it. "Even the missionaries are filthy," I
thought to myself. Within two weeks, everything I owned smelled the
same way, and I lived with that odor for the remainder of the fieldwork.
My own habits of personal cleanliness reached such levels that I didn't
even mind being examined by the Indians, as I was not much cleaner
than they were after I had adjusted to the circumstances.

So much for my discovery that primitive man is not the picture of      16
nobility and sanitation I had conceived him to be. I soon discovered that
it was an enormously time-consuming task to maintain my own body in
the manner to which it had grown accustomed in the relatively antiseptic
environment of the northern United States. Either I could be relatively
well fed and relatively comfortable in a fresh change of clothes and do
very little fieldwork, or, I could do considerably more fieldwork and be
less well fed and less comfortable.

It is appalling how complicated it can be to make oatmeal in the      17
jungle. First, I had to make two trips to the river to haul the water. Next, I
had to prime my kerosene stove with alcohol and get it burning, a tricky
procedure when you are trying to mix powdered milk and fill a coffee
pot at the same time: the alcohol prime always burned out before I could
turn the kerosene on, and I would have to start all over. Or, I would turn
the kerosene on, hoping that the element was still hot enough to vapor-
ize the fuel, and start a small fire in my palm-thatched hut as the liquid
kerosene squirted all over the table and walls and ignited. It was safer to
start over with the alcohol. Then I had to boil the oatmeal and pick the
bugs out of it. All my supplies, of course, were carefully stored in
Indian-proof, rat-proof, moisture-proof, and insect-proof containers, not
one of which ever served its purpose adequately. Just taking things out of
the multiplicity of containers and repacking them afterward was a minor
project in itself. By the time I had hauled the water to cook with,
unpacked my food, prepared the oatmeal, milk, and coffee, heated water
for dishes, washed and dried the dishes, repacked the food in the containers, stored the containers in locked trunks and cleaned up my mess,
the ceremony of preparing breakfast had brought me almost up to lunch
time!

Eating three meals a day was out of the question. I solved the      18
problem by eating a single meal that could be prepared in a single
container, or, at most, in two containers, washed my dishes only when
there were no clean ones left, using cold river water, and wore each
change of clothing at least a week to cut down on my laundry problem, a
courageous undertaking in the tropics. I was also less concerned about
sharing my provisions with the rats, insects, Indians, and the elements,
thereby eliminating the need for my complicated storage process. I was
able to last most of the day on café con leche, heavily sugared espresso
coffee diluted about five to one with hot milk. I would prepare this in the
evening and store it in a thermos. Frequently, my single meal was no

more complicated than a can of sardines and a package of crackers. But at least two or three times a week I would do something sophisticated, like make oatmeal or boil rice and add a can of tuna fish or tomato paste to it. I even saved time by devising a water system that obviated the trips to the river. I had a few sheets of zinc roofing brought in and made a rain-water trap; I caught the water on the zinc surface, funneled it into an empty gasoline drum, and then ran a plastic hose from the drum to my hut. When the drum was exhausted in the dry season, I hired the Indians to fill it with water from the river.

19       I ate much less when I traveled with the Indians to visit other villages. Most of the time my travel diet consisted of roasted or boiled green plantains . . . that I obtained from the Indians, but I always carried a few cans of sardines with me in case I got lost or stayed away longer than I had planned. I found peanut butter and crackers a very nourishing food, and a simple one to prepare on trips. It was nutritious and portable, and only one tool was required to prepare the meal, a hunting knife that could be cleaned by wiping the blade on a leaf. More importantly, it was one of the few foods the Indians would let me eat in relative peace. It looked too much like animal feces to them to excite their appetites.

20       I once referred to the peanut butter as the dung of cattle. They found this quite repugnant. They did not know what "cattle" were, but were generally aware that I ate several canned products of such an animal. I perpetrated this myth, if no for no other reason than to have some peace of mind while I ate. Fieldworkers develop strange defense mechanisms, and this was one of my own forms of adaptation. On another occasion I was eating a can of frankfurters and growing very weary of the demands of one of my guests for a share in my meal. When he asked me what I was eating, I replied: "Beef." He then asked, "What part of the animal are you eating?" to which I replied, "Guess!" He stopped asking for a share.

21       Meals were a problem in another way. Food sharing is important to the Yą̧nomamö in the context of displaying friendship. "I am hungry," is almost a form of greeting with them. I could not possibly have brought enough food with me to feed the entire village, yet they seemed not to understand this. All they could see was that I did not share my food with them at each and every meal. Nor could I enter into their system of reciprocities with respect to food; every time one of them gave me something "freely," he would dog me for months to pay him back, not with food, but with steel tools. Thus, if I accepted a plantain from someone in a different village while I was on a visit, he would most likely visit me in the future and demand a machete as payment for the time that the "fed" me. I usually reacted to these kinds of demands by giving a banana, the customary reciprocity in their culture—food for food— but this would be a disappointment for the individual who had visions of that single plantain growing into a machete over time.

22       Despite the fact that most of them knew I would not share my food

with them at their request, some of them always showed up at my hut during mealtime. I gradually became accustomed to this and learned to ignore their persistent demands while I ate. Some of them would get angry because I failed to give in, but most of them accepted it as just a peculiarity of the subhuman foreigner. When I did give in, my hut quickly filled with Indians, each demanding a sample of the food that I had given one of them. If I did not give all a share, I was that much more despicable in their eyes.

A few of them went out of their way to make my meals unpleasant,      23
to spite me for not sharing; for example, one man arrived and watched me eat a cracker with honey on it. He immediately recognized the honey, a particularly esteemed Yąnomamö food. He knew that I would not share my tiny bottle and that it would be futile to ask. Instead, he glared at me and queried icily, "Shaki![4] What kind of animal semen are you eating on that cracker?" His question had the desired effect, and my meal ended.

Finally, there was the problem of being lonely and separated from      24
your own kind, especially your family. I tried to overcome this by seeking personal friendships among the Indians. This only complicated the matter because all my friends simply used my confidence to gain privileged access to my cache of steel tools and trade goods, and looted me. I would be bitterly disappointed that my "friend" thought no more of me than to finesse our relationship exclusively with the intention of getting at my locked up possessions, and my depression would hit new lows every time I discovered this. The loss of the possession bothered me much less than the shock that I was, as far as most of them were concerned, nothing more than a source of desirable items; no holds were barred in relieving me of these, since I was considered something subhuman, a non-Yąnomamö.

The thing that bothered me most was the incessant, passioned, and      25
aggressive demands the Indians made. It would become so unbearable that I would have to lock myself in my mud hut every once in a while just to escape from it: Privacy is one of Western culture's greatest achievements. But I did not want privacy for its own sake; rather, I simply had to get away from the begging. Day and night for the entire time I lived with the Yąnomamö I was plagued by such demands as: "Give me a knife, I am poor!"; "If you don't take me with you on your next trip to Widokaiya-teri I'll chop a hole in your canoe!"; "Don't point your camera at me or I'll hit you!"; "Share your food with me!"; "Take

---

[4]"Shaki," or, rather, "Shakiwä," is the name they gave me because they could not pronounce "Chagnon." They like to name people for some distinctive feature when possible. *Shaki* is the name of a species of noisome bee; they accumulate in large numbers around ripening bananas and make pests of themselves by eating into the fruit, showering the people below with the debris. They probably adopted this name for me because I was also a nuisance, continuously prying into their business, taking pictures of them, and, in general, being where they did not want me.

me across the river in your canoe and be quick about it!"; "Give me a cooking pot!"; "Loan me your flashlight so I can go hunting tonight!"; "Give me medicine . . . I itch all over!"; "Take us on a week-long hunting trip with your shot-gun!"; and "Give me an axe or I'll break into your hut when you are away visiting and steal one!" And so I was bombarded by such demands day after day, months on end, until I could not bear to see an Indian.

26    It was not as difficult to become calloused to the incessant begging as it was to ignore the sense of urgency, the impassioned tone of voice, or the intimidation and aggression with which the demands were made. It was likewise difficult to adjust to the fact that the Yąnomamö refused to accept "no" for an answer until or unless it seethed with passion and intimidation — which it did after six months. Giving in to a demand always established a new threshold; the next demand would be for a bigger item or favor, and the anger of the Indians even greater if the demand was not met. I soon learned that I had to become very much like the Yąnomamö to be able to get along with them on their terms: sly, aggressive, and intimidating.

27    Had I failed to adjust in this fashion I would have lost six months of supplies to them in a single day or would have spent most of my time ferrying them around in my canoe or hunting for them. As it was, I did spend a considerable amount of time doing these things and did succumb to their outrageous demands for axes and machetes, at least at first. More importantly, had I failed to demonstrate that I could not be pushed around beyond a certain point, I would have been the subjects of far more ridicule, theft, and practical jokes than was the actual case. In short, I had to acquire a certain proficiency in their kind of interpersonal politics and to learn how to imply subtly that certain potentially undesirable consequences might follow if they did such and such to me. They do this to each other in order to establish precisely the point at which they cannot goad an individual any further without precipitating retaliation. As soon as I caught on to this and realized that much of their aggression was stimulated by their desire to discover my flash point, I got along much better with them and regained some lost ground. It was sort of like a political game that everyone played, but one in which each individual sooner or later had to display some sign that his bluffs and implied threats could be backed up. I suspect that the frequency of wife beating is a component of this syndrome, since men can display their ferocity and show others that they are capable of violence. Beating a wife with a club is considered to be an acceptable way of displaying ferocity and one that does not expose the male to much danger. The important thing is that the man has displayed his potential for violence and the implication is that other men better treat him with respect and caution.

28    After six months, the level of demand was tolerable in the village I used for my headquarters. The Indians and I adjusted to each other and knew what to expect with regard to demands on their part for goods,

favors, and services. Had I confined my fieldwork to just that village alone, the field experience would have been far more enjoyable. But, as I was interested in the demographic pattern and social organization of a much larger area, I made regular trips to some dozen different villages in order to collect genealogies or to recheck those I already had. Hence, the intensity of begging and intimidation was fairly constant for the duration of the fieldwork. I had to establish my position in some sort of pecking order of ferocity at each and every village.

For the most part, my own "fierceness" took the form of shouting 29 back at the Yąnomamö as loudly and as passionately as they shouted at me, especially at first, when I did not know much of their language. As I became more proficient in their language and learned more about their political tactics, I became more sophisticated in the art of bluffing. For example, I paid one young man a machete to cut palm trees and make boards from the wood. I used these to fashion a platform in the bottom of my dugout canoe to keep my possessions dry when I traveled by river. That afternoon I was doing informant work in the village; the long-awaited mission supply boat arrived, and most of the Indians ran out of the village to beg goods from the crew. I continued to work in the village for another hour or so and went down to the river to say "hello" to the men on the supply boat. I was angry when I discovered that the Indians had chopped up all my palm boards and used them to paddle their own canoes[5] across the river. I knew that if I overlooked this incident I would have invited them to take even greater liberties with my goods in the future. I crossed the river, docked amidst their dugouts, and shouted for the Indians to come out and see me. A few of the culprits appeared, mischievous grins on their faces. I gave a spirited lecture about how hard I had worked to put those boards in my canoe, how I had paid a machete for the wood, and how angry I was that they destroyed my work in their haste to cross the river. I then pulled out my hunting knife and, while their grins disappeared, cut each of their canoes loose, set it into the current, and let it float away. I left without further ado and without looking back.

They managed to borrow another canoe and, after some effort, recov- 30 ered their dugouts. The headman of the village later told me with an approving chuckle that I had done the correct thing. Everyone in the village, except, of course, the culprits, supported and defended my action. This raised my status.

Whenever I took such action and defended my rights, I got along 31 much better with the Yąnomamö. A good deal of their behavior toward me was directed with the forethought of establishing the point at which I would react defensively. Many of them later reminisced about the early days of my work when I was "timid" and a little afraid of them, and they could bully me into giving goods away.

[5]The canoes were obtained from missionaries, who, in turn, got them from a different tribe.

32    Theft was the most persistent situation that required me to take some sort of defensive action. I simply could not keep everything I owned locked in trunks, and the Indians came into my hut and left at will. I developed a very effective means for recovering almost all the stolen items. I would simply ask a child who took the item and then take that person's hammock when he was not around, giving a spirited lecture to the others as I marched away in a faked rage with the thief's hammock. Nobody ever attempted to stop me from doing this, and almost all of them told me that my technique for recovering my possessions was admirable. By nightfall the thief would either appear with the stolen object or send it along with someone else to make an exchange. The others would heckle him for getting caught and being forced to return the item.

33    With respect to collecting the data I sought, there was a very frustrating problem. Primitive social organization is kinship organization, and to understand the Yąnomamö way of life I had to collect extensive genealogies. I could not have deliberately picked a more difficult group to work with in this regard: They have very stringent name taboos. They attempt to name people in such a way that when the person dies and they can no longer use his name, the loss of the word in the language is not inconvenient. Hence, they name people for specific and minute parts of things, such as "toenail of some rodent," thereby being able to retain the words "toenail" and "(specific) rodent," but not being able to refer directly to the toenail of that rodent. The taboo is maintained even for the living: One mark of prestige is the courtesy others show you by not using your name. The sanctions behind the taboo seem to be an unusual combination of fear and respect.

34    I tried to use kinship terms to collect genealogies at first, but the kinship terms were so ambiguous that I ultimately had to resort to names. They were quick to grasp that I was bound to learn everybody's name and reacted, without my knowing it, by inventing false names for everybody in the village. After having spent several months collecting names and learning them, this came as a disappointment to me: I could not cross-check genealogies with other informants from distant villages.

35    They enjoyed watching me learn these names. I assumed, wrongly, that I would get the truth to each question and that I would get the best information by working in public. This set the stage for converting a serious project into a farce. Each informant tried to outdo his peers by inventing a name even more ridiculous than what I had been given earlier, or by asserting that the individual about whom I inquired was married to his mother or daughter, and the like. I would have the informant whisper the name of the individual in my ear, noting that he was the father of such and such a child. Everybody would then insist that I repeat the name aloud, roaring in hysterics as I clumsily pronounced the name. I assumed that the laughter was in response to the violation of the name taboo or to my pronunciation. This was a reason-

able interpretation, since the individual whose name I said aloud invariably became angry. After I learned what some of the names meant, I began to understand what the laughter was all about. A few of the more colorful examples are: "hairy vagina," "long penis," "feces of the harpy eagle," and "dirty rectum." No wonder the victims were angry.

I was forced to do my genealogy work in private because of the horseplay and nonsense. Once I did so, my informants began to agree with each other and I managed to learn a few new names, real names. I could then test any new informant by collecting a genealogy from him that I knew to be accurate. I was able to weed out the more mischievous informants this way. Little by little I extended the genealogies and learned the real names. Still, I was unable to get the names of the dead and extend the genealogies back in time, and even my best informants continued to deceive me about their own close relatives. Most of them gave me the name of a living man as the father of some individual in order to avoid mentioning that the actual father was dead. 36

The quality of a genealogy depends in part on the number of generations it embraces, and the name taboo prevented me from getting any substantial information about deceased ancestors. Without this information, I could not detect marriage patterns through time. I had to rely on older informants for this information, but these were the most reluctant of all. As I became more proficient in the language and more skilled at detecting lies, my informants became better at lying. One of them in particular was so cunning and persuasive that I was shocked to discover that he had been inventing his information. He specialized in making a ceremony out of telling me false names. He would look around to make sure nobody was listening outside my hut, enjoin me to never mention the name again, act very nervous and spooky, and then grab me by the head to whisper the name very softly into my ear. I was always elated after an informant session with him, because I had several generations of dead ancestors for the living people. The others refused to give me this information. To show my gratitude, I paid him quadruple the rate I had given the others. When word got around that I had increased the pay, volunteers began pouring in to give me genealogies. 37

I discovered that the old man was lying quite by accident. A club fight broke out in the village one day, the result of a dispute over the possession of a woman. She had been promised to Rerebawä, a particularly aggressive young man who had married into the village. Rerebawä had already been given her older sister and was enraged when the younger girl began having an affair with another man in the village, making no attempt to conceal it from him. He challenged the young man to a club fight, but was so abusive in his challenge that the opponent's father took offense and entered the village circle with his son, wielding a long club. Rerebawä swaggered out to the duel and hurled insults at both of them, trying to goad them into striking him on the head with their clubs. This would have given him the opportunity to strike them on the head. His 38 opponents refused to hit him, and the fight ended. Rerebawä had won a moral victory because his opponents were afraid to hit him. Thereafter, he swaggered around and insulted the two men behind their backs. He was genuinely angry with them, to the point of calling the older man by the name of his dead father. I quickly seized on this as an opportunity to collect an accurate genealogy and pumped him about his adversary's ancestors. Rerebawä had been particularly nasty to me up to this point, but we became staunch allies: We were both outsiders in the local village. I then asked about other dead ancestors and got immediate replies. He was angry with the whole group and not afraid to tell me the names of the dead. When I compared his version of the genealogies to that of the old man, it was obvious that one of them was lying. I challenged his information, and he explained that everybody knew that the old man was deceiving me and bragging about it in the village. The names the old man had given me were the dead ancestors of the members of a village so far away that he thought I would never have occasion to inquire about them. As it turned out, Rerebawä knew most of the people in that village and recognized the names.

39    I then went over the complete genealogical records with Rerebawä, genealogies I had presumed to be in final form. I had to revise them all because of the numerous lies and falsifications they contained. Thus, after five months of almost constant work on the genealogies of just one group, I had to begin almost from scratch!

40    Discouraging as it was to start over, it was still the first real turning point in my fieldwork. Thereafter, I began taking advantage of local arguments and animosities in selecting my informants, and used more extensively individuals who had married into the group. I began traveling to other villages to check the genealogies, picking villages that were on strained terms with the people about whom I wanted information. I would then return to my base camp and check with local informants the accuracy of the new information. If the informants became angry when I mentioned the new names I acquired from the unfriendly group, I was almost certain that the information was accurate. For this kind of checking I had to use informants whose genealogies I knew rather well: they had to be distantly enough related to the dead person that they would not go into a rage when I mentioned the name, but not so remotely related that they would be uncertain of the accuracy of the information. Thus, I had to make a list of names that I dared not use in the presence of each and every informant. Despite the precautions, I occasionally hit a name that put the informant into a rage, such as that of a dead brother or sister that other informants had not reported. This always terminated the day's work with that informant, for he would be too touchy to continue any further, and I would be reluctant to take a chance on accidentally discovering another dead kinsman so soon after the first.

41    These were always unpleasant experiences, and occasionally dangerous ones, depending on the temperament of the informant. On one

occasion I was planning to visit a village that had been raided about a week earlier. A woman whose name I had on my list had been killed by the raiders. I planned to check each individual on the list one by one to estimate ages, and I wanted to remove her name so that I would not say it aloud in the village. I knew that I would be in considerable difficulty if I said this name aloud so soon after her death. I called on my original informant and asked him to tell me the name of the woman who had been killed. He refused, explaining that she was a close relative of his. I then asked him if he would become angry if I read off all the names on the list. This way he did not have to say her name and could merely nod when I mentioned the right one. He was a fairly good friend of mine, and I thought I could predict his reaction. He assured me that this would be a good way of doing it. We were alone in my hut so that nobody could overhear us. I read the names softly, continuing to the next when he gave a negative reply. When I finally spoke the name of the dead woman he flew out of his chair, raised his arm to strike me, and shouted: "You son-of-a-bitch! If you ever say that name again, I'll kill you!" He was shaking with rage, but left my hut quickly. I shudder to think what might have happened if I had said the name unknowingly in the woman's village. I had other, similar experiences in different villages, but luckily the dead person had been dead for some time and was not closely related to the individual into whose ear I whispered the name. I was merely cautioned to desist from saying any more names, lest I get people angry with me. . . .

## Evaluating the Text

1. What was Chagnon's purpose in going to study the Yąnomamö Indians of Brazil, the largest known culturally intact native tribe in the Americas?
2. What incidents reveal the major part that aggression plays in Yąnomamö culture? Does the way aggression is expressed toward Chagnon seem to differ from the way they express it toward each other?
3. What is the phenomena known as "culture shock," and what details does Chagnon give that most effectively illustrate it? Specifically, what contrasts can you discover between Chagnon's expectations and the experience of his first encounter with the Yąnomamö?
4. What is kinship, and why is it so important to the Yąnomamö?
5. What features of the Yąnomamö's examination of Chagnon made it so distasteful for him?
6. Which of all the difficulties Chagnon faced in regard to food preparation did you find the most interesting? What were some of the ingenious solutions Chagnon thought of to prevent the Yąnomamö from taking his food?
7. How do the Yąnomamö try to use reciprocal gift-giving to extract Chagnon's prized possessions?
8. To what extent did Chagnon's experiences lead him to question his taken-for-granted assumption that friendship is a universal human

concept? How did he have to readjust his thinking in order to deal with the reality of Yąnomamö culture? How did he change his behavior in order to function among the Yąnomamö? For example, how does the incident involving the floor boards of Chagnon's canoe illustrate his adaptation?

9. Discuss how the taboo involving revealing tribal names, of the living as well as the dead, presented an obstacle to Chagnon's research on the Yąnomamö's genealogy.

10. How does the case history of Rerebawä illustrate the kinds of difficulties Chagnon had to overcome in pursuing his research? How did Chagnon use Rerebawä's information to cross-check the information given to him by the old man?

11. From Chagnon's account, what do you infer about the role of women in Yąnomamö society?

12. What role does wife-beating play in Yąnomamö culture?

13. Discuss how the strange etiquette that rules ritualized aggression among the Yąnomamö is designed to demonstrate fierceness without actually leading to real violence. What correspondences can you discover in different sports? For example, hard-checking is allowed in hockey, but high-sticking is not. What would be the equivalences in football and baseball?

## Exploring Different Perspectives

1. Compare Chagnon's need to be aggressive to win the respect of the Yąnomamö with methods used by Wade Davis (in Gino Del Guercio's "The Secrets of Haiti's Living Dead") to gain access to the secrets of voodoo during his research in Haiti.

2. In what respects is the methodology used by Chagnon, an anthropologist, similar to the scientific methods used by Wade Davis, an ethnobotonist, in Haiti (described by Del Guercio)? How do both these articles alert you to the kinds of research procedures and perspectives characteristic of anthropology? How do both these differ from the approach taken by Paul Fussell as a traveler/tourist in "Taking It All Off in the Balkans"?

3. To what extent is the Yąnomamö's view that anyone outside their society is a stranger who can be lied to, tricked, and exploited, similar to and different from the attitude the Japanese have toward foreigners that Pico Iyer discusses in "Perfect Strangers"?

4. Discuss the similarities between the Haitian belief that a voodoo priest can gain power over the essential part of the self (see Del Guercio, "The Secrets of Haiti's Living Dead") and the naming taboo that governs under what circumstances a Yąnomamö can be called by his or her given name.

## Extending Viewpoints through Writing

1. Have you ever experienced what might be called "culture shock"? Describe the circumstances and discuss what about the experiences was so unsettling and challenged your expectations. What about this experience enables you to better understand Chagnon's reaction to the Yąnomamö?

2. For a research project, you might look into the explorations of Colin M. Turnbull's study of the Ituri Pygmies (1965, 1983) and/or his research on the Ik (1972). To what extent was Turnbull's interaction with the peoples he studied similar to or different from that of Chagnon?

3. To what extent does the psychology underlying reciprocal gift-giving operate in contemporary American society among your family and friends? What are some of the similarities and differences from the way it operates in Yąnomamö culture?

4. Have you ever tried to construct a family tree? Describe your experiences. To what extent did you hit on the same methods of cross-confirmation that Chagnon used?

5. Chagnon discovered that the academic training he received hardly prepared him for the experience he faced in real-life anthropological research. Have you or anyone you know had a corresponding experience? If so, describe it.

6. The subtitle for Chagnon's book on the Yąnomamö is *The Fierce People*, a phrase that sums up the overwhelmingly important role aggression plays in every aspect of Yąnomamö life. If you were to adopt the perspective of an anthropologist in regard to a group you know, what phrase would you use to express its single most distinctive quality?

# Raymonde Carroll

# *Minor Accidents*

---

*Raymonde Carroll was born in Tunisia and was educated in France and the United States. She was trained as an anthropologist and studied the culture of Micronesia while she lived for three years on a Pacific atoll. She presently teaches in the Department of Romance Languages at Oberlin College. "Minor Accidents" is a chapter from her book,* Cultural Misunderstandings: The French-American Experience *(translated by Carol Volk, 1988). This fascinating investigation of misunderstandings between the French and Americans discloses how implicit cultural presuppositions shape our perception of the world.*

1   A commercial on American television shows a mother and daughter (twelve or thirteen years old) trying to resolve the problem of a stain on a blouse. The daughter is frantic; her mother promises to do her best to help her. Thanks to a miracle detergent, the blouse is returned to its former beautiful state. In order to understand the depth of the crisis resolved by the detergent in question, one must know that the stained blouse does not belong to the girl on the screen but to her older sister, who lent it to her. The situation is serious enough for the mother to enter the picture, and for us to be relieved (and thankful for the magic detergent) when the blouse, unharmed, is put in its proper place just before the arrival of its owner, who, as it turns out, wants to wear it that very evening. The crisis has been averted; the heroines smile.

2   Things are not so rosy in the "Dear Abby" column, which millions of Americans read every day in the newspaper. The same problem often appears in many forms: "X borrowed my thingamajig, returned it damaged, and offered neither to replace it nor to repair it. What should I do?"

3   Are Americans frightened by their older siblings (the first case), or incapable of resolving the slightest problem (the second case)? The list of "adjectives" and of "explanations" can go on, according to one's tastes and culture. What interests me here is the fact that in both "cases" there was a "minor accident." In the first case, the "guilty" party knows what to do while in the second the "victim" does not know what to do, which indicates that an expectation was not met.

4   For a French person, it is likely that both cases would serve as

(For further background on France, see pp. 182 and 265.)

additional proof of the "keen sense of proprietorship characteristic of Americans." But why lend one's property if one feels that way about it? It seems, here again, that the nature of the problem lies elsewhere. Before going any further, however, it would be useful to review a few French cases of "minor accidents." Some of these cases are taken from personal experience. They seemed completely "normal" to the French woman in me but slightly "strange" to the anthropologist in me, who considered them with a voluntarily "foreign" eye.

F (a French woman), her husband, and her daughter, who are pre- 5 paring to leave a party, are standing in the foyer saying goodbye. As she leaves, F has a "minor accident": while putting on her coat, her hand brushes against a small painting, which, dislodged by the movement, falls to the ground. The lacquered wooden frame breaks, but the damage is reparable. F says to her host, from whom she was just taking leave: "Oh, sorry, I had a little accident." Then, suddenly joking: "But what an idea to put a painting in such a place! My word, you must have done it on purpose!" Not knowing what to do with the little painting which she now has in her hands, she turns it over, probably to examine the damage, and cries out joyously, "Oh, you see, it must have already been broken, since it has been glued." Upon saying this, she points to a piece of sticky paper which appears to have nothing to do with the frame itself. Everyone present clearly sees this, but they all act if they hadn't noticed, and the host (who is French) hurriedly takes the painting from her and says "Don't worry about it, it's nothing, I'll take care of it." As F attempts to joke some more about the accident, her husband drags her toward the door, saying, "Listen, if you keep this up you'll never be invited here again." Everyone laughs. Exeunt all.

Not once did F offer to have the frame repaired. Rather, it seemed as 6 if all her efforts tended toward minimizing the gravity of the accident by making a joke of it. She thus started recounting another incident: her daughter, when she was still a baby in her mother's arms, had unhooked a signed (she insists) plate from the wall behind her mother, and threw it on the floor. "Well that was a real catastrophe, I didn't know what to do with myself . . ." In other words, the "truly" serious incident, that of the valuable (signed) plate, was the fault of the baby (and at the same time not her fault, since she was a baby?). In comparison, the incident with the frame appears (or should appear?) negligible.

Does the comparison of these two incidents also imply that F is not 7 responsible either? Like the baby? The fact that she did not offer to repair the frame (which would be a recognition of her responsibility) seems to indicate that this is a plausible interpretation of this comparison. Of course, we can say that F was so embarrassed that in the second case, as in the first, she "didn't know what to do with herself" and that joking was a way to hide her embarrassment. But one can just as easily be sorry or embarrassed, and joke around to relax the atmosphere, while at the same time offering to repair the damage.

8    While at a party at the home of friends of her friends, D, twenty-two years old, Parisian, spills red wine (a full glass) on the carpet. She grabs a small paper napkin to wipe it up. The friend who had invited her quickly returns from the kitchen with enough paper towels to really soak up the large quantity of wine; someone else brings salt. D, while her friend is cleaning, says, "My God, L (the host) is not going to be happy . . . but can you imagine. . . . That's the trouble with light-colored carpeting, it's so difficult to clean!" D made an effort, although insufficient, to repair the damage. But her commentary is strangely similar to that of F. The "victim" seems to be transformed into the truly responsible party, that is, into the person who is ultimately responsible for the accident: if the painting hadn't been placed there . . . if the carpet hadn't been chosen in such a light color . . .

9    Monsieur T, while visiting his son in the United States, discovers the existence of window shades, which are placed between the window panes and the curtains in the great majority of American homes and which serve to block out the sun. These shades are spring-loaded, which allows one to lower or raise them to any degree at will and thereby to adjust the quantity of light let in. In order to do this, one must learn to accompany the shade with one's hand, or else it winds itself up suddenly with a snap. The son demonstrates this for Monsieur T, insisting particularly on the fact that he must never release the shade and "let it roll up by itself" (which the French in the United States are endlessly tempted to do, even if they have been living here for more than twenty years, as I have). The next day, the son briefly reminds him of his instructions and only succeeds in exasperating Monsieur T ("Do you think I am a fool?"). A few days later, the son hears a snap, which sounds like a shot, followed by an exclamation. He runs over and finds his father in front of the window; as soon as he sees him come in, his father says, "This is horrible, you'd think you were in the devil's den. My word! Can't have a weak heart at your place. . . . It's not surprising that Americans all go to psychiatrists. . . . That gave me a terrible fright, and yet I did exactly as you said, I don't understand what happened."

10    L, twenty-eight years old, from the Bordeaux region, shares an apartment with V, approximately the same age, from Normandy. L burns one of her good saucepans while V is out. Upon V's return, L confesses, apologizes, and, in the course of her explanation adds, "because, you know, for me, a good saucepan or a bad saucepan are the same, because I'm not at all materialistic, I don't get attached to objects." In other words, if this is considered an "accident," it is only because it is V's nature to regret the loss of a simple saucepan, a mere object.

11    M, from Midi, lends his projector to S, who returns it, jammed, with these words: "Your projector is strange, it makes a funny noise." S later

discovers a slide which is part of M's collection wedged in the slide mechanism.

S, from the Basque coast, borrows R's car, brings it back the next day, 12 and asks with a sly smile: "Are you sure your car works well? Because it stalled twice. Once, I was even stuck in the middle of the road because I was trying to turn, and I was afraid a car would hit me." R, who is S's friend, adds, upon relating to me this incident: "S is a very nice guy, but he can't drive to save his life."

B, from Paris, returns the typewriter he borrowed from me, and, 13 wearing the mischievous smile of a naughty child who knows he will be excused, tells me, "You know, your typewriter was very mean to me, it must not like me very much because it was skipping letters constantly. . . . I had to be very careful as I typed."

The preceding examples seem to indicate that French people do not offer to repair things when there has been an accident. Yet this is not the case. Among the cases I collected, offers to repair the damage were just as common as those mentioned above. Thus L, who had already burned V's saucepan, had also, at another time, accidentally broken a hand-crafted pitcher which V had brought back from France. In this case, L, who did indeed understand the sentimental value of pitchers if not the material value of saucepans, offered, or rather promised, to replace the broken object ("I'll buy you one exactly like that"). Over a year later, V tells me, the pitcher had not been replaced, or even mentioned.

This same V, G tells me, borrowed an electronic, programmable 14 calculator to do "a few simple calculations." The calculations were apparently too simple for the delicate mechanism of the instrument because it became "mysteriously" blocked. V offered to share the cost of repairing it with G, thus implying that there must have been something wrong with the machine before she borrowed it (or else she would have offered to pay all the costs). According to G, the cost of repairing it turned out to be so astronomical that he preferred to buy another inexpensive calculator, "just in case." In the meantime, according to G, V never mentioned sharing the costs and never asked for news of the wounded calculator. The last I heard, G and V are still friends.

A variation on this case consists of saying what one would have liked 15 to do, but did not do, to repair an accident. For instance, a white tablecloth which K borrowed from a friend for a holiday meal was irreparably stained. "I thought of buying a tablecloth to replace yours, but I didn't know what you'd like," says K, several years after the accident. The friend asserts that she has never been compensated and that it never put their friendship on the line.

Finally, there are certain cases in which the repair was made. Yet the 16 comments differ depending on whether one talks to the person who cased the "minor accident" and repaired the damage or to the person who was the "victim." I have on occasion heard the former say things such as "I paid a great deal to have a worthless rug cleaned," whereas the latter, whose car was dented and repaired by the friends who had borrowed it made the following comment: "Of course, they paid for the repairs, but now the car is totally ruined."

We might conclude from the preceding examples that the French break everything and repair or replace nothing. Certain French people think so, and, as a result, "do not lend anything to anyone" and "do not ask anything of anyone," because "they never give it back in the state you lent it." As we know from having learned La Fontaine's fables, "Madame Ant is slow to lend\The last thing, this, she suffers from."[1] But there are obviously many French people who do not hold this attitude, as is proven by the accident cases cited earlier. How then can we interpret the various ways in which the actors treated these accidents? As we have seen, the reactions ranged from playful jokes to reproachful jokes, and from reproachful jokes to disguised accusations. Offers of repair were not made, made but never followed up on, mentioned as something one had thought of, or else made and followed up on but to no one's satisfaction.

17      In other words, when I have a "minor accident," it is not really my fault. It is because an object was in a bad place (I might almost say "in my way"), because a carpet was too light to hide stains, because a machine was too delicate to function normally, because to have shades in a house is aberrant, and so on. In fact, I acted in all innocence and nothing would have happened if the others had correctly played their parts. It becomes clear that by joking and "taking things lightly," I place responsibility where it belongs, on the person who committed the error of poorly placing his painting, of choosing an insane color for a carpet, of buying an overly complicated calculator . . . and who, most of all, made the mistake of not sufficiently protecting his possession if he cared about it so much.

18      By pushing this logic to its extreme, I would say that when entertaining me, X runs the risk of having his good crystal broken if he chooses to use it ("accidents can happen") and that when lending me an object, he should warn me of its fragility. In fact, he should not lend, or put within my reach, an object which is fragile, and certainly not an object about which he cares a great deal. If he does this, X is obviously the one who should assume ultimate responsibility for the accident. Similarly, if I offer to repair or to pay for the damage ("tell me how much I owe you"), I have done my part, I have fulfilled my duty; it is up to X to request the necessary sum when required since I told him I would give it to him. Thus, I force the other to take responsibility for some of my acts, and in

[1]From "The Ant and the Grasshopper," in *A Hundred Fables from La Fontaine*, trans. Philip Wayne (Doubleday).

doing so I propose or reaffirm a relationship. If X refuses this relationship, he will never again invite me to his house or lend me anything more. And this does happen. But if X accepts the relationship, he reinforces it by placing more value on it than on the damaged object, as valuable as that object may be. Hence the "leave it, it's not important," which erases the accident. And as we more or less tacitly honor the same code, we each have a chance to be both victim and perpetrator of an accident, thus becoming linked to one another and affirming, sometimes against our wishes, the importance of these bonds.

Needless to say, an American would be completely baffled by such [19] conduct. It is, in fact, this type of behavior that provokes the "Dear Abby" letters mentioned at the beginning of this chapter.

An informant described to me the "American general rule" as fol- [20] lows: "If I lend X my car, the minimum I can expect is that, before returning it, he will fill it with more gas than he consumed. If I lend him my car for a fairly long period, he will make a point of returning it to me in a better state than when I lent it to him (washed, waxed, vacuumed, etc.) He will not do this in order to point out my negligence but, in a sense, to repay me for my generosity. He will take responsibility for any necessary repairs, and I will hold him to this (unless it is an old wreck, in which case I would refuse to lend it to him so as to spare him some very predictable, but difficult to attribute, expenses)." Let us then look at some American cases, such as they have been reported to me.

At an elegant dinner, J breaks a crystal glass. She asks the hostess to [21] lend her a glass of the same set, so that she can find a perfect replacement. The hostess honors her request.

P, fourteen or fifteen years old, meets a group of friends at D's house. [22] They go to play basketball at the school basketball court and return, tired from the game, to D's house, where his mother serves them lunch. P, drawn without knowing why to a carafe on the buffet, picks up the stopper, which slips from his hands, falls back on the carafe, and chips it. P, confused, apologizes to D's mother for his clumsiness, and without hesitating offers to replace the carafe. P is over forty today, yet he remembers this scene very clearly. He remembers that at the very moment when he offered to replace the carafe he knew that he did not have, but would have to find, the necessary sum, and he also remembers that D's mother left him an escape route ("I'll let you know when I find one"), but not without her having expressed concern and regret over the accident. That is to say, according to him, D's mother was willing to be generous, but without diminishing P's responsibility.

A dinner with friends. M spills a glass of wine. His wife quickly runs [23] to the kitchen, returns with the necessary products, and sponges up the wine—in short, does everything to repair the accident. M thanks his wife with a look of gratitude and apologizes for his clumsiness. Note: in this case, M's wife has repaired his clumsiness because she forms a couple with him and therefore shares responsibility for the accident, takes responsibility for it as well. This does not preclude the possibility that some couples have "sexist" habits, but it gives the gesture a deeper meaning, as is shown by the fact that the inverse is just as possible: a woman spills some wine and her husband tries to repair the damage. . . .

24    An informal evening. Guests are seated on the carpet, their drinks by their sides. An accident quickly occurs: N spills a glass of tomato juice. The same efforts to clean it, as well and as quickly as possible, are made. N asks if his hosts have a carpet cleaning foam. They respond in the negative. N offers to pay the cost of the cleaning. "Thanks, but don't worry, we'll take care of it, no problem." The difficulty seems to be resolved. Yet later in the evening, on several occasions, N makes allusion to his clumsiness ("Don't give it to me, you know how klutzy I am"; "Oh God, this stain is looking at me"; "I feel so bad, such a beautiful carpet").

25    A meeting of the members of our block association, held at the house of one of my neighbors. The sofa and chairs are fitted with slip covers, the furniture with cloths to protect the wood, and the table with an oilcloth. Coffee and cake are served in paper cups and on paper plates. Everyone is relaxed, there is no chance of an irreparable accident, everything has been foreseen.

26    Another meeting, at the far more elegant home of one of my colleagues. C, who is about to place his glass of white wine on the coffee table in front of us, stops his gesture halfway and asks our host if the wooden table (modern, elegant) has been treated, "protected." Despite our host's affirmative response, another colleague comes to the rescue and passes C a wooden coaster from a small stack which had been discreetly placed on a table nearby. The glass of cold white wine will leave no trace of its dampness.

The recital of cases could go on indefinitely. Those which I have mentioned suffice to illustrate the implicit rules governing American interpersonal exchanges in case of a "minor accident." I will summarize them as follows:

27    1. If I borrow an object from someone, I have an obligation to return it in the very same state as when it was lent to me. If it is a machine that breaks down in my hands, I must repair it, so as to erase all traces of the mishap. (I don't do this in order to hide the accident, which I must mention in any case, but in order to return the object to its previous condition.)

28    2. If the damage is irreparable, I must replace the object by an identical one, no matter how much time and searching are required. I can, however, ask the owner of the object where it was purchased. I must not replace it by an "equivalent," which would mean brushing off as unimportant all the reasons for the owner's choice, or the meaning which a certain object has come to have for its owner. Nor can I replace

the object by another similar — but more or less expensive — one (a glass for a glass, for example), because in both cases I would be suggesting that all that counts in my eyes is the price of the object.

3. If I have an accident at someone's home, the situation is even more delicate. If I have even slightly damaged a valuable object (an art object or one with sentimental value), I must be grieved by my clumsiness without finding any excuse for myself; I must immediately offer to take the object and to have it repaired (while showing that I know where to go and that I am not going to worsen the damage by leaving the object with nonprofessionals); I must insist on being allowed to do this, if only to relieve my feelings of guilt ("I feel so bad. I wouldn't be able to sleep"). If my host does not wish to signal the end of our relationship, he or she will, out of kindness, allow me to take the object with me, in order to "let me off the hook." 29

If the accident is of a common sort and not very serious, I must do everything in my power to repair the damage then and there, but I must be careful not to insult my host by offering to replace a common item or to pay the cost of cleaning a tablecloth, for instance, because in doing so I would be suggesting that I do not think he or she has the means to take care of it. In this case, I show that I take the accident seriously by mentioning it several times, by berating myself for my clumsiness, by making fun of myself — in short, by taking total responsibility for the accident. 30

All this might seem strange, if not "heavy-handed," to a French person. Why make such a fuss? Why put on such an act? Is this yet another example of American "hypocrisy" and "puritanism"?

It is nothing of the kind, of course. On the contrary, although their conduct may be completely different from that of the French people mentioned above (in fact it is exactly opposite), the Americans I have focused on sent a message very similar to that expressed by the French people. Indeed, when I (an American) borrow an object from X, I create or confirm a tie with X (I do not borrow things from just anyone). The care I take with this object will therefore be proportionate to the importance I place on my relationship to the person who lent it to me. Similarly, when I accidentally disturb a home to which I have been invited, my reaction will be interpreted as a conscious commentary on the relationship between my host and myself. If I do everything possible to clean a carpet, it is not for the sake of the endangered carpet (or because my host and I are "materialistic" because we are American) but out of respect for my host. In other words, our relationship does not presuppose that we will "weather difficulties" together (as it does in the French context); it presupposes a tacit pact between the borrower and the lender, the host and the guest, to preserve an equilibrium, without which all relationships of this kind would become impossible. For if I show little concern for something belonging to X which he has put within my reach 31 or at my disposal (thereby trusting me), X has the right to feel wounded, scorned, and to refuse further dealings with me. Meanwhile, the expectation that one will honor this pact is so strong that any avoidance or refusal on my part risks leaving X bewildered, "not knowing what to do," just like the Dear Abby correspondents mentioned earlier. This is, in a sense, because for Americans it is not in the cards that others will behave in ways other than expected (without being criminals, louts, or other types with whom X would not maintain relations).

32     If my "accident" is really major and X refuses to allow me to free myself, as far as is possible, from my debt, X transforms this bond into a shackle, and I have no reason to maintain a relationship with someone so unconcerned with my feelings.

33     In many circumstances, intercultural misunderstandings spring from the fact that surface resemblances and behavioral similarities conceal profound differences in meaning. It is interesting to see here that the inverse is also true.

## *Evaluating the Text*

1. Which of the examples cited by Carroll (the broken painting, the spilled red wine, the window shade incident, the burned saucepan, the jammed projector, the stalled car, the broken typewriter) seems to most effectively support her thesis that the French have a different attitude toward minor accidents in terms of who is responsible for repairing the damage. For example, would an American have responded as did D, when she spilled red wine on the carpet?
2. In Carroll's view, what cultural differences come into play to explain why Americans tend to respond to "minor accidents" with apologies and self-deprecating remarks, whereas the French barely stop short of "blaming the victim"?
3. How does the selection of a commercial on American TV and reference to "Dear Abby" columns suggest this is a value that predominates in American culture? To what extent do advertisers understand how Americans feel about personal property and play on these fears to sell their products? Evaluate the use of these examples. Do they seem to be typical or atypical, representative or unrepresentative? Would generalizations based on this kind of evidence about all of American culture seem well-founded?
4. Why does Carroll present many more cases illustrating French attitudes than those of Americans in beginning her analysis?
5. In the example of D, why is it significant that people other than the one responsible for spilling the glass of red wine on the carpet make real efforts to clean up the stain? Is it conceivable that D at another time (had someone else spilled red wine on a carpet) would have helped clean up the stain instead of standing by and seeming to blame the carpet's owner for the choice of light-colored carpeting? How does this incident show that one's response in the situation is guided by unstated, but very real, underlying cultural assumptions and expectations?

6. From an American point of view, why is it doubly intolerable that someone who damages another's property (whether a picture, carpet, saucepan, projector, car, or typewriter) would not only disclaim responsibility but attempt to shift the blame by implying there is something wrong with the positioning of the object or choice of the item? How is a situation like this for an American guided by different expectations? How might American responses lead the French to think Americans were overly materialistic?

7. Before you were aware of Carroll's hypothesis to explain the differences between the way the French and Americans view "minor accidents," what did you think of the behavior of the French in each of the situations? What explanation did you give yourself for their behavior?

8. If G and V were Americans, how do you think the episode of the broken calculator, considering the past episodes (burned saucepan, broken handcrafted pitcher) would have turned out? For example, would V's consistent lack of care taken with G's possessions be interpreted as a negative message regarding the state of their friendship?

9. How does Carroll's examples of situations when repairs were made and paid for imply that both parties were angrier and unhappier than when nothing was done? Why, for the French, would a friendship be endangered when repairs are made, whereas when nothing is done, the friendship stays intact? How could attempts to repair the object be interpreted as undercutting the important French cultural value that friendship is above such petty concerns?

10. Identify specific words and phrases that reveal how each culture verbalizes reactions to "minor accidents." In what way are American reactions characterized by expressions of guilt and self-deprecation, whereas French reactions disclaim responsibility, express no guilt, and even turn the situation around so that the "victim" is in the wrong by virtue of faulty placement or a history emphasizing defects in the object?

11. What does the episode of C, the white wine and discreetly placed coasters, reveal about the values most important in American households? Consider all the precautions that Americans take to avoid the broken plate, cracked saucer, or stained coffee table. How does the meeting of the block association (where everything is served on paper plates) reveal the same values?

12. Why would being denied the chance to make amends, repair, or replace an object you had damaged in an American home be interpreted by both parties to mean that the friendship was over? How would the same circumstance for the French be a reaffirmation of the friendship?

## Exploring Different Perspectives

1. Compare and contrast Carroll's findings with the discoveries Napoleon A. Chagnon ("Doing Fieldwork among the Yąnomamö") made in circumstances where his relationship to the Yąnomamö was reflected by their attitude toward his possessions (e.g., their attitude toward his food, floorboards of his canoe, machetes, etc.).

2. Drawing on the interpretive framework provided by Carroll, discuss the extent to which the social values of the Japanese (see Pico Iyer's "Perfect

Strangers") more nearly resemble those of the French or those of the Americans.

3. In what ways do the attitudes of the Kiowa Indians (see Gretel Ehrlich's "To Live in Two Worlds") toward material possessions and friendship resemble those of the French?

## *Extending Viewpoints through Writing*

1. Have you ever borrowed or lent an item (favorite record, cassette, item of clothing, etc.) that was accidentally broken or damaged? What offer of restitution was made? Are you still friends with the borrower or lender of that item? How did the episode involving this object affect your friendship?

2. Choose one of Carroll's examples and speculate how the same "minor accident" would be treated if all parties were Americans instead of French. What would have been said in the same circumstances?

3. To what extent do American attitudes reveal what might be called an investment psychology in which taking good care of objects is a way of showing others one is credit-worthy?

4. Discuss a situation (e.g., showing affection in public, interactions between parents and children, conceptions of privacy, telephone manners) where it was obvious to you that people from different cultures relied on their respective assumptions in interpreting the same action very differently.

# Gretel Ehrlich

# *To Live in Two Worlds*

---

*Gretel Ehrlich was born and raised in California, educated at Bennington College, UCLA Film School, and the New School for Social Research, and first went to Wyoming as a documentary film maker. Her work has appeared in* The New York Times, The Atlantic, *and* Harper's. *She has worked on ranches, branding cattle and herding sheep, and currently lives with her husband on a ranch in Shell, Wyoming. "To Live in Two Worlds" is her fascinating first hand account of the Kiowa Indian Sun Dance, from her book* The Solace of Open Spaces *(1986).*

*The Kiowas are North American Indians of the plains. After being forced from the Black Hills in South Dakota by the Cheyenne and the Sioux, they joined the Commanche in raiding parties as far south as Mexico. In the nineteenth century, they actively opposed white settlers until 1874, when the U.S. Army was brought in. Traditionally a nomadic tribe, the largest group of Kiowa (about four thousand) lives in Oklahoma today. The language of the Kiowa is thought to derive from that spoken by the ancient Aztecs.*

1   July. Last night from one in the morning until four, I sat in the bed of my pickup with a friend and watched meteor showers hot dance over our heads in sprays of little suns that looked like white orchids. With so many stars falling around us I wondered if daylight would come. We forget that our sun is only a star destined to someday burn out. The time scale of its transience so far exceeds our human one that our unconditional dependence on its life-giving properties feels oddly like an indiscretion about which we'd rather forget.

2   The recent news that astronomers have discovered a new solar system in-the-making around another sun-star has startled us out of a collective narcissism based on the assumption that we dominate the cosmic scene. Now we must make room for the possibility of new life—not without resentment and anticipation—the way young couples make room in their lives for a baby. By chance, this discovery came the same day a Kiowa friend invited me to attend a Sun Dance.

3   I have Indian neighbors all around me—Crow and Cheyenne to the north, Shoshone and Arapaho to the south—and though we often ranch, drink, and rodeo side by side, and dress in the same cowboy uniforms—Wrangler jeans, tall boots, wide-brimmed, high-crowned

hats — there is nothing in our psyches, styles, or temperaments that is alike.

4        Because Christians shaped our New World culture we've had to swallow an artificial division between what's sacred and what's profane. Many westerners, like Native Americans, have made a life for themselves out in the raw wind, riding the ceremony of seasons with a fine-tuned eye and ear for where the elk herd is hidden or when in fall to bring the cattle down. They'll knock a sage hen in the head with a rock for dinner and keep their bearings in a ferocious storm as ably as any Sioux warrior, but they won't become visionaries, diviners, or healers in the process.

5        On a Thursday I set off at two in the morning and drove to the reservation. It was dark when I arrived and quiet. On a broad plain bordered in the west by mountains, the families of the hundred men who were pledging the dance had set up camps: each had a white canvas tipi, a wall tent, and a rectangular brush arbor in a circle around the Lodge, where for the next four days the ceremony would take place. At 5 A.M. I could still see stars, the Big Dipper suspended in the northwest as if magnified, and to the east, a wide band of what looked like blood. I sat on the ground in the dark. Awake and stirring now, some of the "dancers" filed out of the Lodge, their star quilts pulled tightly over their heads. When they lined up solemnly behind two portable johns, I thought I was seeing part of the dance. Then I had to laugh at myself but at the same time understood how the sacredness of this ceremony was located not just in the Lodge but everywhere.

6        Sun Dance is the holiest religious ceremony of the Plains tribes, having spread from the Cheyenne to the Sioux, Blackfoot, Gros Ventre, Assiniboine, Arapaho, Bannock, and Shoshone sometime after the year 1750. It's not "sun worship" but an inculcation of regenerative power that restores health, vitality, and harmony to the land and all tribes.

7        For the hundred dancers who have volunteered to dance this year (the vow obligates them to dance four times during their lives) Sun Dance is a serious and painful undertaking; called "thirsty standing," they eat no food and drink no water for four days. This year, with the hundred-degree heat we've been having, their suffering will be extreme. The ceremonies begin before dawn and often last until two or three in the morning. They must stay in the Lodge for the duration. Speaking to or making eye contact with anyone not dancing is forbidden, and it's considered a great disgrace to drop out of the dance before it is over.

8        Sun Dance was suppressed by the government in the 1880s, and its full revival has only been recent. Some tribes practiced the ceremony secretly, others stopped. George Horse Capture, a Gros Ventre who lives near me and has completed one Sun Dance, has had to read the same sources I have — Dorsey, Kroeber, and Peter Powell — to reeducate himself in his tradition.

9        "Did you sleep here last night?" an old man, one of the elders of the

tribe, asked. Shrunken and hawk-nosed, he wore a blue farmer's cap and walked with a crudely carved pine cane. "No, I drove from Shell," I answered, sounding self-conscious because I seemed to be the only white person around. "Oh . . . you have a very good spirit to get up so early and come all this way. That's good . . . I'm glad you are here," he said. His round eyes narrowed and he walked away. On the other side of the shed where the big drum was kept he approached three teenage girls. "You sober?" he asked. "Yes," they replied in unison. "Good," he said. "Don't make war on anyone. If you're not drunk, there's peace." He hobbled past me again out into the parched field between the circle of tents and the Lodge. Coleman lanterns were being lighted and the tipis behind him glowed. He put both hands on top of the cane and, in a hoarse voice that carried far across the encampment, sang an Arapaho morning song: "Get up, Everyone get up . . . ," it began, followed by encouragements to face the day.

The sky had lightened; it was a shield of pink. The new moon, white    10
when I had arrived, now looked blue. Another voice—sharp, gravelly, and less patient, boomed from the north, his song overlapping that of the first Crier's. I looked: he was a younger man but bent at the shoulders like a tree. He paced the hard ground as he sang, and the tweed jacket he wore, which gave him a Dickensian look, hung from him and swayed in the breeze. Now I could hear two other Criers to the south and west. The four songs overlapped, died out, and started again. The men, silhouetted, looked ghostlike against the horizon, almost disembodied, as though their age and authority were entirely in the vocal cords.

First light. In the Lodge the dancers were dressing. Over gym shorts    11
(the modern substitute for breechclouts), they pulled on long, white, sheath skirts, to which they fastened, with wide beaded belts, their dance aprons: two long panels, front and back, decorated with beads, ribbons, and various personal insignias. Every man wore beaded moccasins, leaving legs and torsos bare. Their faces, chests, arms, and the palms of their hands were painted yellow. Black lines skittered across chests, around ankles and wrists, and encircled each face. Four bundles of sage, which represents healing and breath, were tucked straight up in the apron fronts; thin braided wreaths of it were slipped onto the dancer's wrists and ankles, and a crown of sage ending in two loose sprays looked like antennae.

Light begets activity—the Lodge began filling up. It's a log arbor,    12
forty yards across, covered with a thatchwork of brush. Its sixteen sides radiate from a great center pole of cottonwood—the whole trunk of a hundred-year-old tree whose forked top looked like antlers. A white cloth was tied with rope around the bark, and overhead, on four of the pine stringers, tribal members had hung bandanas, silk cowboy scarves, and shawls that all together form a loose, trembling hieroglyph spelling out personal requests for health and repair.

Alongside the dancers, who stood in a circle facing east, a group of    13 older men filed in. These were the "grandfathers" (ceremonially related, not by blood) who would help the younger dancers through their four-day ordeal.

14    The little shed against which I had leaned in the premorning light opened and became an announcer's stand. From it the drum was rolled out and set up at the entrance to the Lodge.

15    Light begets activity begets light. The sky looked dry, white, and inflammable. Eleven drummers who, like "the grandfathers," were probably ranchers sat on metal folding chairs encircling the drum. A stream of announcements in both Arapaho and English flooded the air. Friends and relatives of the dancers lined up in front of the Lodge. I found myself in a group of Indian women. The drumming, singing, and dancing began all at once. It's not really a dance with steps but a dance of containment, a dance in place. Facing east and blowing whistles made of eagle wing bones in shrill unison, the men bounced up and down on their heels in time to the drumbeat. Series after series of songs, composed especially for Sun Dance, were chanted in high, intense voices. The ropey, repeating pulse was so strong it seemed to pull the sun up.

16    There were two important men at the back of the Lodge I hadn't noticed. That their faces were painted red, not yellow, signified the status of Instructor, Pledger, or Priest. The taller of the two held a hoop (the sun) with eagle feathers (the bird of day) fastened around it. The "grand-father" standing in back of him raised the hoop-holding hand and, from behind, pushed the arm up and down in a wide, swinging arc until it took flight on its own.

17    I felt warmth on my shoulder. As the sun topped the horizon, the dancers stretched their arms straight out, lifting them with the progress of the sun's rising. Songs pushed from the backs of the drummers' throats. The skin on the dancer's chests bounced as though from some interior tremor. When the light hit their faces, they looked as if they were made of sun.

18    The sunrise ceremony ended at eight. They had danced for nearly two hours and already the heat of the day was coming on. Pickups rambled through camps, children played quietly everywhere. Walking to a friend's camp, I began to understand how the wide ampleness of the Indian body stands for a spirit of accommodation. In the ceremony I had just witnessed, no one—dancer, observer, child, priest, or drummer—had called attention to himself. There was no applause, no frivolousness. Families ambled back to their camps as though returning from a baseball game. When I entered my friend's brush arbor (already a relief from the sun) and slid behind the picnic table bench she handed me the cup of coffee I'd been hoping for. "They're dancing for all of us," she said. Then we drained our cups in silence.

19    Though I came and went from the Sun Dance grounds (it was too hot to stand around in the direct sun) the ceremonies continued all day and most of each night. At nine the "runners" drove to the swamp to cut

reeds from which they fashioned beds for the dancers. The moisture in the long, bladelike leaves helped cool the men off. At ten, special food eaten by the dancers' families was blessed in the Lodge, and this was surely to become one of the dancers' daily agonies: the smell of meat, stew, and fry bread filling the space, then being taken away. The sunrise drummers were spelled by new ones, and as the songs began again those dancers who could stood in their places and danced. Each man was required to dance a certain number of hours a day. When he was too weak or sick or reeling from hallucination, he was allowed to rest on his rush mat.

"What happens if it rains during Sun Dance?" I asked my Kiowa [20] friend. "It doesn't," she answered curtly. By eleven, it was ninety-nine degrees. We drove west away from the grounds to the land she owned and went skinny-dipping in the river. Her brown body bobbed up and down next to my white one. Behind us a wall of colored rock rose out of the water, part of a leathery bluff that curved for miles. "That's where the color for the Sun Dance paints comes from," my friend's husband said, pointing to a cave. He'd just floated into view from around an upstream bend. With his big belly glinting, he had the complacent look of a man who lords over a houseful of women: a wife, two daughters, a young tutor for his girls. The night before, they'd thrown an anniversary party at this spot. There were tables full of Mexican food, a five-piece Mexican band whose members looked like reformed Hell's Angels, a charro with four skinny horses and a trick-riding act, two guests who arrived from the oil fields by helicopter, and a mutual friend who's Jewish and a Harvard professor who popped bikini-clad out of a giant plywood cake.

The men in the Rabbit Lodge danced as late as the party-goers. The [21] next morning when I arrived at four-thirty the old man with the cane walked directly to me. "Where's your coat? Aren't you cold?" he asked gruffly, though I knew he was welcoming me. The dancers spit bile and shuffled back and forth between the johns and the Lodge. A friend had asked one of them how he prepared for Sun Dance. He replied, "I don't. There's no way to prepare for pain." As the dancers began to look more frail, the singing became raucous. The astounding volume, quick rises in pitch, and forays into falsetto had an enlivening effect on all of us. Now it was the drummers who made the dancers make the sun rise.

Noon. In the hottest midday sun the dancers were brought out in [22] front of the Lodge to be washed and freshly painted. The grandfathers dipped soft little brooms of sage in water and swabbed the men down; they weren't allowed to drink. Their families gathered around and watched while the dancers held their gaze to the ground. I couldn't bring myself to stand close. It seemed a violation of privacy. It wasn't nudity that rendered the scene so intimate (they still had their gym shorts on), but the thirst. Behind me, someone joked about dancing for rain instead of sun.

23      I was wrong about the bathing scene. Now the desolation of it struck me as beautiful. All afternoon the men danced in the heat—two, eight, or twenty of them at a time. In air so dry and with their juices squeezed out, the bouncing looked weightless, their bodies thin and brittle as shells. It wasn't the pain of the sacrifice they were making that counted but the emptiness to which they were surrendering themselves. It was an old ritual: separation, initiation, return. They'd left their jobs and families to dance. They were facing physical pain and psychological transformation. Surely, the sun seared away preoccupation and pettiness. They would return changed. Here, I was in the presence of a collective hero. I searched their faces and found no martyrs, no dramatists, no antiheroes either. They seemed to pool their pain and offer it back to us, dancing not for our sins but to ignite our hearts.

24      Evening. There were many more spectators tonight. Young Indian women cradling babies moved to the front of the Lodge. They rocked them in time with the drums and all evening not one child cried. Currents of heat rose from the ground; in fact, everything seemed to be rising: bone whistles, arms, stars, penises, the yeast in the fry bread, the smell of sage. My breasts felt full. The running joke in camp was about "Sun Dance Babies." Surely the expansive mood in the air settled over the tipis at night, but there was more to it than that. Among some tribes a "Sacred Woman" is involved in the ceremony. The sun is a "man power" symbol. When she offers herself to the priest, their union represents the rebirth of the land, water, and people. If by chance a child is conceived, he or she is treated with special reverence for a lifetime.

25      Dawn. This morning I fainted. The skinny young man dancing in front of me appeared to be cringing in pain. Another dancer's face had been painted green. I'm not saying they made me faint—maybe I fainted for them. With little ado, the women behind me picked me up. Revived and feeling foolish, I stood through to the end. "They say white people don't have the constitution to go without water for so many days," a white friend commented later. It sounded like a racist remark to me. She'd once been offered a chance to fast with a medicine man and refused. "I think it has more to do with one's concepts of hope and fear," I mumbled as she walked through the field to her car.

26      Afternoon. At five, only two dancers were standing. Because of the heat, the smell of urine had mixed with the sage.

27      Later in the evening I stood next to two teenage boys from Oklahoma. Not realizing I was old enough to be their mother, they flirted with me, then undercut the dares with cruelty. "My grandmother hates white tourists," the one who had been eyeing my chest said to me. "You're missing the point of this ceremony," I said to him. "And racism isn't a good thing anywhere." They walked away, but later, when I bumped into them, they smiled apologetically.

28      When I had coffee in a friend's brush arbor during a break in the dancing, the dancer's wife looked worried. "He looks like death warmed

over," she said. A young man with black braids that reached his belt buckle was dangling a baby on each knee; I've never seen men so gentle and at ease with children. A fresh breeze fanned us. The round-the-clock rhythm of drumbeats and dancing made day and night seem the same. Sleeping became interchangeable with waiting, until, finally, there was no difference between the two.

Sunday. Two American flags were raised over the Lodge today — 29 both had been owned by war veterans. The dance apron of a man near me had U.S. Navy insignias sewn into the corners. Here was a war hero, but he'd earned his medal far from home. Now the ritual of separation, initiation, and return performed in Vietnam, outside the context of community, changes into separation, benumbment, and exile.

Throughout the afternoon's dancing there was a Give-Away, an 30 Indian tradition to honor friends, relatives, and admirers with a formal exchange of gifts. In front of the announcer's stand there was a table chock-full of food and another stacked high with Pendleton blankets, shawls, and beadwork. The loudspeaker overwhelmed the drumming until all the gifts were dispersed. Pickups streamed through the camps and a layer of dust muted the hard brightness of the day. After his first Sun Dance one old man told me he had given nearly everything he owned away: horse, wagons, clothes, winter blankets. "But it all comes back," he said, as if the day and night rhythm of this ceremony stood for a bigger tidal cadence as well.

Evening. They've taken the brush away from the far side of the 31 Lodge. Now the dancers face west. All hundred men, freshly painted with a wild dappling of dots, stripes, and crooked lines, bounced up and down vigorously and in short strokes waved eagle fans in front of their bodies as if to clear away any tiredness there.

When I asked why the Sun Dance ended at night, my friend said, "So 32 the sun will remember to make a complete circle, and so we'll always have night and day." The sun drained from the dancers' faces and sank into a rack of thunderclouds over the mountains. Every movement coming from the Lodge converged into a single trajectory, a big "V" like a flock of birds migrating toward me. This is how ritual speaks with no words. The dancing and whistling surged; each time a crescendo felt near, it ebbed. In the southwest, the first evening star appeared, and the drumming and singing, which had begun to feel like a hard dome over my head, stopped.

Amid cries of relief and some clapping I heard hoarse expulsions of 33 air coming from dancers, like whales breaching after being under water too long. They rushed forward to the front of the Lodge, throwing off the sage bracelets and crowns, knelt down in turn by wooden bowls of chokecherry juice, and drank their first liquid in four days.

The family standing next to me approached the Lodge cautiously. 34 "There he is," I heard the mother say. They walked toward the dancer, a big, lumbering man in his thirties whose waist, where rolls of fat had been, now looked concave. The man's wife and father slid their arms around his back, while his mother stood in front and took a good look at him. He gave her the first drink of sweet water from his bowl. "I tried to be there as much as possible today. Did you see me?" his wife asked. He nodded and smiled. Some of the young children had rushed into the Lodge and were swinging the flattened reeds that had been the dancers' beds around and around in the air. One of the drummers, an energetic man with an eccentric, husky voice, walked up to a group of us and started shaking our hands. He didn't know us but it didn't matter. "I'm awfully glad you're here," he kept saying, then walked away laughing ecstatically. The dancer I had been watching was having trouble staying on his feet. He stumbled badly. A friend said he worked for Amoco and tomorrow he'd be back in the oil fields. Still supporting him with their arms, his family helped him toward their brush arbor, now lit with oil lamps, where he would vomit, then feast.

## Evaluating the Text

1. What is the Sun Dance designed to accomplish?
2. Ehrlich's account appears in the form of a journal entry for July. What is the thematic relationship between the entries based on her observation of meteor showers and the underlying imagery of the Sun Dance?
3. Describe the preparation of the dancers for taking part in the Sun Dance. What is the significance of the different elements of the costume and the kinds of colors worn as it relates to the purpose of the dance?
4. How are different stages of the dance designed to mimic events in the natural world? For example, how is the sun "pulled up"?
5. What provisions are made for the dancers to rest between "shifts"?
6. What can you infer about Ehrlich's relationship with her Kiowa friend? What encounters does Ehrlich have with different people in the camp? At which moments does she feel more like an insider and less like an outsider?
7. How is the ritual conducted so as to progress through phases of separation, initiation, and return?
8. Why is it important that the dancers not make eye contact with each other or the crowd?
9. What kind of events occur on the third day that seem, to Ehrlich, to reveal the regenerative effects of the Sun Dance?
10. Ehrlich's account takes the form of a first-person narrative, of the kind that might be found in a journal or diary. Yet her account has been refined from initial notes and observations. At what points do you think Ehrlich is attempting to make her original account "more literary"? What specific words and phrases can you cite that support this?
11. How would you characterize Ehrlich's attitude toward the events she describes? How does she seem to have been changed by the experience of witnessing the Sun Dance of the Kiowas?

## Exploring Different Perspectives

1. In what way are the rituals conducted in the Sun Dance of the Kiowa Indians in Wyoming and in Bessie Head's story set in Botswana (see

"Looking for a Rain God") based on tribal religious assumptions that human activities can influence the natural world? How does the attitude toward the sun differ between these two selections? How is this different attitude reflected in the differences between the two rituals?

2. In what way are rituals in the Sun Dance of the Kiowas and fiestas in Mexico described by Octavio Paz in "The Day of the Dead" based on the principle that if you give away or divest yourself of worldly possessions or use all the money you have for religious festivals, the original amounts and more will be returned to you? Discuss the psychology of sacrifice that underlies this belief.

3. Compare the role of specific herbs and plants in the religious ceremony of the Sun Dance and in the voodoo rituals in Haiti described by Gino Del Guercio in "The Secrets of the Living Dead." Can you think of any other ceremonies that are based on sacramental attributes of particular herbs or plants?

## Extending Viewpoints for Writing

1. Were you ever invited by someone from another culture to witness or take part in a ceremony or ritual that was important to them? Describe your experiences, and tell how the actual event was different from what you had expected.

2. What is the longest period of time you have ever gone without food and water? Have you ever fasted for religious or spiritual reasons? Write a narrative explaining how you felt before, during, and after your fast.

3. How is the Sun Dance similar to and different from what we usually call dancing? Discuss as many significant similarities and differences as you can discover (e.g., how are differences in eye contact or lack of it between the dancers and the crowd, apparel, makeup, musical accompaniment, movement of the dancers, eating and drinking while dancing, all related to different purposes of the Sun Dance versus regular dancing?)

4. Ehrlich observes that although she and her Indian neighbors "often ranch, drink, and rodeo side by side, and dress in the same cowboy uniforms . . . there is nothing in our psyches, styles, or temperaments, that is alike." Unlike secular culture, American Indian culture does not segregate the sacred from everyday life. Discuss how the details in the performance of the Sun Dance reveal this lack of separation.

5. In an essay, discuss the cultural impact of religious beliefs of Islam in Egypt (Nawal El-Saadawi, "Circumcision of Girls," Chapter 2); Iran (Salman Rushdie, "A Pen against the Sword," Chapter 7); and the Sudan (Tayeb Salib, "A Handful of Dates, Chapter 2); Voodoo in Haiti (Gino del Guercio, "The Secrets of Haiti's Living Dead," Chapter 8); Animism in Bali (Clifford Geertz, "Of Cocks and Men," Chapter 3); Buddhism in Vietnam (Robert Santos, "My Men," Chapter 9) and Singapore (Catherine Lim, "Paper," Chapter 4); the Mennonite religion of the Amish (Gene Logsdon, "Amish Economics," Chapter 4), Roman Catholicism in Ireland (William Trevor, "Teresa's Wedding," Chapter 1); and the Sikh and Hindu religions in India (Krishnan Varma, "The Grass-Eaters," Chapter 5; and Bharati Mukherjee, "The Management of Grief," Chapter 7).

# Paul Fussell

# *Taking It All Off in the Balkans*

---

*Paul Fussell is Donald T. Reagan Professor of English at the University of Pennsylvania and the author of* Class: A Guide Through the American Status System *(1983),* Abroad: British Literary Traveling Between the Wars *(1980),* Thank God for the Atomic Bomb *(1988), and many books on eighteenth-century and modern British culture. His book* The Great War and Modern Memory *(1985) won the National Book Award in 1976. "Taking It All Off in the Balkans" first appeared in* Gentlemen's Quarterly *(April 1987). This eye-opening account of nudism along the Adriatic coast demonstrates how the concept of modesty is culturally determined.*

*Yugoslavia on the Balkan peninsula in southeast Europe is a federation of six republics — Serbia, Croatia, Bosnia, Macedonia, Slovenia, and Montenegro — that came into existence after World War I in 1918. Since its inception, Yugoslavia has been plagued by tensions between its different ethnic and religious groups, including Roman Catholics, Serbian Orthodox, and Muslims. At the end of World War II, in 1945, Yugoslavia became a communist state under the leadership of Josip Broz or "Tito." In 1948, Tito broke with Russian leadership and developed a form of "national" communism, independent from the Soviet Union. When he died in 1980, his authority was transferred into a collective state presidency, where the head of government would rotate among the six republics. The calls for democracy in Yugoslavia resulted in the communist party giving up its constitutional monopoly on power in January 1990. Fears that Yugoslavia could face internal war between the republics increased when the Slovenian and Croatian Republics voted, on June 25, 1991, to secede from the federation. The section of Yugoslavia discussed by Fussell lies along its western border, the island-studded Adriatic coast, known as Dalmatia, to which sun-seekers from many countries flock each summer.*

1    If enjoying the beach is the most common contemporary enactment of the pastoral urge, enjoying the beach nude is the ultimate form. What could more conveniently constitute an antidote to civilization and a celebration of Golden Age honesty, freedom, and simplicity than casting off your dearest disguises? And casting off as well that sly, niggling, self-conscious, crypto-porno sexualism which is as telling a stigma of

Modernism as free verse or anthropology? You don't believe you slough off sexual obsession when you take off your clothes in public? Come with me to the Balkans.

"Yugoslavia," a state tourist official said recently, "is becoming one 2 great nude beach." But it hasn't reached that goal yet — there are still other attractions: Sarajevo, with its minarets and the bridge where a few pistol shots started the First World War; the town of Cetinje, capital of the former midget country of Montenegro, its once pretentious British and Russian and Turkish embassies fallen into ironic ruin. And of course Belgrade, Split, Zagreb, and the superb walled city of Dubrovnik. Once it was named Ragusa, and its merchant marine was the rival of Venice. The word *argosy* comes from its former name. But finally you're bound to wander up and down the coast, and it's there you can sense what the tourist-industry spokesman is getting at. It's a good place to experience, if you haven't already, the manners and unwritten rules governing communal naturism. Or nudism, as it used to be called when there seemed something naughty and furtive about it. Once, no more than twenty-five years ago, people who went to "nudist camps" were careful to use only their first names. Now, no such caution.

If you're curious, the best place in the whole world to take the pulse 3 of international naturism is the Adriatic Coast — totaling 3,700 miles, islands and inlets included — of the Socialist Federal Republic of Yugoslavia. It has been in the nude-beach business (*nudizma*, in Serbo-Croat) for over twenty-five years, less to set a good example of personal liberty to other communist countries than to earn lots of foreign exchange. Chiefly Deutsche Marks. For the past few years West Germany has supplied the bulk of visitors to Yugoslavia, followed by Britain, France, Czechoslovakia, Belgium, Holland, and Italy. Afflicted with sexual anxieties as they are known to be, nice Republican middle-class Americans —those, that is, with the money and the motive to travel around Europe —have not responded wildly to the naturist invitation. You almost never see Yanks in take-it-all-off Yugoslavian settings, although in their baggy shorts and frilly one-pieces they can sometimes be observed glancing wistfully toward areas designated FOR NUDISTS ONLY: ALL OTHERS KEEP AWAY.

Actually the naturist beaches are so German that they seem all but 4 exclusively so, and the local socialist barkeeps and waitresses and windsurfing instructors have learned long ago that *Bier* means *pivo; Weisswein, belo vino;* and *bitte, molim.* The vast throngs of German naturists are assisted by their own guidebooks to Dalmatian *Naktkultur*, like *Naktfakte*, a work listing the best naturist beaches, hotels, camp sites, and resorts. Driving, the German tourist has only to follow the signs reading FKK to find the right beaches. FKK, a term which may sound a bit suggestive to English speakers, is simply an abbreviation of *Freikörperkultur*, a word invented around the 1920s by the Germans to invest the whole nudist operation with an air of the therapeutic and the innocent-educational.

The FKK sign will lead the traveler to some thirty naturist sites along the coast, ranging from simple unimproved tent sites and trailer camps to elaborate hotels and even small towns. From a distance, these towns appear quite ordinary, but when you come closer you see everyone going around stark naked, shopping at the supermarket and the drugstore, sipping apéritifs at the café, going to the hairdressers, renting sailboats for the day, or driving off in the family car for a picnic.

5      For a typical naturist experience you might go to the Hotel Osmine, near the small town of Slano, twenty-five miles north of Dubrovnik. This is a standard, moderate-priced family resort hotel of some three hundred rooms, with the usual dining room, bar, and game room. As you register you may notice that virtually every passport in the cubbyholes is West German. The nice elderly woman at the desk reminds you — a bit gingerly, since you are American and thus, doubtless, in her view a puritan and moral dogmatist, quite ready to be shocked — that this is a naturist hotel. Any doubt on this score will vanish as you walk down a long stairway and approach the beach, where all normal activity — swimming and sailing lessons, beer drinking, or lunching at the café — is taking place without bathing suits and with no self-consciousness or visible sexual awareness whatever. Ages range from one to eighty-five years, and everyone is brown. All over.

6      Is only the beach naturist, or is the whole hotel? Officially, the whole hotel is, but you notice that as people return from the beach, they gradually begin covering up, and only a rare naturist (an impudent one, some would say) arrives back at the public rooms with nothing on. I did see two middle-aged men nude at the bar, but it didn't look right, and even they seem embarrassed. When the sun disappears, so does naturism. In the dining room at evening and for dancing on the patio at night, everyone is dressed, just as if the place were a normal hotel. But in the morning, off it all comes again as you head for the sand and the water. The boys in the dance band, nicely dressed for their performance the night before, are seen on the beach the next day, politely greeting everyone. They are now nude.

What does it feel like, taking it all off in public? At first, to be sure, there's a terrible shyness, and you spend a lot of effort worrying about the most decent way to disrobe. (This is before you come to understand that the term *decent* belongs to an anxious world which is not this one.) Should your shorts or your shirt be the last thing you remove? Experience will inform you that removing shorts or bathing suit *first* is the more honorable way. Once stripped, you sense a momentary impulse to Look Your Best — stand straight, shoulders back. Pull in that stomach. But after a few minutes of this, you understand that you've missed the whole point, and you relax as the genuine naturist feeling begins to flood over you. The naturist feeling? A new and lovely sense of perfect freedom, not just from jocks and waistbands and bras but from social fears and niggling gentilities. You quickly overcome your standard anxieties about what the neighbors or the boss will think. The illusion, which naturists recognize as an illusion, is that all evil has been for the moment banished from the beach. Including the grave risk of skin cancer, which is never mentioned by naturists.

On naturist premises you notice all sorts of significant things about  7 people. You notice first something easily obscured in artificial or sophisticated circles, namely, that everyone is unequivocally male or female, and that effeminate or butch mannerisms don't do much to define identity and character once the drapes are put aside. You become aware too that the "unisex" concept is a fraud and a delusion, a con useful to merchandising and perhaps to sentimentality but useful nowhere else. To the naturist eye, men are men and women are women, and there's no way to shade or qualify the difference.

Nude, older people look younger, especially when very tan, and  8 younger people look even younger—almost like infants, some of them. In addition fat people look far less offensive naked than clothed. Clothes, you realize, have the effect of sausage casings, severely defining and advertising the shape of what they contain, pulling it all into an unnatural form which couldn't fool anyone. And there's one visual side benefit of naturism that those with taste will appreciate: the eye is repulsed much less than in normal vacation life by those hideous "resort" clothes. No one is got up in bright green pseudo-linen Bermuda shorts or self-humiliating hundred-dollar knit shirts celebrating the male tits of the too-well-fed middle-aged, or horrible "Italian" brown and white shoes with holes and cutouts. Better total nakedness: no one totally nude could look as ugly as someone costumed in current vacation wear, no matter his or her shape. The beginning naturist doesn't take long to master the principle that it is stockings that made varicose veins noticeable, belts that call attention to forty-eight-inch waists, brassieres that emphasize sagging breasts. Not to mention the paradox, familiar to all naturists, that the body clothed is really sexier than the body nude. As one experienced naturist notes, "Much of our clothing . . . tends to accentuate certain areas of the body that it is supposed to hide." That's part of the pleasure of clothes, of course, but there's pleasure also in rejecting that convention in favor of one that proves in practice to involve an unaccustomed sort of innocence.

A further benefit of naturism is this: you regain something of the  9 physical unselfconsciousness and absence of anxiety about your appearance that you had as a young child. A little time spent on naturist beaches will persuade most women that their breasts and hips are not, as they may think when alone, appalled by their mirrors, "abnormal," but quite natural, "abnormal" ones belonging entirely to the nonexistent creatures depicted in ideal painting and sculpture. The same with men: if you think nature has been unfair to you in the sexual anatomy sweepstakes, spend some time among the naturists. You will learn that every man looks roughly the same—quite small, that is, and that heroic fixtures are not just extremely rare, they are deformities.

In their enthusiasm to forward a noble cause in a suspicious, nasty-minded world, naturists have been vigorous devisers of euphemisms. *Naturist* has by now virtually ousted *nudist*, which itself could be supposed a sort of euphemism for *nakedist*. Lest the idea of a *naturist beach* seem too jolting to the conventional, naturists have come up with *free beach*, or *clothing-or-swimsuit-optional beach*. *Sunbathing* is popular as a disarming synonym for *nudism*, and among the cognoscenti no elbow nudge is needed to suggest how it differs from *sunning*, which is what you do with a bathing suit on. Indeed, the diction of nudism could supply material for a good-sized study. In Australia, it is *sunbaking* that means taking the sun nude. *Sunbathing* there means with a bathing suit on. Beaches where cover-up is required are now often referred to, by naturists, as *textile* beaches, as opposed to both *top-free* and simply *free*. Europeans are most likely to use terms involving some form of the word nude. In America, nudist clubs and resorts are united by membership in the American Sunbathing Association or the Naturist Society. But regardless of what you call it, ideas not just of sun but of water seem indispensable to the movement. Even confirmed naturists might feel uncomfortable stripping indoors or in some conventionally unwholesome and unathletic environment like a cocktail lounge, say, or a poolroom.

People don't just (forgive the understatement) look different on a naturist beach. They act different. And actually the code of manners governing naturist behavior is about the most formal to be met with in the current social scene. People accustomed to backslapping, touching, or asking all and sundry "Where you from?" or "Come here often?" will be startled to find the atmosphere of a nude beach as decorous as that of the Back Bay about 1910.

10      The rules are nowhere available for study, but they are apparent to all, and if you don't catch on fast, the naturists will urge you to leave. For one thing, no staring. Or, more accurately, no conspicuous staring. Permitted is genteel staring from behind dark glasses or when looking up occasionally from reading. A more specific visual no-no: when conversing, you look nowhere but at the face of the person addressed. But it's best to address no one but your partner, if any, and you should never go wandering about, in quest of "dates." Cameras are not very popular, and a habitual naturist will recoil from the sight of one the way a good Moslem flinches from a bottle of vodka. But if cameras are frowned upon, so equally is any show of "modesty," which has meaning, after all, only in the world of dress. For the naturist the ideal presentation is the air of everything being quite normal. You should act as if you always go around with no clothes on. You should give the impression that you would be scandalized to hear that the practice strikes some people as odd

or perverse. But there is one crucial, and interesting, exception to the antimodesty convention.

Some philosophes of the eighteenth century, anxious to demonstrate 11 that Whatever Is, Is Right, argued that in planning the human body Nature must have known exactly what she was doing, for she took care to hide from customary view the least prepossessing external body opening. Naturists seem to recognize at least the aesthetic element of this argument, for they seem careful never to let the audience to the rear see them bending down. In fact, that undignified, even comical, part of the body is never knowingly exposed by a naturist, a fact suggesting that even naturism retains its pruderies, for all its pretense of bravely casting them aside.

Contrary to the ordinary frequenter of "textile" beaches, naturists 12 consider their turfs not at all appropriate theaters of eroticism. "Naturism and pornography," one naturist points out recently, "are irreconcilable." A spokesman for Polish naturism has asserted: "With our beach nudity we protest against the perversion of erotic life; that is, against pornography and refined exhibitionism." In the United States there is now an organization called NOPE (Naturists Opposing Pornographic Exploitation) devoted to publicizing the nonerotic element in social naturism. Naturists cannot be compared to exhibitionists either, because of the vigorous contempt they feel for peepers, whether by land, peering down from cliffs through binoculars, or by sea, cutting in too close to the beach in small boats, and giggling lewdly. Naturists regard all such people as sick and in need of treatment. They also deeply resent the presence on their beaches of the clothed, be the clothing ever so slight (except, of course, for the hotel or beach staff, whose clothing makes them easy to spot when you need their services). It's amazing the way a bikini, even if both top and bottom are present, looks grossly obscene in a nude context, nastily coy and flirtatious. To a naturist, the toplessness of French beaches is the ultimate pornography. Jewelry, on the other hand, is permitted so long as, like earrings and crosses on gold chains, it is not trying to conceal anything normally considered sexually meaningful. By the same token hats are allowed, and, on rocky beaches, shoes.

The naturist attitude toward more extensive covering up will suggest 13 the essential nudist emotion and value: "sincerity." It is this that prompts women to leave off makeup: too suggestive of fraud and archness. And in addition to sincerity, and perhaps harder to believe, innocence. A sixteenth-century painting by Lucas Cranach can illustrate that point. It is titled *The Golden Age*, that is, before the fall of humankind into dirtymindedness, and the version in the Alte Pinakothek, Munich, depicts eleven couples disporting nude in a scene that could almost be a naturist beach. They are swimming, chatting, and dancing hand-in-hand around a tree, and the naturalness and innocence of their nudity is underlined by the presence of a "naturist" lion couple and deer couple, both clearly devoid of foul-minded sexual innuendo.

As opposed to its shy beginnings a half century or more ago, naturism 14 currently has acquired strength and purpose and a degree of high privilege from ecological, environmentalist, and conservationist movements, of which naturists easily feel themselves a significant part. All these impulses, after all, constitute votes on behalf of "the natural," to be preserved and valued as a quasi-religious obligation. Littering, thus, is quite unthinkable to naturists, as irreconcilable with social nudity as pornography. As one longtime practitioner says, naturism occupies a central position between purposeless nudism and love-of-outdoor-things naturalism. A naturist, he points out, is not quite a naturalist, but almost. One Italian naturist, describing a nudist lake shore not far from Rome, says, "Here, people seek naturism. They don't disturb or pollute. The lake keeps its integrity."

15      Sooner or later, anyone reading about this topic is bound to wonder about what one may call the Male Response. The fact is that if one pursues one's naturism correctly, it's no problem at all. Dealing with it, making sure it doesn't happen, is precisely a part of the naturist exercise, indeed, one of its benefits, if one may go so far as that. The naturist rule, No Love in Public, helps keep one on the right track. Naturists agree that, given the cascades of sexual stimuli poured over us by contemporary civilization, at stated times and places a little contrived, conscious sexlessness is good for you.

16      For all its essential charm and harmlessness, not everyone is enthusiastic about naturism in Yugoslavia. The prim British travel writer J. A. Cuddon has produced a *Companion Guide of Jugoslavia* whose 480 pages do not once mention that naturism is an attraction, although he includes sections on Principal Coastal Resorts, Hotels, Entertainment, Spas, and Costumes, and devotes 162 pages to a description of the Dalmatian Coast. (It may be worth noting that when it comes to priggish, self-righteous, "middle-class" disapproval of naturism, it is likely that British lips are doing the uttering. Like Valerie Grove's, who recently deplored, in the *Spectator*, the growing popularity of naturism in the Mediterranean. Argument failing her, she descends to physical insult, assuming that the main naturist motive is simple exhibitionism:

> As for the full frontal men lying stretched out, what poor bare fork'd things indeed. It was my mother-in-law who declared that the problem here is one of visibility. Perhaps some sort of magnifying glass could be provided, she suggests?

It's pleasant to observe that such smirking, self-satisfied puritanism becomes rarer each year, although it doubtless disappears more slowly from the former Anglo-Saxon empires than elsewhere. Valerie Grove's reaction nicely illustrates Orwell's point about geographical righteousness, which applies as well to Canadians, Americans, and Mexicans, in that order. "When nationalism first became a religion, the English looked at the map, and, noticing that their island lay very high in the Northern Hemisphere, evolved the pleasing theory that the further north you live the more virtuous you are.")

From J. A. Cuddon and his like you'd never gather that several travel agencies, like Yugotours (see any big-city Yellow Pages), offer complete naturist package tours to Yugoslavia. For example, Lister International Travel advertises a seventeen-day tour attractively named The Adriatic Escapade. This conveys people "with an insatiable sense of curiosity to try new things" to a number of the naturist coastal resorts, "the ideal place to acquire the ultimate suntan."   17

The naturist coast is largely a Roman Catholic area. I wondered about the attitude of the faithful and others who might be thought to disapprove of all this, and I sought some illumination from the Director of Tourism for the Dubrovnik area. He assured me that the Church gave no trouble, and couldn't even if it wanted to, because, thanks to socialism —i.e., communism—the Church was no longer a power in Yugoslavia. He pointed out that even in Greece, where at least in rural areas the Orthodox Church is still potent, the Church has been unable to reverse the modern trend to touristic naturism. Why expect the Church to have greater power in a socialist country? Yes,but how does naturism square with socialism? (I was thinking of the quasi-capitalistic cynical profit-making behind the whole operation.) It squares perfectly, he said, rather heatedly: socialism is founded upon mutual respect among human beings, and if you want to take your clothes off, who am I to object, so long as you don't force me to look at the spectacle?   18

He pointed out also that socialism concerns itself with the public health and that naturism has been held to have distinct therapeutic value. Indeed, he went on, some Yugoslavian physicians prescribe swimming at naturist resorts as a cure for barrenness in women. It is the therapeutic benefits of naturism that are specified in the official 24-page pamphlet *Jugoslavia Naturism*, issued by the National Tourist Office. Yugoslavia, it says, was among the first countries to encourage naturists to pursue "their useful cause which contributes to a person's spiritual and physical well-being." So important is Yugoslavia in the whole naturist movement that in 1972 the World Naturist Congress chose to hold its convention there, the equivalent, we are to assume, of the American Medical Association deciding to meet in Boston or Rochester, Minnesota, or the Medieval Academy of America deciding to meet in Canterbury. Whatever the reason, there's something about European communism in general that seems interestingly hospitable to naturism. The reason is probably in part communism's readiness to do things that annoy religious institutions and other survivals of "feudal" values. Hungary, for example, seems rapidly catching up to Yugoslavia as a naturist paradise, and a large gathering of international naturists chose to honor it by assembling there in 1987. Even Poland, despite the troubles communism encounters there from the Church and the citizenry, goes in for a sur-   19 prising amount of naturism, the total number of devotees there being estimated as between 100,000 and 200,000.

20    I left the Director of Tourism quite buoyed up about the future of naturism. Since Yugoslavia already has some naturist towns, would there ultimately be naturist cities? And how about naturist countries? There dirty shows might consist of women on sleazy platforms slowly and slyly putting on clothes.

21    "Yugoslavia's 1,000-island Dalmatian Coast is the most beautiful in the world." So says the Lister Tours naturist holiday brochure, and for once a travel agency is not lying, or even exaggerating. Naturism is a success along the Balkan Adriatic because there nature is a success. The coastline is incredibly lovely — low hills, pine trees and palms, unpolluted water, benign dark blue sea, brilliant skies, caressing sun. There the squalid, which might threaten naturism, seems drained away, leaving only innocent beauty. You get the feeling that if naturism is grand and even (permit me) ennobling near Slano, it would be degrading near Camden or Detroit.

22    Sea and sky and sun, and after swimming and browning all day, all over, in the evening cold lobster with mayonnaise and the local light white wine. And never any wet bathing suits to hang up. Not a bad formula for something like heaven, an attainable version of super-pastoral.

## Evaluating the Text

1. Evaluate the reasons Fussell offers to explain why Americans are few and far between on the nude beaches of the Adriatic coast. What nationalities are the most frequent habituees of these beaches?
2. What dos and don'ts govern personal interactions while on a nude beach or at naturist resorts? What assumptions about embarrassment underlie these generally accepted, if never stated, codes of behavior?
3. How does Fussell take into account assumptions his readers might have about the kind of people who would want to frequent nude beaches? What evidence, details, and examples does Fussell offer to refute these assumptions?
4. How does Fussell's initial reaction to "taking it all off' reveal exactly the kind of mentality naturists wish to avoid? To what extent does Fussell seem to be aware of this?
5. Discuss the assumptions underlying the connotative and denotative meanings of the words having to do with nude beaches. For example, why is "naturist" preferred over "nudist"? What distinct meanings do the words "sunbathing," "sunning," and "sunbaking" have in the context of the cultures who use them? What implications does Fussell draw from the fact that Americans tend to favor euphemisms over Europeans — who more readily use the word *nude*? How do euphemisms function in the same way clothes do to conceal rather than reveal what is really taking place?

6. Explain the reasons why wearing jewelry or makeup is discouraged by naturists. What is the rationale behind this?
7. What connection does Fussell observe between naturism and activism on behalf of the environment or ecology? In your opinion, why would naturists also be environmental activists?

## Exploring Different Perspectives

1. Discuss the ritual overtones of separation, initiation, and return (found in the ceremony of the Kiowa's Sun Dance described in Gretel Ehrlich's "To Live in Two Worlds") as it governs the behavior of people who go to nude beaches along the coasts of the Adriatic Sea.
2. If faced with the choice of experiencing the "culture shock" of Fussell or that of Napoleon A. Chagnon (see "Doing Fieldwork among the Yąnomamö"), which would you choose and why?

## Extending Viewpoints through Writing

1. How do you feel about the phenomena Fussell is discussing? Is your reaction closer to that of Americans or to that of Europeans?
2. Have you ever had an occasion to "take it all off" on a beach? What was the experience like? If you have not, how do you think you would feel about being nude on a beach? If you knew the people on the beach, would it make you more or less reluctant to "take it all off"? Would it change your decision if the beach were inhabited only by members of your own sex?
3. Fussell, Natsume Soseki (*I Am a Cat*, Chapter 1); Amy Tan ("Jing-Mei Woo: Two Kinds," Chapter 1); Margaret Atwood ("Happy Endings," Chapter 3); and Josef Škvorecký ("An Insolvable Problem of Genetics," Chapter 5) all write with a sense of humor. In an essay, discuss how humor plays a part in revealing the authors' attitudes toward their subjects and toward themselves.

# Octavio Paz

# *The Day of the Dead*

---

*Octavio Paz, born on the outskirts of Mexico City in 1914, is a poet, essayist, and unequalled observer of Mexican society. He served as a Mexican diplomat in France and Japan and as Ambassador to India before resigning from the diplomatic service to protest the Tlatelolco Massacre (government massacre of 300 students in Mexico City) in 1968. His many volumes of poetry include* Sun Stone *(1958), a new reading of the Aztec myths;* Marcel Duchamp *(1968);* The Children of the Mire *(1974); and* The Monkey Grammarian *(1981). In 1990, Paz was awarded the Nobel Prize for Literature. As an essayist whose works have helped redefine the concept of Latin American culture, Paz wrote* The Other Mexico *(1972) and* The Labyrinth of Solitude, *translated by Lysander Kemp (1961), from which "The Day of the Dead" is taken.*

*Mexico was inhabited as far back as 20,000 B.C. Before the arrival of the Spanish in the early sixteenth century, great Indian civilizations, such as the Aztecs and Mayas, flourished. A wave of Spanish explorers, including Hernán Cortés, arrived in the 1500s, overthrew the Aztec empire, and turned Mexico into a colony of Spain, until Mexico achieved its independence in 1821. Although recently Mexico's economy has been on the rebound, previous cycles of economic instability and the earthquake that devastated Mexico City (one of the largest cities in the world with a population of nearly 17 million) in 1985, have led many to cross the border into the United States in hopes of finding work. In the following essay, Paz offers insight, conveyed with his typical stylistic grace and erudition, into the deep psychological needs met by fiestas in Mexican culture.*

1    The solitary Mexican loves fiestas and public gatherings. Any occasion for getting together will serve, any pretext to stop the flow of time and commemorate men and events with festivals and ceremonies. We are a ritual people, and this characteristic enriches both our imaginations and our sensibilities, which are equally sharp and alert. The art of the fiesta has been debased almost everywhere else, but not in Mexico. There are few places in the world where it is possible to take part in a spectacle like our great religious fiestas with their violent primary colors, their bizarre costumes and dances, their fireworks and ceremonies and their

inexhaustible welter of surprises: the fruit, candy, toys and other objects sold on these days in the plazas and open-air markets.

Our calendar is crowded with fiestas. There are certain days when the whole country, from the most remote villages to the largest cities, prays, shouts, feasts, gets drunk and kills, in honor of the Virgin of Guadalupe or Benito Juárez. Each year on the fifteenth of September, at eleven o'clock at night, we celebrate the fiesta of the *Grito*[1] in all the plazas of the Republic, and the excited crowds actually shout for a whole hour . . . the better, perhaps, to remain silent for the rest of the year. During the days before and after the twelfth of December,[2] time comes to a full stop, and instead of pushing us toward a deceptive tomorrow that is always beyond our reach, offers us a complete and perfect today of dancing and revelry, of communion with the most ancient and secret Mexico. Time is no longer succession, and becomes what it originally was and is: the present, in which past and future are reconciled.

But the fiestas which the Church and State provide for the country as a whole are not enough. The life of every city and village is ruled by a patron saint whose blessing is celebrated with devout regularity. Neighborhoods and trades also have their annual fiestas, their ceremonies and fairs. And each one of us — atheist, Catholic, or merely indifferent — has his own saint's day, which he observes every year. It is impossible to calculate how many fiestas we have and how much time and money we spend on them. I remember asking the mayor of a village near Mitla, several years ago, "What is the income of the village government?" "About 3,000 pesos a year. We are very poor. But the Governor and the Federal Government always help us to meet our expenses." "And how are the 3,000 pesos spent?" "Mostly on fiestas, señor. We are a small village, but we have two patron saints."

This reply is not surprising. Our poverty can be measured by the frequency and luxuriousness of our holidays. Wealthy countries have very few: there is neither the time nor the desire for them, and they are not necessary. The people have other things to do, and when they amuse themselves they do so in small groups. The modern masses are agglomerations of solitary individuals. On great occasions in Paris or New York, when the populace gathers in the squares or stadiums, the absence of people, in the sense of *a* people, is remarkable: there are couples and small groups, but they never form a living community in which the individual is at once dissolved and redeemed. But how could a poor Mexican live without the two or three annual fiestas that make up for his poverty and misery? Fiestas are our only luxury. They replace, and are perhaps better than, the theater and vacations, Anglo-Saxon weekends and cocktail parties, the bourgeois reception, the Mediterranean café.

[1]Padre Hidalgo's call-to-arms against Spain, 1810. — *Tr.*
[2]Fiesta of the Virgin of Guadalupe. — *Tr.*

5      In all of these ceremonies—national or local, trade or family—the Mexican opens out. They all give him a chance to reveal himself and to converse with God, country, friends or relations. During these days the silent Mexican whistles, shouts, sings, shoots off fireworks, discharges his pistol into the air. He discharges his soul. And his shout, like the rockets we love so much, ascends to the heavens, explodes into green, red, blue, and white lights, and falls dizzily to earth with a trail of golden sparks. This is the night when friends who have not exchanged more than the prescribed courtesies for months get drunk together, trade confidences, weep over the same troubles, discover that they are brothers, and sometimes, to prove it, kill each other. The night is full of songs and loud cries. The lover wakes up his sweetheart with an orchestra. There are jokes and conversations from balcony to balcony, sidewalk to sidewalk. Nobody talks quietly. Hats fly in the air. Laughter and curses ring like silver pesos. Guitars are brought out. Now and then, it is true, the happiness ends badly, in quarrels, insults, pistol shots, stabbings. But these too are part of the fiesta, for the Mexican does not seek amusement: he seeks to escape from himself, to leap over the wall of solitude that confines him during the rest of the year. All are possessed by violence and frenzy. Their souls explode like the colors and voices and emotions. Do they forget themselves and show their true faces? Nobody knows. The important thing is to go out, open a way, get drunk on noise, people, colors. Mexico is celebrating a fiesta. And this fiesta, shot through with lightning and delirium, is the brilliant reverse to our silence and apathy, our reticence and gloom.

6      According to the interpretation of French sociologists, the fiesta is an excess, an expense. By means of this squandering the community protects itself against the envy of the gods or of men. Sacrifices and offerings placate or buy off the gods and the patron saints. Wasting money and expending energy affirms the community's wealth in both. This luxury is a proof of health, a show of abundance and power. Or a magic trap. For squandering is an effort to attract abundance by contagion. Money calls to money. When life is thrown away it increases; the orgy, which is sexual expenditure, is also a ceremony of regeneration; waste gives strength. New Year celebrations, in every culture, signify something beyond the mere observance of a date on the calendar. The day is a pause: time is stopped, is actually annihilated. The rites that celebrate its death are intended to provoke its rebirth, because they mark not only the end of an old year but also the beginning of a new. Everything attracts its opposite. The fiesta's function, then, is more utilitarian than we think: waste attracts or promotes wealth, and is an investment like any other, except that the returns on it cannot be measured or counted. What is sought is potency, life, health. In this sense the fiesta, like the gift and the offering, is one of the most ancient of economic forms.

7      This interpretation has always seemed to me to be incomplete. The fiesta is by nature sacred, literally or figuratively, and above all it is the advent of the unusual. It is governed by its own special rules, that set it

apart from other days, and it has a logic, an ethic and even an economy that are often in conflict with everyday norms. It all occurs in an enchanted world: time is transformed to a mythical past or a total present; space, the scene of the fiesta, is turned into a gaily decorated world of its own; and the persons taking part cast off all human or social rank and become, for the moment, living images. And everything takes place as if it were not so, as if it were a dream. But whatever happens, our actions have a greater lightness, a different gravity. They take on other meanings and with them we contract new obligations. We throw down our burdens of time and reason.

In certain fiestas the very notion of order disappears. Chaos comes back and license rules. Anything is permitted: the customary hierarchies vanish, along with all social, sex, caste, and trade distinctions. Men disguise themselves as women, gentlemen as slaves, the poor as the rich. The army, the clergy, and the law are ridiculed. Obligatory sacrilege, ritual profanation is committed. Love becomes promiscuity. Sometimes the fiesta becomes a Black Mass. Regulations, habits and customs are violated. Respectable people put away the dignified expressions and conservative clothes that isolate them, dress up in gaudy colors, hide behind a mask, and escape from themselves. 8

Therefore the fiesta is not only an excess, a ritual squandering of the goods painfully accumulated during the rest of the year; it is also a revolt, a sudden immersion in the formless, in pure being. By means of the fiesta society frees itself from the norms it has established. It ridicules its gods, its principles, and its laws: it denies its own self. 9

The fiesta is a revolution in the most literal sense of the word. In the confusion that it generates, society is dissolved, is drowned, insofar as it is an organism ruled according to certain laws and principles. But it drowns in itself, in its own original chaos or liberty. Everything is united: good and evil, day and night, the sacred and the profane. Everything merges, loses shape and individuality and returns to the primordial mass. The fiesta is a cosmic experiment, an experiment in disorder, reuniting contradictory elements and principles in order to bring about a renascence of life. Ritual death promotes a rebirth; vomiting increases the appetite; the orgy, sterile in itself, renews the fertility of the mother or of the earth. The fiesta is a return to a remote and undifferentiated state, prenatal or presocial. It is a return that is also a beginning, in accordance with the dialectic that is inherent in social processes. 10

The group emerges purified and strengthened from this plunge into chaos. It has immersed itself in its own origins, in the womb from which it came. To express it in another way, the fiesta denies society as an organic system of differentiated forms and principles, but affirms it as a source of creative energy. It is a true "re-creation," the opposite of the "recreation" characterizing modern vacations, which do not entail any rites or ceremonies whatever and are as individualistic and sterile as the world that invented them. 11

Society communes with itself during the fiesta. Its members return to 12 original chaos and freedom. Social structures break down and new relationships, unexpected rules, capricious hierarchies are created. In the general disorder everybody forgets himself and enters into otherwise forbidden situations and places. The bounds between audience and actors, officials and servants, are erased. Everybody takes part in the fiesta, everybody is caught up in its whirlwind. Whatever its mood, its character, its meaning, the fiesta is participation, and this trait distinguishes it from all other ceremonies and social phenomena. Lay or religious, orgy or saturnalia, the fiesta is a social act based on the full participation of all its celebrants.

13    Thanks to the fiesta the Mexican opens out, participates, communes with his fellows and with the values that give meaning to his religious or political existence. And it is significant that a country as sorrowful as ours should have so many and such joyous fiestas. Their frequency, their brilliance and excitement, the enthusiasm with which we take part, all suggest that without them we would explode. They free us, if only momentarily, from the thwarted impulses, the inflammable desires that we carry within us. But the Mexican fiesta is not merely a return to an original state of formless and normless liberty: the Mexican is not seeking to return, but to escape from himself, to exceed himself. Our fiestas are explosions. Life and death, joy and sorrow, music and mere noise are united, not to re-create or recognize themselves, but to swallow each other up. There is nothing so joyous as a Mexican fiesta, but there is also nothing so sorrowful. Fiesta night is also a night of mourning.

14    If we hide within ourselves in our daily lives, we discharge ourselves in the whirlwind of the fiesta. It is more than an opening out: we rend ourselves open. Everything—music, love, friendship—ends in tumult and violence. The frenzy of our festivals shows the extent to which our solitude closes us off from communication with the world. We are familiar with delirium, with songs and shouts, with the monologue . . . but not with the dialogue. Our fiestas, like our confidences, our loves, our attempts to reorder our society, are violent breaks with the old or the established. Each time we try to express ourselves we have to break with ourselves. And the fiesta is only one example, perhaps the most typical, of this violent break. It is not difficult to name others, equally revealing: our games, which are always a going to extremes, often mortal; our profligate spending, the reverse of our timid investments and business enterprises; our confessions. The somber Mexican, closed up in himself, suddenly explodes, tears open his breast and reveals himself, though not without a certain complacency, and not without a stopping place in the shameful or terrible mazes of his intimacy. We are not frank, but our sincerity can reach extremes that horrify a European. The explosive, dramatic, sometimes even suicidal manner in which we strip ourselves, surrender ourselves, is evidence that something inhibits and suffocates us. Something impedes us from being. And since we cannot or dare not confront our own selves, we resort to the fiesta. It fires us into the void; it

is a drunken rapture that burns itself out, a pistol shot in the air, a sky-rocket.

*Translated by Lysander Kemp*

## Evaluating the Text

1. What factors contribute to the popularity of fiestas in Mexico, especially in relationship to the Mexican national character, as described by Paz?
2. In what way are people's experience of time during the fiesta period qualitatively different from their experience of time during the rest of the year?
3. How would you characterize Paz's understanding of the underlying psychological and cultural motivations for Mexican fiestas? For example, how is the love of fiestas related to what Paz calls the "solitude" of Mexicans?
4. How does Paz's use of economic information as to the cost and frequency of fiestas help explain the extraordinary importance they play in Mexican life?
5. In what sense does a fiesta provide an opportunity for the solitary individual to be "at once resolved and redeemed"? What do you think Paz means by this?
6. Evaluate the explanation for fiestas offered by French sociologists. In your opinion, what would be an "American" version of such conspicuous squandering of money ill-afforded? Would the interpretations be the same? If not, in what ways might they differ?
7. How do Paz's comparisons between Mexican attitudes toward celebrations, life, and death with those of Europeans and North Americans make it easier for his readers to understand his analysis?

## Exploring Different Perspectives

1. In what ways does the fiesta create its own world, set off from time, demarcated in space, and encourage forms of behavior normally not permitted in everyday life? To what extent are fiestas (involving as they do costumes, dances, ceremonies, and expenditure of material possessions and energy) similar to and different from the Kiowa Indian Sun Dance (see Gretel Ehrlich's "To Live in Two Worlds")? In what sense are the goals of both of these ritual celebrations the same?
2. Drawing on the research of Robert Levine and Ellen Wolff ("Social Time: the Heartbeat of Culture"), explore how the experience of time during the fiesta period (what might be termed "ritual time") qualitatively differs from "clock time" (normal time as it is experienced during the rest of the year).
3. Discuss the psychology of sacrificing what normally would be conserved, to placate the gods and attract abundance, as it is revealed in Paz's essay and in Bessie Head's "Looking for a Rain God."

# Extending Viewpoints through Writing

1. Have you ever been at a party that came close in spirit to the Mexican fiesta where people use the occasion to renew friendships, get drunk together, and discover kinships? If so, describe your experiences and discuss the similarities and differences in terms of emotional transformation such celebrations encourage.
2. If you are familiar with Mardi Gras in Brazil or in New Orleans, or the Ash Wednesday Celebration in Trinidad, describe how it serves many of the same purposes as the Mexican fiesta.
3. To what extent do celebrations such as weddings, baptisms, bar mitzvahs, and vacations serve much the same function in the United States as fiestas do in Mexico? Discuss the similarities and differences.

# Gino Del Guercio

# *The Secrets of Haiti's Living Dead*

*Gino Del Guercio is a national science writer for United Press International and was a MACY fellow at Boston's television station WGBH. "The Secrets of Haiti's Living Dead" was first published in* Harvard Magazine *(January/February 1986). In 1982, Wade Davis, a Harvard-trained ethnobotanist, whose exploits formed the basis for this article, traveled into the Haitian countryside to investigate accounts of Zombies—the infamous living dead of Haitian folklore. Davis's research led him to obtain the poison associated with the process. His findings were first presented in* The Serpent and the Rainbow *(1988), a work that served as the basis for the movie of the same name, directed by Wes Craven, and later in* Passage of Darkness *(1988). Davis is currently research associate in ethnobotany at the New York Botanical Garden.*

*The Republic of Haiti in the West Indies occupies the western third of the island of Hispaniola, which it shares with the Dominican Republic. French rule of Haiti lasted from 1697, until Toussaint l'Ouverture, a former slave, led Haiti to become the second independent nation in the Americas, in 1804. For the most part, Haiti's history has been fraught with intrigue and violence. In 1957, François "Papa Doc" Duvalier established a dictatorship and was succeeded by his son Jean Claude ("Baby Doc"), who fled the country in 1986. A commitment to restoring democracy, despite attempts at military coups, has characterized successive governments since 1988. In December 1990, the Reverend Jean Bertrand Aristide, a champion of the poor, was elected head of the government in Haiti's first democratic elections. Guercio's report reveals the extent to which Haitian life is controlled by voodoo, a religious belief, West African in origin, that is characterized by induced trances and magical rituals. Until this century, Voodoo was the state religion and continues to flourish despite opposition from Roman Catholicism, the other major religion in Haiti.*

Five years ago, a man walked into l'Estère, a village in central Haiti, approached a peasant woman named Angelina Narcisse, and identified himself as her brother Clairvius. If he had not introduced himself using a boyhood nickname and mentioned facts only intimate family members knew, she would not have believed him. Because, eighteen years earlier, Angelina had stood in a small cemetery north of her village and watched as her brother Clairvius was buried.

2    The man told Angelina he remembered that night well. He knew when he was lowered into his grave, because he was fully conscious, although he could not speak or move. As the earth was thrown over his coffin, he felt as if he were floating over the grave. The scar on his right cheek, he said, was caused by a nail driven through his casket.

3    The night he was buried, he told Angelina, a voodoo priest raised him from the grave. He was beaten with a sisal whip and carried off to a sugar plantation in northern Haiti where, with other zombies, he was forced to work as a slave. Only with the death of the zombie master were they able to escape, and Narcisse eventually returned home.

4    Legend has it that zombies are the living dead, raised from their graves and animated by malevolent voodoo sorcerers, usually for some evil purpose. Most Haitians believe in zombies, and Narcisse's claim is not unique. At about the time he reappeared, in 1980, two women turned up in other villages saying they were zombies. In the same year, in northern Haiti, the local peasants claimed to have found a group of zombies wandering aimlessly in the fields.

5    But Narcisse's case was different in one crucial respect; it was documented. His death had been recorded by doctors at the American-directed Schweitzer Hospital in Deschapelles. On April 30, 1962, hospital records show, Narcisse walked into the hospital's emergency room spitting up blood. He was feverish and full of aches. His doctors could not diagnose his illness, and his symptoms grew steadily worse. Three days after he entered the hospital, according to the records, he died. The attending physicians, an American among them, signed his death certificate. His body was placed in cold storage for twenty hours, and then he was buried. He said he remembered hearing his doctors pronounce him dead while his sister wept at his bedside.

6    At the Centre de Psychiatrie et Neurologie in Port-au-Prince, Dr. Lamarque Douyon, a Haitian-born, Canadian-trained psychiatrist, has been systematically investigating all reports of zombies since 1961. Though convinced zombies were real, he had been unable to find a scientific explanation for the phenomenon. He did not believe zombies were people raised from the dead, but that did not make them any less interesting. He speculated that victims were only made to *look* dead, probably by means of a drug that dramatically slowed metabolism. The victim was buried, dug up within a few hours, and somehow reawakened.

7    The Narcisse case provided Douyon with evidence strong enough to warrant a request for assistance from colleagues in New York. Douyon wanted to find an ethnobotanist, a traditional-medicines expert, who could track down the zombie potion he was sure existed. Aware of the medical potential of a drug that could dramatically lower metabolism, a group organized by the late Dr. Nathan Kline — a New York psychiatrist

and pioneer in the field of psychopharmacology—raised the funds necessary to send someone to investigate.

The search for that someone led to the Harvard Botanical Museum, one of the world's foremost institutes of ethnobiology. Its director, Richard Evans Schultes, Jeffrey professor of biology, had spent thirteen years in the tropics studying native medicines. Some of his best-known work is the investigation of curare, the substance used by the nomadic people of the Amazon to poison their darts. Refined into a powerful muscle relaxant called D-tubocurarine, it is now an essential component of the anesthesia used during almost all surgery.

Schultes would have been a natural for the Haitian investigation, but he was too busy. He recommended another Harvard ethnobotanist for the assignment, Wade Davis, a 28-year-old Canadian pursuing a doctorate in biology.

Davis grew up in the tall pine forests of British Columbia and entered Harvard in 1971, influenced by a Life magazine story on the student strike of 1969. Before Harvard, the only Americans he had known were draft dodgers, who seemed very exotic. "I used to fight forest fires with them," Davis says. "Like everybody else, I thought America was where it was at. And I wanted to go to Harvard because of that Life article. When I got there, I realized it wasn't quite what I had in mind."

Davis took a course from Schultes, and when he decided to go to South America to study plants, he approached his professor for guidance. "He was an extraordinary figure," Davis remembers. "He was a man who had done it all. He had lived alone for years in the Amazon." Schultes sent Davis to the rain forest with two letters of introduction and two pieces of advice: wear a pith helmet and try ayahuasca, a powerful hallucinogenic vine. During that expedition and others, Davis proved himself an "outstanding field man," says his mentor. Now, in early 1982, Schultes called him into his office and asked if he had plans for spring break.

"I always took to Schultes's assignments like a plant takes to water," says Davis, tall and blond, with inquisitive blue eyes. "Whatever Schultes told me to do, I did. His letters of introduction opened up a whole world." This time the world was Haiti.

Davis knew nothing about the Caribbean island—and nothing about African traditions, which serve as Haiti's cultural basis. He certainly did not believe in zombies. "I thought it was a lark," he says now.

Davis landed in Haiti a week after his conversation with Schultes, armed with a hypothesis about how the zombie drug—if it existed—might be made. Setting out to explore, he discovered a country materially impoverished, but rich in culture and mystery. He was impressed by the cohesion of Haitian society; he found none of the crime, social disorder, and rampant drug and alcohol abuse so common in many of the other Caribbean islands. The cultural wealth and cohesion, he believes, spring from the country's turbulent history.

During the French occupation of the late eighteenth century, 370,000

African-born slaves were imported to Haiti between 1780 and 1790. In 1791, the black population launched one of the few successful slave revolts in history, forming secret societies and overcoming first the French plantation owners and then a detachment of troops from Napoleon's army, sent to quell the revolt. For the next hundred years Haiti was the only independent black republic in the Caribbean, populated by people who did not forget their African heritage. "You can almost argue that Haiti is more African than Africa," Davis says. "When the west coast of Africa was being disrupted by colonialism and the slave trade, Haiti was essentially left alone. The amalgam of beliefs in Haiti is unique, but it's very, very African."

16      Davis discovered that the vast majority of Haitian peasants practice voodoo, a sophisticated religion with African roots. Says Davis, "It was immediately obvious that the stereotypes of voodoo weren't true. Going around the countryside, I found clues to a whole complex social world." Vodounists believe they communicate directly with, indeed are often possessed by, the many spirits who populate the everyday world. Vodoun society is a system of education, law, and medicine; it embodies a code of ethics that regulates social behavior. In rural areas, secret vodoun societies, much like those found on the west coast of Africa, are as much or more in control of everyday life as the Haitian government.

17      Although most outsiders dismissed the zombie phenomenon as folklore, some early investigators, convinced of its reality, tried to find a scientific explanation. The few who sought a zombie drug failed. Nathan Kline, who helped finance Davis's expedition, had searched unsuccessfully, as had Lamarque Douyon, the Haitian psychiatrist. Zora Neale Hurston, an American black woman, may have come closest. An anthropological pioneer, she went to Haiti in the Thirties, studied vodoun society, and wrote a book on the subject, *Tell My Horse*, first published in 1938. She knew about the secret societies and was convinced zombies were real, but if a powder existed, she too failed to obtain it.

18      Davis obtained a sample in a few weeks.

19      He arrived in Haiti with the names of several contacts. A BBC reporter familiar with the Narcisse case had suggested he talk with Marcel Pierre. Pierre owned the Eagle Bar, a bordello in the city of Saint Marc. He was also a voodoo sorcerer and had supplied the BBC with a physiologically active powder of unknown ingredients. Davis found him willing to negotiate. He told Pierre he was a representative of "powerful but anonymous interests in New York," willing to pay generously for the priest's services, provided no questions were asked. Pierre agreed to be helpful for what Davis will only say was a "sizable sum." Davis spent a day watching Pierre gather the ingredients — including human bones — and grind them together with mortar and pestle. However, from his knowledge of poison, Davis knew immediately that nothing in the formula could produce the powerful effects of zombification.

20      Three weeks later, Davis went back to the Eagle Bar, where he found

Pierre sitting with three associates. Davis challenged him. He called him a charlatan. Enraged, the priest gave him a second vial, claiming that this was the real poison. Davis pretended to pour the powder into his palm and rub it into his skin. "You're a dead man," Pierre told him, and he might have been, because this powder proved to be genuine. But, as the substance had not actually touched him, Davis was able to maintain his bravado, and Pierre was impressed. He agreed to make the poison and show Davis how it was done.

The powder, which Davis keeps in a small vial, looks like dry black  21
dirt. It contains parts of toads, sea worms, lizards, tarantulas, and human bones. (To obtain the last ingredient, he and Pierre unearthed a child's grave on a nocturnal trip to the cemetery.) The poison is rubbed into the victim's skin. Within hours he begins to feel nauseated and has difficulty breathing. A pins-and-needles sensation afflicts his arms and legs, then progresses to the whole body. The subject becomes paralyzed; his lips turn blue for lack of oxygen. Quickly — sometimes within six hours — his metabolism is lowered to a level almost indistinguishable from death.

As Davis discovered, making the poison is an inexact science. Ingre-  22
dients varied in the five samples he eventually acquired, although the active agents were always the same. And the poison came with no guarantee. Davis speculates that sometimes instead of merely paralyzing the victim, the compound kills him. Sometimes the victim suffocates in the coffin before he can be resurrected. But clearly the potion works well enough often enough to make zombies more than a figment of Haitian imagination.

Analysis of the powder produced another surprise. "When I went  23
down to Haiti originally," says Davis, "my hypothesis was that the formula would contain *con̆combre zombi*, the 'zombie's cucumber,' which is a *Datura* plant. I thought somehow *Datura* was used in putting people down." *Datura* is a powerful psychoactive plant, found in West Africa as well as other tropical areas and used there in ritual as well as criminal activities. Davis had found *Datura* growing in Haiti. Its popular name suggested the plant was used in creating zombies.

But, says Davis, "there were a lot of problems with the *Datura*  24
hypothesis. Partly it was a. question of how the drug was administered. *Datura* would create a stupor in huge doses, but it just wouldn't produce the kind of immobility that was key. These people had to appear dead, and there aren't many drugs that will do that."

One of the ingredients Pierre included in the second formula was a  25
dried fish, a species of puffer or blowfish, common to most parts of the world. It gets its name from its ability to fill itself with water and swell to several times its normal size when threatened by predators. Many of these fish contain a powerful poison known as tetrodotoxin. One of the most powerful nonprotein poisons known to man, tetrodotoxin turned up in every sample of zombie powder that Davis acquired.

Numerous well-documented accounts of puffer fish poisoning exist,  26 but the most famous accounts come from the Orient, where *fugu* fish, a species of puffer, is considered a delicacy. In Japan, special chefs are licensed to prepare *fugu*. The chef removes enough poison to make the fish nonlethal, yet enough remains to create exhilarating physiological effects — tingles up and down the spine, mild prickling of the tongue and lips, euphoria. Several dozen Japanese die each year, having bitten off more than they should have.

27    "When I got hold of the formula and saw it was the *fugu* fish, that suddenly threw open the whole Japanese literature," says Davis. Case histories of *fugu* poisoning read like accounts of zombification. Victims remain conscious but unable to speak or move. A man who had "died" after eating *fugu* recovered seven days later in the morgue. Several summers ago, another Japanese poisoned by *fugu* revived after he was nailed into his coffin. "Almost all of Narcisse's symptoms correlated. Even strange things such as the fact that he said he was conscious and could hear himself pronounced dead. Stuff that I thought had to be magic, that seemed crazy. But, in fact, that is what people who get *fugu*-fish poisoning experience."

28    Davis was certain he had solved the mystery. But far from being the end of his investigation, identifying the poison was, in fact, its starting point. "The drug alone didn't make zombies," he explains. "Japanese victims of puffer-fish poisoning don't become zombies, they become poison victims. All the drug could do was set someone up for a whole series of psychological pressures that would be rooted in the culture. I wanted to know why zombification was going on," he says.

29    He sought a cultural answer, an explanation rooted in the structure and beliefs of Haitian society. Was zombification simply a random criminal activity? He thought not. He had discovered that Clairvius Narcisse and "Ti Femme," a second victim he interviewed, were village pariahs. Ti Femme was regarded as a thief. Narcisse had abandoned his children and deprived his brother of land that was rightfully his. Equally suggestive, Narcisse claimed that his aggrieved brother had sold him to a *bokor*, a voodoo priest who dealt in black magic; he made cryptic reference to having been tried and found guilty by the "masters of the land."

30    Gathering poisons from various parts of the country, Davis had come into direct contact with the vodoun secret societies. Returning to the anthropological literature on Haiti and pursuing his contacts with informants, Davis came to understand the social matrix within which zombies were created.

31    Davis's investigations uncovered the importance of the secret societies. These groups trace their origins to the bands of escaped slaves that organized the revolt against the French in the late eighteenth century. Open to both men and women, the societies control specific territories of the country. Their meetings take place at night, and in many rural parts of Haiti the drums and wild celebrations that characterize the gatherings can be heard for miles.

Davis believes the secret societies are responsible for policing their 32
communities, and the threat of zombification is one way they maintain
order. Says Davis, "Zombification has a material basis, but it also has a
societal logic." To the uninitiated, the practice may appear a random
criminal activity, but in rural vodoun society, it is exactly the opposite—
a sanction imposed by recognized authorities, a form of capital punishment. For rural Haitians, zombification is an even more severe punishment than death, because it deprives the subject of his most valued
possessions: his free will and independence.

The vodounists believe that when a person dies, his spirit splits into 33
several different parts. If a priest is powerful enough, the spiritual aspect
that controls a person's character and individuality, known as *ti bon ange*,
the "good little angel," can be captured and the corporeal aspect, deprived of its will, held as a slave.

From studying the medical literature on tetrodotoxin poisoning, 34
Davis discovered that if a victim survives the first few hours of the
poisoning, he is likely to recover fully from the ordeal. The subject
simply revives spontaneously. But zombies remain without will, in a
trance-like state, a condition vodounists attribute to the power of the
priest. Davis thinks it possible that the psychological trauma of zombification may be augmented by *Datura* or some other drug; he thinks
zombies may be fed a *Datura* paste that accentuates their disorientation.
Still, he puts the material basis of zombification in perspective: "Tetrodotoxin and *Datura* are only templates on which cultural forces and
beliefs may be amplified a thousand times."

Davis has not been able to discover how prevalent zombification is in 35
Haiti. "How many zombies there are is not the question," he says. He
compares it to capital punishment in the United States: "It doesn't really
matter how many people are electrocuted, as long as it's a possibility."
As a sanction in Haiti, the fear is not of zombies, it's of becoming one.

Davis attributes his success in solving the zombie mystery to his 36
approach. He went to Haiti with an open mind and immersed himself in
the culture. "My intuition unhindered by biases served me well," he
says. "I didn't make any judgments." He combined this attitude with
what he had learned earlier from his experiences in the Amazon.
"Schultes's lesson is to go and live with the Indians as an Indian." Davis
was able to participate in the vodoun society to a surprising degree,
eventually even penetrating one of the Bizango societies and dancing in
their nocturnal rituals. His appreciation of Haitian culture is apparent.
"Everybody asks me how did a white person get this information? To ask
the question means you don't understand Haitians—they don't judge
you by the color of your skin."

As a result of the exotic nature of his discoveries, Davis has gained a 37
certain notoriety. He plans to complete his dissertation soon, but he has
already finished writing a popular account of his adventures. To be
published in January by Simon and Schuster, it is called *The Serpent and*

*the Rainbow*, after the serpent that vodounists believe created the earth and the rainbow spirit it married. Film rights have already been optioned; in October Davis went back to Haiti with a screenwriter. But Davis takes the notoriety in stride. "All this attention is funny," he says. "For years, not just me, but all Schultes's students have had extraordinary adventures in the line of work. The adventure is not the end point, it's just along the way of getting the data. At the Botanical Museum, Schultes created a world unto itself. We didn't think we were doing anything above the ordinary. I still don't think we do. And you know," he adds, "the Haiti episode does not begin to compare to what others have accomplished—particularly Schultes himself."

## *Evaluating the Text*

1. To what extent does Guercio's account gain credibility because he begins with the mysterious case of Clairvius Narcisse? How is Narcisse's identification by his sister intended to put the case beyond all doubt and leave the process of zombification as the only possible explanation for his otherwise inexplicable "death"?

2. Why is it important to Guercio's account that he mentions physicians from the United States as well as Haitian doctors certified the "death" of Clairvius Narcisse? What is Guercio's attitude toward this phenomena? How is this attitude revealed in the way he constructs his report?

3. What motivations played a part in the quest to find an answer to this mystery? What was Wade Davis's situation at the time Richard Evans Schultes selected him to go to Haiti? Why would an ethnobotanist be required for research of this kind?

4. What is the relationship between the vodoun religion and African tribal customs? Why is it important that Haiti was the only independent black republic in the Caribbean, populated by a people who launched one of the few successful slave revolts in history?

5. What is the relationship between the process by which zombies are made and the Haitian religious belief that at death the soul splits into several parts and that powerful vodoun priests can control a person if they can capture the part known as the *ti bon ange* (the "good little angel")? Why is one of the crucial elements of the process of zombification a belief on the part of the victim that he or she no longer has free will?

6. How does the threat of zombification serve as a preventative measure that ensures social control in deterring crimes against the community? How did it operate in the cases of Clairvius Narcisse and "Ti Femme"? In what ways is the reality of the social mechanism of zombification quite different from how it has been presented in movies and popular culture?

7. What kinds of independent confirmation of the effects of tetrodotoxin, a potent neurotoxin that drastically reduces metabolism and produces paralysis, did Davis discover in his research on the effects of Japanese victims of *fugu* fish poisoning?

## *Exploring Different Perspectives*

1. After reading Pico Iyer's "Perfect Strangers," speculate on the differences between Japanese and Haitian cultures that would explain why those

Japanese who have been lucky enough to recover from their dining encounters with *fugu* fish, containing the powerful poison tetrodotoxin, do not become zombies, and usually resume a normal life. How do the social processes and different religious beliefs concerning the control of a person's soul produce in Haiti what would not be produced in Japan?

2. Compare and contrast the experiences of Davis to those of Napoleon A. Chagnon (see "Doing Fieldwork among the Yąnomamö") in terms of the persistence, adaptability, and imagination that both researchers displayed in pursuing their respective objectives. Compare the difficulties Chagnon and Davis faced in terms of physical conditions, unwillingness of people to help, and the vast cultural differences between the Yąnomamö and the Haitians.

## *Extending Viewpoints through Writing*

1. If you are familiar with or interested in the processes by which various religious cults enlist and program their members, you might compare their methods to those of the vodoun priests in terms of positive and negative reinforcement of psychological, sociological, and physiological conditioning.

2. If you have had the opportunity to see the movie *The Serpent and the Rainbow* (1988), directed by Wes Craven, you might wish to compare its representation of the events described in this article or Wade Davis's book *The Serpent and the Rainbow* (1985). For further research on this subject, you might consult Wade Davis, *Passage of Darkness: The Ethnobiology of the Haitian Zombie* (1988), an in-depth study of the political, social, and botanical mechanisms of zombification.

3. For a research project, you might pursue the fascinating interconnections between François Duvalier's rise to political power (president from 1957 until his succession by his son, Jean-Claude Duvalier) in Haiti and his prior activities as a physician, voudoun priest, and well-regarded anthropologist.

# Bessie Head

# *Looking for a Rain God*

---

*Bessie Head was born of mixed parentage in Pietermaritzburg, South Africa, in 1937. She was taken from her mother at birth, raised by foster parents until she was thirteen, and then placed in a mission orphanage. In 1961, newly married, she left South Africa to escape apartheid and settled on an agricultural commune in Serowe, Botswana, where she lived until her death in 1986. Among her publications are the novels* When Rain Clouds Gather *(1969);* Maru *(1971);* A Question of Power *(1974), acclaimed as one of the first psychological accounts of a black woman's experience; and* A Collector of Treasures and Other Botswana Village Tales *(1977), from which "Looking for a Rain God" is taken. She is also the author of two histories,* Serowe: Village of the Rain Wind *(1981) and* A Bewitched Crossroad *(1985). "Looking for a Rain God" is based on a shocking local newspaper report that dramatizes the enduring power of ancient tribal rituals and their conflict with contemporary codes of behavior in African life.*

*Located in South-Central Africa, Botswana became independent from British rule in 1966. Because of its land-locked location, Botswana continues to be economically dependent on South Africa (whose apartheid policy it denounces, see p. 412) and Zimbabwe, which controls railroad routes through Botswana. Religious practices are equally divided between Christianity and traditional tribal beliefs. The conditions of drought so graphically described by Bessie Head in her 1977 story were again confronted by the country during six successive years of drought between 1981 and 1987.*

1      It is lonely at the lands where the people go to plough. These lands are vast clearings in the bush, and the wild bush is lonely too. Nearly all the lands are within walking distance from the village. In some parts of the bush where the underground water is very near the surface, people made little rest camps for themselves and dug shallow wells to quench their thirst while on their journey to their own lands. They experienced all kinds of things once they left the village. They could rest at shady watering places full of lush, tangled trees with delicate pale-gold and purple wildflowers springing up between soft green moss and the children could hunt around for wild figs and any berries that might be in season. But from 1958, a seven-year drought fell upon the land and even

the watering places began to look as dismal as the dry open thornbush country; the leaves of the trees curled up and withered; the moss became dry and hard and, under the shade of the tangled trees, the ground turned a powdery black and white, because there was no rain. People said rather humorously that if you tried to catch the rain in a cup it would only fill a teaspoon. Toward the beginning of the seventh year of drought, the summer had become an anguish to live through. The air was so dry and moisture-free that it burned the skin. No one knew what to do to escape the heat and tragedy was in the air. At the beginning of that summer, a number of men just went out of their homes and hung themselves to death from trees. The majority of the people had lived off crops, but for two years past they had all returned from the lands with only their rolled-up skin blankets and cooking utensils. Only the charlatans, incanters, and witch doctors made a pile of money during this time because people were always turning to them in desperation for little talismans and herbs to rub on the plough for the crops to grow and the rain to fall.

The rains were late that year. They came in early November, with a 2 promise of good rain. It wasn't the full, steady downpour of the years of good rain but thin, scanty, misty rain. It softened the earth and a rich growth of green things sprang up everywhere for the animals to eat. People were called to the center of the village to hear the proclamation of the beginning of the ploughing season; they stirred themselves and whole families began to move off to the lands to plough.

The family of the old man, Mokgobja, were among those who left 3 early for the lands. They had a donkey cart and piled everything onto it, Mokgobja — who was over seventy years old; two girls, Neo and Boseyong; their mother Tiro and an unmarried sister, Nesta; and the father and supporter of the family, Ramadi, who drove the donkey cart. In the rush of the first hope of rain, the man, Ramadi, and the two women, cleared the land of thornbush and then hedged their vast ploughing area with this same thornbush to protect the future crop from the goats they had brought along for milk. They cleared out and deepened the old well with its pool of muddy water and still in this light, misty rain, Ramadi inspanned two oxen and turned the earth over with a hand plough.

The land was ready and ploughed, waiting for the crops. At night, the 4 earth was alive with insects singing and rustling about in search of food. But suddenly, by mid-November, the rain flew away; the rain clouds fled away and left the sky bare. The sun danced dizzily in the sky, with a strange cruelty. Each day the land was covered in a haze of mist as the sun sucked up the last drop of moisture out of the earth. The family sat down in despair, waiting and waiting. Their hopes had run so high; the goats had started producing milk, which they had eagerly poured on their porridge, now they ate plain porridge with no milk. It was impossible to plant the corn, maize, pumpkin, and watermelon seeds in the dry earth. They sat the whole day in the shadow of the huts and even stopped thinking, for the rain had fled away. Only the children, Neo and Boseyong, were quite happy in their little-girl world. They carried on with their game of making house like their mother and chattered to each other in light, soft tones. They made children from sticks around which they tied rags, and scolded them severely in an exact imitation of their own mother. Their voices could be heard scolding the day long: "You stupid thing, when I send you to draw water, why do you spill half of it out of the bucket!" "You stupid thing! Can't you mind the porridge pot without letting the porridge burn!" And then they would beat the rag dolls on their bottoms with severe expressions.

5      The adults paid no attention to this; they did not even hear the funny chatter; they sat waiting for rain; their nerves were stretched to break-ing-point willing the rain to fall out of the sky. Nothing was important, beyond that. All their animals had been sold during the bad years to purchase food, and of all their herd only two goats were left. It was the women of the family who finally broke down under the strain of waiting for rain. It was really the two women who caused the death of the little girls. Each night they started a weird, high-pitched wailing that began on a low, mournful note and whipped up to a frenzy. Then they would stamp their feet and shout as though they had lost their heads. The men sat quiet and self-controlled; it was important for men to maintain their self control at all times but their nerve was breaking too. They knew the women were haunted by the starvation of the coming year.

6      Finally, an ancient memory stirred in the old man, Mokgobja. When he was very young and the customs of the ancestors still ruled the land, he had been witness to a rain-making ceremony. And he came alive a little, struggling to recall the details which had been buried by years and years of prayer in a Christian church. As soon as the mists cleared a little, he began consulting in whispers with his youngest son, Ramadi. There was, he said, a certain rain god who accepted only the sacrifice of the bodies of children. Then the rain would fall; then the crops would grow, he said. He explained the ritual and as he talked, his memory became a conviction and he began to talk with unshakable authority. Ramadi's nerves were smashed by the nightly wailing of the women and soon the two men began whispering with the two women. The children continued their game: "You stupid thing! How could you have lost the money on the way to the shop! You must have been playing again!"

7      After it was all over and the bodies of the two little girls had been spread across the land, the rain did not fall. Instead, there was a deathly silence at night and the devouring heat of the sun by day. A terror, extreme and deep, overwhelmed the whole family. They packed, rolling up their skin blankets and pots, and fled back to the village.

8      People in the village soon noted the absence of the two little girls. They had died at the lands and were buried there, the family said. But people noted their ashen, terror-stricken faces and a murmur arose.

What had killed the children, they wanted to know? And the family replied that they had just died. And people said amongst themselves that it was strange that the two deaths had occurred at the same time. And there was a feeling of great unease at the unnatural looks of the family. Soon the police came around. The family told them the same story of death and burial at the lands. They did not know what the children had died of. So the police asked to see the graves. At this, the mother of the children broke down and told everything.

Throughout that terrible summer the story of the children hung like a   9
dark cloud of sorrow over the village, and the sorrow was not assuaged when the old man and Ramadi were sentenced to death for ritual murder. All they had on the statute books was that ritual murder was against the law and must be stamped out with the death penalty. The subtle story of strain and starvation and breakdown was inadmissible evidence at court; but all the people who lived off crops knew in their hearts that only a hair's breadth had saved them from sharing a fate similar to that of the Mokgobja family. They could have killed something to make the rain fall.

## Evaluating the Text

1. Why doesn't Head withhold knowledge of the ending in telling this story? How does knowing what happened shift the focus of the story into an attempt to try to understand how it happened?

2. Why is it significant that the events in this brief story actually occurred over a period of seven years? How does knowing this change your initial reaction?

3. Why is it important that the events described in this story take place, for the most part, far from the original village where Mokgobja and his family had lived?

4. When the potions and talismans bought as offerings for the gods, in exchange for rain, fail, why is it significant that some of the men in the village hang themselves? What insight does this give you into the depths of desperation and despair that have befallen everyone in the village?

5. How does the author lay the psychological groundwork for what otherwise would come as a shock—the choice of the two young girls in the family as sacrificial victims? Look carefully at how the girls must appear to everyone else in the family, especially in a culture where everyone, in order to survive, must contribute to the welfare of all. Looked at in this way, how do details such as their sloppiness (spilling food or water) and disobedience contribute to the family's decision to kill them in exchange for rain? How do the games Neo and Boseyong play provide further insight into how they are already being treated by the adults?

6. How does overwhelming stress reactivate a belief in rituals that lie just below the surface of collective tribal memory? From the details concerning the slaughter and dismemberment of the girls, how, in your opinion, was this ritual supposed to have worked?

7. How does the story involve a conflict between the two opposite value

systems of latent tribal beliefs and a superficial adherence to Christian religious practices?

8. Despite the fact that the police respond, as representatives of Neo and Boseyong and the social order, and execute Mokgobja and Ramadi for killing their children, why is it significant that Head ends the story with the statement that the other villagers "could have killed something to make the rain fall"? What does this tell you about Head's attitude toward the events in the story?

## Exploring Different Perspectives

1. How in both this story set in Botswana and in Guercio's account of voodoo in Haiti are officially unsanctioned rituals resorted to in times of extreme political, environmental, and psychological stress—in situations where faith in the powers that be fails?

2. Explore the assumptions in this story and in Gino Del Guerico's "The Secrets of Haiti's Living Dead" that the bones of the dead, especially those of children, are imbued with extraordinary magical powers.

3. How is the tribal notion of time in Botswana different from ordinary "clock time"? For example, why is the season rather than the day the basic unit of measurement? You may wish to compare the concept of what is considered early (as in early in the planting season) with the results of inquiries by Robert Levine and Ellen Wolff in Brazil and Japan in "Social Time: the Heartbeat of Culture."

## Extending Viewpoint through Writing

1. To what extent does "Looking for a Rain God" give you insight into situations that are so extreme (such as a soccer team stranded in a snow-filled mountain pass becoming cannibals in order to survive) that the normal conceptions of what is right or wrong give way to the question of survival?

2. To what extent does this story give you insight into the lives of people who live in colonized nations where Western Christian values are superimposed on tribal customs and beliefs? As a follow-up research project, you might wish to investigate the practice of Santería, a religion originating in Africa, brought to the United States by Cuban emigrees. See Joseph M. Murphy's *Santería: An African Religion in America* (1988); Judith Gleason's *Santería, Bronx* (1975); and Migene Gonzalez-Wippler's *The Santería Experience* (1982) and *Rituals and Spells of Santería* (1984).

3. Did your family have a secret that they either kept from someone in the family or from the outside world? If it can now be revealed, tell what it was. Does the secret seem as significant as it did at the time?

4. Works by Head; Henri Lopes ("The Esteemed Representative," Chapter 3); and Ngũgĩ wa Thiong'o ("Decolonising the Mind," Chapter 6) explore the tension between native African heritages and colonial European influences. In an essay, discuss what elements represent indigenous traditions and what elements represent colonial influences within each of the three societies of Botswana, Republic of the Congo, and Kenya. Which appears to have achieved the best fit between traditional African and European heritages?

# CONNECTING CULTURES

## Robert Levine with Ellen Wolff, "Social Time: The Heartbeat of Culture"

1. After reading Rigoberta Menchu ("Birth Ceremonies" Chapter 1), analyze the social significance of the number of days allotted to various aspects of the birth ceremony ritual. For example, you might observe the number of days the newborn baby is left alone with his mother, how this varies with the sex of the infant, and what happens when the child is forty days old.
2. To what extent are Levine and Wolff's observations about "social time" in Japan borne out by John Burgess's portrayal of a typical day in the life of a salaryman ("A Day in the Life of 'Salaryman'," Chapter 4)?
3. Relate Levine and Wolff's observations regarding the culturally determined expectations attached to time in Bharati Mukherjee's story ("The Management of Grief," Chapter 7). What inferences can you draw about the lengths of time considered appropriate for grieving in each of the cultures referred to in her story? How are these varying lengths of time related to the values of each culture?
4. How does "social time" for a culture differ from "psychological time" for an individual as dramatized in Panos Ioannides's story "Gregory" (Chapter 9)?

## Pico Iyer, "Perfect Strangers"

5. Discuss similarities in attitude between the people gathered in Asado Park in Hiroshima on the fortieth anniversary of the atomic bombing with those of the women gathered for the reunion portrayed in Kyōko Hayashi's "The Empty Can" (Chapter 9). How is the idea of collective mourning, in which individuals mourn personal losses without forgetting the losses of one another, an important value for the Japanese?
6. After reading Bruce Dollar ("Child Care in China," Chapter 1), evaluate the Chinese attitude toward individualism with that of the Japanese as described by Iyer. How is the idea of the "star" performer alien to both these cultures? How does Amy Tan's story ("Jing-Mei Woo: Two Kinds," Chapter 1) show that this attitude is a culturally acquired value?
7. How is the Japanese attitude toward sports similar to their attitude toward work as revealed in John Burgess's report ("A Day in the Life of 'Salaryman'," Chapter 4)?
8. How do both Iyer's account and Natsumi Soseki's chapter from *I Am a Cat* (Chapter 1) reveal the characteristic Japanese fondness for assimilating admired aspects of Western culture into Japanese life? What particular details in Soseki's description of the hobbies of the schoolmaster illustrate this most clearly?

## Napoleon A. Chagnon, "Doing Fieldwork among the Yąnomamö"

9. What are the similarities and differences between the ritualized aggression of the Yąnomamö in Brazil and how it is used to shape recruits into Marines as described by Henry Allen ("The Corps," Chapter 2)?

10. In your opinion, what unique qualities distinguish the Yąnomamö from the Iban of Borneo as described by Douchan Gersi ("Initiated into an Iban Tribe of Headhunters," Chapter 2)?

11. How do the Yąnomamö in Brazil differ from the Maasai in Kenya as described by Tepilit Ole Saitoti ("The Initiation of a Maasai Warrior," Chapter 2) in their attitudes toward aggression and the relationship between the sexes?

## Raymonde Carroll, "Minor Accidents"

12. After reading Kyōko Hayashi's "The Empty Can" (Chapter 9), discuss why Kinuko's behavior in bringing her parents' bones in a can to school conflicts with Japanese cultural norms. How does this story illustrate how conflicting expectations within a culture can create conflicts that are similar to the kinds of intercultural misunderstandings discussed by Carroll?

13. How does Mark Salzman's account ("Lessons," Chapter 4) illustrate that Americans and Chinese bring entirely different expectations to bear in defining what constitutes a situation in which one should feel "shame"?

14. Which of Jamaica Kincaid's examples ("A Small Place," Chapter 7) most effectively dramatizes the different meanings tourists versus native Antiguans attach to almost every aspect of Antiguan life (e.g., lack of rain, expensive Japanese cars used as taxis, etc.)? Which instances most clearly illustrate the kinds of intercultural misunderstandings described by Carroll?

## Gretel Ehrlich, "To Live in Two Worlds"

15. How are the various rituals described by Rigoberta Menchu ("Birth Ceremonies," Chapter 1) and Ehrlich designed to persuade supernatural powers to influence the outcome of human events?

16. What similarities and differences can you discover between Douchan Gersi's situation ("Initiated into an Iban Tribe of Headhunters," Chapter 2) and Ehrlich's? How do their expectations differ?

17. How are the ritual dances performed by the Kiowa designed to accomplish the same kinds of objectives as those performed by the Maasai as described in Tepilit Ole Saitoti ("The Initiation of a Maasai Warrior," Chapter 2)?

## Paul Fussell, "Taking It All Off in the Balkans"

18. What different attitudes toward modesty and sexuality emerge from Francine Du Plessix Gray's account ("Sex and Birth," Chapter 1) and that

of Fussell? Keep in mind that both Yugoslavia and Russia are socialist countries.

19. How does the practice of going to a nude beach conform to a three-part ritual of separation, initiation, and return, in ways that are reminiscent of all ritual initiations, as for example, those described by Tepilit Ole Saitoti ("The Initiation of a Maasai Warrior," Chapter 2); Rigoberta Menchu ("Birth Ceremonies," Chapter 1); and Henry Allen ("The Corps," Chapter 2)?

20. After reading Nawal El Saadawi ("Circumcision of Girls," Chapter 2), discuss how Islamic attitudes toward concealment of the female body reflect underlying cultural values in ways that are opposite to those described by Fussell.

21. How do the questions of modesty, privacy, and self-respect appear in Krishnan Varma's portrayal of the couple in "The Grass-Eaters" (Chapter 5)? How would you explain the importance of these values in Indian culture when so many people live in such close quarters as compared with the opposite situation described by Fussell?

22. Compare Jamaica Kincaid's description ("A Small Place," Chapter 7) of tourists who go to the beaches of Antigua with Fussell's portrayal of people who frequent nude beaches in the Balkans. What differences in attitude and tone can you discover between the authors' treatments of their respective subjects?

## Octavio Paz, "The Day of the Dead"

23. What differences in outlook, based on different cultural values, can you discover between the Amish attitude toward celebrations as described by Gene Logsdon ("Amish Economics," Chapter 4) and the Mexican attitude toward fiestas?

24. What insight do you gain into the psychology of celebrations from Paz's analysis and Joan Didion's description ("Miami: The Cuban Presence," Chapter 7) of quinces (coming-out parties for fifteen-year-old Cuban girls)?

## Gino Del Guercio, "The Secrets of Haiti's Living Dead"

25. What differences can you discover between the Haitian use of zombification as a form of social control with methods used to condition and control citizens in communist China as described by Bruce Dollar ("Child Care in China," Chapter 1)?

26. What important differences can you discover between the methods and goals of Wade Davis and those of Douchan Gersi ("Initiated into an Iban Tribe of Headhunters," Chapter 2)?

27. How does the circumcision of females act as a form of social control in Islamic societies, as described by Nawal El Saadawi ("Circumcision of Girls," Chapter 2)? Why is it significant that this procedure is performed to forestall rather than to punish any deviation from social norms in those cultures? How does this differ from situations where the practice of

voodoo in Haiti comes into play? In what way does the practice of voodoo also serve to forestall as well as to punish social deviance?

28. How do the methods used to punish social deviance among the Balinese (see Clifford Geertz, "Of Cocks and Men," Chapter 3) differ from those used by the voodoo priests in Haiti? How do the methods of each society reflect different underlying cultural values?

## Bessie Head, "Looking for a Rain God"

29. How do both Head's story and Ngũgĩ wa Thiong'o's account ("Decolonising the Mind," Chapter 6) reveal the dual nature of tribal society in Botswana and Kenya? What attitude do both works reveal toward the recently imposed layer of colonial "civilization"?
30. How do both Head's story and Nicholasa Mohr's "A Very Special Pet" (Chapter 7) dramatize the breakdown of human relationships under conditions of extraordinary stress?
31. Compare the literal meaning in Head's story of "drought" with its figurative use by Jan Rabie ("Drought," Chapter 6).
32. How does the behavior of the family described by Krishnan Varma ("The Grass-Eaters," Chapter 5) differ, under conditions of extreme stress, from that of the family in "Looking for a Rain God"? In your opinion, are these differences due to the personalities of the individuals rather than to differences in cultural values between India and Botswana?
33. Compare the attitude of the narrator toward Gregory in Panos Ioannides's story ("Gregory," Chapter 9) with the attitudes of the parents toward their two daughters. How in both stories must the misdeeds of both Gregory and the two little girls be exaggerated in order to make it easier to kill them?

# 9

# *The Impact of War*

In a century in which humanity has been faced with the choice of extinction or survival, the voices of those who testify to the human consequences of war—whether from the point of view of soldier, victim, survivor, journalist, or historian—provide some of the most compelling and moving literature imaginable. In Cyprus, Panos Ioannides explores the question of conscience in wartime in his startling story "Gregory," based on a true incident that occurred during the Greek Cypriot Liberation struggle against the British in the late 1950s. Everett C. Hughes, in "Good People and Dirty Work," offers a sociological perspective on war in his analysis of the psychological and social mechanisms that allowed the German people to deny knowledge of atrocities performed by the Nazi SS acting in their name.

The works in this chapter speak across time and national boundaries, from George Orwell's graphic firsthand experiences in the Spanish Civil War in 1937 in "Homage to Catalonia," to Robert Santos's gripping account in "My Men" of his experiences as a young Hispanic Army lieutenant during the 1968 Tet Offensive in Vietnam. We read the touching, thinly fictionalized story "The Empty Can" by Kyōko Hayashi of attending a reunion of atomic bomb survivors at Nagasaki Girl's High School in 1975. A remarkable interview by Maurizio Chierici in "The Man from Hiroshima" with Claude Eatherly, the lead pilot of the squadron that dropped the atomic bomb on Hiroshima, provides a complementary perspective to Hayashi's narrative. So too, Kate Wilhelm's nightmarish parable, "The Village," begins where Santos's true-life account leaves off. The chapter ends with Trevor N. Dupuy's analysis of the quick victory of the Allied coalition (led by the United States) over the Iraqi forces in the 1991 war in the Persian Gulf.

# George Orwell

# *Homage to Catalonia*

---

*George Orwell was the pen name taken by Eric Blair (1903–1950), who was born in Bengal, India. Educated on a scholarship at Eton, he served as a British official in the police in Burma, and became disillusioned with the aims and methods of colonialism. He describes the next few years in his first book* Down and Out in Paris and London *(1933), a gripping account of life on the fringe. In 1936, Orwell went to Spain to report on the Civil War and joined the Communist P.O.U.M. militia to fight against the Fascists. His account of this experience, in which he was severely wounded, titled* Homage to Catalonia *(1938), is a graphic account of the bleak and comic aspects of trench warfare on the Aragon front. Disillusioned with how the Communist party turned against the P.O.U.M. and tried to exterminate their members, Orwell became a sardonic observer of Communism. In* Animal Farm *(1945), he satirized the Russian Revolution and the machinations of the Soviet bureaucracy. In his acclaimed novel* 1984 *(1949), his distrust of totalitarianism emerged as a grim prophecy of a bureaucratic, regimented England of the future whose citizens are constantly watched by "big brother." The selection that follows, Chapter 3 from* Homage to Catalonia, *illustrates Orwell's statement that "in trench warfare five things are important: firewood, food, tobacco, candles and the enemy."*

*Spain, located in southwestern Europe, was indisputably the world's greatest power during the sixteenth century. The destruction of the Spanish Armada by the English fleet in 1588 signalled the decline of Spanish influence. The election of a Leftist coalition in 1936 precipitated the Spanish Civil War (1936–1939), the conflict that Orwell describes from his position as a soldier fighting on the side of the pro-Republican Loyalist forces against Fascists led by General Francisco Franco. Franco's victory began his thirty-six year dictatorship that ended with his death in 1975, when Juan Carlos I was crowned king and established a constitutional monarchy and free elections.*

1    In trench warfare five things are important: firewood, food, tobacco, candles and the enemy. In winter on the Zaragoza front they were important in that order, with the enemy a bad last. Except at night, when a surprise-attack was always conceivable, nobody bothered about the

enemy. They were simply remote black insects whom one occasionally saw hopping to and fro. The real preoccupation of both armies was trying to keep warm.

I ought to say in passing that all the time I was in Spain I saw very little fighting. I was on the Aragon front from January to May, and between January and late March little or nothing happened on that front, except at Teruel. In March there was heavy fighting round Huesca, but I personally played only a minor part in it. Later, in June, there was the disastrous attack on Huesca in which several thousand men were killed in a single day, but I had been wounded and disabled before that happened. The things that one normally thinks of as the horrors of war seldom happened to me. No aeroplane ever dropped a bomb anywhere near me, I do not think a shell ever exploded within fifty yards of me, and I was only in hand-to-hand fighting once (once is once too often, I may say). Of course I was often under heavy machine-gun fire, but usually at longish ranges. Even at Huesca you were generally safe enough if you took reasonable precautions.

Up here, in the hills round Zaragoza, it was simply the mingled boredom and discomfort of stationary warfare. A life as uneventful as a city clerk's, and almost as regular. Sentry-go, patrols, digging; digging, patrols, sentry-go. On every hill-top, Fascist or Loyalist, a knot of ragged, dirty men shivering round their flag and trying to keep warm. And all day and night the meaningless bullets wandering across the empty valleys and only by some rare improbable chance getting home on a human body.

Often I used to gaze round the wintry landscape and marvel at the futility of it all. The inconclusiveness of such a kind of war! Earlier, about October, there had been savage fighting for all these hills; then, because the lack of men and arms, especially artillery, made any large-scale operation impossible, each army had dug itself in and settled down on the hill-tops it had won. Over to our right there was a small outpost, also P.O.U.M., and on the spur to our left, at seven o'clock of us, a P.S.U.C. position faced a taller spur with several small Fascist posts dotted on its peaks. The so-called line zigzagged to and fro in a pattern that would have been quite unintelligible if every position had not flown a flag. The P.O.U.M. and P.S.U.C. flags were red, those of the Anarchists red and black; the Facists generally flew the monarchist flag (red-yellow-red), but occasionally they flew the flag of the Republic (red-yellow-purple).[1] The scenery was stupendous, if you could forget that every mountain-top was occupied by troops and was therefore littered with tin cans and crusted with dung. To the right of us the sierra bent south-eastwards and made way for the wide, veined valley that stretched across to Huesca. In

[1]An errata note found in Orwell's papers after his death: "Am not now completely certain that I ever saw Fascists flying the republican flag, though I *think* they sometimes flew it with a small imposed swastika."

the middle of the plain a few tiny cubes sprawled like a throw of dice; this was the town of Robres, which was in Loyalist possession. Often in the mornings the valley was hidden under seas of cloud, out of which the hills rose flat and blue, giving the landscape a strange resemblance to a photographic negative. Beyond Huesca there were more hills of the same formation as our own, streaked with a pattern of snow which altered day by day. In the far distance the monstrous peaks of the Pyrenees, where the snow never melts, seemed to float upon nothing. Even down in the plain everything looked dead and bare. The hills opposite us were grey and wrinkled like the skins of elephants. Almost always the sky was empty of birds. I do not think I have ever seen a country where there were so few birds. The only birds one saw at any time were a kind of magpie, and the coveys of partridges that startled one at night with their sudden whirring, and, very rarely, the flights of eagles that drifted slowly over, generally followed by rifle-shots which they did not deign to notice.

5     At night and in misty weather patrols were sent out in the valley between ourselves and the Fascists. The job was not popular, it was too cold and too easy to get lost, and I soon found that I could get leave to go out on patrol as often as I wished. In the huge jagged ravines there were no paths or tracks of any kind; you could only find your way about by making successive journeys and noting fresh landmarks each time. As the bullet flies the nearest Fascist post was seven hundred metres from our own, but it was a mile and a half by the only practicable route. It was rather fun wandering about the dark valleys with the stray bullets flying high overhead like redshanks whistling. Better than nighttime were the heavy mists, which often lasted all day and which had a habit of clinging round the hill-tops and leaving the valleys clear. When you were any-where near the Fascist lines you had to creep at a snail's pace; it was very difficult to move quietly on those hill-sides, among the crackling shrubs and tinkling limestones. It was only at the third or fourth attempt that I managed to find my way to the Fascist lines. The mist was very thick, and I crept up to barbed wire to listen. I could hear the Fascists talking and singing inside. Then to my alarm I heard several of them coming down the hill towards me. I cowered behind a bush that suddenly seemed very small, and tried to cock my rifle without noise. However, they branched off and did not come within sight of me. Behind the bush where I was hiding I came upon various relics of the earlier fighting — a pile of empty cartridge-cases, a leather cap with a bullet-hole in it, and a red flag, obviously one of our own. I took it back to the position, where it was unsentimentally torn up for cleaning-rags.

6     I had been made a corporal, or *cabo*, as it was called, as soon as we reached the front, and was in command of a guard of twelve men. It was no sinecure, especially at first. The *centuria* was an untrained mob com-posed mostly of boys in their teens. Here and there in the militia you came across children as young as eleven or twelve, usually refugees from

Fascist territory who had been enlisted as militiamen as the easiest way of providing for them. As a rule they were employed on light work in the rear, but sometimes they managed to worm their way to the front line, where they were a public menace. I remember one little brute throwing a hand-grenade into the dug-out fire 'for a joke.' At Monte Pocero I do not think there was anyone younger than fifteen, but the average age must have been well under twenty. Boys of this age ought never to be used in the front line, because they cannot stand the lack of sleep which is inseparable from trench warfare. At the beginning it was almost impossible to keep our position properly guarded at night. The wretched children of my section could only be roused by dragging them out of their dug-outs feet foremost, and as soon as your back was turned they left their posts and slipped into shelter; or they would even, in spite of the frightful cold, lean up against the wall of the trench and fall fast asleep. Luckily the enemy were very unenterprising. There were nights when it seemed to me that our position could be stormed by twenty Boy Scouts armed with air-guns, or twenty Girl Guides armed with battledores, for that matter.

At this time and until much later the Catalan militias were still on the same basis as they had been at the beginning of the war. In the early days of Franco's revolt the militias had been hurriedly raised by the various trade unions and political parties; each was essentially a political organization, owing allegiance to its party as much as to the central Government. When the Popular Army, which was a 'non-political'' army organized on more or less ordinary lines, was raised at the beginning of 1937, the party militias were theoretically incorporated in it. But for a long time the only changes that occurred were on paper; the new Popular Army troops did not reach the Aragon front in any numbers till June, and until that time the militia-system remained unchanged. The essential point of the system was social equality between officers and men. Everyone from general to private drew the same pay, ate the same food, wore the same clothes, and mingled on terms of complete equality. If you wanted to slap the general commanding the division on the back and ask him for a cigarette, you could do so, and no one thought it curious. In theory at any rate each militia was a democracy and not a hierarchy. It was understood that orders had to be obeyed, but it was also understood that when you gave an order you gave it as comrade to comrade and not as superior to inferior. There were officers and N.C.O.'s, but there was no military rank in the ordinary sense; no titles, no badges, no heel-clicking and saluting. They had attempted to produce within the militias a sort of temporary working model of the classless society. Of course there was not perfect equality, but there was a nearer approach to it than I had ever seen or than I would have thought conceivable in time of war.

But I admit that at first sight the state of affairs at the front horrified me. How on earth could the war be won by an army of this type? It was what everyone was saying at the time, and though it was true it was also unreasonable. For in the circumstances the militias could not have been much better than they were. A modern mechanized army does not spring up out of the ground, and if the Government had waited until it had trained troops at its disposal, Franco would never have been resisted. Later it became the fashion to decry the militias, and therefore to pretend that the faults which were due to lack of training and weapons were the result of the equalitarian system. Actually, a newly raised draft of militia was an undisciplined mob not because the officers called the privates 'Comrade' but because raw troops are *always* an undisciplined mob. In practice the democratic 'revolutionary' type of discipline is more reliable than might be expected. In a workers' army discipline is theoretically voluntary. It is based on class-loyalty, whereas the discipline of a bourgeois conscript army is based ultimately on fear. (The Popular Army that replaced the militias was midway between the two types.) In the militias the bullying and abuse that go on in an ordinary army would never have been tolerated for a moment. The normal military punishments existed, but they were only invoked for very serious offences. When a man refused to obey an order you did not immediately get him punished; you first appealed to him in the name of comradeship. Cynical people with no experience of handling men will say instantly that this would never 'work,' but as a matter of fact it does 'work' in the long run. The discipline of even the worst drafts of militia visibly improved as time went on. In January the job of keeping a dozen raw recruits up to the mark almost turned my hair grey. In May for a short while I was acting-lieutenant in command of about thirty men, English and Spanish. We had all been under fire for months, and I never had the slightest difficulty in getting an order obeyed or in getting men to volunteer for a dangerous job. 'Revolutionary' discipline depends on political consciousness — on an understanding of *why* orders must be obeyed; it takes time to diffuse this, but it also takes time to drill a man into an automation on the barrack-square. The journalists who sneered at the militia-system seldom remembered that the militias had to hold the line while the Popular Army was training in the rear. And it is a tribute to the strength of 'revolutionary' discipline that the militias stayed in the field at all. For until about June 1937 there was nothing to keep them there, except class loyalty. Individual deserters could be shot — were shot, occasionally — but if a thousand men had decided to walk out of the line together there was no force to stop them. A conscript army in the same circumstances — with its battle-police removed — would have melted away. Yet the militias held the line, though God knows they won very few victories, and even individual desertions were not common. In four or five months in the P.O.U.M. militia I only heard of four men deserting, and two of those were fairly certainly spies who had enlisted to obtain information. At the beginning the apparent chaos, the general lack of training, the fact that you often had to argue for five minutes before you could get an order obeyed, appalled and infuriated me. I had British Army ideas, and certainly the Spanish militias were very unlike the British Army. But considering the circumstances they were better troops than one had any right to expect.

Meanwhile, firewood — always firewood. Throughout that period 9 there is probably no entry in my diary that does not mention firewood, or rather the lack of it. We were between two and three thousand feet above sea-level, it was mid-winter and the cold was unspeakable. The temperature was not exceptionally low, on many nights it did not even freeze, and the wintry sun often shone for an hour in the middle of the day; but even if it was not really cold, I assure you that it seemed so. Sometimes there were shrieking winds that tore your cap off and twisted your hair in all directions, sometimes there were mists that poured into the trench like a liquid and seemed to penetrate your bones; frequently it rained, and even a quarter of an hour's rain was enough to make conditions intolerable. The thin skin of earth over the limestone turned promptly into a slippery grease, and as you were always walking on a slope it was impossible to keep your footing. On dark nights I have often fallen half a dozen times in twenty yards; and this was dangerous, because it meant that the lock of one's rifle became jammed with mud. For days together clothes, boots, blankets, and rifles were more or less coated with mud. I had brought as many thick clothes as I could carry, but many of the men were terribly underclad. For the whole garrison, about a hundred men, there were only twelve great-coats, which had to be handed from sentry to sentry, and most of the men had only one blanket. One icy night I made a list in my diary of the clothes I was wearing. It is of some interest as showing the amount of clothes the human body can carry. I was wearing a thick vest and pants, a flannel shirt, two pull-overs, a woollen jacket, a pigskin jacket, corduroy breeches, puttees, thick socks, boots, a stout trench-coat, a muffler, lined leather gloves, and a woollen cap. Nevertheless, I was shivering like a jelly. But I admit I am unusually sensitive to cold.

Firewood was the one thing that really mattered. The point about the 10 firewood was that there was practically no firewood to be had. Our miserable mountain had not even at its best much vegetation, and for months it had been ranged over by freezing militiamen, with the result that everything thicker than one's finger had long since been burnt. When we were not eating, sleeping, on guard or on fatigue-duty we were in the valley behind the position, scrounging for fuel. All my memories of that time are memories of scrambling up and down the almost perpendicular slopes, over the jagged limestone that knocked one's boots to pieces, pouncing eagerly on tiny twigs of wood. Three people searching for a couple of hours could collect enough fuel to keep the dug-out fire alight for about an hour. The eagerness of our search for firewood turned us all into botanists. We classified according to their burning qualities every plant that grew on the mountain-side; the various heaths and grasses that were good to start a fire with but burnt out in a few minutes, the wild rosemary and the tiny whin bushes that would burn when the fire was well alight, the stunted oak tree, smaller than a gooseberry bush, that was practically unburnable. There was a kind of dried-up reed that was very good for starting fires with, but these grew only on the hill-top to the left of the position, and you had to go under fire to get them. If the Fascist machine-gunners saw you they gave you a drum of ammunition all to yourself. Generally their aim was high and the bullets sang over-head like birds, but sometimes they crackled and chipped the limestone uncomfortably close, whereupon you flung yourself on your face. You went on gathering reeds, however; nothing mattered in comparison with firewood.

11    Beside the cold the other discomforts seemed petty. Of course all of us were permanently dirty. Our water, like our food, came on mule-back from Alcubierre, and each man's share worked out at about a quart a day. It was beastly water, hardly more transparent than milk. Theoreti-cally it was for drinking only, but I always stole a pannikinful for washing in the mornings. I used to wash one day and shave the next; there was never enough water for both. The position stank abominably, and outside the little enclosure of the barricade there was excrement everywhere. Some of the militiamen habitually defecated in the trench, a disgusting thing when one had to walk round it in the darkness. But the dirt never worried me. Dirt is a thing people make too much fuss about. It is astonishing how quickly you get used to doing without a handker-chief and to eating out of the tin pannikin in which you also wash. Nor was sleeping in one's clothes any hardship after a day or two. It was of course impossible to take one's clothes and especially one's boots off at night; one had to be ready to turn out instantly in case of an attack. In eighty nights I only took my clothes off three times, though I did occa-sionally manage to get them off in the daytime. It was too cold for lice as yet, but rats and mice abounded. It is often said that you don't find rats and mice in the same place, but you do when there is enough food for them.

12    In other ways we were not badly off. The food was good enough and there was plenty of wine. Cigarettes were still being issued at the rate of a packet a day, matches were issued every other day, and there was even an issue of candles. They were very thin candles, like those on a Christmas cake, and were popularly supposed to have been looted from churches. Every dug-out was issued daily with three inches of candle, which would burn for about twenty minutes. At that time it was still possible to buy candles, and I had brought several pounds of them with me. Later on the famine of matches and candles made life a misery. You do not realize the importance of these things until you lack them. In a night-alarm, for instance, when everyone in the dug-out is scrambling for his rifle and treading on everybody else's face, being able to strike a light may make the difference between life and death. Every militiaman

possessed a tinder-lighter and several yards of yellow wick. Next to his rifle it was his most important possession. The tinder-lighters had the great advantage that they could be struck in a wind, but they would only smoulder, so that they were no use for lighting a fire. When the match famine was at its worst our only way of producing a flame was to pull the bullet out of a cartridge and touch the cordite off with a tinder-lighter.

It was an extraordinary life that we were living — an extraordinary way to be at war, if you could call it war. The whole militia chafed against the inaction and clamoured constantly to know why we were not allowed to attack. But it was perfectly obvious that there would be no battle for a long while yet, unless the enemy started it. Georges Kopp, on his periodical tours of inspection, was quite frank with us. "This is not a war," he used to say, "it is a comic opera with an occasional death." As a matter of fact the stagnation on the Aragon front had political causes of which I knew nothing at that time; but the purely military difficulties — quite apart from the lack of reserves of men — were obvious to anybody. 13

To begin with, there was the nature of the country. The front line, ours and the Fascists', lay in positions of immense natural strength, which as a rule could only be approached from one side. Provided a few trenches have been dug, such places cannot be taken by infantry, except in overwhelming numbers. In our own position or most of those round us a dozen men with two machine-guns could have held off a battalion. Perched on the hill-tops as we were, we should have made lovely marks for artillery; but there was no artillery. Sometimes I used to gaze round the landscape and long — oh, how passionately! — for a couple of batteries of guns. One could have destroyed the enemy positions one after another as easily as smashing nuts with a hammer. But on our side the guns simply did not exist. The Fascists did occasionally manage to bring a gun or two from Zaragoza and fire a very few shells, so few that they never even found the range and the shells plunged harmlessly into the empty ravines. Against machine-guns and without artillery there are only three things you can do: dig yourself in at a safe distance — four hundred yards, say — advance across the open and be massacred, or make small-scale night-attacks that will not alter the general situation. Practically the alternatives are stagnation or suicide. 14

And beyond this there was the complete lack of war materials of every description. It needs an effort to realize how badly the militias were armed at this time. Any public school O.T.C. in England is far more like a modern army than we were. The badness of our weapons was so astonishing that it is worth recording in detail. 15

For this sector of the front the entire artillery consisted of four trench-mortars with *fifteen rounds* for each gun. Of course they were far too precious to be fired and the mortars were kept in Alcubierre. There were machine-guns at the rate of approximately one to fifty men; they were oldish guns, but fairly accurate up to three or four hundred yards. 16

Beyond this we had only rifles, and the majority of the rifles were scrap-iron. There were three types of rifle in use. The first was the long Mauser. These were seldom less than twenty years old, their sights were about as much use as a broken speedometer, and in most of them the rifling was hopelessly corroded; about one rifle in ten was not bad, however. Then there was the short Mauser, or *mousqueton*, really a cavalry weapon. These were more popular than the others because they were lighter to carry and less nuisance in a trench, also because they were comparatively new and looked efficient. Actually they were almost useless. They were made out of reassembled parts, no bolt belonged to its rifle, and three-quarters of them could be counted on to jam after five shots. There were also a few Winchester rifles. These were nice to shoot with, but they were wildly inaccurate, and as their cartridges had no clips they could only be fired one shot at a time. Ammunition was so scarce that each man entering the line was only issued with fifty rounds, and most of it was exceedingly bad. The Spanish-made cartridges were all refills and would jam even the best rifles. The Mexican cartridges were better and were therefore reserved for the machine-guns. Best of all was the German-made ammunition, but as this came only from prisoners and deserters there was not much of it. I always kept a clip of German or Mexican ammunition in my pocket for use in an emergency. But in practice when the emergency came I seldom fired my rifle; I was too frightened of the beastly thing jamming and too anxious to reserve at any rate one round that would go off.

17        We had no tin hats, no bayonets, hardly any revolvers or pistols, and not more than one bomb between five or ten men. The bomb in use at this time was a frightful object known as the 'F.A.I. bomb,' it having been produced by the Anarchists in the early days of the war. It was on the principle of a Mills bomb, but the lever was held down not by a pin but a piece of tape. You broke the tape and then got rid of the bomb with the utmost possible speed. It was said of these bombs that they were 'impartial'; they killed the man they were thrown at and the man who threw them. There were several other types, even more primitive but probably a little less dangerous — to the thrower, I mean. It was not till late March that I saw a bomb worth throwing.

18        And apart from weapons there was a shortage of all the minor necessities of war. We had no maps or charts, for instance. Spain has never been fully surveyed, and the only detailed maps of this area were the old military ones, which were almost all in the possession of the Fascists. We had no range-finders, no telescopes, no periscopes, no field-glasses except a few privately-owned pairs, no flares or Very lights, no wire-cutters, no armourers' tools, hardly even any cleaning materials. The Spaniards seemed never to have heard of a pull-through and looked on in surprise when I constructed one. When you wanted your rifle cleaned you took it to the sergeant, who possessed a long brass ramrod which was invariably bent and therefore scratched the rifling. There was

not even any gun oil. You greased your rifle with olive oil, when you could get hold of it; at different times I have greased mine with vaseline, with cold cream, and even with bacon-fat. Moreover, there were no lanterns or electric torches—at this time there was not, I believe, such a thing as an electric torch throughout the whole of our sector of the front, and you could not buy one nearer than Barcelona, and only with difficulty even there.

As time went on, and the desultory rifle-fire rattled among the hills, I began to wonder with increasing scepticism whether anything would ever happen to bring a bit of life, or rather a bit of death, into this cock-eyed war. It was pneumonia that we were fighting against, not against men. When the trenches are more than five hundred yards apart no one gets hit except by accident. Of course there were casualties, but the majority of them were self-inflicted. If I remember rightly, the first five men I saw wounded in Spain were all wounded by our own weapons—I don't mean intentionally, but owing to accident or carelessness. Our worn-out rifles were a danger in themselves. Some of them had a nasty trick of going off if the butt was tapped on the ground; I saw a man shoot himself through the hand owing to this. And in the darkness the raw recruits were always firing at one another. One evening when it was barely even dusk a sentry let fly at me from a distance of twenty yards; but he missed me by a yard—goodness knows how many times the Spanish standard of marksmanship has saved my life. Another time I had gone out on patrol in the mist and had carefully warned the guard commander beforehand. But in coming back I stumbled against a bush, the startled sentry called out that the Fascists were coming, and I had the pleasure of hearing the guard commander order everyone to open rapid fire in my direction. Of course I lay down and the bullets went harmlessly over me. Nothing will convince a Spaniard, at least a young Spaniard, that fire-arms are dangerous. Once, rather later than this, I was photographing some machine-gunners with their gun, which was pointed directly towards me.

"Don't fire," I said half-jokingly as I focused the camera.

"Oh, no, we won't fire."

The next moment there was a frightful roar and a stream of bullets tore past my face so close that my cheek was stung by grains of cordite. It was unintentional, but the machine-gunners considered it a great joke. Yet only a few days earlier they had seen a mule-driver accidentally shot by a political delegate who was playing the fool with an automatic pistol and had put five bullets in the mule-driver's lungs.

The difficult passwords which the army was using at this time were a minor source of danger. They were those tiresome double passwords in which one word has to be answered by another. Usually they were of an elevating and revolutionary nature, such as *Cultura—progreso*, or *Seremos—invencibles*, and it was often impossible to get illiterate sentries to remember these highfalutin words. One night, I remember, the pass-

19

20

21

22

23

word was *Cataluña—heroica*, and a moon-faced peasant lad named Jaime Domenech approached me, greatly puzzled, and asked me to explain.

24      "Heroica—what does heroica mean?"

25      I told him that it meant the same as *valiente*. A little while later he was stumbling up the trench in the darkness, and the sentry challenged him:

26      "Alto! Cataluña!"

27      "Valiente!" yelled Jaime, certain that he was saying the right thing.

28      Bang!

29      However, the sentry missed him. In this war everyone always did miss everyone else, when it was humanly possible.

## *Evaluating the Text*

1. Summarize Orwell's situation in terms of the problems created by the physical conditions of trench warfare. How does Orwell's account of what actually occurred run contrary to your expectations as to what a civil war would be like? Why do taken-for-granted items assume extraordinary importance?

2. Discuss the differences between the way armies are usually run and how Orwell's military unit arrived at and carried out command decisions. What unexpected challenges did not having a traditional chain-of-command create?

3. What are some of the specific words and phrases Orwell uses to appeal to each of the five senses in his description of the environment? How does his choice of similes and metaphors not only put the reader into the scene (hearing the sounds the soldiers heard, etc.) but imply what Orwell's attitude is toward what he describes? For example, what attitude toward war is implied by his description that "the houses look like the throwing of dice"?

4. Pinpoint places in the chapter where Orwell employs irony or humor to make a point. Analyze one or two of these episodes. For example, how does Orwell illustrate Georges Kopp's statement that "this is not a war . . . it is a comic opera with an occasional death"?

5. How does Orwell's analysis of praiseworthy character traits support his claim that the ability to endure inconveniences rather than brute courage and bravery is the most important virtue for a soldier to have?

6. Orwell states that he liked night patrol. What does this tell you about his personality? What distinctive appeal did it have for him? Would it have appealed to you? Why or why not? How does Orwell's reticence about portraying himself as a hero contribute to the effectiveness of this chapter in puncturing illusions people may have about warfare?

7. What important detail informs the reader that Franco was supported by Hitler?

8. How did the ideals expressed in the passwords reflect the aspirations of the militia?

## *Exploring Different Perspectives*

1. Compare and contrast Orwell's attitude as leader of the unit toward the men he was responsible for with Robert Santos's (see "My Men").

2. Do you think Orwell would have been capable of taking the kind of action described by Panos Ioannides in "Gregory"? Why or why not? Does Orwell discuss any situations that suggest that he was aware of conflicts between individual conscience and the need to perform one's military duty?

## Extending Viewpoints through Writing

1. If you were a soldier, which of the two kinds of military organizations would you want to belong to and why—one based on equality, for which getting orders obeyed requires discussion and agreement for each decision, or the traditional army, based on hierarchy, for which soldiers simply obey the orders of those above them? What are the advantages and disadvantages of each type of military organization? In what situations (everyday routine or actual battle) would one type of military organization be better than the other?

2. How does Orwell's analysis of the differences between armies based on social equality versus armies based on hierarchy illuminate his political beliefs during this time? As a research project, compare Orwell's attitude in this selection with his change of mind described in later chapters of *Homage to Catalonia* (1952). You might wish to explore the relationship between Orwell's disillusionment with communism and his political satires *Animal Farm* (1946) and *1984* (1949).

3. Compare and contrast the circumstances under which Orwell fought in the Spanish Civil War with desert fighting conditions faced by U.S. infantry soldiers stationed in the Middle East.

4. Analyze any section you consider to be an especially effective description. What principle of organization does Orwell use: dominant impression surrounded by supporting details, left to right, close-up to far, and so on?

5. George Orwell, in "Why I Write" (1946), stated, "My book about the Spanish Civil War, *Homage to Catalonia*, is, of course, a frankly political book, but in the main it is written with a certain detachment and regard for form. I did try very hard in it to tell the whole truth without violating my literary instincts." What elements in the chapter that you read are frankly political and display a feeling of partisanship? Do you think Orwell succeeded in his attempt to write a work that was politically truthful and effective in a literary sense? Discuss your reactions.

# Everett C. Hughes

# Good People and Dirty Work

---

*Most people, if asked "Could the Holocaust happen here?" would deny the possibility. Yet, the idea that the bureaucratic machinery of the state could be used to exterminate a designated group of people would have seemed just as far-fetched in the Germany of a half century ago, an advanced culture in the arts, sciences, technology, and theology. It is precisely this question that Everett C. Hughes set out to answer by exploring the circumstances under which "good" people in any society allow others to do the "dirty work." At the time of his death in 1983, Hughes was professor emeritus of sociology at Boston College and the author of books including* French Canada in Transition *(1943, reprinted in 1963);* The Sociological Eye *(1984);* Men and Their Work *(1958);* Making the Grade: The Academic Side of College Life *(with Howard Saul Becker, 1968); and* Where Peoples Meet: Racial and Ethnic Frontiers *(with Helen M. Hughes, 1952, reprinted in 1981). "Good People and Dirty Work" first appeared in* Social Problems *(Summer 1962).*

*Germany emerged during the latter half of the nineteenth century out of a federation of states under the leadership of Otto von Bismarck. Industrial, colonial, and military moves toward expansion threatened British and French interests and contributed to bringing about World War I, in which Germany was defeated. Mass unemployment, economic instability, and the rhetoric of political extremism paved the way for Adolf Hitler's rise to power, with consequences explored by Hughes in "Good People and Dirty Work." World War II began with Germany's invasion of Poland in 1939 and ended with Germany's defeat in 1945. Thereafter, Germany was divided into four zones occupied by British, French, Soviet, and American forces. In 1989, the Berlin Wall, which had divided the city of Berlin since 1961, was opened to East German citizens and was ultimately dismantled on November 9 in response to massive pro-democracy demonstrations within Soviet-dominated East Germany. October 1990 saw the reunification of East and West Germany under the leadership of the Christian Democratic government headed by Helmut Kohl. The capital shifted from Bonn to Berlin, and national elections were held for the first time on December 2, 1990.*

The National Socialist Government of Germany, with the arm of its 1
fanatical inner sect, the S.S., commonly known as the Brown Shirts or
Elite Guard, perpetrated and boasted of the most colossal and dramatic
piece of social dirty work the world has ever known. Perhaps there are
other claimants to the title, but they could not match this one's combination of mass, speed, and perverse pride in the deed. Nearly all peoples
have plenty of cruelty and death to account for. How many Negro
Americans have died by the hand of lynching mobs? How many more
from unnecessary disease and lack of food or of knowledge of nutrition?
How many Russians died to bring about collectivization of land? And
who is to blame if there be starving millions in some parts of the world
while wheat molds in the fields of other parts?

I do not revive the case of the Nazi *Endloesung* (final solution) of the 2
Jewish problem in order to condemn the Germans, or make them look
worse than other peoples, but to recall to our attention dangers which
lurk in our midst always. Most of what follows was written after my first
postwar visit to Germany in 1948. The impressions were vivid. The facts
have not diminished and disappeared with time, as did the stories of
alleged German atrocities in Belgium in the first World War. The fuller
the record, the worse it gets.

Several millions of people were delivered to the concentration camps, 3
operated under the leadership of Heinrich Himmler with the help of
Adolf Eichmann. A few hundred thousand survived in some fashion.
Still fewer came out sound of mind and body. A pair of examples, well
attested, will show the extreme of perverse cruelty reached by the S.S.
guards in charge of the camps. Prisoners were ordered to climb trees;
guards whipped them to make them climb faster. Once they were out of
reach, other prisoners, also urged by the whip, were put to shaking the
trees. When the victims fell, they were kicked to see whether they could
rise to their feet. Those too badly injured to get up were shot to death,
as useless for work. A not inconsiderable number of prisoners were
drowned in pits full of human excrement. These examples are so horrible
that your minds will run away from them. You will not, as when you
read a slightly salacious novel, imagine the rest. I therefore thrust these
examples upon you and insist that the people who thought them up
could, and did, improvise others like them, and even worse, from day to
day over several years. Many of the victims of the Camps gave up the
ghost (this Biblical phrase is the most apt) from a combination of humiliation, starvation, fatigue, and physical abuse. In due time, a policy of
mass liquidation in the gas chamber was added to individual virtuosity in
cruelty.

This program—for it was a program—of cruelty and murder was 4
carried out in the name of racial superiority and racial purity. It was
directed mainly, although by no means exclusively, against Jews, Slavs,
and Gypsies. It was thorough. There are few Jews in the territories which
were under the control of the Third German Reich—the two Germanys,

Holland, Czechoslovakia, Poland, Austria, Hungary. Many Jewish Frenchmen were destroyed. There were concentration camps even in Tunisia and Algeria under the German occupation.

5    When, during my 1948 visit to Germany, I became more aware of the reactions of ordinary Germans to the horrors of the concentration camps, I found myself asking not the usual question, "How did racial hatred rise to such a high level?" but this one, "How could such dirty work be done among and, in a sense, *by* the millions of ordinary, civilized German people?" Along with this came related questions. How could these millions of ordinary people live in the midst of such cruelty and murder without a general uprising against it and against the people who did it? How, once freed from the regime that did it, could they be apparently so little concerned about it, so toughly silent about it, not only in talking with outsiders — which is easy to understand — but among themselves? How and where could there be found in a modern civilized country the several hundred thousand men and women capable of such work? How were these people so far released from the inhibitions of civilized life as to be able to imagine, let alone perform, the ferocious, obscene, and perverse actions which they did imagine and perform? How could they be kept at such a height of fury through years of having to see daily at close range the human wrecks they made and being often literally spattered with the filth produced and accumulated by their own actions?

6    You will see that there are here two orders of questions. One set concerns the good people who did not themselves do this work. The other concerns those who did do it. But the two sets are not really separate; for the crucial question concerning the good people is their relation to the people who did the dirty work, with a related one which asks under what circumstances good people let the others get away with such actions.

7    An easy answer concerning the Germans is that they were not so good after all. We can attribute to them some special inborn or ingrained race consciousness, combined with a penchant for sadistic cruelty and unquestioning acceptance of whatever is done by those who happen to be in authority. Pushed to its extreme, this answer simply makes us, rather than the Germans, the superior race. It is the Nazi tune, put to words of our own.

8    Now there are deep and stubborn differences between peoples. Their history and culture may make the Germans especially susceptible to the doctrine of their own racial superiority and especially acquiescent to the actions of whoever is in power over them. These are matters deserving of the best study that can be given them. But to say that these things could happen in Germany simply because Germans are different — from us — buttresses their own excuses and lets us off too easily from blame for what happened there and from the question whether it could happen here.

Certainly in their daily practice and expression before the Hitler 9
regime, the Germans showed no more, if as much, hatred of other racial
or cultural groups than we did and do. Residential segregation was not
marked. Intermarriage was common, and the families of such marriages
had an easier social existence than they generally have in America. The
racially exclusive club, school, and hotel were much less in evidence than
here. And I well remember an evening in 1933 when a Montreal
businessman—a very nice man, too—said in our living room, "Why
don't we admit that Hitler is doing to the Jews just what we ought to be
doing?" That was not an uncommon sentiment, although it may be said
in defense of the people who expressed it that they probably did not
know and would not have believed the full truth about the Nazi program
of destroying Jews. The essential underlying sentiments on racial matters
in Germany were not different in kind from those prevailing throughout
the western, and especially the Anglo-Saxon, countries. But I do not wish
to overemphasize this point. I only want to close one easy way out of
serious consideration of the problem of good people and dirty work, by
demonstrating that the Germans were and are about as good and about
as bad as the rest of us on this matter of racial sentiments and, let us add,
their notions of decent human behavior.

But what was the reaction of ordinary Germans to the persecution of 10
the Jews and to the concentration camp mass torture and murder? A
conversation between a German schoolteacher, a German architect, and
myself gives the essentials in a vivid form. It was in the studio of the
architect, and the occasion was a rather casual visit, in Frankfurt am
Main in 1948.

**The architect:** "I am ashamed for my people whenever I think of it. But
we didn't know about it. We only learned about all that later. You
must remember the pressure we were under; we had to join the party.
We had to keep our mouths shut and do as we were told. It was a
terrible pressure. Still, I am ashamed. But you see, we had lost our
colonies, and our national honor was hurt. And these Nazis exploited
that feeling. And the Jews, they *were* a problem. They came from the
east. You should see them in Poland; the lowest class of people, full of
lice, dirty and poor, running about in their Ghettos in filthy caftans.
They came here, and got rich by unbelievable methods after the first
war. They occupied all the good places. Why, they were in the proportion of ten to one in medicine and law and government posts!"

At this point the architect hesitated and looked confused. He continued: "Where was I? It is the poor food. You see what misery we are
in here, Herr Professor. It often happens that I forget what I was
talking about. Where was I now? I have completely forgotten."

(His confusion was, I believe, not at all feigned. Many Germans
said they suffered losses of memory such as this, and laid it to their
lack of food.)

I said firmly: "You were talking about loss of national honor and how the Jews had got hold of everything."

**The architect:** "Oh, yes! That was it! Well, of course that was no way to settle the Jewish problem. But there *was* a problem and it had to be settled some way."

**The schoolteacher:** "Of course, they have Palestine now."

I protested that Palestine would hardly hold them.

**The architect:** "The professor is right. Palestine can't hold all the Jews. And it was a terrible thing to murder people. But we didn't know it at the time. But I am glad I am alive now. It is an interesting time in men's history. You know, when the Americans came it was like a great release. I really want to see a new ideal in Germany. I like the freedom that lets me talk to you like this. But, unfortunately this is not the general opinion. Most of my friends really hang on to the old ideas. They can't see any hope, so they hang on to the old ideas."

11    This scrap of talk gives, I believe the essential elements as well as the flavor of the German reaction. It checks well with formal studies which have been made, and it varies only in detail from other conversations which I myself recorded in 1948.

12    One of the most obvious points in it is unwillingness to think about the dirty work done. In this case — perhaps by chance, perhaps not — the good man suffered an actual lapse of memory in the middle of this statement. This seems a simple point. But the psychiatrists have shown that it is less simple than it looks. They have done a good deal of work on the complicated mechanisms by which the individual mind keeps unpleasant or intolerable knowledge from consciousness, and have shown how great may, in some cases, be the consequent loss of effectiveness of the personality. But we have taken collective unwillingness to know unpleasant facts more or less for granted. That people can and do keep a silence about things whose open discussion would threaten the group's conception of itself, and hence its solidarity, is common knowledge. It is a mechanism that operates in every family and in every group which has a sense of group reputation. To break such a silence is considered an attack against the group; a sort of treason, if it be a member of the group who breaks the silence. This common silence allows group fictions to grow up; such as, that grandpa was less a scoundrel and more romantic than he really was. And I think it demonstrable that it operates especially against any expression, except in ritual, of collective guilt. The remarkable thing in present-day Germany is not that there is so little reference to something about which people do feel deeply guilty, but that it is talked about at all.

13    In order to understand this phenomenon we would have to find out who talks about the concentration camp atrocities, in what situations, in what mood, and with what stimulus. On these points I know only my own limited experiences. One of the most moving of these was my first

postwar meeting with an elderly professor whom I had known before the Nazi time; he is an heroic soul who did not bow his head during the Nazi time and who keeps it erect now. His first words, spoken with tears in his eyes, were:

"How hard it is to believe that men will be as bad as they say they 14 will. Hitler and his people said: 'Heads will roll,' but how many of us—even of his bitterest opponents—could really believe that they would do it."

This man could and did speak, in 1948, not only to the likes of me, 15 but to his students, his colleagues, and the public which read his articles, in the most natural way about the Nazi atrocities whenever there was occasion to do it in the course of his tireless effort to reorganize and to bring new life into the German universities. He had neither the compulsion to speak, so that he might excuse and defend himself, nor a conscious or unconscious need to keep silent. Such people were rare; how many there were in Germany I do not know.

Occasions of another kind in which the silence was broken were 16 those where, in class, public lecture, or informal meetings with students, I myself had talked frankly of race relations in other parts of the world, including the lynchings which sometimes occur in my own country and the terrible cruelty visited upon natives in South Africa. This took off the lid of defensiveness, so that a few people would talk quite easily of what happened under the Nazi regime. More common were situations like that with the architect, where I threw in some remark about the atrocities in response to Germans' complaint that the world is abusing them. In such cases, there was usually an expression of shame, accompanied by a variety of excuses (including that of having been kept in ignorance) and followed by a quick turning away from the subject.

Somewhere in consideration of this problem of discussion versus 17 silence we must ask what the good (that is, ordinary) people in Germany did know about these things. It is clear that the S.S. kept the more gory details of the concentration camps a close secret. Even high officials of the government, the army, and the Nazi party itself were in some measure held in ignorance, although of course they kept the camps supplied with victims. The common people of Germany knew that the camps existed; most knew people who had disappeared into them; some saw the victims, walking skeletons in rags, being transported in trucks or trains or being herded on the road from station to camp or to work in fields or factories near the camps. Many knew people who had been released from concentration camps; such released persons kept their counsel on pain of death. But secrecy was cultivated and supported by fear and terror. In the absence of a determined and heroic will to know and publish the truth, and in the absence of all the instruments of opposition, the degree of knowledge was undoubtedly low, in spite of the fact that all knew that something both stupendous and horrible was going on; and in spite of the fact that Hitler's *Mein Kampf* and the utterances of his aides said that no fate was too horrible for the Jews and other wrong-headed or inferior people. This must make us ask under what conditions the will to know and to discuss is strong, determined, and effective; this, like most of the important questions I have raised, I leave unanswered except as answers may be contained in the statement of the case.

18　　But to return to our moderately good man, the architect. He insisted over and over again that he did not know, and we may suppose that he knew as much and as little as most Germans. But he also made it quite clear that he wanted something done to the Jews. I have similar statements from people of whom I knew that they had had close Jewish friends before the Nazi time. This raises the whole problem of the extent to which those pariahs who do the dirty work of society are really acting as agents for the rest of us. To talk of this question one must note that, in building up his case, the architect pushed the Jews firmly into an out-group; they were dirty, lousy, and unscrupulous (an odd statement from a resident of Frankfurt, the home of old Jewish merchants and intel-lectual families long identified with those aspects of culture of which Germans are most proud). Having dissociated himself clearly from these people, and having declared them a problem, he apparently was willing to let someone else do to them the dirty work which he himself would not do, and for which he expressed shame. The case is perhaps analo-gous to our attitude toward those convicted of crime. From time to time, we get wind of cruelty practiced upon the prisoners in penitentiaries or jails; or, it may be, merely a report that they are ill-fed or that hygienic conditions are not good. Perhaps we do not wish that the prisoners should be cruelly treated or badly fed, but our reaction is probably tempered by a notion that they deserve something, because of some dissociation of them from the in-group of good people. If what they get is worse than what we like to think about, it is a little bit too bad. It is a point on which we are ambivalent. Campaigns for reform of prisons are often followed by counter-campaigns against a too high standard of living for prisoners and against having prisons run by softies. Now the people who run prisons are our agents. Just how far they do or could carry out our wishes is hard to say. The minor prison guard, in boastful justification of some of his more questionable practices, says, in effect: "If those reformers and those big shots upstairs had to live with these birds as I do, they would soon change their fool notions about running a prison." He is suggesting that the good people are either naïve or hypo-critical. Furthermore, he knows quite well that the wishes of his em-ployers, the public, are by no means unmixed. They are quite as likely to put upon him for being too nice as for being too harsh. And if, as sometimes happens, he is a man disposed to cruelty, there may be some justice in his feeling that he is only doing what others would like to do, if they but dared; and what they would do, if they were in his place.

19　　There are plenty of examples in our own world which I might have picked for comparison with the German attitude toward the concentration camps. For instance, a newspaper in Denver made a great scandal out of the allegation that our Japanese compatriots were too well fed in the camps where they were concentrated during the war. I might have mentioned some feature of the sorry history of the people of Japanese background in Canada. Or it might have been lynching, or some aspect of racial discrimination. But I purposely chose prisoners convicted of crime. For convicts are formally set aside for special handling. They constitute an out-group in all countries. This brings the issue clearly before us, since few people cherish the illusion that the problem of treating criminals can be settled by propaganda designed to prove that there aren't any criminals. Almost everyone agrees that something has to be done about them. The question concerns what is done, who does it, and the nature of the mandate given by the rest of us to those who do it. Perhaps we give them an unconscious mandate to go beyond anything we ourselves would care to do or even to acknowledge. I venture to suggest that the higher and more expert functionaries who act in our behalf represent something of a distillation of what we may consider our public wishes, while some of the others show a sort of concentrate of those impulses of which we are or wish to be less aware.

Now the choice of convicted prisoners brings up another crucial point 20 in intergroup relations. All societies of any great size have in-groups and out-groups; in fact, one of the best ways of describing a society is to consider it a network of smaller and larger in-groups and out-groups. And an in-group is one only because there are out-groups. When I refer to *my* children I obviously imply that they are closer to me than other people's children and that I will make greater efforts to buy oranges and cod-liver oil for them than for others' children. In fact, it may mean that I will give them cod-liver oil if I have to choke them to get it down. We do our own dirty work on those closest to us. The very injunction that I love my neighbor as myself starts with me; if I don't love myself and my nearest, the phrase has a very sour meaning.

Each of us is a center of a network of in- and out-groups. Now the 21 distinctions between *in* and *out* may be drawn in various ways, and nothing is more important for both the student of society and the educator than to discover how these lines are made and how they may be redrawn in more just and sensible ways. But to believe that we can do away with the distinction between *in* and *out*, *us* and *them* in social life is complete nonsense. On the positive side, we generally feel a greater obligation to in-groups; hence less obligation to out-groups; and in the case of such groups as convicted criminals, the out-group is definitely given over to the hands of our agents for punishment. That is the extreme case. But there are other out-groups toward which we may have aggressive feelings and dislike, although we give no formal mandate to anyone to deal with them on our behalf, and although we profess to believe that they should not suffer restrictions or disadvantages. The greater their social distance from us, the more we leave in the hands of others a sort of mandate by default to deal with them on our behalf. Whatever effort we put on reconstructing the lines which divide in- and out-groups, there remains the eternal problem of our treatment, direct or delegated, of whatever groups are considered somewhat outside. And here it is that the whole matter of our professed and possible deeper unprofessed wishes comes up for consideration; and the related problem of what we know, can know, and want to know about it. In Germany, the agents got out of hand and created such terror that it was best not to know. It is also clear that it was and is easier to the conscience of many Germans not to know. It is, finally, not unjust to say that the agents were at least working in the direction of the wishes of many people, although they may have gone beyond the wishes of most. The same questions can be asked about our own society, and with reference not only to prisoners but also to many other groups upon whom there is no legal or moral stigma. Again I have not the answers. I leave you to search for them.

22      In considering the question of dirty work we have eventually to think about the people who do it. In Germany, these were the members of the S.S. and of that inner group of the S.S. who operated the concentration camps. Many reports have been made on the social backgrounds and the personalities of these cruel fanatics. Those who have studied them say that a large proportion were "gescheiterte Existenzen," men or women with a history of failure, of poor adaptation to the demands of work and of the classes of society in which they had been bred. Germany between wars had large numbers of such people. Their adherence to a movement which proclaimed a doctrine of hatred was natural enough. The movement offered something more. It created an inner group which was to be superior to all others, even Germans, in their emancipation from the usual bourgeois morality; people above and beyond the ordinary morality. I dwell on this, not as a doctrine, but as an organizational device. For, as Eugen Kogon, author of the most penetrating analysis of the S.S. and their camps, has said, the Nazis came to power by creating a state within a state; a body with its own counter-morality, and its own counter-law, its courts and its own execution of sentence upon those who did not live up to its orders and standards. Even as a movement, it had inner circles within inner circles; each sworn to secrecy as against the next outer one. The struggle between these inner circles continued after Hitler came to power; Himmler eventually won the day. His S.S. became a state within the Nazi state, just as the Nazi movement had become a state within the Weimar state. One is reminded of the oft-quoted but neglected statement of Sighele: "At the center of a crowd look for the sect." He referred, of course, to the political sect; the fanatical inner group of a movement seeking power by revolutionary methods. Once the Nazis were in power, this inner sect, while becoming now the recognized agent of the state and, hence, of the masses of the people, could at the same time dissociate

itself more completely from them in action, because of the very fact of having a mandate. It was now beyond all danger of interference and investigation. For it had the instruments of interference and investigation its own hands. These are also the instruments of secrecy. So the S.S. could and did build up a powerful system in which they had the resources of the state and of the economy of Germany and the conquered countries from which to steal all that was needed to carry out their orgy of cruelty luxuriously as well as with impunity.

Now let us ask, concerning the dirty workers, questions similar to those concerning the good people. Is there a supply of candidates for such work in other societies? It would be easy to say that only Germany could produce such a crop. The question is answered by being put. The problem of people who have run aground (gescheiterte Existenzen) is one of the most serious in our modern societies. Any psychiatrist will, I believe, testify that we have a sufficient pool or fund of personalities warped toward perverse punishment and cruelty to do any amount of dirty work that the good people may be inclined to countenance. It would not take a very great turn of events to increase the number of such people, and to bring their discontents to the surface. This is not to suggest that every movement based on discontent with the present state of things will be led by such people. That is obviously untrue; and I emphasize the point lest my remarks give comfort to those who would damn all who express militant discontent. But I think study of militant social movements does show that these warped people seek a place in them. Specifically, they are likely to become the plotting, secret police of the group. It is one of the problems of militant social movements to keep such people out. It is of course easier to do this if the spirit of the movement is positive, its conception of humanity high and inclusive, and its aims sound. This was not the case of the Nazi movement. As Kogon puts it: "The SS were but the arch-type of the Nazis in general." But such people are sometimes attracted, for want of something better, to movements whose aims are contrary to the spirit of cruelty and punishment. I would suggest that all of us look well at the leadership and entourage of movements to which we attach ourselves for signs of a negativistic, punishing attitude. For once such a spirit develops in a movement, punishment of the nearest and easiest victim is likely to become more attractive than striving for the essential goals. And, if the Nazi movement teaches us anything at all, it is that if any shadow of a mandate be given to such people, they will—having compromised us—make it larger and larger. The processes by which they do so are the development of the power and inward discipline of their own group, a progressive dissociation of themselves from the rules of human decency prevalent in their culture, and an ever growing contempt for the welfare of the masses of people.

The power and inward discipline of the S.S. became such that those who once became members could get out only by death; by suicide, murder, or mental breakdown. Orders from the central offices of the S.S. were couched in equivocal terms as a hedge against a possible day of judgment. When it became clear that such a day of judgment would come, the hedging and intrigue became greater; the urge to murder also became greater, because every prisoner became a potential witness.

25      Again we are dealing with a phenomenon common in all societies. Almost every group which has a specialized social function to perform is in some measure a secret society, with a body of rules developed and enforced by the members and with some power to save its members from outside punishment. And here is one of the paradoxes of social order. A society without smaller rule-making and disciplining powers would be no society at all. There would be nothing but law and police; and this is what the Nazis strove for, at the expense of family, church, professional groups, parties, and other such nuclei of spontaneous control. But apparently the only way to do this, for good as well as for evil ends, is to give power into the hands of some fanatical small group which will have a far greater power of self-discipline and a far greater immunity from outside control than the traditional groups. The problem is, then, not of trying to get rid of all the self-disciplining, protecting groups within society, but one of keeping them integrated with one another and as sensitive as can be to a public opinion which transcends them all. It is a matter of checks and balances, of what we might call the social and moral constitution of society. . . .

## Evaluating the Text

1. Why did Hughes go to Germany in 1948? Why was he interested in answering the question "how could these millions of ordinary people live in the midst of such cruelty and murder without a general uprising against it and against the people who did it"?
2. What purpose is served by beginning his analysis with examples that "show the extreme of perverse cruelty reached by the SS guards in charge of the camps"? How do these examples bring home the need to investigate how such bestial events could occur without protest of any kind by the German people?
3. How does Hughes's investigation of the circumstances under which people will let others do their "dirty work" for them illustrate the assumptions that guide sociologists? Rather than accepting the hypothesis that the Germans are innately evil, how does Hughes's analysis assume the existence of social mechanisms that could produce the same results in any group? Does Hughes create an effective case for his theory?
4. How does Hughes's conversation with the architect in Frankfurt illustrate the process of denial and collective amnesia that Hughes has discovered elsewhere as well? Explain what this process involves, and discuss those few occasions where Hughes got people to speak on an issue about which they were normally silent.
5. Evaluate Hughes's hypothesis that the Nazis acted as agents to carry out the wishes of most Germans in a way that allowed the general population

to deny knowledge of what was happening. According to Hughes, what kinds of social pressures operated to keep knowledge of what was going on in the concentration camps from being widely discussed?

6. Why does Hughes compare the knowledge Germans had of activities in the concentration camps with the general population's awareness of prison conditions in the United States? How effective is the analogy Hughes draws between prison guards in the United States and guards in the concentration camps?

7. Summarize Hughes's thesis about the existence of "in" and "out" groups. What is the nature of their relationship in delegating and performing "dirty work"? How does Hughes illustrate his claim with a discussion of how the SS (which was formerly an "out" group) became an "in" group by agreeing to be the agents for persecuting other "out" groups?

## Exploring Different Perspectives

1. Explore the psychology of a soldier designated to perform "dirty work" during the Cypriot rebellion in "Gregory" by Panos Ioannides. What additional insights does Ioannides's characterization provide beyond the sociological analysis offered by Hughes?

2. Examine the repercussions of performing "dirty work" by Claude Eatherly, the lead pilot of the squadron that dropped the first atomic bomb on Hiroshima (as described in Maurizio Chierici's article "The Man from Hiroshima"). What differences can you discover between Eatherly's reactions and those of the guards in the concentration camps and those Germans whom Hughes interviewed?

3. How does the same process Hughes discovered by which the German population distanced itself from knowledge of what was happening to various "out" groups operate in Kate Wilhelm's story ("The Village")? That is, to what extent do people in the village condone what is happening so long as it is happening "over there"?

## Extending Viewpoints through Writing

1. To what extent did the public nature of the Vietnam war, seen on TV every night, distinguish it from World War II in terms of people being able to deny knowledge of what was happening, as they did in Germany?

2. How might the reunification of East and West Germany affect the kinds of information Germans receive about the concentration camps? Given the fact that East Germany was dominated by Russia since World War II, why might East Germans' impressions of what went on be very different from those of West Germans?

# Kyōko Hayashi

# *The Empty Can*

---

*Kyōko Hayashi was born in 1930 in Nagasaki and spent the years from 1931 to 1945 in Shanghai. After returning to Japan, she was enrolled in the third year of Nagasaki Girl's High School and was exposed to the atomic bomb while working as a recruit in the Mitsubishi Munitions factory. Her first published work, "Ritual of Death," in which she describes her experiences as an atomic bomb victim, was awarded the 73rd Akutagawa Prize. "The Empty Can," translated by Margaret Mitsutani, appeared in* The Crazy Iris and Other Stories of the Atomic Aftermath, *edited by Kenzaburō Ōe (1985). The story is a thinly fictionalized account of her class reunion with other survivors thirty years later.*

*Following the annilihation of Hiroshima on August 6 and Nagasaki on August 9 of 1945, Emperor Hirohito agreed to an unconditional surrender on August 14. The military administration of occupied Japan ended in 1951, and full Japanese sovereignty was restored in 1952. By some estimates, 1,800,000 Japanese died during the war, during which 40 percent of Japanese towns and cities were destroyed. Within twenty years of this devastation, Japan became the world's fastest growing economy and today is a principal trading partner and political ally of the United States.*

1    The school was a four storied, U-shaped building. The five of us were standing in about the center of the yard it enclosed. It was past 1:30 in the afternoon. The sun had begun to shift toward the west, and the school building cast its shadow across the yard. The place where the five of us were standing was already in shadow. But the auditorium, which faced toward the west, was still flooded with sunlight.

2    "And now a word about the use of the lavatories," said Oki, facing the other four, hands on hips. "Who was it who always used to say that?" Nishida asked, pointing at Oki, trying to remember. Who was that anyway? There was definitely one teacher who was always lecturing us about the use of the lavatories. "Scrub brush!" I shouted, remembering his nickname. Hara gave the sleeve of my overcoat a tug, and warned me in the gentle way so characteristic of the Nagasaki dialect. "Careful—

(For more background on Japan, see pp. 35, 250, and 525.)

they'll hear you in the faculty room." But the teachers of thirty years ago couldn't be in the faculty room now. Not only the teachers of thirty years ago. There was no one left in the faculty room now.

Our alma mater was to be closed at the end of next year. The students 3 had already moved to the new school, which had been built on a height overlooking the city of Nagasaki. The phoenix palm that was once planted by the circular driveway at the entrance had been dug up, and lay with its roots wrapped in straw matting—we had seen it when we entered the school gate a little while before. There had been a phoenix palm by the circular driveway when we were high school girls. Judging from the shape of the branches, this was probably the same tree. In thirty years' time this phoenix, which branched off into three trees near the root, had grown to a height of 7 or 8 meters. Would it, too, be transplanted to the grounds of the new school?

We were the only ones on the school grounds. The school had 4 absorbed all sound into its concrete surface, and stood in silence like a castle wall.

We were often called together in this yard when there was a special 5 announcement. The teacher Oki had imitated was a man science teacher. When the announcement was over, he would turn, and with a "Well now . . . " begin to address the students, bustling over to climb the platform the faculty used when we had our morning exercises. Then, in just the tone of Oki's imitation, he would start, "And now a word about the use of the lavatories." The correct way to dispose of sanitary napkins, and to flush the toilets; he would explain in great detail all the rules of proper usage. Especially during the winter, when the pipes of the toilets would freeze, the water would overflow on the outside, making a white water stain on the outside wall of the building which severely detracted from the aesthetic appearance of the school. He would point at the stain in admonition. Those were the rough days just after the war, but we were young girls after all, and we were embarrassed by such talk. That was probably why this was the first memory to come to Oki as she stood in the school yard—embarrassment must have left a deep impression. The white stain where the water had overflowed was still there, even wider than before.

First floor, second floor, following the floors up along the surface of 6 the wall, I turned my eyes toward the sky. The patch of clear blue sky cut into the shape of a U was right above my face. The light of the sun, which gave off a warmth unusual for early winter, gleamed along the straight concrete edge. I lowered my eyes once again to the fourth floor, then the third. The windows of the building were all closed. For a deserted school building, the glass was well polished. And there was a perfect pane of glass in each window on every floor. That was what looked strange to me.

From the time the A-bomb was dropped on August 9, 1945, until I 7 graduated two years later, there wasn't a single pane of glass in the school. In the corners of the window frames, which the blast had warped into bowlike curves, only fragments had remained here and there, pointed like shark's teeth.

8    Pieces of board had been nailed over the dressing rooms and toilets, where a screen of some kind was needed, but that was only in the places where the steel window frames were straight.

9    How had they mended each warped window frame? The window frames, divided vertically and horizontally into many sections, were perfectly straight, and panes of transparent glass were fitted into them, just as they had been then. If you looked carefully you could see that the now popular aluminum type sash had been installed in five or six of the windows on the auditorium side. The windows were divided into two parts, upper and lower, and only in those places the frames caught the western sun, gleaming silver in its lights. They must have been put in to replace the windows that were damaged beyond repair, but their flashy newness stuck out next to the white water stain and the rusty iron window frames smeared with putty.

10    "Was the yard really this small?" said Nishida, looking around.

11    "I was just thinking the same thing," said Hara, glancing around the yard along with Nishida.

12    "Want to take a look inside?" asked Noda, who was dressed in kimono.

13    "Yeah, let's go in," said Oki. "I want to get a last look at the auditorium." I, too, wanted to see the auditorium one more time before it was torn down.

14    We walked toward the student entrance. There was an iron lock on the entrance. We cut through the yard, and through the main entrance, dirty with the earth from the uprooted phoenix palm, we entered the school.

15    The instant that we stood in the entrance of the auditorium, the five of us stopped our chattering. Each one stood stock still, as if nailed to the spot. There was nothing in the auditorium. The wooden benches and long narrow tables where we students had sat during ceremonies and assemblies were gone. Only one bench, its back broken, its days of usefulness long past, had been left in the center of the auditorium.

16    The curtain of the stage had been torn away, and the whitewashed wall was exposed to plain view. The piano, the blackboard on which the order of the school ceremonies had been written, and all the other paraphernalia had been taken away, and on the lusterless, splintery floor, one dried up rag lay where someone had thrown it. I looked up at the ceiling. The ceiling, lined with narrow boards, was painted pale green. The shade of the green paint, and the grain of the wooden boards, each one 10 centimeters wide, appeared before my eyes, just as they had been thirty years ago. And the milk colored chandelier in the shape of a globe—it was there too, just as it had been.

It was bright inside the auditorium, and perfectly silent. "Makes you 17
sad just to think of it," Hara whispered. "The memorial service," I said,
also in a whisper. Oki and Noda nodded in silence. I turned to the stage,
naked without its curtain, and gave a silent prayer.

This was the first time I had seen the auditorium since I had gradu- 18
ated. It was neither the memory of school concerts nor of graduation
ceremonies that had nailed me to the spot as I stood at the entrance of
the auditorium. It was the memory of the ceremony that had been held
in October of the year the war ended in memory of the students and
teachers who had died in the bombing. The silent prayer I had given was
for the spirits of my friends for whom the service had been held. Oki and
the others must have been thinking of the same thing. Especially Hara
and Oki, for they had had the experience of lying on this auditorium
floor, seriously injured after having been exposed to the A-bomb at a
munitions factory in Uragami. Hara and Oki, their wounds healed, had
both survived, but many other girls had died on this floor under the
watchful eyes of teachers and friends. Out of a student body of thirteen
or fourteen hundred, nearly three hundred had died between August 9th
and the day of the memorial service. Some had been recruited to work in
the munitions factories in the Uragami district, and had died instantly
there; others had died in their own homes—death had come in various
ways. The names of the students were written with a brush on rice paper
and put up on the whitewashed wall in four or five rows, each row
reaching from one side of the wall to the other.

The homeroom teacher of each class read the names of his or her 19
students. The names of students whose homeroom teacher had been
killed in the bombing were read by another teacher of the same grade. As
the name of each student was read, there was a stirring among the
students who had survived. Then after a while all was quiet, and we sat
on the benches, shoulders drooping, as though stupefied. The parents of
the students who had died sat along the three walls. The parents were in
tears before the memorial service began. The tears turned to sobs, and
the sobs drifted steadily toward the center of the room where the students were sitting. "Makes you sad just to think of it," Hara had whispered. Her words plainly expressed the thoughts of that day that had
come to life again in each of our hearts. I went into the auditorium and
walked over to the window that looked out onto the central yard. With
my back to the window, through which the western sun was shining, I
looked at the auditorium once again. Nishida and Oki came over.

Leaning against the low window sill, Nishida said, "I feel so awk- 20
ward when you talk about the bombing. It makes me feel guilty." Of
course, merely hearing the words "memorial service" was enough to tell
Nishida what we were thinking about. Nishida had not been exposed to
the bombing. Like me, she was a transfer student. She was not one of the
"bona-fide" students of N Girls' High School, who had taken the entrance examination after grade school, and been specially chosen to

enter. The students of N Girls' High were selected by examination, and they were proud of their school's reputation. They therefore tended to look down on transfer students, even though they were all students of the same N Girls' High. But although we were both transfer students, there was a subtle distinction between Nishida and me.

21    I entered N Girls' High as a transfer student in March of 1945. On the following August 9th, I was exposed to the A-bomb while working as a labor recruit. Nishida had transferred in October of the year the war ended, on the day of the memorial service. The difference between having been exposed to radiation or not, bore even upon our relationships with Oki and the other "bona-fide" N High girls.

22    When Nishida said she felt awkward, she was referring to this question of the relationships among us. The distinction between having been exposed or not was what made her feel guilty. Oki laughed and said, "You must be joking! Of course it's better not to have been exposed— that's only natural."

23    "No, it's not that," said Nishida, "it's not a question of good or bad, it's an emotional thing—emotionally, I want to have been exposed like you." She then went on. "For instance, both you and I were transfer students, so we can't really speak Nagasaki dialect properly, and if we try too hard, it sounds awkward. It's that awkwardness—you know what I mean?" she said to me.

24    "I still feel it, even now," Nishida continued. "Just now when the four of you were standing at the entrance to the auditorium and you all looked as though you were about to cry. I know what you were thinking about just then—it was the memorial service, wasn't it? But I was thinking of something else." Nishida told us that the scene that had come to her mind was the all school student speech contest that had been held soon after she had transferred to N Girls' High.

25    "Remember?" Nishida asked me. Around that time I was running a fever from radiation sickness, and stayed at home as much as possible on days when there weren't regular classes. I probably hadn't been at school on the day of the speech contest. I had no memory of it. "I feel mortified just to think of it!" said Oki, covering her face with her hands in embarrassment like a young girl.

26    "What happened?" asked Hara and Noda, coming over to see what was the matter.

27    For the contest, each student had been asked to write a speech expounding her views on a topic of her own choosing. The best speech was chosen from each class, and the students chosen to represent their classes delivered their speeches on the stage of the auditorium. It seemed that Nishida and Oki had each been chosen as class representatives, and had thus been rivals for first place in the competition.

28    Nishida's topic was "On Woman Suffrage," while Oki's was "Careers for Women." In her speech, Oki had vigorously asserted that women should be freed from the task of child bearing, and that was

apparently what was making her feel mortified now. "A lucky guess that was—I've never had any children yet," Oki said jokingly. After graduating from a women's university in Tokyo, Oki had come back to Nagasaki, and taken up a career as a junior high school teacher, working for Nagasaki Prefecture. Since then, for no special reason, she had remained single. Expecting to marry someday, she had simply waited, until at last she was over forty.

"But the best place for a woman who doesn't marry is in government service, isn't it?" said Nishida.

"That's right, and besides, you can draw a pension in your old age," added Noda. "Now if my husband dies, I'm out—right then and there," she added, making motions of hanging herself. "Oh no you're not," said Oki, a look of gloom coming over her face.

The problem of education on the outlying islands of Nagasaki Prefecture had recently begun to draw a good deal of public attention. Nagasaki Prefecture has a great number of outlying islands, and the education of the children living on them is a longstanding problem. To Oki, the problem was a most personal one, for it involved the question of whether or not she herself would be assigned to a teaching post on one of the outlying islands. In fact, it seemed very likely that she would be. One of the conditions for taking such a post was that the person be unmarried. Furthermore, during her more than twenty years as a teacher, Oki had never been assigned to a post outside of the city of Nagasaki. Until now, she had been transferred only to junior high schools within the city limits. This was unusual for a teacher in Nagasaki Prefecture, with all its outlying islands. But it was almost certain that she would be ordered to an island post next spring. It wasn't that Oki objected to being transferred. What she was worried about was a recurrence of radiation sickness.

When the list of names of students killed was posted by the school gate immediately after the bombing, the name "Oki" was near the top. Until the day of the memorial service, we had thought that Oki had died after the bombing. The fragments of glass embedded in her arms and back had caused her to lose a lot of blood, and she had lost consciousness from time to time while she was being cared for on the auditorium floor. Carried in the arms of her parents, who had come for her, Oki had gone home, but the way she had looked at that time seems to have been responsible for the theory that she had died. Now she looked healthy enough, but it was as though she was carrying an unexploded bomb around inside her. "As old as I am, I ought to be ready to die, but when it comes right down to it, it's awfully scary," said Oki. There were doctors on the outlying islands, but if radiation sickness was to appear, Oki—I, too, for that matter—wanted to enter the Hospital for Atomic-Bomb Victims in Nagasaki. If we became ill with any kind of disease, we wanted to enter the Hospital for Atomic-Bomb Victims, where the doctors who treated us would have the possibility of radiation sickness in mind. If possible, we wanted to live in a city or town near the Hospital for Atomic-Bomb Victims. Oki's anxiety arose from the thought of crossing the water to some isolated island, separating herself from the Hospital. But a history of exposure to the A-bomb was not acceptable as a reason for refusing a post on one of the outlying islands. Supposing it was—every teacher in Nagasaki Prefecture was probably connected to the bomb in some way. There would be no teachers left to go to the outlying islands. Still, as a fellow A-bomb victim, I could understand Oki's feeling of uncertainty.

33     "It may sound brutal to say so," Nishida said, "but once you have your plans set, you have to go ahead with them—that's life, isn't it? Even if you are sick."

34     It's no use standing still in one spot. The present, where we are right now, has always got to be a starting point. That's what Nishida was saying.

35     Half a year ago, Nishida had lost her husband. He had died after only two or three days in bed, without so much as a parting word. Fortunately, Nishida had made a name for herself as a fashion designer. Unlike Noda, her husband's death did not mean that she would have to hang herself. Her work had an established reputation, and she seemed to have secured a place for herself in the world of fashion. "You've got to keep going forward no matter what—they're all just waiting to see when you'll trip up," she said. Then she turned to Hara. "Excuse me for being blunt, but are you married?" she asked. Hara shook her head, and answered, "Same as Miss Oki." Compared to Oki, who was rather stout, Hara looked quite sickly.

36     Her arms and legs were thin, and her face, with its finely chiselled features, like those of a Japanese doll, was a pale, lifeless color. She had been suffering from pernicious anemia since her exposure to the A-bomb, and didn't look as though she could bear up physically under the strain of married life. Oki's parents had died several years ago, one after the other, but Hara's parents were well, and she was living under their care.

37     "Then the only one of us with a husband is Mrs. Noda," I said. "How about you?" Noda asked me.

38     "I'm alone," was all I said in answer.

39     Five of us, once young girls; and now the only one among us who was living a peaceful married life was Noda. Death, divorce, and then Hara and Oki, who had remained single to this day. We stood a while in silence in the spot of sunlight by the window.

40     "Thirty years; I feel as though I've just been living and that's all," said Hara. "Are we making too much of the bomb?" said Oki in a whisper.

41     "What about Kinuko? Couldn't she come today?" asked Noda, changing the subject. Oki gave a wild cry. "Oh, I forgot!" Kinuko, who lived in Shimabara, had called Oki that morning. Kinuko knew that

Nishida and I were coming from Tokyo for a week's stay in Nagasaki, and she had been planning to come along on today's visit to our alma mater. Then suddenly something had come up, and she hadn't come.

"She'd had her name in for a bed in the A-bomb Hospital. There's an empty bed now, so she said she's going into the hospital tomorrow." At these words of Oki's, Hara furrowed her brow and said, "Radiation sickness?" "No," said Oki, shaking her head, "to have some glass taken out of her back." 42

Kinuko was an elementary school teacher in Shimabara, in charge of a class of second graders. She had first felt the pain of the fragments of glass in her back during gym class. Kinuko, past forty but still full of energy, was demonstrating a somersault for the children. She had felt it when her rounded back hit the mat — a prickle of pain like the glimmer of an electric light. "I'm getting too old for this sort of thing," she had thought, but nevertheless did another somersault for her pupils. This time, the pain was a sharp one. After school, Kinuko had stopped at the hospital to have it checked. The doctor pressed her back here and there with his fingertips, and then asked Kinuko, "Were you around when the A-bomb was dropped? It might be glass from the time of the bombing, you know." An X-ray was taken, and when they opened her back in one place a week later, they found glass, just as the doctor had said. The skin was hard in that place, and there were several other places like it. They apparently showed up on the X-ray film as shadows. Kinuko was going into the hospital tomorrow for an operation to have all the glass removed, Oki explained. 43

"Kinuko. I'm not sure I remember her, but wasn't she one of the girls in the speech contest with us?" asked Nishida. "That's right, she was in it," answered Noda. "She was bald then, wasn't she?" It seemed that after the bombing, Kinuko's hair had fallen out, leaving her bald. I had no memory of Kinuko standing bald on the platform in the auditorium, nor did I remember her at all when she was a high school student. 44

"She talked about the importance of life," Hara remembered. "That's right — her mother and father were killed instantly," said Oki. "Was she an only child?" I asked. "Just like me — a teacher, and all her life alone," said Oki, turning to us with a laugh. 45

Having no memory of Kinuko as a student, my association with her had begun when we met at a class reunion, or some such sort of meeting. Then, last year, I had seen her for the first time in ten years. 46

One of our teachers at high school was a young woman named Miss T. Twenty-four or five at the time, she was the daughter of K Temple in Kamimachi in the city of Nagasaki. A graduate of N Girls' High School, she was beautiful; fair skinned, with downy golden hair that shone across her cheeks to her earlobes. Her eyes were bluish-grey, and her chestnut hair was fine; only slightly coarser than a baby's. There are many men and women in Nagasaki who look as though they could be of 47 racially mixed parentage, and Miss T was one of them. Miss T had accompanied the students who had been recruited to work in the munitions factories, and on August 9th, had been killed instantly in the precision machine factory where she and Kinuko had been working.

48    Having found out that Miss T was buried in the graveyard of K Temple, her birthplace, I had called Kinuko, and in October of last year, we had gone to visit her grave for the first time in the thirty years since her death.

49    After paying our respects at the grave, we sat down by the roots of the oak tree on the grounds of K Temple, overlooking the city, and talked about our memories of Miss T. Kinuko had been there when Miss T died. She hadn't actually identified the body, but she had witnessed the moment when Miss T, struck in the forehead by the blinding flash, had melted into the light and disappeared. Just at that instant, Miss T had opened her mouth wide, and yelled something to Kinuko. Of course she hadn't been able to hear the words. It might simply have been a scream, but Kinuko had never stopped thinking that somehow she wanted to understand Miss T's last words. She had sketched the shape of those open lips in her mind over and over again, until at last Miss T had become fixed in Kinuko's brain, like a picture stuck fast to a wall.

50    The burden of the words that she hadn't been able to hear weighed on Kinuko's heart, and lately she had begun to doubt the reality of that scene, even of Miss T's death. She told me that she had come to K Temple to assure herself of the past that was becoming more and more vague in her mind, and to confirm the fact of Miss T's death. "The priest's wife said that they cremated Miss T under this oak tree," she said, citing the words of the priest's wife as proof.

51    "That's right. The priest's wife was saying that they'd cremated her here," I answered, tapping the gnarled root of the oak tree.

52    "She said they collected the bones after the cremation. It's best to forget about people who are dead," said Kinuko, tapping the gnarled root as I had done. Just then, Kinuko gave a sharp cry of pain and rubbed the palm of her hand. There was neither blood nor any sign of a wound on the palm of her hand. Puzzled, I asked her if she'd been pricked by a thorn.

53    "No, glass," she had answered simply. The flatness of Kinuko's words came back to me now.

54    "You know, the human body's really amazing," Oki said. Four or five years ago, Oki too had had a piece of glass taken out of her back. After the doctor had made the incision, he had removed a lump of fat like a ball of floss silk. Several small fragments of glass, four or five milimeters long, formed the kernel of the fat, and the fat had covered them over like a white, round pearl.

55    We left the auditorium. Outside the auditorium, the corridor went off to the right and left with the staircase in the center. To the right, there

were special classrooms. The classrooms we had used immediately after the war were to the left. As we walked down the hall, we asked each other which class we had been in, and who our homeroom teachers had been. The corridor we were walking down formed the base of the U. The classroom at the corner of the U had only one entrance.

The other classrooms each had a front and a back door. In the corner 56 classroom, a door had been made in the wall leading to the classroom next door, in case of emergency. I remembered the door in the corner classroom. "This was my class," I said to Nishida. Peeking into the classroom through the window in the corridor, Nishida asked, "Which one?" Just as she had often done as a high school girl, Nishida leaned both elbows on the railing, poked her head and shoulders into the room and looked around. "This was my class," she said. Nishida too remembered the doorknob in the wall. Both of our memories of the knob itself were probably correct, but was the knob we remembered in the corner classroom, with only one entrance, or in the classroom on the other side of the wall; the one with the common door? Whichever it was, it seemed certain that my class and Nishida's had been next to each other.

Nishida and I had been drawn together by the loneliness of being 57 transfer students, but we had never once been in the same class. It was strange that we both had memories of the same classroom.

Oki came up beside Nishida and looked into the room. "Kinuko was 58 in this class. Were you in the same class?" she asked me. I said no. Nishida said that she didn't remember having been in the same class with Kinuko either. "There was a big hole in this wall," Oki said, walking into the classroom. Oki remembered everything in detail. Just as in the auditorium, in the semi-darkness of the classroom there were neither chairs nor desks. The blackboard, its surface covered with chalk dust, was hanging on the wall on the corridor side.

This blackboard, which had hung on the side wall of the classroom, 59 had served as a student bulletin board. The door I mentioned earlier was to the right of the blackboard. The hole Oki had referred to was in the wall between the blackboard and the door. The hole was toward the back of the classroom. It was big enough for two high school girls to pass through side by side, and through it we could see what was going on in the classroom next door. When I became bored with my own class, I would turn around and, within the limits of what I could see through the hole, I would wink to my friends in the classroom next door. The hole was soon repaired, but as I traced my memories, it seemed more and more to me as though the corner classroom had been my classroom after all. Because I was short, I had sat in the front of the class. The corner classroom was the only one where you could see into the next room through the hole in the wall from the front seat.

"Remember?" Oki asked. "Remember Kinuko's empty can?" she 60 asked again. "What was she doing with an empty can?" asked Noda.

"You know—she put her mother and father's bones in an empty can 61 and brought it to school with her every day," Oki said. "Ah!" I cried.

That girl—was that Kinuko? If it was, then Kinuko and I were class-mates. I remembered the girl who came to school with the bones of her parents in her school bag. The girl had kept the bones in a lidless empty can that had been seared red by the flames. To keep the bones from falling out, she had covered the top with newspaper, and tied it with red string. When the girl arrived at her seat, she took her textbooks out of her school bag. Then she took out the empty can, picking it up carefully with both hands, and placed it on the right side of her desk. When classes were over, she would put it back into the bottom of her school bag, again with both hands, and go home. At first, none of us had known what was in the empty can. And the girl did not show any sign of wanting to tell us, either. After our exposure to the A-bomb, the number of things we couldn't talk about openly had increased, so although it weighed on our minds, no one questioned her about it. The love we could see in the girl's fingertips when she handled the can made us feel all the more reluctant to ask.

62    It had happened during calligraphy class. One day the young callig-raphy teacher, who had been discharged from military service and come back, noticed the empty can on her desk. The top of the desk was covered with writing paper, an ink stone, and the textbook.

63    "What's that can doing there? Put it away in your desk," said the teacher from the platform. The girl hung her head, and held the can on the knees of her workpants. Then, she began to cry. The teacher asked her why.

64    "It's the bones of my mother and father," the girl answered. The calligraphy teacher took the can from the girl's hands, and placed it in the center of the desk on the platform. "May your parents rest in peace. Let us have a moment of silent prayer in their memory," he said, and closed his eyes. After a long silence, the teacher handed the can back to the girl and said, "After this, leave it at home. Your parents will be waiting there for you. It's better that way."

65    The girl that day was Kinuko. The incident of the empty can had stayed with me—a pain in the heart, as though an awl had been driven into the midst of my girlhood. It wasn't so much the owner of the can as the incident itself that had made such a deep and lasting impression. The figure of Kinuko as a child, standing in the ruins of her home, bending over to pick up the bones of her mother and father from beneath the white ash, appeared before me in the dim light of the classroom.

66    Where was that empty can now?

67    Did Kinuko still keep the bones of her parents in that rusty red can? Was the can on the desk in the room where she lived alone?

68    Last year, when I had met her at K Temple, Kinuko hadn't mentioned her parents. She had said nothing about her past life or her present life. Perhaps the glass in her back had already begun to hurt around that time.

69    Kinuko was to enter the hospital tomorrow. How many fragments of

glass from thirty years ago would come out of Kinuko's back? What kind of a glow would those smooth white pearls of fat cast when they were brought out into the light?

*Translated by Margaret Mitsutani*

## Evaluating the Text

1. What occasion draws the former students together to revisit the Nagasaki High School in 1975? What do these women have in common, and why would it promote the reminiscences Hayashi dramatizes?
2. How would you characterize the personalities of each of the girls Hayashi describes? What character traits distinguish Oki, Nishida, Hara, and Noda from each other?
3. What importance do the panes of window glass play in Hayashi's story? How does she introduce this theme? In what way does the significance of the glass fragments give you a different perspective on the effects of atomic bombing?
4. In your opinion, why does Nishida "feel guilty" about not having been exposed to radiation? How is her reaction related to feelings of guilt over not having suffered as much as the others? What insight does this give you into Japanese cultural values?
5. How have each of the girls been affected by the atomic bombing of Nagasaki? Try to mention as many different kinds of effects as you can (e.g., psychological, physiological, desire or ability to marry and have children, choice of job location, etc.).
6. What might you infer about the kind of life a woman could expect who was solely dependent on her husband and who had no marketable skill in the event her husband should die. What conclusions can be drawn about the role of women in Japanese culture?
7. As schoolmates do at class reunions, the four girls remember a classmate, Kinuko, who had planned to attend but did not. What importance does the story of Kinuko assume in the context of the overall narrative? To what extent is Kinuko's reaction more shocking because it differs so greatly from those of the other girls? How does her reaction violate Japanese cultural norms illustrated by the behavior of the other girls?

## Exploring Different Perspectives

1. Compare and contrast Hayashi's story with the different perspective offered by Maurizio Chierchi's interview, "The Man from Hiroshima." In what respects are Eatherly's reactions unexpectedly similar to those of Nishida?
2. In what ways does the theme of remembering and forgetting play an important role in this story and in the analysis by Everett C. Hughes ("Good People and Dirty Work")? What factors seem to determine whether war survivors wish to remember or forget the past?
3. To what extent do both Hayashi and Kate Wilhelm ("The Village")

involve the reader by telling their stories from the vantage point of victims of war?

## Extending Viewpoints through Writing

1. What insight does Hayashi's story give you about Japanese culture? For example, you might discuss themes of selflessness, the feeling of guilt for not suffering as much as fellow countrymen, women's dependency on husbands, the choice of suicide in the event of the husband's death, nationalism, the need to live through common experiences together, or the value of exhibiting composure in the face of disaster.

2. How would you compare the reactions of U.S. citizens to those of the Japanese in the face of disaster? To what extent might these differences be culturally based?

3. What are the most important differences between the kinds of life led by those who were exposed to the bomb and those who were not? You might wish to read John Hersey's *Hiroshima* (1946) and compare it with his 1974 account of what happened to the survivors of the atomic bomb.

4. Create a dialogue between Claude Eatherly (see Maurizio Chierici, "The Man from Hiroshima") and any one of the four women in Hayashi's story. What might they say to one another?

# Maurizio Chierici

# *The Man from Hiroshima*

---

*Maurizio Chierici is a special correspondent for the Milan newspaper*
Corriere della Sera. *"The Man from Hiroshima," translated from the*
*Italian by Wallis Wilde-Menozzi, first appeared in* Granta *(Autumn*
*1987). Chierici's interview with Claude Eatherly, the lead pilot whose*
*decision regarding weather conditions allowed the atomic bomb to be*
*dropped on Hiroshima, reveals the extent to which feelings of guilt*
*have taken over Eatherly's life. Fourteen months after this interview,*
*Eatherly committed suicide.*

*Comprising four major islands, Japan was cut off from contact*
*with the rest of the world until 1854, when an American Naval*
*Officer, Matthew C. Perry, persuaded the government to open trade*
*with the West. The lack of natural resources, overpopulation, and the*
*growing influence of the military led Japan to invade northern China*
*in the 1930s and to form a military alliance with Germany and Italy in*
*World War II. The dropping of the atomic bombs by the United States*
*on Hiroshima and Nagasaki led to Japan's surrender in August 1945*
*and subsequent occupation by U.S. forces. Full Japanese sovereignty*
*was restored in 1952. Japan is now a major power in the fields of*
*electronics, automobile manufacturing, and shipbuilding. Despite*
*continuing problems stemming from an imbalance in foreign trade,*
*Japan is a political ally of the United States.*

The protagonists of Hiroshima have no nostalgia. Even those people 1
only remotely connected with the event have had difficult lives. All
except one: Colonel Paul Tibbets, pilot of the *Enola Gay*, the plane that
carried the atom bomb. On TV, serene under his white locks, he was
unrepentant: 'I did my duty; I would do it again.' Tibbets is the only one
to have passed these years without so much as a shiver. One of the pilots
in the formation which flew over Hiroshima that day was unable to
participate in the victory celebrations; he took his life three days before
the official ceremony.

I knew another pilot full of problems; it wasn't at all easy to arrange 2
to meet him. Everyone said: 'You'll need patience. But if he gave you his
word, you'll hear from him sooner or later.' For days I waited and no one
came. Then the pilot called to apologize. There was fog at the airport: the
plane couldn't take off. Or: he had no money and the banks were closed.
He would buy the ticket tomorrow. Tomorrow came and went; there was

(For further information on Japan, see pp. 35, 250, 525, and 632.)

always a different story. Eventually I made a proposal: 'Eatherly, in five days it will be Christmas. I want to be back home in Italy before then. So I'll come to see you. It's much warmer where you are than in New York, and I've never been to Texas. I'll leave this afternoon.'

3    'No, stay where you are,' Eatherly interrupted. 'It's hard to talk here. Being in Texas blocks me; the people inhibit me. They know me too well, and there's no love lost between us. I plan to spend the holidays in New Jersey with a friend — I'd go out of my mind staying in Waco for Christmas — so I'll come and see you.'

4    I waited. Hours and hours in the lobby of the Hotel St Moritz, Central Park south. Behind windows the city is grey. Great lighted clocks scan the seconds at the tops of skyscrapers. Soon it will start to snow. People rush past who have come to New York on business, and who are going home laden with presents in coloured packages, their ribbons fluttering to the ground. In this festive atmosphere I find it strange to be meeting a man who contributed to the deaths of 60,000 people and turned their city into a monument for all time.

5    Three hours later the man sits down on the other side of the table, a glass in his hands. He is thin; his eyes are deeply marked, making his glance look old. But his hands are calm. When we shook hands I could feel they were cold and dry. He speaks first.

6    'How do I look?'

7    'I couldn't say. I've only seen your photographs. In them you seem older. And more tired and down on your luck.'

8    'I'm not old, or tired; only tormented. But not all the time. They have taken care of my nightmares. Right there in Waco; a doctor by the name of Parker. Grey-haired man; thin. It was heavy treatment. I don't know if their methods have changed, but the one they used with me was useless. "Give it up, Claude," Parker said, "you're not guilty. It just fell to you to pilot a plane over Hiroshima. How many other Claudes were there in the air force who would have carried out an order as important as that one? The war finished; they went home. And what was the order anyway? Look at the sky and say: *Too many clouds here. Can't see Kokura and Nagasaki. Better do Hiroshima.*" Every day for fourteen months Doctor Parker gave me more or less the same speech. In the end I had to ask not to see him any more. I'd got worse.'

9    'There are a lot stories, Mr Eatherly. Some people say you're a fake. Why?'

10    He doesn't answer immediately. Instead he asks if he can take advantage of my hospitality: would I have another drink with him? I wouldn't like to give the impression that Eatherly was an alcoholic. He could hold a bottle of whisky without any trouble and his eyes never clouded over. They remained alert and cold, just as they had been when he entered, bringing in a little of the wind from the city.

11    'You mean what Will Bradfort Huie wrote? He's a journalist who spent two days with me and then wrote a book — a whole book — about

my life. Who am I? I don't know. But no one can describe himself in a minute. If I asked you point blank: "Do you think of yourself as an honest person, or someone who works at giving others an impression to suit your own needs?" would you be able to demonstrate either in a minute? I doubt it. I didn't know how to answer him either.'

'Are you a pacifist as you've claimed for years?'                    12

'I am, and sincerely so, as is any American of good will. If I were    13
religious, I would say that pacifism springs from a Jewish or Christian consciousness, but I'm not religious, and I don't want to look a fool expounding my philosophy. I can't be religious after Hiroshima. When someone makes a trip like mine and returns alive, he either kills himself or he lives like a Trappist monk. Cloistered; praying that the world changes and that the likes of Claude Eatherly and Paul Tibbets and the scientists who worked on the bomb are never born again.'

Claude grew up in Texas, where discourse is uninformed by Edwar-    14
dian whispers from New England. Hearty laughter and loud voices; every sensation seems amplified. After the Japanese bombed Pearl Harbor, Texas offered more volunteers than any other state—the yellow devils had to be punished. Eatherly was among the volunteers. The youngest of six children, and a tackle on the Texas North College football team, he had a level head and a solid way of bringing them down. He didn't miss in the air either: he shot down thirty-three planes and his career took off. After three years he became a major, and a brilliant future seemed to await the handsome man with two bravery medals on his chest. The medals were what dug his grave. In the summer of 1945, he got orders to return home, but first he had to carry out one more mission. Just one.

You don't send a soldier home for the pleasure of giving him a little    15
of the good life. In the letter he posted to his mother announcing his imminent return, Claude wrote, 'This will be the last cigarette they stick in this prisoner's mouth.' Nothing to get worried about. He went to New Mexico and joined a formation of supermen: the best, bravest, most famous pilots, all being trained in secret. They assigned him to a Boeing B-29 Superfortress that Claude christened *Straight Flush*.

The account of that morning some weeks later belongs to history.    16
Three planes take off during the night of 6 August from Tinian in the Mariana Islands. Paul Tibbets is the group's commander. Eatherly opens the formation. There are no bombs in his plane; as for the others, no one suspects what a terrible device is hidden inside the *Enola Gay*. A bigger contrivance, they think, nothing more. Eatherly's job is to pinpoint the target with maximum accuracy. He must establish whether weather conditions allow for the centre to be Hiroshima, Kokura or Nagasaki, or whether they should continue towards secondary targets. He tells the story of that morning's events in a voice devoid of emotion which suggests that the recitation is the thousandth one.

17      'I had command of the lead plane, the *Straight Flush*. I flew over Hiroshima for fifteen minutes, studying the clouds covering the target — a bridge between the military zone and the city. Fifteen Japanese fighters were circling beneath me, but they're not made to fly above 29,000 feet where we were to be found. I looked up: cumulus clouds at 10,000, 12,000 metres. The wind was blowing them towards Hiroshima. Perfect weather. I could see the target clearly: the central span of the bridge. I laugh now when I think of the order: "I want only the central arch of the bridge, *only* that, you understand?" Even if I'd guessed that we were carrying something a bit special, the houses, the roads, the city still seemed very far away from our bomb. I said to myself: This morning's just a big scare for the Japanese.

18      'I transmitted the coded message, but the person who aimed the bomb made an error of 3,000 feet. Towards the city, naturally. But three thousand feet one way or the other wouldn't have made much difference: that's what I thought as I watched it drop. Then the explosion stunned me momentarily. Hiroshima disappeared under a yellow cloud. No one spoke after that. Usually when you return from a mission with everyone still alive, you exchange messages with each other, impressions, congratulations. This time the radios stayed silent; three planes close together and mute. Not for fear of the enemy, but for fear of our own words. Each one of us must have asked forgiveness for the bomb. I'm not religious and I didn't know who to ask forgiveness from, but in that moment I made a promise to my self to oppose all bombs and all wars. Never again that yellow cloud . . . '

19      Eatherly raises his voice. It is clear the yellow cloud accompanies him through his life.

20      'And what did Tibbets say?'

21      'Tibbets has nerves of steel, but the evening afterwards he explained how he spent those minutes. They had told him to be extremely careful: he was most at risk. So when the machine gunner yelled that the shock waves were on their way, he veered to take photographs; but the aeroplane just bounced like a ping-pong ball held up by a fountain. Calm returned and Tibbets felt tired; he asked to be relieved, and fell asleep. But he talked about it that evening when the number of victims was just beginning to be known. He kept on saying: "I'm sorry guys, I did my duty. I've no regrets." And I don't have his nerves. A year later I asked to be discharged.'

22      'What reason did you give?'

23      'Exhaustion. I was exhausted. And I wanted to get married. It's risky to bring matters of conscience into it when you're in the forces. They were astounded — how could I throw away such a promising future? The day of my discharge they waved a sheet of paper in front of me. It said I would receive 237 dollars a month pension. That was good money in those days, but I turned it down. And since the regulations didn't allow me to refuse, I put it in writing that the sum was to go to war widows. The end of my relationship with flying.'

He didn't tell the rest of the story willingly. He returns to Texas 24
where his family doesn't recognize him: thin, nervous, irascible, 24 years
old. He marries the Italian girl he met in New Mexico while he was
training for the final mission. Concetta Margetti had tried Hollywood
and finally been reduced to selling cigarettes in a local nightclub—not
perhaps the ideal wife for someone in Claude's state. But they write to
each other, they get married. A war story, yes; but the war had shredded
Eatherly's nerves. In the middle of the night he wakes his wife, breathless and in tears: 'Hit the ground, the yellow cloud's coming!' It goes on
like this for four years. His family finally convince him to enter the
psychiatric hospital in Waco as a voluntary patient. He can take walks in
the park any time of the day or night. He plays golf and receives visitors.
Concetta keeps him company on Sunday. His brother brings him books
and a pair of running shoes.

Then the problems start. Claude forges a cheque to send to the 25
victims of Hiroshima. He enters a bank with a toy pistol; for a few
minutes the employees are terrified until Eatherly bursts out laughing.
One day his move succeeds; he threatens a department store clerk with a
fake gun and makes her turn over the money, which he throws from a
balcony before escaping. They catch him and take him back to Waco.
He's no longer a voluntary patient: now they lock him in. They accuse
him of behaving in an antisocial way. (This euphemism is the last show
of respect for his heroic war record.) He is confined to his room.

After fourteen months in the mental hospital he leaves, a ghost. His 26
wife abandons him. His brother closes his bank account. Claude cannot
look after himself or his money. And now the protest smoulders again.
He enters a bar in Texas, armed. He threatens the people inside and gets
them to put their money into the sack he is holding, just like he's seen in
films. But it comes to nothing. He is handcuffed and taken to gaol in a
police car. The sergeant accompanying him doesn't know who he is, only
that he's an ex-pilot. I asked Eatherly how it felt to be facing a prison
sentence for the first time.

'I should say terrible, but it wasn't. Nothing mattered to me. I'd been 27
in prison all the time; the door was inside me. In the police car the
sergeant was staring at me. He was curious. He was thinking about some
famous criminal . . . It was a long trip. I was quiet, but his staring eyes
bothered me. "Where do you come from, sergeant?" I asked him. "From
Chicago." And I: "I knew you came from somewhere." I wanted to
unfreeze the atmosphere, but he wasn't having it. He asked me: "It's not
strictly legal, but can you talk, here in the car?" I made a yes sign.

'"Where are you from?"                                                      28
'"From here."                                                              29
'"Where were you based during the war?"                                    30
'"In the Pacific."                                                         31
'"I was in the Pacific too. Where did they land you?"                      32
'"Tinian, in the Marianas, special group 509."                            33
'He looked at me, stunned. "I know who you are. You're Major              34

Eatherly! Good God, Major, how did you end up like this? You're sick, right? I read that somewhere. I'll give you a hand."

35    'Then they locked me up in the loony bin again.'

36    His torment went on: a poor soul, incapable of getting on with the business of life. No one understands his drama. People's aversion to him grows. Let's not forget that Eatherly lived out this difficult period in the America of Senator McCarthy — the Grand Inquisitor of frustrated nationalism. McCarthy fomented a type of suspicion which reflected the cold war: the witch hunt. Eatherly becomes a witch. His passionate, if slightly naïve, criticism of the mechanisms of war is considered a threat to national security. The judges disagree over his case. The biography confected by William Bradfort Huie from less than two days of interviews weakens his defence. For Bradfort, the Major 'never saw the ball of fire, nor was he aware of the yellow wave. By the time of the explosion, he and his gunner were 100 kilometres from the site.' Returning to base he was surprised by the journalists and photographers crowding the runway where the *Enola Gay* had landed. 'If Eatherly is mad,' writes Bradfort, 'then his madness was hatched on 6 August, 1945, not from horror but from jealousy.'

37    'When I knew him,' Bradfort Huie continues implacably, 'he was already a fraud. Right off he asked me for five hundred dollars. He had never once attempted suicide. I spent a long time with him, and I looked at his wrists: there were no scars.'

38    'Is that true Claude?'

39    'These are not the kind of things you want to brag about. Look at my arms.' He turns up the sleeves of his jacket and unbuttons his cuffs. Two purple scars, deep and unpleasant, run towards his hands. 'I don't want you to pity me. I'm happy to have been able to talk. Now I've got to go.'

40    He disappeared as he had appeared, with the same suddenness. Before passing through the bar door and turning out into the hall he looked back, as if he had forgotten something. 'I want to apologize for being late. And thanks for these . . .' He gestured towards the row of glasses on the table.

41    'It was my pleasure to meet you. Merry Christmas.'

42    Fourteen months later Claude Eatherly took his life.

*Translated from the Italian by Wallis Wilde-Menozzi*

## Evaluating the Text

1. How is Chierici's account shaped by the fact that he is a foreign journalist attempting to get a behind-the-scenes interview with the American pilot whose decision regarding weather conditions allowed the atomic bomb to be dropped on Hiroshima?

2. What details suggest the importance Chierici attached to getting the

interview with Eatherly? From Chierici's perspective, why would Eatherly be an especially good subject for an interview?

3. How do the kinds of treatment Eatherly received and comments by doctors suggest that in society's view Eatherly should not feel a sense of personal guilt? Why is it ironic that Eatherly's feelings of guilt were diagnosed as evidence of mental illness? What does this tell you about the prevailing cultural values in the United States at that time?

4. What actions by Eatherly suggest that guilt feelings are ruining his life? How do his actions imply that he feels progressively more guilty as time goes on? What details suggest that Eatherly's reactions were not atypical of pilots who took part in the mission?

5. How is Eatherly's reluctance to be interviewed by Chierici related to the way he was treated by journalists previously? What relationship do Chierici and Eatherly seem to have? How is Chierici's attitude evident in the dominant impression that emerges from the interview?

6. Discuss the significance of Eatherly's statement, "When someone makes a trip like mine and returns alive, he either kills himself or he lives like a Trappist monk."

7. Were you surprised to discover that Eatherly volunteered for military service and was not drafted? What accomplishments in his military career might have made it seem unlikely he would have reacted as he did?

8. What does Eatherly's refusal of his pension and his decision to turn it over to war widows tell the reader about his state of mind at the time and about how he felt about what he had done?

## Exploring Different Perspectives

1. What similarities can you discover between Eatherly's predicament and the situation in which the narrator finds himself in "Gregory" by Pano Ioannides? How do both accounts turn on the key question of unexpected remorse involved with actions carried out as a result of military orders?

2. In what respects is Eatherly's situation similar to those cited by Everett C. Hughes, ("Good People and Dirty Work")—of German officers who wished to leave the SS once they discovered what would be required of them, but could not?

3. How do both this interview and Hughes's account provide insight into the societal mechanisms that require soldiers to perform actions for which they are not supposed to feel a sense of guilt or remorse? What is the main difference between what Eatherly did and what was done by the SS?

## Extending Viewpoints through Writing

1. Write a short essay exploring how you think you would have reacted and what you would have felt if you were in Eatherly's position. To what extent was Eatherly's disillusionment a result of not being told by his superiors what to expect after the bomb had been dropped?

2. As a research project, read Paul Fussell's *Thank God for the Atom Bomb and Other Essays* (1988), and evaluate the argument Fussell makes for having dropped the bomb on Hiroshima and Nagasaki.

3. What questions would you have asked Eatherly that Chierici did not? Explain what you would have hoped to find out from the answers to these questions.

4. Write a report drawing on Chierici's interview as well as information on the front pages and editorial pages of newspapers for the period of August 6–10, 1945. You might wish to interview relatives and friends who are old enough to remember the bombing of Hiroshima and Nagasaki. Compare the attitudes toward the bombings that you find with those expressed by Claude Eatherly.

# Panos Ioannides

# *Gregory*

---

*Panos Ioannides was born in Cyprus in 1935 and was educated in Cyprus, the United States, and Canada. He has been the head of TV programs at Cyprus Broadcasting Corporation. Ioannides is the author of many plays, which have been staged or telecast internationally, and has written novels, short stories, and radio scripts. "Gregory" was written in 1963 and first appeared in* The Charioteer, a Review of Modern Greek Literature *(1965). The English translation is by Marion Byron and Catherine Raisiz. This compelling story is based on a true incident that took place during the Cypriot Liberation struggle against the British in the late 1950s. Ioannides takes the unusual approach of letting the reader experience the torments of a soldier ordered to shoot a prisoner, Gregory, who had saved his life and was his friend.*

*Cyprus is an island republic with a population of nearly 700,000 situated in the eastern Mediterranean south of Turkey and west of Syria and has been inhabited since 6500 B.C. Seventy-seven percent of the people are of Greek origin, living mainly in the south, and the remaining population, situated in the north, is of Turkish descent. Cyprus came under British administration in 1878 and was annexed by Britain in 1914. The quest among Greek Cypriots for self-rule and union with Greece has been a source of continuous civil discord, erupting in 1955 into a civil war. The conflict was aggravated by Turkish support of Turkish Cypriot demands for partition of the island. A settlement was reached in 1959 including provisions for both union with Greece and partition. In 1960, Makarios III, leader of the Greek Cypriot Nationalists was elected president, a development that did not prevent continued fighting. A United Nations peace-keeping force was sent to Cyprus in 1965. In 1974, in response to the overthrow by Greek Army officers of the Makarios regime, Turkey invaded Cyprus. Since then, Cyprus has remained a divided state, and little progress has been made toward reunification.*

My hand was sweating as I held the pistol. The curve of the trigger was biting against my finger. 1

Facing me, Gregory trembled. 2

His whole being was beseeching me, "Don't!" 3

4    Only his mouth did not make a sound. His lips were squeezed tight. If it had been me, I would have screamed, shouted, cursed.

5    The soldiers were watching . . .

6    The day before, during a brief meeting, they had each given their opinions: "It's tough luck, but it has to be done. We've got no choice."

7    The order from Headquarters was clear: "As soon as Lieutenant Rafel's execution is announced, the hostage Gregory is to be shot and his body must be hanged from a telegraph pole in the main street as an exemplary punishment."

8    It was not the first time that I had to execute a hostage in this war. I had acquired experience, thanks to Headquarters which had kept entrusting me with these delicate assignments. Gregory's case was precisely the sixth.

9    The first time, I remember, I vomited. The second time I got sick and had a headache for days. The third time I drank a bottle of rum. The fourth, just two glasses of beer. The fifth time I joked about it, "This little guy, with the big pop-eyes, won't be much of a ghost!"

10    But why, dammit, when the day came did I have to start thinking that I'm not so tough, after all? The thought had come at exactly the wrong time and spoiled all my disposition to do my duty.

11    You see, this Gregory was such a miserable little creature, such a puny thing, such a nobody, damn him.

12    That very morning, although he had heard over the loudspeakers that Rafel had been executed, he believed that we would spare his life because we had been eating together so long.

13    "Those who eat from the same mess tins and drink from the same water canteen," he said, "remain good friends no matter what."

14    And a lot more of the same sort of nonsense.

15    He was a silly fool—we had smelled that out the very first day Headquarters gave him to us. The sentry guarding him had got dead drunk and had dozed off. The rest of us with exit permits had gone from the barracks. When we came back, there was Gregory sitting by the sleeping sentry and thumbing through a magazine.

16    "Why didn't you run away, Gregory?" we asked, laughing at him, several days later.

17    And he answered, "Where would I go in this freezing weather? I'm O.K. here."

18    So we started teasing him.

19    "You're dead right. The accommodations here are splendid . . . "

20    "It's not so bad here," he replied. "The barracks where I used to be are like a sieve. The wind blows in from every side . . . "

21    We asked him about his girl. He smiled.

22    "Maria is a wonderful person," he told us. "Before I met her she was engaged to a no-good fellow, a pig. He gave her up for another girl. Then nobody in the village wanted to marry Maria. I didn't miss my chance. So what if she is second-hand. Nonsense. Peasant ideas, my friend.

She's beautiful and good-hearted. What more could I want? And didn't she load me with watermelons and cucumbers every time I passed by her vegetable garden? Well, one day I stole some cucumbers and melons and watermelons and I took them to her. 'Maria,' I said, 'from now on I'm going to take care of you.' She started crying and then me, too. But ever since that day she has given me lots of trouble — jealousy. She wouldn't let me go even to my mother's. Until the day I was recruited, she wouldn't let me go far from her apron strings. But that was just what I wanted . . . ''

He used to tell this story over and over, always with the same words, 23 the same commonplace gestures. At the end he would have a good laugh and start gulping from his water jug.

His tongue was always wagging! When he started talking, nothing 24 could stop him. We used to listen and nod our heads, not saying a word. But sometimes, as he was telling us about his mother and family problems, we couldn't help wondering, "Eh, well, these people have the same headaches in their country as we've got."

Strange, isn't it! 25

Except for his talking too much, Gregory wasn't a bad fellow. He was 26 a marvelous cook. Once he made us some apple tarts, so delicious we licked the platter clean. And he could sew, too. He used to sew on all our buttons, patch our clothes, darn our socks, iron our ties, wash our clothes . . .

How the devil could you kill such a friend? 27

Even though his name was Gregory and some people on his side had 28 killed one of ours, even though we had left wives and children to go to war against him and his kind — but how can I explain? He was our friend. He actually liked us! A few days before, hadn't he killed with his own bare hands a scorpion that was climbing up my leg? He could have let it send me to hell!

"Thanks, Gregory!" I said then, "Thank God who made you . . . '' 29

When the order came, it was like a thunderbolt. Gregory was to be 30 shot, it said, and hanged from a telegraph pole as an exemplary punishment.

We got together inside the barracks. We sent Gregory to wash some 31 underwear for us.

"It ain't right." 32

"What is right?" 33

"Our duty!" 34

"Shit!" 35

"If you dare, don't do it! They'll drag you to court-martial and then 36 bang-bang . . . ''

Well, of course. The right thing is to save your skin. That's only 37 logical. It's either your skin or his. His, of course, even if it was Gregory, the fellow you've been sharing the same plate with, eating with your fingers, and who was washing your clothes that very minute.

38    What could I do? That's war. We had seen worse things.

39    So we set the hour.

40    We didn't tell him anything when he came back from the washing. He slept peacefully. He snored for the last time. In the morning, he heard the news over the loudspeaker and he saw that we looked gloomy and he began to suspect that something was up. He tried talking to us, but he got no answers and then he stopped talking.

41    He just stood there and looked at us, stunned and lost . . .

Now, I'll squeeze the trigger. A tiny bullet will rip through his chest. Maybe I'll lose my sleep tonight but in the morning I'll wake up alive.

Gregory seems to guess my thoughts. He puts out his hand and asks, "You're kidding, friend! Aren't you kidding?"

What a jackass! Doesn't he deserve to be cut to pieces? What a thing to ask at such a time. Your heart is about to burst and he's asking if you're kidding. How can a body be kidding about such a thing? Idiot! This is no time for jokes. And you, if you're such a fine friend, why don't you make things easier for us? Help us kill you with fewer qualms? If you would get angry — curse our Virgin, our God — if you'd try to escape it would be much easier for us and for you.

So it is *now*.

Now, Mr. Gregory, you are going to pay for your stupidities wholesale. Because you didn't escape the day the sentry fell asleep; because you didn't escape yesterday when we sent you all alone to the laundry — we did it on purpose, you idiot! Why didn't you let me die from the sting of the scorpion?

So now don't complain. It's all your fault, nitwit.

Eh? What's happening to him now?

Gregory is crying. Tears flood his eyes and trickle down over his cleanshaven cheeks. He is turning his face and pressing his forehead against the wall. His back is shaking as he sobs. His hands cling, rigid and helpless, to the wall.

Now is my best chance, now that he knows there is no other solution and turns his face from us.

I squeeze the trigger.

Gregory jerks. His back stops shaking up and down.

I think I've finished him! How easy it is . . . But suddenly he starts crying out loud, his hands claw at the wall and try to pull it down. He screams, "No, no . . . "

I turn to the others. I expect them to nod, "That's enough."

They nod, "What are you waiting for?"

I squeeze the trigger again.

The bullet smashed into his neck. A thick spray of blood spurts out.

Gregory turns. His eyes are all red. He lunges at me and starts punching me with his fists.

"I hate you, hate you . . . " he screams.

I emptied the barrel. He fell and grabbed my leg as if he wanted to hold on.

He died with a terrible spasm. His mouth was full of blood and so 42
were my boots and socks.

We stood quietly, looking at him. 43

When we came to, we stooped and picked him up. His hands were 44
frozen and wouldn't let my legs go.

I still have their imprints, red and deep, as if made by a hot knife. 45

"We will hang him tonight," the men said. 46

"Tonight or now?" they said. 47

I turned and looked at them one by one. 48

"Is that what you all want?" I asked. 49

They gave me no answer. 50

"Dig a grave," I said. 51

Headquarters did not ask for a report the next day or the day after. The top brass were sure that we had obeyed them and had left him swinging from a pole.

They didn't care to know what happened to that Gregory, alive or 52
dead.

*Translated by Marion Byron Raizis and Catherine Raizis*

## *Evaluating the Text*

1. Discuss Ioannides's use of framing techniques in his choice of how to open and close his story. How does his choice of opening the story as Gregory is about to be shot and his use of flashbacks to explore the narrator's relationship with Gregory enhance the effectiveness of the story?
2. Much of the story's action takes place during the few seconds when the narrator must decide whether to pull the trigger. Why do you think Ioannides chooses to tell the story from the executioner's point of view rather than from Gregory's?
3. What in the narrator's past leads his superiors (and the narrator himself) to conclude he is the one best-suited to kill Gregory?
4. What details illustrate that Gregory has become a friend to the narrator and other soldiers rather than just a prisoner? In what way does Gregory embody the qualities of humanity, decency, and domestic life that the soldiers were forced to leave behind? Why is his innocence a source of both admiration and irritation?
5. How does Gregory's decision to marry Maria suggest the kind of person he is and answer the question as to why he doesn't try to escape when he is told he is going to be killed?

6. Discuss the psychological process that allows the narrator to convert his anguish at having to shoot Gregory into a justification to do so.
7. Why didn't Gregory take the opportunity to escape that the soldiers gave him? What insight does Ioannides give the reader into Gregory's character that would explain why he doesn't perceive the real threat to his life even at the moment the narrator is pointing a gun at his head?
8. How does the question "*Why didn't you let me die from the sting of the scorpion?*" reveal the anguish the narrator feels as he is faced with the order to kill his friend Gregory?
9. When the narrator fires the first shot, why does he hope the other soldiers will stop him from firing again; why don't they stop him?
10. At the end, how does the narrator's order not to hang Gregory's body reveal his distress after shooting Gregory? Why is it ironic that the higher-ups never inquire whether their orders have been carried out? What does this imply and why does it make the narrator feel even worse?

## Exploring Different Perspectives

1. How do both Everett C. Hughes's analysis ("Good People and Dirty Work") of collective amnesia among Germans and Ioannides's story shed light on the psychological mechanism of "denial"?
2. In what sense do both Eatherly in Maurizio Chierici's report ("The Man from Hiroshima") and the narrator in this story find themselves in similar circumstances? To what extent are their reactions similar?
3. How does Ioannides accomplish the difficult task of getting readers to understand, and perhaps even sympathize with someone who, in Hughes's terminology, performs the "dirty work" in response to military orders?

## Extending Viewpoints through Writing

1. In your opinion, is Gregory a good person or just a fool who is stupid enough to get killed when he does not have to die?
2. If you were in the narrator's shoes, what would you have done? Do you think you would have had to make yourself hate Gregory, as the narrator did, in order to be able to kill him?
3. In an essay, explore the effects of British colonialism in Cyprus, Antigua (see Jamaica Kincaid's "A Small Place," Chapter 7), and Kenya (see Ngũgĩ wa Thiong'o's "Decolonising the Mind," Chapter 6).

# Robert Santos

# *My Men*

---

*Robert Santos was Rifle Platoon Leader in the 101st Airborne Division at Hue, November 1967 to November 1968. He is among New York state's most decorated veterans. After returning from Vietnam, he graduated from the University of Michigan Law School in 1978. His account originally appeared in* Everything We Had: An Oral History of the Vietnam War by Thirty-Three American Soldiers Who Fought It, *edited by Al Santoli (1981). In the tradition of Studs Terkel, Santoli is well-known for his best-selling oral histories,* To Bear Any Burden *(1985) and* New Americans: An Oral History, Immigrants & Refugees in the U.S. Today *(1988). "My Men" is Santos's ironic and deeply moving account of how his experiences during the 1968 Tet Offensive as a young Hispanic army lieutenant led him to the realization "I tried to think of what I would be like if this took place in my hometown. This may have been a turning point in my life, at least in terms of the war."*

*The Vietnam War in Southeast Asia 1954–1975 was waged between communist North Vietnam and noncommunist South Vietnam. Following France's defeat in the French Indochina War, 1946–1954, Vietnam was divided into North and South Vietnam by the Geneva Convention (1954). War broke out as communist-led guerrillas (the Vietcong) attempted to take over South Vietnam. From 1961 on, the United States supplied support troops to South Vietnam and after the Tonkin Gulf resolution in 1964, American military support escalated until U.S. troops numbered 550,000 by 1969. American involvement in the war divided the country between supporters and those who opposed it through mass demonstrations or by refusing to serve in the Armed Forces. Increased opposition to the war resulted from the communist's 1968 Tet Offensive, a series of major attacks at the time of the lunar New Year (or "Tet"), which created doubt whether the combined forces of the United States and South Vietnam could prevail. Santos's narrative relates his experiences as a commanding officer during the Tet Offensive.*

(For additional information on Vietnam, see pp. 457, 466, and 666.)

1    I was drafted in March 1966. It wasn't my intention to go into combat, but to go to Office Candidate School, and quit a month before OCS ended. It wouldn't be held against me and I'd have less than a year left. But the way it worked out, a friend did that ahead of me and he went to 'Nam, anyway. So I decided that based on what I had seen and my own feelings about myself, I should complete OCS.

2    I went over to 'Nam with two other guys as part of an advance party for the 101st Airborne, mainly to handle logistics and to make sure all the equipment was there. The rumors were that advance parties were being wiped out. When my company got there, they were under the impression that I had already died, which was a really weird feeling, to meet the company commander, who I didn't get along with, and the first words out of his mouth are "I thought you were dead." My response was "Too bad, huh?"

3    The 101st were mostly West Point officers. I was the first guy to come there from OCS, and was not well received. They had a camaraderie. Most of the lieutenants out of West Point graduated from the same class. They graduated through Airborne school, Ranger school, and all came there as a unit.

4    We were part of the Hue liberation force in the Tet offensive. The North Vietnamese Army had taken the city. So the Marine Corps, the South Vietnamese, the 101st and the 1st Cavalry went in from different angles to liberate the city.

5    I was twenty-one. But I was young in terms of commanding men in combat. I didn't know anything. I was the kind of lieutenant that they'd say, "Oh, shit, here's another green lieutenant." That's what I was. You don't know what to do, your mind races over the training you've taken in how to deal with these kinds of situations. I was naïve and really took what they said at face value.

6    We operated for maybe two weeks with only minor contact. I was working the whole time, spreading the platoon out, doing it right. I was lead platoon on our way into Hue. We came past the paddies, the trees, came around the green. I looked up and saw an NVA flag flying over the next open space. I couldn't believe it. I just . . . I guess I just freaked. I got on the horn right away and called the CO. I was stuttering and stammering: "I see it. I see the flag! I . . . My God, they're finally there."

7    All I knew at that point was "My God! I'm scared shitless. Holy shit. This is the real thing." I never expected to see a flag. I expected to get shot at. But they were so brazen. They were there. Dug in. The CO said, "Move out." I've heard that before: "Follow me." But I was in the bottom of the infantry. He didn't say "Follow me," he said "Move out." I said, "Now I know what 'Follow me' means—Lieutenant says 'Follow me.'" And that's what we did.

8    The strange thing about war, there's always humor. Prior to that, when I was walking around I was your typical "asshole lieutenant."

Everyplace I walked something got caught. You know, guys could walk right through a bush. My helmet would fall off, my pack would get snagged. And although no one ever told me, I had a reputation as the wait-a-minute-lieutenant. "Hold up, hold up, the lieutenant's caught." Here you're trying to lead men in combat and be a tough guy. Most of the guys were bigger than me. I weighed like 130 pounds. And really, always getting snagged was embarrassing.

I remember walking through the rice paddies that opened up and the small stream and the green on both sides. We were walking down the right side, near the trail, and there was another company on my left flank. All of a sudden all hell opened up. You have to understand, I've never been a Boy Scout, I've never been a Cub Scout. The closest I came to that was going to my sister's Campfire Girl meetings. I grew up in New York City and Long Island. Watched a lot of movies and read a lot of books. I never fired a weapon. I never got into fights with my buddies. My RTO was from East Wenatchee, Washington. Grew up a hunter. They opened up fire and Wes started going down. You make a connection real quick that someone's being shot and someone's getting hurt.

The first thing I did was yell, "Follow me," and I turned to the right to run for cover. There was a bamboo thicket. I couldn't walk through a jungle, an open field, without tripping. Somehow I made a hole through those bushes that everyone in the platoon could go through side by side. Got on the other side—my hat was on my head, my rifle was in my hands, I'd lost nothing. There were guys from another platoon that didn't know what they were doing. Everyone was running around crazy.

I said, "Come with me. Follow me." And I didn't know what I was doing. I knew I was supposed to go toward the enemy. I was trained not to stand still. Don't stand in the killing zone. Don't get shot. Move. So I moved, and as I ran forward I heard these noises. Kind of like *ping, ping*—no idea what that noise was. I finally jumped down behind this mound of dirt that turned out to be a grave, which I didn't know at that time. So I jumped behind this mound of dirt with my RTO and we're all kind of hid behind this stuff. I said, "Just climb up, tell them we're in place and we're hooked up with the left flank and the enemy is in front of us." And I started playing the game. I got up and ran around yelling "Move this machine gun over here" and "Do this over there." I mean, all this noise is going past me. I still didn't know what this noise was. *Ping.* Just a little weird, something new. I finally got back after running around, sat down next to the RTO, and he said, "What the fuck are you doing?" I said, "What do you mean?" He said, "Don't you know what's going on?" I said, "Yeah, goddamnit. I know what's going on. Who do you think I am? He says, "Don't you know what that noise is?" I said no. He said, "That's the bullets going over your head." I never knew it. I mean, If I'd known it I probably would've just buried myself and hid. But I didn't know it. I just didn't know it.

The NVA were in the thicket. There was a stream between us and them, and they were dug in on the opposite side. And they nailed us. They had us pinned down all over the place. Everything that day was done by the book. Just incredible. I don't know how I survived that day, because lieutenants had a very short life expectancy and the reason is because they're jerks and they run out and do stupid stuff by the book. That day we took our first casualties in our platoon. Sergeant Berringer, I think his name was, next to me got shot in the arm. And I remember the training again. Here you were a medic. Look for the bullet's exit. So I found the exit and patched him up with his bandage. Then I realized that there's also an entrance. So I took my bandage out. This is a mistake. You're not supposed to take out your bandage and patch someone else up. But I had to do it. I turned around and called the medic, but he was all freaked out. The bullet that went through Berringer's arm killed the guy next to him. It was a very traumatic day for all of us.

13    I had told that guy's squad leader that morning, "Tell him to stay behind with the gear and the chopper will bring him forward later." But he wanted to go out. To this day I still think you can tell ahead of time when someone's going to die. Whether they know it or not, I'm convinced that I can tell. It's not something deliberate. Kind of a blankness comes over their face. It's not like they're already dead. It's like a distance and a softness to their features.

14    But he died and it was a really bad day. We found out how heavy a dead guy could be. The biggest guy in our platoon couldn't pick him up and carry him. So I picked him up, took about three steps, and I couldn't go much farther. But by that time the big guy realized that he could pick him up—It was just mental. We were freaked. And eventually we got out of that mess.

15    From that first time we made contact we proceeded to keep sweeping in toward the city. The way the 101st operated, we sometimes moved as a battalion, but generally the company split off and we did that whole anvil/hammer bit. So although you were working in the battalion operation, you were functioning as a company and sometimes as small a unit as a platoon.

16    I think it's funny how you can rationalize everything while you're there. Everything is justifiable in terms of survival, which is unfortunate. I can criticize people today, like at law school when I went there, for being so competitive, so survival-oriented. They were called "gunners," would do things just to make sure they got a better grade. Seems to me today's perception of how unimportant that all is . . . Whereas you go back there and you're justifying killing someone. I'm not sure which one's worse—whether it's unimportant or the means by which you compete. It's really crazy. But we would chase them every day, they'd shoot at us and we'd shoot at them, never making contact. And then every day, almost like clockwork, in the late afternoon they'd stop and make a stand and we'd fight. Went on for months, literally for months. Even after the city was retaken, they still operated in the area.

17    We overran a base camp on the way into Hue. We called it a base

camp, but it probably wasn't but a staging area—there were packs just like ours lined up on the ground. It's a really freaky thing to think you're chasing someone and then to suddenly show up and there they are taking a break for exercise or going inside a barracks for a class—I don't know what they did. But psychologically it really shook us because shit, they're just as disciplined and efficient as we are. They're so confident they can just walk away and leave their stuff like it was a field exercise, training. Maybe it was. Maybe that's what I was to them. But this time we were using live fire. We opened up their packs and they had sets of civilian clothes, military clothes, personal effects. I really wondered if they were at war, except to know that we fought with them every day.

North Vietnamese, that's all I fought. I went into Hue and saw the  18 civilian bodies lined up. I know I didn't kill them. Americans don't shoot people from a distance and then line the bodies up. So when you walk in and find them lined up there on their stomachs with their hands tied behind their backs, you know it was the NVA who did that. I know no Americans did that because we were the first ones to enter that portion of the village. They killed the water buffalo, everything.

It was civil war and we were in there and they were killing us as we  19 killed them. I mean, the poor victims who had relatives in the North and relatives in the South . . . The only equivalent I can imagine was I was sent to the Detroit riots with the 101st before I went to 'Nam. Coming back, my biggest fear was going to Fort Dix, because even though I wanted to be close to home, I didn't want to be stuck on riot duty. I said, "I'll be damned if I come all the way back here from Vietnam to go on riot duty and have someone throw a bottle or a brick and split my head open." What's your reaction going to be? Pull that trigger? Shoot my own countrymen?

Patriotism is just loyalty to friends, people, families . . . I didn't  20 even know those guys in Vietnam until I got there, and it wouldn't have mattered if you came to my platoon tomorrow—if we got hit, I would go out and try to save your ass just as I would've done for anyone else I'd been with for a month, two months, three months. Instant bonding.

One thing I did find out after I went to Hue and came back, which I  21 didn't know at the time because of the cultural gap, was the significance of the pine trees in the middle of the jungle. Every time someone died that was relatively famous, they'd plant a pine tree in his honor so his spirit would live on. I had a teacher who was Vietnamese when I went to school after getting out of the service. His father was a poet laureate of Hue who had a tree planted for him. I never had the heart to tell the teacher, who was a friend, that I used to sling a poncho on those trees. I mean, I thought it was a great place to sleep because the pine needles were nice and it was always clean. I didn't make the connection that there was something special about the area. We used the needles to help start our fires. Dig little holes in the hedges around it—dig in. Sacrilege. In some sense his father's spirit gave me shelter, which is kind of ironic.

It was really a break for us to go to the rice hovels because we hadn't  22 cooked for so many months. A little boy came out and wanted some C-rations. When they want C-rations, you know they're hurting, the food's just terrible. He was going to share his dinner with us and he brought out some fish. The hottest damn thing I ever had. I can still to this day remember them being fuming hot. We shared our food and we asked him where he lived. He pointed to this house in the clearing. He said he was there with his sister, and we said, "Well, why doesn't your sister come out and join us for dinner?" And he said, "She can't. The VC will see her with us, they'll kill her." We said, "What about you? They'll see you." He said it didn't matter because they know he's getting food.

23 So it's just like everything else: you leave and they're back, and people have to live with that. They have to deal with the fact that we're going to be gone and leave them behind. But what struck me that day when I was looking at that kid — and I didn't know how old he was, but he had to be under ten — was that all his life he knew war. And then when we're gone he's going to know that Americans may have come through and raped his sister. The VC may have raped his sister because she allowed the Americans to do this. And if the Americans had conceivably seen her with the VC, they would've . . . the whole thing was just . . . it was certainly a statement. It was a tragedy and it was so horrifying. I tried to think of what I would be like if this took place in my hometown. This may have been a turning point in my life, at least in the terms of the war.

## Evaluating the Text

1. Did the training Santos received at Officer Candidate School before he arrived in Vietnam prepare him for what he actually experienced?
2. How did Santos's first experience in combat give him a new perspective on the words "follow me?" How does Santos' description of the sound bullets make enable the reader to see the extent of his combat inexperience?
3. What personal attributes and limitations did Santos have to overcome now that he was in charge of his own platoon?
4. What specific changes in a soldier's appearance, according to Santos, lead him to believe that he can tell who is going to die?
5. Why did Santos find it unnerving to walk into a camp at which the enemy had left their packs as if their earlier firefights had been merely a training session?
6. Why would Santos's concept of patriotism have made it difficult for him to have been stationed on riot duty back in the states?
7. Santos mentions that previously he did not have much of a sense of humor. What evidence can you cite that illustrates that he has acquired a sense of humor? For example, look at his description of how he was unable to walk through the jungle without getting snagged?
8. How did the episode of the pine trees play a crucial role in giving Santos insight into the Vietnamese culture and how his actions might appear from their perspective? How might what he did have been comparable to resting on a hammock slung between two grave stones in a cemetery?

9. Discuss how his encounter with the little boy who came out for food, in a clearing between U.S. troops and the Vietcong, was a turning point for Santos? How did this change his attitude toward himself and the war? How would you characterize the nature of this change?

## Exploring Different Perspectives

1. Compare Santos's account with Panos Ioannides's "Gregory" in terms of what they show you about how difficult it is to kill someone whom you see as another human being. What insight do you gain into the process by which military language creates the distance between people that makes killing possible?
2. To what extent do Santos in Vietnam and George Orwell ("Homage to Catalonia") in the Spanish Civil War offer similar pictures of themselves? In what ways are both self-deprecating?
3. How did Santos's experiences with the boy who came out to get C-rations lead him to a realization of what the war was like for the Vietnamese people? How did this insight become a turning point in his life at that time? What is the relationship of this insight to the premise and structure of Kate Wilhelm's "The Village"?

## Extending Viewpoints through Writing

1. Evaluate Santos's discovery about people's ability to rationalize whatever was necessary on the battlefield as it relates to the behavior of students in law school. To what extent do your own experiences in school confirm Santos's observations about what people will do to get higher grades?
2. If you were in a platoon, would you want Santos to be your commanding officer? Why or why not?
3. Have you had the experience of very quickly forming emotional bonds in a new group within a short period of time? Discuss how the bonds were stronger if they were formed to achieve a common objective or in response to a common enemy.
4. Much of Santos's account has to do with the changes he had to make to become a leader. If you have ever been put into a leadership position, describe the adjustment you had to make.
5. Contrast the wars in Vietnam and Iraq in terms of any of the following: Congressional approval, public support, draftee versus all-volunteer army, international backing, objectives, natural resources, economic factors, media coverage, treatment of P.O.W.s, weaponry, terrain, duration, military and civilian casualties, cultural differences, role played by drugs and alcohol, refugees, public attitude toward veterans, political and military leaders, and issues left unresolved.

# Kate Wilhelm

# *The Village*

---

*Kate Wilhelm was born in 1928 in Toledo, Ohio. In 1968, her science-fiction story, "The Planners" won a Nebula Award. She won another Nebula, the Hugo Award, and the Jupiter Award for her novel* Where Late the Sweet Birds Sang *(1977). A prolific novelist, her works include* City of Cain *(1973) and* The Clewiston Test *(1976). Many of her short stories have been collected in* The Infinity Box *(1976) and* Somerset Dreams and Other Fiction *(1978). "The Village" was first published in* Bad Moon Rising *(1973) and appeared in* The Field of Fire *(1987), edited by Jeanne Van Buren Dann and Jack Dann. This shocking story looks at the effects of a land war in an unnamed country in Asia on the soldiers who fought it and on the civilians back home from a most unusual perspective.*

1    Mildred Carey decided to walk to the post office early, before the sun turned the two blocks into a furnace. "They've done something to the weather," she said to her husband, packing his three sandwiches and thermos of lemonade. "Never used to be this hot this early."

2    "It'll get cooler again. Always does."

3    She followed him to the door and waved as he backed out of the drive. The tomato plants she had set out the day before were wilted. She watered them, then started to walk slowly to town. With a feeling of satisfaction she noticed that Mrs. Mareno's roses had black spot. Forcing the blooms with too much fertilizer just wasn't good for them.

4    Mike Donatti dozed as he awaited orders to regroup and start the search-and-clear maneuver. Stilwell nudged him. "Hey, Mike, you been over here before?"

5    "Nope. One fuckin' village is just like the others. Mud or dust. That's the only fuckin' difference."

6    Stilwell was so new that he was sunburned red. Everyone else in the company was burned black. "Man, could we pass," they liked to say to Latimore, who couldn't.

7    Mr. Peters was sweeping the sidewalk before the market. "Got some good fresh salami," he said. "Ed made it over the weekend."

8    "You sure Ed made it, Not Buz? When Buz makes it, he uses to much garlic. What's he covering up is what I want to know."

9    "Now Miz Carey, you know he's not covering up. Some folks like it hot and strong."

666

"I'll stop back by after I get the mail."  10

The four Henry children were already out in the street, filthy, chasing  11
each other randomly. Their mother was not in sight. Mildred Carey
pursed her lips. Her Mark never had played in the street in his life.

She dropped in the five-and-dime, not to buy anything but to look  12
over the flats of annuals — petunias, marigolds, nasturtiums. "They sure
don't look healthy," she said to Doris Offinger.

"They're fine, Miz Carey. Brother bought them fresh this morning  13
from Connor's down at Midbury. You know Connor's has good stock."

"How's Larry getting along? Still in the veterans' hospital at Lake-  14
view?"

"Yes. He'll be out in a couple of weeks, I guess." Doris' pretty face  15
remained untroubled. "They've got such good doctors down there, I hate
to see him get so far from them all, but he wants to come home."

"How can these people stand this heat all the time?" Stilwell said  16
after a moment. The sun wasn't up yet, but it was eighty-six degrees,
humidity near one hundred percent.

"People," he says. "Boy, ain't you even been briefed? People can't  17
stand it, that's the first clue." Mike sighed and sat up. He lighted a
cigarette. "Boy, back home in August. You know the hills where I come
from are cold, even in August?"

"Where's that?"  18

"Vermont. I can remember plenty of times it snowed in August.  19
Nights under a blanket."

"Well, he can help out here in the store. With his pension and the  20
store and all, the two of you are set, aren't you? Isn't that Tessie Hetherton going in Peters' market?"

"I didn't notice her. Did you want one of those flats, Miz Carey?"  21

"No. They aren't healthy. Connor's must have culled the runts and  22
set *them* out." She stood in the doorway squinting to see across the way
to Peters' market. "I'm sure it was. And she told me she's too arthritic to
do any more housework. I'll just go talk to her."

"I don't think she will, though. Miz Avery wanted her on Wednes-  23
days and she said no. You know Mr. Hetherton's got a job? With the
paper mill."

"Shtt. That won't last. They'll pay off a few of last winter's bills and  24
then he'll start to complain about his liver or something and she'll be
hustling for work. I know that man." She left the store without looking
back, certain that Doris would be eyeing the price tags of the flats. "You
take care of yourself, Doris. You're looking peaked. You should get out in
the sun.

"Mrs. Hetherton, you're looking fit again," Mildred Carey said, cor-  25
nering the woman as she emerged from the store.

"Warm weather's helped some."  26

"Look, can you possibly come over Thursday morning? You know  27
the Garden Club meets this week, and I can't possibly get ready without
some help."

28     "Well, I just don't know . . . Danny's dead set against my going out to work again."

29     "But they're going to have to close down the mill. And then where will he be?"

30     "Close it down? Why? Who says?"

31     "It's been in the papers for weeks now. All those dead fish, and the stink. You know that committee came up and took samples and said they're the ones responsible. And they can't afford to change over the whole process. They're going to move instead."

32     "Oh, that. Danny said don't hold your breath. They're making a study, and then they'll have to come up with a plan and have it studied, and all in all it's going to take five years or even more before it all comes to a head."

33     "Hm. Another big kill and the Department of Health . . ."

34     Mrs. Hetherton laughed and Mildred Carey had to smile too. "Well, anyway, can you come over just this time? For this one meeting?"

35     "Sure, Miz Carey. Thursday morning? But only half a day."

36     The school bus turned the corner and rolled noisily down the broad new street. The two women watched it out of sight. "Have you seen the Tomkins boys lately?" Mildred Carey asked. "Hair down to here."

37     "Winona says they're having someone in to talk about drugs. I asked her point blank if there are drugs around here and she said no, but you never can tell. The kids won't tell you nothing."

38     "Well, I just thank God that Mark is grown up and out of it all."

39     "He's due home soon now, isn't he?"

40     "Seven weeks. Then off to college in the fall. I told him that he's probably safer over there than at one of the universities right now." They laughed and moved apart. "See you Thursday."

41     "Listen, Mike, when you get back, you'll go through New York, won't you? Give my mother a call, will you? Just tell her . . ."

42     "What? That you got jungle rot the first time out and it's gone to your brain?"

43     "Just call her. Say I'm fine. That's all. She'll want to have you over for dinner, or take you to a good restaurant, something. Say you don't have time. But it'd mean a lot to her to have you call."

44     "Sure. Sure. Come on, we're moving."

45     They walked for two hours without making contact. The men were straggling along in two uneven columns at the sides of the road. The dirt road was covered with recent growth, no mines. The temperature was going to hit one hundred any second. Sweat and dirt mixed on faces, arms, muddy sweat trickled down shirts.

46     The concrete street was a glare now. Heat rose in patterns that shifted and vanished and rose again. Mildred Carey wondered if it hadn't been a mistake to rebuild the street, take out the maples and make it wide enough for the traffic that they predicted would be here in another year or two. She shrugged and walked more briskly toward the post office.

That wasn't her affair. Her husband, who should know, said it was necessary for the town to grow. After being in road construction for twenty-five years, he should know. Fran Marple and Dodie Wilson waved to her from outside the coffee shop. Fran looked overdue and miserable. Last thing she needed was to go in the coffee shop and have pastry. Mildred Carey smiled at them and went on.

Claud Emerson was weighing a box for Bill Stokes. Bill leaned against 47 the counter smoking, flicking ashes on the floor. "Don't like it here, get out, that's what I say. Goddamn kids with their filthy clothes and dirty feet. Bet they had marijuana up there. Should have called the troopers, that's what I should have done."

"They was on state land, Bill. You had no call to run them off." 48

"They didn't know that. You think I'm going to let them plop them- 49 selves down right outside my front door? Let 'em find somewhere else to muck about."

Claud Emerson stamped the box. "One seventy-two." 50

Stilwell and Mike were following Laski, Berat, and Humboldt. Berat 51 was talking.

"You let it stick out, see, and come at them with your M-16 and you 52 know what they watch! Man, they never seen nothing like it! Scared shitless by it. Tight! Whooee! Tight and hot!"

Stilwell looked as if he saw a green monster. Mike laughed and lit 53 another cigarette. The sun was almost straight up when the lieutenant called for a break. He and Sergeant Durkins consulted a map and Humboldt swore at great length. "They've got us lost, the bastards. This fuckin' road ain't even on their fuckin' map."

Mildred Carey looked through the bills and advertising in her box, 54 saving the letter from Mark for last. She always read them twice, once very quickly to be sure that he was all right, then again, word for word, pausing to pronounce the strange syllables aloud. She scanned the scrawled page, then replaced it in its envelope to be reread at home with coffee.

Bill Stokes' jeep roared outside the door, down the street to screech to 55 a halt outside the feed store.

Mildred shook her head. "He's a mean man." 56

"Yep," Claud Emerson said. "Always was, always will be, I reckon. 57 Wonder where them kids spent the night after he chased them."

Durkins sent out two scouts and the rest of them waited, cursing and 58 sweating. A helicopter throbbed over them, drowned out their voices, vanished. The scouts returned.

Durkins stood up. "Okay. About four miles. The gooks are there, all 59 right. Or will be again tonight. It's a free-fire zone, and our orders are to clean it out. Let's go."

Loud voices drifted across the street and they both looked toward the 60 sound. "Old Dave's at it again," Claud Emerson said, frowning. "He'll have himself another heart attack, that's what."

61     "What good does arguing do anyway? Everybody around here knows what everybody else thinks and nobody ever changes. Just what good does it do?" She stuffed her mail into her purse. "Just have to do the best you can. Do what's right and hope for the best." She waved good-bye.

62     She still had to pick up cottage cheese and milk. "Maybe I'll try that new salami," she said to Peters. "Just six slices. Don't like to keep it more than a day. Just look at those tomatoes! Sixty-nine a pound! Mr. Peters, that's a disgrace!"

63     "Field-grown, Miz Carey. Up from Georgia. Shipping costs go up and up, you know." He sliced the salami carefully, medium thick.

64     A new tension was in them now and the minesweepers walked gingerly on the road carpeted with green sprouts. Stilwell coughed again and again, a meaningless bark of nervousness. Durkins sent him to the rear, then sent Mike back with him. "Keep an eye on the fuckin' bastard," he said. Mike nodded and waited for the rear to catch up with him. The two brothers from Alabama looked at him expressionlessly as they passed. They didn't mind the heat either, he thought, then spat. Stilwell looked sick.

65     "Is it a trap?" he asked later.

66     "Who the fuck knows?"

67     "Company C walked into an ambush, didn't they?"

68     "They fucked up."

69     Mildred Carey put her milk on the checkout counter alongside the cottage cheese. Her blue housedress was wet with perspiration under her arms and she could feel a spot of wetness on her back when her dress touched her skin. That Janice Samuels, she thought, catching a glimpse of the girl across the street, with those shorts and no bra, pretending she was dressing to be comfortable. Always asking about Mark. And him, asking about her in his letters.

70     "That's a dollar five," Peters said.

71     They halted again less than a mile from the village. The lieutenant called for the helicopters to give cover and to close off the area. Durkins sent men around the village to cover the road leading from it. There was no more they could do until the helicopters arrived. There were fields under cultivation off to the left.

72     "What if they're still there?" Stilwell asked, waiting.

73     "You heard Durkins. This is a free-fire zone. They'll be gone."

74     "But what if they haven't?"

75     "We clear the area."

76     Stilwell wasn't satisfied, but he didn't want to ask the questions. He didn't want to hear the answers. Mike looked at him with hatred. Stilwell turned away and stared into the bushes at the side of the road.

77     "Let's go."

78     There was a deafening beating roar overhead and Mildred Carey and Peters went to the door to look. A green-and-brown helicopter hovered over the street, then moved down toward the post office, casting a

grotesque shadow on the white concrete. Two more of the monstrous machines came over, making talk impossible. There was another helicopter to the north; their throb was everywhere, as if the clear blue sky had loosened a rain of them.

From the feed-store entrance Bill Stokes shouted something lost in the din. He raced to his jeep and fumbled for something under the seat. He straightened up holding binoculars and started to move to the center of the street, looking through them down the highway. One of the helicopters dipped, banked, and turned, and there was a spray of gunfire. Bill Stokes fell, jerked several times, then lay still. Now others began to run in the street, pointing and shouting and screaming. O'Neal and his hired hand ran to Bill Stokes and tried to lift him. Fran Marple and Dodie Wilson had left the coffee shop, were standing outside the door; they turned and ran back inside. A truck rounded the corner at the far end of the street and again the helicopter fired; the truck careened out of control into cars parked outside the bank. One of the cars was propelled through the bank windows. The thunder of the helicopters swallowed the sound of the crash and the breaking glass and the screams of the people who ran from the bank, some of them bleeding, clutching their heads or arms. Katharine Ormsby got to the side of the street, collapsed there. She crawled several more feet, then sprawled out and was still.

Mildred Carey backed into the store, her hands over her mouth. Suddenly she vomited. Peters was still on the sidewalk. She tried to close the door, but he flung it open, pushing her toward the rear of the store.

"Soldiers!" Peters yelled. "Soldiers coming!"

They went in low, on the sides of the road, ready for the explosion of gunfire, or the sudden eruption of a claymore. The helicopters' noise filled the world as they took up positions. The village was small, a hamlet. It had not been evacuated. The word passed through the company: slopes. They were there. A man ran into the street holding what could have been a grenade, or a bomb, or anything. One of the helicopters fired on him. There was a second burst of fire down the road and a vehicle burned. Now the company was entering the village warily. Mike cursed the slopes for their stupidity in staying.

Home was all Mildred Carey could think of. She had to get home. She ran to the back of the store and out to the alley that the delivery trucks used. She ran all the way home and, panting, with a pain in her chest, she rushed frantically through the house pulling down shades, locking doors. Then she went upstairs, where she could see the entire town. The soldiers were coming in crouched over, on both sides of the road, with their rifles out before them. She began to laugh suddenly; tears streaming, she ran downstairs again to fling open the door and shout.

"They're ours," she screamed toward the townspeople, laughing and crying all at once. "You fools, they're ours!"

Two of the khaki-clad GIs approached her, still pointing their guns at her. One of them said something, but she couldn't understand his words. "What are you doing here?" she cried. "You're American soldiers! What are you doing?"

86 The larger of the two grabbed her arm and twisted it behind her. She screamed and he pushed her toward the street. He spoke again, but the words were foreign to her. "I'm an American! For God's sake, this is America! What are you doing?" He hit her in the back with the rifle and she staggered and caught the fence to keep her balance. All down the street the people were being herded to the center of the highway. The soldier who had entered her house came out carrying her husband's hunting rifle, the shotgun, Mark's old .22. "Stop!" she shrieked at him. "Those are legal!" She was knocked down by the soldier behind her. He shouted at her and she opened her eyes to see him aiming the rifle at her head.

87 She scrambled to her feet and lurched forward to join the others in the street. She could taste blood and there was a stabbing pain in her jaw where teeth had been broken by her fall. A sergeant with a notebook was standing to one side. He kept making notations in it as more of the townspeople were forced from their houses and stores into the street.

88 Mike Donatti and Stilwell herded a raving old woman to the street; when she tried to grab a gun, Mike Donatti knocked her down and would have killed her then, but she was crying, obviously praying, and he simply motioned for her to join the others being rounded up.

89 The sun was high now, the heat relentless as the people were crowded closer together by each new addition. Some of the small children could be heard screaming even over the noise of the helicopters. Dodie Wilson ran past the crowd, naked from the waist down, naked and bleeding. A soldier caught her and he and another one carried her jerking and fighting into O'Neal's feed store. Her mouth was wide open in one long unheard scream. Old Dave ran toward the lieutenant, clutching at him, yelling at him in a high-pitched voice that it was the wrong town, damn fools, and other things that were lost. A smooth-faced boy hit him in the mouth, then again in the stomach, and when he fell moaning, he kicked him several times about the head. Then he shot him. Mildred Carey saw Janice Samuels being dragged by her wrists and she threw herself at the soldiers, who fought with her, their bodies hiding her from sight. They moved on, and she lay in a shining red pool that spread and spread. They tied Janice Samuels to the porch rail of Gordon's real-estate office, spread her legs open, and half a dozen men alternately raped and beat her. The sergeant yelled in the gibberish they spoke and the soldiers started to move the people as a lump toward the end of town.

90 Mike Donatti took up a post at the growing heap of weapons and watched the terrorized people. When the order came to move them out, he prodded and nudged, and when he had to, he clubbed them to make sure they moved as a unit. Some of them stumbled and fell, and if they didn't move again, they were shot where they lay.

The filthy Henry children were screaming for their mother. The 91
biggest one, a girl with blond hair stringing down her back, darted away
and ran down the empty street. The lieutenant motioned to the troops
behind the group and after an appreciable pause there was a volley of
shots and the child was lifted and for a moment flew. She rolled when
she hit the ground again. Marjory Loomis threw herself down on top of
her baby, and shots stilled both figures.

The people were driven to the edge of town, where the highway 92
department had dug the ditch for a culvert that hadn't been laid yet. The
sergeant closed his notebook and turned away. The firing started.

The men counted the weapons then, and searched the buildings 93
methodically. Someone cut down a girl who had been tied to a rail. She
fell in a heap. Fires were started. The lieutenant called for the helicopters
to return to take them back to base camp.

Berat walked with his arm about Stilwell's shoulders, and they 94
laughed a lot. Smoke from the fires began to spread horizontally, head
high. Mike lighted another cigarette and thought about the cool green
hills of Vermont and they waited to be picked up.

## Evaluating the Text

1. How does the description of the intense heat serve to alert the reader that
   something unusual may be taking place in the town?
2. How does the variety of ethnic backgrounds suggested by names of the
   characters underscore the universality of the story?
3. How does the sudden juxtaposition of soldiers on a mission "over here"
   with the small talk between Mildred Carey and Mr. Peters suggest that
   these two scenes are somehow related to each other? How do
   conversations on similar topics suggest a possible relationship?
4. How does the title of the story, "The Village," shift its meaning as the
   point of view shifts within the story so that it acquires multiple
   connotations?
5. How is the effectiveness of the story enhanced by showing the
   townspeople as mainly conservative and antagonistic to marijuana
   smoking, long-haired hippies, and the like?
6. In light of what the reader discovers later, why is it in keeping with a
   transposed southeast Asian scene that most of the conversations revolve
   around agricultural matters?
7. What is the significance of the fact that Mildred Carey cannot understand
   the language of the soldiers when they are Americans? How effective is
   this in communicating the soldier's view that these people are "slopes?"
8. At what point did you begin to suspect that the story intended to
   counterpoint the life of soldiers in southeast Asia with the wholesome
   small-town atmosphere they had left behind in the United States? What
   clues alerted you that they were in the same country?
9. How does the conversation of the G. I.'s about "these people standing
   the heat" raise the issue that the enemy has to be perceived of as being
   subhuman? What function does dehumanizing the villagers (by finding

their toleration of the heat and language incomprehensible) serve for the soldiers?

10. How does the reference to disabled veterans make you realize that both sides in a war experience tragedy in the same human terms?

11. Did you find the characterization of the language, attitudes, and behavior of the soldiers more offensive because of the situation in which Wilhelm puts them, that is, in an American town? Would the same language, attitudes, and behavior have been less offensive to you if it had been described in the context of Vietnam? What does your answer reveal to you about your feelings on this issue?

## Exploring Different Perspectives

1. How does Wilhelm's story dramatize the statement by Robert Santos (in "My Men"), "I tried to think of what I would be like if this took place in my hometown"? In what way does her fictional treatment allow you to look at this event from a different perspective?

2. How do both Wilhelm in this story and Panos Ioannides in "Gregory" use dramatic contrast (between one place and another, the past and the present, and what is going on inside someone's mind compared with what is going on around him) to generate and maintain suspense?

3. How do both Wilhelm and Everett C. Hughes ("Good People and Dirty Work") direct the reader's attention to how language used to describe the enemy can provide the justification for atrocities because the victims are not perceived as human beings? What insights do Wilhelm and Hughes provide about societal backing for agents who perform the "dirty work"?

## Extending Viewpoints through Writing

1. Describe any experience that is usually looked at from only one side without being examined from the perspective of people suffering the consequences. Try to describe the experience from the opposite perspective, that is, from the victim's point of view, without telling the reader that this is what you are doing. For example, you might describe an abortion from the fetus's point of view.

2. Discuss the extent to which the public nature of the Vietnam war, which was seen on TV every night, made it different from past wars.

3. What function does a military euphemism such as "free-fire" zone serve in describing an area in which anything can be shot? Why do you think the military uses a relatively neutral-sounding expression instead of describing the situation as it really is? What insight does this give you into how changing language makes it possible to change perceptions of reality in order to allow actions to be performed without guilt?

4. Works by Wilhelm, Danny Santiago ("Famous All Over Town," Chapter 2); Kyōko Hayashi ("The Empty Can"); Christy Brown ("The Letter 'A',"

Chapter 2); Toi Derricotte ("The Black Notebooks," Chapter 5); Josef Škvorecký ("An Insolvable Problem of Genetics," Chapter 5); Jo Goodwin Parker ("What is Poverty?" Chapter 5); and David Whitman ("Trouble for America's 'Model' Minority," Chapter 7) deal with the consequences of being different (in terms of race, ethnicity, physical disabilities, social class). In high school, was there an individual or a group of people who were regarded as being "different" and were ostracized? Describe that person or group. How did you feel toward them at the time? Has your attitude changed? If so, discuss what brought about the change.

# Trevor N. Dupuy

# *How the War Was Won*

---

*Trevor N. Dupuy is a retired Colonel of the United States Army. He is the author of ninety books, including* The Encyclopedia of Military History, *with R. Ernest Dupuy, 2nd ed. rev. (Harper & Row, 1986),* Understanding War: History and Theory of Combat *(Paragon House, 1987), and* Understanding Defeat: How Loss in Battle Can Provide Victory in War *(Paragon House, 1990). On December 13, 1990, he offered extensive testimony before the House of Representatives Arms Services Committee that included an analysis of possible military strategies that military planners, including General Norman Schwarzkopf, might use in the event of a Persian Gulf war. This testimony became the basis of his widely read* How to Defeat Saddam Hussein: Scenarios and Strategies for the Gulf War *(Warner Books, 1991). "How the War was Won" first appeared in* National Review, *April 1, 1991. In this article, Dupuy analyzes the military strategy used by General Schwarzkopf to produce "one of the most stunning and one-sided victories in the history of warfare."*

1    A preliminary analysis of the Kuwait War suggests that of the components of the remarkable outcome, seven were particularly significant. While some might disagree, I rank these in relative order of importance as follows:

1.  Air-power superiority of the UN forces.
2.  Relative combat effectiveness of UN and Iraqi forces.
3.  Leadership and planning (or professionalism).
4.  Logistical virtuosity.
5.  Technological superiority.
6.  Intelligence competence.
7.  Intelligence denial.

Except for the first two, I would not quarrel with any change in the order of relative importance. These factors are, of course, essentially descriptive of the performance of the U.S. forces. The *political* significance of the international composition of the coalition forces cannot be over-

(For information on Iraq, see p. 389.)

stated. With all due respect to some exceptional contributions by most of our allies, however, militarily all aspects of this war were dominated by U.S. forces.

Let's look at each of these factors in some detail.          2

**1. Air-Power Superiority.** The single most significant aspect of the          3
victory was the role played by air power, from beginning to end. The circumstances were extremely favorable to the employment of air power. These included the size and excellence of the allies' air forces in comparison with the Iraqis', the geography favoring target acquisition, and the limited road and rail networks in Iraq. Before the war I predicted that these and other special circumstances "just might" permit the allied air forces to win the war without any significant employment of ground forces. And if time, ammunition, patience, and human tolerance had all been unlimited, eventually the air campaign alone could have compelled an Iraqi surrender.

As it was, this war proved, as never before, that air forces alone          4
cannot defeat a ground enemy in any except the most unusual circumstances. Few airmen had claimed that they could, although there were probably few who did not hope that they might.

But if the war demonstrated a clear limitation on the capability of air          5
power, it also demonstrated its vital importance in modern military conflict, and its pre-eminence under some circumstances. In this war air power was without question the most important single component of the UN victory, and it was the principal reason for the most astonishing aspect of that outcome: incredibly low casualties on the part of the forces supported by overwhelming air power.

Let me digress briefly on this aspect of the war. The table presents          6
"Selected Comparative Casualty Statistics." I have included the Battle of the Little Big Horn in that comparison because the U.S. 7th Cavalry Regiment lost more than twice as many men killed on the first day of that engagement as the 530,000 personnel of the U.S. Army, Navy, Air Force, and Marines lost in the entire 43 days of the Kuwait War.

Note that not only were our casualties in this war fewer than in our          7
previously least costly war, the Spanish–American War, but the casualty *rate* was less than *one-tenth* the rate in the Spanish–American War.

Before the war, using a computerized combat simulation, I estimated          8
that U.S. casualties in a war to liberate Kuwait would be about 5,800, of whom about 1,150 would be killed. That is a daily rate of 0.025 percent, or a rate midway between the Spanish–American and the Vietnam wars. This was far lower than the rates projected by models in use in and for the Pentagon, and I was widely criticized for underestimating casualties. Yet my low estimate was 15 times higher than what actually occurred.

There were two reasons for this unusually low casualty rate. One is          9
that the terrible pounding Iraqi troops received from our air forces degraded their effectiveness even more than I had allowed for in my model. Secondly, the normal Iraqi combat effectiveness was probably

SELECTED COMPARATIVE CASUALTY STATISTICS

| War or battle | Theater strength | KIA | WIA | Total casualties | Casualties per day* |
|---|---|---|---|---|---|
| Civil War (4 years) | 400,000 | 69,000 | 318,200 | 387,200 | 0.07 |
| Little Big Horn (2 days) | 600 | 257 | 44 | 301 | 25.08 |
| Spanish–American (8 months) | 50,000 | 272 | 1,600 | 1,872 | 0.02 |
| World War I (6 months) | 990,000 | 37,568 | 224,089 | 261,657 | 0.45 |
| World War II (3 years) | 1,500,000 | 175,407 | 625,328 | 800,735 | 0.05 |
| Korean War (3 years) | 220,000 | 19,453 | 77,788 | 97,241 | 0.04 |
| Vietnam War (5 years) | 240,000 | 23,373 | 104,032 | 127,405 | 0.03 |
| Kuwait War (6 weeks) | 530,000 | 111 | 256 | 367 | 0.0016 |

*As a percentage of theater strength.

even lower than I had projected. Which brings us to the second of my seven major components of victory.

10    **2. Combat Effectiveness.** Iraqi forces had been engaged in five conflicts in the half-century before the Kuwait War, and had performed poorly in each. In the 1973 Arab–Israeli War, for instance, a comparison with respect to Israeli forces showed that 100 Israeli soldiers were the combat-effectiveness equivalent of about 330 Iraqi soldiers with comparable equipment. The average for the other Arab armies was about 100 Israelis for 200 Arabs. I had assumed that eight years of battle experience against Iran had brought the Iraqis' capability up to the Arab average. So I gave them this standard combat effectiveness in comparison to American troops, who I assumed were at least the equal of the Israelis. Clearly, I have overestimated their capability.

11    **3. Leadership and Planning.** When things go wrong on the battlefield, this is usually because of poor planning, poor execution, and/or enemy interference with execution of plans. When things go well on the battlefield it means that the plans were good, the execution was good, and there was minimal enemy interference with the operation. This, of course, was the case with Operation Desert Storm.

12    The United States Armed Forces operate in a fashion consistent with the General Staff system introduced in Prussia in 1809, which attracted the world's attention by its stunning victories over Austria in 1866 and France in 1870. In a General Staff system it is rarely possible to determine whether good performance in planning—and in execution—is due to the staff system and the quality of the people on the staff, or due

to the genius of the commander. But since the commander is responsible, and would be blamed in case of failure, it is only proper that he be given the credit for success. Thus General Schwarzkopf must be given credit for one of the most stunning and one-sided victories in the history of warfare.

He and his staff applied a doctrine which the U.S. Army and Air 13 Force adopted about ten years ago: the AirLand Battle Doctrine. The doctrine is both new and old. It is new to the extent that it endeavors to take maximum advantage of the most modern developments in technology, in terms of firepower, mobility, and electronics. It is old because it emphasizes the application of the new technologies in accordance with the classic Principles of War, which characterized the successful battles of such great captains as Alexander the Great and Hannibal [see "Principles of War" table].

All nine of the "Principles of War" were employed to good effect in 14 the brief ground campaign of Desert Storm, but two stand out: Maneuver and Surprise.

Maneuver was the hallmark of the great strategic envelopment car- 15 ried out by the U.S. XVIII Airborne and VII Corps.

Surprise contributed to this remarkably successful maneuver. One 16 aspect was deception, in the feints in which two Marine Expeditionary Brigades (MEBs) afloat in the Persian Gulf threatened an amphibious invasion of the Kuwaiti coast. As a result, six or seven Iraqi divisions were kept on constant alert along that seacoast, and were unable to help deal with the massive envelopment of western Kuwait by the U.S. VII Corps.

Another manifestation of surprise was the quiet, unobstrusive move- 17 ment of the VII Corps and XVIII Airborne to positions just south of the Saudi–Iraqi border, far to the west of Kuwait.

## PRINCIPLES OF WAR

1. *Objective.* Every military operation must be directed toward a decisive, obtainable objective.

2. *Offensive.* Only offensive action achieves decisive results.

3. *Simplicity.* Simplicity must be the keynote of military operations.

4. *Unity of Command.* The decisive application of full combat power requires unity of command.

5. *Mass.* Maximum available combat power must be applied at the point of decision.

6. *Economy of Forces.* Minimum essential means must be employed at points other than that of decision.

7. *Maneuver.* Maneuver must be used to alter the relative combat power of militay forces.

8. *Surprise.* Surprise may decisively shift the balance of combat power in favor of the commander who achieves it.

9. *Security.* Security is essential to the application of the other principles of war.

18    **4. Logistical Virtuosity.** That great two-corps envelopment would
not have been possible without logistical performance that was little
short of miraculous. The movement of supplies — particularly fuel and
ammunition — enabled the nine divisions of those corps not only to go
swiftly across the trackless desert in an extremely bold maneuver, but
also to maintain the momentum of their advance for four days. It was a
logistical achievement that has never been surpassed, and it is worthy of
comparison with the even larger — but no more successful — logistical
effort that supported the allied cross channel assault in Operation Overlord in June 1944.

19    This, however, was merely the culmination of a seven-month logistical effort which began with the first movement of U.S. and allied troops
to Saudi Arabia in early August 1990. It was an accomplishment which is
at least worthy of comparison with the vast buildup in Great Britain
before Overlord. The quantities in Desert Storm were not so great,
but the time available was much shorter, and there was no indigenous production capability or industrial and transportation infrastructures
such as existed in Britain.

20    **5. Technological Superiority.** Some may believe that I have under-
rated the contribution of technology to the victory. They may be right. I
cannot deny the significance of the U.S. technological edge with such
"smart" weapons as Tomahawk, Hellfire, and Patriot; such versatile
mobile systems as the M1A1 Abrams Tank and the Bradley Infantry
Fighting Vehicle; and the amazing variety of sophisticated, computer-
controlled electronic systems. However, these weapons would have been
meaningless without trained and capable men to employ them to their
maximum potential, and leadership to commit them at the right time and
place.

21    There is no doubt in my mind that if the U.S. forces had fought with
the weapons and equipment of the Iraqi forces, and if the Iraqis had
fought with ours, the outcome would have been exactly the same; although the war probably would have lasted longer than 43 days, and our
casualties would have been greater.

22    **6. Intelligence Competence.** It is no exaggeration to say that the
results of Operation Desert Storm could not have been achieved without
highly skilled intelligence systems at all levels, and linked from top to
bottom. Acquiring targets, assessing bomb damage, identifying and locating enemy units are only a few of the myriad means by which
intelligence staffs provide their commanders with reasonably accurate
and comprehensive pictures of enemy capabilities. The unvarying success of the air and ground efforts of UN forces testify to the quality of the
detailed information compiled by the intelligence staffs about the terrain,
and about enemy dispositions and capabilities.

23    **7. Intelligence Denial.** Possibly equally important — and some believe more so — was the denial of intelligence capability to the enemy.
This was in large part, of course, an automatic result of the destruction of

the Iraqi communications facilities and network. By the time the land campaign began, the Iraqi ground forces were virtually blind. They had little or no idea of the location of the UN forces, or of the movements that might have given them some inkling of the U.S. strategy. Thanks to intelligence denial, they were sitting ducks.

A final word. One might ask: If we so outclassed the enemy, how can 24 this be considered a great victory?

There are no great victories in war unless one side has a significant 25 superiority in one or more respects, *and is able to take advantage of that superiority*. There are no great victories when evenly matched armies and commanders face each other. The 1864 campaign between Grant and Lee in Northern Virginia is only one example. No one has better explained this phenomenon of great victories better than the renowned German military theorist, Count Alfred von Schlieffen. In his classic book *Cannae*, he wrote: "A complete battle of Cannae is rarely met in history. For its achievement, a Hannibal is needed on the one side, and a Terentius Varro on the other, both cooperating for the attainment of the great goal."

## Evaluating the Text

1. Why in Dupuy's opinon were "air-power superiority" and "relative combat effectiveness of UN and Iraqi forces" decisive in ensuring a quick victory for the United States-led coalition?
2. How does Dupuy use comparisons of casualties in past wars to emphasize the "incredibly low casualties" of the Kuwait war? To what does he credit the unusually low casualty figures for the UN coalition?
3. How is the form Dupuy's assessment takes well-suited to explore the relative importance of particular factors in accounting for such a one-sided victory?
4. What insight do you gain into how a military scholar and historian looks at the key features of any battle against the framework of past military campaigns? How does Dupuy's analysis of the "AirLand Battle Doctrine" point out its up-to-date application of crucial "Principles of War"? Which of the nine principles he identifies played an especially important role?
5. In what way does Dupuy's assessment of the role played by "smart" weapons differ from the view conveyed by the media? Do you agree or disagree with the reasons he offers to support his view?
6. What role did "denial of intelligence capability to the enemy" play in allowing the maneuver of envelopment to proceed unopposed?
7. What features other than those identified by Dupuy do you think played a significant role in determining the outcome?

## Exploring Different Perspectives

1. What similarities and differences can you observe between Dupuy's analysis and the account of Robert Santos in "My Men"? What factors

might help explain any difference in the author's attitudes towards the respective conflicts?

2. After reading Kate Wilhelm's story "The Village," discuss whether it would be likely or even possible for a fiction writer to create an analogous story based on the circumstances of the Persian Gulf war.

3. The "air-power superiority of the UN forces" caused casualties in Iraq among soldiers and civilians that were comparable to those caused by the bombing of Hiroshima. Why, in your view, do the circumstances of the Persian Gulf war make it less likely that any pilot might react as Claude Eatherly did? Explain you reaction after reading Maurizio Chierici's "The Man From Hiroshima."

## Extending Viewpoints through Writing

1. In an essay, discuss the features that distinguish the Persian Gulf war from previous conflicts in which the United States was involved, such as the Vietnam war. You might discuss the reasons for the differences in the public attitudes toward these conflicts.

2. In an essay, discuss your personal reaction to the Persian Gulf war, including your evaluation of the reasons why it took place and your assessment of the outcome. For a more in-depth analysis, you might wish to read Dupuy's *How to Defeat Saddam Hussein: Scenarios and Strategies for the Gulf War* (1991, Warner Books).

# CONNECTING CULTURES

## George Orwell, "Homage to Catalonia"

1. What common features do Orwell's account and those of Tepilit Ole Saitoti ("The Initiation of a Maasai Warrior," Chapter 2) and Christy Brown ("The Letter 'A'," Chapter 2) share as autobiographical narratives? How does each writer use highly descriptive and evocative language to recreate the feelings of what it was like to be in each of these different situations? In each case, what words and images are designed to appeal to specific senses?
2. How do both Orwell's account and that of Beryl Markham ("West with the Night," Chapter 4) give you insight into the state of mind necessary to make clear decisions of life and death under harrowing circumstances? What common elements can you identify?
3. What insight does Orwell offer as to whether a completely egalitarian army could function as effectively as could the Marines described by Henry Allen ("The Corps," Chapter 2)?

## Everett C. Hughes, "Good People and Dirty Work"

4. How are the techniques used to train recruits described by Henry Allen ("The Corps," Chapter 2) similar to the methods used to recruit soldiers to do the "dirty work" as described by Hughes?
5. Why does the phenomena of labeling (assigning meaning by stereotyping) become a crucial issue during wartime or civil insurrection? You might discuss this idea as it emerges in the narratives of Armando Valladares ("A Nazi Prison in the Caribbean," Chapter 6); Alicia Partnoy ("The Little School: Tales of Disappearance and Survival in Argentina," Chapter 6); and Shen Tong's account "Bloody Sunday in Tiananmen Square" (Chapter 6).

## Hyōko Hayashi, "The Empty Can"

6. How do Hayashi's story and Christy Brown's narrative ("The Letter 'A'," Chapter 2) provide insight into how society treats those who have something wrong with them? What insight do you get into what it was like to be a survivor of atomic radiation or to have been stricken by cerebral palsy?
7. How would Marilyn French's ("Gender Roles," Chapter 3) observations about the culturally determined nature of gender roles have to be modified to account for the picture you get of the status of women in Japan from Hayashi's point of view?
8. Discuss the issue of scapegoating in both Hayashi's story and Bessie Head's "Looking for a Rain God" (Chapter 8). Explain why the psychology of scapegoating requires an individual to involuntarily assume the burden of the collective.

## Maurizio Chierici, "The Man from Hiroshima"

9. How are questions of conscience involved in Chierici's interview with Eatherly, Francine du Plessix Gray's interview with Dr. K ("Sex and Birth," Chapter 1) on Soviet health care for women, and in Tayeb Salih's story ("A Handful of Dates," Chapter 2)?
10. How are Eatherly's reactions and Shaila's dilemma in Bharati Mukherjee's "The Management of Grief" (Chapter 7) examples of conscience that pit the individual against the group?

## Panos Ioannides, "Gregory"

11. How do both David K. Shipler's report ("The Sin of Love," Chapter 3) and "Gregory" illustrate how personal relationships can be overwhelmed by societal and political pressures?
12. To what extent did the kind of possibility for disobeying military orders arise among Chinese troops in Tiananmen Square, according to Shen Tong ("Bloody Sunday in Tiananmen Square," Chapter 6) as it did for the narrator in "Gregory"?
13. How do both Studs Terkel's interview with C. P. Ellis ("Why I Quit the Klan," Chapter 5) and "Gregory" depend on the idea of developing empathy with those normally seen as the enemy?

## Robert Santos, "My Men"

14. What common elements connect the life of soldiers as revealed in Santos's account with the societal expectations and responsibilities of Maasai warriors in Kenya as described by Tepilit Ole Saitoti ("The Initiation of a Maasai Warrior," Chapter 2)?
15. How do both Santos and C. P. Ellis ("Why I Quit the Klan," Chapter 5) have the experience of seeing their own situations from an entirely different perspective?
16. Contrast Santos's unwillingness to serve on riot duty, where he would be faced with the prospect of shooting other Americans, with the behavior of the soldiers in Beijing who shot the demonstrators in Tiananmen Square (see Shen Tong, "Bloody Sunday in Tiananmen Square," Chapter 6)? What factors might explain the difference in their reactions?

## Kate Wilhelm, "The Village"

17. In your opinion, would the kind of training Marines receive according to Henry Allen ("The Corps," Chapter 2) have made the events described in Wilhelm's story more or less likely to occur?
18. How do both Wilhelm's story and David K. Shipler's account ("The Sin of Love," Chapter 3) illustrate that stereotyping always leads to dehumanization?
19. How does Wilhelm's story present an imaginative account of events in the kind of village to which Le Ly Hayslip ("Sisters and Brothers," Chapter 7) returned after living in America for thirty years?

## *Trevor N. Dupuy, "How The War Was Won"*

20. How does Henry Allen in "The Corps" (Chapter 2) spell out the distinctive features of training received by Marines that might shed light on the high degree of combat effectiveness of U.S. soldiers as compared to those of the Iraqi Army? To what extent does Allen's analysis support Dupuy's contention that the quality of the soldiers is more important than technological sophistication?
21. What insight does Samir al-Khalil's account "Authority" (Chapter 6) give you into the means Saddam Hussein uses to maintain his hold on power that might explain the worldwide reaction against his invasion of Kuwait?

# Geographical Index

## AFRICA

**Botswana**    Bessie Head, "Looking for a Rain God"
                Marjorie Shostak, "Memories of a !Kung Girlhood"
**Congo**    Henri Lopes, "The Esteemed Representative"
**Kenya**    Ngũgĩ wa Thiong'o, "Decolonising the Mind"
**South Africa**    Jan Rabie, "Drought"
**Sudan**    Tayeb Salih, "A Handful of Dates"
**Tanzania**    Tepilit Ole Saitoti, "The Initiation of a Maasai Warrior"

## ASIA

**China**    Chen Jo-hsi, "The Big Fish"
         Shen Tong, "Bloody Sunday in Tiananmen Square"
         Bruce Dollar, "Child Care in China"
         Mark Salzman, "Lessons"
**Cyprus**    Panos Ioannides, "Gregory"
**India**    Krishnan Varma, "The Grass-Eaters"
         Bharati Mukherjee, "The Management of Grief"
**Japan**    John Burgess, "A Day in the Life of 'Salaryman'"
         Kyōko Hayashi, "The Empty Can"
         Natsume Soseki, "I Am a Cat"
         Pico Iyer, "Perfect Strangers"
**Pakistan**    Talat Abbasi, "Facing the Light"
**Soviet Union**    Boris Yeltsin, "Childhood in Russia"
         Francine du Plessix Gray, "Sex and Birth"

## EUROPE

**Czechoslovakia**    Josef Škvorecký, "An Insolvable Problem of Genetics"
         Václav Havel, "The Velvet Hangover"
**England**    Beryl Markham, "West with the Night"
**France**    Simone de Beauvoir, "The Married Woman"
         Raymonde Carroll, "Minor Accidents"
         Daniel Boulanger, "The Shoe Breaker"
**Germany**    Everett C. Hughes, "Good People and Dirty Work"
**Ireland**    Christy Brown, "The Letter 'A'"
         William Trevor, "Teresa's Wedding"
**Italy**    Dino Buzzati, "The Falling Girl"
**Poland**    Slawomir Mrożek, "The Elephant"

# Rhetorical Index

## DESCRIPTION

| | |
|---|---|
| Rigoberta Menchu | "Birth Ceremonies" |
| Douchan Gersi | "Initiated into an Iban Tribe of Headhunters" |
| Tepilit Ole Saitoti | "The Initiation of a Maasai Warrior" |
| Talat Abbasi | "Facing the Light" |
| Beryl Markham | "West with the Night" |
| Mark Salzman | "Lessons" |
| Toi Derricotte | "The Black Notebooks" |
| Dino Buzzati | "The Falling Girl" |
| Armando Valladares | "A Nazi Prison in the Caribbean" |
| Alicia Partnoy | "The Little School: Tales of Disappearance and Survival in Argentina" |
| Joan Didion | "Miami: The Cuban Presence" |
| Jamaica Kincaid | "A Small Place" |
| Pico Iyer | "Perfect Strangers" |
| Napoleon A. Chagnon | "Doing Fieldwork among the Yąnomamö" |
| Gretel Ehrlich | "To Live in Two Worlds" |
| Octavio Paz | "The Day of the Dead" |
| George Orwell | "Homage to Catalonia" |

## NARRATION (Personal)

| | |
|---|---|
| Boris Yeltsin | "Childhood in Russia" |
| Christy Brown | "The Letter 'A'" |
| Douchan Gersi | "Initiated into an Iban Tribe of Headhunters" |
| Tepilit Ole Saitoti | "The Initiation of a Maasai Warrior" |
| Talat Abbasi | "Facing the Light" |
| Marjorie Shostak | "Memories of a !Kung Girlhood" |
| Cha Ok Kim | "The Peddler" |
| Beryl Markham | "West with the Night" |
| Mark Salzman | "Lessons" |
| C. P. Ellis | "Why I Quit the Klan" |
| Toi Derricotte | "The Black Notebooks" |
| Armando Valladares | "A Nazi Prison in the Caribbean" |
| Shen Tong | "Bloody Sunday in Tiananmen Square" |
| Someth May | "The Field behind the Village" |
| V. S. Naipaul | "Prologue to an Autobiography" |
| Le Ly Hayslip | "Sisters and Brothers" |
| Robert Santos | "My Men" |

## IRONY, HUMOR, AND SATIRE

## AUTOBIOGRAPHY

# Acknowledgments

TALAT ABBASI, "Facing the Light." Copyright © 1989 by Talat Abbasi. "Facing the Light" first appeared in *Sudden Fiction International*, W. W. Norton, 1989. Reprinted by permission of the author.

SAMIR AL-KHALIL, "Authority" from *Republic of Fear: The Inside Story of Saddam's Iraq*, 1988. Reprinted with permission from The University of California Press.

HENRY ALLEN, "The Corps," March 5, 1972. *The Washington Post*, © 1972 *The Washington Post*. Reprinted with permission.

MARGARET ATWOOD, "Happy Endings," from *Murder in the Dark* by Margaret Atwood, published by Coach House Press (Toronto). Copyright © 1983 by Margaret Atwood. Reprinted by permission of the author. This story first appeared in *Ms.* magazine.

SIMONE DE BEAUVOIR, "The Married Woman." From *The Second Sex* by Simone de Beauvoir, translated and edited by H. M. Parshley. Copyright © 1952 by Alfred A. Knopf, Inc. Reprinted by permission of the publisher.

DANIEL BOULANGER, "The Shoe Breaker," from *Les Noces Du Merle* by Daniel Boulanger. Copyright © 1963 by Daniel Boulanger, published by Editions de la Table Ronde. English translation copyright © 1989 by Penny Million Pucelik and Maryjo Despreaux Schneider. Copyright © 1985 by Editions Gallimard. Reprinted with permission of Editions Gallimard.

CHRISTY BROWN, "The Letter 'A'," from *My Left Foot*, 1955. Reprinted by permission of Martin Secker and Warburg Limited.

JOHN BURGESS, "The Ultimate Company Man: A Day in a Life in Japan." *The Washington Post*, September 4, 1987. © 1987, *The Washington Post*. Reprinted with permission.

DINO BUZZATI, "The Falling Girl." Excerpt from *Restless Nights* by Dino Buzzati, translation copyright © 1983 by Lawrence Venuti. Published by North Point Press and reprinted by permission.

RAYMONDE CARROLL, "Minor Accidents," from *Cultural Misunderstandings* (1988). Reprinted with permission from The University of Chicago Press and the author.

NAPOLEON A. CHAGNON, "Doing Fieldwork Among the Yąnomamö." Excerpt from *Yąnomamö: The Fierce People*, second edition, by Napoleon A. Chagnon. Copyright © 1977 by Holt, Rinehart and Winston, Inc., reprinted by permission of the publisher.

ANDREW CHERLIN and FRANK FURSTENBERG, JR., "The American Family in the Year 2000." Reprinted, with permission, from *The Futurist*, June 1983, published by the World Future Society, 4916 Saint Elmo Avenue, Bethesda, Maryland 20814.

MAURIZIO CHIERICI, "The Man from Hiroshima." From GRANTA, #22 Autumn 1987. Reprinted with permission of GRANTA.

TOI DERRICOTTE, "From the Black Notebooks," from *Ariadne's Thread*, Harper & Row, 1982. Reprinted with permission of the author.

JOAN DIDION, "Miami: The Cuban Presence." Copyright © 1987 by Joan Didion. Reprinted by permission of Simon & Schuster, Inc.

BRUCE DOLLAR, "Child Care in China." From the *Saturday Review*, May 1973. Reprinted with permission of Omni Publications International.

TREVOR N. DUPUY, "How the War Was Won." © 1991 *National Review*, Inc., 150 East 35th Street, New York, N.Y. 10016. Reprinted by permission.

GRETEL EHRLICH, "To Live in Two Worlds." Excerpt from "To Live in Two Worlds: Crow Fair and Sundance." From *The Solace of Open Spaces* by Gretel Ehrlich. Copyright © 1985 by Gretel Ehrlich. Reprinted by permission of Viking Penguin, a division of Penguin Books USA, Inc.

NAWAL EL SAADAWI, "Circumcision of Girls." From *The Hidden Face of Eve: Women in the Arab World*, 1980. Reprinted with permission of Beacon Press.

C. P. ELLIS, "Why I Quit the Klan." From *American Dreams Lost and Found* by Studs Terkel. Copyright © 1980 by Studs Terkel. Reprinted by permission of Pantheon Books, a division of Random House, Inc.

MARILYN FRENCH, "Gender Roles," from *Beyond Power: On Women, Men, and Morals*. Copyright © 1985 by Belles Lettres, Inc. Reprinted by permission of Summit Books, a division of Simon & Schuster, Inc.

PAUL FUSSELL, "Taking it All Off in the Balkans." From *Thank God for the Atom Bomb*. Copyright © 1988 by Paul Fussell. Reprinted by permission of Summit Books, a division of Simon & Schuster, Inc.

CLIFFORD GEERTZ, "Of Cocks & Men," from "Deep Play: Notes on the Balinese Cockfight." Reprinted by permission of *Daedalus, Journal of the American Academy of Arts and Sciences*, "Myth, Symbol, and Culture," Winter, 1972, Volume 101, Number 1. Reprinted by permission.

Douchan Gersi, "Initiated into an Iban Tribe of Headhunters," from *Explorer* (1987), Jeremy P. Tarcher, Inc., Los Angeles, California. Reprinted with permission.

Francine du Plessix Gray, "Sex and Birth." Excerpt from *Soviet Women: Walking the Tightrope* by Francine du Plessix Gray, copyright © 1990 by Francine du Plessix Gray. Originally published in *The New Yorker Magazine*. Used by permission of Doubleday, a division of Bantam Doubleday Dell Publishing Group, Inc.

Gina Del Guercio, "The Secrets of Haiti's Living Dead." February 1986, *Harvard Magazine*. Reprinted with permission from *Harvard Magazine*.

Václav Havel, "The Velvet Hangover." Originally appeared in *Harper's* Vol. 281, No. 1685 (October 1990). Reprinted by permission.

Kyōko Hayashi, "The Empty Can," from *The Crazy Iris and Other Stories of the Atomic Aftermath* (1985). Edited and with an Introduction by Kenzaburo Oe. Reprinted by permission of Grove Weidenfeld. Copyright © 1985 by Kenzaburo Oe.

Le Ly Hayslip, "Sisters and Brothers." Excerpt from *When Heaven and Earth Changed Places*, by Le Ly Hayslip and Charles Jay Wurts, 1989. Used by permission of Doubleday, a division of Bantam Doubleday Dell Publishing Group, Inc.

Bessie Head, "Looking for a Rain God," from *The Collector of Treasures*. Copyright © 1977 by Bessie Head. Reprinted by permission of Heinemann Educational Books Ltd. and the author's agent, John Johnson, Ltd. Reprinted with permission.

Everett C. Hughes, "Good People and Dirty Work," (1962). © 1962 by the Society for the Study of Social Problems. Reprinted from *Social Problems*, Vol. 10, No. 1, Summer 1962, pp. 3–11, by permission.

Panos Ioannides, "Gregory," first published in *The Charioteer, A Review of Modern Greek Literature*. Copyright © 1989 by Panos Ioannides. English language translation © 1989 by Marion Byron and Catherine Raizis. Reprinted by permission of Pella Publishing.

Pico Iyer, "Perfect Strangers." From *Video Night in Kathmandu and Other Reports From The Not-So-Far East* by Pico Iyer. Copyright © 1988 by Pico Iyer. Reprinted by permission of Alfred A. Knopf Inc.

Chen Jo-Hsi, "The Big Fish," from *The Execution of Mayor Yin and Other Stories* (1979). Reprinted with permission of the University of Indiana Press.

Ivan Karp, "Good Marx for the Anthropologist," 1981. Reprinted with permission from the author.

Cha Kim, "The Peddler." From *New Americans: An Oral History* by Al Santoli. Copyright © 1988 by Al Santoli. Reprinted by permission of the publisher, Viking Penguin, a division of Penguin Books USA Inc.

Jamaica Kincaid, "A Small Place." Excerpt from *A Small Place* by Jamaica Kincaid. Copyright © 1988 by Jamaica Kincaid. Reprinted by permission of Farrar, Straus and Giroux, Inc.

Robert Levine and Ellen Wolff, "Social Time: The Heartbeat of Culture." Reprinted with permission from *Psychology Today* Magazine. Copyright © 1985 (PT Partners, L. P.).

CATHERINE LIM, "Paper," from *Little Ironies: Stories of Singapore*, 1978. Reprinted with permission of Heinemann Asia, a division of Octopus Publishing Asia PTE Ltd.

GENE LOGSDON, "Amish Economics: A Lesson in Modern Economics," 1986. Originally appeared in *Whole Earth*, 27 Gate Five Road, Sausalito, California 94965. Subscriptions $20.00 per year. Reprinted with permission of the author.

HENRI LOPES, "The Esteemed Representative," from *Tribaliks: Contemporary Congolese Stories*. Reprinted with permission of Heinemann (Oxford) and Cle.

BERYL MARKHAM, "West with the Night." Excerpt from *West with the Night*, copyright © 1983 by Beryl Markham. Published by North Point Press and reprinted by permission.

SOMETH MAY, "The Field Behind the Village," from *Cambodian Witness* (1986). Reprinted by permission of Sterling Lord Literistic, Inc. Copyright © 1986 by Someth May.

RIGOBERTA MENCHU, "Birth Ceremonies." From *I . . . Rigoberta Menchu: An Indian Woman in Guatemala*. Edited by Elisabeth Burgos-Debray, 1984. Reprinted with permission of Verso Publications.

NICHOLASA MOHR, "A Very Special Pet," from *El Bronx Remembered: A Novella and Stories* by Nicholasa Mohr, 1975. Reprinted by permission of HarperCollins Publishers.

SLAWOMIR MROŻEK, "The Elephant," from *The Elephant* by Slawomir Mrożek. Copyright © 1962 by Grove Press. English language translation copyright © by Konrad Syrop. Reprinted by permission of Grove Weidenfeld.

BHARATI MUKHERJEE, "The Management of Grief," from *The Middleman and Other Stories*. Reprinted by permission of Grove Weidenfeld. © 1988 by Bharati Mukherjee.

V. S. NAIPAUL, "Prologue to an Autobiography." From *Finding the Center: Two Narratives* by V. S. Naipaul. Copyright © 1984 by V. S. Naipaul. Reprinted by permission of Alfred A. Knopf Inc.

GEORGE ORWELL, "Homage to Catalonia," from *Homage to Catalonia* (1952). Chapter 3 from *Homage to Catalonia* by George Orwell, copyright 1952 and renewed by Sonia Brownell Orwell, reprinted by permission of Harcourt Brace Jovanovich, Inc.

JO GOODWIN PARKER, "What Is Poverty?" (1965). Reprinted with permission from University of Oklahoma Press.

ALICIA PARTNOY, "Introduction" and "A Conversation Under the Rain" (1986) are reprinted from *The Little School, Tales of Disappearance and Survival in Argentina*, by Alicia Partnoy, with the permission of the author and Cleis Press, Pittsburgh, PA. Copyright © 1986 by Alicia Partnoy. To order book please write to Cleis Press, Pittsburgh, PA.

OCTAVIO PAZ, "The Day of the Dead," from *The Labyrinth of Solitude*, translated by Lysander Kemp. Reprinted by permission of Grove Weidenfeld. Copyright © 1961 by Grove Press, Inc.

JAN RABIE, "Drought" (1962). Reprinted with permission from author.

SALMAN RUSHDIE, "A Pen Against the Sword: In Good Faith." From *Newsweek*, February 12, 1990. Reprinted with permission of Wylie, Aitken & Stone, Inc.

# Index of Authors and Titles

INDEX OF AUTHORS AND TITLES

.

.

(U.S.)

Canada

United States

*Atlantic Ocean*

Cuba

Puerto Rico

Mexico

Antigua

Haiti

Guatemala

Trinidad

Brazil

*Pacific Ocean*

Argentina

Only countries mentioned in
selections are labeled on this map.